America's Political System

RANDOM HOUSE New York

America's Political System

Peter Woll
Brandeis University

Robert H. Binstock
Brandeis University

Peter Woll, Ph.D., has been a professor of political science at Brandeis University, Waltham, Massachusetts since 1964. He has also taught politics at the University of California at Los Angeles (UCLA). He has written numerous articles and books in the field of political science including *American Bureaucracy* and *American Government: Readings and Cases.*

Robert H. Binstock, Ph.D., has also been a professor of political science at Brandeis University since 1964. He was a member of a White House Task Force in 1967 and 1968, and is an active consultant to federal, state, and local governments. His books include *The Politics of the Powerless* and *Feasible Planning for Social Change.*

ISBN: 0–394–31300–3

Library of Congress Catalog Card Number: 79–37746

Manufactured in the United States of America
Printed by Halliday Lithograph Corp., West Hanover, Mass.
Bound by The Book Press, Inc., Brattleboro, Vt.

First Edition

987654321

Preface

No political system can survive if it does not have the support of the community that it serves. How is this support developed and maintained in a democratic system? A critical first step is for its citizens to gain an understanding of how their government works so that they can participate meaningfully in making those political decisions that affect their lives.

America's Political System is designed to explain in a realistic manner all of the facets of the American political system. While containing a full exposition of the formal institutions of government, the book places particular emphasis on the informal workings of the political process. These informal aspects lend excitement to the drama of politics. On the other hand, the realities of political decision-making are not always pleasant from the standpoint of those who do not receive what they feel they deserve from the government. Compromise thus is a keystone of the democratic process because of the numerous political forces seeking to advance their own particular interests. In order to influence government decisions, therefore, a citizen must understand how to maximize his or her power within the system.

This book contributes to such an understanding of politics by viewing American government as part of a "system" in which "inputs" flow from a variety of sources—such as the electorate, political parties, and interest groups—to the decision-making structures: Congress, the Presidency, the bureaucracy, and the judiciary. These branches of government respond to the various inputs by producing public policy "outputs" affecting almost every citizen. As students will readily observe while reading the book, there is nothing mysterious about the systems approach. It is primarily a way of organizing material and presenting the subject matter. It helps to identify the various parts of the political process and thereby enables students to fit the pieces of the political puzzle together. Rather than presenting a series of isolated descriptions of parts of the political process, the systems approach used in this book stresses the relationships among these parts. This approach will give readers an integrated view of the nature of American politics.

The case studies that appear at the end of each chapter provide a unique feature of the book. Most of the case studies deal with contemporary issues and problems, and all of them have been selected to complement and illuminate the analysis presented in the text. Students will find these case studies unusually interesting and, by drawing on the groundwork material presented in the chapters, will be able to approach the case study readings from a critical point of view.

A project of this scope necessarily involves many people. We would particularly like to thank Walter Kossmann, Mollie Cohen, and Jane Marx of Random House, without whose creative talents, dedication, and encouragement this book could not have been completed. Mary Woll and Jutta Binstock cheered the authors at various critical stages of the project. Bob and Cindy Woll helped the completion of the book by demonstrating continual interest in what would be the nature of the authors' output.

Peter Woll
Weston, Massachusetts

Robert H. Binstock
Cambridge, Massachusetts

July 19, 1971

Contents

UNIT FOUR

The Conversion Structures of the National Government

255

UNIT FIVE

Outputs of the Political System

465

UNIT SIX

The System in Transition   **625**

List of Tables

Diagrams, Maps, and Graphs

Introduction

The foundations of the American political system may have been shaken severely during the nineteen sixties. By the end of the decade public opinion surveys revealed that a large majority of the people felt that the country was in deep trouble, because of its involvement in Vietnam, racial strife, the generation gap, pollution of the environment, a steadily rising crime rate, and other maladies. A central problem was that expectations about public institutions were not being fulfilled. The rules of the game of our democratic system, widely accepted in previous decades, suddenly seemed to be questioned on many fronts.

What were the causes of these dramatic shifts in popular feeling about political institutions? Certainly one major cause was the ubiquitous nature of the mass media, which reached into every home in the nation, making it virtually impossible for political leaders to hide behind ambiguous language and actions. For example, the publication of *The Pentagon Papers* in 1971 revealed the duplicity of many Administrations in leading the country gradually into a major war in Vietnam. Individuals were able to read for themselves the various memoranda of close advisers of Presidents, Cabinet Secretaries, and military leaders, some of which openly suggested the use of disception in dealing not only with foreign governments but also with the American people. The evidence of *The Pentagon Papers* suggested that at least some members of the Johnson Administration, if not the President himself, were preparing to bomb North Vietnam and escalate the war even while President Johnson during the election campaign of 1964 was promising to keep "the boys" at home.

About the same time as the revelations of *The Pentagon Papers* appeared in print, the Kennedy Papers were opened to the public. In some respects they were also disquieting to those who wanted to believe in the integrity of their political leaders. For example, after a Cabinet level review of the Vietnam situation in 1963, Pierre Salinger, Press Secretary to President

Kennedy, wrote a communique for the press explaining what had transpired. A marginal note was penciled in by McGeorge Bundy, a close adviser to President Kennedy, in which he stated: "Pierre: Champion! Excellent Prose. No Surprise. 'A communique should say nothing in such a way as to fool the Press without deceiving them.'" As more and more of this type of information is revealed to the public it should not surprise anyone that an "information-gap" develops between people and government. This may lead to a serious lack of confidence and support in political institutions, which can undermine the entire system.

Extensive media coverage has also made people more aware of the gap between government promises and reality. The media have not only conveyed to the public the repeated assertions by political leaders of broad public goals for achieving social justice, but also have shown everyone the distressing conditions of life experienced in all segments of our society. Equality of opportunity in education, equal employment opportunity, and a war on poverty are constantly being promised but seldom realized in practice. In other areas as well, promises and reality do not coincide. Promised withdrawl from Vietnam is agonizingly slow in coming. Full employment seems a distant goal. Control over crime appears to be a losing battle. In these and other areas the government has raised popular expectations of solutions that it has not been able to achieve. And it is no longer possible for any of us to remain insulated from these problems, pretending that they do not exist.

The contrast between promise and reality is also evident in the widening gap between, on the one hand, constitutional and democratic theory that is an integral part of our heritage, and, on the other hand, actual political practice. Constitutional theory emphasizes the importance of the separation of powers among legislative, executive, and judicial branches in order to prevent the arbitrary exercise of political power. The separation of powers is buttressed by checks and balances among the three branches of government. This is the theory, but what is the reality of the political system?

First, there is little doubt that an excessive amount of power has accrued to the President, particularly in the military sphere. Although the President was to be Commander-in-Chief under the terms of Article II of the Constitution, the war power was to reside in Congress. It would have been unthinkable to the framers of the Constitution that the President could lead the country into major foreign wars, such as Korea and Vietnam. But the reality of American politics of the twentieth century is that Presidents from Wilson through Franklin D. Roosevelt, Truman, and Lyndon Johnson have guided the country into major foreign involvements. Although Congress did declare war in World Wars I and II, the action of the President led to American entry into those wars. Even if one feels all the wars of the Twentieth Century were justified, the fact is clear that it is the Presidency and not Congress that in fact has the power to declare war. This violates a fundamental constitutional principle. Political support for the constitutional rules of the game depends upon governmental adherence to the Constitution. If Presidents embark upon foreign wars under the mask of involving the country in "police actions," the faith of citizens in the constitutional system will be diminished. Although it is clearly a Presidential prerogative to be dominant in foreign affairs, some balance between the legislature and the executive must be restored in the military area.

A second major dilemma of our constitutional system is the fact that the growth of the bureaucracy as a fourth branch of government is not taken into account in constitutional theory. Administrative agencies have developed to meet the enlarged scope of responsibilities that have been placed upon government. In order to meet these responsibilities the administrative branch has been given legislative and judicial power, which it exercises with a great deal of discretion. Often operating under vague Congressional mandates, administrators fill in the details of skeleton legislation. By giving legislation definition they determine the true substantive content of the law. Yet the bureaucracy is not controlled within the framework of traditional constitutional limits. The balance of power between Congress and the President obscures lines of control over administrative agencies and leaves them free to go their own way, in combination with private interest groups that form the most important parts of their constituencies. The delegation of substantial legislative authority to administrative agencies is one of the most critical problems of our political system.

How can administrative agencies be kept accountable within the framework of our constitutional government? Traditional approaches to the problem of administrative accountability include giving Congress more authority over the agencies. An important first step in this process would be to force Congress to define its laws more fully so that administrative agencies would not have such wide latitude in filling in the details of legislation. As long as the primary legislative authority resides in Congress, constitutional conditions are met and administrative agencies are acting only as agents of the legislative branch.

In reality, the nature of the political process, and the tremendous scope of governmental activity, necessitates broad Congressional delegation of authority. Politically, Congressmen often find it in their interests to remain ambiguous on touchy issues of public policy. They can accomplish this by passing on the burden of reconciling divergent political demands to administrative agencies that they create to act for them. It is the tendency of Congress to enact statutes mandating administrative agencies to adhere to the "public interest" in policy making and adjudication of disputes. No one can disagree with the principle of "the public interest," but it is very difficult to define, which means that the agencies are the ones that have to make the concrete decisions that will raise the ire of those who do not feel they are being treated fairly. In the final analysis a broad delegation of power to the administrative branch is inevitable, and all that Congress can do is to oversee sporadically the activities of the bureaucracy.

Another proposed solution to the dilemma of administrative power is to make the bureaucracy accountable to the President. In this way the fourth branch of the government will merge into a constitutionally legitimate branch, the Presidency. Administrative accountability will then be to the President, and he will be responsible for the activities of the administrative agencies. However, the scope of the administrative branch precludes total Presidential domination. Moreover, the jealousy between Congress and the President often prevents the legislature from authorizing Presidential supervision over administrative agencies. Realistically, Presidential domination of the bureaucracy is only a partial solution to the problem of administrative discretion.

Finally, constitutional legitimacy can be partially obtained by making the bureaucracy accountable to the judiciary for its quasijudicial decisions. The bureaucracy is deeply involved in settling cases and controversies arising within its jurisdiction, and this means that it is exercising judicial functions outside of the traditional arena of the courts. Judicial review of agency action is possible within limits, but most administrative decisions of a judicial nature are informal in character and not subject to review by courts. Even where cases are appropriate for judicial review, going to court is a time consuming and an expensive process not readily available to most citizens. Judicial review, then, like other suggestions for curtailing administrative discretion, is only a partial solution.

The great constitutional dilemmas of our system arise out of the emphasis of the Constitution itself upon the need to limit the power of government. But government must also be capable of taking positive action; otherwise it will not be able to meet the requirements of the community, particularly at this time when there are so many urgent problems pressing for solution. It is necessary to balance the desirability of limiting governmental power with the necessity for creating a government that is capable of taking effective action.

Ideal democratic theory suggests that government should reflect the will of the people, as expressed through a representative legislature and executive. Adherents to the democratic process have an underlying faith in the will of the people, and in government as long as it reflects that will. But translating popular feeling into governmental action is not nearly as simple as is commonly assumed. The mass of people often do not have any particular feelings about public policies and are disinterested in involving themselves in the political process unless they can perceive a direct connection between politics and their individual lives. Political apathy is an inevitable ingredient of all political systems. And some would argue that it is not always undesirable, especially if it is a reflection of satisfaction with the policy outputs of the system. A totally activated electorate places stress upon the system because of a high level of expectations concerning what government should be doing. If government cannot meet these expectations a lack of support for the system develops that ultimately can produce a breakdown. There is little doubt that political activism is becoming far more common today than in the past, because of higher levels of education, economic status, and the pervasiveness of the mass media, which tends to agitate people about political issues.

There is little doubt that the "will of the people" is shaped in the political realm primarily through intermediaries between the government and the people. The elites of government, political parties, and interest groups shape the political information that reaches the community. The scope and quality of public debate about issues of government policy is largely dependent upon these elites. The public cannot be expected to vote intelligently in Presidential election campaigns unless the candidates themselves have a respect for the people and raise issues that are relevant to the concerns of the community. The leaders of political parties have a key role to play in this area, for it is through them that issues are developed and debated initially before they are finally presented to the public at large.

The tendency at all levels of government has been for candidates and party organizations to engage in deceptive and nonissue-oriented tactics to garner votes. The quality of public debate often degenerates into meaningless carping about political personalities, rather than about the way in which candidates might deal with important issues once they are elected. This causes a great deal of disillusionment among large segments of the public, who are not fooled by the political game but who nevertheless are often confused because they are unable to sort out what is going on. This increases their cynicism about the nature of government, and reinforces the age-old belief in American folklore that "politics is dirty business." In the past, when the functions of government were far less ubiquitous then they are today, people were willing to tolerate something below excellence and honesty in government, just as they tolerated it in the private sector. As society has become more interdependent, and the responsibilities of government have assumed major significance, ineptitude in government has a profound and highly visible adverse impact upon the community as a whole. Unless political institutions can positively respond to popular demands for capable government action, people withdraw their support and the entire system is placed in jeopardy.

Perhaps the most important set of intermediaries between people and government are interest group leaders. One of the oldest and most original theories in our political heritage is the "theory of concurrent majority." This was devised by John C. Calhoun several decades before the Civil War and was published in 1854 in his famous book entitled *A Disquisition On Government.* Although full of ambiguities, inconsistencies, and a lack of logic, Calhoun's thesis basically is that the only way in which arbitrary government can be prevented is to give to the major interests in society a veto power over legislation enacted by government which affects the spheres in which they operate. The premise of Calhoun's theory is that individual political interests are fully subsumed within the framework of interest groups. He suggested that individuals naturally either join or are represented by interest groups, because they cannot exist alone in society.

To Calhoun, then, the democratic process is not one in which individuals exercise independent judgment and select representatives to do their will in government. Rather, the governmental process is a group process in which all of the interests of individuals are represented by interest groups. Public policy should be a reflection of the compromises worked out among interest groups and each interest group should have a veto over policy affecting it.

Calhoun's theory became the basis of democratic group theory, which is widely accepted by political scientists as a proper and realistic description of the way in which the political process operates. Group theorists believe that society is naturally "pluralistic"—composed of many groups that together reflect the "will of the people." The democratic process is a group process in which public policy outputs of government are primarily a reflection of the interaction of interest groups. The economic theory of capitalism posits that individual pursuit of self-interest naturally produces "the public interest" in the economic sphere. Similarly, interest group theorists suggest that the free operation of interest groups is not only a natural phenomenon, it is desirable and produces the only "public interest" capable of being defined within a democratic political system. The public interest cannot be separated from the interests of groups within society, whether these groups be organized or simply "potential" interest groups that will surface and become organized if their interests are not adequately taken into account by government.

Capitalistic theory has been modified to recognize the fact that in order for the nation to survive there must be some broader public interest that will from time to time take precedence over the interests of private firms. For example, if capitalism were not regulated in any way, it would be only natural for each firm to pollute the waters and the atmosphere in order to dispose of waste products and increase profits. The pursuit of self-interest in such cases is clearly not in the public interest. Government must step in to reflect the interests of a broad segment of society and regulate the firms involved in order to bring about environmental pollution controls.

Just as unbridled capitalism is not desirable, uncontrolled operation of interest groups within the political sphere clearly is not always in the public interest. A perfect example of excessive interest group power can be observed in the "military-industrial complex," where the armaments industry, in conjunction with the Defense Department and key Congressional committees, has succeeded in sustaining a war machine of staggering proportions. This situation has not only drained our economy, but has created a threat to the stability of the nation and the world. Is it possible to define a "public interest" in the military security field beyond that which is produced by the military-industrial complex? This is a major question of democratic theory today, and one that has not adequately been solved.

It is the primary hope of the authors of this book to introduce students to the realities of the political process, which include not only the formal institutions of the government, but also the myriad informal forces that tend to determine who gets what, when, and how. Students should do their utmost to shun simple solutions to what are in fact very complex problems. There are no easy answers to the dilemmas that have arisen in our society. Constitutional and democratic theory, the foundation of our political system, must be understood, analyzed, and adapted to the changing needs of the community. The future success of our political system depends upon a truly enlightened citizenry, one that not only understands the nature of the political process but also takes a pragmatic and constructive view toward it. It is neither trite nor meaningless to say that change can and must take place within the framework of the system. This means that those seeking change must locate the avenues of power and gain influence within the system. It is hoped that this book will make a small contribution to the achievement of this goal.

One of the major problems facing our nation—and in fact, the entire world—is the poisoning of our atmosphere and environment by pollution of both air and water. How can we solve this dilemma that man has created for himself? Should we rely on a humanitarian private company or research foundation to develop methods and devices that will clean the air and water for us? Or should we demand that the government establish regulatory measures that will force industrial plants, private automobiles, and public utilities to stop contaminating us and our environment?

If the latter method seems to be a more reliable means of obtaining results, how can we make our demands known to the legislators who can devise the effective means of solving the problem? What public officials and institutions, private citizens and organizations will react to the threat of pollution so that pressures will be placed on legislators to act? What forces, philosophies, and behaviors will come into play behind the scenes in the evolvement of our demands into a beneficial policy? These demands, pressures, and forces make up the essence of politics.

The special interests and aspirations of private citizens and their public representatives are not spelled out in constitutions or in lawbooks. And yet, these basic elements of human behavior play a large role in determining what is achieved by democratic government. They explain why some appeals are made into laws and others are not; why certain governmental regulations are vigorously enforced at some times and almost totally ignored at others; why a President, governor, or mayor may make a decision that either goes against or coincides with the will of the people.

These unofficial events and considerations underlie the official actions of government. No government can be understood without an examination of the political forces that shape its operation. Therefore, American government should be examined as a political system. That is, its study should focus, not on a series of abstract laws and gray, granite buildings, but on the colorful, true-to-life panorama of struggle, compromise, and agreement that is the basis for all human behavior.

UNIT ONE
Government and Political Systems

CHAPTER 1

The Nature of Political Systems

Pick up the daily newspaper any morning, or tune in the news on your radio or TV any evening. What do you hear? "The President has called a press conference to explain the new tax-reform measure." "A new ambassador has been selected to represent the United States in Iran." "The state is asking for bids on the construction of a new highway intersection." "The election of the Board of Education will be held." All of these news items are really reports on the governmental process in action. How do these things happen? Who decides when and where they will happen? What procedures are involved? These are some of the questions the study of government should answer.

Government and the Forces Behind It

Throughout history, men have tried to understand why governments are established. From the time of Plato in the fifth century B.C. to the present, political philosophers have disagreed on how civil societies originate and function. So far, complete agreement has eluded them. Most philosophers, however, have been able to accept two basic reasons for setting up government.

The need for government. First, political philosophers agree that government is based on man's need for collective or group action to accomplish those things which one man could not accomplish alone. This basic need is illustrated by the Aztecs in Mexico, who built a magnificent city, Tenochtitlán, on a high plateau in the middle of their empire. Archeologists have found the remains of pyramids, floating gardens, and systems of irrigation, all of which attest to a high level of civilization. The Aztecs could not have accomplished these feats without a means of organizing laborers to construct the pyramids, without a military system to conquer slaves and defend the city, and without a method of group-

What does the small personal government that has been developed on a desert island have in common with the large complex governments that have evolved in most of the major nations of the world?

ing people to build irrigation dams and to farm. Such organization of laborers, soldiers, and farmers required some efficient collective action by a government.

The second point on which political thinkers agree is that government is needed to set standards by which members of a society must live. Certainly this job is complicated when different religious, language, and racial groups live under the same government. Each group will have its own values to be taken into consideration. Disputes and differences, which arise when these values conflict, must also be settled by government. On another plane, governments themselves must also agree to certain rules of conduct and settle disputes which arise between them. When one nation shoots at another's fishing boats because it feels they are encroaching on national waters, the dispute should be settled by the two nations themselves, or by an international organization. Otherwise, the two nations might resort to war.

Government, then, is established by men to organize themselves for accomplishing those things that would otherwise be unachievable. It is also the instrument by which men within a society can establish standards so that the various elements will be regulated by the same general rules. Constitutions and laws, regulations and procedures, offices and institutions, and the official actions of government are all part of the formal process by which this instrument accomplishes the goals of a society.

Informal forces. The purposes for which a government establishes its authority and the scope of that authority are determined by political behavior. People react to situations and problems in various ways, because they have different motives for doing things and many varied interests and concerns. They also have different standards on which they base their lives. Some people are religious, some scorn material things, and some place high value on social position. These are all personal factors that influence people when they ask the government to do something for them or when they select representatives to act for them. These representatives, too—whether they be mayors, governors, congressmen, or the President—are subject to the same personal factors as the rest of the people.

It is these *informal forces* of politics which activate, restrain, and reshape the government and its authority. Indeed, the informal forces frequently have more to do with the nature and impact of government than the formal attributes. Therefore, these informal forces should be examined carefully, along with the formal structure of government.

■ *Unequal representation in elections.* The importance of informal forces can be seen in the difficulties that will arise when a government attempts to set up a *formal mechanism* guaranteeing each citizen equal representation. Such a mechanism is important to a *democracy* such as ours, where the authority to govern, or *sovereignty,* is shared equally, in principle, by all of the people. If this theory were carried out to the letter in the United States, it would mean that 200 million people would decide just how the government should act in every instance. To make government a practical operation in this country and still enable the people to retain ultimate authority, a mechanism of representation has been devised by which the people delegate their authority to a few men.

Consider a simple example of such a formal mechanism, a popular election for instance, in which all the citizens of a community select a single chief executive invested with all the powers to run the community's government. If each citizen has the same opportunity to participate in the election, equal representation has been accomplished. All the citizens have had the same chance to determine who will exercise the government's powers on their behalf.

The informal forces that play on a voter as well as on a candidate will almost immediately confront this simple mechanism and could cause it to break down. Because of his own personal mo-

Drawing by D. Fradon; © 1968 The New Yorker Magazine, Inc.

"How many times have you asked yourself, 'What can I, as a single person, possibly do to help shape the destiny of mankind?' Well, I'll tell you what you can do. You can vote for me."

(Each person's wishes, wants, and needs should be the principal concern of his elected representative.)

tives, each person is going to want different criteria for setting up the election procedure. Are all the people to have a voice in the selection of candidates? If so, is it not possible then, that there will be too many candidates? Perhaps one for each group of citizens? In an extreme case each citizen might even select himself. If there is to be a nominating committee to select candidates, then what are the qualifications for such special members of the community? Are all citizens to vote, regardless of age?

■ *Unequal influence on governmental decisions.* To carry the example a step further, once a candidate has been elected and is in office, what guarantee is there that he will do what the people expect of him? And when he has decided what to do, how will he carry out his decision?

It should be clear to everyone, from the items in the news or from personal experience, that the citizens of a community (local or nationwide) do not all participate in the decision-making process of government. There are few formal arrangements in our country, or anywhere in the world, for the direct participation of the people in making or applying governmental decisions. The candidate for a position in the government usually makes many vague promises, and some specific ones, as to decisions he will make if elected. But commitments made in the heat of an election campaign are rarely fulfilled and are soon forgotten by most voters; in any event, they are certainly not binding.

The participation of citizens in governmental decisions is apt to be haphazard, unpredictable, and unregulated. Some people are invited by government officials to participate in policy deliberations. Others seek to inject themselves into the governmental process and do influence the decisions of legislators and admin-

istrators. Still others, the vast majority of citizens, do not participate at all and, in many cases, they do not even want to.

□ *Expert citizen participation.* In 1966, the United States Senate Subcommittee on Executive Reorganization held many hearings on the problems of America's urban areas. A few private citizens were invited to these hearings to give their opinions on what government should do. Most of these people were invited because they were regarded as experts on the subject by the members of the subcommittee. No doubt, there were other citizens, equally knowledgeable on the subject, who were unknown to the subcommittee and thus not asked to participate. Still thousands of other citizens would have liked to express their own views if they had been asked. A great many others who knew about the hearings would not have had any views to express, even if they had been invited. Still countless others were unaware that the hearings were taking place.

Here is an example, then, in which the participation of citizens in the governmental decision-making process was unequal. The invited persons, because they were regarded as experts, were able to participate in policy deliberations and possibly to influence a major congressional decision. Yet, no one can claim that these were the best experts on urban problems; they merely happened to be known to those on the subcommittee.

□ *Organized citizen participation.* Another type of unequal representation takes place when private individuals or groups feel that their vital interests are affected by the government's action. Unlike the situation in which officials seek out the participation of citizens, these private citizens inject themselves into the process by trying to alter, block, or encourage official decisions.

The factors that determine what type of informal influence is needed to obtain a desired government action, of course, vary from one situation to the next.

Much of this activity is undertaken by organized groups representing economic, professional, social, and ideological interests. Labor unions, like the United Auto Workers (UAW), attempt to influence government decisions affecting wages, working conditions and hours, fringe benefits, strike regulations, collective-bargaining procedures, and other such matters which are of importance to them. While members of the UAW talk with congressmen, administrative officials, and White House aides, the Washington representatives of the auto manufacturers try to sway the same people with their own point of view.

Organizations that represent professional groups—the American Medical Association, the American Bar Association, the National Education Association, and others—also try to influence government decisions which may have an effect on the practice of their respective professions. One notable example has been the continuing interest of the American Medical Association (AMA) in the federal government's Medicare program. Under this program, established through legislation in 1965, many of the nation's older people are reimbursed by the government for a substantial portion of their medical expenses. Naturally, physicians would be vitally concerned about such a program, and the AMA was actively involved, on their behalf, in the deliberations and legislative debates that took place before Medicare's enactment.

Other organizations, working on behalf of social and ideological causes, are continually aware of governmental policy that might concern their members. The National Association for the Advancement of Colored People, the Congress of Racial Equality, the National Urban League, and other groups working to better the lot of black Americans, try to affect policy, too. The American Legion, the Daughters of the American Revolution, the Veterans of Foreign Wars, and other patriotic organizations become active when they feel, for one reason or another, that fundamental American values and ideals are being threatened. Because of its concern over the methods of some laboratories, the Society for Prevention of Cruelty to Animals is asking, among other things, for legislation regulating the use of animals in scientific experiments. The Sierra Club, a group of conservationists, became involved in the mid-1960's when it was proposed that the federal government help finance a hydroelectric project in the Grand Canyon.

There are thousands of organized groups, representing almost every conceivable cause, interest, or concern, seeking to influence governmental policy. By gathering vocal and concerned people together, these organizations have a greater influence on policy than an equal number of unorganized individuals might have.

□ *Group versus individual influence.* Private individuals, of course, also attempt to influence governmental policy. But groups usually have far greater impact in shaping decisions, because they tend to possess more powerful resources for swaying government officials.

Imagine, for example, that in an election year, the Mayor is debating whether to submit a proposal for a skating rink to the Town Council. An organization with a membership of two thousand ice skaters is trying to encourage him, while a half-dozen individuals are opposed to the proposal. The Mayor may have one meeting with a single representative of the large organization, and he may have six separate meetings with the half-dozen individuals. For a number of reasons, the one meeting may have a far greater impact on the Mayor's thinking than the six separate ones, added together. The Mayor will realize, whether or not the organization's representative reminds him, that the group has two thousand potential votes for the next election. As the local leader of his political party and, possibly, as a candidate for reelection, he may consider the support of this group more important than that of the six individuals. Moreover, the Mayor can anticipate that the group might express appreciation for his favorable action by making a sizable contribution to his campaign fund. All of these factors could carry a great deal of weight when he makes his decision.

On the surface, it appears that such informal forces of influence help to preserve the government as a democratic instrument because more weight is given to the wishes of two thousand people than to the preferences of six individuals. The wish of the majority of concerned people has been served. The government is acting as a democratic instrument functioning in a truly representative fashion. Actually, the matter is not so simple.

Only a very small proportion of citizens are represented by organizations which express their views on any given issue. Few individuals spend much time wondering how governmental policies could, or do, affect them. Most of those who do think about these matters do not want to express themselves or do not know how to go about it. Consequently, a small minority of persons who do know how and who are organized to pressure officials has a far better chance of achieving its purposes through governmental processes. Such groups, which put pressure on public officials to make certain decisions, are re-

ferred to as "pressure groups" or "interest groups." The men who represent these pressure groups and who wait around in the lobbies and corridors of government buildings in Washington, or of state capitols, city halls, and county seats, are known as "lobbyists." Since lobbyists are well-organized and are constantly alert for opportunities to buttonhole government officials, they are more able to influence governmental decisions than the majority of citizens who are unorganized and do not express their views.

■ *Unequal applications of decisions.* Just as citizens are represented unequally in the formulation of policy, it is also true that policy, in turn, may be applied unequally to the citizens. Once again, the informal forces are working upon the structure of government.

Sometimes policy is applied unevenly because officials succumb to motives and pressures that may not coincide with those of the decision-makers. Consider the case of a man who has had too much to drink and is wandering the streets at 3:00 A.M., singing loudly. If the man is neatly dressed, a policeman will probably see that he gets home safely so he can "sleep it off." If instead, the man is unshaven and poorly dressed, he may very well be charged with disorderly conduct, escorted to the "cooler," and released the following morning after he has sobered up. In the second case, the policeman may assume from the man's appearance that he does not have a home. The policeman may make an overnight arrest in one case where he would not in the other. The two citizens may receive different treatment under the same law.

It is easy to see that many political arguments can result from the way that policy is applied by government officials. When the Federal Communications Commission (FCC), for example, refuses to renew a television station's license, the denied applicant may feel the Commission is prejudiced when it renews the licenses of other stations. The Supreme Court and other courts throughout the nation are constantly settling disputes that involve individual claims of inequitable actions taken by the government.

Although government policy is most frequently applied unevenly without any conscious or deliberate intent, at other times unequal treatment is actually sought and received by private citizens. Usually, these are attempts to have officials overlook the law. Everyone has heard of someone who had a traffic ticket "fixed." It may have been done by offering a bribe, by making a threat, by asking for a favor, or simply by drawing upon a personal friendship.

The use of influence to secure special application of the law is more apt to occur in local government, and it extends beyond traffic violations to violations of gambling, sanitation, building, and fire codes, and so on. This kind of activity flourishes because the vast majority of citizens are usually indifferent to or uninformed about these matters. When, however, an official has been too obvious in granting special favors, or in his relations with underworld characters, informed citizens who have been following the case through the news media (newspapers, magazines, radios, and television) can express their displeasure at the ballot box.

Because government is, in part, an instrument for setting standards that the community must follow, it is natural to expect that government officials will avoid occasions of fraud, bribery, and favoritism which result in the unequal application of laws. In general, the federal government has been less tainted in this regard than other government bodies. This may be due to the tradition of "fair play" that has been instilled over the

"I guess he must have a lot of political pull."

(If personal influence were allowed to be carried to extremes, such exaggerations might be more common.)

years within agencies of national government. But it may also be true because the federal government is more exposed to the spotlight of the nation's press. While local governments may be able to cover up suspicious situations, members of the federal government are less able to hide their dealings from the constant vigilance of the press.

In the late 1950's, it was suggested that Sherman Adams, President Eisenhower's Special Assistant, used his governmental influence on behalf of a New England industrialist who had given him some expensive gifts. There was never any evidence that Adams had done anything improper to favor the industrialist, but the matter remained in the press for many months and Adams retired from public life shortly thereafter. Obviously, the American people regard the national government with a special respect that makes wrong-doing, or suspicion of it, at the highest level of government intolerable.

While it is easy to understand that citizens may overlook the government's reluctance to enforce a law, it is less easy to comprehend why many citizens do not take advantage of their own privileges. This unconcern results in other unequal applications of governmental policy.

Those citizens who know about their rights usually acquire the benefits that are offered. Some know, for example, that certain expenses can be deducted from their income tax, that when apprehended by a policeman they have the right to a lawyer, or that they are eligible for social security when they retire, or workmen's compensation when they are disabled. Others do not know these things. They do not fully enjoy the benefits they are entitled to, simply because they have never been informed about these opportunities at all. Other citizens may be unable, owing to the lack of money or personal connections, to take advantage of their rights in the courts. The man who can afford a highly skilled lawyer has an advantage over the man who can not. Many people do not even vote and thus deprive themselves of any representation in the system.

Review questions

1. Governments have evolved because of people's needs. Why?
2. How do "expert citizen participation" and "organized citizen participation" influence government decision-making?
3. What effects do pressure groups have on the democratic process?

The Significance of Politics

So far, just a few of the informal forces of the governmental process have been examined, and these have been considered only superficially. They should make it clear, however, that even the most fundamental ideal of a democracy—equal representation in government for all citizens—can not be achieved by writing constitutions, establishing legislatures, or composing administrative regulations.

The study of government must include not only the formal governmental structures but also the broad range of human activities which affect the government and which are affected by it. The general name given to this broad range of human affairs is *politics*. The term is derived from the Greek word *polis,* meaning "city-state," which was a form of government in ancient Greece. The combined study of government and politics is called *political science,* and the scholars devoted to this study are known as *political scientists.*

From time to time, political scientists do broaden their sights and examine other elements in the society besides government, such as families, schools, business firms, and even sports organizations. They do this for two basic reasons. First, they want to know how these elements in the society relate to the government in general. Second, they hope to gain insights into the government itself by seeing how politics work within these smaller units.

Almost every group has an assortment of human contacts. Some people are leaders, some are followers; some are passive, and some are vocal. The reactions of these people to one another form the politics of the group. A study of the politics of the National Football League, for example, should reveal why certain cities have teams and others do not; or why a coach is fired in Cleveland, and another is hired in San Diego.

Basic concepts of political science. To make the study of politics easier to understand, political scientists have identified and defined certain concepts which are basic to most political activity. While these concepts are useful in the study of all politics, they are especially useful in the study of government.

■ *Authority.* One fundamental concept is that of *authority,* which is the legal or assumed right to give commands, enforce obedience, take action, and impose decisions. Sources of authority are found in most areas of human existence, but in each case, authority has definite limits beyond which it does not operate. A father, for example, may exercise authority in a family, but his authority will not extend beyond that family. A school principal has authority over the teachers and students in his school; and a teacher has authority over his students; but neither has authority over teachers or students in another school.

The study of politics, however, focuses on the sources, scope, and limitations of *governmental authority.* By determining what the authority within a government is, the operation of that government's structure can be understood. Therefore, political scientists concentrate on such questions as the following:

(1) Who has authority in the government and who does not?

(2) How do those in authority get and maintain their position?

(3) Who or what determines the limits of this authority?

(4) What effect does the use of this authority have on society?

Once these questions are answered, then another question can be asked:

(5) Does the government do what it was set up to do?

■ *Influence.* Another fundamental concept of political science is that of *influence.* Edward Banfield, in his book entitled *Political Influence,* defines influence as the "ability to get others to act, think, or feel as one intends." Political influence, then, is the ability to get governmental authority "to act . . . as one intends."

What is the difference between governmental authority and influence? Usually, governmental authority is based on such formal sources as constitutions, statutes, administrative regulations, and legal customs. Influence, on the other hand, comes from the informal forces of politics. It can be acquired through expert knowledge, superior physical force, wealth, friendships and obligations, and a variety of other sources.

Sometimes, it is difficult to separate governmental authority from influence, for governmental authority can be a source of influence, as well as the target of influence. If a person is in a position to exercise governmental authority, he is also in a position of political influence. The authority of the President of the United States, for instance, fortifies his role as the leader of his political party. Much of politics, then, consists of an interplay between authority and influence.

During this study, these basic concepts of authority and influence as well as the role of informal forces will be used to explain how the American government works. But a method or system for organizing the study of politics and government is still needed.

Review questions

1. Why is the concept of authority so important to the study of government?
2. Which is more important in the running of government—authority or influence? Why?

The Components of Systems

If you were asked to discuss the major features of the automobile, how would you approach your topic? First, you would decide which major feature you wanted to describe—the design, the mechanics, or the function. Suppose you wanted to analyze the mechanics of the automobile. Superficially, you might describe the parts that constitute the car's mechanics—its engine, crankshaft, and transmission. But a simple description of the automobile's mechanical parts does not explain what they do. For this, it is necessary to describe how the various pieces are connected together to form a *system* that makes the car go.

Mechanical and biological systems. The automobile, like any mechanical system, is designed to produce certain results. Every system includes *inputs* and *structures* which convert inputs to *outputs*. Once produced, the outputs have a *feedback* effect that alters the nature and flow of further inputs. In the automobile, an input—gasoline—is poured into a tank and then transmitted to a structure—the engine—where it is converted to an output—energy—that turns the wheels. As the car moves, gasoline is burned. This is one feedback effect, or reaction to the pro-

duction of energy. In this case, more input, gasoline, is needed to keep the system running. Any reaction by the parts of the system to the output is *feedback*. Another feedback effect is wear and tear on various parts of the car which require replacement.

Another type of system is a biological one. The human organism, for example, consumes inputs of food and air which are converted, through the biological structure of the body, to energy output. The use of energy requires additional food, a feedback effect.

Social systems. Social systems, which include political systems, can be analyzed much like mechanical and biological systems. The major features of social systems, though, are composed not of parts but of people who play input, conversion, and output roles.

The family is a simple type of social system in which parents and children interact within the framework of a definite structure. Children make certain *demands* on parents. These demands are converted by the parental structure through certain accepted procedures, rules, and compromises. Each demand is an input filtered through the family structure to produce an output such as an allowance, rights

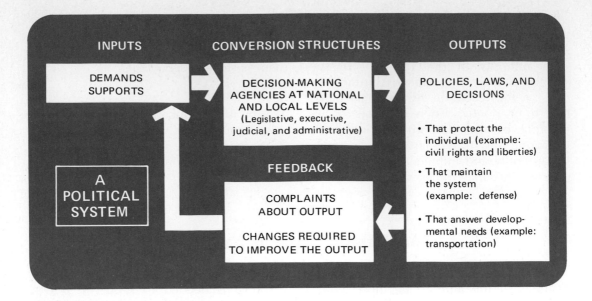

INPUTS	CONVERSION STRUCTURES	OUTPUTS

INPUTS

DEMANDS
SUPPORTS

CONVERSION STRUCTURES

DECISION-MAKING
AGENCIES AT NATIONAL
AND LOCAL LEVELS
(Legislative, executive,
judicial, and administrative)

OUTPUTS

POLICIES, LAWS, AND
DECISIONS

- That protect the
  individual (example:
  civil rights and liberties)

- That maintain
  the system
  (example: defense)

- That answer develop-
  mental needs (example:
  transportation)

A POLITICAL SYSTEM

FEEDBACK

COMPLAINTS
ABOUT OUTPUT

CHANGES REQUIRED
TO IMPROVE THE OUTPUT

to the family car, dating privileges, and use of the television. All of these outputs will produce feedback. And feedback will consist of two kinds. If the children accept the amount of allowance, they *support* the decision. Then no more demands will be made. As soon as a change is thought by the children to be required in the allowance, the feedback effect is one of new demands.

Other social systems, such as clubs, labor unions, and farm cooperatives function in a similar way. In all social systems, certain procedures exist for transforming various demands into results.

Social as well as mechanical and biological systems are composed of *inputs, conversion structures,* and *outputs.* Any change, or alteration, in the character or flow of any one of these three main features will result in a change in the whole system. But, unlike mechanical and biological systems, social systems can adapt themselves to radical alterations in the nature and extent of inputs. The structure of an automobile could not convert inputs of water to energy. Social

systems, however, are more flexible and constantly maintain their power to function by adapting to new demands.

Another curious factor of social systems is that individuals can switch from one social system to another. When a judge takes off his judicial robes and goes home for dinner, he is leaving the judicial system and entering the family system. When a housewife votes, or attends political meetings, she leaves the family system and enters the political system. Each person, then, functions within several social systems, and he affects the inputs and is affected by the outputs of each system.

The unique make-up of political systems. A political system is composed of the same elements as other social systems. It converts demands or inputs of its members through the governmental structure to various actions and policies, or outputs. In the United States, people ask for things through representatives or organizations, or express their opinions in actions. These are demands. The Presidency, Congress, the courts, state legislatures, and city councils are the conversion structures. And the policies, laws, and regulations adopted by the government, are the outputs. Feedback consists of the reaction to these outputs in the form of new demands and supports. As in all social systems, supports, or acceptance, of specific outputs and for the rules of the system are important inputs. Creation of new demands, as well as supports, through feedback completes the system's cycle.

Political systems, however, are unlike other social systems in one important aspect. They have greater power to impose their decisions on all members of the community. A government can expect its authority and policies to be respected and obeyed because it can enforce its decisions by means of a police force, a court system, or the regulations of an administrative agency. A private organization can not enforce its policies to the extent that a government can.

■ *Boundaries of a political system.* While the impact of authority in a political system is stronger than that of other social systems, it does have its limitations. A political system, for example, can not legally impose its authority on the members of other political systems. Within the political system itself, there may be definite areas of activity—social, economic, religious, family, and so forth—into which its authority does not extend.

The boundaries of political systems are not rigidly fixed. Because people and their demands and attitudes are continually fluctuating, the boundaries of a political system should reflect the flux that occurs in the whole community. During the past

"THE MAN TO HEAD THE LINE"

Carmack

(This cartoon, drawn during Harry Truman's Presidency, shows the extent of demands in the presidential subsystem.)

few decades, for example, the federal government in the United States has played an increasingly important role in the nation's economic life. As demands for more welfare programs and other regulations affecting business and labor matters have multiplied, the government has found it necessary to become more involved. This increase in government activity, in turn, has expanded the boundaries of the national political system. During wartime, in particular, the national government usually enters many fields and takes on a variety of tasks that return to private hands when hostilities end.

■ *Roles in the political system.* Every individual and group within a system performs *roles,* or functions. These roles are private when they are related to the family, a religion, and other non-political systems. They are political when they involve the individual or group in making demands on the formal structure of government, or in supporting the government by paying taxes or voting. A man has a political role, an economic role, or a family role, depending on what he is doing at a specific moment.

Just as there are many different roles in society, there are several types of political roles within a political system. A person can make demands. He can be employed by the government and therefore be a part of the conversion structure. And he can belong to an agency which administers policy; thus he is involved in output. It is also possible for an individual to perform more than one of these roles. The President of the United States, for example, receives demands and acts as a conversion structure. He is also a source of demands when he tries to influence other sectors of the governmental structure, such as Congress. Other government sectors, in turn, are going to make demands on him.

The legislative and the administrative branches of government also play dual roles. They act as conversion structures when they convert demands into laws and policies; at the same time, each is a source of demands on other government branches. The judicial branch is an exception. It is barred from the role of initiating demands. The Constitution requires that it can become involved only in cases or controversies that are brought before it.

Review questions

1. What are the common characteristics shared by mechanical, biological, and social systems? How do these systems differ?
2. When do the boundaries of a political system change?

Characteristics of a Political System

Included in the basic components of the political system of inputs, conversion structures, outputs, and feedback, there are certain fundamental characteristics that must be considered by the political scientist. These characteristics contribute to the way that the various pieces of the system work with and against each other.

The channels of demands. In all political systems, demands are made on the government. Although the sources of demands will vary from one system to another, similarities exist among the types of demands made. People in a non-democratic state desire the same things as those in a democratic state—housing, medical care, good working conditions, and so forth—but they will go about getting them in a different way.

Consider a democratic political system, such as the American, where people are allowed to join together to obtain their desires. Interest groups have been organized to represent the special concerns of many segments—labor, business, or professional—of the community. Each of these groups forms a source of demands on government. Political parties provide another vital source of demands within the American political system. If a party is to capture and retain political office, it must agree to champion the broad interests of the voters. The individual citizen acting alone, however, is somewhat ineffective in making his demands. To be effective, he must channel his demands through a political party or another interest group.

In a nondemocratic system, the private citizen is even less effective in making his demands felt. Private interest groups do not exist to the extent allowed in a democracy or may not exist at all. There is usually no more than one political party, and the party and the government tend to be inseparable. Both are relatively unresponsive to the demands originating outside them.

Flexibility in the conversion structure. All political systems must be able to adjust to constant changes. This requirement for adaptability must be considered when the formal structures of government are established. If it is not, the system will fail.

One of the major advantages of a democratic system is that it can readily adjust to political change. Each part of the system is flexible enough to reflect new developments. In the United States, new political demands can be expressed through elections, constitutional amend-ments, and judicial interpretations of the Constitution. The reorganization of a government's formal structures, other than a change in administration, is a more radical means of responding to political demands. An example of this occurs when a city replaces a mayor with a council-manager system.

When, in the early days of the American Republic, liberal interpretations of the Constitution won out over strict interpretations, it was a victory for flexibility in the political system. On the other hand, the Civil War represented a total breakdown in the flexibility of the political system. At that time, part of the system was unwilling to adapt to changing conditions. The system itself could not reconcile the sharply opposing demands that were being made on it.

The ability to adjust to change determines whether a political system can maintain itself and continue to exist. The system is maintained by adjusting to internal conflicts and by meeting external threats. Effective domestic and foreign policy outputs that are geared to maintaining the system, such as increased voting rights and peaceful international relations, then, are keystones in the preservation of any political system.

Ideology. The maintenance of a political system relies largely on the attitudes of the citizens. Do they want to keep it as it is, or do they want it changed? Every political system is based on certain ideas, or concepts, about how government should function in relation to society. If the system is to survive, then the citizens must accept the system's basic values; otherwise, they will ignore them and finally destroy the system.

These values are often grouped into a set of doctrines, or an *ideology* such as democracy, communism, or fascism. These ideologies are founded on such broad philosophical concepts that they are easily adapted to the needs of various nations. For example, the democratic ideology is a basis for government in both Great Britain and the United States. Each of these countries adds a dimension to the ideology developed from its own history and unique circumstances. Thus, the head of government in Great Britain is a prime minister who is the leader of the majority party in Parliament and is designated by the monarch to form a cabinet. In the United States, the head of government is a president, chosen and elected by the people. Yet both countries do accept the broad dogmatic principles of popular sovereignty and participation in government.

Communism, as an ideology, has been accepted by both the Soviet Union and the People's Republic of China; but the ideology practiced in the Soviet Union is vastly different from that in China. This is because each country adds its particular nationalistic elements to the ideology. Similarly, before World War II, fascism in Germany differed considerably from that in Italy.

Importance of political socialization. In order for a political system to be preserved, its ideology must be passed on to and accepted by younger generations and new citizens. The process of passing on political values is called *political socialization.* This is ordinarily accomplished through education, through exposure to community problems by mass media, or just through involvement in the community. The aim is to enable young adults and new citizens to become responsive to and appreciative of the common needs of the political community. Successful political socialization convinces the new entrants that the political ideology is worth preserving and, thus, encourages them to support the rules of the system and the system itself.

In the United States, such socialization has been difficult because of the large numbers of immigrants who have had to adjust to their adopted system after having been schooled in other systems. Political ideas and theories of all kinds have been imported by the immigrants and have been absorbed into a system based on Anglo-American concepts of democracy. This process of absorption, or *assimilation,* has strengthened some of the system's original values. It has, in particular, emphasized the political equality of all citizens.

Another difficulty in political socialization arises when citizens come into conflict over different interpretations of the system's basic values. In the United States everyone accepts "democracy," a "government of law and not of man," equal rights, federalism, and so forth. But since these concepts do not mean the same thing to everyone, sharp political disagreements often arise.

Still, strict political conformity should not be one of the goals of political socialization. Instead, healthy argumentation exposing the conflicts that exist in a democratic system should be the goal of a successful socializing process. When the Supreme Court overrules an act of Congress, when the President and Congress disagree over policy, and when the various agencies take opposing sides to enforce a policy, the system is merely displaying its ability to allow contrasting views within the structure. At the same time, while general acceptance of some political values binds the political community together, if there is too much disagreement the system will break down. For the system to work well therefore, some effort must be made to restrict the inevitable tendency toward fragmentation that results if too much emphasis is placed on specific roles. A successful system is delicately balanced. The judge needs the congressman, and both need the President, even if all three disagree.

Subsystems. Political systems are made up of many *subsystems,* each of which has *specialized* demands and supports, governing structures, and outputs. A political subsystem gets its demands and supports from a narrower group of interests than the total system does. Whenever demands are acted on by a conversion structure and outputs result, one of the political subsystems has been in operation. Political subsystems may be classified according to the category of demands—such as agricultural or urban—that they satisfy, or by the conversion structure that demands are being made on.

When groups of farmers make demands on the President, on their congressional representatives, or on any administrative

SUBSYSTEMS OF THE NATIONAL GOVERNMENT

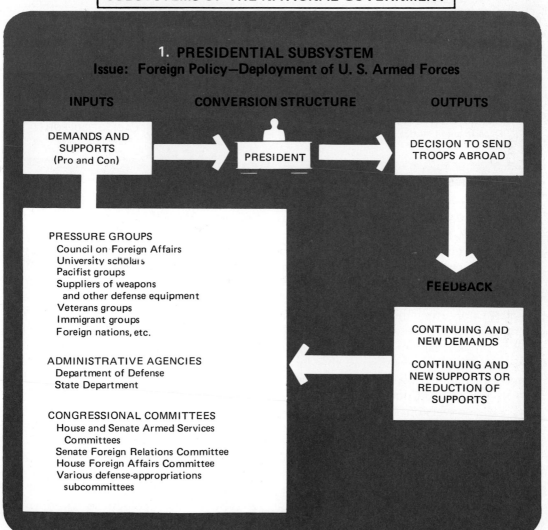

1. PRESIDENTIAL SUBSYSTEM
Issue: Foreign Policy—Deployment of U. S. Armed Forces

INPUTS   CONVERSION STRUCTURE   OUTPUTS

DEMANDS AND SUPPORTS (Pro and Con) → PRESIDENT → DECISION TO SEND TROOPS ABROAD

FEEDBACK

CONTINUING AND NEW DEMANDS

CONTINUING AND NEW SUPPORTS OR REDUCTION OF SUPPORTS

PRESSURE GROUPS
Council on Foreign Affairs
University scholars
Pacifist groups
Suppliers of weapons
  and other defense equipment
Veterans groups
Immigrant groups
Foreign nations, etc.

ADMINISTRATIVE AGENCIES
Department of Defense
State Department

CONGRESSIONAL COMMITTEES
House and Senate Armed Services
  Committees
Senate Foreign Relations Committee
House Foreign Affairs Committee
Various defense-appropriations
  subcommittees

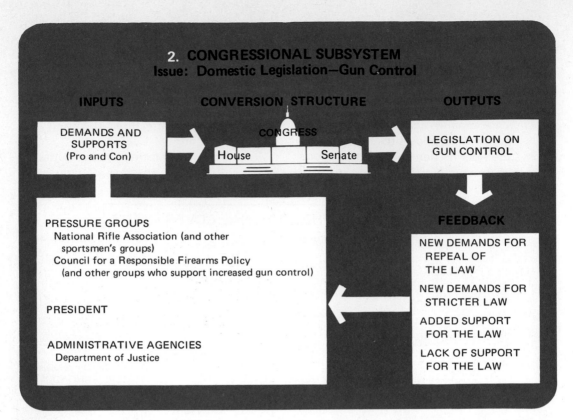

2. CONGRESSIONAL SUBSYSTEM
Issue: Domestic Legislation—Gun Control

INPUTS

CONVERSION STRUCTURE

OUTPUTS

DEMANDS AND
SUPPORTS
(Pro and Con)

CONGRESS

House   Senate

LEGISLATION ON
GUN CONTROL

FEEDBACK

PRESSURE GROUPS
  National Rifle Association (and other
    sportsmen's groups)
  Council for a Responsible Firearms Policy
  (and other groups who support increased gun control)

PRESIDENT

ADMINISTRATIVE AGENCIES
  Department of Justice

NEW DEMANDS FOR
REPEAL OF
THE LAW

NEW DEMANDS FOR
STRICTER LAW

ADDED SUPPORT
FOR THE LAW

LACK OF SUPPORT
FOR THE LAW

agency, they are acting within an agricultural subsystem on the national level. In this example, the President, the congressional representative, or the administrative agency is acting as a conversion structure. On a broader range, if a great number of citizens make a demand on the President alone, then they become a source of inputs for the presidential subsystem.

In a similar manner, Congress and the Supreme Court also serve as the focal points of separate subsystems. Thus, whenever the Supreme Court or the Congress acts as a conversion structure and converts a demand into a policy, either as legislation or as a judicial decision, it is acting within the political subsystem concerned with that demand.

On the state level, citizens have numerous roles in subsystems similar to those on the national level. As members of local communities, they are part of dozens of other political subsystems. They make demands on the governor, on the state legislature, on county, city, town, borough, and village governments, asking whichever conversion structure is appropriate to make policy to solve special problems.

A school system is a good example of a subsystem within a political system. It is bounded geographically by the borders of the township, city, or district. Politically, it is bounded by the demands placed on it, and the nature of its outputs—in this case "education."

Review questions

1. What are the most important sources of demands and supports in the American political system?
2. Why is an ideology so vital to the maintenance of any political system?

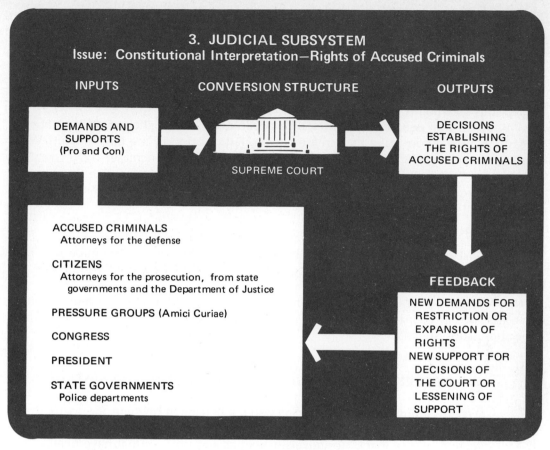

3. JUDICIAL SUBSYSTEM
Issue: Constitutional Interpretation—Rights of Accused Criminals

INPUTS   CONVERSION STRUCTURE   OUTPUTS

DEMANDS AND SUPPORTS (Pro and Con)

SUPREME COURT

DECISIONS ESTABLISHING THE RIGHTS OF ACCUSED CRIMINALS

ACCUSED CRIMINALS
Attorneys for the defense

CITIZENS
Attorneys for the prosecution, from state governments and the Department of Justice

PRESSURE GROUPS (Amici Curiae)

CONGRESS

PRESIDENT

STATE GOVERNMENTS
Police departments

FEEDBACK

NEW DEMANDS FOR RESTRICTION OR EXPANSION OF RIGHTS
NEW SUPPORT FOR DECISIONS OF THE COURT OR LESSENING OF SUPPORT

Chapter Review

Terms you should know

authority	ideology	political science
conversion structures	influence	political socialization
demands	informal forces	sovereignty
democracy	inputs	subsystem
feedback	interest group	supports
government	outputs	

Questions about the chapter

1. Are interest groups and pressure groups compatible with the basic premises of a democratic government? What arguments would you give for or against the continuation of such groups?
2. Identify some social systems. Describe their input, conversion, and output functions.
3. If you wanted to influence government decision-making, how would you do it?
4. Why is the private citizen less effective than a pressure group in making demands felt by the government?

5. Why is the process of political socialization vital to a society? How successful has the American political system been in socializing its citizens?

Thought and discussion questions

1. It has been stated by various groups in America that the present political structure is not capable of adjusting to the demands being made on it today. Do you agree with this viewpoint?

2. Why do so few people in America take advantage of the right to vote? What suggestions would you make to increase citizen participation in the government? What consequences might occur if citizen participation does not increase?

3. What are the weaknesses of a democratic system? Would you imagine that passage of a bill would take longer in a democracy or in a communist regime? Give reasons for your answer.

Class projects

1. Make a list of the organized groups in your community. Try to determine which of these groups is most likely to be successful in getting its viewpoint adopted by the local government.

2. The American political system is composed of many political subsystems. Identify at least five in your local area. What roles do your parents or people you know play in these subsystems?

Case Study: The university as an example of a system

Universities and colleges are social systems that have become the focus of attention throughout the country. Widespread campus protest is a reflection of "feedback" to university actions and policies that have been unable to meet the expectations and aspirations of a growing number of students. Universities, as part of the larger community, have also borne the brunt of discontent that students have felt regarding the policy outputs of the political system in general. University administrators have been placed in an extraordinarily difficult position because they are not fully in control of those matters that have resulted in campus protest and violence. Responses of the governing bodies of universities cannot fully deal with all of the dissatisfactions expressed by students. Within universities important decisions require a broad consensus of such groups as faculty, trustees, and students. Even if administrators succeed in reaching an internal consensus, their jurisdiction does not extend beyond the boundries of the university community to enable them to deal with external causes of discontent. For example, it is well recognized that the Vietnam war is a major cause of student protest, but this is not something that university leaders can deal with directly. But, students feel that university authorities are often implicated because they are a part of a broader "establishment" that has not raised its voice against the actions of the government. One example of student protest occurred in Berkeley, California, in the latter 1960s, which seriously threatened the foundations of the university system as well as the broader community surrounding it.

As you read this case study, consider the following:

1. Why is it necessary to understand the make-up of a community before analyzing its problems?
2. As a result of the People's Park crisis, did university leaders become more responsive to the university community?
3. How did administrators and faculty attempt to handle the disturbances described by the authors?
4. Identify the major inputs of the university community as revealed by this case study, as well as the conversion structures, and the outputs. What was the nature of the feedback?

Berkeley: The Battle of People's Park
SHELDON WOLIN—JOHN SCHAAR

Shortly before 5:00 A.M., on Thursday, May 16 [1969], a motley group of about fifty hippies and "street-people" were huddled together on a lot 270 by 450 feet in Berkeley. The lot was owned by the Regents of the University of California and located a few blocks south of the Berkeley campus. Since mid-April this lot had been taken over and transformed into a "People's Park" by scores of people, most of whom had no connection with the university. Now the university was determined to reassert its legal rights of ownership. A police officer approached the group and announced that it must leave or face charges of trespassing. Except for three persons, the group left and the area was immediately occupied and surrounded by about 200 police from Berkeley, Alameda county, and the campus. The police were equipped with flak jackets, tear gas launchers, shotguns, and telescopic rifles. At 6:00 A.M. a construction crew arrived and by mid-afternoon an eight-foot steel fence encircled the lot.

At noon a rally was convened on campus and about 3,000 people gathered. The president-elect of the student body spoke. He started to suggest various courses of action that might be considered. The crowd responded to the first of these by spontaneously marching toward the lot guarded by the police. (For this speech, the speaker was charged a few days later with violating numerous campus rules, and, on the initiative of University officials, indicted for incitement to riot.) The crowd was blocked by a drawn police line. Rocks and bottles were thrown at the police, and the police loosed a tear gas barrage, scattering the crowd. Elsewhere, a car belonging to the city was burned. Meanwhile, police reinforcements poured in, soon reaching around 600. A rock was thrown from a roof-top and, without warning, police fired into a group on the roof of an adjacent building. Two persons were struck in the face by the police fire, another was blinded, probably permanently, and a fourth, twenty-five-year-old James Rector, later died. Before the day was over, at least thirty others were wounded by police gunfire, and many more by clubs. One policeman received a minor stab wound and six more were reported as having been treated for minor cuts and bruises.

. . .

Reprinted with permission from *The New York Review of Books.* Copyright © 1969, The New York Review.

The next day, May 17, 2,000 National Guardsmen appeared in full battle dress, armed with rifles, bayonets, and tear gas. They were called into action by the Governor, but apparently the initiative came from local authorities acting in consultation with University administrators. Helicopters weaved back and forth over the campus and city. Berkeley was occupied. . . .

. . .

On Tuesday, May 20, the pattern and tempo changed. Previously the police had sought to break up gatherings on the campus, so now the protesters left the campus and began a peaceful march through the city. This was promptly stopped by the police. The marchers then filtered back to campus and a crowd of about 3,000 assembled. The group was pressed toward the Plaza by the police and Guardsmen and, when solidly hemmed in, was attacked by tear gas. A little later a helicopter flew low over the center of the campus and spewed gas over a wide area, even though the crowd had been thoroughly scattered. Panic broke out and people fled, weeping, choking, vomiting. Gas penetrated the University hospital, imperiling patients and interrupting hospital routines. It caused another panic at the University recreation area, nearly a mile from the center of campus, where many people, including mothers and children, were swimming. The police also threw gas into a student snack bar and into an office and classroom building.

The next day, May 21, was a turning point. More than 200 faculty members announced their refusal to teach; a local labor council condemned the police action; some church groups protested; and the newspapers and television stations began to express some criticism. Controversy arose over the ammunition which the police had used the previous Thursday. Sheriff Madigan was evasive about the size of birdshot issued, but the evidence was clear that buckshot had killed James Rector. The tear gas was first identified as the normal variety (CN) for crowd disturbances, but later it was officially acknowledged that a more dangerous gas (CS) was also used. The American army uses CS gas to flush out guerrillas in Vietnam. It can cause projectile vomiting, instant diarrhea, and skin blisters, and even death, as it has to the VC, when the victim is tubercular. The Geneva Conventions outlaw the use of CS in warfare.

. . .

The next day, May 22, a peaceful march and flower planting procession began in downtown Berkeley. With little warning, police and Guardsmen converged on the unsuspecting participants and swept them, along with a number of shoppers, newsmen, people at lunch, and a mailman, into a parking lot, where 482 were arrested, bringing the week's total near 800. As those arrested were released on bail, disturbing stories began to circulate concerning the special treatment accorded "Berkeley types" in Santa Rita prison.

. . .

After the mass arrests, the Governor lifted the curfew and the ban on assemblies, saying "a more controlled situation" existed. But he warned that no solution was likely until the trouble-making faculty and students were separated from the University. "A professional revolutionary group," he said, was behind it all. Charles Hitch, the President of the University of California, issued his first statement. (Much earlier, his own staff issued a statement protesting campus conditions of "intolerable stress" and physical danger.) The President ventured to criticize "certain tactics" of the police, but noted that these "were not the responsibility of university authorities."

In a television interview, the Chancellor agreed with the President, but added that negotiations were still possible because "we haven't stopped the rational process." A published interview (May 22) with the principal Vice-Chancellor found him saying, "Our strategy was to act with humor and sensitivity. For instance, we offered to roll up the sod in the park and return it to the people. . . . We had no reason to believe there would be trouble." . . .

. . .

On Friday, May 23, the Faculty Senate met. It listened first to a speech by the Chancellor in which he defined the occupation of the lot as an act of "unjustified aggression" against the University, and declared that the "avoidance of confrontations cannot be the absolute value." He said that the fence would remain as long as the issue was one of possession and control, and, pleading for more "elbow room," he asserted that the faculty should support or at least not oppose an administrative decision once it had been made. The faculty then defeated a motion calling for the Chancellor's removal (94 voted for, 737 against, and 99 abstained). It approved, by a vote of 737 to 94, a series of resolutions which condemned what was called "as irresponsible a police and military reaction to a civic disturbance as this country has seen in recent times."

The resolutions demanded withdrawal of "the massive police and military presence on campus"; the "cessation of all acts of belligerency and provocation by demonstrators"; an investigation by the Attorney General of California and the Department of Justice; and the prompt implementation of a plan whereby part of the lot would become "an experimental community-generated park" and the fence would be simultaneously removed. The faculty also resolved to reconvene in a few days to reassess the situation.

. . .

What brought on this crisis? Like many of its sister institutions, the Berkeley campus has been steadily advancing its boundaries into the city. . . .

. . . For many years, Telegraph Avenue and "the south campus area" have constituted a major irritant to the University, the City fathers, and the business interests. It is the Berkeley demi-monde, the place where students, hippies, drop-outs, radicals, and run-aways congregate. . . . It is no secret that the University has long considered the acquisition of land as a means of ridding the area not of substandard housing, but of its human "blight." . . .

Around mid-April, a movement was begun by street-people, hippies, students, radicals, and a fair sprinkling of elderly free spirits to take over the parking lot and transform it. Many possibilities were discussed: a child care clinic; a crafts fair; a baseball diamond. Soon grass and shrubs were planted, playground equipment installed, benches built, and places made for eating, lounging, and occasional speechmaking. About 200 people were involved in the beginning, but soon the Park was intensively and lovingly used by children, the young, students and street-people, and the elderly. A week after the Park began, the University announced its intention to develop a playing field by July 1, and the Park people responded by saying that the University would have to fight for it. Discussions followed, but not much else. The University said, however, that no construction would be started without proper warning and that it was willing to discuss the future design of the field.

On May 8 the Chancellor agreed to form a committee representing those who were using the lot as well as the University. But he insisted as "an essential condition" of discussions about the future of the land that all work on the People's Park cease. In addition he announced certain guidelines for his committee: University control and eventual use must be assured; the field must not produce "police and other control problems"; and no political or public meetings were to be held on the land. Suddenly, on May 13, he announced his decision to fence in the area as the first step toward developing the land for intramural recreation. "That's a hard way to make a point," he said, "but that's the way it has to be. . . . The fence will also give us time to plan and consult. Regretfully, this is the only way the entire site can be surveyed, soil tested, and planned for development . . . hence the fence."

Why did it have to be this way? Because, as the Chancellor explained, it was necessary to assert the University's title to ownership. Concerning the apparent lack of consultation with his own committee, he said that a plan could not be worked out because the Park people had not only refused to stop cultivating and improving the land, but they had "refused to organize a responsible committee" for consultative purposes. In addition, he cited problems of health, safety, and legal liability, as well as complaints from local residents.

The first response came from the faculty chairman of the Chancellor's committee. He declared that the Chancellor had allowed only two days (the weekend) for the committee to produce a plan and that the "University didn't seem interested in negotiations." On May 14 a protest rally was held and the anarchs of the Park, surprisingly, pulled themselves together and formed a negotiating committee. Although rumors of an impending fence were circulating, spokesmen for the Park people insisted that they wanted discussion, not confrontation.

. . .

Why did the making of a park provoke such a desolating response? . . .

. . .

What needs comment is the increasingly ineffectual quality of the University's responses, particularly when its organizational apparatus attempts to cope with what is spontaneous, ambiguous, and disturbingly human. It is significant that the Berkeley administration repeatedly expressed irritation with the failure of the Park people to "organize" a "responsible committee" or to select "representatives" who might "negotiate." The life-styles and values of the Park people were forever escaping the categories and procedures of those who administer the academic plant.

Likewise the issue itself: the occupants of the Park wanted to use the land for a variety of projects, strange but deeply natural, which defied customary forms and expectations, whereas, at worst, the University saw the land as something to be fenced, soil-tested, processed through a score of experts and a maze of committees, and finally encased in the tight and tidy form of a rational design. At best, the most imaginative use of the land which the University could contemplate was as a "field-experiment station" where faculty and graduate students could observe their fellow beings coping with their "environment." In brief, the educational bureaucracy, like bureaucracies elsewhere, is experiencing increasing difficulty, because human life is manifesting itself in forms which are unrecognizable to the mentality of the technological age.

This suggests that part of the problem lies in the very way bureaucracies perceive the world and process information from it. It was this "bureaucratic epistemology" which largely determined how the University responded to the People's Park. Bureaucracy is both an expression of the drive for rationality and predictability, and one of the chief agencies in making the world ever more rational and predictable, for the bureaucratic mode of knowing and behaving comes to constitute the things known and done themselves.

. . .

On the other side we see an assertion of spontaneity, self-realization, and do-your-own-thing as the sum and substance of life and liberty. And this assertion, in its extreme form, does approach either madness or infantilism, for the only social institutions in which each member is really free to do his own thing are Bedlam and the nursery, where the condition may be tolerated because there is a keeper with ultimate control over the inmates. The opposing forces were not quite that pure in the confrontation over the People's Park, but the University and public officials nearly managed to make them so. That they could not do so is a comforting measure of the basic vitality of those who built the Park and who have sacrificed to preserve it.

But this still does not account for the frenzy of violence which fell on Berkeley. To understand that, we must shift focus.

Clark Kerr was perceptive when he defined the multiversity as "a mechanism held together by administrative rules and powered by money." But it is important to understand that the last few years in the University have seen more and more rules and less and less money. The money is drying up because the rules are being broken. The rules are being broken because University authorities, administrators and faculty alike, have lost the respect of very many of the students. When authority leaves, power enters—first in the form of more and tougher rules, then as sheer physical force, and finally as violence, which is force unrestrained by any thought of healing and saving, force whose aim is to cleanse by devastation.

. . .

. . . Demands for a different future have been welling up in this society for some years now, and while those demands have not been unheard they have gone unheeded. Vietnam, racism, poverty, the degradation of the natural and manmade environment, the bureaucratization of the academy and its active collaboration with the military and industrial state, unrepresentative and unreachable structures of domination—all these grow apace. It seems increasingly clear to those who reject this American future that the forces of "law and order" intend to defend it by any means necessary. It becomes increasingly clear to the forces of law and order that extreme means will be necessary, and that the longer they are delayed the more extreme they will have to be.

Those two futures met at People's Park. It should be clear that what is happening this time is qualitatively different from 1964 and the Free Speech Movement. The difference in the amount of violence is the most striking, but this is largely a symptom of underlying differences. In 1964, the issues centered around questions of civil liberties and due process within the University. The issues now are political in the largest sense.

End questions

1. What did the authors identify as the basic causes of this disturbance at Berkeley?
2. Compare your university or college community to that of Berkeley. What similarities and differences exist?
3. Do you feel that the responses of the governing authorities of the university were adequate to meet the situation that arose? What different responses might have been tried?
4. What institutions outside of the university were involved in this case? How did university authorities attempt to deal with problems created beyond the boundries of the immediate university community?

Some of the most characteristic features of the American political system are its complexity, its restraint on authority, and its pluralism. The system consists not of one government but of many governments. Some lie completely within other governments. Some contain many governments within their own boundaries. And some cut across the boundaries of other governments. Each of these governments serves as the conversion structure of a political subsystem.

Overseeing this complex structure is the national government. But, the national government does not have unlimited authority to do whatever it likes. It has been restrained by certain limiting factors such as those cited in the Constitution which are then interpreted by the legal branch.

Added to this structural complexity, there are all the informal forces, stemming from the concerns and interests of the people, that play on the politics of the nation and its leaders. They are as complex and varied as the structures they feed their demands into. All of this gives the American political system its very *pluralistic,* or many-sided, nature.

America's Many Kinds of Governments

There are about 80,000 distinct governments in the United States, or about one government for every twenty-five hundred Americans. The national government—with all the grandeur, dignity, and authority of the President, the Congress, and the Supreme Court—is only one of these. The fifty state governments, plus the governments of counties, cities, towns, villages, and townships account for thousands more. Then, there are the public school districts and other special district governments. The latter have been created mainly to manage airports, bridges, tunnels, mass transportation systems, health services, and sanitation within specified regions.

An example of a special district government is the Port of New York Authority, set up in 1921 by New York and New Jersey to oversee transportation facilities and to promote commerce between the two states. Another example is the Metropolitan Water District of Southern Cali-fornia, which supervises the transfer of water more than three hundred miles from the Colorado River to the inhabitants of the three counties between Los Angeles and San Diego.

The boundaries of governments. The geographical boundaries of these governments add to the overall complexity of the American political system. Except for the national government, each of the governments in the United States is located within the geographical boundaries of another government. Every state government, as well as the Commonwealth of Puerto Rico and the territorial governments —such as the Panama Canal Zone, Guam, the Virgin Islands, and American Samoa— falls within the jurisdiction of the national government. So do all the more local governments. These governments may also lie completely within the boundaries of a state, as do city and county governments.

To add to the territorial complexity, the authority of some of these governments may overlap the authority of other governments. The authority of a district government, for example, may cut across state boundaries. Or a regional school district

Could the pluralist system in the United States work, if the several different levels of government vying for power were not restrained by the limits imposed on them by the constitutional law?

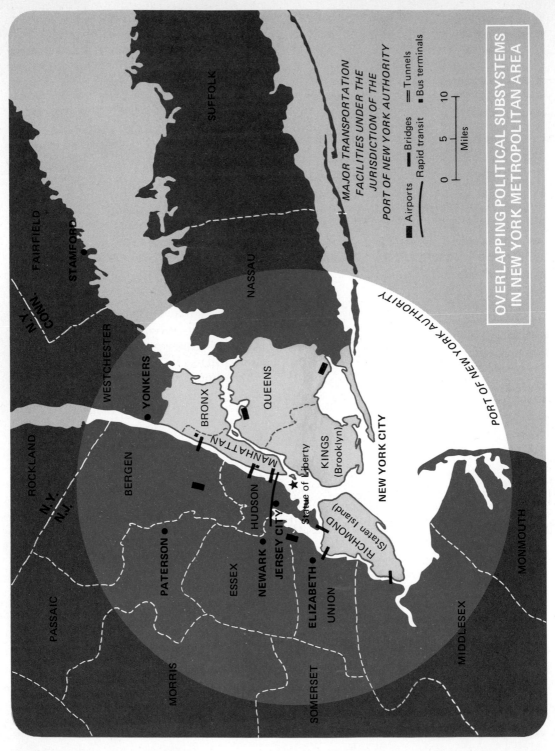

MAJOR TRANSPORTATION
FACILITIES UNDER THE
JURISDICTION OF THE
PORT OF NEW YORK AUTHORITY

■ Airports ▬ Tunnels
— Bridges ■ Bus terminals
▬ Rapid transit

Miles
0   5   10

OVERLAPPING POLITICAL SUBSYSTEMS
IN NEW YORK METROPOLITAN AREA

may cut across the lines of two or more town governments.

The existence of all of these thousands of governments is one of the reasons why the American political system is called *pluralistic,* which means composed of many parts. Demands and supports come from many sources and are directed toward the several governmental units among which legal authority is divided. The outputs of each unit result from both the interaction of people with government and the relationships of various governments with each other.

Some of these governments affect the lives of Americans far more than others do. But at one time or another, any one of them can have an important effect upon every citizen subject to its authority. More than nine out of ten of these governments have the potential authority to tax citizens living within their boundaries or using their services. Consider the position of a man who lives in his own house in a New Jersey suburb and who works in New York City. He pays a local real estate tax on his house and a sales tax to the New Jersey state government when he shops in local stores. He also pays a toll to the Port of New York Authority every time he uses a bridge or tunnel to drive across the Hudson River to get to or from work. When he shops in New York, he pays sales taxes to the governments of both New York City and New York State. In addition, he pays income taxes to New York City, New York State, and the federal government.

The dilemma of political subsystems. The pluralistic nature of government is intensified by the fact that most governments, whether they be national, state, or local, are composed of many political subsystems. Legislative bodies, courts, and administrative agencies all serve as conversion structures within their respective national, state, and local subsystems.

At the national level alone, each branch of government may serve a number of political subsystems as a conversion structure. Each branch responds to a different mixture of inputs, and thus yields different outputs.

BICYCLE BUILT FOR TWO

From *The Herblock Gallery* (Simon & Schuster, 1900)

(Sometimes even the President and key members of the administration seem to pull against each other.)

■ *Conflict of branches within a subsystem.* It is also possible for a number of branches to be involved in the same subsystem. The news media often report situations in which the President, members of Congress, justices of the Supreme Court, and high-level administrative officials have opposing views on the same matters. Sometimes, the different branches are even sharply critical of each other.

In 1967, both Congress and the Department of Health, Education, and Welfare (HEW) reviewed a federal welfare program. The program, Aid For Dependent Children (AFDC), was set up to provide money for mothers too poor to buy enough food, clothing, and other essentials for their children. HEW administered the program, but the money to pay for it came from tax funds authorized by Congress.

In the process of reviewing the program, many members of the House of Representatives concluded that all mothers receiving financial aid should be required to take part in a job-training program. These Congressmen hoped that eventually the mothers would be able to earn enough money on their own to purchase essentials for their children and would cease to be dependent on federal funds. Meanwhile, high-level officials in HEW were planning the program's revision. They wanted to make sure that children would receive governmental help regardless of their mothers' abilities to take part in job-training programs or to hold jobs.

Both HEW and Congress initiated separate policies. In August 1967, HEW reorganized the administration of the program to make it easier for mothers to receive financial aid for their children without having to take part in any service or training program. And the following December, Congress enacted a law requiring mothers to enroll in a job-training program if they wanted financial help.

Each of the opposing views expressed by the two branches had its own supporters throughout the country. HEW could depend on the support of the poor families that needed the funds delegated to dependent children, and Congress was trying to appease irate taxpayers not content with what they considered "handouts." Since each of the structures was responding to different sources of demands and support, each produced an output somewhat different from the other. Thus, two opposing policies were enacted on a single issue by separate branches of the same government. Only by identifying and examining the differences within the political subsystems is it possible to understand how the subsystems and the total system function as they do.

Review questions

1. What do all the various political subsystems have in common?
2. How do conflicts that arise within the various subsystems affect the government?

The Sources and Nature of American Governmental Authority

In the United States, governmental authority is conferred and limited by law—that is, by the Constitution, through legislation, or both. But the meaning of these laws is not always clear. Judicial interpretation is therefore a necessity and an important source of legal authority.

In addition to the boundaries set by law, informal factors can sometimes set limitations on governmental authority. For example, consider the situation of the President as Commander in Chief. He has the constitutional authority to direct most of the activities of the armed forces, but a number of factors reduce this power. He may have to deal with reluctant generals who oppose his views. His information is sometimes limited which forces him to rely on the advice of subordinate staff members. Or, he may be restrained by popular feeling. His authority thus depends on many extralegal elements, as well as the laws that have defined the scope of presidential power.

Law as a limit to governmental authority. All the pieces of the American governmental structure function within specific limits defined by the Constitution and by the *statutes,* or legislation, which supplements it. This is what is meant by the *rule of law.* To determine the authority of any governmental unit, Americans look first to the Constitution and statutes, and then to their interpretation by the various units of government.

Setting the limits of authority, however, does not necessarily establish an effective control over power. More often than not, laws are worded in general terms. This is done because they must cover such a wide range of conduct. It is not evident though from the Constitution, nor from most statutes, exactly how the law is to be applied in specific cases. Thus, while boundaries are set, governmental power can be exercised quite broadly within these limits. Governmental power as it is employed depends, then, more on judicial interpretation of the law than on the wording of the law itself.

The final word on the nature and limitations of governmental authority is generally supplied by the judicial branch of the United States through *judicial review.* This is the power of the courts to determine that a statute or other act of government is unconstitutional—that it does not conform to the limits set by the Constitution. If any of the legislative, executive, or administrative offices of government exceed the limits of their authority, an appeal may be made in the courts.

■ *Constitutional law.* In America, the limits of authority set for the various branches of the government are largely outlined in the Constitution, but amendments and judicial decisions may enlarge or diminish this authority. Judicial decisions interpreting or applying a point made in the Constitution constitute what is known as *constitutional law.* Usually, interpretation of the Constitution involves defining, or limiting, power and the rights of individuals. Final interpretation of the Constitution's meaning rests with the Supreme Court.

The Court's interpretation of the Constitution may be based on a logical analysis of the document's wording. It may also be based on precedents set earlier by the judiciary in related cases, on new knowledge about the matter being reviewed, or on a combination of these. Regardless of how the Court arrives at its decision, the decision is binding on all lower federal and state courts.

Article I, Section 8 of the Constitution, for example, stipulates that Congress shall have the power to lay and collect taxes. It also states that Congress shall have power to provide for the common defense and general welfare of the United States and to regulate commerce with foreign nations and among the states. But the wording, like that in the rest of the Constitution, is general. It must be clarified, and this is accomplished by judicial interpretation.

The Constitution's commerce clause, which was clarified in 1824 in the case of *Gibbons v. Ogden,* is a notable example of this procedure. The state of New York had granted a license to Aaron Ogden which gave him the exclusive right to navigate in the state's waters. But Congress had passed a statute authorizing the federal licensing of all vessels using coastal waters. When a New York court ordered Thomas Gibbons, who had obtained a federal license, to stop operating his vessels in the state's waters between New York and New Jersey, Gibbons took the case to the Supreme Court.

Chief Justice John Marshall, in the opinion he wrote for the Court, concluded that the constitutional authority of Congress to regulate commerce "among the several states" meant that it could regulate commerce *intrastate* (within the boundaries of the states) whenever *interstate* commerce (commerce crossing state boundaries) had, in turn, been affected. Through the process of interpretation, Marshall had defined the meaning of the "commerce clause."

■ *Statutory law.* Another legal means of establishing governmental authority is through *statutory law.* This body of law includes all legislation enacted by both Congress and state legislatures. Sometimes statutory law defines the application of governmental authority in very specific terms. For example, it may establish immigration quotas, extend social security or veterans' benefits, and adjust rates and regulations for farm subsidies. Often, however, statutory law merely sets general policy and then delegates authority to other governmental units to devise means of taking action.

For example, the Trade Expansion Act of 1962 provided that the President may raise and lower tariffs in accordance with various economic and political considerations. Instead of requiring the President to set tariffs at a particular level, Congress delegated authority in this vague manner because it could not possibly foresee all the problems that would be encountered when the law was administered.

Of course, there are still limits on presidential authority regarding trade. But because of such broad congressional delegation of authority, the President and his administrators can act more freely. As a result, the President's proposals can be a more significant indication of United States trade policy than are the statutes of Congress.

Judicial interpretation. The need for interpretation of statutory law by the courts can be illustrated by the history of antitrust laws. On the basis of its constitutional power to "regulate Commerce . . . among the several States," Congress has enacted several antitrust statutes which include the Sherman Antitrust Act of 1890, the Clayton Antitrust and Federal Trade Commission Acts of 1914, and numerous acts and amendments added later. These laws are worded so generally that the many supervisory authorities which must interpret them—the Justice Department, Federal Trade Commission, Federal Communications Commission, Civil Aeronautics Board, and so forth—are unable to agree on their enforcement. The Sherman Antitrust Act states:

"Section 1. Every contract, combination in the form of trust or otherwise, or conspiracy, in restraint of trade or commerce among the several States, or with foreign nations, is hereby declared to be illegal. . . .

"Section 2. Every person who shall monopolize, or attempt to monopolize, or combine or conspire with any other person or persons, to monopolize any part of the trade or commerce among the several States, or with foreign nations, shall be deemed guilty of a misdemeanor. . . ."[1]

Several points in these sections are obscure, and the rest of the Act does not make them any clearer. For example, what is a contract, trust, or conspiracy? What exactly is "restraint of trade"? What constitutes a restraint of trade "among the several states"? And when is a combination of persons considered a "monopoly"? As the agencies began to administer this Act, such questions and the nature of

[1] *26 Stat. 209, 15 U.S.C. 1-7 (1890). This designation means Volume 26 of the United States Statutes at Large, page 209, Title 15 of the United States Code, Sections 1-7.*

interstate commerce had to be clarified.

■ *Developing an antitrust policy.* Since Congress gave the courts responsibility for enforcement, the task of clarification fell to them. During the 1890's, the Justice Department initiated suits against several large corporations for violating the Act. By assigning a limited meaning to "interstate commerce," however, the Supreme Court failed to uphold the Justice Department's application of the Act.

The Court held that the firms involved had insufficient connections with interstate commerce. In the case of *United States v. E.C. Knight Company* (1895), it made what was soon to be considered an artificial distinction between manufacturing and commerce. In this case, the American Sugar Refining Company was accused of acquiring a nationwide monopoly on sugar refining. But the Court stated that widespread control over "manufacturing" involving many separate states did not necessarily involve interstate "commerce." The Sherman Antitrust Act therefore was not applicable in such instances.

But in 1911, after the decision of the Supreme Court in *Standard Oil Company v. United States,* judicial interpretation gave the Sherman Antitrust Act new meaning. Here the Court upheld a lower court's decision to dissolve a large trust in accordance with the Sherman Act. In its opinion, the Court discussed the meaning of the Act. It concluded that, although there were precedents to be relied on, it was up to the Court to judge each case separately by applying a "rule of reason."

The "precedents" of earlier opinions had held that all restraints of trade violated the Sherman Act. But in applying the "rule of reason" in the *Standard Oil* case, Chief Justice Edward D. White asserted that the Act forbade only "unreasonable" restraints. According to White, the Sherman Act did not clearly specify the kinds of restraints it prohibited. Some restraints, White felt, were justifiable. He even suggested that, although the parent New Jersey company was an unreasonable restraint of trade, its subsidiary companies might be able to form, through combinations, "reasonable" restraints over commerce.

There Seems To Be No Letup

Partymiller—York (Pa.) Daily Record

(Interpretation of regulation and law is still a problem today with the new wave of conglomerate mergers.)

Justice John Marshall Harlan vigorously dissented from Chief Justice White's rule of reason. Such judicial discretion, he wrote, could lead to nothing less than rewriting the law. This, Harlan contended, would be a "usurpation by the judicial branch of the government of the functions of the legislative department."[2]

Harlan's objection to judicial legislation may seem valid on the theoretical level. Yet, because of the vagueness of statutory

[2] Standard Oil Co. v. United States, *221 U.S. 103* (1911). *This designation means Volume 221 of the United States Supreme Court official report, page 103. This citation form will be followed throughout the book.*

law, as illustrated by the Sherman Act, it is impossible for the judiciary to avoid "legislating" through its interpretation of law.

■ *Changes in judicial interpretation.* Because interpretation is affected by many factors, it changes to some degree as the factors change. Obviously, the attitudes of members of the judiciary are very important and judicial interpretations change with alterations in court membership.

The President, too, plays a role in the way that the Court may interpret. His opinions are mirrored in his appointments to the Supreme Court, the Justice Department, and the various regulatory agencies.

Review questions

1. Why is statutory law worded in very general terms?
2. In what way did Chief Justice Marshall's decision in *Gibbons v. Ogden* establish governmental authority by clarifying a section of the Constitution?

The Source of Inputs: Political Constituencies

Pluralism as a characteristic of the American political system is not restricted to the existence of political subsystems. It is also obvious in the variety of inputs (demands and supports) and of ways in which they are received by the government and converted into policy outputs. Most demands and supports come from the *political constituencies* within the many different political subsystems. A political constituency is composed of those groups and individuals whose demands and supports are considered by an elected representative or a government official before he makes a decision. In the case of an elected delegate, a Senator or a Representative, the constituency is made up of the voters in his district. A government administrator also has a political constituency. It is composed of all the individuals and special interest groups concerned about the matters with which his agency deals. Thus, the constituencies of the elected official and the administrator overlap because members of special interest groups—teachers or steelworkers—are also voters.

Electoral constituencies. Since constituency demands and supports greatly in-

fluence the formulation of policies, it is important to understand how they affect the formal governmental processes. The average person uses the term political constituency with reference to electoral constituencies only. When he refers to the constituency of the President or of a member of Congress, a governor, or a mayor, he means the voters who support the elected official. The electoral constituency is also framed by a geographical boundary—the United States in the case of the President, a state for a Senator, an electoral district for a Representative, a city for a mayor, and so forth.

Every elected official must respond to the requests of his constituents (the individuals who comprise his constituency) if he wants to be reelected. He must heed, in particular, the requests of those individuals and groups who have supported him with their votes and their influence within the constituency.

The attitudes of elected officials toward their constituents vary widely. This is because these attitudes depend on such factors as personality, political party, issues, and the location of the constituency. Regardless of differences between an

INPUTS

ELECTORAL CONSTITUENCIES

Make demands directly
by voting

ADMINISTRATIVE AND JUDICIAL
CONSTITUENCIES (Interest
groups and individuals
who are also members
of the electorate)

CONVERSION STRUCTURES

Electoral constituencies
make indirect demands on
the bureaucracy and the
courts through the President,
who appoints administration
officials and Supreme Court
judges, and through Congress,
which approves presidential
appointments and
agency budgets.

PRESIDENT

CONGRESS

Interest groups make
demands directly through
active support of
agencies and in cases
before the courts.

ADMINISTRATIVE
AGENCIES

JUDICIARY

"IF THEY'D STOP WASTING MONEY ON MOON SHOTS AND POVERTY PROGRAMS, WE COULD FINISH THE WAR!"

"IF THEY'D STOP WASTING MONEY ON WARS AND POVERTY PROGRAMS, WE COULD GET THERE."

"IF THEY'D STOP WASTING MONEY ON WAR, POVERTY PROGRAMS AND MOON SHOTS, THEY COULD CURE POLLUTION!"

"I HOPE THEY HURRY WITH THEIR MOON SHOT—WE COULD USE A GOOD POVERTY PROGRAM!"

(Each constituent's demand is affected by and must be weighed against the other constituent demands.)

elected official and his constituents, he is always responding to their demands and supports. And they, in turn, are dependent on and influenced by his decisions.

Administrative and judicial constituencies. Elected officials are not the only officials who are affected by electoral constituents. Appointed officials such as administrators and judges are also affected indirectly by these same constituents. When voters elect an official, that official, in turn, brings the demands and supports of the electorate to bear on the appointed officials. In this way, representative government is extended through the elected official to the administrative agencies and the judiciary. For example, the President— elected by the people—appoints the heads of the administrative agencies and departments as well as Supreme Court judges; the Congress, also elected by the voters, verifies the President's appointments by approving them.

In addition, when a voter belongs to a special interest group, spokesmen for the group carry that voter's demands directly to appointed officials. The political constituencies of administrative agencies and the judiciary, then, are made up of the general electorate and special interests within and outside of government. Appointed officials, like elected ones, can not ignore the opinions of these constituents.

Usually an electoral constituency makes demands on these appointed officials through the elected representative. For example, at a Senate committee hearing, an appointed official from the Department of Transportation may be called on by Senators from urban areas to explain why funds have not been assigned for rapid transit systems in urban areas. If Transportation's spokesman does not give an adequate reason for the lack of funds, the vote of some urban constituencies may go to the opposing party in the next election, and the man who appointed the spokesman may lose. The spokesman, in turn, would lose his own position.

Appointed officials and others who work in the administrative subsystem of government are, of course, better protected from the immediate impact of electoral-constituency interests than are elected representatives. This is because an appointed official does not have to face reelection. Nonetheless, he is indirectly responsible to those constituents because they do elect the officials who can appoint or dismiss him from his job.

At the same time, the appointed official must also react to the demands made on him by other governmental agencies. The Department of Defense, for example, may insist that these same transportation funds are needed to improve facilities at a port used to ship military goods, while the President may want them diverted to the highway program. Thus, the Department of Transportation official must respond to a number of opinions, each of which reflects the thinking of a political constituency.

The administrative agencies and the judiciary are also aware of the demands made by private groups or individuals vitally interested in the outcome of a particular issue or policy. These groups and individuals also make up constituencies. The members of the National Education Association, for example, make up one constituency of HEW, and the members of the National Association for the Advancement of Colored People (NAACP) make up a constituency for a particular court deciding a case on school desegregation. Almost every public and private group in American society, therefore, belongs to the constituency of some part of the government. And some of these groups are even more influential because they belong to several constituencies.

Changing boundaries of constituencies. A constituency may increase or decrease according to what is at stake. This is even true of electoral constituencies, which have definite geographical boundaries. Rarely do all potential voters within an electoral district help to elect or defeat a particular candidate, nor do they always disclose their views on particular issues. Some constituents will do so if sufficiently aroused; others will take no active part at all in the political process.

An official, whether elected or appointed, usually has little interest in passive, inactive, constituents. An elected official, however, has to be far more concerned with that part of the active or potentially active electorate that will give him a majority vote. In the constituencies of the bureaucracy and judiciary, there are groups and individuals whose levels of interest also depend on the issue at stake. When an issue is of great importance to them, they will actively press their demands before the appropriate agency or court. If they are only moderately interested in an issue, they will put forward their demands with something less than full vigor. And if an issue is not important to them, they may not even express their concern.

Because of these variations among constituencies, the President, a member of Congress, a bureaucrat, or a judge must try to measure or at least guess the amount and intensity of support he may receive for the decisions he is contemplating.

Examples of constituency inputs. The complexity of the constituency picture should suggest the tremendous intricacy of the governmental process. This intricacy can be illustrated by showing how a particular constituency influences appointed officials. To define a constituency that is not an electoral constituency, it is necessary first to identify the agency or court involved and second, to determine what type of decision will be made and to whom or what this decision will be applied. The recent history of the civil rights issue illustrates how the Supreme Court justices must respond to political constituents when exercising the power of judicial review. The make-up of the Court's constituency on this issue is shown in the diagram on this page.

Not all of the political constituencies listed in the diagram are equally concerned with desegregation, but they do represent all shades of opinion on the issue. Some groups favor a strong stand on civil rights.

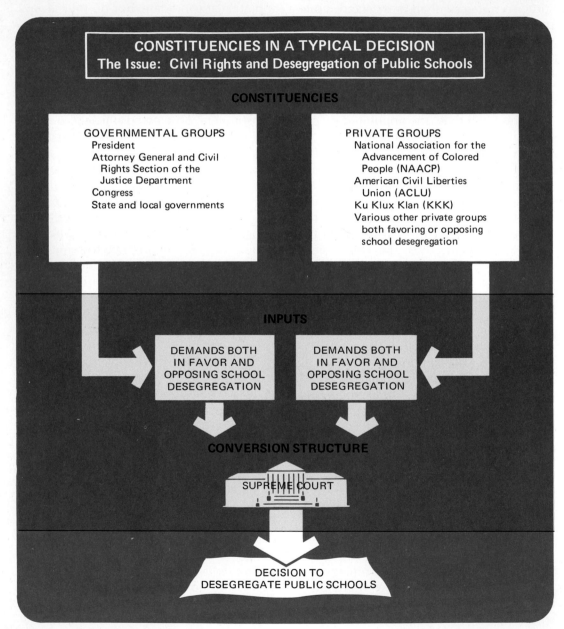

CONSTITUENCIES IN A TYPICAL DECISION
The Issue: Civil Rights and Desegregation of Public Schools

CONSTITUENCIES

GOVERNMENTAL GROUPS
  President
  Attorney General and Civil
    Rights Section of the
    Justice Department
  Congress
  State and local governments

PRIVATE GROUPS
  National Association for the
    Advancement of Colored
    People (NAACP)
  American Civil Liberties
    Union (ACLU)
  Ku Klux Klan (KKK)
  Various other private groups
    both favoring or opposing
    school desegregation

INPUTS

DEMANDS BOTH
IN FAVOR AND
OPPOSING SCHOOL
DESEGREGATION

DEMANDS BOTH
IN FAVOR AND
OPPOSING SCHOOL
DESEGREGATION

CONVERSION STRUCTURE

SUPREME COURT

DECISION TO
DESEGREGATE PUBLIC SCHOOLS

Some favor a weak program or none at all.

Moreover, these groups will express their interest in a Supreme Court's civil rights decision differently. An example is the *Brown v. Board of Education* case of 1954, which made segregation in public schools unconstitutional. The NAACP was directly involved because it insisted that the case on behalf of Linda Brown, a black student, against the Board of Education of Topeka, Kansas be brought to trial. The state and local authorities were also directly involved. Other interested groups—such as the Justice Department, the American Jewish Congress, the American Civil Liberties Union, the American Federation of Teachers, the Congress of Industrial Organizations (CIO), and the American Veterans Committee—expressed interest in the case by filing amicus curiae briefs. *Amicus curiae* (plural: *amici curiae*) is a Latin term meaning "friend of the court." An amicus curiae is not a direct party to a case before a court, but he is concerned with the decision and feels that it will affect his interests. The Justice Department often makes its policies known to the court involved, whether it is federal or state, by means of an amicus curiae brief

Some constituencies remain inactive in a case, or do not attempt to intervene directly, even though they will be affected by the decision that is made. Although the interests of these constituencies are not immediate and direct, and perhaps not very well expressed, they do have potential force. Thus, some thought will be given to their interests when the decision is made.

The members of the Senate Judiciary Committee, for example, did not participate directly in the 1954 and 1955 Supreme Court decisions desegregating public schools. But Senator James O. Eastland of Mississippi, who became the committee's chairman in 1956, was fond of asking new Presidential appointees to the Court how they felt about the *Brown* decision and the Court's subsequent moves to advance the cause of civil rights. While he could not change the course of the Court's decisions, he did make these appointees conscious of the anti-desegregation sentiments of a particular constituency. He thus added to the intensification of hostility to the Court.

Measurement of constituency power. It is difficult to measure the effect of various constituencies on governmental decisions. For example, in 1954 the Supreme Court ruled that segregated schools violated the "equal protection of the laws" clause contained in the Fourteenth Amendment to the Constitution. Following this decision, pro-civil-rights groups demanded that the Court rule directly and immediately for integration of the schools. Anti-civil-rights groups, meanwhile, pressured the Court to reverse its decision. Labeling the decision "drastic" and "revolutionary," they contended that the Court had ignored the political desires and constitutional rights of a large section of the country.

Faced with extreme pressure from both sides, the Court found it necessary in 1955 to compromise the interests of both groups. It declared that the public schools would not have to be fully and instantly integrated. Under supervision of the lower federal courts—the district courts—a transitional program was to be worked out that would lead "with all deliberate speed" to desegregated school systems.

It was then argued by pro-civil-rights critics of the Court, that the Court's backtracking in the 1955 decision indicated that it had been intimidated by the powerful conservative interests in its constituency. Actually what the Court had done was to balance the opposing interests of its constituencies. It had arrived at a compromise. Such balancing of interests is characteristic of the democratic process. If the process is to succeed, it must be able to hold together different interests within the community.

Government as a countervailing force. The balance between constituency interests could not be maintained, however, if the most powerful interests always had their way. To prevent certain private interests from having excessive weight in official decisions, the government itself can serve as a *countervailing,* or opposing force, so that a balance between all interests can be achieved.

All governmental regulatory agencies, for example, are charged with the responsibility of protecting the public interest, and in so doing, they frequently counter private interests. The Federal Trade Commission (FTC) acted as a countervailing force against powerful private tobacco interests when it nudged Congress into taking action about the labeling of cigarettes as hazardous to an individual's health.

The fragmentation of policy-making. One final observation should be added to the discussion of the Supreme Court, civil rights, and desegregation. Many important ingredients seem to be missing from the story. Neither the role of the President nor that of Congress has been indicated. And the role of the two major political parties is also unstated.

The truth is that the President, Congress, and the political parties played a very small part in formulating the school desegregation policy. This is not unusual. In the American political system, the policy-formulating process is always fragmented. Rarely does the entire governmental apparatus become involved in making a policy decision. When it does, different parts of the government, because of opposing constituency demands and supports, are apt to conflict with each other.

Review questions

1. Why must every elected official respond to the demands and support of those in his constituency?
2. Which group or individual would have more influence on the decision-making of a federal administrative agency, such as the Federal Communications Commission: the citizen of a state, the Senator from that state, the Pentagon, the Supreme Court, the president of a television network? Give reasons for your decision.

The Politics of Policy Formulation

What happens to a constituent demand once it has been expressed to the proper policy-making authority? How does it get transformed into policy output? Obviously when the demand has been made, it is only the beginning of the governmental process. The next step is the conversion of the input through the various governmental structures until a policy has been formulated which responds to the demand.

Most Americans are familiar with the major national policy-making structures of government—the executive, the legislature, and the judiciary. Policy is also made by the *bureaucracy,* or the administrative branch which includes all of the executive departments and the independent regulatory agencies.

The bureaucracy in policy formulation. It is often assumed that the federal bureaucracy is part of the executive branch and that the President, with the aid of the Cabinet, has complete control over the bureaucracy. Such a view, however, disregards many of the complexities of the administrative structure.

Actually the bureaucracy does not function solely as part of the executive branch. While all of the executive departments and most of the regulatory agencies have some responsibilities to the President, they are also responsible to the courts and to congressional committees. The administrative structure depends on the courts to uphold decisions when a policy is applied, and it depends on Congress for funds. Despite this dual responsibility, many officials in the bureaucracy act as if they held basic authority rather than delegated power. Frequently, these officials themselves formulate policy for their respective areas of concern. In so doing they are of course responding directly to demands and supports of their relatively unique constituencies. (For further exploration of the bureaucracy, see Chapters 15 and 16.)

■ *Antitrust policy as an example.* Administrative policy formulation can be understood by examining a specific policy issue. Since the government is often faced with antitrust problems—those that arise from company mergers, trusts, or monopolies which prevent competition—it might be best to explore such a problem here.

One of the nation's recent antitrust problems was caused by mergers between transportation companies in the early 1960's. Neither Congress nor President John F. Kennedy had a policy regarding trusts. To develop one, the President appointed a four-man team composed of members from the Council of Economic Advisers and the Departments of Justice, Commerce, and Labor. In March 1963, the White House issued a statement containing the team's recommended guidelines for mergers and competitive practices in the railroad and airline industries.

These guidelines, encouraging competition whenever possible, contained three major points. First, both railroad and airline mergers and practices should be prevented if they curtailed competition. Second, mergers should be disapproved if they created too much unemployment in sections of the country or in local communities. Third, mergers for financial efficiency should not be approved if savings expected from the proposed mergers could be achieved by less binding agreements among firms within an industry.

After this report, the casual observer might have said: "That's that. The White House has given its guidelines. Any merger in the transportation industry, unless it is unquestionably in the public interest, seems to be ruled out." The policy-making process, however, is never so simple.

■ *The regulatory agency's power.* A number of important factors interfered with the implementation of President Kennedy's guidelines. Congress had delegated the authority to approve or disapprove merger applications to two agencies: the Interstate Commerce Commission (ICC) for the railroads, and the Civil Aeronautics Board (CAB) for the airline industry. These are both *independent regulatory agencies,* established outside the major executive departments.

Created by Congress, these independent regulatory agencies are given the power, within the areas of the economy that they regulate, to make rules and prosecute violators. Presidential authority to interfere with the independent regulatory agencies is strictly limited. While the President appoints new commission members, he may not, according to congressional statutes, legally remove a member except for "inefficiency, neglect of duty, or malfeasance [wrongdoing] in office." Because of such statutory limitations on presidential interference, the independent regulatory agencies are often called *arms of Congress.*

As is true for other governmental units, the regulatory agencies have to maintain a balance between various constituent interests when they formulate policy. The support they obtain, in turn, gives them political strength that increases their access to, and support by, both Congress and the President.

The ICC and the CAB have carefully cultivated political support. But their constituencies are, of necessity, rather limited. As with most regulatory agencies, their major support has been found within the regulated industries themselves and, thus, differs substantially from the more broad-based constituency of the President. It is

From *The Herblock Gallery* (Simon & Schuster, 1968)

(The merger of the New York Central and the Pennsylvania railroads along with the New Haven as a poor stepchild was upheld by the Supreme Court in 1968.)

therefore only natural that policies of such agencies will also tend to differ on many points from those of the President. Although administrative units have to take presidential standards into account in formulating policies, they are not bound by these standards. The ICC and CAB are expected to maintain healthy railroad and airline industries. If these agencies believe that mergers will help achieve this goal, they will approve them, regardless of the President's antitrust guidelines.

■ *Disagreement over guidelines.* At the time President Kennedy announced his guidelines for mergers, several important cases were pending before both the ICC and the CAB. The ICC was considering several railroad-merger applications—including one for the New York Central and Pennsylvania railroads, and one for the Great Northern and Northern Pacific railroads. It was also examining applications submitted by the Southern Pacific Railroad and the Atchison, Topeka, and Santa Fe Railway to gain control of the Western Pacific Railroad.

The ICC chose to take a stand independent of the President's. An early indication of this came soon after the White House guidelines were announced when an ICC official gave the Santa Fe control of the Western Pacific. Despite the Justice Department's expression of opposition to this move, the ICC said that it favored other mergers. Such an attitude is to be expected. The railroads are a dominant element within the ICC's political constituency. To the ICC, the "public interest," naturally and perhaps properly, tends to be whatever furthers the economic health of the railroads.

■ *In fighting over air routes.* The CAB soon asserted its independence from the President's guidelines also. It turned down an application from Northeast Airlines for permission to continue flying the New

York-to-Florida route, thus reducing competition. The CAB had permitted Northeast to enter this market in 1956, hoping to strengthen what was then a small New England carrier. But by 1963, Northeast's financial position was shaky again. The CAB felt that the airline could not compete with Eastern and National, the other carriers on the route. In the interests of the stockholders, and of financially sound air transportation, the CAB took the Florida route away from Northeast. The CAB then offered to subsidize Northeast for the losses it would necessarily suffer on its New England route.

Reaction to the CAB's decision was immediate and vigorous. The Justice Department, in agreement with the first guidelines of the President's policy, felt that the decision would unnecessarily reduce competition on the New York-to-Florida route; but it was unable to secure a hearing before the CAB to advance its case. The CAB said that the Department had entered the proceedings too late. Other groups opposed to the decision used every device at their command to secure a reversal. Their most formidable tactic in such a fight, they soon recognized, was to muster political support for their position.

Northeast Airlines and New England labor unions and city governments, among others, also sought to have the decision reversed by exerting pressure on members of Congress. Many of these lawmakers had great influence at the White House, in the Justice Department, and within Congress itself. But they could not move the CAB from its ruling. They even went so far as to introduce a bill overriding the decision. But once power had been delegated and the administrative unit had established its lines of influence and support, it was difficult for only a few individual members of Congress to exercise significant control over the unit's outputs. At this point, only

a large bloc of congressional members working together would have been able to take legislative action restraining the CAB's action.

Individual members of Congress from New England tried to get the entire Congress to act to reverse the CAB's decision. But their colleagues from other areas of the country were only slightly concerned with the Northeast Airlines decision. In short, Congress had delegated the decision-making authority in this type of case to the CAB. Since the constituents of most congressmen were not affected, they felt the CAB should keep this authority. Even though the CAB demonstrated its relative independence, the case of the Northeast Airlines route actually dragged on into the late 1960's, when the airline finally won the right to keep the route.

Pluralism in governmental policy. The conflicts of the ICC and the CAB with the Justice Department, the President, and various members of Congress illustrate the effects of different constituencies in shaping the outputs of the American political system. These conflicts also demonstrate the pluralistic nature of the United States government's policy-making mechanism. Governmental policy on any issue can come from almost any source in the governmental structure. It can come from the President, the Congress, the Supreme Court, or the bureaucracy. When speaking of governmental policy, it is therefore important to identify which governmental unit is involved.

This pluralistic character of the American governing process, however, does not necessarily produce disagreement in policy-making. Still, there can never be complete agreement on what is in the national interest, except where the vaguest of generalities are concerned. Even during a crisis, there is usually much disagreement among governmental units as well as among groups within the general public. During World War II, when unified points of view within the national government might have been expected, the conflict among departments and agencies was so intense that it was often referred to as "the Battle of Washington."

Complete unity in a society as complex as the United States is unnatural. It could be attained, but only by an excessively powerful and unified governmental authority. Critics of the American political system often say that its failure to achieve unity leads to inefficiency. But if a free democratic society is to be achieved, policy outputs must result from the interplay of clashing viewpoints.

Review questions

1. How are independent regulatory agencies able to retain some freedom in their actions?
2. How did the Civil Aeronautics Board's decision regarding Northeast Airlines illustrate the pluralism in the government's policy-making structure?

American Pluralism and the Impact of Immigration

The great number and the variety of viewpoints that interact within the governmental process, as well as the multiplicity of formal governmental authorities, comprise the fundamental characteristic of the American political system today—its pluralism. Consider the hundreds of economic, social, religious, occupational, intellectual, and artistic differences there are among just the people you know. All these people have varied interests and concerns, and many of them will express their feelings whenever they have a chance—at the ballot box, town meetings, neighborhood political gatherings, parent-teacher's meetings, and so forth. There are therefore innumerable informal forces that initiate the inputs of the system.

Significance of immigration. One of the most important, and perhaps unique, historical elements contributing to the pluralistic character of the American system is the diversity of backgrounds from which the nation's citizens come. Immigrants from almost every corner of the world have decided to leave their ancestral homes and to make a new life in America. Except for the American Indians, Eskimos, and native Hawaiians, every American is either an immigrant or a descendant of immigrants.

The flow of people to what is now the United States began in the sixteenth century. It continued largely unrestricted until 1921 when Congress enacted legislation setting quotas for the number of persons who could annually enter the United States. Above all, this continuing immigration made a tremendous and dramatic contribution to the size of the population of the United States. Most historians estimate that the pre-revolutionary population of the thirteen British colonies was fewer than 3 million persons. By the time of the first national census in 1790, the population had risen to slightly under 4 million. Since the end of the eighteenth century, 45 to 50 million immigrants have entered the United States. Exact figures are impossible to give because no official records of immigration were kept before 1820.

But the impact of immigration on the development of the United States goes far beyond its effect on the size of population. The tide of immigrants that began to swell in the 1840's, and crested at the end of the nineteenth century, made possible the astounding industrial and commercial growth of the United States as well as its territorial expansion.

Another startling feature of American immigration has been the ethnic, economic, and religious diversity of the immigrants. Other nations can trace their development to mass influxes of immigrants. Canada, the countries of Latin America, as well as South Africa and Australia have all attracted large numbers of immigrants. But none of these is comparable to the United States in the variety of countries and walks of life from which the immigrants came. United States citizens today can trace their heritages to virtually every part of the globe.

Conditions abroad and in America caused these people to arrive here in great waves. Almost all of the African immigrants came prior to the Civil War, but, unlike most other immigrants, they did not come of their own free will. Chinese immigrants in large numbers settled on the West Coast in the 1850's and 1860's. Many people from Northern and Western Europe came before 1880. At the end of the nineteenth and beginning of the twentieth century, others from Southern, Eastern, and Central Europe arrived in such large numbers that the annual immigration total went over the million mark for several years. More recently, Hungarians and Cubans have fled their homelands to escape communism.

Immigrants in politics. The ethnic diversity caused by immigration to the United States has enriched American music, literature, art, and the whole fabric of the nation's society. It has also had a noticeable effect on the American political system.

One of the most notable aspects of the American experience for most immigrants, —with the exception of Africans and most Mexican-Americans—has been a virtually unlimited opportunity to take part in American life despite the newcomer status. After five years' residence and the passing of a series of tests on the principles of government and law in the United States, any adult—male or female—now can become a fully qualified citizen. The interests and needs of these naturalized citizens, of course, have provided inputs for the American political system.

As the number of potential immigrant voters increased, politicians began searching for ways to win their electoral support. One sure way was to pay more attention to events occurring in countries from which large numbers of immigrants had come. For, while American immigrants engaged wholeheartedly in the life of their new country, they also retained family, cultural, and sentimental attachments to the lands of their origin. In an attempt to appeal to new voters during the nineteenth century, the national political parties began to support causes related to events in other countries. Among these causes were Irish independence and Italian nationalism.

The emergence of ethnic politics. Far more important, however, was the impact that immigrant groups had on the American political system as they became active in the governmental process. A great many immigrants had been peasant farmers in their native lands. They had little, if any, formal education and little or no training in crafts, trades, or professions. Politics thus provided them with one of the few avenues for getting ahead in American life.

Many immigrants soon found that if they ran for public office, they could attract a substantial number of votes from members of their own immigrant groups. They could do so simply on the basis of national identity and the prospect of a symbolic triumph for the immigrant group in its new and alien environment.

As immigrant groups made up larger and

THE MODERN ARK.—Drawn by Sol Eytinge, from a Sketch by E. S. Bisbee.

Harper's Weekly

(In 1871 this cartoonist depicted the arrival of immigrants in the United States as a modern Noah's ark. Recognizable are people from many parts of the world: Britain, Africa, China, Turkey, Russia, and others.)

larger concentrations of voters in the urban centers, they were increasingly successful in electing their members to public office. Their representatives, in turn, responded to this support by doing all they could to help members of the group get ahead. The immigrant politician tried to find jobs for members of his ethnic group. Just as importantly, he helped them cope with the laws, regulations, and responsibilities of citizenship in a place where, for most, the language was unfamiliar and difficult to master. In return for jobs, favors, legal help, and the satisfaction of seeing a compatriot reach prominence, the immigrant voters contributed continued political support. This style of politics, which emerged during the second half of the nineteenth century, profoundly influenced the nature of the American political system.

Ethnic politics and American pluralism. One of the most important effects of immigration on American political life has been the continuation of ethnic identity in American politics. This loyalty to national origins is of great importance when a candidate is nominated for public office. It also affects the casting of votes, the framing of issues, the filling of public jobs, and many other matters in the governmental process. In some situations it is a strong force while in others it is a minor one or does not operate at all.

The continuance of ethnic identity is especially significant because it reinforces the pluralistic character of the American political system. It adds to the complexity of forces influencing the activities of government. And it helps to ensure that political influence will be widely shared. Because there are so many ethnic differences, no one group is able to get control of the machinery of American government.

In spite of this persistence in keeping ethnic identity, most ethnic groups have become sufficiently *assimilated,* or absorbed into American society, so as to subordinate this identity to their identity as Americans. This has been due, in large part, to the ability of the political system and other segments of the society to accept the newcomers into the political and social processes.

The black in the American situation. Unlike other ethnic groups, black Americans, who have been here since before the inception of the Republic, have not been able to participate fully in the political and social processes. Despite their familiarity with the language, their ties to early American history, and their common religious beliefs with the majority of Americans, the blacks have been kept outside the general framework of American so-

ciety. The weakening of ethnic ties that has allowed other groups to assimilate has not worked in the case of the black American. He could not change the color of his skin and, therefore, has remained conspicuously different. Laws, statutes, and traditions were stacked against him, keeping him from voting, from equal schooling, from the right to live where he pleased even if he could afford it.

It is only within the past few decades that the black has begun to win a few basic rights of citizenship that were previously denied him. Ironically, recent outspoken quests by blacks for these rights may actually have deepened the cleavage between blacks and whites in the United States.

Many blacks are still frustrated at their inability to contribute to the inputs of the political system. They feel that there are no receptive officials through whom they can channel their demands, or who will represent their interests within the conversion structure. Some believe their only recourse is violence to counteract this ineffectiveness in the political system. To some black Americans, it may appear that the stability of the society is really not worth preserving.

Ethnic diversity, then, can be both a blessing and a challenge. In many cases, it tends to weaken and prevent any group from gaining control, thus allowing all the groups to participate in the democratic procedure. On the other hand, as in the case of black Americans, when any single group is not included in the process, the democratic ideals are not being fulfilled.

Review questions

1. How have ethnic groups used politics to improve their situation in American society?
2. Why has the black American not been able to enter the American scene fully?

Chapter Review

Terms you should know

amicus curiae
antitrust
bureaucracy
constitutional law
countervailing force

independent regulatory
  agencies
interstate commerce
intrastate commerce
judicial review

pluralism
political constituency
rule of law
rule of reason
statutory law

Questions about this chapter

1. Why is the American political system called "pluralistic"?
2. What was the significance of the ruling made by the Supreme Court in the *Gibbons v. Ogden* case?
3. When does a government agency act as a countervailing force?
4. How did the Civil Aeronautics Board's decision regarding Northeast Airlines bring about the participation of constituency groups in the situation?
5. What kind of power do judges wield when they are called upon to interpret the Constitution?
6. Explain the following paradox as exhibited in the Sherman Antitrust Act and other legislation: Government intervention in the free economy is essential for the preservation of free enterprise.
7. Why have politics been viewed by the immigrant as a means of "getting ahead" in America?

Thought and discussion questions

1. How is it possible for two conversion structures to come into conflict with each other? Does this affect the operation of government? Explain.
2. How does a legislator act as an intermediary in the relationship between the average citizen and his "big government"?
3. What part does the judiciary play in making the Constitution flexible to meet changing economic and social conditions?
4. The only way to maintain a free democratic society is to allow the interplay of clashing viewpoints. Discuss the truth of this statement.
5. What role have ethnic groups played in making the American political system pluralistic? Can you cite any examples of the continuation of this role?

Class projects

1. If you wanted to become involved in a political subsystem in your community how would you go about it? Diagram the different political subsystems in your community; find out who the members of these subsystems are. Is there any overlapping in membership? Is there any conflict between these subsystems over policy?
2. Trace the history of one ethnic group which came to America. How was it possible for the American system to assimilate these immigrants? Did this group actively enter politics? If so, how successful were they in seeking public office? Do they still vote in an ethnic bloc? If so, why?

Case Study: "Chicano Power"

The United States has always been a nation of immigrants. For decades, ethnic minorities have been absorbed into the social fabric of the nation. Yet a few have remained outside American society. Recently, one such minority has stepped onto the American political stage, demanding their equal rights as citizens and the correction of long held injustices. The Mexican-Americans (or "Chicanos" as they call themselves) have become aware of their group power and are trying to gather their forces to correct the obvious inequalities that they have suffered.

As you read this study of the Chicano movement, consider the following:
1. According to Mr. Bigart, what are the objectives of the Chicano movement?
2. Why are the Chicanos suddenly so angry with the American political system?
3. Which tactics will prove most successful for this minority?
4. How optimistic is Mr. Bigart about realization of Chicano goals?

THE NEW YORK TIMES.   SUNDAY, APRIL 20, 1969

A New Mexican-American Militancy

By HOMER BIGART

LOS ANGELES—Five million Mexican-Americans, the nation's second largest minority, are stirring with a new militancy. The ethnic stereotype that the Chicanos are too drowsy, too docile to carry a sustained fight against poverty and discrimination is bending under fresh assault. . . .

Some Mexican-Americans, notably in New Mexico, claim descent from Spanish explorers. Others say they were derived from the ancient Aztecs, and stress their Indianness. But the vast majority describe themselves as mestizos, people of mixed Spanish and Indian blood.

They all have a common complaint: they say the Anglos treat Chicanos as a conquered people by suppressing their Spanish language in the schools and discriminating against them in jobs, housing and income.

Consigned in the main to menial jobs, they earn a little more money than the Negro, but because their families are larger, the per capita income is generally lower: $1,380 for Mexican-Americans, against $1,437 for nonwhites in the Los Angeles area.

The worst-off Chicanos are the farm workers. Testifying last December before the Civil Rights Commission in San Antonio, the local Roman Catholic Archbishop, the Most Rev. Robert E. Lucey, observed that migrant farm workers lived "in the awful reality of serfdom."

Like other ethnic groups, the Chicanos are drawn to cities. The crowded urban barrios are usually adjacent to the Negro ghettos, and the rising ferment among Mexican-Americans has been stimulated in part by the . . . civil rights movement.

In the Spanish-speaking ghetto of East Los Angeles, barrio toughs boast of grenades and other explosives cached for the day of revolt against the gringo [the white man].

In Denver, Rodolfo (Corky) Gonzales . . . a former prize fighter, claims total victory in last month's strike at a high school in the west side barrio, a strike marred by violence in which, Corky says, a dozen police cars were disabled.

Quixotic Courthouse Raider

In New Mexico, Reies Lopez Tijerina, the quixotic former evangelist who raided a courthouse two years ago to make a "citizen's arrest" of a district attorney, takes a visitor on a tour of a "pueblo libre," a proposed free city-state in the wilderness where Chicanos will control their own destiny.

Unfortunately, 90 per cent of the pueblo is national forest. This does not bother Tijerina's followers. They claim the land under Spanish royal grants made prior to American sovereignty. They have chopped down the boundary

This condensation from "A New Mexican-American Militancy," by Homer Bigart, The New York Times, April 20, 1969, p. 1. © 1969 by The New York Times Company. Reprinted by permission.

47

markers and other signs of gringo occupation.

They have even held a mock trial for a couple of forest rangers who fell into their hands. Tijerina himself is under a two-year Federal sentence for aiding and abetting an assault on a ranger. His conviction is under appeal. . . .

A Diverse People

. . . [Cesar] Chavez ["the sad-eyed director of the California grape strike"] has been called the spiritual leader of the Chicano moderates. His tiny bedroom at Delano, Calif., where he spends most of his time (he is afflicted with muscular spasms) is adorned with photos of his heroes—Gandhi and Martin Luther King, both apostles of nonviolence—and of his political mentor, the late Senator Robert F. Kennedy.

His belief in nonviolence seems unshakeable. He told a visitor: "Those of us who have seen violence never want to see it again. I know how it tears people apart. And in the end we lose.

"I'm not saying we should lay down and die. I think I'm as radical as anyone. But I think we can force meaningful change without the short cut of violence."

The strength of the militants is impossible to gauge. Tijerina contends he has 35,000 members in his Alianza; Corky Gonzales says he can muster 2,500 for a demonstration in Denver. Barrio militants in Los Angeles say they have "gone underground" and refuse to discuss strength.

"Our people are still frightened, but they are moving," commented Mr. Chavez, who said he had no wish to become a national leader. "I'm at most a leader of our union, and that union is very small," he said.

Three years ago, the Mexican-American community had no staff-funded organization except Mr. Chavez's organizing committee. Today there are several, including the Mexican-American Legal Defense and Educational Fund (which resembles the N.A.A.C.P. Legal Defense and Educational Fund, Inc.) and the Southwest Conference of La Raza (The People), both of which are supported by the Ford Foundation. . . .

The grievances of the Mexican-Americans, most of whom live in California, Texas, New Mexico, Arizona and Colorado, with sizable colonies in the Middle West (founded in the last century by construction gangs for the Santa Fe Railroad) sound familiar: job discrimination, miserable housing, social isolation,

lack of political power (the result of gerrymandering the urban barrios) and exposure to a school system completely insensitive to Mexican-American history and cultures.

In only one respect is the Mexican-American better off than the Negro. Provided he is not too swarthy and provided he has money, the Chicano can escape from the barrio and move into Anglo middle-class districts.

He is worse off in other respects. Of all the minorities, only the American Indian makes less money than the Chicano. A linguistic and cultural gap separates the Mexican-American from the Anglo. Proud of his ancient Spanish-Indian heritage, the Chicano is less eager for assimilation than the Negro.

Most Speak Little English

Most Chicano children speak only a few words of English when they enter school. It can be a traumatic experience, especially in districts where Chicano pupils are spanked if they are overheard using Spanish in the halls and on the playground. . . .

Besides being confronted with a foreign language, the Chicano pupil finds that the attitudes, social relationships and objects depicted in his lessons are entirely outside his home experience. He is constantly admonished that if he wants to be an American, he must not only speak American but think American as well.

Their school dropout rate (34 per cent for Chicano children enrolled in Grades 7–12 in Texas) is the highest for any minority group.

In San Antonio, which has the second largest Mexican-American colony (about 350,000; Los Angeles is first with about one million), a hearing conducted last December by [the] United States Civil Rights Commissioner . . . disclosed subtle forms of discrimination.

School officials admitted, according to [the Commissioner], that junior high school counselors tended to steer Chicanos into predominantly Mexican-American vocational high schools. This betrayed the counselors' ethnic stereotype of the Chicano as an individual inherently equipped only for vocational training and unsuited for the Anglo college preparatory schools, he said. . . .

School strikes and boycotts in the Southwest are becoming an almost daily occurrence. In Texas, Chicano pressure has obliged the school districts of San Antonio, Austin, El Paso and Edcouch-

Elsa (adjacent towns in the lower Rio Grande Valley) to stop the punishment of children using Spanish in schools or playgrounds. . . .

Corky Gonzales, 40 years old, father of eight children, was one of the top 10 featherweights from 1947 to 1955. A former Democratic district captain in the [Denver] barrio, he gave up politics because, he said, "I was being used." Then he founded a militant organization, "Crusade for Justice."

On a recent warm April day, a visitor to Corky's headquarters, a former Baptist church in the decaying Capitol Hill district of Denver, was led upstairs to a barnlike room. . . .

Accompanied by Guard

Corky, when he arrived with a bodyguard, went directly to his office, a musty cluttered room that had been the minister's study. He was no longer a featherweight, but he still looked trim and tough. He had grown a bushy black mustache, and he wore a pendant symbol of his movement—a three dimensional head representing Spanish father, Indian mother and mestizo offspring, mounted on an Aztec calendar plaque.

"How can there be justice," he demanded bitterly, "if we don't have our people on the jury system and the draft boards?" . . .

Corky said he believed the best way to unify Mexican-Americans was through nationalism.

To foster Chicano nationalism Corky held a five-day conference in Denver at the end of March. About 1,000 youths from five southwestern states showed up, and they represented an ideological spectrum that included the New Left, Communists and liberals.

Coalition in Dispute

The convention nearly broke up on the issue of coalition with Negroes. Some barrio youths, resentful of Negro dominance in the civil rights movement, insisted on maintaining racial separateness.

Corky, who had quarreled with the black leadership of the Poor People's March on Washington a year ago, preached a modified ethnic nationalism, and he prevailed. Coalition with the blacks might be feasible later, he said, but meanwhile the Chicano must first achieve enough self-reliance to "do his thing alone."

As a first step toward liberating the Chicanos, Corky told the youths to go home and prepare a nationwide walkout of Mexican-American students. . . .

"Brown Power" in Texas

The new Chicano militancy, with its cry of "Brown Power," can be heard even in Texas, where Mexican-Americans have long complained of brutal suppression by the Texas Rangers and by the state and local police.

[Recently] more than 2,000 Chicanos paraded through the border town of Del Rio, ostensibly to protest Gov. Preston Smith's decision to shut down the local projects of VISTA, the domestic Peace Corps, but also to cry out against discrimination.

Normally such demonstrations are small and sedate, the Chicanos parading behind a priest carrying the banner of the Virgin of Guadelupe.

But this time the priest and the Virgin were forced to yield the front of the line to militants of the Mexican-American Youth Organization (MAYO), and they tacked a manifesto on the courthouse door warning that violence might erupt if demands for equality were not met.

One of the founders of MAYO, José Angel Gutierrez, 22, said the organization's goals were the formation of political units independent of the Republican and Democratic parties ("only Mexicans can really represent Mexican interests") gaining control of schools, and the building of economic power through the weapon of boycott.

But the cause has had serious setbacks in the Rio Grande Valley. Attempts to organize farm labor have failed completely. Unemployment is high. And a powerful friend of the Chicanos, the Rev. Ed Krueger, was recently dismissed by the Texas Conference of Churches as its field representative in the lower valley.

Mr. Krueger said he had been under pressure from conference officials to "work with the establishment instead of with the poor," and that his superiors were also displeased because he refused to withdraw a suit against the Texas Rangers, a suit alleging that the Rangers manhandled Mr. Krueger and his wife when they tried to photograph a farm strike in Starr County two years ago.

The dismissal of Mr. Krueger was investigated by a panel headed by Dr. Alfonso Rodriguez, in charge of the Hispanic-American ministry of the National Council of Churches. The panel reported "tragic conditions of alienation, polarization, conflict and tension" in the valley, adding that the tension had been aggravated by Mr. Krueger's dismissal.

Farther west, El Paso and Phoenix show scant signs of Chicano militancy, despite their teeming barrios. In El Paso, where thousands of Mexican-Americans still live in squalid, rat-infested, barrack-like "presidios," some of which have only one outhouse for 20 families, about the only recent demonstrations have been peaceful "prayer-ins" on the lawn of a slumlord's agent.

In Phoenix a Roman Catholic priest, the Rev. Miguel Barragan, field representative of the Southwest Conference of La Raza, said it was difficult to involve the older Chicanos because they were prejudiced against political solutions, recalling the turmoil in Mexico. And the newer migrants feared police harassment and loss of jobs.

Yet the priest warned:

"If there are no immediate changes in the Southwest, no visible improvement in the political and economic status of the Mexican-American, then I definitely foresee that our youths will resort to violence to demand the dignity and respect they deserve as human beings and as American citizens.

"I see the barrios already full of hate and self-destruction. I see an educational system doing psychological damage to the Mexican-American, creating a self-identity crisis by refusing to recognize his rich cultural heritage and by suppressing his language.

"And therefore, to me, burning a building and rioting is less violent than what is happening to our youth under a school system that classes as 'retarded and inferior' those with a language difficulty."

California Chicano Demands

In California Mexican-American demands for larger enrollments of Chicanos at the Berkeley and Los Angeles campuses of the University of California were receiving sympathetic attention. And Berkeley was planning a Department of Ethnic Studies in which Mexican history and culture would be taught.

But in East Los Angeles and Boyle Heights, these concessions were taken as insignificant crumbs.

"Basically, people are tired of talking," said a youth in the Boyle Heights barrio. "A confrontation is inevitable. It's not unusual to see people going around with grenades and TNT. The tension is here; the weapons are here. The new underground organizations of ex-cons, addicts and dropouts make the Brown Berets look like Boy Scouts."

Across town, on the U.C.L.A. campus, a neutral observer gave a pessimistic but somewhat milder assessment. Prof. Leo Grebler, a German-born economist who directed a four-year study of Mexican-Americans for the Ford Foundation, [a study which has since been published], recalled how Gunnar Myrdal in his classic study of the Negro in the United States had been over-optimistic about the nation's ability to cope with the racial crisis. . . .

The study [has concluded] that the Anglo Establishment must quickly remove obstacles to the socio-economic development of the Mexican-Americans and broaden its understanding of this minority.

End questions

1. What is an "ethnic group"? How is it identifiable?

2. How does the political, social, and economic position of the Chicanos compare with other groups that you are familiar with?

3. What ethnic groups are readily discernible in your community? Do they have any grievances? How can these ethnic groups make their opinions felt in the local political systems?

4. Compare the Black Power movement with the Brown Power one. Which group do you think has a better chance for success?

Supplementary Reading

GIBSON, JOHN S. *Ideology and World Affairs.* Boston: Houghton, Mifflin, 1964. This book, which is based on a series of television broadcasts, examines the impact of extreme ideologies of both the right and the left on democracy. It answers and explains the basic questions about the origin of extremist ideologies, and also gives a good explanation about the origins of our own democratic beliefs.

HANDLIN, OSCAR. *The Uprooted.* New York: Grosset & Dunlap, 1957. A rousing narrative that describes the waves of immigration tossed up on America's shores and the immigrants' first encounters with their new way of life.

LERNER, MAX. *America as a Civilization.* 2 vols. New York: Simon & Schuster, 1961. The author makes an attempt to review the innumerable possible factors that have contributed to the culture and institutions that can now be categorized as truly American.

LIPPMANN, WALTER. *The Public Philosophy.* Boston: Little, Brown, 1955. The venerable journalist concludes that government by mass movement has replaced government by moral principle. He calls for a revival of the Public Philosophy—The Natural Law, which alone can bring the government and the governed back into their proper relationship with each other.

PACKARD, VANCE. *The Status Seekers.* New York: David McKay, 1959. Packard examines America in terms of its class structure—but it is a class structure that we have not really been aware of. In addition, he examines what happens to the class structure after a period of unparalleled prosperity and material abundance. Does life become better? Are opportunities for leadership made easier? These are only a few of the provocative questions that this book answers.

SORAUF, FRANCIS J. *Political Science: An Informal Overview.* Columbus, Ohio: C. E. Merrill, 1967. Designed as a guide for teachers, this study can also be of great benefit to students searching for a concise introduction to a sometimes confusing topic. The author suggests that political science is drifting away from the traditional, institutional approach to a behavioral approach which examines the predictable and unpredictable reactions to politics.

STONE, CHUCK. *Black Political Power in America.* Indianapolis: Bobbs-Merrill, 1968. With a humerous and direct style, Mr. Stone traces the development of the Afro-Americans' role in the American political system. While presenting some personal viewpoints on the roles of other ethnic groups, the author touches on the political experience of black Americans at local, state, and national levels.

WITTKE, CARL F. *We Who Built America.* Rev. ed. Cleveland: Press of Case Western Reserve, 1964. A collection of essays that reveal the role that immigrants have played in the development of America.

It must not be assumed that the American political system blossomed overnight in a flurry of activity and debate during the Constitutional Convention at Philadelphia in 1787. The heritage from which Americans drew the ideas for their government was an old one—beginning with Plato and continuing through John Locke and Baron de Montesquieu. The Framers of the Constitution, thus, had a fairly well-developed knowledge of political theory from which they took the ideas they incorporated into the Constitution.

Although the American democratic system is partly a product of the Revolution and of the political philosophies prevalent at that time, it has been developing ever since. With a remarkably flexible Constitution as its cornerstone, the American system has been constantly expanding to meet the needs of the people. Yet most of the basic principles that are still adhered to in the present system were born of solutions to the problems of the new nation. Federalism, for example, seemed to be a more than satisfactory response to the desires of the new states to retain some of the sovereignty they enjoyed when they first broke away from Britain. Defenders of states' rights today trace the origins of their arguments back to these early battles for state sovereignty.

Other features of American democracy as it is known today were fed by changes in the political climate of the nation. The expansion of the suffrage, for instance, came about in two steps. First, the Constitution was strengthened by adding certain amendments granting the vote to all citizens regardless of color or sex. But this was not enough. The right to vote was guaranteed only after the passage of legislation enforcing these amendments.

Almost two hundred years have passed since the American Constitution was written. Yet, the document is still workable. Some amendments have been added for the purpose of defining phrases or statements in the original work. Others have been added in response to the changes in American life. One amendment, the Twenty-first, was even added to negate a previous amendment, the Eighteenth, which was the product of a social outcry—Prohibition. Despite all these changes, the basic principles of the Constitution still stand.

UNIT TWO
The Setting of the American System

CHAPTER 3

The Ideological Foundations: Philosophies of Constitutional Democracy

The American democratic system is generally credited with having certain characteristics. Some of the more familiar ones are majority rule, government by the people, government conducted by delegates of the people, and a society that accepts the principle of equality and practices it. But no one of these characteristics, nor all of them together, can adequately suggest even the broad outlines of American democracy. Thus, the American political system should be regarded as a blend of many features that cannot be labeled with a single term.

The Meaning of Constitutional Democracy

The most accurate phrase describing the American political system is *constitutional democracy*. Each term in this phrase suggests a complex set of ideas. To understand effectively the meaning of this phrase each word should be considered separately.

A definition of democracy. The distinguishing feature of a democratic society is that sovereignty rests equally among all the people. (Democracy comes from the Greek word *dēmokratía; demos* meaning "people," and *kratos* meaning "power.") This does not mean that popular consent is required for every law, amendment to the Constitution, administrative regulation, or other action of government. It means that the whole structure of government rests on a foundation of popular support.

The practical effect of having sovereignty rest with the people is that governmental decisions are tested and evaluated by how well they meet the people's interests. Since a democratic government is established to meet the needs of the people, it acts properly and/or legitimately only if its actions are directed toward those needs.

There are, however, other ways for a government to act and still get results.

Some societies, during times of religious fervor, have accepted the actions of their king and his government because they were certain that the king acted in accordance with the word of God. Other governments have succeeded by threatening the people with physical force. In the United States though, the government's performance is measured by the people according to how well it meets their needs.

The political systems of many other modern nations are also structured on this principle of satisfying the people's wishes. Scholars from the Soviet Union, for example, will declare that democratic principles are set forth in the Soviet Constitution and practiced by the government. Whether these principles are truly carried out in the same fashion as in the United States is the subject of constant dispute between Soviet and American scholars.

Even if democratic principles were carried out identically by these two political systems, another important question has to be answered to make an effective comparison. What is the extent of the government's authority over the people in its quest to meet their collective needs? American scholars maintain that the Soviet government is *totalitarian*—that it has total control over its people and unlimited authority to achieve what it thinks their needs are. This control is exercised by censoring the press, by denying freedom

◀ Are the ingredients for the constitutional stew constantly being changed, or have they remained the same since the original recipe was incorporated into the 1787 Constitution?

53

"We Now Bring You More Late Election Returns"

Norris – Vancouver Sun, Canada

"...TOMORROW A CITIZEN CAN WALK INTO THIS HUMBLE STATION, PROUD IN HIS DEMOCRATIC RIGHT TO CHOOSE HIS GOVERNMENT, SECURE IN THE PRIVACY OF HIS CHOICE, PROFOUNDLY THANKFUL FOR THIS HARD-WON FREEDOM.....AND LOUSE UP HIS BALLOT."

(A basic democratic right—the right to vote—may operate differently under contrasting political systems.)

of religion, assembly, or speech, by completely directing economic life, and by rigidly dominating education.

In contrast, America's system is called *constitutional* because governmental authority is limited first by the Constitution and then by other factors. These limitations prevent the government from controlling the people. While the Soviet Union also has a constitution, in practice the document does not serve to restrain the government's control over its people.

An explanation of constitutionalism. To call the American system simply a democracy, then, is to neglect one of its key, distinguishing features—*constitutionalism.* A constitutional system is one in which the power of the government is kept in check by certain principles inherent in the system. These principles may be based on unwritten customs, traditions, and social facts—as in Great Britain—or they may be set forth in a written document—as in the United States.

One of the major checks on the power of American government is the guarantee of certain rights to individual citizens. Some of these rights were set down in the Bill of Rights—the first ten amendments to the Constitution—which guarantee such basic freedoms as speech and press. The Constitution erects numerous obstacles to governmental action so that citizens are free to pursue most activities without interference from or control by the government. Moreover, there are only a few circumstances when the government can deny an American his full rights as a citizen. Prisoners, for example, can be denied the right to vote.

Another important restraining feature of American constitutionalism is the *separation of powers* among the different branches of the national government. As powerful as the President is, there are many things which he is not authorized to do. Even in those areas where he *is* authorized to act, he can be checked by the

54

actions of Congress or the Supreme Court. The same is true, of course, with respect to the other two branches of the national government.

Similarly, the power of the national government is restrained by the *federal structure* of the political system with its division of authority between the national government and the fifty state governments. In fact, the national government's authority is limited to those powers expressly enumerated or reasonably implied in the Constitution; all other powers remain with the states.

Each of these checks on governmental authority does, in turn, prevent any abuse of governmental power by a majority. The separation of powers and the federal structure serve to keep the representatives of a majority from misusing the authority of government.

The purpose of these restrictions, however, is not only to protect the minority from being tyrannized by the majority but also to make governmental policy reflect a balanced expression of popular preferences. Thus, a narrow majority—such as fifty-one percent of the votes in Congress—can not easily commit the society to a course of action that is severely in conflict with the wishes of a large minority.

Constitutional restraints also tend to check the swift execution of a policy that may have the backing of virtually everyone in the nation. This is sometimes desirable because the policy may be an expression of emotionalism that could be regretted when passions have cooled and new information and ideas have become available. If the government were able to commit itself easily to popular courses of action, it would often have to reverse policies and try to correct mistakes.

Despite the basic importance of these constitutional restraints on governmental activity, the term "constitutional" by itself is inadequate to describe the American system. Constitutionalism can be *monarchical,* as it was for many centuries in Great Britain when authority was divided between the king and parliament, and restrained by some guaranteed rights such as those expressed in the Magna Carta. Constitutionalism can also be aristocratic, as it was in certain states during the American Republic's early years when only adult males who were not slaves and who owned a certain amount of property could vote.

"Constitutional" and "democracy" are both needed to portray adequately the complexities, strengths, and weaknesses of the American political system. The American system is a constitutional one because of its sources of limitation; it is a democracy because it responds, within limits, to the needs of the people.

The dilemma of a constitutional democracy. In a constitutional democracy, people evaluate the government's performance by asking: How well does it accomplish the public interest or work for the common good? Since each person has many interests that might conflict with those of others, it is hard, if not impossible, to know how all these personal elements combine to form a "public interest" on any given matter. The most severe challenge to a constitutional democracy is that it must preserve the individual's freedoms and interests, while it is convincing them to act collectively for the benefit of all. This dilemma is at the core of the philosophy of any constitutional democracy. And the success of a constitutional democracy is measured by its ability to solve this dilemma.

This challenge is particularly difficult because it is impossible for both basic objectives to be fully realized at the same time. No action can be taken on behalf of the public interest without sacrificing someone's private interest or freedom. On the other hand, it would be impossible for any public policy to be so broad that it could answer every individual's demands.

This perpetual dilemma of a constitutional democracy is solved only by compromise. The numerous demands and supports of citizens are converted by the structure of the political system into policy outputs that reflect a balance between private sacrifices and benefits to the public. Thus, most citizens give up part of their money in taxes so that other citizens will have sufficient food, shelter, and clothing. As long as the balance reflected by most of these policy outputs remains tolerable to the majority of people, the system remains workable.

Styles of representation. The mechanism of representation is probably the most important device for ensuring that tolerable balances are expressed by policy outputs. There are two styles of representation employed by elected officials, and the combined use of these styles makes balanced policies possible.

■ *Direct representation.* One style of representation commonly used by congressmen and other legislators might be called *direct,* or *transmission-belt, representation.* Here, the congressman votes or expresses views in accordance with the dominant desires of his constituents. He serves as a direct conveyor of these interests to the representative assembly. In the assembly, these interests are registered and weighed against the preferences of the other represented constituencies.

If this method were employed by all congressmen, the output of the legislative subsystem would be policies that are consistently weighted in favor of the interests of some constituents and that almost totally ignored the interests of others. Overall balance among the many different needs and interests of the citizens would be difficult to achieve, and no one would be paying attention to matters of general concern.

■ *Indirect representation.* The other style of representation used in the American political system is *indirect,* or *virtual, representation.* Here, a representative does not simply register the dominant views of his constituents. Instead, he assumes that they have chosen him as a representative on the basis of his judgments as a politician, and not because of his reliability as a transmission belt. He interprets his responsibility as requiring him to weigh carefully all issues of public policy and to decide which course of action is in the best interests of the total society.

This concept of indirect representation was described particularly well by Edmund Burke in a speech to his electors in Bristol, while he was campaigning for election to the British Parliament in the late eighteenth century:

"To deliver an opinion is the right of all men; that of constituents is a weighty and respectable opinion, which a representative ought always to rejoice to hear; and which he ought always most seriously to consider. But authoritative instructions; mandates issued, which the member is bound blindly and explicitly to obey, to vote and to argue for, though contrary to the clearest conviction of his judgment and conscience; these are things utterly unknown to the laws of this land, and which arise from a fundamental mistake of the whole order and tenor of our constitution. Parliament is not a congress of ambassadors from different and hostile interests; which interests each must maintain, as an agent and advocate, against other agents and advocates; but parliament is a deliberative assembly of one nation, with one interest, that of the whole; where not local purposes, not local prejudices

ought to guide, but the general good . . .

"*Certainly gentlemen, it ought to be the happiness and glory of a representative, to live in the strictest union, the closest correspondence, and the most unreserved communication with his constituents. Their wishes ought to have great weight with him; their opinion high respect; their business unremitted attention. . . . But his unbiased opinion, his mature judgment, his enlightened conscience, he ought not to sacrifice to you, to any man, or to any set of men living.*"[1]

■ *Mixture of styles.* The operation of both of these styles on all levels of the political system results in a reasonable balance of public and private interests. Specialized needs and desires as well as the welfare of the entire community are both taken into consideration. The direct representative helps his own, smaller constituency achieve goals which might otherwise be overlooked, while protecting rights that might otherwise be violated. The indirect representative, on the other hand, helps to produce policies that are designed to benefit the total community regardless of the fact that any single constituency, including his own, may not favor them.

A good example of a representative who has adopted both styles over the years is Senator J. William Fulbright of Arkansas. On issues concerning race relations, Senator Fulbright has acted as a direct representative, responding to the dominant views of his constituents. On issues concerning foreign affairs, however, he operates as an indirect representative, working for what he considers the best interest of the total society.

[1] *Edmund Burke,* Burke's Politics: Selected Writings and Speeches of Edmund Burke on Reform, Revolution, and War, *eds. J.S. Hoffman and Paul Levack (New York: Alfred A. Knopf, 1949), pp. 115–116.*

"Here, consensus! Here, consensus! Here, boy!"

(No matter which style of representation a delegate chooses, can he discover what the public is thinking?)

Government officials who are not legislators also employ two styles of representation. The President, for example, continually acts as both a direct and an indirect representative. On the one hand, he tries to pursue policies that coincide with national public opinion. On the other hand, he has the responsibility of doing whatever he feels is best for the nation, regardless of the action's immediate popularity. Naturally, each President, as each congressman, develops his own mixture of these two styles, his goals, and his understanding of public needs.

In many ways, it is remarkable that American constitutional democracy has survived and flourished in spite of the dilemmas which challenge it. The Americans who framed the Constitution deserve much credit for the strength and endurance of our political system. They embodied certain principles into the Constitution that have enabled the system to work effectively throughout the varied stages of America's growth and development.

1. What checks and restraints are incorporated in the American political system to prevent the government from becoming totalitarian?
2. Distinguish between a constitutional state and a totalitarian state.

The Origins of American Political Philosophy

Throughout history, there are examples of political systems that have evolved without the guidance or adoption of any particular set of ideas or systematic philosophy. Governments established by force or by a personal claim to power have often been justified later by a philosophy created solely to support the already existent government. In the case of the United States, the government was deliberately designed by men who had already given a certain amount of consideration to the writings of others about the philosphy of government.

Historical influences. Since the beginning of Western civilization, political philosophers have been concerned with an extensive range of questions about the processes of government. They have considered such matters as the nature of the state, the role of constitutions and other forms of law, the relationship between the people and their government, the best form of government to attain various goals, and the meaning of concepts like "the public interest" and "the common good."

Most of the issues of political philosophy were raised in one form or another as early as the fifth century B.C. first by Plato, and later by Aristotle. And almost all of these issues remain important today. The emphasis of concern has shifted, of course, throughout history, fluctuating in accordance with economic and social changes.

The issue of the relationship between church and state, for example, formed the core of much medieval philosophy, especially in the writings of Saint Augustine and Saint Thomas Aquinas. During this long period of Western history, most political thought was expressed as theology. Later, when the bond between religion and politics was weakened by the Reformation, political philosophy took on a more secular aspect.

The American political tradition was strongly influenced by European political philosophy of the seventeenth and eighteenth centuries. This era was marked by a decline in the influence of spiritual values. Human conduct was guided by a new reliance on reason and an increase in material values. The emphasis on the use of reason to solve problems contributed to the development of a scientific approach to politics.

The science of politics. Americans of the eighteenth century applied the scientific approach when composing the Constitution in 1787. This approach was also used by Alexander Hamilton, James Madison, and John Jay in a series of eighty-five newspaper articles, written during 1787 and 1788 to champion the cause of the Constitution. Addressed principally to the voters of New York, these papers were later published as a book, *The Federalist,* in the spring of 1788. Hamilton and Madison took this opportunity to advance numerous arguments and to cite evidence supporting the principles embodied in the Constitution.

Much political writing in eighteenth-century America was political science in the sense that the term is used today. The evidence used to support and justify political propositions was often crude, consisting of vague and unconvincing references to history and philosophers. At the same time, American political thinking could also be persuasive and logical, especially when it was based on the practicality of the colonial experience. Fundamental principles of the American Constitution, such as the separation of powers, came from a combination of philosophy and experience.

Because American political thought is derived from many sources, it is a mixture of viewpoints. Thus, it is difficult to speak of a unified American approach to political theory. The frontier environment, the maturing political life of the colonies, and the ensuing struggles with Great Britain and its agents in the colonies all produced lively political discussion leading to the evolvement of an American philosophy.

A universe governed by science. Among the more widespread political ideas in eighteenth-century America was the concept that men can shape their governments, their societies, and their communities in accordance with the laws of nature. The source of this idea was the belief in the superiority of science and the scientific nature of the universe.

The American revolutionaries were particularly optimistic. They were men like Thomas Jefferson who believed that man can better himself through education and that societies can and should form governments which will preserve liberty and the natural rights of all men.

The Declaration of Independence clearly illustrated the prevailing assumptions. Even though the document was drafted by one man, Jefferson, it strongly mirrored the views of the period about government, the nature of the universe, and even the nature of man. Consider the opening paragraph:

"When in the Course of human events, it becomes necessary for one people to dissolve the political bonds which have connected them with another, and to assume among the Powers of the earth, the separate and equal station to which the Laws of Nature and of Nature's God entitle them, a decent respect to the opinions of mankind requires that they should declare the causes which impel them to the separation."

Note in this passage the phrases "Laws of Nature" and "Nature's God." They show a belief in a law of nature higher than that of man. The central position is given to the idea of a god who is the source of that law. This "Nature's God" is not, however, a specific supreme being worshiped through a particular religious sect or institution.

Natural rights. What is the content of the natural law that Jefferson mentions in the Declaration of Independence? This is clearly set forth in the second paragraph. "All men are created equal . . . they are endowed by their Creator with certain unalienable Rights, that among these are Life, Liberty, and the pursuit of Happiness."

Since the composition of the Declaration of Independence, there has been controversy over why Jefferson included "happiness" and not "property" among the natural rights. Clinton Rossiter, a modern historian, claims that Jefferson

"was more than a felicitous penman when he proclaimed the 'pursuit of happiness'

A FINE OLD AMERICAN FAMILY

(This 1930's cartoon shows the right of personal property as one of the American system's fundamental ideals.)

to be a natural right of man, for by the time of the Declaration most thinkers agreed with him on this point. He was, however, something of a non-conformist in substituting this right for that of property. He alone flirted seriously with the advanced view that property was a social rather than a natural right."[2]

It would probably be a more accurate reflection of eighteenth century America if "property" instead of "happiness" had been included as one of these rights. For property rights have always been considered by Americans to be among the most fundamental of all rights. Despite Jefferson's reasons for including "happiness" in the Declaration of Independence, the Founding Fathers did recognize the importance of the concept of private property. In the Fifth Amendment to the Constitution, adopted in 1791, it was stipulated that private property can not be taken by undue governmental action. Property was, thus, placed on an equal level with "life" and "liberty." And, again in the Fourteenth Amendment, adopted in 1868, the right of all citizens to "life, liberty, and property" was reaffirmed.

■ *The influence of John Locke.* The American concern for property is definitely traceable to the philosophy of John Locke, the seventeenth-century English political theorist. Locke based his theory of government on similar sources to those used by other political theorists of the time, and he formulated his opinions during a period when the English were fighting for parliamentary supremacy.

A similar urgency to overthrow what was felt to be a despotic British govern-

[2]*Clinton Rossiter*, Seedtime of the Republic (*New York: Harcourt, Brace & World, 1953*), p. 380.

ment existed later in Revolutionary America. It was thus quite natural that Locke be read by educated colonial Americans, although he probably did not enjoy as wide an audience as was suspected by some historians. In any case, the colonists drew on the same tradition of political thought and experience that underlay Locke's thinking.

Regardless of the extent to which Locke was actually read by the colonists, the similarity of his ideas to those of eighteenth-century America is striking. Certainly Jefferson and a number of his contemporaries studied Locke. In fact one of Locke's works, entitled *Second Treatise of Civil Government* (1690), was used by Jefferson when he drafted the Declaration of Independence.

A summary of Locke's treatise reveals the parallels between Locke and Jefferson. Locke believed that all men were reasonable enough to recognize a general principle, which he termed "the Natural Law," that no one ought to harm the life, liberty, or property of any other man. In the absence of government, Locke thought, each man would be continually exposed to uncertainties and fears for his safety, liberty, and possessions. Each man would then apply these principles to suit himself when his own interests were involved. Without government there would be no recognized, unbiased judge to turn to for an impartial settlement of disputes among men. Men would establish governments, then, for their mutual protection and to settle their differences.

The real influence of Locke goes far beyond the impact he had on Thomas Jefferson. There is little question that American political life has adhered to the fundamental principles contained in Locke's theories about relations among men, society, and government. For example, Locke emphasized the sanctity of private property. The strength of this principle in the American political tradition undoubtedly accounts in large measure for the fact that this nation has rejected communism's central principle of collective ownership.

Of particular importance is the extent to which Americans share Locke's views on the nature of man. All of our governmental institutions, processes, and traditions are based on these views. Such concepts as the primacy of the individual, man's inborn ability to exercise reason to discern truth and to arrive at the higher principles of order and justice, and the political and social equality among men are all values which Americans accept as Locke did. While these values have not always been borne out by experience and practice, America is theoretically committed to these ideals.

■ *The Baron de Montesquieu.* Eighteenth-century Americans admired many other political philosophers in addition to Locke. Probably the most influential one was the French Baron de Montesquieu, who wrote in the early eighteenth century, during the reigns of Louis XIV and Louis XV. Clinton Rossiter says that "every literate colonist could quote [Montesquieu] to advantage, and . . . [his] exposition of the separation of powers was already making perfect sense to American minds."[3]

The most prominent feature of Montesquieu's political theory, the separation of powers, is contained in his famous *Spirit of the Laws.* In this work, Montesquieu points out the need for a government of law, incorporating a separation of powers to protect individual liberty. Montesquieu argued that by granting some authority to each branch of government— legislative, executive, and judicial—the power of one branch would offset, or

[3]Ibid., p. 359.

check, the power of the other branches. In such a system, liberty would be protected from the excesses of government. He assumed that since those who governed would use the power in their possession to the fullest, tyranny would be prevented by distributing governmental power.

Although Montesquieu attempted to use the British constitution as a model for his book, the example was not a successful one. The British did not have the kind of separation of powers about which Montesquieu wrote. Still his concept of a constitutional government founded on a separation of powers was important to the Americans.

■ *Basic acceptance of the theorists.* Although many political philosophers had an impact upon the American political tradition, Locke and Montesquieu can be considered the two principal exponents of the political philosophy adopted by Revolutionary America. Certainly there have been various divergent trends in American political thought. For example, Alexander Hamilton, James Madison, and John Adams—three major figures in the construction and development of the political system—did not share the optimistic Lockean view of the nature of man with Jefferson. Still they did share a faith in the effectiveness of constitutional democracy and that faith has been maintained since the formulation of the Constitution. Essentially this is a belief in government by the people under law.

In accordance with both Locke and Montesquieu, Americans have recognized that government can be too big, and that some restraints have to be imposed, both on the will of the majority and on the government, to preserve individual rights. Principally, these rights are expressed in the Constitution, which also provides that neither the power of government, nor that of the people expressed through government, should be absolute.

Review questions

1. How does the Declaration of Independence illustrate that Americans were optimistic about the nature of man?
2. How does Locke show that governments are necessary?

Constitutional Restraints on Popular Sovereignty

The American constitutional system is based on ideas, tradition, and political experience. These three factors have enabled the complex but flexible system to meet its many challenges successfully. On the one hand, the constitutional system has served as a potent instrument for the execution of the popular will. On the other hand, it has been sufficiently fragmented and restrained to avoid the dangers of unchecked governmental power.

The merits of the American system can be assigned in part to the wisdom and judgment of the Framers of the Constitution. These men blended their knowledge of political philosophy with their own experience to compose a complex legal mechanism as the basis of a constitutional democracy.

The Federalist Papers reveal the thinking that went into the process of justifying the Constitution. By examining some of these ideas, it is possible to come to a better understanding of the fundamental structure of American government.

The problem of faction. The reasoning employed by some of the Framers is illustrated by James Madison in *The Federalist,*

No. 10, when he explores the problem of faction.

In this paper, Madison defined "faction" as "a number of citizens, whether amounting to a majority or minority of the whole, who are united and actuated by some common impulse of passion, or of interest, adverse to the rights of other citizens, or to the permanent and aggregate [collective] interests of the community." In other words Madison was implying that a faction was a special interest group. He foresaw the development of factions because he anticipated the inevitable conflict between individual interests and the public interest. He wished to construct a system of popular government which would promote the general welfare. At the same time he recognized the persistence of faction as an obstacle to the realization of the general welfare. "The friend of popular governments," he said, "never finds himself so much alarmed for their character and fate, as when he contemplates their propensity to this dangerous vice [faction]."

One of the sources of faction that Madison recognized in eighteenth-century America was the unequal distribution of property. In *The Federalist*, No. 10, he said:

"Those who hold, and those who are without property, have ever formed distinct interests in society. Those who are creditors, and those who are debtors, fall under a like discrimination. A landed interest, a manufacturing interest, a mercantile interest, a moneyed interest, with many lesser interests, grow up of necessity in civilized nations, and divide them into different classes, actuated by different senti-

Burr Schafer. Copyright © 1965. Saturday Review, Inc.

THROUGH HISTORY WITH J. WESLEY SMITH
"But I have my own well; why should I be taxed for Croton Reservoir?"

(Of concern to all factions and interest groups, taxes have often been a source of political division.)

ments and views. The regulation of these various and interfering interests forms the principal task of modern legislation, and involves the spirit of party and faction in the necessary and ordinary operations of government."

According to Madison, once faction was able to influence government, serious consequences would result. This was because faction, as defined by Madison, was opposed to the national interest. He felt that legislators and other members of the government would naturally act in accordance with the interests that they represented and which gave them support. Madison clung to a skeptical view of human nature—namely, that politicians strive for maximum power and their own interests.

Controlling the effects of faction. It occurred to Madison that there were two possible ways to remove the causes of faction: first, "by destroying the liberty" which faction needs in order to survive; and, second, by making every citizen conform in their opinions, passions, and interests. But he rejected both alternatives. The first method was, of course, unsatisfactory for Madison because he was committed to freedom and popular government. The second was unsatisfactory because Madison was a realist who believed that the "causes of faction"—man's fallibility, and his "self-love"—were inherent in the nature of man.

Having determined that "the *causes* of faction could not be removed," Madison concluded that "relief is only to be sought in the means of controlling its *effects*." One way to control the effects of faction, as he saw it, was to federate a number of popularly governed communities into one large representative republic. By bringing a sufficient number of divergent factions into one large republic, Madison thought the strength of any single faction would be diluted, and they would balance out each other. He reasoned that some "factious leaders may kindle a flame within their particular states" but would "be unable to spread a general conflagration through the other states." In like manner, "a malady" might be contained within a county or district without spreading to the whole state.

In addition, Madison felt that a government of representatives would further control the effects of faction by refining and enlarging the views of the public. He thought that special interests would be watered down "by passing them through the medium of a chosen body of citizens, whose wisdom may best discern the true interest of their country, and whose patriotism and love of justice, will be least likely to temporary or partial considerations."

It is clearly not enough though, Madison continued, to rely only on the federal structure and on the principle of representation to protect against faction. For "men of factious tempers, of local prejudices, or of sinister designs, may by intrigue, by corruption, or by other means, first obtain the suffrages, and then betray the interests of the people."

Madison thus recognized that factions could develop within the government itself as well as among the citizens of the nation. What was to be done to check the power of special interests within the federal government itself? Consideration of this problem led Madison to support a separation of powers among the executive, legislative, and judicial branches of the national government.

Review questions

1. Why was faction so feared by Madison?
2. Why did Madison reject both ways of removing the causes of faction?

The Doctrine of the Separation of Powers

Although it had been tested somewhat during the colonial and post-Revolutionary periods, the doctrine of the separation of powers was accepted largely on faith. Its effectiveness had not been proven. In *The Federalist*, No. 51, Madison noted that

"the great security against a gradual concentration of the several powers in the same department [of government], consists in giving to those who administer each department, the necessary constitutional means, and personal motives, to resist encroachment of the others. . . . If men were angels, no government would be necessary. If angels were to govern men, neither external or internal controls on government would be necessary. In framing a government, which is to be administered by men over men, the great difficulty lies in this: You must first enable a government to control the governed; and in the next place, oblige it to control itself."

The government then, according to Madison, should have two characteristics. First it should have the power to govern the people, and secondly, it should be motivated to control itself. The delegates to the Constitutional Convention of 1787 had to decide what fundamental powers the government would need to govern the people, and how these powers would be divided among the branches of government.

The Framers developed the practical arrangement of the separation of powers. First, the government had to be able to make laws, to legislate. This power was given to the legislature—the Congress. Second, it had to be able to administer, or enforce the laws once they were made. This power was given to the executive— the President. And third, the government had to be able to settle disputes that might arise, either between the branches of government or between the people and the government. This judicial power was given to the Supreme Court and the inferior courts. All of this was not accomplished, however, without some debate among the Framers over just how the separation of powers was to be incorporated in the American government.

Importance of the legislative branch. Of the three branches of government—executive, legislative, and judicial—set up in the Constitution, the legislative branch received the most attention from American political theorists in the eighteenth century. This attention was an outgrowth of the emphasis placed on legislative bodies in Great Britain and in the colonies. The principle of parliamentary supremacy had been firmly established in Great Britain. And although the colonies were initially subject to strong executives (the royal governors), colonial assemblies had assumed more and more power during the eighteenth century.

The belief that great power should be invested in legislative bodies was heightened when the state constitutions, written after the Revolution, granted even more formal power to the legislatures than had been acquired by the colonial assemblies. In many instances, the new state constitutions merely recognized legally what had already been practiced in fact.

After the Revolution began, it soon became obvious that some form of national government would be necessary. But the Articles of Confederation, which set up a national government in 1781, reflected the strong belief in legislative power, and established a weak structure in which there was no executive or judicial branch. While most legislative authority was retained by the states during this period from 1781 to 1787, the central government did manage to obtain some power in the national legislature.

(The original contest between the executive and the legislature over power is an ever-present struggle.)

When forming the federal constitution of 1787, it was clear to the Framers that significant authority had to be assigned to an executive if the new government was to have any strength at all. A great deal of effort was spent on convincing the populace within the various states that the new executive branch would not usurp essential power from the legislature. Since the power to govern had only recently been acquired by the states, they were jealously guarding their hard-won right.

Balance of legislative and executive power. Eighteenth-century attitudes about appropriate balance of power between the legislature and the executive were unclear. On the one hand, some of the Framers felt that the legislature should have a great portion of governmental authority. Since it would have the widest range of representation possible, the legislature would be the branch continuously responsive to the wishes of the people. On the other hand, some Framers of the Constitution felt that the amount of authority required by any legislature for a popular form of government would almost certainly result in an abusive exercise of power.

There were, then, conflicting opinions among different groups at the Constitutional Convention over the extent of legislative and executive authority. Sometimes even the same person would have a conflict in his own mind about the role of the legislature and executive in government.

Thomas Jefferson, who did not attend the Convention but who held ideas similar to those of many delegates, for example, was known for his cautious approach to executive authority. One of his principal objections to the Constitution was that it did not limit the number of terms a President could serve. Without such a limit, Jefferson feared that any one man holding the office for a long time could make the executive far too strong. At the same time, Jefferson was wary of placing too much power in the hands of the legislature. In his *Notes on Virginia,* finished in 1782, five years before the Constitutional Convention met, Jefferson expressed his dissatisfaction with what he considered to be a defect of the Virginia Constitution. "All the powers of government, legislative, executive, and judiciary result to the legislative body. The concentrating of these in the same hands is precisely the definition of despotic government. . . . One hundred and seventy-three despots would surely be as oppressive as one."

Jefferson was concerned, then, with the possibility that too much power would be delegated to the legislature by the Constitution. He believed in a separation of powers as a means to control the legislature.

The best eighteenth-century expression of the view that a constitutional democracy would have a dominant legislative branch is found in *The Federalist Papers.* Although both Madison and Hamilton favored a strong executive in these letters, they also explained the strength of the legislature. After all, they were trying to sell the Constitution to the newly formed states where opposition to the document was largely centered on the fear of a powerful executive.

While emphasizing the power of the legislature, the authors of *The Federalist* also stressed the need for a strong and independent executive authority to balance this power. They coupled their emphasis on this need to control the legislature with an argument for the desirability of an independent and unified executive.

Over the years many statements made in *The Federalist,* especially those regarding the potential of the legislative and executive branches, have been invalidated. Yet, Madison and Hamilton, regardless of whether they believed in what they said, did mirror the opinions of many of their contemporaries.

In *The Federalist,* No. 48, Madison expressed the view that legislative power is based on the fact that the legislature represents the people both directly and indirectly. The people are, ultimately, the greatest source of power. But according to Madison, there are also important reasons why legislative power is to be feared in a representative republic. The constitutional authority of the legislature is necessarily extensive. Tradition dictated, for example, that it would have control of the purse strings. Thus, the legislature both appropriated money and possessed the authority to levy taxes. Madison thought these powers could not be taken from the legislature without subverting the very firmly established principles of constitutional democracy.

Contrast of the three branches. A highly revealing passage in *The Federalist,* No. 48, contrasted the potential powers of the legislature with those of the executive and judicial branches. In this passage, Madison states that since the constitutional authority of the legislature is more extensive than that of the other government branches and "less susceptible to precise limits, it can, with the greater facility, mask, under complicated and indirect measures, the encroachment which it makes on the [other branches]." Essentially, the separation of powers doctrine was devised to check this ability of the legislature to enlarge its area of influence.

The fascinating question posed today is whether or not the separation of powers, devised mainly as a limitation on the legislature, can effectively limit power in a situation where there is tremendous growth in executive, administrative, and judicial power. For in the contemporary American political system, these other branches have obviously developed far greater strength than was anticipated by the Framers of the Constitution.

Review questions

1. Why was the legislature viewed as such an important branch of government in the first years of the American Republic?
2. Jefferson's *Notes on Virginia* and Madison's comments in *The Federalist,* No. 48, show some interesting similarities in their approach to the legislative branch. What are they?

Chapter Review

Terms you should know

constitutional democracy
constitutionalism
direct representation
faction
federal structure

Federalist Papers
indirect representation
monarchical
natural law

natural rights
public interest
separation of powers
totalitarian

Questions about this chapter

1. According to Edmund Burke, what is the responsibility of the representative to his constituents?
2. How does direct, or transmission-belt representation differ from indirect, or virtual, representation? Why do most members of the legislature use a mixture of these styles?
3. Why is it difficult to give an accurate definition to the word "democracy" as it is practiced in America?
4. Which basic concepts of American democracy are traceable to Locke's philosophy? Which is traceable to Montesquieu?
5. How does Madison's concept of factions, found in *The Federalist,* No. 10, compare with the organization and function of interest groups today?
6. The legislative branch received the greatest attention from the eighteenth-century American political theorists. Why?
7. Why did Jefferson believe that legislative authority should be carefully controlled?

Thought and discussion questions

1. In a constitutional democracy, how can citizens express their dissatisfaction with the government?
2. The powers of the legislative branch have seemed to decrease, while those of the executive branch have increased since the framing of the Constitution. How do you account for this?
3. What changes in the Constitution do you foresee in the coming years? Why?
4. *The Federalist* is often regarded as the best single commentary on the American Constitution. Do you consider this statement true? Why?

Class projects

1. Investigate the voting records of your local political representatives. See if you can conclude whether or not they meet Edmund Burke's definition of the role of a representative. Do you think that a legislator should be a "transmission-belt"?
2. Examine a recent vote in your state legislature. What factions can you identify? Do these factions help or hinder democratic ideals? Does your examination show that the competition of diverse interests helps the public interest?
3. Choose a recent presidential election and analyze the various factions within each party. Can you determine which programs these factions supported? Compare the unity of one political party for that year with its unity during a previous campaign, when there was no contest for President. During which campaign was the party more unified?

Case Study: The way democracy works in America

In the 1830's Alexis de Tocqueville, a French statesman and aristocrat, visited the United States. Imbued with liberal ideas, he came to find out and write about American democracy. Everything he saw went into his two-volume masterpiece, *Democracy in America*.

According to Tocqueville, political equality was the way of the future. At the same time, he was frightened by what he saw in Europe—the disintegration of the traditional social restraints of Church, crown, and class. He was fearful that Americans as well as Europeans, hungry for the promises of the new democratic age, would create a "tyranny of the majority" far worse than the injustices of the old regime in France.

As you read these excerpts from Tocqueville, consider the following:
1. Does Tocqueville favor a democratic government over an aristocratic one?
2. Determine how Tocqueville warns against imposing the standards of the majority on society.
3. Which of Tocqueville's observations are still applicable today?

Unlimited Power of the Majority in the United States, and Its Consequences

In my opinion, the main evil of the present democratic institutions of the United States does not arise, as is often asserted in Europe, from their weakness, but from their irresistible strength. I am not so much alarmed at the excessive liberty which reigns in that country as at the inadequate securities which one finds there against tyranny.

When an individual or a party is wronged in the United States, to whom can he apply for redress? If to public opinion, public opinion constitutes the majority; if to the legislature, it represents the majority and implicitly obeys it; if to the executive power, it is appointed by the majority and serves as a passive tool in its hands. The public force consists of the majority under arms; the jury is the majority invested with the right of hearing judicial cases; and in certain states even the judges are elected by the majority. . . .

If, on the other hand, a legislative power could be so constituted as to represent the majority without necessarily being the slave of its passions, an executive so as to retain a proper share of authority, and a judiciary so as to remain independent of the other two powers, a government would be formed which would still be democratic while incurring scarcely any risk of tyranny.

These excerpts are from Democracy in America, *by Alexis de Tocqueville, published originally in 1835 in French and translated by Phillips Bradley in 1944 for Alfred A. Knopf, Inc. Copyright © 1945 by Alfred A. Knopf, Inc. Reprinted by permission of the publishers.*

I do not say that there is a frequent use of tyranny in America at the present day; but I maintain that there is no sure barrier against it, and that the causes which mitigate the government there are to be found in the circumstances and the manners of the country more than in its laws. . . .

In the United States the omnipotence of the majority, which is favorable to the legal despotism of the legislature, likewise favors the arbitrary authority of the magistrate. The majority has absolute power both to make the laws and to watch over their execution; and as it has equal authority over those who are in power and the community at large, it considers public officers as its passive agents and readily confides to them the task of carrying out its designs. The details of their office and the privileges that they are to enjoy are rarely defined beforehand. It treats them as a master does his servants, since they are always at work in his sight and he can direct or reprimand them at any instant. . . .

. . . But in a nation where democratic institutions exist, organized like those of the United States, there is but one authority, one element of strength and success, with nothing beyond it.

In America the majority raises formidable barriers around the liberty of opinion; within these barriers an author may write what he pleases, but woe to him if he goes beyond them. . . . he is exposed to continued obloquy [censor] and persecution. His political career is closed forever, since he has offended the only authority that is able to open it. . . . and those who think as he does keep quiet and move away. . . . He yields at length, overcome by the daily effort which he has to make, and subsides into silence, as if he felt remorse for having spoken the truth.

Fetters and headsmen were the coarse instruments that tyranny formerly employed. . . . Such is not the course adopted by tyranny in democratic republics; there the body is left free, and the soul is enslaved. The master no longer says: "You shall think as I do or you shall die"; but he says: "You are free to think differently from me and to retain your life, your property, and all that you possess; but you are henceforth a stranger among your people. You may retain your civil rights, but they will be useless to you, for you will never be chosen by your fellow citizens if you solicit their votes; and they will affect to scorn you if you ask for their esteem. You will remain among men, but you will be deprived of the rights of mankind. Your fellow creatures will shun you like an impure being; and even those who believe in your innocence will abandon you. . . ."

Absolute monarchies had dishonored despotism; let us beware lest democratic republic should reinstate it and render it less odious and degrading in the eyes of the many by making it still more onerous to the few.

. . . But the ruling power in the United States is not to be made game of. The smallest reproach irritates its sensibility, and the slightest joke that has any foundation in truth renders it indignant. . . . The majority lives in the perpetual utterance of self-applause, and there are certain truths which the Americans can learn only from strangers or from experience. . . .

It is important not to confuse stability with force, or the greatness of a thing with its duration. In democratic republics the power that directs society is not stable, for it often changes hands and assumes a new direction. But whichever way it turns, its force is almost irresistible. The governments of the American republics appear to me to be as much centralized as those of the absolute monarchies of Europe, and more energetic than they are. I do not, therefore, imagine that they will perish from weakness.

If ever the free institutions of America are destroyed, that event may be attributed to the omnipotence of the majority, which may at some future time urge the minorities to desperation and oblige them to have recourse to physical force. Anarchy will then be the result, but it will have been brought about by despotism.

Mr. Madison expresses the same opinion in *The Federalist,* No. 51. "It is of great importance in a republic, not only to guard the society against the oppression of its rulers, but to guard one part of the society against the injustice of the other part. Justice is the end of government. It is the end of civil society. It ever has been, and ever will be, pursued until it be obtained, or until liberty be lost in the pursuit. In a society, under the forms of which the stronger faction can readily unite and oppress the weaker, anarchy may as truly be said to reign as in a state of nature, where the weaker individual is not secured against the violence of the stronger: and as, in the latter state, even the stronger individuals are prompted by the uncertainty of their condition to submit to a government which may protect the weak as well as themselves, so, in the former state, will the more powerful factions be gradually induced by a like motive to wish for a government which will protect all parties, the weaker as well as the more powerful. . . ."

Jefferson also said: "The executive power in our government is not the only, perhaps not even the principal, object of my solicitude. The tyranny of the legislature is really the danger most to be feared, and will continue to be so for many years to come. The tyranny of the executive power will come in its turn, but at a more distant period."[1]

I am glad to cite the opinion of Jefferson upon this subject rather than that of any other, because I consider him the most powerful advocate democracy has ever had.

What Are the Real Advantages Which American Society Derives from a Democratic Government

The political Constitution of the United States appears to me to be one of the forms of government that a democracy may adopt; but I do not regard the American Constitution as the best, or as the only one, that a democratic people may establish. In showing the advantages which the Americans derive from the government of democracy, I am therefore very far from affirming, or believing, that similar advantages can be obtained only from the same laws. . . .

Democratic laws generally tend to promote the welfare of the greatest possible number; for they emanate from the majority of the citizens, who are subject to error, but who cannot have an interest opposed to their own advantage. The laws of an aristocracy tend, on the contrary, to concentrate wealth and power in the hands of the minority; because an aristocracy, by its very nature, constitutes a minority. It may therefore be asserted, as a general proposition, that the purpose of a democracy in its legislation is more

---

[1] Letter from Jefferson to Madison, March 15, 1789

useful to humanity than that of an aristocracy. This, however, is the sum total of its advantages.

Aristocracies are infinitely more expert in the science of legislation than democracies ever can be. They are possessed of a self-control that protects them from the errors of temporary excitement; and they form far-reaching designs, which they know how to mature till a favorable opportunity arrives. Aristocratic government proceeds with the dexterity of art; it understands how to make the collective force of all its laws converge at the same time to a given point. Such is not the case with democracies, whose laws are almost always ineffective or inopportune. The means of democracy are therefore more imperfect than those of aristocracy, and the measures that it unwittingly adopts are frequently opposed to its own cause; but the object it has in view is more useful.

. . . The great advantage of the Americans consists in their being able to commit faults which they may afterwards repair.

. . . It is easy to perceive that American democracy frequently errs in the choice of the individuals to whom it entrusts the power of the administration; but it is more difficult to say why the state prospers under their rule. . . . As the people in democracies are more constantly vigilant in their affairs and more jealous of their rights, they prevent their representatives from abandoning that general line of conduct which their own interest prescribes. . . . If the democratic magistrate is more apt to misuse his power, he possesses it for a shorter time. . . . It is no doubt of importance to the welfare of nations that they should be governed by men of talents and virtue; but it is perhaps still more important for them that the interests of those men should not differ from the interests of the community at large; for if such were the case, their virtues might become almost useless and their talents might be turned to a bad account. I have said that it is important that the interests of the persons in authority should not differ from or oppose the interests of the community at large; but I do not insist upon their having the same interests as the *whole* population, because I am not aware that such a state of things ever existed in any country.

No political form has hitherto been discovered that is equally favorable to the prosperity and the development of all the classes into which society is divided. These classes continue to form, as it were, so many distinct communities in the same nation; and experience has shown that it is no less dangerous to place the fate of these classes exclusively in the hands of any one of them than it is to make one people the arbiter of the destiny of another. . . . The advantage of democracy does not consist, therefore, as has sometimes been asserted, in favoring the prosperity of all, but simply in contributing to the well-being of the greatest number.

The men who are entrusted with the direction of public affairs in the United States are frequently inferior, in both capacity and morality, to those whom an aristocracy would raise to power. But their interest is identified and mingled with that of the majority of their fellow citizens. . . .

The maladministration of a democratic magistrate, moreover, is an isolated fact, which has influence only during the short period for which he is elected. Corruption and incapacity do not act as common interests which may connect men permanently with one another. . . . The vices of a magistrate in democratic states are usually wholly personal. . . .

In the United States, where public officers have no class interests to promote, the general and constant influence of the government is beneficial, although the individuals who conduct it are frequently unskillful and sometimes contemptible. . . . In aristocratic governments public men may frequently do harm without intending it; and in democratic states they bring about good results of which they have never thought.

. . . But I maintain the most powerful and perhaps the only means that we still possess of interesting men in the welfare of their country is to make them partakers in the government. At the present time civic zeal seems to me to be inseparable from the exercise of political rights. . . .

How does it happen that in the United States, where the inhabitants have only recently immigrated to the land which they now occupy, and brought neither customs nor tradition with them there; where they met one another for the first time with no previous acquaintance; where, in short, the instinctive love of country can scarcely exist; how does it happen that everyone takes as zealous an interest in the affairs of his township, his county, and the whole state as if they were his own? It is because everyone, in his sphere, takes an active part in the government of society.

The lower orders in the United States understand the influence exercised by the general prosperity upon their own welfare; simple as this observation is, it is too rarely made by the people. Besides, they are accustomed to regard this prosperity as the fruit of their own exertions. . . .

. . . As the American participates in all that is done in his country, he thinks himself obliged to defend whatever may be censured in it; for it is not only his country that is then attacked, it is himself. . . .

After the general idea of virtue, I know no higher principle than that of right; or rather these two ideas are united in one. The idea of right is simply that of virtue introduced into the political world. . . . The man who submits to violence is debased by his compliance; but when he submits to that right of authority which he acknowledges in a fellow creature, he rises in some measure above the person who gives the command. There are no great men without virtue; and there are no great nations—it may almost be added, there would be no society—without respect for right; for what is a union of rational and intelligent beings who are held together only by the bond of force.

. . . In America, the lowest classes have conceived a very high notion of political rights, because they exercise those rights; and they refrain from attacking the rights of others in order that their own may not be violated. While in Europe the same classes sometimes resist even the supreme power, the American submits without a murmur to the authority of the pettiest magistrate.

. . . The government of a democracy brings the notion of political rights to the level of the humblest citizens, just as the dissemination of wealth brings the notion of property within the reach of all men; to my mind, this is one of its greatest advantages. I do not say it is easy to teach men how to exercise political rights, but I maintain that, when it is possible, the effects which result from it are highly important; and I add that, if there ever was a time at which such an attempt ought to be made, that time is now. . . . When I am told that the laws are weak and the people are turbulent, that passions are excited and the authority of virtue is paralyzed, and therefore no measures must be taken to increase the rights of the democracy, I reply that for these very reasons some measures of the kind ought to be taken; and I believe that governments are still more interested in taking them than society at large, for governments may perish, but society cannot die.

But I do not wish to exaggerate the example that America furnishes. There the people were invested with political rights at a time when they could not be abused, for the inhabitants were few in number and simple in their manners. As they have increased, the Americans have not augmented the power of the democracy; they have rather extended its domain. . . .

It cannot be repeated too often that nothing is more fertile in prodigies than the art of being free; but there is nothing more arduous than the apprenticeship of liberty. It is not so with despotism: despotism often promises to make amends for a thousand previous ills; it supports the right, it protects the oppressed, and it maintains public order. The nation is lulled by the temporary prosperity that it produces, until it is roused to a sense of its misery. Liberty, on the contrary, is generally established with difficulty in the midst of storms; it is perfected by civil discord; and its benefits cannot be appreciated until it is already old. . . .

In the United States, except slaves, servants, and paupers supported by the townships, there is no class of persons who do not exercise the elective franchise and who do not indirectly contribute to make the laws. Those who wish to attack the laws must consequently either change the opinion of the nation or trample upon its decision.

A second reason, which is still more direct and weighty, may be adduced: in the United States everyone is personally interested in enforcing the obedience of the whole community to the law; for as the minority may shortly rally the majority to its principles, it is interested in professing that respect for the decrees of the legislator which it may soon have occasion to claim for its own. . . .

. . . Among civilized nations, only those who have nothing to lose ever revolt; and if the laws of a democracy are not always worthy of respect, they are always respected; for those who usually infringe the laws cannot fail to obey those which they have themselves made and by which they are benefited; while the citizens who might be interested in their infraction are induced, by their character and station, to submit to the decisions of the legislature, whatever they may be. Besides, the people in America obey the law, not only because it is their own work, but because it may be changed if it is harmful; a law is observed because, first, it is a self-imposed evil, and secondly, it is an evil of transient duration. . . .

It is not impossible to conceive the surprising liberty that the Americans enjoy; some ideas may likewise be formed of their extreme equality; but the political activity that pervades the United States must be seen in order to be understood. No sooner do you set foot upon American ground than you are stunned by a kind of tumult; a confused clamor is heard on every side, and a thousand simultaneous voices demand the satisfaction of their social wants. . . .

The great political agitation of American legislative bodies, which is the only one that attracts the attention of foreigners, is a mere episode, or a sort of continuation, of that universal movement which originates in the lowest classes of the people and extends successively to all the ranks of society. It is impossible to spend more effort in the pursuit of happiness.

It is difficult to say what place is taken up in the life of an inhabitant of the United States by his concern for politics. To take a hand in the regulation of society and to discuss it is his biggest concern and, so to speak, the only pleasure an American knows. This feeling pervades the most trifling habits of life; even the women frequently attend public meetings and listen to political harangues as a recreation from their household labors. . . .

In some countries the inhabitants seem unwilling to avail themselves of the political privileges which the law gives them; it would seem that they set too high a value upon their time to spend it on the interests of the community; and they shut themselves up in a narrow selfishness, marked out by four sunk fences and a quickset hedge. But if an American were condemned to confine his activity to his own affairs, he would be robbed of one half of his existence; he would feel an immense void in the life which he is accustomed to lead, and his wretchedness would be unbearable. I am persuaded that if ever a despotism should be established in America, it will be more difficult to overcome the habits that freedom has formed than to conquer the love of freedom itself. . . .

When the opponents of democracy assert that a single man performs what he undertakes better than the government of all, it appears to me that they are right. The government of an individual, supposing an equality of knowledge on either side, is more consistent, more persevering, more uniform, and more accurate in details than that of a multitude, and it selects with more discrimination the men whom it employs. If any deny this, they have never seen a democratic government, or have judged upon partial evidence. . . . Democracy does not give the people the most skillful government, but it produces what the ablest governments are frequently unable to create: namely, an all-pervading and restless activity, a superabundant force, and an energy which is inseparable from it and which may, however unfavorable circumstances may be, produce wonders. These are the true advantages of democracy.

. . . If, in short, you are of the opinion that the principal object of a government is not to confer the greatest possible power and glory upon the body of the nation, but to ensure the greatest enjoyment and to avoid the most misery to each of the individuals who compose it—if such be your desire, then equalize the conditions of men and establish democratic institutions.

End questions

1. How does the McCarthy era in American history reflect Tocqueville's ideas on majority rule? Why did this occur in a country where freedoms are guaranteed in the Constitution?

2. Why is James Madison, in *The Federalist,* No. 51, so concerned with justice? What do you think are other aims of government?

3. What do you suppose Tocqueville means by majority rule? Can you think of any contemporary situation where a majority has imposed its will on a minority? Do you approve? Why?

4. What does Tocqueville mean when he says, "Among civilized nations, only those who have nothing to lose ever revolt"? Do you agree with him? Support your answer.

5. Tocqueville wrote, "If the laws of a democracy are not always worthy of respect, they are always respected." How does this apply when you register for selective service?

The core of a nation's political philosophy is usually expressed in its constitution. In some countries, such as the United States, the nation's political philosophy has been set down in a single written document. In other countries, such as Great Britain, the substance of the nation's political philosophy consists of separate laws enacted over hundreds of years. Thus Britain's constitution is a compilation of all those laws that are still in force. The "constitution" is really unwritten. Regardless of whether a country's constitution is found in a single document, or in many, it is usually extended through interpretation, and through customs and traditions.

To endure over a period of time, a written document must contain language so flexible that it can be interpreted differently by succeeding generations to meet new governmental requirements, changes in social customs, and technological advancements. This does not mean that a principle stated in the constitution will be ignored when it is no longer needed. It means that the statement made in the constitution will simply be redefined to fit the new situation as it exists. For this reason, interpretation of the constitution is often as important as the formal document itself.

The United States Constitution is a frugal document that has been expanded substantially through judicial interpretation and political practice. It has withstood the test of time! It is the oldest written constitution in existence.

The Constitutional Convention of 1787

Although an examination of the constitutional document itself will not yield an understanding of our system today, it is helpful to view the Constitution in its original historical context. The lesson to be learned from such historical analysis is that there was no obvious, clear-cut goal prior to the Constitutional Convention of 1787. Rather there were many conflicting ideas about what should be included in the nation's system. These divergent interests were compromised through a series of hard-bargaining sessions, making the final product a patchwork of many views.

Autonomy of the states. American politics in the period immediately before the Constitutional Convention was characterized by a firmly embedded tradition of state sovereignty. The states had been accustomed to self-government. Even before they became independent they had exercised a substantial amount of autonomy within the loose framework of British controls. One of the major causes of the American Revolution was the fact that the tightening of the British mercantile system clashed head-on with the spirit of self-government that had developed in the colonies. And during the Revolution, each state tended to regard itself as a separate entity, recruiting its own militia, and negotiating separate treaties.

This condition continued throughout the period when the national government was under the Articles of Confederation. Having no authority to raise taxes or duties, to provide a national currency, to regulate interstate commerce and trade, or to enforce its laws, Congress had little power

◄ How has the Constitution been able to endure all the changes that have occurred in the United States since its inception nearly two hundred years ago at the 1787 Constitutional Convention in Philadelphia?

"It is unthinkable that the citizens of Rhode Island should ever surrender their sovereignty to some central authority located way off in Philadelphia."

(The issue of states' rights has been a perennial problem in American politics.)

over the states or the American people. In 1786 Daniel Shays led a rebellion of Massachusetts debtors, irate about being placed in prison and losing their property. The rebellion had to be put down by a private army supported by individual contributions. A stronger national government was evidently the only way to avoid complete anarchy.

The desire for state sovereignty, however, was still prevalent when the Constitutional Convention met in 1787. In fact, this belief in state autonomy continued throughout the eighteenth and nineteenth centuries, causing innumerable problems for those who wished to solidify the strength of the national government.

Convention disputes. Although the Framers of the Constitution were primarily dedicated to the establishment of a stronger national government, there were also regional interests that had to be incorporated into a governmental system. The Constitution, drafted in 1787 and subsequently ratified, was an attempt to satisfy the needs for a strong central government without offending regional interests and those who supported state sovereignty.

The key to the drafting of the Constitution was compromise. Without this meeting of interests between personal, political, and economic motives, the national organization would never have been possible.

Because each state had interests that it wanted to protect against encroachment by the others, disputes arose at the Convention over the proper structure and powers of the new government. The large states were pitted against the small states, the southern slave states opposed the northern free states, and the merchant states were in conflict with the agrarian states.

■ *Large versus small states.* Delegates from the large states thought that representation in the legislative body should be apportioned according to the size of the resident population of each state. Led by Edmund Randolph of Virginia, these delegates proposed a plan to organize the government along these lines. Under the Virginia Plan, there was to be a *bicameral,* or two-house, legislature. Representation in the lower house would be according to each state's resident population. The upper house was to be selected by the members of the lower house. This arrangement would have given the larger states such as Virginia, which was the most populated, a dominant role in the new government.

The interests of the smaller states were stated in the New Jersey Plan, devised under the direction of William Paterson. Whereas the Virginia Plan was designed to establish a strong national government, the New Jersey Plan would have allowed continuation of a government more akin to the confederation already established. Under the New Jersey Plan, the Articles of Confederation would have been maintained with a few amendments that would have only slightly increased the powers of the national government. The *unicameral,* or one-house, legislature of the Articles of Confederation was to be retained, with each state having the same number of representatives. Paterson also proposed that the legislature be authorized to request state revenues in proportion to the population of the states and to regulate commerce among the states. The New Jersey Plan would have resulted undoubtedly, in a weak national government with real power retained by the states.

Amazingly enough, in light of the emphasis given to the separation of powers doctrine eventually written into the Constitution, both of the original plans advocated selection of the executive by the legislature. Supporters of the New Jersey Plan reasoned that a weak executive would mean increased power for the small states, since these states would have a disproportionate share of power in the legislature. Backers of the Virginia Plan contended likewise that if their plan was accepted, the large states would hold sway in the legislature and thereby control the executive.

■ *Economic disputes.* The other two basic arguments during the Convention set the northern states against the southern states. Since most of the northern states were concerned with manufacturing, they needed to import raw materials for their factories. They wanted imports to be favored. Southern plantation owners, however, wanted the government to favor exports, and to allow continuation of the slave trade as a source of cheap labor, so that their products would be advantageous to overseas buyers. Naturally each region wanted to control the government that would make the decisions about treaties and taxes.

■ *Slave versus non-slave.* The South was also concerned about how slaves would be counted in the population. It would make a tremendous difference if representation in the new government were based on population. Northerners, who did not possess the high number of slaves that the southerners did, disagreed with this viewpoint. They did not want the slaves counted except as property for tax purposes.

The Compromises. To reconcile these many interests, one Convention delegate from each state was assigned to a committee to settle the disputes. Inspired by Oliver Ellsworth of Connecticut, this committee arrived at a compromise known as the "Great Compromise," or the "Connecticut Compromise."

The compromise included a bicameral legislature, which most of the Framers had already accepted. Delegates to the lower house would be elected by the people from each state in proportion to the population. To arrive at a compromise between northern and southern interests, each slave was to be counted as three-fifths of a person for representation and taxation purposes. All states would have equal representation in the upper house, with two members elected from each state.

Other compromises were required to settle the controversies between the commercial interests of the North and the agrarian South. These controversies involved the powers to regulate commerce and to tax, as well as the procedure for admitting new states. The "commerce compromise" provided that the national government would have the power to regulate commerce, but that it could not tax exports nor could the states tax imports. The South exported agricultural products and feared that federal power to tax exports would be harmful to southern economic interests. This part of the commerce compromise thus answered a regional need.

Those who favored a strong national union, on the other hand, won a victory in this compromise by adding the provision prohibiting state taxation of imports from other states or from abroad. Undoubtedly, such a power would have been used by many states against the products of their neighbors, as well as against foreign goods. The ability of Congress to regulate commerce later became a potent weapon in the arsenal of those who favored the expansion of national power over the states.

Opposing views over the ability of the national government to tax were finally settled by providing that direct taxation would be apportioned according to population, and all excise taxes were to be uniform. Arguments over methods for admitting new states were resolved, by passing the problem on to the new Congress.

Finally there was the issue of slavery. In addition to the three-fifths compromise of the Great Compromise, a series of other accords dealt with this issue. The Framers agreed that the slave trade could continue until 1808 without interference, that fugitive slaves would be returned to their masters, and that the issue of slavery in new states would be determined by Congress.

Ratification. After the Constitution was drafted and accepted by the Framers, it had to be ratified by the states that would make up the new Republic. Ratification by nine states was required to put the document into operation. Conventions were called in twelve of the thirteen states in 1787 and 1788. Rhode Island was the only state that refused to call a ratifying convention at the time. Once the Constitution had become operable, Rhode Island gave in to the inevitable and ratified it in 1790.

Extensive debates took place within the states over ratification. Objections were made that the Constitution lacked a list of individual freedoms, that the executive was too powerful, and that the proposed new national government would be able to submerge state interests. But supporters of a strong national government, the Federalists, were able to swing the votes needed by promising to add certain amendments. The ninth state convention (New Hampshire) ratified the Constitution on June 21, 1788.

Review questions

1. Why had most states agreed by 1787 that a stronger national government was needed?
2. What was the significance of the Connecticut Compromise?

The Machinery of Constitutional Limitation

While the Constitution was primarily seen as an instrument to strengthen the national government, the Framers were wise enough to realize that certain provisions would have to be made to protect individual rights from an overwhelmingly powerful government. The power of the government, then, would have to be divided, and no one branch would be allowed to gain an excess of power over the others.

As conceived by the Founding Fathers, the mainstay of constitutional limitation was to be the separation of powers. For this reason, they set up three distinct branches of government with independent constituencies. One of these branches, the Congress, was further divided into two parts—each with a different constituency and, in some instances, separate authority.

A system of checks and balances. The Framers of the Constitution did not think it would be sufficient, however, to separate the legislative, executive, and judicial functions of government into three branches. They felt that despotic or arbitrary government could be prevented only through a system of *checks and balances* by which each branch possessed the ability to curtail excessive power by either of the other two. Consequently, an essential ingredient of the separation of powers was the sharing of some powers among the branches of the government. Without some shared functions, it was feared that each branch would possess unlimited authority in its respective sphere.

For example, with a complete separation of powers, an uncontrolled judicial system could be unjust in deciding cases and controversies. Likewise, the legislature could make laws and expect them to be obeyed, even if they deprived some citizens of their freedoms. And the President could appoint incompetent ambassadors or negotiate unreasonable treaties without any restraints.

The Constitution, then, created a relationship of restraints among the three branches of the government. In *The Federalist,* No. 47, Madison outlined the arguments that were made against the Constitution by those who thought that it blended the functions of government too much. He answered these arguments in this same paper and elsewhere in *The Federalist.*

First, Madison recognized that "the accumulation of all powers, legislative, executive, and judiciary, in the same hands, whether hereditary, self-appointed, or elective, may justly be pronounced the very definition of tyranny." He then went on to point out the debt that the Framers owed to Montesquieu, whom he thought should be credited with the authorship of the doctrine of separation of powers. According to Madison, the French theorist never envisioned that the three branches of government should be completely separated. Rather, he interpreted Montesquieu as implying that the principles of a "free constitution" would be lost only in the extreme situation where "the *whole* power of one department is exercised by the same hands which possess the *whole* power of another department." Some interlinking of responsibility, or sharing of functions, between the branches of government had to be expected.

■ *Illustrations of shared functions.* The sharing of governmental functions among the branches can be demonstrated in several ways. The President's power to *veto,* or refuse to sign, a bill, for example, is essentially a legislative function. It means the President can stop a bill from becom-

SHARED FUNCTIONS OF GOVERNMENT
(Checks and Balances)

SHARED LEGISLATIVE FUNCTIONS

- Vetoes bills
- Suggests legislation
- Calls special sessions

SHARED EXECUTIVE FUNCTIONS

- Declares actions of President or officials unconstitutional
- Interprets treaties
- Reviews administrative-agency cases

PRESIDENT

Administrative agencies

SHARED EXECUTIVE FUNCTIONS

- Overrides vetoes
- Impeaches and removes officials including President
- Approves or denies appointments and treaties
- Sets up agencies and programs

SHARED JUDICIAL FUNCTIONS

- Appoints judges
- Grants pardons for federal offenses

CONGRESS

JUDICIARY

SHARED LEGISLATIVE FUNCTIONS

- Determines constitutionality of laws
- Interprets laws and treaties

SHARED JUDICIAL FUNCTIONS

- Impeaches and removes judges
- Fixes number of justices who sit on Supreme Court
- Sets up lower courts
- Regulates types of appeals
- Approves and rejects presidential appointments

ing law. Presidential responsibility for recommending legislation and providing general information about the state of the union are other examples of the executive's legislative function. Through the years, the responsibilities and powers of the President in these areas have increased.

Likewise, Congress can interfere at many points with the exercise of the executive function. For example, while the President has the authority to write treaties and appoint ambassadors, the Senate must approve all treaties and appointments.

Congress is also empowered to decide the nature of the federal judiciary's organization—the number of courts and judges, their location, and the way they operate. And Congress can decide which types of decisions made by the lower courts can be appealed to the Supreme Court. Thus Congress shares some of the judicial function.

All of these provisions set up the machinery by which legislative, executive, and judicial branches check and balance each other's power. No one branch can dominate the government.

Implications of the separation of powers. It is easy enough to understand the concept of separation of powers with its system of checks and balances. But how has the doctrine actually worked?

■ *Legislative implications.* For many observers, the most potent limitation that has resulted from the Constitution is the Supreme Court's power to overrule Congress through judicial review. However, historically this power has not been enforced too often. Since the drafting of the Constitution, the Supreme Court has ruled only about eighty acts of Congress unconstitutional. Since 1937, the Court has so ruled only once. This unusual case involved congressional removal of American citizenship from draft evaders going to other countries.

As far as the law-making process itself is concerned, the most significant constitutional limitation has been the requirement that the President and Congress agree on major legislation. If they do not, the President can use his veto, and the Congress can use a number of delaying tactics. This has caused many stalemates in the legislative process. The nature of their legislative functions alone—with the President asking for the passage of certain legislation and the Congress debating its value—frequently puts the two branches at loggerheads.

In addition, the separate branches of government draw their support and demands from different constituencies. As a result they often work for separate interests. The President represents the interests of the nation as a whole, while the Senators are responsible for the interests of their states, and the Representatives are responsible to local interests within their states.

There may even be more disagreement between the President and Congress when they represent opposing political parties. Republican President Dwight D. Eisenhower was unable to influence much legislation during the two-year period from 1958 to 1960 when the Congress was heavily Democratic. It is difficult to say therefore to what degree the conflict between the executive and the legislative bodies is caused by the separation of powers rather than by simple political maneuvering. At any rate, the separation of the two branches does aid somewhat in preventing any single faction from acquiring the power of both branches.

■ *The bureaucracy as an outgrowth.* There is little doubt that separation of powers has encouraged the development of the federal bureaucracy, which consists of the many administrative and regulatory agencies that enforce most government legislation. Ordinarily it is thought that since the President appoints commission members, the administrative agencies are under his legal control. Since he also has the power to appoint Cabinet members and is Commander in Chief of the armed forces, it would appear that an agency such as the Defense Department would be obligated to him. This is not entirely true.

The Constitution endowed Congress with the power to create and structure the organization of the bureaucracy. When this right is coupled with the jealousy that Congress feels about the President's power, it is only natural that Congress should place the administrative agencies outside the direct supervision of the White House.

Top Hat

Copyright © 1963 by Chicago Sun-Times.
Reproduced by permission of Wil–Jo Associates, Inc. and Bill Mauldin.

(While it is under civilian control, the Pentagon does make some decisions on military matters by itself.)

Actually, Congress can provide for agency control by the President, but it has relinquished its power only in special circumstances. In any case, Congress retains control of the agencies' budgets and can call for investigations whenever it feels that the agencies are overstepping their bounds. In addition, the decisions of independent agencies are subject to court review. The judiciary can overturn agency decisions which it considers unconstitutional or beyond the legal authority of the agency in question. So, the administrative agencies are checked by two other branches of the government.

Over the years, the presidential-congressional separation has brought about the development of a well-diversified bureaucracy without very definite lines of responsibility. Some commissions are considered agents of Congress; some are directly under Presidential supervision; and some are a combination of both.

The freedom of administrative agencies to act within their own spheres of authority stems directly from this uncertainty in the line of control. The Constitution did not establish any clear lines of authority over the bureaucracy. Instead it empowered the Congress to oppose the President in this and other areas. As a result, the bureaucracy is not clearly responsible to any one of the three branches. In effect the bureaucracy has become a "fourth branch" of the government often acting in a semi-independent fashion. The creation of this semi-autonomous bureaucracy is undoubtedly one of the most far-reaching consequences of the separation of powers.

Review questions

1. How does the system of "checks and balances" strengthen the government?
2. What are some of the implications of the separation of powers as it works in the American government?

Constitutional Obstacles to Majority Rule

A very important benefit of the separation of powers is its tendency to prevent the accumulation of political strength by an overpowering majority or faction on the national level. If a political party, or faction, or even a popular majority acquired too much power, it might monopolize the government and suppress any disagreeing minorities.

Because the various branches of the government are based on different constituencies and have been given different sources of authority, each branch has reason for, and the means of, resisting encroachments by the other branches. There are several constitutional obstacles in the path of superiority of the majority, or *majority rule,* whether it be by a party, a particularly large interest group, or a popular majority.

Passage of legislation. First, the bicameral nature of the legislature itself has been an important limitation to majority rule. A bill has to pass both houses of the Congress. Two majorities, one in each house, are needed for passage. Since the House of Representatives and the Senate have different constituencies, passage is not always an easy matter. Often the two houses are in sharp disagreement.

The President's veto power. Second, once a bill is passed by both houses of Congress, it must be signed by the President to become law. If he vetoes it, the chances of the bill becoming law are slim. A veto can be overridden only by a two-thirds majority in both houses; thus it is rare that a veto is overruled.

Obtaining passage of vetoed legislation requires the coalition of many varied interests. Since most Congressmen are reluctant to compromise, such a meeting of interests is very difficult to achieve. Furthermore, it does not take long for issues that were in hot debate for a short time to become less intense and to disappear.

Under the terms of Article I, Section 7 of the Constitution, the President must return a bill to the Congress within ten days after it is passed if he wishes to veto it. The only exception to this rule is if Congress adjourns within ten days after the passage of legislation. In such cases the President can resort to a *pocket veto.* This means that he can refuse to take action on the bill, or "pocket" it, and it automatically dies.

In recent years, the pressure of business in Congress has been so great that much legislation has not been passed until the end of a session. This situation substantially increases the ability of the President to control the outcome of legislation by making use of the pocket veto.

During the eight-year term of Dwight D. Eisenhower, Congress overrode only two of the more than two hundred bills he vetoed. The success President Eisenhower had in vetoing bills illustrates that this presidential power is today a strong check on any majority that might try to express its strength through Congress.

The administration of laws. Third, in almost all cases, after legislation is approved by both Congress and the President, the authority to carry it out is delegated to an administrative agency. Since administrative agencies have acquired a certain amount of independent responsibility, they are generally able to interpret policy without referring back to the Congress or the President for guidance. Thus an administrative agency is more able to ignore the broad constituencies of the branches which originally approved the legislation, the bill may be given a shape by the agency that was not foreseen by the original proponents of a particular policy. While majority rule may have been expressed on the presidential or congressional level, it may be ignored by the administrative agency which responds to its own particular constituency.

Administrative constituencies, therefore, may actually limit the effectiveness of majority rule. The implementation of policy requires support not only from presidential and congressional constituencies, but also from the constituencies of the agencies that will enforce the laws. When implementing defense policy, for example, the Department of Defense must heed the demands of its own constituency (the military-industrial complex that provides the matériel of war), as well as the constituencies of the Congress and the President (the voters).

Extraordinary majorities. The Constitution also limits majority rule under certain circumstances by insisting on *extraordinary majorities,* or majorities well above 50 percent. The Presidential veto of legislation can be overridden only by a two-thirds majority in both houses of Congress. An impeached President can be convicted in the Senate only on the approval of a two-thirds majority. Amendments to the Constitution can be proposed by Congress only if there is a two-thirds majority in favor, or upon the application of two-thirds of the state legislatures. To be ratified, amendments must have the approval of three-fourths of the state legislatures or conventions (depending upon what method of ratification is specified by Congress). Finally, the President can make treaties only with the approval of two-thirds of the Senate.

Such constitutional insistence on extraordinary majorities has occasionally defied the will of the simple majority in some important instances. Certainly the im-

peachment of President Andrew Johnson in 1868 would have resulted in his removal from office if a simple majority of the Senate had been permitted. In fact, the vote in the Senate was 35 to 19, one vote short of the two-thirds majority required for conviction. Another historical example was President Woodrow Wilson's unsuccessful attempt to get Senate approval for United States membership in the League of Nations in 1920. Acceptance of League membership required ratification of a treaty by a two-thirds majority in the Senate. Even though a majority in the Senate approved of the League, the two-thirds requirement was unattainable and the United States never became a member.

The effect of the extraordinary majority provisions in the amendment process is more difficult to determine. Amendments with substantial congressional support have usually been ratified quite easily. On the other hand, the provisions for extraordinary majorities have prevented the ratification of some amendments. The controversial Bricker Amendment, for example, which would have limited the President's authority to make treaties and executive agreements, failed by only one vote to get the necessary two-thirds majority in the Senate in 1954.

Civil liberties. Fifth, the Constitution restrains the will of the majority by establishing some "hands-off" areas where even the government is not allowed to interfere. The most notable of these are the freedoms listed in the Bill of Rights. Although these first ten amendments to the Constitution were not of particular significance until the Civil War, since that time they have been cited more and more frequently to limit any tyranny of the majority over individuals.

In the last few decades, the Supreme Court has made many "unpopular" decisions expanding civil rights and civil liberties. Although the opposition to these decisions can not be measured precisely, it is generally assumed that the Supreme Court is not in agreement with the majority of the American people. Even though the Supreme Court is proceeding slowly in the advancement of civil rights, there is no doubt that the Court is committed to protecting the freedoms listed in the Bill of Rights. This line of intepretation has favored minorities generally and has run counter to the will of a large portion of the populace.

Besides the Bill of Rights, the Constitution contains other specific prohibitions on governmental exercise of power over individuals. Most of these prohibitions have to do with criminal law. For example, Congress is not permitted, except in the case of rebellion or invasion, to suspend the right to a *writ of habeas corpus.*

This right directs that an official must show the reason for detaining or holding a person in custody.

In addition, neither Congress nor a state government can pass a *bill of attainder*—that is, condemn and punish a person without a trial. The Constitution also prohibits the passage of an *ex post facto* law—which makes an act a crime after it has been committed. These provisions clearly place obstacles in the way of a majority insisting on measures that might cost an individual his freedom.

Review questions

1. What are some of the constitutional limitations on majority rule?
2. If only a simple majority were required to change the Constitution, do you imagine that there would have been more changes? Why?

Constitutional Expansion of National Power

While many features of the Constitution were originally intended to limit the power of the national government, the document has been the foundation for expansion of government on the national level as well. The Constitution listed all the powers that each branch of the government would possess. While this listing may have been thought of originally as limiting the power of each branch, it has, in fact, allowed the branches to expand in certain areas. For example, the Framers never imagined that giving Congress the power to tax would eventually allow the legislature to establish a social security tax on personal incomes.

The powers of Congress in Article I. Article I of the Constitution, which defines the powers of Congress, is the most extensive prescription of authority contained in

the Constitution. It is, thus, reflective of the emphasis on legislative power that the Framers of the Constitution felt was all-important. At the same time, the careful *enumeration of the powers* delegated to Congress exposed the Founding Fathers' suspicion, that the legislature itself might try to encroach on the rights of other branches. If the rights of Congress were carefully listed, there would be no such expansion of authority they thought.

Article I of the Constitution states that Congress has the following powers:

To lay and collect Taxes, Duties, Imposts, and Excises, to pay the Debts and provide for the common Defense and general Welfare of the United States . . . ;

To borrow Money on the credit of the United States;

To regulate Commerce with foreign Na-

tions, and among the several States . . . ;

To establish a uniform Rule of Naturalization . . . ;

To coin Money, regulate the Value thereof, and of foreign Coin . . . ;

To provide for the punishment of counterfeiting . . . ;

To establish Post Offices and post Roads;

To promote the Progress of Science and useful Arts . . . ;

To constitute Tribunals inferior to the supreme Court;

To define and punish Piracies and Felonies committed on the high Seas, and Offences against the Law of Nations;

To declare War . . . ;

To raise and support Armies . . . ;

To provide and maintain a Navy;

To make Rules for the Government and Regulation of the land and naval Forces;

To provide for calling forth the Militia to execute the Laws of the Union, suppress Insurrections and repel Invasions;

To provide for organizing, arming, and disciplining the Militia, and for governing such Part of them as may be employed in the Service of the United States . . . ;

To exercise exclusive Legislation . . . over such district . . . as may . . . become the Seat of the Government of the United States . . . ;

To make all Laws which shall be necessary and proper for carrying into execution the foregoing Powers, and all other Powers vested by this Constitution in

'What it says isn't always what it means'

(Even though Congress has certain stipulated powers, the Supreme Court can still reinterpret them.)

the Government of the United States, or in any Department or office thereof.

■ *The problem of interpretation.* There are two ways of looking at the enumeration of powers in the Constitution. First, they can be seen as giving Congress the authority to accomplish certain things. Second, they can be regarded as restraining legislative action within definite boundaries. Because the language employed to express these stated powers is limited, the expansion or contraction of these congressional powers depends on the way in which they are interpreted.

■ *Commerce clause as an example.* The *commerce clause* of Article I (the third one in the list above) offers a prime example of how constitutional interpretation has worked. When the Framers stated that Congress could regulate commerce "among the several States," there was no general agreement as to what this really implied. It could be interpreted narrowly to mean commerce when it crossed a state's borders, or it could be construed broadly to include commerce conducted within a state that eventually affected interstate commerce.

Chief Justice John Marshall, in the famous case of *Gibbons v. Ogden* (1824), chose to give it the latter interpretation. (See Chapter 2, pages 29–30.) In his opinion, Marshall concluded that "the power of Congress . . . comprehends navigation within the limits of every state in the Union, so far as that navigation may be, in any manner, connected with 'commerce with foreign nations, or among the several States, or with the Indian tribes.' " Thus, through broad interpretation, the commerce clause has become an important stone in the edifice of national power. It has generally been cited as an example of how the authority of the national government has been increased at the expense of the states.

In general, Article I has proved flexible enough to permit Congress to increase its own power within the government. There are instances, however, when some of the provisions of Article I have been used to limit the national authority of Congress. During the New Deal period of the 1930's, major legislation passed by Congress was ruled unconstitutional when the Supreme Court reasoned that Congress had exceeded its enumerated powers. Congress has fared well in this respect though, and usually a broad interpretation of its powers has prevailed.

The nature of the Presidency. Article II of the Constitution, detailing the President's duties and powers, also furnishes several important elements that add to the strength of the central government and in particular to the executive. Certainly, it was intended by the Framers that executive power should be concentrated in the hands of one man rather than split up amongst a group. Early in the proceedings of the Constitutional Convention, an attempt of Virginia to create a plural executive was quickly outmaneuvered by the proponents of strong executive leadership.

■ *A fixed term.* Besides unifying the Presidency in one person, the Constitution strengthened the office by denoting a fixed term of four years. During this term, the President cannot be removed except through impeachment, a procedure so cumbersome that it has only been attempted once. Even then, in the extreme case of President Andrew Johnson, when the Congress was more united against the President than at any other time in history, the procedure failed.

Not only was the President given a fixed term, but he was able to repeat his tenure in office as often as he liked. There were proposals at the Constitutional Convention to limit the President to one term, but like those for creation of a plural execu-

Rollin Kirby. Reprinted by permission of the *New York Post*.

"—THRICE PRESENTED HIM A KINGLY CROWN, WHICH HE
DID THRICE REFUSE"—Julius Caesar

March 24, 1928

(The refusal of a third term by a President was virtually a foregone conclusion until 1940.)

tive, they did not succeed. While no constitutional limit was set for the number of terms a President could serve, there was an unwritten tradition, until 1940, that a President would serve no more than two terms. This tradition was broken by Franklin D. Roosevelt under the extraordinary circumstances of a threatening war, World War II.

It was not until March 1951 that the states ratified the Twenty-second Amendment which provides that

"No person shall be elected to the office of the President more than twice, and no person who has held the office of President, or acted as President, for more than two years of a term to which some other person was elected President shall be elected to the office of the President more than once."

■ *Election of the President.* Having placed the executive power in the hands of one man, and having given him a fixed term that could be repeated, the Framers of the Constitution then went on to grant the President independence from the legislature. The Convention did this by developing a separate means of selecting the President—through a system of electors.

Each state was allowed the same number of electors as it had members of Congress. The method of appointing these electors was left to the individual state legislatures. By discarding the proposals of both the Virginia and New Jersey Plans to have the President elected by the Congress, the Founding Fathers completed the work of making the President independent of the national legislature.

■ *Effect of separating President and Congress.* By assigning the election of the President to electors rather than to Congress, the Framers gave the President an independent constituency. Thereby they increased his ability to muster political support and further augmented his political power. This strength of the President, has, in turn, increased the strength of the national government.

If, instead, Congress had been empowered to select the President, the United States probably would have developed some form of parliamentary government. In a parliamentary government, the legis-

A COMPARISON OF CONSTITUTIONAL SYSTEMS

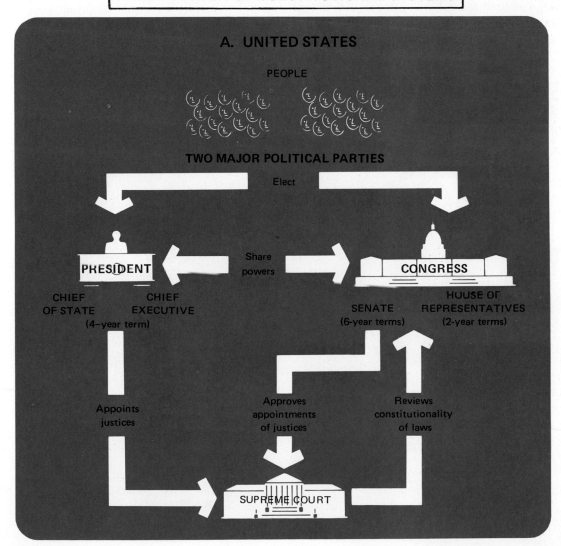

A. UNITED STATES

PEOPLE

TWO MAJOR POLITICAL PARTIES

Elect

PRESIDENT

Share powers

CONGRESS

CHIEF OF STATE   CHIEF EXECUTIVE
(4–year term)

SENATE
(6-year terms)

HOUSE OF REPRESENTATIVES
(2-year terms)

Appoints justices

Approves appointments of justices

Reviews constitutionality of laws

SUPREME COURT

lature dominates by selecting the prime minister. He is nearly always a member of the party that is in control of the parliament. This system is effective in a country that has a disciplined two-party system, where either one party or the other dominates the legislature. Great Britain, for example, has a powerful legislature whose power is reflected by the executive. But, if a country is composed of diverse economic, political, and regional interests, these in turn may be mirrored in the national legislature by a number of political parties. Such a variety of interests weakens the legislature because of perpetual and often irreconcilable conflict. If the legislature is thus fragmented, and if it chooses the executive, the executive will be weak for he will have to respond to a number of parties that control the legislature and elect him. There may even be frequent changes of the executive. This was the situation in France until the Fifth Republic, when the selection of Premier was placed in the hands of the President.

■ *The President's legal authority.* Besides fixing his term and giving him a separate constituency, the Constitution also listed special powers that the President would have. He is the Commander in Chief of the armed forces. He is Chief Executive, and in this regard he "may require the

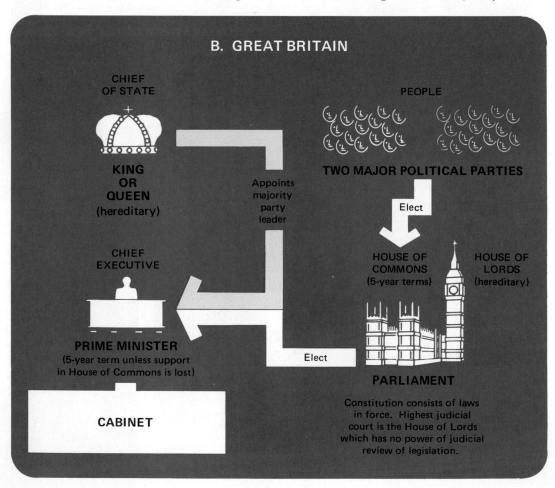

B. GREAT BRITAIN

CHIEF OF STATE

KING OR QUEEN (hereditary)

Appoints majority party leader

PEOPLE

TWO MAJOR POLITICAL PARTIES

Elect

CHIEF EXECUTIVE

PRIME MINISTER (5-year term unless support in House of Commons is lost)

CABINET

Elect

HOUSE OF COMMONS (5-year terms)

HOUSE OF LORDS (hereditary)

PARLIAMENT

Constitution consists of laws in force. Highest judicial court is the House of Lords which has no power of judicial review of legislation.

opinion, in writing, of the principal officer in each of the executive departments, upon any subject relating to the duties of their respective office. . . . " Moreover, Section 3 of Article II provides that he is to give to the Congress

"information of the state of the Union, and recommend to their consideration such measures as he shall judge necessary and expedient; he may, on extraordinary occasions, convene both Houses, or either of them, and in case of disagreement between them with respect to the time of adjournment, he may adjourn them to such time as he shall think proper; he shall receive ambassadors and other public ministers;

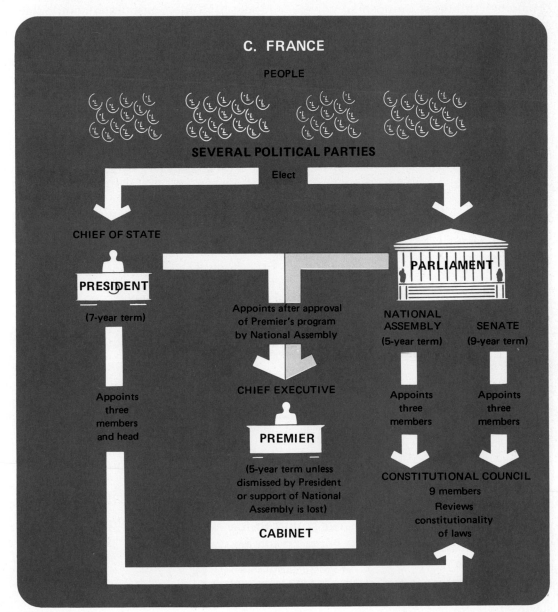

C. FRANCE

PEOPLE

SEVERAL POLITICAL PARTIES

Elect

CHIEF OF STATE

PRESIDENT

(7-year term)

Appoints after approval
of Premier's program
by National Assembly

Appoints
three
members
and head

CHIEF EXECUTIVE

PREMIER

(5-year term unless
dismissed by President
or support of National
Assembly is lost)

CABINET

PARLIAMENT

NATIONAL
ASSEMBLY
(5-year term)

SENATE
(9-year term)

Appoints
three
members

Appoints
three
members

CONSTITUTIONAL COUNCIL
9 members
Reviews
constitutionality
of laws

he shall take care that the laws be faithfully executed, and shall commission all the officers of the United States."

Although the President has never used his power to adjourn Congress, all of the other provisions of Article II, vesting him with extensive and independent legal authority, have been employed at one time or another to bolster Presidential power. Most of the constitutional provisions for executive authority are now generally accepted and continuously used by the President to maintain and increase the political power of his office.

The powers of the judiciary. The evolution of a dynamic Supreme Court was the most unexpected expansion of the government's power. Although there is some evidence to suggest that the Framers feared the legislature more than any other branch of the national government, they probably did not foresee the strength that the Supreme Court would eventually acquire. Article III of the Constitution contributed in its own way—and to a considerable extent unintentionally—to the development of judicial authority.

Article III instituted only one Supreme Court. Its members were to be chosen by the President, "with the advice and con-

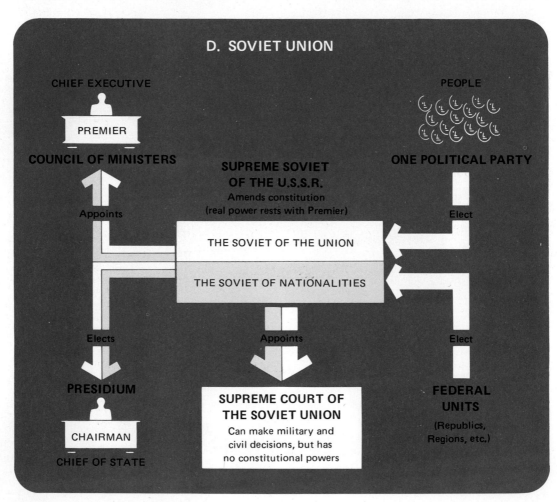

D. SOVIET UNION

CHIEF EXECUTIVE

PREMIER

COUNCIL OF MINISTERS

Appoints

Elects

PRESIDIUM

CHAIRMAN

CHIEF OF STATE

SUPREME SOVIET OF THE U.S.S.R.
Amends constitution
(real power rests with Premier)

THE SOVIET OF THE UNION

THE SOVIET OF NATIONALITIES

Appoints

SUPREME COURT OF THE SOVIET UNION
Can make military and civil decisions, but has no constitutional powers

PEOPLE

ONE POLITICAL PARTY

Elect

Elect

FEDERAL UNITS
(Republics, Regions, etc.)

sent" of the Senate. The judges "both of the Supreme and inferior courts, shall hold their offices during good behavior, and shall, at stated times, receive for their services, a compensation, which shall not be diminished during their continuance in office."

Beyond the simple establishment of a Supreme Court, however, Article III did not, in fact, provide explicitly for some of the more significant powers the Court soon assumed. In particular, it did not expressly give the Court the power of judicial review.

Because of the vagueness of Article III, it has been necessary for the Supreme Court itself to interpret the precise meaning of such terms as "judicial power," "cases," and "controversies." This is another instance of the continued need for interpreting the Constitution. In *Marbury v. Madison* (1803), Chief Justice Marshall held that the "judicial power" included the power of judicial review which could nullify those laws considered not in keeping with the Constitution. Certainly this power could not be inferred merely from the language of Article III. Marshall had to rely on logic and historical evidence to support his conclusion.

Moreover, the Court has often had to redefine what is meant by "cases" and "controversies." It has decided it will not hear cases set up to test the Court's opinions, but will hear only cases in which there are adversaries with adequate interests at stake. All of the Court's many rules pertaining to the definitions of cases and controversies have been formulated through judicial interpretation.

■ *Judicial restraint.* It might be asked: If the courts are so free to interpret as they wish, why have they not become the real force in the country? History has shown, though, that judicial self-restraint is as common as judicial excess. Still, there have been periods when the courts seized the initiative and acted in opposition to the desires of Congress and the President. During the New Deal period of the 1930's, the Supreme Court boldly turned down programs supported by both President Franklin D. Roosevelt and Congress.

On the whole, however, the courts have been relatively restrained. After all, they have to answer, in the long run, to the desires of Congress and the President, which in turn reflect general public sentiment.

Review questions

1. Why are the powers of the Congress so carefully enumerated in the Constitution?
2. What is the difference between the constituency that elects the President and the constituency that elects a Congressman?

Chapter Review

Terms you should know

bicameral
bill of attainder
checks and balances
commerce clause
Connecticut Compromise

enumerated powers
ex post facto law
extraordinary majority
fourth branch
majority rule

pocket veto
shared functions
unicameral
veto
writ of habeas corpus

Questions about the chapter

1. How did the Constitution preserve the interests of small states? of large states?
2. Compare the Virginia Plan with the New Jersey Plan. Why was it essential to reach a compromise between these two plans?
3. Why did Congress oppose much of President Eisenhower's legislation between 1958 and 1960? Does this illustrate a weakness or a strength in the American form of constitutional democracy?
4. How can administrative agencies ignore both presidential and congressional constituencies?
5. How was the power of the Supreme Court increased by the *Marbury v. Madison* decision?
6. How did separation of powers help to create the federal bureaucracy as "the fourth branch" of the government?
7. How have the powers of Congress been increased by constitutional interpretation?

Thought and discussion questions

1. Can a government be considered democratic if it does not have a written constitution? Give reasons for your answer.
2. Is it contradictory to support both state sovereignty and the supremacy of a national government? Why?
3. Why is it difficult to amend the Constitution? Do you think it should be made easier? Explain your answer.
4. Does the Supreme Court create public opinion or follow it? Choose several Supreme Court cases which prove your position.

Class projects

1. Consider a bill that is being brought before Congress. How could the executive, legislative, and judicial branches alter this bill? What effect would the administrative agencies have on its contents? What chance is there that the bill will pass if the President should veto it?
2. Examine the United States Constitution on pages i–xvii of this book. What purpose do the amendments serve? Are there any amendments that you feel are unnecessary for the maintenance of American democracy? Are there any amendments you might suggest to improve American democracy?

Case Study: Taxes—a shared function

By 1967 the war in Vietnam had put considerable strain on the American economy; the resulting wage-price spiral was having its effects on the consumer. In August, President Lyndon Johnson asked Congress for a 10 percent surcharge on individual and corporate incomes in the hope of curbing inflation. But any tax bill, before it can be debated in Congress, must first be approved by the House Ways and Means Committee. This procedure enables the Chairman of the Ways and Means Committee to stall executive requests for tax reform. The Committee's Chairman at this time was Representative Wilbur D. Mills of Arkansas. During his more than ten years as Committee Chairman, Mills had amassed so much power that no tax legislation could pass without his support.

Mills had been a Congressman since 1939 and had witnessed the increase in the federal budget from less than $9 billion to more than $140 billion. Now he was adamant that there would be no consideration of the surcharge unless there was a substantial reduction in the federal budget. Aware of all this, President Johnson lavished attention on Mills in the form of telephone calls, informal meetings, and conferences, seeking Mills' advice and support for the 10 percent surcharge. This case study illustrates how the sharing of legislative functions between the executive and legislative branches can produce a stalemate.

Watch for answers to the following questions as you read this case study:
1. How does the separation of powers enable the House Ways and Means Committee to block executive decisions?
2. What constituency does Mills represent when he tries to check executive power? Why can Mills be called "the people's economist?"

Capitol Hill's "Show Me" Economist

by Gilbert Burck, Board of Editors, Fortune Magazine.

Two days after Christmas [1967], Secretary of the Treasury Henry Fowler and a few Administration experts in economics and foreign trade took off for the LBJ Ranch in a presidential JetStar. During December alone, the U.S. had lost $925 million of its gold stock, or at the appalling rate of $11 billion a year, and the time had come to formulate a resolute scheme for dealing with the nation's balance-of-payments problem. Two hours after leaving Washington, [and before going to LBJ's ranch] the plane touched down . . . at Little Rock. . . . They had an appointment with Representative Wilbur Mills, who was at home in Kensett [Arkansas] for the holidays. . . .

As chairman (since 1958) of the powerful House Ways and Means Committee, which originates all revenue bills and has jurisdiction over legislation and the bonded U.S. debt, tariffs, taxation, trade, and social security, Wilbur Daigh Mills has made himself the most influential Congressman in what might be called the federal economic establishment. Now, as the second session of the Ninetieth Congress opens, the fate of its most important legislation largely depends on him. For more than a year Mills has blocked every Administration attempt to "prevent" inflation by levying a surcharge on corporate and personal income taxes, and he is deciding whether a tax bill will be presented to Congress this session. . . .

Mills is much more than a man lucky

FORTUNE MAGAZINE

FEBRUARY 1968

enough to ascend by seniority to the chairmanship of the Ways and Means Committee at a time when it is becoming more important than ever. He not only possesses a genius for establishing rapport with almost any kind of person, he is among the most diligent of men. . . . His combination of political acumen and expertise has made him enormously effective at "reading" the mood of the House, shaping a bill acceptable to the majority, and leading it on to final triumph. . . .

. . . He believes that a dynamic economy cannot depend on government spending, and that the private sector of the economy must expand faster than the public sector. "My philosophy," he says, "is that government is not entitled to all of the increment that comes from a tax system when the economy is booming. In periods of normal growth we generate $4 billion to $5 billion in additional tax revenue each year. Some people think that belongs to government for new programs, and the President's economic advisers seem to feel that way. But I think there should be periodic tax reductions of these increments, and they should go back to the private sector. Why? Simply because I believe it generates more and better economic activity than the government can."

De Gaulle of the Ozarks

Precisely because of this carefully considered bias against excessive federal spending and the deficits that have accompanied it, Mills finds himself in the role of a people's economist, constantly auditing the economic policies of the federal government. The U.S. Constitution provides a vast array of specific checks and balances on political power. Although the economic power of the reigning Administration in these days of $135-billion budgets is colossal, there are no well-defined checks and balances to call it to account. Wilbur Mills is remedying this shortcoming. He and his committee, ably seconded by the congressional Joint Economic Committee, are subjecting both Administration policies and the data and forecasts on which it bases those policies to an informed, hardboiled skepticism. Some annoyed Administration men are beginning to look on him as a kind of de Gaulle of the Ozarks. . . .

By early 1967, even while the deficit was piling up and the engine of inflation was pumping away, the economy began to falter. The Administration nevertheless had predicted a "continuous" strong 1967, and indeed the President's [Johnson] 1967 State of the Union

Message proposed a 6 percent corporate and individual tax surcharge, effective at mid-year, to finance the war and "prevent" inflation. But Mills and his staff and advisers felt a tax would slow down an already hesitant economy. Moreover, Mills had long insisted, in keeping with his principles, that he would cooperate in no general tax increase unless the President promised him to cut domestic spending.

The rapport between the executive department and the Ways and Means Committee, already strained, was not helped by two days of angry hearings late in January, when Secretary Fowler and former Budget Director Charles Schultze came running over to Mills with the news that the war was costing much more than they had figured. . . . Fowler was being pressed to meet commitments such as pensions and unemployment benefits, and he and Schultze pleaded that the temporary debt limit be increased. . . .

During the first half of 1967 the economy practically stood still, as Mills had predicted it would; and so did Mills on taxes. . . . Nevertheless, in early August [of 1967] President Johnson formally asked Congress for a 10 percent surcharge on corporate and individual incomes. The alternative, he said, was a potential deficit for fiscal 1968 (ending June 30, 1968) in excess of $28 billion, which would lead to "inflation, tight money, and shortages that would tax the American people cruelly and capriciously."

Not the season for tax increases

Nonchalantly fingering a small cigar, Mills opened hearings on the proposed legislation [in] August in the large, ornate Ways and Means Committee room of the old House Office Building. His greeting to the Administration troika of Fowler, Schultze, and Ackley [former Chairman—Council of Economic Advisers] was not reassuring: "I regret exceedingly the circumstances that bring you here." Thereafter the three fired salvo after salvo at Mills and the committee in an attempt to convince them, in the blithe words of Fowler, that there is a time and a season for everything, and now is the time for a tax increase. . . .

During the hearings, dozens of leading businessmen testified in favor of an increase. Some 320 economists . . . were rounded up and persuaded to sign an endorsement of an increase. . . . But Mills insisted that there would be a rise only if the President reduced expenditures by $7.4 billion. "If I am going to be for an increase," he added, "I want some degree of assurance that the action is going to be temporary, and I know it's not going to be temporary unless federal spending is cut back." . . .

. . . In early October the committee shocked the Administration—and by implication repudiated its arguments—by voting twenty to five to suspend action, pending on agreement between Congress and the Administration on "more effective expenditure reduction and controls."

Three days later, Mills seemed to raise his ante. He went to some length to explain that a mere promise to reduce fiscal-1968 spending by so many dollars was not enough, and that the Administration completely misunderstood him if it thought it was enough. . . . Mills now demanded a long-term program that would spell out priorities, with some older programs weeded out and others redirected. We cannot, he has pointed out, raise enough money fast enough to police the world, live well, and go to the moon without building up unacceptable deficits. . . . President Johnson was not impressed. In a subsequent televised press conference, he remarked that Mills and Representative Ford "would live to rue the day" they set aside the tax measure.

The administration makes concessions

For a month or more, the tax-increase issue seemed dead. Then, just as Mills was preparing to fly home to Arkansas on a fence-mending trip, Fowler personally delivered to him a brief, outlining new expenditure cuts and postponements . . . Mills still wasn't particularly impressed. . . .

But on November 18 the British devalued the pound; and the next day the Federal Reserve raised the rediscount rate to 4.5 percent. The Administration saw its chance. Using the pound crisis as a lever, it put the pressure on Mills. While the President talked to the press about a deficit of $35 billion, Fowler called Mills with the news that the Administration had some new proposals, and from Arkansas, Mills announced that his committee would meet . . . to consider them. . . .

. . . The day before the committee met . . . Mills declared that the hearings would concern expenditure reductions, not tax revenues; and in any event it would be too late to formulate a bill and get it through Congress before the end of the year. It was as bitter a defeat as Lyndon Johnson had ever suffered. . . .

Early in January, at home in Arkansas, Mills received Administration data predicting a boom in 1968, and asking for reconsideration of a tax measure. He was not enthusiastic. "I've been misled by rosy predictions in the past," he said. . . .

Mills hasn't changed his mind about a tax increase. Unless the government cuts its spending more than it seems about to do, Mills is against it. . . . Mills insists on a considered program of spending cuts as the price of any tax increase. That goes not only for fiscal 1968, but for 1969 and the years to come. And that, in his view, is the best way to preserve the American business system.

THE WALL STREET JOURNAL

Mills Renews Demand for Spending Cuts, Terms Senate Tax-Rise Bill Unacceptable

CHICAGO [April 24, 1968]. . . . Mr. Mills, the pivotal figure in the tax struggle, declared flatly that a spending-limit and tax-increase plan passed by the Senate is unacceptable to him. He demanded reductions in old and new Federal activities going well beyond what President Johnson has hinted he may give for a tax bill; the President has balked even at the Senate plan to cut $6 billion from his proposed budget. . . .

The Ways and Means chairman all but scuttled hopes he might be persuaded to accept a Senate-passed tax increase and spending-reduction plan. That plan would couple a 10% surtax with a spending limit designed to cut $6 billion from the Administration's proposed $186.1 billion budget for the fiscal year that begins July 1.

Mr. Mills and other House neogtiators

These excerpts from The Wall Street Journal, *dates as indicated, are reprinted with permission of* The Wall Street Journal.

are scheduled to resume discussions today with Senate conferees who have been pressing for acceptance of their fiscal package. But without Mr. Mills' acquiescence, there's almost no chance House negotiators will accept the Senate's plan.

And Mr. Mills declared: "I do not feel that I can agree to anything until I am convinced that the House prerogatives in revenue-raising matters have been fully recognized, honored and preserved, and until we can be sure that real and meaningful expenditure-control measures . . . have been set in motion. . . . In my judgment, the present provisions of the Senate version of the bill do not rise to that stature."

. . . His reference to "preserving House prerogatives" apparently means he will insist that the House be allowed its Constitutional right to initiate any tax-increase and spending-cut package. . . .

Mr. Mills said, "I have never said flatly that I was opposed to the 10% surcharge per se, anymore than I have said flatly that I was for the 10% surcharge per se."

But, Mr. Mills continued, the Ways and Means Committee shares his belief that "before we can, in good faith, go to the American people and to American business and ask them to tighten their belts and come up with additional taxes, it will be necessary for the Federal Government to also tighten its belt."

While the Vietnam war lasts, Mr. Mills said, the economy can't tolerate the expansion of "nonessential expenditure programs." Nonetheless, "this is what has been done and we are today suffering the economic consequences of such unwise action," he stated. . . .

Mills Says Many Problems Stand in Way of Tax-Increase, Spending-Cut Package

WASHINGTON—[May 3, 1968] . . . Mr. Mills declined to specify how much he thinks spending should be cut next year. But he said there are sharp differences between the Senate-passed plan to cut $6 billion and the Administration's proposal to cut $4 billion. He said the problem goes beyond the $2 billion difference.

The Senate plan would achieve the cut by placing a ceiling on most Federal spending, he said, while it's "unclear" whether the Administration proposal actually would put a ceiling on spending or merely represent an expression of intent. If a tax bill is going to be passed, Mr. Mills said, he would want a ceiling on spending next fiscal year and he "assumes" the House also would want one.

He said he'll continue to "try to get some kind of spending limitation to attract enough votes," one that would generate "acceptance throughout the country to a tax increase." . . .

Mills Sees $6 Billion Spending Cut, 10% Tax Rise Clearing House

WASHINGTON [May 24, 1968]—(AP)— Chairman Mills of the House Ways and Means Committee said he expects the House to pass the proposal for a 10% income-tax surcharge and a $6 billion spending cut "when all the fanfare is over." . . .

Rep. Mills told newsmen Senate conferees on the tax bill wouldn't accept a spending reduction of less than $6 billion. He added that if the House were to insist on it, the result probably would be to kill the income-tax bill. "I have never known the House not to face up to its responsibilities," . . . he said. . . .

House Approved Tax Boost, Spending Cut; Senate To Vote June 21, Passage Seen Certain: President Reaffirmed He Will Sign Measure

[June 21, 1968]

THE WALL STREET JOURNAL

Mills Again Suggests Surtax
May Be Kept Beyond Next June 30

WASHINGTON [September 24, 1968]— For the second time in recent weeks, the chairman of the House Ways and Means Committee suggested that a new Administration may want the 10% income-tax surcharge retained beyond next June 30, when it's slated to lapse under current law.

Rep. Mills (D. Ark.) commented on the income-tax outlook in an interview with a U.S. Chamber of Commerce publication.

He avoided a flat prediction about the surtax, but said it's "entirely possible" that the fiscal situation early next year may be similar to the one that finally forced enactment of the surtax this year. "If we face another enormous budget deficit, the new Administration [coming into office in 1969] may want to extend the surtax," Mr. Mills said. . . .

THE WALL STREET JOURNAL

Mr. Nixon, Meet Mr. Mills

[November 20, 1968]

Wilbur Mills, chairman of the tax-writing Ways and Means Committee, is nothing if not forthright. More than two months before Richard Nixon assumes office, he has reaffirmed his opposition to the President-elect's tax-credit ideas.

At the least, then, any tax-credit proposals seem sure to face searching scrutiny in Congress.

End questions

1. Why did Mills try to block the surcharge suggested by President Johnson? Why did the President demand it at this particular time?
2. How has the House Ways and Means Committee, along with the Joint Economic Committee, acted as a check on the executive branch? Has this check expanded the concept of democracy?
3. Does the Chairman of the Ways and Means Committee have a right to all the power that he automatically acquires when he assumes the Chairmanship? What other men in the House or Senate have similar power?
4. Are there any examples of separation of power in your local government? How might a town or city council oppose a mayor? Is there any individual in your local government who has comparable power to Representative Mills?

The political situation that existed in the American colonies, and for a short time after the Revolutionary War, virtually cried out for the creation of some form of centralized government. This was not recognized in 1781 by those who set up the Articles of Confederation—the first attempt at self-government by the new American states. But the loose organization of sovereign states, which had relinquished little real power to the central government, was not successful.

Even at the Constitutional Convention in 1787, it would have been almost unthinkable, given the state of political affairs in America, to establish a really centralized system. The states had enjoyed a great deal of autonomy under the Articles and were unwilling to give up their hard-earned sovereignty. Thus, a federal form of government was the only solution that would permit the states to maintain some autonomy and would also allow the establishment of a stronger, more effective central government. Like many other fundamentals of the new Republic, federalism was not necessarily adopted because of its theoretical merits, but because of its political suitability to the situation that existed at that moment.

The Theory of American Federalism

Once it had been accepted that the new federal government would be composed of two parts—the national, or central, government and the state governments—other questions had to be resolved. What was to be the relationship between the new central government and the states that had joined to create it? What authority would the states yield to the national government? What authority would be retained by the states? On what matters would the authority of the states and the national government overlap? The structure of American federalism was forged as the delegates to the Constitutional Convention responded to these questions.

Characteristics of federalism. Unlike a unitary centralized system where some power is delegated by the central government to regions, *federalism* is a method of governmental organization where authority is divided between the central government and the constituent governments. Historically, federalism has been a recognized form of government since the leagues of ancient Greece. Switzerland, Mexico, Canada, and Australia are other examples of modern federal systems.

One characteristic of federalism is that the constituent governments usually are endowed with more than a trivial amount of authority. Naturally, the amount of power held by the constituent governments depends on how strong they are at the time of union. A second characteristic of federalism is the equal distribution of power between the constituents. Usually, constituent governments possess equal authority on their own levels and yield equal amounts of authority to the central government. In the United States authority is divided between the national government and the fifty states that now comprise the federation.

The Constitution, however, does not specifically mention federalism. The system is implied rather than stipulated. Some

Is the federal form of government as fundamental to the preservation of the nation in the latter half of the twentieth century as it was when the Constitution was originally debated and written?

scholars, therefore, have suggested that because federalism is not outlined in the Constitution, perhaps the Framers intended to set up a stronger central government than they did. In fact, there is little in the Constitution that would prohibit the federal government from vastly expanding its power over the states. Nevertheless, whether it was an afterthought or not, the Tenth Amendment to the Constitution, ratified in 1791, does clarify the issue. The amendment states that "the powers not delegated to the United States by the Constitution, nor prohibited by it to the States, are reserved to the States respectively, or to the people."

Initial arguments for a stronger central government. The discussions today about the merits and deficiencies of the federal system are not unlike those that took place in 1787. Such discussions have focused on the encroaching power of the national government over the states. Supporters of a stronger national government in the eighteenth and nineteenth centuries, however, did not advocate a complete unitary form of government as today's supporters often do. Rather, they felt that federalism, because of its vigorous national government, had advantages over the loose confederation they had already tried.

While the Constitution was being drafted, the states were the dominant powers. Thus, when Alexander Hamilton discussed the merits of a federal government over a confederacy, he was making his arguments against a background of overwhelming state power. Because the states were concerned with maintaining their sovereignty in 1787, Hamilton had to convince the states that a federal government would not usurp state power. This was not an easy task. It was to be expected that the states would zealously guard their powers to raise militias, levy taxes, and regulate commerce.

(This cartoon of the federal chariot being drawn by thirteen states appeared on the cover of a 1788 almanac.)

Courtesy of the American Antiquarian Society

In *The Federalist,* No. 16, Hamilton carefully explained that the central government would possess only limited powers under the Constitution and it would be foolhardy to imagine it could ever completely dominate the states. Since power continued to be lodged in the states, Hamilton reasoned, the only way the central government could ever control the states would be through the recruitment and maintenance of a large and powerful national army. But Hamilton felt this was unlikely because the states would certainly continue to exert a great deal of authority. In any case, Hamilton wrote,

"The resources of the Union would not be equal to the maintenance of an army considerable enough to confine the larger States within the limits of their duty; nor would the means ever be furnished of forming such an army in the first instance. Whoever considers the populousness and strength of these States singly at the present juncture, and looks forward to what they will become, even at the distance of half a century, will at once dismiss as idle and visionary any scheme which aims at regulating their movements by law . . . ".

Hamilton's argument was not to convince those who supported the Constitution and a stronger central government. It was to gain support from those who wanted state power, and who were worried about real domination by the national government. Another element of discontent among the political factions of 1787 was expressed by those who favored a very strong central government and were unable to recognize the document's potential for establishing a dominant national government.

In *The Federalist,* No. 16, Hamilton went on to defend the strengthening of the central government. He pointed out that the weakness of the central government under the Articles of Confederation had led to the chaos that required a new Constitution. Some form of central government capable of regulating the mutual concerns of the states was definitely needed. To do this, Hamilton felt the central government would have to be able to enforce its legislation without any "intermediate legislation." In other words, that it "must itself be empowered to employ the arm of the ordinary magistrate [law officer] to execute its own resolutions." The courts and other means of enforcing national authority, Hamilton thought, should be entrusted to the national rather than the state governments.

Penalties of nullification. Hamilton also argued that the states should not be allowed to evade federal laws. If that were the case, he said, there would be no point in having a central government. But the doctrine of *nullification,* whereby states could invalidate federal laws within their own jurisdictions, was accepted practice during the early Republic. The Kentucky and Virginia Resolutions of 1798 and 1799 even stated that "nullification" was the "rightful remedy" for the states to follow whenever they felt that the central government had overstepped its bounds. Hoping to end this practice, Hamilton explained that in the proposed Constitution the authority of the national government would be superior to that of the states. According to Hamilton, nullification of federal law by individual states could not take place "without an open and violent exertion of unconstitutional powers." It would thus constitute an act of rebellion. Hamilton's predictions were borne out by the Civil War.

National versus state power. While Hamilton argued in *The Federalist,* No. 16 that the national government probably would not be able to maintain an army strong enough to keep the states in line, he also believed that the states would find it difficult to go beyond the boundaries of their own jurisdictions. But this presented another problem. If restraints were placed on the states, would that not allow the national government to take over the authority that resided with the states?

In *The Federalist,* No. 17, Hamilton made the distinction between national and local matters. He argued that politicians controlling government at the national level would have sufficient ways in which to exert their authority without having to turn to the local sphere. Hamilton concluded this argument by stating that "It will always be far more easy for the State governments to encroach upon the national authorities, than for the national government to encroach upon the State authorities." He was confident that as long as the states acted with "uprightness and prudence" in their relations with the people, they would enjoy greater influence than the national government, which would be too diverse in its objectives and interests.

When Hamilton suggested that the states had nothing to fear from the constitutional authority granted to the national government, in the opinion of his contemporaries he was making a logical point. He was emphasizing that regardless of the legal division of authority in the Constitution between the national and state governments, other factors, such as the attachment of the individual to his home locale, would prevent the national government from completely dominating the political system. As long as so many interests remained local, people would turn to their state and local governments for redress of grievances, and would give these governments their support.

Of course it was not realized then that with the growth of the national economy, interests that were regarded in the eighteenth century as purely local would eventually expand into the interests of the federal government. As this extension of nationalization occurred, federalism as the protector of local interests was undermined. When the focus of political interests changed from the local to the national scene, the balance of governmental power also shifted in the same direction.

"In Two Words, Yes And No"

From *The Herblock Book* (Beacon Press, 1952)

(Sometimes a state's position within the federal system appears to be two-faced, as is shown in this cartoon.)

Review questions

1. Why was there opposition to a strong central government for the United States?
2. In *The Federalist,* No. 16, how did Hamilton prove that a strong central government did not mean one with unlimited power?

The Twilight Zone Between National and State Power

The Framers of the Constitution devoted considerable attention to how much strength should be given the central government. And the Constitution did provide for a fairly strong national government as well as a division of authority between the federal government and the states. Still, many practical issues were not anticipated by the Founding Fathers. These issues had to be resolved, as they emerged, after the federal system began to operate.

Judicial expansion of national authority. One of the early landmarks in resolving the nature and limits of national authority was the famous Supreme Court case, *McCulloch v. Maryland* (1819). It was in this decision that Chief Justice John Marshall stated the doctrine of national supremacy. Two extremely important constitutional questions were raised in this case. First, should the Constitution be interpreted broadly or narrowly? Second, in areas where they shared authority, was the national government supreme over the states?

The case of *McCulloch v. Maryland* arose from a dispute between a bank, incorporated under a congressional law, and the state of Maryland, which wished to tax a Baltimore branch of the bank. McCulloch was a cashier of the Baltimore branch of the Second Bank of the United States. He had refused to pay the state tax, justifying his action on the assumption that an instrumentality of the national government could not be taxed by a state. The state of Maryland contended, on the other hand, that Congress had no authority to incorporate a bank. Where was this explicitly stated in the Constitution? Certainly, Maryland argued, even if Congress did have this power, a sovereign state would be able to tax a branch of a na-

tional bank within the state boundaries.

The Supreme Court had to decide whether the Constitution was to be construed broadly enough to permit Congress to incorporate a bank. The Court also had to decide whether the national government or the state governments had priority in a conflict where both levels of government had some jurisdiction, such as the power to tax. Chief Justice Marshall's opinion emphatically decided these issues in favor of the national government.

■ *Implied powers.* First, Marshall held that even though the enumerated powers of Congress did not explicitly grant it power to charter a national bank, this authority was *implied* by the powers listed in Article I. The Chief Justice argued that

"although, among the enumerated powers of government, we do not find the word 'bank,' or 'incorporation,' we find the great powers to lay and collect taxes; to borrow money; to regulate commerce; to declare and conduct a war; and to raise and support armies and navies. The sword and the purse, all the external relations, and no inconsiderable portion of the industry of the nation, are entrusted to its government. . . . It may, with great reason, be contended, that a government, entrusted with such ample powers, on the due execution of which the happiness and prosperity of the nation so vitally depends, must also be entrusted with ample means for their execution."[1]

The Constitution, Marshall went on to note, "does not profess to enumerate the means by which the powers it confers may

[1] *4 Wheaton 316 (1819). Early Supreme Court cases were collected annually under the name of this report editor.*

107

be executed; nor does it prohibit the creation of a corporation, if the existence of such a being be essential to the beneficial exercise of those powers." Stating the theory of implied powers, Marshall concluded that if the result were "legitimate," then any means of achieving that result—as long as it was not prohibited by the Constitution, but was "consistent with the letter and spirit of the Constitution"—was constitutional. The Chief Justice had, thus, decided that the Congress could incorporate a bank on the basis of its general enumerated powers. While this power was not specifically stated in the Constitution, it was *implied* by the powers Congress did have to regulate commerce and to borrow money.

■ *National supremacy.* Having determined that the national government could incorporate a bank, Marshall then dealt with the question of whether the state of Maryland could tax a branch of the bank within its own boundaries. Speaking first of the general supremacy of the national government, the Chief Justice stated, "If any one proposition could command the universal assent of mankind, we might expect it to be this: that *the government of the Union,* then, though limited in its powers, *is supreme within its sphere of action.*" [Italics added.] The Constitution, because it is the basis for the national government then, is the "supreme law of the land."

Building on this principle of national supremacy, Marshall considered the legitimacy of a state tax on a national bank. "The power to tax," Marshall said, "involves the power to destroy," and can not be used by the states against a legitimate agency of national authority. The Court's opinion concluded that "the states have no power, by taxation or otherwise, to retard, impede, burden, or in any manner control, the operations of the constitutional laws enacted by Congress to carry

into execution the powers vested in the general government."

By using the implied powers doctrine, the national government has been able to expand its supremacy over the states in several areas. This acquisition of power has been accomplished through Congress' enumerated powers to tax, to provide for the general welfare, to regulate commerce among the states, and to declare and wage war.

Concurrent powers. The sphere of national supremacy is not always as easy to determine as it was in *McCulloch v. Maryland.* In that case, there was a clear conflict of issues between federal and state law. In other cases, the lines are not so clearly drawn.

There are many areas in which both the states and the national government have jurisdiction within their own spheres—that is, they have *concurrent power.* For example, both the states and the national government have the power to regulate commerce. The states have jurisdiction over intrastate commerce, while the federal government regulates interstate commerce.

The police power to protect the health, morals, and safety of the community is also a concurrent power of the states and the federal government. Treasury agents and agents of the Federal Bureau of Investigation (FBI) are representatives of the national government, while state police are responsible for law enforcement within the states.

Many parts of the Constitution do clearly designate exclusive power to the national government in certain areas—naturalization, regulation of commerce with foreign nations, the setting of the value of money, and so forth. In those areas, however, where there is no clear designation of authority to the national government by the Constitution, the power to legislate

THE AMERICAN FEDERAL SYSTEM
Division of Powers Between the National Government and the State Governments

POWERS DELEGATED TO THE NATIONAL GOVERNMENT

DELEGATED

- TO LEVY AND COLLECT TAXES
- TO BORROW MONEY
- TO REGULATE COMMERCE
- TO COIN MONEY
- TO ESTABLISH POST OFFICES
- TO DECLARE WAR
- TO ADMIT NEW STATES
- TO GOVERN TERRITORIES
- TO CONDUCT FOREIGN RELATIONS
- TO RAISE AND SUPPORT MILITARY SERVICES

IMPLIED

"TO MAKE ALL LAWS WHICH SHALL BE NECESSARY AND PROPER FOR CARRYING INTO EXECUTION THE FOREGOING POWERS, AND ALL OTHER POWERS VESTED BY THIS CONSTITUTION IN THE GOVERNMENT OF THE UNITED STATES, OR IN ANY DEPARTMENT OR OFFICER THEREOF."
(Article 1, Section 8, 18.)

CONCURRENT POWERS

- TO LEVY AND COLLECT TAXES
- TO BORROW MONEY
- TO MAKE AND ENFORCE LAWS
- TO ESTABLISH COURTS
- TO PROVIDE FOR THE GENERAL WELFARE

POWERS RESERVED TO THE STATES

- TO REGULATE INTRASTATE COMMERCE
- TO CONDUCT ELECTIONS
- TO SET UP QUALIFICATIONS OF VOTERS
- TO INCORPORATE BUSINESSES
- TO ISSUE LICENSES
- TO SET UP LOCAL GOVERNMENTS
- TO PROVIDE FOR PUBLIC SAFETY AND MORALS

---

is concurrently shared between the national government and the states. In these cases, where the division of power is not clearly drawn, the limits of concurrent powers have to be determined by the Supreme Court.

■ *National preemption.* Generally, when cases involving concurrent jurisdiction are brought before the Supreme Court, the Court holds that congressional action takes precedence, or *preempts,* in the area. This was exemplified by the Court's ruling in the case of *Pennsylvania v. Nelson* in 1956. A Pennsylvania court had convicted Steve Nelson, an acknowledged member of the Communist Party, of violating a Pennsylvania statute by threatening to violently overthrow the federal government.

When the case was appealed to the state supreme court, it was ruled that Nelson could not be convicted under the state statute because Congress had already preempted the field with the Smith Act of 1940. Like the Pennsylvania law, the Smith

109

Act made it a crime to advocate the violent overthrow of the United States government. The Pennsylvania court inferred that if the threat had been made against the government of Pennsylvania it probably would have been proper for the state

"Pardon Me, But I Think That's My Hat"

From *Herblock's Special for Today* (Simon & Schuster, 1958)

(The Supreme Court's decision in 1956 concerning the Pennsylvania state sedition law evoked this cartoon.)

to prosecute. But the Supreme Court held that the Smith Act, together with other federal subversive control statutes (Internal Security Act of 1950 and the Communist Control Act of 1954), outlawed advocacy of violent overthrow of any government, whether federal, state, or local. On the basis of all the federal statutes in the sedition field, the Court concluded that "Con-

gress has intended to occupy the field of sedition. Taken as a whole, they [the statutes] evince a congressional plan which makes it reasonable to determine that no room has been left for the States to supplement it. Therefore, a state sedition statute is superseded regardless of whether it purports to supplement the federal law. . . ."[2] The Pennsylvania law, along with the sedition acts of other states, was therefore void.

■ *Exception to the preemption rule.* Although the national government has exclusive authority in some areas, such as interstate commerce, it may decide to step aside if the situation warrants. It is possible, under unusual circumstances, for the states to pass laws affecting interstate commerce which passes through their boundaries. In this case, jurisdiction becomes concurrent with the permission of the national government.

An interesting decision of the Supreme Court was rendered in 1963 in the case of *Colorado Anti-Discrimination Commission v. Continental Air Lines.* At issue was a state law, the Colorado Anti-Discrimination Act, which made it an unfair practice to refuse employment to qualified individuals because of race, creed, color, national origin, or ancestry. Under the terms of this act, a commission was established to investigate complaints.

Marlon D. Green, a black pilot, applied for a job with Continental Air Lines, an interstate carrier whose route passes through Colorado. Refused a position with the airline, Green filed a complaint with the Colorado Anti-Discrimination Commission, claiming that he was not hired because of his race. The Commission held extensive hearings to determine whether or not the complaint was valid, upheld the applicant, and ordered Continental to

[2] *350 U.S. 497 (1956).*

cease and desist from this and other discriminatory practices. It directed the airline to enroll Mr. Green in the line's pilot training school when a new vacancy occurred.

Through a series of appeals, the state courts of Colorado held that the decision by the Anti-Discrimination Commission was nullified by the exclusive federal jurisdiction over interstate commerce. When the case reached the United States Supreme Court, however, the authority of the state of Colorado to affect interstate commerce through its Anti-Discrimination statute was upheld.

In its opinion the Court pointed out that "the line separating the powers of a state from the exclusive power of Congress is not always distinctly marked; courts must examine closely the facts of each case to determine whether the dangers and hardships of diverse regulations justify foreclosing a state from the exercise of its traditional powers." Using this criterion, the Court went on: "We are not convinced that commerce will be unduly burdened if Continental is required by Colorado to refrain from racial discrimination in its hiring of pilots in that state."[3] It noted that the state law, while upholding an important civil right, would not harass interstate commerce.

Replying to the assertion that Congress had already legislated with respect to hiring policies in interstate transportation, the Court determined that the Anti-Discrimination statutes of Colorado did not conflict with federal laws. In fact, the state went further than the national government in its requirements for nondiscrimination in hiring. The Court noted: "We are satisfied that Congress in the Civil Aeronautics Act and its successor [the Federal Aviation Act] had no express or implied intent to bar state legislation in this field and that

[3] 372 U.S. 714 (1963).

the Colorado statute . . . will not frustrate any part of the purpose of the federal legislation." Since there were no explicit statements about barring state legislation in this field, the Court upheld the constitutionality of the Colorado Anti-Discrimination law.

It might appear that in the *Continental Air Lines* case, the Court upset its previous decision on federal preemption. Supreme Court decisions may vary, however, sometimes substantially, from case to case. The facts of each case differ, even though the law may remain the same. Besides, the political climate of the nation is in constant flux. The prevailing characteristic of most law, however, is its vagueness. This means that a court, or any other body authorized to interpret law, can base decisions on a number of subjective factors. In the *Continental* case, there is little doubt that the decision of the Court reflected its strong advocacy of civil rights. Had Colorado passed a law with a contrary effect, it would probably have been held invalid.

When confronted with resolving the boundary lines of federal and state power, the Supreme Court bases its judgment on many factors. There are precedents the Court can follow, but these are not always applicable and they are often disregarded. Sometimes the states are not permitted to enter a field that has been preempted by the federal government. Or, as indicated in the *Continental Air Lines* case, the Court may permit concurrent legislation to be passed if there is no direct conflict with the national government. The doctrine of national preemption, however, usually prevails.

Review questions

1. Why is *McCulloch v. Maryland* considered a landmark case?
2. How can national preemption be qualified?

National Supremacy in Foreign Affairs

There is one area of governmental responsibility that the states are definitely forbidden to enter—foreign affairs. But while the Constitution gave the national government exclusive authority in this area, it did not define the boundaries of the power. This is a basic dilemma of federalism. How far could the national government go, in the name of foreign affairs, before it ran into obstacles set up by the state governments? A series of Supreme Court cases were required to broaden and anchor the federal government's authority.

Definition of scope. Article II of the Constitution gave the President the authority to make foreign policy, but the scope of that power had to be determined. In 1936 the extent of Presidential authority in foreign affairs was formally challenged in the case of *United States v. Curtiss-Wright Export Corporation.*

President Franklin D. Roosevelt had prohibited the sale of arms to the nations of Argentina and Bolivia which were then in the midst of a territorial dispute. Curtiss-Wright had been charged with conspiring to sell machine guns to Bolivia. A New York district court ruled that there was insufficient evidence and also disputed the Presidential power to prohibit the sale of arms. When the case reached the Supreme Court, Justice George Sutherland had the opportunity of clarifying the scope of the President's authority in foreign policy matters: "In this vast external realm with its important, complicated, delicate, and manifold problems, the President alone has the power to speak or listen as a representative of the nation."[4]

Justice Sutherland also pronounced on the national government's power in foreign affairs as compared to its limits in internal affairs. He held that in the realm of internal affairs, certain powers were taken away from the states and given to the national government by the Constitution. Those powers not enumerated in the Constitution remained with the states. In the realm of foreign affairs, however, Sutherland argued, where the states never possessed any substantial power, the power of the national government to act came from other sources.

The *Curtiss-Wright* decision made it obvious that the authority of the federal government in international affairs was more complete than its power in the domestic field. According to the Supreme Court, even if the powers "to declare and wage war, to conclude peace, to make treaties, to maintain diplomatic relations with other sovereignties" had not been included in the Constitution, they would have naturally belonged to the national government.

Federal-state conflict. In the *Curtiss-Wright* case, the Supreme Court supported the concept of sweeping national authority, from Congress to the President, in the area of foreign affairs. There was no question of states infringing on the prerogatives of the national government. On several other occasions though, the Supreme Court did have to resolve how far a state could go in taking action that would conflict with national foreign policy.

A classic case involving federal-state conflict in foreign affairs was *United States v. Pink,* decided by the Supreme Court in 1942. In this case, it was held that an executive agreement took precedence over state action. Executive agreements have the same legal status as treaties but do not require the Senate's approval.

[4] *299 U.S. 304 (1936).*

The case arose when the state of New York authorized the payment of claims to creditors by a Russian insurance company that had been nationalized by the Soviet government. Since the company's assets had also been nationalized, the Soviet government tried to stop this distribution of the company's funds. But, the United States did not recognize the Soviet Union at the time, so it was impossible for the Russians to take action.

A New York court, meanwhile, in 1931 had directed the state Superintendent of Insurance, Louis H. Pink, to dispose of the balance that remained by paying the claims of certain foreign creditors and giving the rest to members of the company's board of directors. Pink had proceeded to do this, but he was stopped, pending disposition of a United States claim against the company. After the United States recognized the Soviet Union in 1933, by means of an executive agreement, the assets of the company's New York branch were assigned to the United States. The national government later claimed the assets that had been deposited with Superintendent Pink.

The essential question to be decided by the Supreme Court was whether an international agreement between the United States and a foreign nation took precedence over a state court decision. The answer was clear. The Supreme Court held that New York had, in essence, rejected a foreign policy of the United States, and that "such power is not accorded to a state in our constitutional system. To permit it would be to sanction a dangerous

The Hartford Convention or *LEAP NO LEAP.*

(Frustrated by foreign policy—the War of 1812 and the embargo—some states almost seceded in 1814.)

113

invasion of federal authority. . . . " The court went on to state that "There are limitations on the sovereignty of states. No state can rewrite our foreign policy to conform to its own domestic policies. Power over external affairs is not shared by the states; it is vested in the national government exclusively."[5]

The supremacy of treaties. While the Pink case did settle the question of whether foreign agreements took precedence over state actions, another question had not been clarified. Could a foreign agreement take precedence over the Constitution when that treaty contained provisions contrary to part of the Constitution? Here the "supremacy clause" in Article VI of the Constitution comes into play. It states:

"The Constitution, and the laws of the United States which shall be made in pursuance thereof; and all treaties made, or which shall be made, under the authority of the United States shall be the supreme law of the land; and the judges in every state shall be bound thereby, anything in the Constitution or laws of any state to the contrary notwithstanding."

This provision indicates that both the Constitution and treaties carry equal weight as the supreme law of the land.

The Supreme Court defined the scope of the treaty-making power in the famous case of *Missouri v. Holland* (1920). The issue to be decided was whether Congress, in pursuance of the terms of a treaty, could pass a law that normally would have been unconstitutional if it were not part of a treaty.

The Constitution gives Congress the power to make laws not only to execute its own enumerated powers, but also to implement "all other powers vested by

this Constitution in the Government of the United States, or in any department or officer thereof." Thereby, Congress can draw power from authority that is delegated to *other* branches of the government. This means, for example, that it can pass laws to enforce a treaty, negotiated by the executive branch. The *Missouri v. Holland* case involved a law that Congress had passed in accordance with a treaty but which was not within the scope of Congress' enumerated powers.

In 1913 Congress had passed a law restricting the killing of certain birds migrating between Canada and the United States. Two lower federal courts held this unconstitutional because, they said, Congress has no enumerated power from which the authority to control bird life could be inferred. Therefore, the control over migratory birds fell within the sphere of the powers reserved for the states.

But in 1916, a treaty was negotiated between the United States and Great Britain (the latter acting as an agent for Canada), which set strict standards for the protection of birds migrating between the United States and Canada. Both nations agreed to propose to their legislatures the necessary measures to enforce the treaty. In 1918 Congress passed an act implementing the treaty's provisions, and regulations were enacted. Believing that the state's reserved powers had been invaded, the state of Missouri tried to stop a United States game warden named Holland from enforcing the regulations.

In its *Missouri v. Holland* opinion, the Supreme Court first turned to the question of whether the treaty was valid. If the treaty was valid, then a subsequent law of Congress passed in compliance with it would also be valid. The Court noted that while acts of Congress are supreme law of the land only when made pursuant to the Constitution, treaties are supreme law

[5] *315 U.S. 203 (1942).*

when "made under the authority of the United States." The Court added, further, that the treaty between the United States and Great Britain did not contradict the Constitution in any way nor was it limited by the Tenth Amendment. The Court concluded that "the subject matter is only transitorily within the state and has no permanent habitat therein. But for the treaty and the statute there might soon be no birds for any powers to deal with."[6]

Thus, the decision in *Missouri v. Holland* established that Congress could make a law to enforce a treaty, even in an area that was not included in the enumerated powers. It established, furthermore, that in matters of foreign affairs, the national government could supersede the powers reserved to the states.

Treaties and citizens' rights. On the other hand, there are some constitutional prohibitions, such as those prescribed in the Bill of Rights, that can not be violated, even by a treaty. For example, in *Reid v. Covert* (1957) the Supreme Court overruled an earlier decision by holding that the wives of soldiers stationed abroad could not be denied the protections of the Bill of Rights. (Courts-martial deny many procedural safeguards considered essential by regular civilian law courts.)

Mrs. Covert had been tried by an Army court-martial and convicted of murdering her soldier-husband. The crime had been committed in Great Britain, and the United States had an executive agreement with Britain which provided that offenses committed against British laws by American servicemen were subject to military jurisdiction. On the first appeal, the Supreme Court had upheld Mrs. Covert's conviction, saying that the court-martial had jurisdiction over such cases because it came under the international agreement.

In 1957 the Supreme Court reversed its original verdict in the *Reid v. Covert* case. It held that "We reject the idea that when the United States acts against citizens abroad it can do so free of the Bill of Rights." Even though Article VI gave the Constitution and treaties equal weight as supreme law of the land, the Court determined that the executive agreement could not legitimately violate constitutional prohibitions. The Court noted that

"It would be manifestly contrary to the objectives of those who created the Constitution, as well as those who were responsible for the Bill of Rights—let alone alien to our entire constitutional history and tradition—to construe Article VI as permitting the United States to exercise power under an international agreement without observing constitutional prohibitions."[7]

The opinion in *Reid v. Covert* clearly establishes the principle that a treaty can not override those individual rights that are specified in the Constitution. This opinion illuminates the earlier decision of *Missouri v. Holland* where the Court ruled that a law was valid if it did not contradict any provision of the Constitution. As long as treaties do not violate the Constitution, they are the supreme law of the land. To this extent, treaties do give the national government some flexibility in dealing with international problems that it does not enjoy when it tries to answer domestic problems.

Review questions

1. What was the significance of the *Curtiss-Wright* case?
2. Why is the federal government more flexible in international matters than in domestic affairs?

[6] *252 U.S. 416 (1920).*

[7] *351 U.S. 487 (1956).*

Advantages and Disadvantages of Federalism

Obviously, there were many legal points that had to be worked out gradually between the states and the central government to make federalism really work. Some of these points were not solved through judicial decisions until long after the Constitution had been ratified.

The development of the legal basis for federalism, however, is only part of the story. Does the system function smoothly? Or do the outputs of the national political system come into direct conflict with the outputs of the state subsystems? Naturally there are some strengths and weaknesses in American federalism.

Advantages according to Bryce. Probably the most famous discussion of American federalism was by the British scholar, James Bryce, in his near-classic work, *The American Commonwealth,* published in 1888. Bryce's outline of the merits and limitations of the American form of government still provide an excellent starting point for an analysis of federalism. First, Bryce noted eight advantages of a federal system of government.

■ *One nation with state identities.* The first advantage of federalism, according to Bryce, is that it "furnishes the means of uniting the commonwealth into one nation under one national government without extinguishing . . . separate administrations, legislatures, and local patriotisms."[8] Thus, without destroying the identity of the states, the federal form of government permitted America to become one nation.

■ *Internal flexibility.* A second advantage of federalism, according to Bryce, is that it allows a flexibility required to answer a variety of needs that naturally arise in a nation that is expanding rapidly in territory. "Thus the special needs of a new region are met by the inhabitants in a way they find best: its special evils are cured by special remedies. . . . " This argument by Bryce in favor of federalism is still valid today. Although American federalism is essentially based on state units, there are new frontiers that do not conform to the state boundaries. The whole realm of regional associations opens up vistas for a new type of federalism.

■ *Prevention of despotism.* Third, Bryce argued that federalism "prevents the rise of despotic central government, absorbing other powers, and menacing the private liberties of the citizen. . . . " This argument is not completely valid, for a central government is not necessarily despotic. France, the Netherlands, Norway, Sweden, Denmark, and Japan all have central governments that are not despotic.

The necessary conditions of democracy can be met both by a unitary form of government and by the federal system. Nor can it be argued that the federal system will be a greater protector of individual liberties than centralized governments. Actually, the reverse is somewhat true in the United States. When the history of the struggle for civil liberties and civil rights in America is examined, it is clear that the state governments tend to curtail these rights far more than the national government. By permitting a state to adopt whatever policies conform to the wishes of the majority dominant within its boundaries, federalism sometimes condones government action that would not be tolerated by a national majority.

■ *Interest in local government.* A fourth advantage, Bryce noted, is that "self-gov-

[8] *This and all subsequent quotes in this section are taken from James Bryce,* The American Commonwealth *(London: The Macmillan Co., 1888).*

ernment stimulates the interest of people in the affairs of their neighborhood. . . ." Bryce's point here was probably more valid in the nineteenth century than today. Although people's awareness of local conditions may be desirable, it is not necessary to have a federal system in order to have local self-government. Moreover, public interest can be activated by many things, such as the effect of legislative action on the individual citizen, or the attention paid to governmental affairs in the newspaper, on the radio, and television. As a result, the citizen often becomes more interested in the national government than in his local community.

■ *Better local government.* The fifth argument advanced by Bryce in favor of federalism is that through federalism, "self-government secures the good administration of local affairs by giving the inhabitants of each locality due means of overseeing the conduct of their business." . . . Here again, Bryce's argument can be countered somewhat by the reality of the present day situations. There is no guarantee that citizens are able to participate more directly and effectively in local than in national affairs. Conditions have changed radically since the framing of the Constitution. Where it still exists, the town meeting is often a sparsely attended function. And local elections rarely attract as many voters as national ones.

■ *Political experimentation.* A sixth advantage of federalism noted by Bryce is that it "enables a people to try experiments in legislation and administration which could not be safely tried in a large centralized country. A comparatively small commonwealth like an American state easily makes and unmakes its laws; mistakes are not serious, for they are soon corrected; other states profit by the experience of a law or a method which has worked well or ill in the state that has

tried it." Here Bryce is expressing an argument that has been used frequently in favor of federalism and of greater decentralization of power among the states in general.

"The Mean Old Federal Courts Are Trying To Impose Their Will On Others"

From *Herblock's Special for Today* (Simon & Schuster, 1958)

(This cartoon shows how the federal system allows one level of government to exercise authority over others.)

But it must be remembered that Bryce was speaking from the vantage point of the nineteenth century. Although a number of measures such as gun control, divorce laws, voting regulation, and experiments in urban government have taken place at the state level, most states have been very conservative in their approaches to new governmental problems.

Few original experiments in state legis-

117

lation have had an important effect on the nation as a whole, or even on other states. At the level of national government, however, many experiments are easily discernible: the development of regulatory commissions, the establishment of government corporations such as the Federal National Mortgage Association, the creation of regional bodies such as the Tennessee Valley Authority, the establishment of a social security system, the use of fiscal controls to expand or contract the economy, and so forth. Some of these were based in part on state experience, as in the case of the independent regulatory commissions which were first developed in the states. Still, on the whole, more governmental experiments have taken place at the national level than at the state level.

■ *Resistance to radicalism.* In the seventh place, Bryce pointed out that although federalism may diminish the collective force of the nation, it also reduces

"the risks to which its size and the diversities of its parts expose it. A nation so divided is like a ship built with watertight compartments. When a leak is sprung in one compartment, the cargo stowed away there may be damaged, but the other compartments remain dry and keep the ship afloat. So if social discord or an economic crisis has produced disorders or foolish legislation in one member of the federal body, the mischief may stop at the state frontier instead of spreading through and tainting the nation at large."

There is much validity in this argument. However, the problem is that a nation with a federal system is not composed entirely of "watertight compartments." The compartments may leak, and thus actually expose the nation as a whole to greater danger than would be the case if the national government could marshal the nation's resources to plug up the leaks as soon as they are found.

Bryce himself was writing during the period when an extreme political movement for the time, Populism, was gaining enthusiastic adherents to its policies of free silver; nationalization of transportation, and telephone and telegraph lines; income tax; direct election of United States Senators; the secret ballot; and limitations on immigration. Though most of these reforms are mild-sounding by today's standards, they were considered quite radical at the end of the nineteenth century. Dominant in the Rocky Mountain states, the Dakotas, Kansas, Nebraska, as well as in the rural South, the Populists had a broad enough base in the election of 1892 to get 22 electoral votes. But by 1896, they were forced to align with the Democrats. Although such radical movements do "leak" from one state to another, the size, diversity, and the various levels of government have tended to dilute them.

■ *Efficient government.* Finally, Bryce claimed that federalism, "by creating many local legislatures with wide powers, relieves the national legislature of a part of that large mass of functions which might otherwise prove too heavy for it. Thus business is more promptly dispatched, and the great central council of the nation has time to deliberate on those questions which most nearly touch the whole country. . . . " This is probably Bryce's most valid point. It is impossible to imagine the national government handling the innumerable concerns such as marriage and divorce laws, traffic regulations, motor vehicle inspection, liquor licenses, and so forth that face state and local governments. It is a job beyond the capabilities of the central government.

The disadvantages of federalism. From the arguments that have been set forth to

THE SUPREME COURT,—"AS IT MAY HEREAFTER BE CONSTITUTED"

(A cartoonist in 1896 depicted a supposed Populist Supreme Court as a ragtag group of homespun characters.)

underline the advantages of federalism, it is obvious that there should be counter arguments which would demonstrate the disadvantages of federalism. James Bryce found that there were six weaknesses, generally attributed to American federalism, that would not exist under a unified system. He listed these as follows:

(1) Weakness in the conduct of foreign affairs;

(2) Weakness in home government through a lack of authority over the states and individual citizens;

(3) Threat of secessions or rebellion of states;

(4) Threat of division into groups and factions by the formation of separate alliances among the states;

(5) Lack of uniformity among the states in legislation and administration;

(6) Trouble, expense, and delay due to the complexity of a double system of legislation and administration.

Bryce noted that the first four weaknesses of any federal system could be the result of one cause: the sapping of the central government by various local centers of force (the states). These centers, Bryce said, are more effective in directing opposition to the national government than individuals would be because they each have "a government, a revenue, a militia [the state police or the National Guard], a local patriotism to unite them." . . .

■ *Weakness in foreign affairs.* Bryce's argument that federalism makes a nation

119

ineffective in foreign affairs has not been borne out by the facts of American history. Although the states do have conflicting interests among themselves and the national government with respect to trade policies, they do not have such conflicts in general foreign policies. In any case, the Constitution avoided any intergovernmental rivalry in this area by clearly stating that the national government is supreme in foreign affairs.

The Constitution provided that states can not enter into treaties, alliances, or confederations; nor can they lay any imposts or duties on imports or exports, unless absolutely necessary to execute inspection laws. Moreover, states can not, without the consent of Congress, "lay any duty of tonnage, keep troops, or ships of war in time of peace, enter into any agreement or compact with another state, or with a foreign power, or engage in war, unless actually invaded, or in such imminent danger as will not admit of delay." (Article I, Sec. 10) These prohibitions on the states in the area of foreign affairs have strengthened rather than weakened the federal government's conduct of foreign affairs in the United States.

■ *Weakness in home government.* Certainly it could be argued that even in a unitary system there is some significant opposition by local communities against national power. Such opposition might not be as frequent and as vigorous as in a federal system. A unitary form of government would require a stronger central administration, and create a more centralized system of patronage—appointments to government jobs—thereby strengthening the hold of the dominant political party on the national level.

Political patronage would surely encourage the loyalty of local officials who would actively support the dominant party to guarantee their own jobs. Government funds would also be allocated in accordance with the amount of support given to government programs by the local politicians. While political patronage now exists in the national government somewhat, it is less effective because the states can control substantial patronage within their own boundaries and thus create their own sources of loyalty and support.

■ *Threat of rebellion.* This weakness is somewhat linked with Bryce's disadvantage above. The Civil War bears out Bryce's contention that secession and rebellion are threats to the federal structure. While the secession movement failed, however, the states as units of government still have the potential to resist national policy. Both Presidents Eisenhower and Kennedy had to call out the National Guard to quell violent southern opposition to school integration. As Bryce would have said, these southern states were legal entities, with their own governments, revenues, and local patriotisms, enabling and indeed even encouraging them to resist national power. Ordinarily, though, in these clashes between national and state power, national power usually emerges victorious.

■ *Threat of division into groups and alliances.* Again, the Civil War serves as an illustration of Bryce's point. The Confederacy, however, lost in its attempt to establish a separate alliance of states, and there has been no other attempt by American states to follow its example.

■ *Lack of uniformity in legislation and administration.* The lack of uniformity in policy and administration among the states, which was noted by Bryce, is a fact of American federalism. Whether this is desirable or not is largely a matter of opinion, but there is little doubt that it is often troublesome. When traveling from state to state or changing state residences, individuals are confronted with different

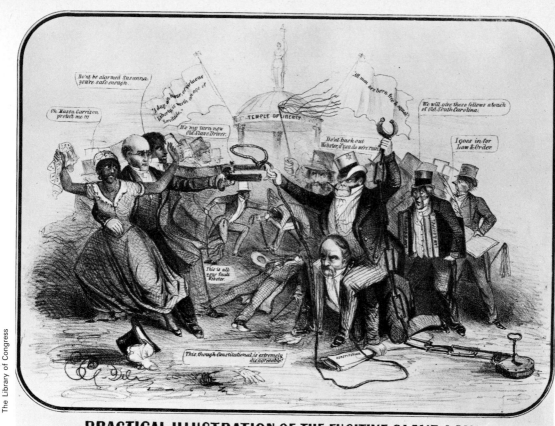

PRACTICAL ILLUSTRATION OF THE FUGITIVE SLAVE LAW.

(This 1851 cartoon shows the northern states defying the federal law allowing pursuit of fugitive slaves.)

laws governing such matters as motor vehicle registration and operation, divorce, education, taxation, civil rights, civil liberties, and so forth. In some of these matters it would be highly desirable to have some kind of national uniformity, or at least some consistency among the states.

■ *Double system of legislation.* Although in some federal systems, two sets of legislative subsystems might lead to conflict, it has not done so in the United States. Authority over most matters has been carefully divided, so that while there is some overlapping of governmental functions, it has not disrupted the system too much.

On the whole, it appears that in the case of the United States, the advantages of federalism have outweighed its disadvantages. The system has its noticeable flaws, but ordinarily, compromises have been reached in those areas where the problems of the two levels of government seemed to be insolvable.

Review questions

1. According to Bryce, what are the benefits of a federal system of government?
2. Are all of Bryce's reasons still valid today? Explain.

Chapter Review

Terms you should know

concurrent power

exclusive authority

federalism

implied powers

McCulloch v. Maryland

national preemption

national supremacy

nullification

unitary system

Questions about the chapter

1. Why did the Founding Fathers adopt a federal structure for the American Republic?
2. How does the theory of nullification coincide with the doctrine of state sovereignty?
3. How did Hamilton make it clear that the proposed Constitution had to be the supreme law of the land?
4. The theory of "implied powers" gained strength from the decision handed down by Chief Justice John Marshall in the case of *McCulloch v. Maryland.* Explain the decision and how it led to the concept of "national supremacy."
5. Give some examples of concurrent power in the government.
6. How was the *Continental Air Lines* case a contradiction of the concept of national preemption?
7. How was Presidential authority challenged in the case of *United States v. Curtiss-Wright Export Corporation?*
8. Has legislative experimentation been carried out more by the federal or by the state governments? Give some examples.
9. What methods have been used to reaffirm national supremacy in foreign affairs?

Thought and discussion questions

1. National supremacy is crucial to the successful operation of the federal system, because the national government is the government of all the people; a state speaks only for some of the people. How do you feel about this statement?
2. Contemporary American society is far more complex today than in the days of the early Republic. In light of this, do you think the federal structure should be replaced with a unitary one? Give reasons for your decision.
3. Because of the existing federal structure in the United States, it has been possible for state governments to circumvent national legislation, especially in the fields of civil liberties and civil rights. Is this a justified criticism of federalism? Why?
4. Do you think laws should be written in specific terms or in general ones? Which method allows the courts the greatest interpretative freedom?

Class projects

1. Imagine that you are a southern political leader and you have been asked to speak at a local political dinner on the subject of "Nullification and Civil Rights Legislation." In your speech, how would you support the state's right to nullify federal legislation? Could you use the ideas of Alexander Hamilton as a basis for your position? Could you base your position on a specific event in American history?
2. Both Presidents Eisenhower and Kennedy called out the National Guard to quell southern opposition to school desegregation. Examine the record of Eisenhower in

his last term in office, and the three years Kennedy was President. In your investigation consider the following: What was each President's reason for taking over the National Guard to enforce federal legislation? Were the final results the same? Why did the governors of the respective states not call up their own state troopers to enforce the federal legislation? How was this action a precedent for the nation as well as the states?

Case Study: Abbeville and the nation

A natural, but obviously unavoidable ingredient in the American federalist concept is the division between national and state sovereignty. This separation of power and interests is most evident when a state or a locality within a state openly defies a national institution or the laws promulgated by it.

In 1954 the Supreme Court ruled segregated public schools unconstitutional, and the federal courts became the administrators of the decision. But ten years later, only 1.17 percent of the blacks in eleven southern states were attending schools alongside whites. Massive school desegregation began to take place only after the passage of the 1964 Civil Rights Act which provided that any state that did not comply with the federal ruling would be ineligible for federal funds. In 1965, the Department of Health, Education, and Welfare drew up guidelines for the enforcement of the 1964 Act.

Still some localities, supported by state laws and by state representatives in Congress, continued to defy the law. They contended that the original interpretation of the desegregation order offered children a "freedom of choice" in the selection of the school they would attend; and there was no mention of local enforced integration.

The success of local resistance has varied. In Abbeville County, South Carolina, 89.2 percent of the black school children still attended all-black schools in 1969. The story of Abbeville's fight to maintain its dual school system is a case study of how a locality can oppose a federal law. In this case, the community denied itself educational aid in the form of funds from the federal government.

As you read, consider the following items:
1. What are the concerns of the national government in this case? What do you think are the concerns of the state governments?
2. What has been termed "inherently unequal" in the Abbeville school system?
3. How does the present busing system reinforce the dual school system? Does this occur in other parts of the United States?
4. What is the "freedom of choice" policy, and why aren't more blacks taking advantage of it?

School Segregation in Abbeville
Federal Guidelines Vs. John C. Calhoun

By REESE CLEGHORN

Abbeville, S.C.

When the Nixon Administration announced at the end of January that it was giving five Southern school districts an unprecedented 60 days beyond deadline to retain their Federal funds, Government negotiators were sent immediately to the districts. . . .

The confrontations in Abbeville, where John C. Calhoun practiced law, and Jefferson Davis held a Confederate Cabinet meeting after losing Richmond, [was] curious. . . .

. . . Abbeville County did not move to end its dual school system. When its 60-day extension ran out in March [1969], Federal school funds that total about $200,000 a year were cut off. The action was taken under Federal guidelines for the enforcement for the Civil Rights Act of 1964, which calls for withdrawal of Federal moneys from any Federally assisted program in which racial discrimination is practiced. The Abbeville cutoff was among the first moves in this area made by the Nixon Administration.

. . . A close look at Abbeville County tells, in miniature, much of the story of . . . resistance in the South to school integration—the conditions that have led to Federal intervention. . . .

Secession Hill, for example, is not far from the school system's administrative offices. The street rises past a long wooden sign: "Secession Hill, The Site of First Meeting of Secession, Nov. 1860." . . .

The county's population of 21,300 is 31 percent Negro, and Negroes make up between a fourth and a fifth of the town's 5,436 people. Publicly, though, all the history is white and much of it is Confederate. . . . "So strongly drawn is the line between the races," John C. Calhoun once said, ". . . and so strengthened by the form of habit and educa-

tion, that . . . no power on earth can overcome the difficulty." In Abbeville County, many people think Calhoun was right. . . .

On school desegregation, Abbeville is among neither the best nor the very worst in the South. Three years ago it adopted the freedom-of-choice desegregation approach which, ironically, has become the battle cry of segregation minded Southern politicians who once thought freedom of choice would be intolerable.

No matter where he lives, an elementary school pupil in Abbeville is free to seek enrollment in any of the 11 elementary schools in the county. A high school student may attend any of the four high schools. Parents are notified that they have this freedom of choice. So far, school officials say, all requests have been honored. . . .

Abbeville is not like some southern freedom-of-choice districts where officials have been tricky about transfers, and Negro children encounter great hostility in the white schools. Negro children in formerly all-white Abbeville High School say, for instance, that they met no harassment this year (though some came from fellow students last year) and they have been fairly treated. . . .

However, the Federal courts and the Department of Health, Education and Welfare have said that freedom-of-choice plans in formerly segregated school systems are unconstitutional unless they undo the dual school system. In Abbeville County, as in almost every Southern district that has adopted it, freedom of choice never has and never could end the dual system.

White students simply do not choose to exercise their freedom to attend Negro schools, which remain what the Supreme Court called them 15 years ago "inherently unequal." The inequality applies to faculties and school facilities alike. Thus the burden for integrating schools falls entirely upon the Negroes, who are still locked in a debilitating structure of segregation. School officials acknowledge that if all the students attending the Negro high school in Abbeville suddenly requested transfer to the town's white high school, they could not be accommodated: the freedom-of-choice plan would have to be abandoned and some kind of zone attendance system instituted. In short, the freedom-of-choice system breaks down exactly at the point at which it might abolish the dual school system.

Southern politicians have long decried the use of buses to "artificially" integrate schools, but the bus system in Abbeville has an opposite effect. The 15 yellow buses parked in front of Wright, the county's only Negro high school, transports students from all over the county; no other school has this county-wide bus system. If the Wright buses served only that school's area, most Negroes would simply take buses to the nearest county high school. As it is, most go to Wright—though some spend as many as two hours in transit each way—and thus the kind of busing done in Abbeville County, as in many other Southern freedom-of-choice districts, reinforces the dual school system. . . .

[Chester] Miller, a leader in the Negro community for many years, is a vocal, friendly man. He greets a visitor, begins to tell him how things are in Abbeville and soon is conducting a seminar. . . . "My boy Steve, who's in the 11th grade, is in a white school now." . . . "Nobody bothers him. But his marks are lower. He has homework for the first time. At Wright High he played all the time and got top marks. He makes passing marks now, and he's had to go to summer school twice." Many Negroes don't seem to be aware how much difference in quality there is between white and black schools, Miller adds.

There is another reason why the Negroes are not taking advantage of freedom of choice. "I used to hear my mother talk about a lynching about 50 years ago." . . . Miller says. . . . Others mention more recent killings of Negroes by white men. . . . All this comes out vaguely, but these are cases that all present have heard something about, and which clearly are embedded in the thinking of black Abbeville. . . .

. . . Black separatism, like the Afro haircut, has not yet won favor in Abbeville—not, at least, among black people. There is no talk of

going a separate way. There is even a perhaps surprising residual confidence that the Federal Government will prevail, that the law ultimately will be enforced.

The principal black "radical" in the eyes of Abbeville whites is Willie H. Cameron, Chester Miller's 25-year-old son-in-law. He was named president when a chapter of the N.A.A.C.P. was organized in Abbeville following a disturbance that arose over the arrest of a Negro. He has led an N.A.A.C.P. "selective buying" campaign against downtown merchants. The purpose was to persuade the merchants to bring pressure on the school board to comply with desegregation requirements. He thinks the N.A.A.C.P. has made headway. . . .

Why doesn't the black middle class lead the way? One reason is that it is so small; in this county, as in scores of others, there is not one Negro physician, lawyer, newspaper publisher or corporate executive. Teachers and school administrators constitute the only large middle-class group among Negroes, and their jobs may be at stake if they speak out strongly. Not one teacher is active in the local N.A.A.C.P. No system of terror is necessary to produce this result. No organized "white power structure" has to enforce it. It is the product of history, and of what history has done to hundreds of individuals' sense of their place and worth (and still does, in classrooms where black children see pictures only of the great white men of history).

H.E.W. has prodded the county to move to a geographical attendance plan, closing some schools. A study made by H.E.W. and the University of South Carolina, using Federal funds that assist school districts with desegregation problems, offered eight alternative plans whereby the county might comply with the law. They called for school consolidations that would produce broader curricula and more varied faculties, as well as ending the dual system. One plan would have brought about a single central high school. The Abbeville school board rejected all eight plans. Few people in the county even knew of the alternatives: the school board regularly bars the press from its meetings and keeps the minutes secret.

R. H. Gettys, the school superintendent, and Duncan Carmichael, a young chemist with a textile firm who serves as school board president, were known to favor a change to keep the Federal funds. But on the nine-man board, five members have steadily resisted; most of them are from outside the town of

Abbeville. For them, integration is tied inextricably to school consolidation, with the probable loss of predominantly white high schools in the small towns of Due West and Calhoun Falls, and the closing of some elementary schools whose sizes range downward to, in one case, 85 pupils. . . .

"You don't fight the Federal Government and win," [the superintendent] says. "If it says we have to eliminate the dual school system, we will have to. I haven't seen any signs they're going to let up on the schools."

He feels that he has smoothly overseen the desegregation that has taken place to date. The first 49 Negro students entered Abbeville's white schools in 1965. For the 1966–67 school year, 156 Negroes enrolled in white schools. The next year the figure declined to 151, and in 1968–69 it was 221. During the 1968–69 school year the county had 2,039 black students and 2,854 whites.

The superintendent wants to regain the Federal funds, and some time ago he proposed school consolidation which probably would have been extensive enough to end the dual system. . . .

The attitudes that have prevailed on the Abbeville school board are represented by Charles Hawthorne, . . . who [can be] found at the one-room town hall in Due West (population 1,166), twelve miles from Abbeville. When some town service needs attention in Due West, Hawthorne is the man who takes care of it. . . .

During the 60 days which H.E.W. gave Abbeville one more chance to come into compliance, Hawthorne was not convinced that the funds would be lost, even if the board did nothing. He found encouragement in some statements by H.E.W. Secretary Robert Finch, especially one indicating new efforts to work things out with local school districts. Like many resistant school board members in the South, he felt that the new Administration might soften enforcement and he saw the 60-day extension as evidence of this softening. (Superintendent Gettys sees it differently. "The Federal Government did not do us a favor," he says. By delaying compliance, he suggests, the extension made matters more difficult.)

Charley Hawthorne wants his small town to keep its too small high school, and he most certainly would oppose any consolidation plan which threatened it even if no racial issue were involved. Beyond that, he is known to favor segregation. Despite what most educators say, he insists students are educated better in small schools. And despite what the courts say, he insists that the county has no legal obligation to eliminate the dual system if it provides freedom of choice. . . .

Federal funds [as late as 1968] totaled more than $200,000 in a school budget of about $2 million, and in future years the total would have been greater. Some of the money stopped coming as soon as H.E.W. made an initial departmental determination late [1968], that Abbeville was not in compliance. Remaining funds stopped at the end of March [1969], after Congress had been notified and after the 60-day extension had passed. . . .

Superintendent Gettys expects that some of the Federal funds will be replaced by local money and that will mean higher taxes. He foresees no curtailment in such programs as adult education and the teaching of agriculture, trade and industry, home economics, and business education; nor in the funds for special personnel such as librarians and secretaries which have been provided for the Negro schools under the Federal Program for Servicing Low Income Families. But funds for free lunches for poor children probably will have to be ended. . . .

What Federal funds have done for Abbeville County comes clearer with a visit to the Branch Street school, the only Negro elementary school in the county seat. . . .

Cornell Reynolds, the black principal of Branch Street, is clearly nervous about talking to a stranger without evidence of the superintendent's approval. . . .

. . . Before Federal money came, there were no funds to pay a secretary for the principal. Reynolds escorts his visitor to the Library to meet [the librarian] . . . [who] is also paid with Federal funds. "We had just about 500 books before we got Federal money for books," she says, "And most of them were old and unsuitable. Now we have 7,062 books." . . .

Reynolds is asked how he thinks his school compares with the white elementary schools. "I think the teachers are as good as the others," he says. "But we have what you call environmental conditions. We're about 100 years behind. Home conditions are a big factor." . . .

Negro students who go on to predominantly white schools see a difference in teachers. JoAnne Wharton, 14, a graduate of Branch Street, is at Abbeville High. "I like it fine here," she says. "At Branch Street they don't get down to the lesson, they don't study so much. Some of the teachers just don't care. Over here they care. They try their best to see that you get it." . . .

. . . [A] young teacher at Branch Street, sees a difference in the motivation of children as well as teachers. At Branch Street, she says, "keeping the children interested is the biggest problem." . . .

Why do so few pupils transfer to white schools? "Most of them are just used to the old ways," says Wanda Thomas. She made the change, but she understands that others have greater fear of failure—or simply fear of the unknown.

The cutoff of Federal funds has not moved the Abbeville school board to comply with the law, but it has forced the white community to confront the school issue.

Since 1899, a Fred D. West has been editor and publisher of the Abbeville Press and Banner. Now it is Fred D. West, Jr., . . . His editorial page is an enigma, offering an abundance of columns by the far right American Way Syndicate along with local editorials that for some time have relentlessly prodded the school board to comply with the law, keep Federal funds and consolidate schools. . . .

What was the public reaction when he advocated extensive school consolidation, including a single senior high school? "Com-plete apathy," he said, "and that goes for the N.A.A.C.P., too." Now, he says, there is similar "complete apathy" about the cutoff of Federal funds. There have been several resolutions deploring the termination, but these have come from groups, such as the American Association of University Professors, that are close to the Erskine College community. "That's not going to change anything," West says. He believes most of the people of Abbeville county do not understand the usefulness of the Federal funds.

It is clear that the Federal policy of stopping funds has had a decisive impact in speeding integration in many Southern school systems. On hundreds of school boards, there are divisions. . . . Yet often it has taken a strong outside force to push such boards and such superintendents toward solutions. They face local constituencies that resist the change; they need counter balancing force to enable them to make the change. . . .

It is to the judges, in fact, that Abbeville school officials now look. The school board majority seems intent upon awaiting a court case. "Privately," Fred West says, "Some of the board members will say they are going to have to be made to comply. They are going to let a judge order it, and then they can say out in the county that they had to do it."

End questions

1. What is the significance of this article's title? You will have to do some research on John C. Calhoun.

2. Is education the responsibility of the state or the federal government? Where would you draw the line between the two? How would you expect a community which had "Secession Hill" as a landmark to react to increased federal involvement? Why? Can you name some communities in other parts of the country where similar attitudes prevail?

3. Compare Charles Hawthorne's attitude toward segregation with that of one person you know who might agree with him and another who disagrees. If you can, determine how these individuals arrived at their opinions. What arguments do they have for their beliefs? Did they make their conclusions by reading, research, hearsay, or experience?

4. What impact would the suspension of federal funds have on the educational structure of a community? Do you know how much your community receives in federal funds? Try to find out.

Representative bodies, the separation of powers, and federalism are key components of the American constitutional system. But these three elements pertain essentially to the structure of government. They do not guarantee the people's involvement in that government.

The discussion of the framework of American government would be incomplete without including the two vital factors that have allowed the people to enter more fully into the political system. These two elements are (1) the amendments that have been made to the Constitution and (2) the changes that have been made in the voting, or electoral, process.

The first of these elements has permitted the Constitution to grow with the needs of the nation. Certain conditions—the expansion of the nation's territory, technological advancements, changes in social requirements—have necessitated alterations in the Constitution that broaden its scope and make it more democratic, or *democratize* it. The electoral process has also been tremendously affected by the demands of the people for more voice in their own government. As a result, the ability of the people to make their voice heard in government has been increased.

Constitutional Amendments

Although the first three articles of the Constitution contained provisions that eventually formed the backbone of a strong national government, the Framers did not presume that these provisions would answer all the problems that might arise in setting up the government. They did not pretend to know how strong a government would emerge in America. Maybe the Framers recognized how difficult it would be to solve the problems of the future, and did not wish to place the newly created government into a legalistic, constitutional straitjacket.

At any rate, the Framers did provide an escape hatch by writing Article V of the Constitution. This Article allows amendments to be made to the document. Congress, "whenever two-thirds of both houses shall deem it necessary," can propose amendments to the Constitution; or Congress, at the request of two-thirds of the state legislatures, can call a convention for the purpose of making amendments. To be ratified, an amendment to the Constitution then requires approval of three-fourths of the state legislatures or conventions. While the Constitution itself outlines the mechanics for its own revision, the formal features of the document have been altered very little over the years, even though vast changes have taken place in the apparatus of national government.

The Bill of Rights. Actually, the first ten amendments—the Bill of Rights—should be considered as part of the original document, for their adoption in 1791 was a condition of ratification by the states. Most of these amendments protect the individual from the government—prohibiting it from quartering military personnel in a person's house without the owner's consent or from searching his personal effects without warrants, guaranteeing the individual the right to "a speedy and public trial," and protecting him from certain criminal procedures such as double jeop-

If the Constitution had been adequately written by the Framers at their convention in 1787, would it have required so many additional amendments in the ensuing years to keep it current and workable?

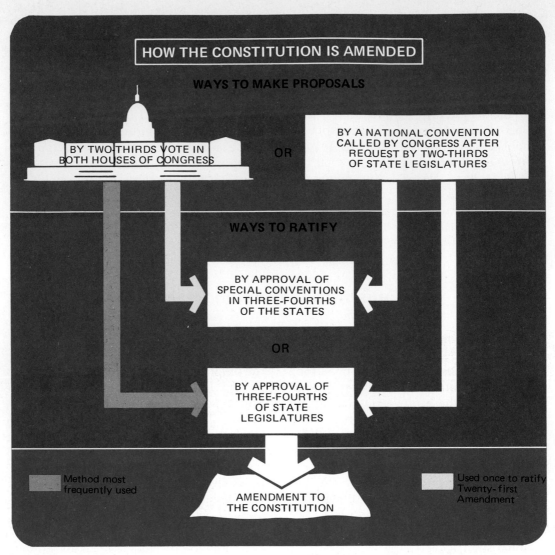

HOW THE CONSTITUTION IS AMENDED

WAYS TO MAKE PROPOSALS

BY TWO-THIRDS VOTE IN BOTH HOUSES OF CONGRESS

OR

BY A NATIONAL CONVENTION CALLED BY CONGRESS AFTER REQUEST BY TWO-THIRDS OF STATE LEGISLATURES

WAYS TO RATIFY

BY APPROVAL OF SPECIAL CONVENTIONS IN THREE-FOURTHS OF THE STATES

OR

BY APPROVAL OF THREE-FOURTHS OF STATE LEGISLATURES

Method most frequently used

Used once to ratify Twenty-first Amendment

AMENDMENT TO THE CONSTITUTION

ardy (being tried twice for the same crime). There are two amendments, though, which broaden substantially the power of the people. The *First Amendment* grants the individual the freedoms of religion, speech, press, and assembly. And the *Tenth Amendment* reserves for the people the powers not delegated to the United States or to the states themselves. Both of these amendments give the people more definite freedom than the original document.

The other amendments. Since 1791, there have been only sixteen additional amendments and one of these—the Twenty-first—cancelled another—the Eighteenth. Thus, there are now only fourteen changes in the formal language of the document of 1791. This is truly a remarkable record, and attests to the durability of the document.

In expanding the Constitution through amendments, some changes, of course, have increased the sense of democracy

DEAD OR NOT

(In the early 1900's, halting the sale of liquor was thought so important, the Constitution was amended.)

more than others. All the amendments, however, have been responses to problems unforeseen by the Framers. The flexibility of the Constitution has permitted them to be incorporated into the document.

■ *Amendments changing the balance of federalism.* Two amendments in particular have clarified somewhat the relations between the national government and the states. One reasserted the sovereignty of the states, and the other redefined the distribution of taxing powers.

□ The *Eleventh Amendment,* adopted in 1798, was the outcome of a suit brought by a private individual against the sovereign state of Georgia. In 1793, in the case of *Chisholm v. Georgia,* the Supreme Court held that a provision of Article III of the Constitution, extending the judicial power to controversies "between a state and citizens of another state" meant that states could be sued by citizens beyond their own boundaries. This interpretation, however, violated the spirit of the *common law* principle, or well-accepted tradition, which held that a sovereign (the state in this case) can not be sued.

Under the federal system, both the national and state governments were thought of as sovereign in their respective spheres. The states could prohibit their own citizens from suing them; but under the ruling of *Chisholm v. Georgia,* they could not extend this prohibition to citizens of other states. Of course, any government can allow itself to be sued if it so chooses, and provisions for private suits against the government exist today at the national, state, and local levels. But in 1793, state authorities were surprised to learn that the Constitution allowed citizens of other states or foreign nations to sue the state governments through the federal courts. Not only did they consider this to be a violation of the long-standing tradition of common law, but they also thought that a number of such suits would threaten their rapidly diminishing financial resources.

The Eleventh Amendment remedied this situation by forbidding suits in federal courts against states by citizens of other states. In order for a citizen to sue a state, the state itself must consent to the suit. A state may be sued, however, by the United States, another state, or a foreign nation.

□ The *Sixteenth Amendment* affects the distribution of the taxing power. It allows Congress to impose an income tax without redistributing the tax to the states.

In 1894 Congress passed a law levying a tax of two percent on incomes over four thousand dollars. Subsequently, this tax was declared unconstitutional because the tax was essentially a "direct" tax which was prohibited by Article 1, Section 9 of the Constitution. This Article stipulates that any direct tax levied by the United States must be redivided among the states according to their apportioned population. If an income-tax law was to be passed, a constitutional amendment was required.

After a substantial amount of political agitation, primarily from groups in the West and South who felt they would benefit from a tax on "eastern wealth," the Sixteenth Amendment was passed by Congress in 1909, and ratified in 1913. It provided that "the Congress shall have power to lay and collect taxes on incomes, from whatever source derived without apportionment among the several states, and without regard to any census or enumeration."

■ *Amendments strengthening individual rights.* There are three amendments which strengthen the rights of individuals. Ratified between 1865 and 1870, these three—the Thirteenth, Fourteenth, and Fifteenth Amendments—are also known as the "Civil War Amendments."

☐ The *Thirteenth Amendment* guarantees individuals their freedom by abolishing all forms of slavery. It provides that "neither slavery nor involuntary servitude, except as a punishment for crime whereof the Party shall have been duly convicted, shall exist within the United States, or any place subject to their jurisdiction." Whereas Abraham Lincoln's Emancipation Proclamation of 1863 abolished slavery in the South, the Thirteenth Amendment extended that abolition to the institution of slavery throughout the country.

☐ The *Fourteenth Amendment* is one of the most significant and controversial changes ever made in the Constitution. It prohibits the states from abridging "the privileges and immunities of citizens of the United States." It adds that no state "shall . . . deprive any person of life, liberty, or property, without due process of law nor deny to any person within its jurisdiction the equal protection of the laws." The most heated controversy surrounding the Fourteenth Amendment has stemmed from this last statement. Opponents to the amendment argued that it was another infringement by the federal government on the rights of the states.

The Fourteenth Amendment was originally drafted to give former slaves full status as citizens and to reapportion the Representatives according to the entire population including former slaves. It also denied public office to any official who had participated in the "rebellion."

Because the Fourteenth Amendment was framed in rather broad terms, the Supreme Court has been able to employ it in the twentieth century to expand the protection of individuals against state encroachment on civil rights and liberties. Through this amendment, the states are limited by the Bill of Rights in the same way that the national government is.

☐ The *Fifteenth Amendment* also gave the Constitution's legal protection in the important area of voting to the citizens of all the states. This amendment declares that "the right of citizens to vote shall not be denied or abridged by the United States or by any State on account of race, color, or previous condition of servitude." Although the language of the Fifteenth Amendment is very clear, state practices such as poll taxes and literacy tests denied many Americans the right to vote until quite recently. Initially, the Supreme Court upheld these practices; but in recent years, it has used the Fifteenth Amendment to hold them unconstitutional.

■ *Amendments clarifying election procedures and terms of the President and Congress.* Several amendments have been added to the Constitution to solve some unforeseen problems in the election system and the maintenance of the government. One removed some of the wrinkles that developed in the original electoral college system. The other three amendments specify when congressional and presidential terms should begin, the number of terms the President can serve, and who is to succeed the President in case of his death or disability. All of these amendments resulted from the inability of the Constitution to come to grips with some of the practicalities of government. □ The history of the events that led to the proposal of the *Twelfth Amendment* reveals why the amendment was needed. When they set up the electoral college system for choosing a President, the Framers of the Constitution had failed to recognize the possibility that political parties would become an active part of the governmental process. James Madison had more foresight than most when he wrote in *The Federalist,* No. 10, that "factions" would be impossible to eliminate completely. Madison was soon proved correct when the debate over ratification of the Constitution produced two opposing groups—the Federalists who wanted to strengthen the national government, and the Antifederalists who wanted to retain a weak central government and greater sovereignty for the states. This debate was just the beginning of developments that led to the establishment of political parties. Shortly, it became evident that the presidential election system, as established in Article II, Section 1 of the Constitution, would not work in a situation where political parties were operating.

In the Constitution, the electoral college system for presidential elections had been set up as follows:

"The electors shall meet in their respective States, and vote by ballot for two per-sons. . . . The person having the greatest number of votes shall be the President, if such number be a majority of the whole number of electors. . . . [I]f there be more than one who have such majority, and have an equal number of votes, then the House of Representatives shall immediately choose by ballot one of them for President; and if no person has a majority, then from the five highest on the list the said House shall in like manner choose the President. . . . In every case, after the choice of the President, the person having the greatest number of votes of the Electors shall be the Vice President. . . . "

As the Framers envisioned this procedure, each elector would cast two votes for the two candidates he thought most qualified. It seemed probable that one person would easily receive a majority of votes and that this person would become President. The person having the second highest number of votes would be Vice President. In practice, this method of selecting the nation's highest officers also made it possible that the President and Vice President would be representatives of opposing factions. This actually occurred in 1796 when John Adams, a Federalist, was elected President and the Vice President was Thomas Jefferson, a Democratic-Republican.

Moreover, once the parties began to nominate candidates for both offices and the electors were divided into party blocs, this simple system did not work. All the electors from one party would vote for both of the candidates nominated by that party for President and Vice President. This guaranteed a tie vote between the two candidates of the majority party. The House of Representatives would always be called upon to choose either the presidential or vice presidential candidate of the majority party for President.

133

The presidential election of 1800 vividly demonstrated this deficiency of the original electoral system. Thomas Jefferson and Aaron Burr were selected by the newly formed Republican party to be candidates for the Presidency and Vice Presidency respectively. The Federalists nominated John Adams to run for a second term. At the time, the candidates for each party were selected by congressional legislators in special meetings known as *caucuses.* There were no political conventions.

Since each elector voted for two men and since each party voted in a bloc, all the Republicans voted for their own candidates. Jefferson and Burr both collected 73 votes; John Adams had 65 votes. With the two top candidates in a tie, and both eligible for the Presidency, the election was thrown into the House of Representatives, then dominated by the opposition party—the Federalists. The vote was deadlocked at first, with many Federalists supporting Burr as the candidate more attuned to their own interests.

Finally, on the thirty-sixth ballot, Alexander Hamilton declared his support for Jefferson. Had Hamilton not made this declaration, it is possible that the Republican vice-presidential candidate, Burr, could have been named President. To prevent this situation from recurring and to avoid having a President and Vice President from different parties, the Twelfth Amendment was ratified in 1804. It remedied both these conditions by requiring that the electors designate their choices for both President and Vice President. The individual receiving the highest vote for each office would be elected. Since the majority party would have a majority of electors, it would be able to select both President and Vice President. The confusion caused by a tie between members of the same party could not occur.

□ The *Twentieth Amendment,* also known

(The electoral college has been under fire as outdated for many generations as shown in this 1969 cartoon.)

as the "Lame-Duck Amendment," states that terms of Senators and Representatives and sessions of Congress should begin on the third of January. The amendment also specifies that the terms of the President and Vice President begin the twentieth of January.

Originally, the Constitution did not designate when elections for Congress and the President should be held nor when the terms of these officials should begin. While Article I did state that Congress should assemble on the first Monday in December each year, it only provided that congressmen would be elected at times determined by the states unless Congress specified otherwise. Article II gave Congress the power to determine only when presidential electors would be chosen and when they would vote for the President.

Since elections were normally held in November for the following year, defeated congressmen still sat in the session of Congress that began in December of the election year. Often a congressman elected in November had to wait a full year before he could assume office. In addition, the President elected in November did not take office until the following March. With this system, there were always many "lame-duck" congressmen and occasionally a "lame-duck" President who knew they would be replaced shortly.

□ The *Twenty-second Amendment* made a fundamental change in the original constitutional conception of the Presidency, by setting a specific limit to the length of time an individual could hold the office. It provided that

"no person shall be elected to the office of the President more than twice, and no person who has held the office of the President, or acted as President, for more than two years of a term to which some other person was elected President shall be elected to the office of the President more than once."

Passed by Congress in 1947, this amendment was ratified by the states in 1951. President Harry S. Truman, who was in office when it was proposed by Congress, was specifically exempted from its terms.

It is sometimes stated sarcastically that the Twenty-second Amendment was a Republican device to get revenge on President Franklin D. Roosevelt, even after his death. Roosevelt, a Democrat, had been the only American President to serve more than two terms, and his political strength and prestige was a constant source of frustration to the Republicans.

Once Roosevelt had broken the two-term tradition, it was feared by some that a future President would also attempt to extend his stay in the White House beyond eight years. A young man, such as President John F. Kennedy, conceivably could have done so. And had it not been for passage of the Twenty-second Amendment, there undoubtedly would have been tremendous pressure on President Dwight D. Eisenhower to run for a third term. A throwback to the two-term tradition that had existed in American politics prior to the Roosevelt era, the Twenty-second Amendment did ensure that no individual could become a semi-permanent holder of the office of the American Presidency.

□ The *Twenty-fifth Amendment,* ratified in 1967, provided for the succession to the Presidency in the event of death, resignation, or disability, and for filling the vacancy in the Vice Presidency after the holder of that office stepped up to the Presidency. Ratification of this amendment filled a major gap in the Constitution which made no clear provisions regarding presidential disability. The illnesses of President Eisenhower and the assassination of President Kennedy highlighted the need for action to ensure the continuation of Presidential functions in the case of future disabilities.

Under the Twenty-fifth Amendment, the Vice President becomes Acting President whenever the President informs Congress that he is unable to perform his functions, or when a majority of the Cabinet or another body appointed by Congress finds the President incapacitated. In both cases the Vice President ceases to be Acting President when the President informs Congress that he is able to take on his responsibilities again. Finally, the amendment states that if the President dies or resigns, the Vice President who becomes President "shall nominate a Vice President who shall take the office upon confirmation by a majority vote of both houses of Congress." (Also see Chapter 14, pages 346–350.)

■ *Amendments extending suffrage.* The remaining amendments to the Constitution deal primarily with the expansion of the voting privilege and the removal of some of the voting limitations imposed by the states. These amendments have increased the democratization of the political system. The Fifteenth Amendment, which has already been explained, extended voting rights to former slaves.

□ The *Seventeenth* and *Nineteenth Amendments* also increased the voice of the people in the government. The Seventeenth Amendment, ratified in 1913, negated the original constitutional provision under which Senators were chosen by state legislatures, and provided that Senators would be elected directly by the people. The Nineteenth Amendment,

ratified in 1920, made it unconstitutional to deprive women of the right to vote.

Perfect examples of "ideas whose time had come," both of these amendments resulted from popular democratic movements of the early twentieth century. Actually, before they were ratified, many states had already adopted practices permitting the popular election of Senators and allowing women to vote.

□ The *Twenty-third Amendment* gave the right to vote in presidential elections to the residents of the District of Columbia. A paradox of compelling interest to observers of American government is the fact that the residents of the seat of government, Washington, D.C., are *disfranchised* —that is, deprived of the right to vote for the officials who govern them. Since the

THE AGE OF BRASS.

(This unflattering caricature of suffragettes campaigning for office was printed by Currier & Ives in 1869.)

Congress was given the right to legislate for the District by Article I, Section 8 of the Constitution, there seemed to be little reason for the residents to exercise the right to vote.

The Twenty-third Amendment, which was ratified in 1961, partially remedies this situation by granting District residents representation in the electoral college "equal to the whole number of Senators and Representatives in Congress to which the District would be entitled if it were a state, but in no event more than the least populous state. . . . " As a result of this amendment, qualified residents of the District participated in a presidential election for the first time in November 1964.

But giving residents of the District the right to vote in a presidential election does not overcome their real status as second-class citizens. They still can not direct their own local government. Instead, it is supervised by members of a congressional committee who have no special interest in the District because they do not represent it directly. In fact, these congressmen do not have to reside in the District while Congress is in session. In addition to this partial disfranchisement, those residents of Washington who work for the government bureaucracy, like their counterparts elsewhere, come under the restriction of the Hatch Act of 1939 which prohibits government employees from entering active politics.

□ Proposed by Congress in 1962 and ratified in 1964, the *Twenty-fourth Amendment* abolished *poll taxes,* or taxes on voting, in elections for federal offices. Two years later, the Supreme Court declared that all state poll taxes, for both federal and state elections, were a violation of the "equal protection" clause of the Fourteenth Amendment and therefore unconstitutional. (See also pages 144–145 in this chapter.)

□ In 1971 the electorate was further expanded with the ratification of the *Twenty-sixth Amendment.* All citizens eighteen years-old and over were made eligible to vote. It was estimated that 11 million new voters had been enfranchised by the amendment.

Review questions

1. How do the amendments to the Constitution illustrate the growth of democracy in the United States?
2. What are the major kinds of changes made to the Constitution since the Bill of Rights was ratified?

The Structure of the Election System

While the constitutional amendments have updated the American governmental system, attuning it to contemporary political needs, other changes have made it more democratic. Of central importance have been those changes made in the election system, which is the principal means by which the people can actively enter into the system. Without the free expression of the people's will, popular democracy loses its meaning.

The Framers of the Constitution recognized that a "due dependence upon the people" was probably the most effective check on the rise of tyrannical government. So, they embedded in the Constitution several basic components of an election system. At the same time, the Framers left most of the details of voting qualifications to the discretion of the states. But the changes in voting procedures, resulting from both national and state action over the past two centuries, have significantly altered the character of our political system.

The election system was a necessary part of the separation-of-powers machinery. By means of the election system, the responsibilities of the elected branches were tied to different constituencies: The House of Representatives was given a local constituency, and Representatives were elected directly by the people; the Senate had a state-based constituency, and Senators were elected by the state legislatures until passage of the Seventeenth Amendment; and the President had a broad national constituency which expressed its choice through the electoral college. These contrasting constituencies made different demands on the branches of government and helped to ensure their separation.

Another important part of the separation of powers was the provision that different elective offices be held for terms of different lengths. Representatives were given two-year terms; Senators, six-year terms; and the President, a four-year term.

Because they are elected at different times and by different constituencies, the President and the majorities in the House and Senate are often from opposing parties and will check each other's power. Even if a party does gain control of both branches for a while, it will not be able to impose its will too long; for as soon as that party loses control, the incoming opposition will undo any legislation it feels is too extreme.

The election system and representative government. The Framers also realized early in the Constitution-making process that *direct democracy,* or participation of all the people, was impossible. So, they opted for a representative form of government—a *republic.* In *The Federalist,* No. 10, Madison explained that in contrast to a democracy, a republic is "the delegation of the government . . . to a small number of citizens elected by the rest. . . . " He defended the establishment of a republican government by noting that it should

"refine and enlarge the public views by passing them through the medium of a chosen body of citizens, whose wisdom may best discern the true interest of their country. . . . Under such a regulation it may well happen that the public voice, pronounced by the representatives of the people, will be more consonant to the public good than if pronounced by the people themselves."

Apparently, Madison and many of the Framers did not have complete faith in the people's ability to direct themselves. At the same time, Madison was less than sure that the representative would always act in the best interests of the people unless he were chosen by a large number of citizens. Madison commented that since "each representative will be chosen by a greater number of citizens in the large than in the small republic, it will be more difficult for an unworthy candidate to practice with success the vicious arts by which elections are too often carried. . . ."

■ *Qualifications of candidates.* Nevertheless, the Framers, like Madison, did express their confidence that the people would choose able delegates. At least, they did not set down very rigid qualifications in the Constitution for those federal officials.

Representatives must be twenty-five years old and citizens of the United States for at least seven years. Moreover, at the time of their election, they must be inhabitants of the states that they are to represent; and during their two-year terms, they can not hold another governmental office. Senators must be thirty years old and citizens for at least nine years, as well as residents of the states that they are to represent. Like Representatives, they cannot hold another post in the government. The President must be at least thirty-five years old, a natural-born citizen, and must have resided in the United States for a minimum period of fourteen years.

■ *Qualifications of voters.* Because of the realities of state power at the time of the Constitutional Convention, the Framers left the determination of voting qualifications largely to the states. The states, however, did have to recognize one constitutional limitation. Those qualified to vote for the most numerous branch of the state legislatures were automatically qualified to select members of the House of Representatives (Article I, Sec. 2).

Initially, the state legislatures were authorized to choose Senators. Since the Senate essentially represented the interests of the states, this was considered appropriate. The House of Representatives was the only national body chosen directly by the people. The Seventeenth Amendment changed this procedure, and in 1913 the people were given the responsibility of choosing members of the Senate as well as the House. Senators, however, are elected at-large within the states, whereas Representatives are still chosen from local districts, called *congressional districts.*

The electoral college system. As a method for selecting the President, the electoral college system has been the subject of continued controversy. Devised by the Framers, the electoral college system is an indirect method of electing a President. Even at the Constitutional Convention, the delegates were incapable of coming to an agreement about a more direct method of electing the President. Alexander Hamilton, in *The Federalist,* No. 68,

"I KNOW IT NEEDS FIXING, BUT RIGHT AT THIS MOMENT I'M SICK OF IT!"

(The shortcomings of the election system come into sharp focus after every presidential election.)

expressed the modest reservation that though the electoral college system "be not perfect, it is at least excellent."

In its final form, the electoral college was organized so that the electors were chosen according to rules set up by state legislatures. Electors were expected to be the more responsible members of the community, capable of making rational and judicious decisions, and removed from the tumult of politics.

The original concept of the Framers was that electors would be independent in judgment, but the inevitable emergence of political parties rendered this system impracticable. By 1800, as political parties developed, states began to apply the *unit rule,* which required electors within a state to vote as a bloc for the candidate whose party had won a majority of the state's votes.

After 1800, independent voting by electors started to vanish and the unit rule became the practice. During the 1830's, presidential electors ceased (except in South Carolina) to be chosen by the state legislatures, and were elected by popular vote. Today, most states insist that the electors pledge their vote to whichever candidate has the majority of the popular vote in that state. Some states, however, like Georgia, allow their electors to remain unpledged and to vote for whichever candidate they like. Still, from 1820 until 1968, only 10 of the 15,092 votes cast by the electoral college were contrary to the instructions given the electors by popular vote.

Both the unit rule and selection of electors by popular vote have modified the electoral college system to meet the needs of an expanded democracy. Objections, though, continue to be raised against the system. Principal among the disadvantages cited is that with the unit rule, it is possible for a candidate to carry a majority of the electors, and still receive only a minority of popular votes. The system has actually permitted the election of three Presidents—John Quincy Adams, Rutherford B. Hayes, and Benjamin Harrison—who obtained fewer popular votes than their opponents. In addition to these *minority* Presidents, twelve other Presidents did not receive a clear majority or more than 50 percent of the total popular vote cast in the elections. (Table 6:1 lists these minority Presidents.)

Table 6:1

Minority Presidents 1824–1968

Year	Elected	Opponents		
1824	Adams 30.54* (84)	Jackson 43.13 (99)	Clay 13.24 (37)	Crawford 13.09 (41)
1844	Polk 49.56 (170)	Clay 48.13 (105)	Birney 2.30	
1848	Taylor 47.35 (163)	Cass 42.52 (127)	Van Buren 10.13	

Year	Elected	Opponents		
1856	Buchanan 45.63 (174)	Fremont 33.27 (114)	Fillmore 21.08 (8)	Smith .01
1860	Lincoln 39.79 (180)	Douglas 29.40 (12)	Breckinridge 18.20 (72)	Bell 12.60 (34)
1876	Hayes 48.04 (185)	Tilden 50.99 (184)	Cooper .97	
1880	Garfield 48.32 (214)	Hancock 48.21 (155)	Weaver 3.35	Others .12
1884	Cleveland 48.53 (219)	Blaine 48.24 (182)	Butler 1.74	St. John 1.49
1888	Harrison 47.86 (233)	Cleveland 48.66 (168)	Fisk 2.19	Streeter 1.29
1892	Cleveland 46.04 (277)	Harrison 43.01 (145)	Weaver 8.53 (22)	Others 2.42
1912	Wilson 41.85 (435)	T. Roosevelt 27.42 (88)	Taft 23.15 (8)	Others 7.58
1916	Wilson 49.26 (277)	Hughes 46.12 (254)	Benson 3.16	Others 1.46
1948	Truman 49.51 (303)	Dewey 45.13 (189)	Thurmond 2.40 (39)	H. Wallace 2.38
1960	Kennedy** 49.71 (303)	Nixon 49.55 (219)	Unpledged .92	Others .27
1968	Nixon 43.42 (301)	Humphrey 42.72 (191)	G. Wallace 13.53 (46)	Others .33

Sources: Congress and the Nation, 1965–68 Vol. II (*Washington, D.C.: Congressional Quarterly Service, Inc., 1969*), p. 425; Seymour Kurtz, ed., The New York Times Encyclopedic Almanac 1970 (*New York: New York Times Co., 1969*), pp. 146–155.

First number indicates percentage of popular vote. Number in parenthesis shows total of electoral votes.

**1960 percentages total more than 100 because of twice-counted Alabama votes under both Kennedy and unpledged columns.*

The number of minority Presidents reveals one major drawback in the electoral college system. Another unfortunate situation arises when no candidate receives a majority of the votes of the electors and the election is referred to the House of Representatives. In such a case, the unit rule prevails, giving each state a single vote. This method, of course, totally disregards the popular will. So far, only two elections—those of 1800 and 1824—have been referred to the House of Representatives. The possibility of election, then, by the House of Representatives has not been a serious obstacle to the proper functioning of the system. On the plus side of the ledger, the electoral college does fortify the two party system. Since the winner takes all, the college discourages splinter- or third-party developments.

■ *Proposals for reform.* Those who feel that the electoral college system does not accurately mirror popular choice frequently make suggestions for reform. One suggestion has been to reapportion the electoral votes among new state subdistricts which would divide the population into equal groupings. The majority within each subdistrict would control the vote of its elector. This would be only a slight modification of the present system.

Another suggested change is to abandon the unit rule entirely. This would enable electors to vote for presidential candidates according to the percentage of popular votes each candidate receives in that state. The most drastic reform would be to abolish the electoral college system altogether and have the President elected by direct popular vote.

In the past, it has been virtually impossible to change the present form of the electoral college system. Powerful state politicians often want to maintain the status quo. By being able to guarantee "delivery" of the state's vote through the unit rule, they wield great influence at party conventions and within the national party organizations.

A proposed amendment providing for direct election of the President passed the House of Representatives in 1969. But passage in the Senate seems doubtful. Moreover, state ratification of the amendment may be difficult to achieve, since many state politicians feel the present system works to their advantage.

Review questions

1. In *The Federalist,* No. 10, how did Madison defend a republican form of government? Is his argument still valid?
2. How can a President with less than 50 percent of the vote win an election?

Suffrage Restrictions and Voters' Rights

The Constitution did not include any complicated list of qualifications for voting. It only said that those qualified to vote for members of the "most numerous branch of the state legislature" would also be permitted to vote for members of the House of Representatives. Presidential electors were to be chosen by methods established by the states, and legal voting requirements were placed almost entirely within the jurisdiction of the states, unless Congress chose to act.

The Fifteenth and Nineteenth Amendments to the Constitution prohibited the national and state governments from discriminating by race or sex in setting up voting regulations. Yet, it was a long time before the Fifteenth Amendment was

UNCLE SAM'S THANKSGIVING DINNER.

(This 1869 cartoon by Thomas Nast depicts universal suffrage as a major American benefit for immigrants.)

interpreted by the Supreme Court so that the blatant devices discriminating against black Americans were made illegal. One of the most offensive discriminatory methods, the poll tax, was made unconstitutional in federal elections by the Twenty-fourth Amendment to the Constitution in 1964.

State requirements for voting. Given the power to establish requirements for voting, the states passed a number of restrictive measures. Voters were required to declare their ages, length of residence, prove their ability to read and write, or pay a tax to vote.

■ *Age limitations.* Although many people do not vote because they are uninterested, qualifications for voting also restrict voter turnout. Until recently, the minimum voting age in most states was twenty-one, although there were some exceptions.

Perhaps reflecting the emphasis on youth in the United States, Congress passed a law that President Nixon signed in June of 1970 which lowered the voting age for all elections throughout the country to eighteen. The Supreme Court later ruled that the law was constitutional *only* for elections of candidates to national offices, not for state or local elections. Congress then proposed an amendment to the Constitution that would make eighteen-year-olds eligible to vote in state and local as well as national elections. The Twenty-sixth Amendment was ratified by three-fourths of the states in 1971, making citizens over eighteen eligible to vote for officials at all levels.

■ *Residency requirements.* America is a nation on the move. Many people change their jobs and shift their residences each year. When they do, they often find it difficult to vote because most states and

143

communities insist that they must reside in a certain locale for a specific time before they are allowed to vote.

Restrictions which prevent new residents of a state or community from voting are instituted because it is felt that new residents, unfamiliar with state and local politics, are not capable of making sound choices. The argument, however, is less defensible in national elections where most people are relatively well-informed on the issues and candidates involved, no matter how short a period they have lived in a particular locale.

While it is almost impossible to estimate how many people are disfranchised each year because of various state residency requirements, it has been suggested that such requirements have kept about eight million voters from voting in recent presidential elections. Recognizing the unjustness of this situation, Congress included a provision in the voting rights law of 1970 that reduced the residency requirement for voting in presidential elections to thirty days throughout the country. The Supreme Court upheld the constitutionality of this provision.

■ *Absentee voting.* Many Americans also travel extensively for business reasons and other purposes. Moreover, the armed services include several million persons stationed away from their home states or abroad. Certainly, a man or woman who is away on duty for the country should not be denied the right to vote.

The states have an assortment of *absentee voting* laws to answer this need. In 1942, Congress passed a law that permitted absentee voting for members of the armed forces, thus preempting the state requirements. This law was replaced by the Federal Voting Assistance Act of 1955 which encouraged, but did not require, the states to adopt a new procedure. Servicemen, federal employees, their dependents, and merchant seamen were permitted to register for voting by means of a simple postcard application. By 1964, all the states had laws that permitted absentee voting by members of the armed services, and forty-seven states allowed civilian employees of the federal government to use absentee ballots.

Absentee voting for those not in military service is far from easy, however. It usually involves finding a notary public, post-office official, or a consular official to witness the placing of the ballot in an envelope. Those who travel abroad a great deal or happen to be out of their home states on the day of an election may still find themselves unable to exercise their franchise.

■ *Poll taxes.* The restrictions of age and residence are relatively inoffensive because they affect people indiscriminately. But other voting restrictions have been used to keep definite segments of the population from voting.

The poll tax, which is nothing more than a fee to vote, has been such a restriction. Set up in the nineteenth century as a substitute for property qualifications, the poll tax was originally regarded as a device to enlarge the electorate. A man would no longer have to possess a certain amount of land or material wealth in order to vote. He could simply pay the tax. It soon became evident, though, that the poll tax was a device which served to restrict, rather than enlarge, the franchise.

By the end of the nineteenth century, all the southern states imposed poll taxes which had the effect of keeping black Americans and poor whites away from the polls. Certainly, the poll tax discouraged those voters who had little motivation to register in the first place.

In 1964, the Twenty-fourth Amendment did away with poll taxes in federal elections, but it did not affect the use of the poll tax in state elections. But in 1966, a

federal court held the Alabama poll tax to be a violation of the Fifteenth Amendment and therefore unconstitutional. By rendering the poll tax invalid for state elections in Alabama, the lower court decision called into question all such taxes that twenty-seven states still levied in 1965.

Using a different point of law in 1966, the Supreme Court held, in *Harper v. Virginia State Board of Elections,* that the poll tax in Virginia was unconstitutional because it was a violation of the "equal protection of the laws" clause of the Fourteenth Amendment. The Court reasoned that since the poor were not as able as the rich to pay a fee to vote, they were not being treated equally. The equal-protection clause is interpreted to mean that state laws must treat everyone in the same manner. With poll taxes rendered unconstitutional in state as well as national elections, the total constitutional elimination of these taxes was completed.

■ *Literacy tests and other voting qualifications.* In the past, the use of literacy tests to qualify voters was widespread. The nature of literacy tests varied from state to state. Many states required that a voter be able to read, write, interpret material, and demonstrate a certain level of education before registering to vote. The Voting Rights Act of 1965 minimized literacy requirements for all citizens. According to this Act, any citizen who has attained a sixth-grade education in a school under the American flag can vote. This means that the language of instruction in the school and that spoken by the citizen need not be English.

In addition, a number of other qualifications, such as good moral character for example, have complemented literacy tests as requirements for voting registration. In Idaho, a moral-character test must be passed, and some "undesirables"—such as bigamists or polygamists—are kept off the rolls. In Alabama, voters have been required to be of "good character" and to be able to read, write, and interpret any article of the United States Constitution. Connecticut and other states insist on "good moral character, which can be interpreted however the state wants."

The real problem has been to determine whether these restrictions are discriminatory. Unless a charge of discrimination can be sustained, it would probably be very difficult for the courts to rule such practices unconstitutional. Under the terms of the Constitution, Congress can act only with respect to federal elections. The Fourteenth and Fifteenth Amendments do provide, though, that Congress has the respon-

From *Straight Herblock* (Simon & Schuster, 1964)

"I THINK THEM FEDS GOT ME, BOYS, BUT I KNOW YOU'LL CARRY ON."

(Since the poll tax became illegal, other devices for limiting voting rights have met the same fate.)

145

sibility and is authorized to legislate to insure equal protection of the laws and to prevent discrimination in voting. It was on the basis of these amendments that Congress finally passed strong voting-rights legislation.

The protection of voting rights. While literacy tests have been "on the books" of most states in the country, they were regarded in the North and West as a mere formality rather than as a barrier to voting. In some southern states, however, literacy tests and other state laws had become conscious instruments of discrimination against blacks.

A report by the United States Commission on Civil Rights in 1965 disclosed some of the practices employed by whites to discourage blacks from entering the polls. This report provided the background for the passage of the 1965 Civil Rights Act.

■ *Discriminatory registration.* The report disclosed that local registrars could administer literacy tests and other voting requirements in any way they saw fit. As a result, they sometimes administered the tests so as to exclude most black and to accept most white applicants. In one southern county, for example, between July 1961 and February 1965, 128 voting applications were submitted by blacks. About 150 whites applied to vote during the same time. It was found that white applicants who took the voting-qualification test were asked to interpret rather simple parts of the state's constitution, such as:

"Section 8. All persons, resident in this state, citizens of the United States, are hereby declared citizens of the state. . . .

"Section 35. The Senate shall consist of members chosen every four years by the qualified electors of the several districts. . . .

"Section 240. All elections by the people shall be by ballot."

Blacks, on the other hand, were given very difficult sections of the state's constitution to interpret. They were asked, for example, about tax exemptions for corporations, judicial sale of land, concurrent jurisdiction of chancery and circuit courts, eminent domain, and habeas corpus.

All 150 white applicants passed their voting-qualification test the first time. Only nine blacks passed, and this was only after repeated attempts were made to satisfy the registrar.

■ *Fear and intimidation.* In addition to discriminatory registration procedures, fear and intimidation were used frequently to discourage blacks from voting. An elderly black woman described her conversation with a local registrar to the United States Commission on Civil Rights:

"Well, when I went to register, the registrar asked me what did I come down there for. I told him 'to register.' He said, 'Register? For what?' And I told him I didn't know what I was coming to vote for. He hollered at me and scared me so I told him I didn't know what I came to vote for. I was just going to vote."

The same woman was asked by the Civil Rights Commission if she had passed the voting test. She replied, "Well, I didn't go back there. I didn't go back. After I went there and he scared me so bad, I didn't go back to see was I passed or no."

Other techniques used by public officials to frighten voters were reported to the Civil Rights Commission at the same time. For example, a sheriff photographed blacks as they attempted to register. He did not photograph whites. When asked about this practice, he replied, "I wanted them for my own use, I take a lot of pictures."

Another technique was the publication in local newspapers of the names and addresses of newly registered voters. This intimidated the potential black voter, who feared harassment of his family and damage to his home. Still another method was to threaten prospective registrants with jail terms for alleged violations of local ordinances. In some cases, registrants were even arrested and put in jail on fictitious charges.

Harassment by public officials has also been practiced in some areas. Should a black succeed in registering, he was likely to confront additional violence at the polling booth.

By 1965, conditions in some areas of the South, and in other parts of the nation, were no longer tolerable. Clearly the passage of federal legislation and the establishment of some form of federal enforcement machinery was necessary to prevent further voter discrimination.

■ *Initiation of a voting-rights bill.* In a television address before the nation on March 15, 1965, President Lyndon B. Johnson announced that he was sending a voting-rights bill to Congress:

"This bill will strike down restrictions to voting in all elections—federal, state, and local—which have been used to deny Negroes the right to vote.

"This bill will establish a simple, uniform standard which can not be abused however ingenious the effort to flout our Constitution.

"It will provide for citizens to be registered by officials of the United States government if the state officials refuse to register them.

"It will eliminate tedious, unnecessary law suits which delay the right to vote.

"Finally, this legislation will insure that properly registered individuals are not prohibited from voting. . . . "

On May 26, by a vote of 77 to 19, the Senate passed a voting rights bill after defeating many crippling amendments

proposed by the southern bloc. The House followed suit and the bill was signed by President Johnson on August 6, 1965.

■ *The Voting Rights Act of 1965.* The 1965 Act gave the Attorney General the power to initiate suits to suspend literacy tests and other devices (in particular, the poll tax) used to discriminate in federal, state, or local elections or in primary elections. A guideline indicating possible discrimination was established. If less than 50 percent of eligible black voters were registered in any particular state or political subdivision, federal investigation could be initiated. When discrimination was definitely demonstrated, federal examiners could be assigned under the terms of the Act to register voters.

One year later, that part of the Act which referred to the poll tax was no longer needed when the Supreme Court, in *Harper v. Virginia State Board of Election,* held that all poll taxes were unconstitutional. Nevertheless, the 1965 Voting Rights Act did enable federal officials to move into Alabama, Georgia, Louisiana, Mississippi, South Carolina, Virginia, some counties in North Carolina and Arizona and one in Idaho for the purpose of watching registration procedures.

The southern bloc quickly raised constitutional objections to the Voting Rights Act of 1965. Some southerners were claiming that the authority to regulate the elections of state and local officials resided in the hands of the states under the terms of the Constitution. The Fifteenth Amendment, however, definitely prohibits racial discrimination in voting—since it states that "the right of citizens of the United States to vote shall not be denied or abridged by the United States or by any state on account of race, color, or previous condition of servitude." Moreover, the Fifteenth Amendment gives Congress the power to enforce the amendment's terms through legislation. The Civil Rights Act of 1965 was explicitly based on this amendment. In 1970 Congress supplemented the 1965 law by banning literacy tests and the Supreme Court upheld it.

Review questions
1. List some of the requirements for voting imposed by the states.
2. How have people been kept from exercising their vote at the ballot box?

Constitutional Government As It Stands Today

A comparison of American government today with the system set up by the Constitution reveals that several important political changes have occurred since the Framers devised the political system. The major requirements of the nation have been altered substantially since 1791.

Some basic changes. Congress today is still tremendously influential and exercises vital functions in the national government. But, it is no longer the primary power in making governmental policy. This change can be traced to several factors.

On any particular subject, congressional leaders have been generally divided and incapable of acting in unison. Because of changes in legislative membership with each session of Congress, the legislature has not always offered the continuity sometimes needed to see programs through. The growth in the nation's economy and the increasing complexity of its society have demanded specialization of knowledge that legislators with their broader overall views could not give.

Specialized committees have developed in Congress to meet these needs. By themselves, however, they have not filled the new requirements of the government. Consequently, the power and prestige of the Presidency and the administrative branch have grown. The need for continued leadership that Congress could not fulfill made people turn to the President, and the need for government specialization and continuity in policy formulation led to a growth in administrative agencies.

Other changes in the constitutional system have been caused by the development of political parties and interest groups. These changes, too, make many of the premises of the Constitution invalid. For example, the Framers introduced the separation of powers and checks-and-balances system into the Constitution largely to hinder the development of factions. Now interest groups and political parties are such an accepted part of the democratic system that there would be no meaningful popular government without them.

Some changes in concepts. Federal and state relationships have also changed. The national government has seen fit to step into some traditionally state areas to protect the rights of individuals. This has happened particularly in such civil rights areas as voting, equal employment opportunities, housing, and public accommodations. The states, in turn, have been less able to cope with such national problems as welfare, health care, and unemployment; and the national government has been assuming some of these burdens.

Moreover, there has been a gradual expansion of popular participation in the government. The Framers did not envision that everyone would be able to vote. Yet, the gradual erosion of state controls over voting rights, and the addition of amendments to the Constitution have led to a truer democracy in the United States.

A new view of government. Whereas the Framers of the Constitution thought more in terms of restraining the national government's powers, today there is a tendency to expand national-government power to its fullest within constitutional limitations. The Framers recognized and met the challenge of creating a national government which had the capacity to resolve the immediate problems of their time.

Fortunately, the Constitution they adopted and the language it contained were extremely flexible. This attribute has allowed this document to survive the onrush of change that has taken place in both the theory and the practice of government since the Constitution's ratification in 1791.

Review questions

1. Which branches of the American federal government have increased in power?
2. List a few changes that have occurred in American constitutional government since its inception.

Chapter Review

Terms you should know

absentee voting	direct democracy	minority President
caucus	disfranchise	poll tax
common law	equal protection of the law	republic
congressional district	lame duck	unit rule
democratization		

Questions about the chapter

1. Why is the Bill of Rights considered an original part of the United States Constitution?
2. How did the presidential election of 1800 show the need for further amendment of the Constitution? What addition was finally made to the Constitution that would prevent this type of presidential election from recurring?
3. Which amendments to the Constitution have increased democratic participation in the American political system? How?
4. How does the Twenty-fifth Amendment provide for continuity of the American Presidency? What events led to the adoption of this amendment?
5. What proposals have been made for reforming the electoral college system?
6. What is the relationship of the Fifteenth Amendment to the Voting Rights Act of 1965?
7. What is the significance of the Supreme Court case of: *Harper v. Virginia State Board of Elections?*
8. How has the attitude toward "faction" changed in the United States since the inception of the Constitution?

Thought and discussion questions

1. Which amendments to the Constitution have the greatest influence on Americans today? Why?

2. Some observers feel that the Nineteenth Amendment to the Constitution has no appreciable effect on elections because "women vote the way their husbands tell them to." How do you feel about this statement? Has campaigning changed at all since women were given the franchise?
3. In the past it has been almost impossible to alter the electoral college system. Has it become more possible today? What changes would you suggest in our electoral system?
4. Have political parties and interest groups played a constructive or destructive role in the American governmental system?
5. A constitution, no matter how well designed, requires adjustment from time to time. The amendment process has been credited with avoiding the violent overthrow of the American government. Do you consider this argument valid? Why?

Class projects
1. Study the presidential election of 1960. What effect did the last minute flood of absentee ballots have on the final electoral vote in the state of California? How can this same situation be avoided in future presidential elections? Compare the procedure for absentee balloting in the state of California with four other states. Why is the procedure simpler in some states? How is absentee voting a form of discrimination?
2. In your opinion, which of the Civil War Amendments has best protected individual rights against the encroachment of the states in the twentieth century? Support your choice by selecting a Supreme Court case that exemplifies the strengthening of the amendment. Why is it necessary for the Supreme Court to defend the rights of the citizens against the power of the states?

Case Study: Black voter registration

Until the 1968 presidential election, voter-registration statistics for southern blacks revealed the effectiveness of discrimination in certain states and the need for reform in voting procedures. With the election of that year, a greater number of black voters registered; this was due, in part, to the 1965 Voting Rights Act and the black man's new-found awareness of his rights as an American citizen.

Throughout America, unfortunately, the poor are less likely to exercise their electoral prerogative than are members of the higher income and educational levels. And many blacks are within the lower economic groups. In addition, as with other citizens, many blacks are indifferent to exercising their right to vote. Civil rights leaders and other activists are trying to dispel citizen apathy. Their success along with the effects of the 1965 Voting Rights Act were clearly evident in the 1968 presidential election.

The following case study, composed of articles and statistics, illustrates the change that has occurred in voter registration since the implementation and enforcement of the federal law. Yet, despite this increase in voter registration, further analysis of the vote has disclosed that the traditional patterns of voting behavior were not broken.

While reading this case study, watch for information in the articles and statistical tables that will help you decide:
1. What types of individuals are least likely to exercise their franchise?
2. What brought about the increase in voter registration in the South?
3. What evidence is there that the blacks in the South are becoming more effective as a political force?

NEGRO VOTE—CAN IT BE DECISIVE?

Facts about the Negro vote, as opposed to theories, will surprise many. Negro voters are increasing, but remain a small minority, often split, in most places.

Once again, the political theory is being advanced that the Negro vote is to be decisive in a presidential election.

Negroes are concentrated in many big cities of the North. Hubert Humphrey, the Democratic nominee, is depending on the electoral votes of the Northern industrial States to win in November. The Negro vote, as a bloc, is counted on to tilt the balance his way.

But what do Census Bureau figures show to be the facts about the relative importance of the white and Negro voters—both North and South?

In the North. Whites of voting age outnumber nonwhites—mostly Negroes—at least 9 to 1 in all of the "big city" States of the Northeast, Midwest and the Pacific Coast.

In these key States, nonwhites make up the following percentages of the total voting-age population:

Illinois, 9.9; Michigan, 8.9; Missouri, 8.2; New York, 8.6; New Jersey, 8.1; Ohio, 7.9; California, 7.7; Pennsylvania, 7.3; and Indiana, 5.4.

Whites outnumber Negroes of voting age by about 25 to 1 in Connecticut, 44 to 1 in Massachusetts, 52 to 1 in Wisconsin, and 90 to 1 in Minnesota.

The only big city in the country where Negroes make up at least half of the voting-age population is the nation's capital—Washington, D.C. In other big cities, whites outnumber nonwhites among potential voters 9 to 1 in San Francisco, 8 to 1 in Boston, 6 to 1 in New York City, 5 to 1 in Los Angeles, 4 to 1 in Chicago, 3 to 1 in Cleveland, Detroit and Philadelphia.

The result is that if bloc voting by Negroes leads to a reaction in the form of bloc voting by whites in the States with big electoral votes, then the candidate favored by white voters obviously would prevail. . . .

In the South. In the 16 States of the South and Border—a region with 174 out of the 538 votes in the Electoral College—voting-age whites outnumber Negroes on an average of 4 to 1.

In major cities, the ratio of voting-age whites to nonwhites ranges from 2 to 1 in Baltimore and New Orleans, to 3 to 1 in St. Louis, 5 to 1 in Dallas and 4 to 1 in Houston. . . .

Negro registration is increasing in the South, as a result of recent civil-rights laws passed by Congress, and voter-registration drives conducted by various groups.

U.S. NEWS & WORLD REPORT

SEPTEMBER 23, 1968

This excerpt from "Negro Vote—Can It Be Decisive?" U.S. News & World Report, September 23, 1968, is reprinted with permission of U.S. News & World Report. Copyright © 1968 by U.S. News & World Report, Inc.

Also, Negroes are becoming more of a political force in State and local elections in the South—particularly where race alone is not a dominant issue.

The U.S. Commission on Civil Rights reports that in the 11 States of the old Confederacy, 57.2 per cent of all Negroes of voting age are registered to vote in the 1968 presidential election—an increase from 43.3 percent who registered four years ago.

The most dramatic gain shows up in Mississippi, where Negro registration jumped from 6.7 to 59.8 per cent. Substantial increases were recorded in four other States covered by the 1965 Voting Rights Act—Alabama, Georgia, Louisiana and South Carolina.

Lesser gains in Negro registration were made in Arkansas, Florida, North Carolina, Tennessee, Texas and Virginia, where the percentage of Negro voting already was relatively high.

There also has been an increasing registration of white voters in the South, and a migration of new white residents from other parts of the country to some areas of the South—notably Florida and Texas.

The Civil Rights Commission's figures show that white voters outnumber Negroes by wide margins. The Negro percentage of total voter registration by States in the South, as reported by the Commission, is as follows:

Alabama, 17 percent; Arkansas, 16.4; Florida, 12.3; Georgia, 18.3; Louisiana, 20.2; Mississippi, 23.5; North Carolina, 14.8; South Carolina, 20.6; Tennessee, 13.6; Texas, 13.3; and Virginia, 17.6.

From this, politicians point out that if there is to be bloc voting along racial lines without regard to other issues, then the Negro vote obviously will be in the minority.

Political Activity. Another element enters into consideration of the Negro electorate at this point, involving the extent and nature of their voting activities.

Census Bureau analysis of the 1966 off-year election showed that, nationwide, 57.1 percent of all whites of voting age went to the polls.

Among Negroes, only 41.8 per cent actually voted.

Studies of voting trends have shown repeatedly that, among the total population, those least likely to register—or vote—are the poor, the undereducated, the unemployed, and the young. The Government's "poverty" definitions indicate that many Negroes fit one or more of these classifications.

Thus, even the voting-age and registration figures do not give an accurate measure of the number of Negroes who actually go to the polls and vote.

Estimates based on census data show that Negroes now constitute around 10 per cent of the total voting-age population. . . .

In the past, the Democratic nominee for President has been the principal beneficiary of the Negro-bloc vote.

A national survey by the Gallup Poll shows that the Democratic candidate received 61 per cent of the Negro vote in 1956, 68 per cent in 1960, and 94 per cent in the 1964 election. . . .

Political soundings in Negro areas of both North and South indicate that many Negroes, in reality, are not enthusiastic about any white candidate this year. Some feel they have been used for political purposes in the past. Many may stay home and simply refuse to vote.

"Black power" groups—who want a separate Negro society—are putting up their own candidates for President on newly formed minority-party tickets which may divert a portion of the Negro vote in some key Northern States.

In addition, there is a growing middle class of educated and property-owning Negroes who have suffered from racial violence. It has been difficult for the Negro "moderates" to stand up in public against . . . the black militants, but many may cast a "silent vote" in favor of "law and order" this year for their own self-protection.

Added to this is a growing conflict between the old city machines, run by white Democrats, and rising Negro political power.

And in the South, some Negroes respond to local groups and officeholders, without regard to national issues.

In sum, the profile of the Negro vote in America shows this:

Voting-age whites greatly outnumber Negroes in both the North and South.

Fewer Negroes register to vote than whites; even fewer actually vote.

The Democratic nominee for President, once again, is likely to get a majority of the Negro vote nationwide.

But Negroes are divided, as never before, over candidates, issues, and the future of the Negro revolution.

More and more, the theory that the Negro vote is decisive in a presidential election appears to be a political myth.

WHO VOTES? THE 1968 FIGURES

WASHINGTON—In the 1968 presidential election, 61 per cent of the resident population of voting age cast ballots—a drop from 62.1 per cent in 1964.

A study by the Census Bureau shows that voter participation varied from 76.1 per cent in Utah to 33.5 per cent in the District of Columbia. Only 15 States showed an increase in voting. Many were in the South, where both Negro and white voting ratios rose from 1964.

In the 1968 election, 51.4 per cent of non-whites in the South reported that they voted, compared with 44 per cent in 1964. White participation in the South rose from 59.5 per cent in 1964 to 61.9 per cent in 1968. Outside the South, the white ratio dropped from 74.7 per cent to 71.8 per cent.

In the predominantly Negro District of Columbia, with no barriers to presidential voting, the ratio of 33.5 per cent was a drop from 39.4 per cent in 1964.

Vote Group Analysis Reflects Traditional Patterns

Despite the racial disturbances and vehement foreign policy arguments which marked the year 1968 and were expected to have a major influence on Presidential voting a surprising pattern of normality emerged from analysis of the vote by city-size, ethnic, occupation or income groupings in all areas except the South, where George C. Wallace received his heaviest vote. The study was based on sample precinct data collected by CBS and NBC News. . . .

Negro, Blue Collar, Farm. In Negro ghetto areas, CBS found Humphrey getting 79 per cent of the vote, Nixon 15 percent and Wallace 6 percent. The Humphrey percentage would probably have been higher and Nixon's and Wallace's lower if the Negro precincts in question had not contained a certain minority of white voters. NBC, which specifically sought out Negro areas rather than accepting those that turned up in a national precinct probability sampling, found the Negro vote for Humphrey even higher—94 percent in New York, for instance, 91.9 percent in Illinois, 90.1 percent in Michigan and 88.1 percent in the . . . Pacific states grouping.

The big surprise of the election came in the blue collar working class areas, which had been expected to be the most sensitive to the racial issue and give heavy support to Wallace. CBS reported that in predominantly white blue-collar worker areas in cities with high Negro populations, or where there had been riots, the vote breakdown was 47 percent for Humphrey, 43 percent for Nixon and just 10 percent for Wallace. Exactly the same vote percentage was reported from all other blue collar precincts around the country. The biggest Wallace vote in any one grouping, in fact, was reported not in or near cities but among farm whites—20 percent in sample precincts, compared to 48 percent for Nixon and 32 percent for Humphrey. Overwhelming farm white support for Wallace in the South helped boost his score in that category, but he also ran an unusually strong race among farm whites in the West.

NBC's sampling of precincts where most breadwinners are union members showed a 60-percent vote for Humphrey and 18 percent for Wallace.

The CBS calculation of the vote in cities which had been hit by racial disturbances in the past few years showed 58 percent for Humphrey, 34 percent for Nixon and 8 percent for Wallace. Democrats lost much less ground in these cities than they did in the country as a whole.

Voter Registration Statistics
REGISTRATION BY STATE—ALL COUNTIES

State	1960 voting age population		Pre-Act Registration				Post-Act Registration				
			Number		Percentage		Number			Percentage	
	White	Nonwhite	White	Nonwhite	White	Nonwhite	White	Nonwhite	Unknown	White	Nonwhite
Alabama	1,353,122	481,220	935,695	92,737	69.2	19.3	1,212,317	248,432	14,297	89.6	51.6
Arkansas	848,393	192,629	555,944	77,714	65.5	40.4	616,000	121,000	....	72.4	62.8
Florida	2,617,438	470,261	1,958,499	240,616	74.8	51.2	2,131,105	299,033	33,694	81.4	63.6
Georgia	1,796,963	612,875	1,124,415	167,663	62.6	27.4	1,443,730	322,496	22,776	80.3	52.6
Louisiana	1,289,216	514,589	1,037,184	164,601	80.5	31.6	1,200,517	303,148	....	93.1	58.9
Mississippi	751,266	422,273	525,000	28,500	69.9	6.7	589,066	181,233	176,099	91.5	59.8
N. Carolina	2,005,955	550,929	1,942,000	258,000	96.8	46.8	1,602,980	277,404	....	83.0	51.3
S. Carolina	895,147	371,104	677,914	138,544	75.7	37.3	731,096	190,017	....	81.7	51.2
Tennessee	1,779,018	313,873	1,297,000	218,000	72.9	69.5	1,434,000	225,000	....	80.6	71.7
Texas	4,884,765	649,512	....	....	....	....	2,600,000	400,000	....	53.3	61.6
Virginia	1,876,167	436,718	1,070,168	144,259	61.1	38.3	1,140,000	243,000	....	63.4	55.6
Total	20,097,450	5,015,933	11,123,816	1,530,634	73.4	35.5	14,750,811	2,810,763	246,866	76.5	57.2

Source: Report of the U.S. Commission on Civil Rights, 1968, Appendix VII, Table 1 (Washington, D.C.: U.S. Government Printing Office, 1968).

FINAL 1968 PRESIDENTIAL ELECTION RESULTS

State	Total Popular Vote				Electoral Vote			Percentages		
	Nixon (R)	Humphrey (D)	Wallace (AIP)	All Others	Nixon	Humphrey	Wallace	Nixon	Humphrey	Wallace
Alabama	146,923	196,579	691,425	14,982			10	14.0	18.7	65.9
Arkansas	190,759	188,228	240,982	—			6	30.8	30.4	38.9
Florida	886,804	676,794	624,207	—	14			40.5	30.9	28.5
Georgia	380,111	334,439	535,550	—			12	30.4	26.8	42.8
Louisiana	257,535	309,615	530,300	—			10	23.5	28.2	48.3
Mississippi	88,516	150,644	415,349	—			7	13.5	23.0	63.5
N. Carolina	627,192	464,113	496,188	—	12		1	39.5	29.2	31.3
S. Carolina	254,062	197,486	215,430	—	8			38.1	29.6	32.3
Tennessee	472,592	351,233	424,792	—	11			37.8	28.1	34.0
Texas	1,227,844	1,266,804	584,269	—		25		39.8	41.1	19.0
Virginia	590,319	442,387	321,833	6,950	12			43.4	32.5	23.6

Source: Congress and the Nation, Vol. II. Reprinted with permission of Congressional Quarterly Service. Copyright © 1969 by Congressional Quarterly, Inc.

The following table shows, for each [Southern] State, the percentage of the total resident population of voting age that voted in 1964 and 1968.

State	1964	1968
Alabama	35.9	50.3
Arkansas	49.9	51.8
Florida	53.3	57.0
Georgia	43.0	42.9
Louisiana	47.2	53.8
Mississippi	33.2	50.6
North Carolina	51.8	53.9
South Carolina	38.7	45.9
Tennessee	51.2	52.7
Texas	44.4	48.5
Virginia	41.1	50.4

Source: U.S. News & World Report, *January 13, 1969.*

End questions

1. Under what conditions will the black vote be more decisive in a presidential election? Why wasn't it a swing factor in the 1968 presidential election? Use both articles and statistics to support your argument.
2. What prevents the black vote from being a solid bloc? Why were there more divisions in the black vote in 1968 than ever before?
3. How can discrimination be determined by federal officials? Is voting discrimination limited only to the southern states?
4. How did the white southern vote affect the 1968 presidential election? Why was this a better example of bloc voting than the black vote?
5. Do you think voter registration will increase in years to come?

Supplementary Reading

ABRAHAM, HENRY J. *Freedom and the Court: Civil Rights and Liberties in the United States.* New York: Oxford Univ. Press, 1967. Paperbound. The author attempts to analyze the conflict between individual rights and community rights. The significance of the judicial branch of the government is given full treatment including the role of the Supreme Court in strengthening our basic rights and liberties.

BECKER, CARL. *The Declaration of Independence: A Study in the History of Political Ideas.* New York: Vintage, 1958. Paperbound. A classic study of the philosophy behind the Declaration of Independence. This history explores the several drafts, and analyzes the literary quality of the document.

BOWEN, CATHERINE DRINKER. *Miracle at Philadelphia.* New York: Bantam, 1968. Paperbound. The reader is deftly transported back in time to that very important Convention of 1787, and is given clear insight into the maneuverings, debates, and decision-making that took place. The tensions, hopes, and aspirations of all those involved in the Convention are vividly evoked. Of added interest are the precise biographies of the participants.

ELAZAR, DANIEL J. *American Federalism: A View From the States.* New York: T. Y. Crowell, 1966. Is the federal concept a political anachronism today? How has cultural and technological change in America influenced and modified our federal system? This book attempts to explain federalism and answer some timely questions.

FROMM, ERICH. *Escape from Freedom.* New York: Avon, 1968. Paperbound. An inquiry into the meaning of freedom for modern man. The author lays stress on the importance of psychology in the social process. He interprets the historical development of freedom in terms of man's awareness of himself as a significant separate being.

GOLDWIN, ROBERT A., ed. *A Nation of States.* Chicago: Rand McNally, 1963. Paperbound. This collection of essays explores both the theoretical and practical aspects of American federalism. It is a readable work in federal-state relations.

HAMILTON, ALEXANDER; JAY, JOHN; MADISON, JAMES. *The Federalist.* New York: Modern Library, 1964. Paperbound. These essays by Hamilton, Jay, and Madison defend the Constitution and were the catalysts for persuading the states to adopt the document. This work should be required reading for anyone who wants to know the fundamental principles upon which the government of the United States was established.

KATZ, WILLIAM L. *Eyewitness: The Negro in American History.* New York: Pitman, 1967. This is an account of the civil rights revolution that began in the mid-1950's and has not stopped. Some of the people who were directly involved in this revolution provide valuable commentary on the movement to achieve equality for the black man.

ROSSITER, CLINTON. *1787: The Grand Convention.* New York: Macmillan, 1966. Rossiter contends that 1787 was one of the most important years for Americans. At the book's end, one can not help but agree with him. The author defends his thesis by providing the setting, background, and struggle behind the writing and the ratification of the Constitution.

WHEARE, K. C. *Federal Government,* 4th ed. New York: Oxford Univ. Press, 1964. Paperbound. This short book is a lasting study of the federal structure. Wheare is not only concerned with federalism as a form of government, but also with the concept and all its ramifications.

W hy should I vote for him? What's he done for me?" "Taxes, taxes—higher and higher!" "Democrats, Republicans, they're all alike! Just a bunch of politicians!" "I think I'll write my Congressman. They're not going to get away with this!" All of these are comments about the way the government is working, and all of these comments or similar ones are heard every day in American homes and streets. The people making these comments are concerned about government and what it is doing for them. It is natural for them to make these comments. It is part of the constitutional democratic system. But what can these citizens really do? How can they make their complaints or support for the actions of their representatives known to the government?

In the complex American political system, direct participation is often more limited than it might be in smaller or less populated democracies where the structures of government tend to be less complicated and where people may have more direct contact with government officials. Everyone, of course, can not participate in government all the time. Therefore, a division of labor is maintained between the public and private spheres of the society. The voter does not sit in the legislature but has a delegate who does. This allows the government to function more efficiently.

The most effective way in which citizens can register their support of, or discontent with, governmental policy is through the ballot box— by retaining or rejecting the representatives who speak for them in the government. But voting is only one means of linking the people with their government. Participation in government can take place on many other levels as well.

Democratic societies have developed several vehicles for achieving participation in government. Among these are the political parties and interest groups that serve as special liaisons between the main body of the electorate and the officials of government. In Unit Three, the formation of political attitudes in general, as well as the nature and role of these parties and interest groups will be explored. All of these elements constitute the sources and channels of the demands and supports that make up the inputs of the political system.

UNIT THREE
Inputs for the Political System: Demands and Supports

CHAPTER 7
Political Attitudes: Their Basis and Formation

In order for government to act on demands from the people, it must know not only what these demands are, but also what percentage of the people feel strongly about them. The latter criterion is the hardest to determine, for *public opinion,* or the accumulation of views regarding any policy goal, is difficult to measure.

Public opinion about any given problem is going to be narrow or broad according to how much of the public is involved. Opinions usually are expressed by individuals who have specific knowledge or are especially affected by the policies under consideration. Thus in most instances, public opinion will only represent a narrow portion of the whole populace. Nationwide public opinion exists only with respect to broad national issues, such as welfare, the economy, defense, and so forth.

Insofar as most political issues are concerned, the public can not be considered as a mass. Instead, it should be thought of in terms of particular groups that interact with the various parts of the government. While the public as a whole is not concerned with many of the complex issues that arise today, interest groups are. These groups often possess an expertise comparable to that found in the government agencies which respond to their needs with policies.

In general, there are interest groups corresponding to most major areas of government policy, such as foreign policy, defense, health, education, welfare, agriculture, communications, transportation, science, and so forth. Interest groups also represent all the segments of society, such as farmers, bankers, doctors, lawyers, teachers, plumbers, and so forth. It is through these specialized interest groups that much public opinion is transmitted to the government.

The Measurement of Public Opinion

Public opinion, whether it is general or specific, must somehow be measured and transmitted to the government. This is both a requirement and a condition of democracy. In order to determine if it is functioning in cooperation with or counter to the will of the people, a democratic government depends on public opinion. If public opinion is to affect the governmental process, the government must be made aware of the broad issues of concern to the public.

Measuring opinion on broad policy issues. Despite the difficulty of pinpointing opinions on broad issues, some attempts have been made to discern what the public is thinking. One of these attempts has been made by the Survey Research Center of the University of Michigan. The Center first tries to decide which issues are of general public concern, and then it conducts surveys to determine how the public feels about these issues. The questions in the surveys focus on such problems as the extent of federal aid to education and to medical care, the amount of government regulation of business, the direction of legislation on housing and labor, the extent of commitments to the free world, and so on.

On recent pre-election questionnaires, the Survey Research Center asked its sample electorate to express its agreement

◀ Which experiences and institutions have the greatest influence in the formation of an individual's political attitudes and opinions? Why do some people refuse to exercise their right to express their opinions?

Robert Day. Copyright © 1967 Saturday Review, Inc.

"Harry only believes in voting in the Gallup, Harris and other public opinion polls. He says the regular elections don't mean so much."

(In most cases, are public opinion polls accurate indications of how the electorate is really thinking?)

or disagreement with a series of statements on broad policy issues. The type of statements the Center used to find out opinions are listed below.[1] They represent the areas of governmental activity about which there is likely to be opinion:

(1) The government in Washington ought to see to it that everybody who wants to work can find a job.

(2) This country would be better off if we just stayed home and did not concern ourselves with problems in other parts of the world.

(3) If cities and towns around the country need help building more schools, the government in Washington ought to give them the money they need.

(4) The United States should give economic help to the poorer countries of the world, even if those countries can't pay for it.

(5) If blacks are not getting fair treatment in jobs and housing, the national government should see to it that they do.

(6) The United States should keep soldiers overseas where they can help countries that are fighting communism.

(7) The national government ought to help people get doctors and hospital care at low cost.

(8) The government in Washington should stay out of the question of whether white and black children go to the same school.

(9) The government in Washington is getting too powerful for the good of the country and the individual person.

These are, of course, all-important questions on which to assess public opinion. Once the data from these questionnaires has been assembled and compiled, the researchers at the Center can tell how the public feels about the problems it has inquired about.

■ *The polls.* The popular public opinion polls, or surveys, conducted by Gallup, Roper, Harris, and other private firms also provide the means of measuring political opinion. The kinds of questions asked often seem rather simple and indefinite. Questions asked by pollsters tend to be fairly broad, so that a wide sampling of the public can be made. For example, a question about the popularity of the President will trigger a "heavy" opinionated response. On the other hand, if a pollster asked individuals how they felt about a recent decision of the Federal Aviation Agency, he would probably receive a heavy "no opinion" response.

Naturally, both the polls and such surveys as those conducted by the Survey Research Center can be misleading. Ques-

[1] *These statements are paraphrased from the "1968 Pre-Election Study" of the Survey Research Center; University of Michigan, Institute for Social Research (Ann Arbor, Sept.–Oct. 1968).*

tions can be so stated that only biased answers can be given. And statistics can be so compiled that they are not true reflections of what the public is really concerned about.

Review questions

1. Why is it difficult to measure public opinion?
2. What are some means of gauging public opinion? How accurate are they?

The Determinants of Political Attitudes

Each individual acquires his attitudes from varied influences on his thinking. Family background, education, income, occupation, and religion all contribute to the formation of an individual's attitudes. The same is also true of his *political attitudes*. He may agree or disagree with more government involvement in education, business, or labor. He may be positive or negative about a political party's program. Or he may disregard politics entirely and concern himself only with the local baseball club. All of these are political attitudes which are formed as a result of many factors.

The family. Just as the family has perceptible influence on a person's attitudes about religion or racial tolerance, it is often the basis for shaping a person's attitude about where he stands politically. This is because the family adopts general attitudes about occupations, education, and economic issues which in turn affect the individual's political attitudes.

It has been shown by some political scientists that there is a direct correlation between the occupation of parents and the attitudes of their children concerning labor, business, governmental participation in the economy, and world affairs. Children most frequently reflect their parents in their thinking on these matters. The degree that children are influenced in their political attitudes by their parents depends largely on the amount of similarity between the interests and attitudes of both parents. If the parents support the same political party and agree about policies, their offspring will probably follow in their footsteps.

Taking this conclusion one step further, it has also been suggested that a basic source of political attitudes, such as the family, determines the intensity of *party loyalty*—the individual's attachment to a particular political party. Political scientists have found that voters who support the party favored by their families develop

Courtesy of The Register and Tribune Syndicate, Inc.

"Son . . . !" "Dad . . . !"

(The political conflicts of the late 1960's revealed the differences between generations within families.)

161

firmer and more consistent habits of party allegiance than voters who renounce the family preference. Since an individual is likely to acquire friends and select a spouse from the same social environment and with the same life style as his own, party loyalties acquired from the family are likely to be strengthened later in life. The family, then, is a force for political stability.

Definite correlations can be drawn between the degree of interest expressed by parents in politics and the political involvement of other family members. There are notable examples of this in politically active families such as the Roosevelts, Lodges, Tafts, and Kennedys who

Reprinted with permission of Los Angeles Times Syndicate.

"Glad To Give You My Opinion. I'm For Disarmament, The Common Market, Foreign Aid, Federal Aid To Education, Medicare, The U.N.—Oh, Yes, And Aid To Teachers Who Get Fired For Expressing Their Opinions!"

(Personal interests are still of primary concern, no matter how political attitudes have been formed.)

have had a substantial effect on national politics. Moreover, on all levels of politics, the family has an important impact in determining which citizens become active or inactive politically.

Indifference to politics, however, must be credited also to other factors, such as a lack of education, an inability to communicate, and other environmental conditions. A person who devotes all of his energy to working for the necessities of life—food and shelter—or who is moonlighting to support his wife and children is less likely to be concerned about politics.

Education, income level, and occupation. Political activity and behavior can also be determined by education, which in turn is largely determined by the parent's occupation and level of income. Data from a Survey Research Center sample of the electorate reveal that of the respondents whose fathers were professionals, 61 percent had a college education, 37 percent had finished high school, and about 2 percent had finished only grade school. On the other hand, when the father's occupation was categorized as unskilled, the proportions of respondents that had completed college, high school, and grade school were 9, 54, and 37 percent respectively.[2] However, as the colleges and universities become more liberal in their admissions policies, and more people are able to continue their education beyond high school, these percentages will change.

Just as the level of education varies in accordance with the parent's occupation and income, the degree of political involvement and the individual's sense of public duty rises in proportion to the level of education. People who have more education are generally more apt to participate

[2] This data is quoted by V. O. Key, Jr., Public Opinion and American Democracy (New York: Alfred A. Knopf, 1961), p. 318.

in politics and to believe in the value of such participation than people with less education. The more education a person has, the more likely he is to have definite opinions about political issues. Those with a college education give far fewer "no opinion" answers to survey questions about international relations, domestic economic policy, or social problems. This pattern of response is to be expected. If those with better education were not better informed about both political and

Table 7:1

Election Year	Religion	Voted Democratic	Voted Republican	Voted Other	
1948		(Truman)	(Dewey)	(Thurmond)	(H. Wallace)*
	Protestant	47	48	3	.8
	Catholic	70	26	1.3	2.2
	Jewish	60	20	1.6	18
1952		(Stevenson)	(Eisenhower)		
	Protestant	37	63		
	Catholic	56	44		
	Jewish	77	23		
1956		(Stevenson)	(Eisenhower)		
	Protestant	37	63		
	Catholic	51	49		
	Jewish	75	25		
1960		(Kennedy)	(Nixon)		
	Protestant	38	62		
	Catholic	78	22		
	Jewish	81	19		
1964		(Johnson)	(Goldwater)		
	Protestant	60	37		
	Catholic	80	17		
	Jewish	91	4.6		
1968		(Humphrey)	(Nixon)	(G. Wallace)	
	Protestant	31.5	54.5	14	
	Catholic	52	41	7	
	Jewish	80	14	3	

*The data for Thurmond and H. Wallace were not tabulated.
Sources: Ivan Hinderaker, ed., American Government Annual 1961–62 (New York: Holt, Rinehart & Winston, 1961), p. 74; and releases of the American Institute of Public Opinion (Gallup Poll); and the Roper Survey.

nonpolitical issues, the educational system would be a striking failure.

Levels of education also can be employed to predict opinions on selected political issues. There are fairly distinct differences of opinion among groups with different levels of education with regard to governmental policies on medical care, guaranteed incomes, aid to education, and private ownership of housing and public utilities. Again, it must be mentioned that the increased capacity of more people to attend college is changing this pattern.

Despite the importance of education, it is still virtually impossible to isolate its influence on political attitudes from the influence of other factors such as family preferences, income, and occupation. In fact, education, like political attitudes, is greatly determined by these other factors.

Religious influences. As with other determinants of political behavior, it is difficult to measure the exact effect of religious influences. Nevertheless, from an analysis of election data, it is possible to detect distinct *voting patterns,* or party preferences in elections, among specific religious groups. Table 7:1 illustrates this tendency in recent presidential elections.

Conclusions about the general relationship between religion and political behavior are difficult to draw from these election statistics. Yet, the statistics do show definite religious voting patterns. The Jewish vote, which is concentrated in urban areas, and the Catholic vote, which is heavily working class, tend to be largely Democratic. A greater proportion of Protestants—who tend to be more suburban or rural and often in higher income brackets—support the Republican party. Thus, to some extent, religious voting patterns reflect economic and social factors and can not be isolated from them.

The biggest problem in such an evaluation is that voters are often influenced profoundly by the personal characteristics of the candidates. For example, in the elections of 1952 and 1956, there was a general shift away from the Democratic party, largely due to the personal popularity of the Republican candidate, Dwight D. Eisenhower. Thus, the shift of the Catholic vote in 1952 and 1956, which tended to be Democratic in other years, is easier to explain in terms of the candidate than in terms of the religious factor alone.

When, however, religion alone overshadows all other public issues in an election, the effect of religious voting patterns is more dramatic. In the presidential elections of 1928 and 1960, voting patterns did not reflect concern over public issues as much as the fact that one of the candidates was a Catholic. The defeat of Al Smith in 1928 was essentially due to his Roman Catholicism and many Protestants voted against him. Likewise in the election of 1960, John F. Kennedy's Catholicism was a widely publicized issue that cost him some Protestant votes. A relatively heavy Catholic vote, though, allowed him to squeak through with a narrow victory. The Jewish vote, too, was more heavily Democratic in 1960 than usual. But this may be accredited more to Jewish support of Kennedy's policies than of his religion.

The fact that Kennedy was elected may indicate that the importance of religion as an issue in the public mind may be declining. The influence of religious differences on political behavior does not remain constant. But this is not unusual. The effect of other forces—education, economic level, and occupation—that shape attitudes also changes in time.

Ethnic groups. Ethnic identity, likewise, tends to have less and less influence on political attitudes. As immigrants become absorbed into the broader society, their separate group identity, as a factor sway-

Racial Voting Patterns				
Election Year	Race	Voted Democratic	Voted Republican	Voted Other
1948	White	53	47	—*
	Black	81	19	—
1952	White	43	57	
	Black	79	21	
1956	White	41	59	
	Black	61	39	
1960	White	49	51	
	Black	68	32	
1964	White	59	41	
	Black	94	6	
1968	White	38	47	15**
	Black	85	12	3

*Percentages for the candidates of the States' Rights and Progressive parties were not tabulated.
**Percentages are for the American Independent Party.
Sources: Ivan Hinderaker, ed., American Government Annual 1961–1962 (New York: Holt, Rinehart & Winston, 1961), p. 74; and releases of the American Institute of Public Opinion (Gallup Poll).

ing the way they vote, recedes into the background. Members of an ethnic group will gradually vote and think more like members of other groups with similar educational, income, and occupational levels. Many Afro-Americans, however, have been prevented from following this trend.

The impact of the black vote in America has been difficult to assess. During the post-Civil-War period, many black people supported the Republican party because it was the party of "freedom." But since the New Deal in the 1930's, blacks have given substantial voter support to the Democratic party. This is due somewhat to a migration of blacks into urban areas and a new identification of the black

voters with the Democratic party already well-established in most urban centers. Table 7:2 breaks down the racial vote for each party in recent presidential elections.

The recent drive to increase black suffrage, which culminated in the Civil Rights Act of 1964 and the Voting Rights Act of 1965, has caused a great deal of speculation about the possible effects of black bloc voting. Where blacks are close to or in a majority, as in some rural sections in Mississippi and Alabama and in large urban areas such as Washington, Newark, Detroit, Cleveland, and Gary, there may be a division of the vote by race into black versus white.

Undoubtedly, if the goals and aspirations of blacks for a political voice continue to be denied them, more and more blacks will look to such unifying slogans as "Black Power" to gather them under one banner. The black community, at present, however, is by no means monolithic. The growing black middle class is developing many of the same political attitudes that their white counterparts have. As has happened with other ethnic groups, political pluralism among blacks will probably become more pronounced as their opportunities for better education and jobs increase.

There are other ethnic groups which, like the blacks, display highly consistent voting patterns. One notable example is the Mexican-American community in the southwestern United States. Most Mexican-Americans vote Democratic. But this is due as much to their income level as to their racial identity.

Review questions

1. Which social determinants have the greatest effect on an individual's political behavior?
2. Has the religion of a presidential candidate ever worked against him? Worked for him? When?

The Impact of Mass Media

The development of the means of communication that reach large numbers of people is one of the most notable changes that has taken place in America during the twentieth century. This has had a profound impact on the political system as well as on other aspects of American life. When people are informed about an event, they also become aware of the event's political aspect. Virtually every adult and child in the nation watched the astronauts walking on the moon, July 20, 1969. The entire nation and much of the world took part in the triumph of the National Aeronautics and Space Administration (NASA), the government agency in charge of the project.

As this historic event clearly demonstrates, television coverage is potentially enormous in terms of the effect such coverage has on Congress and ultimately on the nation's purse strings. It becomes more difficult for Congress to deny funds to NASA if television has convinced the public that space exploration adds to the nation's prestige. Television, then, can be said to have a relatively important impact on the public's political attitudes. Besides television, there are other types of *mass media*—newspapers, magazines, and radio—which help to shape political attitudes by keeping people informed about the nation's politics.

Newspapers and reader selectivity. The impact of a newspaper on readers is measured not only by the size of the paper's circulation but also by the positions of the readers. The kind of readers, their power in the community, and the possibility that these potential decision-makers will be influenced by what they read, hear, or see are more important criteria for measuring the impact of different newspapers than sheer numbers of readers. It is a question of which segment of the public is reached that is important.

Papers such as the *New York Times, Washington Post, Wall Street Journal, St. Louis Post-Dispatch, Los Angeles Times,* and *Louisville Courier-Journal* may reach smaller numbers of readers than a paper like the *New York Daily News.* But the readers of these papers are more likely to be in influential positions in business and government.

The *New York Times* and the *Washington Post* are read by many of the highest officials in Washington. Sometimes these papers even serve as a means of communication within government itself, because officials are not always kept informed about things happening in other departments.

Readers' opinions are, of course, partially shaped by the kind of information that reaches them. Most readers may not be swayed by the editorial page where opinions are definitely expressed. They will, however, be influenced subconsciously by the way in which the paper sifts information and thereby determines the reader's knowledge about a particular subject. A nationwide audience, then, is not a requisite for a newspaper to be influential. In fact, the very opposite may be the case.

Magazine readership. There are also sharp differences in the readerships of different magazines. *Life, Time, Look, Newsweek,* and other news magazines have a very large general readership. Yet, magazines with smaller circulations, such as *Foreign Affairs,* the *New Republic, Forbes, Business Week,* the *National Review, Fortune,* or *Saturday Review,* reach more selective audiences and thus could have more impact on decision-making than a magazine such as *Life* which appeals to a mass audience.

Radio and television. Radio and television probably reach more people than any of the other media. Major television networks—CBS, NBC, and ABC—transmit extensive-coverage news programs to a very broad public. Occasional specialized public-affairs programs, however, necessarily treat issues in a selective way, thereby determining the kind of information the public receives.

Sidney Harris. Copyright © 1969 Saturday Review, Inc.

"Following the President's press conference will be an interpretation, followed by a discussion of the interpretation, followed by an analysis . . ."

(For major news events to be analyzed so that all political bias is removed, such follow-ups might be needed.)

■ *Problem of equal time.* Television stations have to be careful not to exhibit open political bias. Such bias violates the Federal Communications Act of 1934 and the standards established by the Federal Communications Commission (FCC). This does not mean, though, that the stations can not *editorialize,* or give their own viewpoints about the news and condemn policies that they oppose. The FCC's "equal time" rule requires only that if a radio or television station does give one political party air-time to express its viewpoint, it must give equal time to opposition parties so they can present their views.

A strict interpretation of this rule has caused difficulty and has sometimes prevented the scheduling of political programs. During the presidential campaign of 1960, debates between candidates Kennedy and Nixon were able to take place only after the broadcasters were relieved by law from granting equal time to minor party candidates.

The requirement for equal time does not prevent the major networks from sifting information given to the public. Anyone who has watched regular or special news programs on CBS, NBC, or ABC can not help but conclude that the views, however obscure, of the commentators and producers are being aired. Attempts to represent both sides of an issue are frequently quite superficial. The mere selection of topics to be covered in a program shows some political bias. A conservative or liberal point of view is easily exhibited by merely omitting or slanting the "facts" on poverty, sharecropping, unemployment, medical care, or any other subject.

Control over mass media. The variety and diversification of mass media have reduced the chance of centralized control by any one private or governmental group over communications. Obviously, such control would have profound implications on the political system, for it would mean that the news could be "managed" and the public swayed accordingly. Still, the general dispersion and diversity of the mass media has not entirely eliminated the possibility of controlled news. Increasingly, there is a trend toward mergers between newspapers and television stations, between major networks and publishing houses, and between companies within the publishing industry.

■ *Emerging monopolies.* The trend in newspaper publishing is toward greater and greater concentration. This has been caused by high labor costs, a falling off in advertising revenue, and severe competition from television. Metropolitan areas formerly served by several daily newspapers now rely on only one or two which have joined forces with their former competitors to survive. Of all the American cities in which newspapers are published, 42 percent had competing dailies in 1920. But in 1950, this figure had been reduced to less than 10 percent. The smaller the city, the more likely it is to be a one-newspaper town. Newspaper owners comprise an elite, and the increasing concentra-

tion of newspaper publishing creates the possibility that this invaluable source of information will be controlled by a very small and influential group.

The development of monopolies in the mass media is prevalent not only in the newspaper industry but also in radio and television broadcasting. Although there are more than 600 television stations scattered throughout the country, virtually all of these have a network affiliation. The large networks along with the commercial sponsors of programs can determine, to a considerable extent, what the American public hears and sees on radio and television.

To preserve freedom of the airwaves, the Federal Communications Commission has been authorized to delve into the problems of monopoly and network control. Unfortunately, the FCC has met some obstacles in exercising any meaningful power over the networks. It has not succeeded in enlisting enough political support to accomplish any real supervision. This allows a great deal of authority to remain in the private hands of the networks and the sponsors. Although actual determination of program content rests with the networks, the threat of sponsors to withdraw their financial support has occasionally resulted in the cancellation of "controversial" programs.

■ *Managing the news.* Another problem of mass media is the ability of government to withhold information and thus "manage" the news. This charge was leveled against the Kennedy administration during the Cuban missile crisis in 1962, and later against President Johnson for withholding information on the Vietnam war.

When the nation's defense and security are at stake, it is sometimes necessary and understandable that the government operate behind a veil of secrecy. Indeed, to achieve desired results, it may even be necesssary to release deceptive information to the mass media. During the Cuban crisis, for example, when President Kennedy cancelled a political speech in the Midwest and suddenly returned to Washington, the excuse given to the press was that the President had a bad cold. At the time, Kennedy and his advisers felt that it was important to maintain complete secrecy about the projected Cuban blockade. It was hoped that his supposed sickness would throw reporters off the "scent" of a bigger story. A foreign policy emergency such as the Cuban missile crisis, where only a few government officials are cognizant of what is happening, almost demands management of the news.

Government management of the news however, is rare. The pluralistic nature of American government makes it almost impossible to keep information from eventually leaking out to the public. Usually there is some agency or elected official who thinks that it would be best to inform the public about a particular situation.

Mass media and public opinion. Just as with the other factors—family, education, religion, ethnic background—that influence political attitudes, the effect of the mass media on political thinking has to be measured. This is not an easy task. To date, the only major attempts at such measurement have been prior to, during, and after presidential campaigns. Since such measurement is only possible once every four years, it is of limited value in determining the total effectiveness of mass media on political behavior. It does, however, provide a starting point.

■ *The importance of various media.* Some media, of course, command a larger audience than others. So, the first object of research is to determine the degree of popularity enjoyed by each means of communication. To do this, the Survey Research Center asked its respondents a number of questions, similar to those below,[3] after several presidential elections:
(1) Did you read about the campaign in any newspaper?
(2) Did you listen to any speeches or discussions about the campaign on the radio?

[3] These questions based on "1968 Post-Election Study" of the Survey Research Center; University of Michigan, Institute for Social Research (Ann Arbor, Nov.–Dec. 1968).

Table 7:3

Use of Media During Campaigns					
	1952	**1956**	**1960**	**1964**	**1968**
Newspapers	79%	69%	75%	79%	64%
Radio	69	45	39	48	35
Television	49	74	81	89	77
Magazines	40	31	38	39	31

Sources: V. O. Key, Jr., Public Opinion and American Democracy (New York: Alfred A. Knopf, 1961), p. 346; and Survey Research Center, University of Michigan.

(3) Did you watch any programs about the campaign on television?

(4) Did you read about the campaign in any magazines?

(5) Of all of these ways of following the campaign, from which one would you say you got the most information —newspapers, radio, television, or magazines?

Table 7:3 shows the percentages of respondents who followed the campaigns through the various media. Note the decline of radio, the rise of television, and the relative stability of newspapers and magazines as major sources of information on campaign issues. The figures add up to more than 100 percent because most people gathered their information from more than one medium.

When asked which of the media they considered most important to them in acquiring knowledge about campaign issues, the same respondents answered as shown in Table 7:4. Here the percentages do not total 100 because some respondents claimed that none of the media had any impact, or that they did not know which of the media influenced them.

As television has become more common in American households, obviously its impact on voters has increased, virtually replacing that of radio.

■ *The effect of various media.* The impact of the mass media can be measured by correlating the percentages shown in these two tables with such factors as familiarity with issues and the level of political participation. The Survey Research Center measures *issue familiarity* by analyzing the responses of its election sample to a number of questions on prominent issues. *Political participation* is measured by determining the extent to which respondents vote, give money to political parties, go to political meetings and rallies, work for political clubs and parties, wear campaign buttons, put stickers on their cars, and so forth.

It has been found that magazine readers have the greatest issue familiarity and the highest level of political participation. This is a selective audience. Next in line are those who rely on combinations of any two or more media such as newspapers and radio, or magazines and TV. Newspaper readers are third. Those who rely

Table 7:4

Impact of the Various Media					
	1952	1956	1960	1964	1968
Newspapers	22%	24%	21%	24%	16%
Radio	28	10	5	4	2.5
Television	31	49	56	58	45
Magazines	5	5	4	7	4.5

Sources: V. O. Key, Jr., Public Opinion and American Democracy *(New York: Alfred A. Knopf, 1961), p. 346; and Survey Research Center, University of Michigan.*

"You know, I've been keeping a record, and in the last year I've agreed with eight hundred and sixty 'Times' editorials, disagreed with three hundred and thirty-five of them, and had no opinion on two hundred and sixty-five."

(This cartoon presents a basic question: Do people buy newspapers because they agree with the paper's opinions?)

primarily on television or radio alone for information exhibited lower indexes of issue familiarity and political participation.

It would appear from this data that those media that require reading and analysis have more political impact than the others. But, since people with more education tend to read more, it is difficult to measure the effect of these media as an isolated factor.

The role of mass media. The role that the mass media play in the political process depends mostly on how they affect various groups. In most cases, the media are a primary source of information. In others, the media are especially important because they offer contrasting viewpoints on the same subject. National elections would be virtually impossible without exposure of the candidates through the various media. Door-to-door canvassers and mail campaigns can reach only a small number of people. To communicate a candidate's message to a nationwide constituency, the mass media have been better equipped to develop a common language that is easily understood by all the potential voters.

Usually, when media operate on a mass scale, there is a *dilution of information*. That is, the information presented to the public may not be given in its entirety. It may be tailored or slanted so that it appeals to the greatest number of people.

171

Commercial considerations account for some of this dilution. After all, newspapers have to sell to the greatest number of readers to attract advertisers and to remain profitable. And TV broadcasters do not want to anger their viewers who may take out their displeasure by not buying the products advertised.

The mass media can be thought of as the common denominators of ideas. American democracy must span a broad continent, full of many types of people. There must be some common relationship between the people as a whole and the government which is supposed to represent all the divergent subgroups within the nation. The mass media can help to provide a unifying link between the people and their government.

A comparison of recent presidential campaigns with those of the past illustrates this aspect of the mass media quite vividly. Years ago before there were such continent-spanning mass media as television and radio, presidential candidates had to traverse a long campaign trail in order to bring themselves and their programs to the public. While local newspapers and magazines aided in the campaigns by bringing the candidates to the public's attention, it was still impossible for presidential aspirants to come before all the American populace. Thus, many people were not exposed to nationwide problems. Their vote for or against a party was based on how they felt about state or local issues. Television, however, allows the candidate to appear in person in the voter's living room. This adds a new dimension to the campaign.

■ *Television compared to other media.* Television has definitely expanded the public's involvement in politics to some extent. By bringing the candidates, the issues, and some of the details of policy formulation into nearly everyone's home, television has made more people more aware of how the political system works. Still, it has not markedly affected the way they vote. Whether candidates are judged by their makeup or their handshake, the issues remain the same as far as the electorate is concerned. The issues presented through television debates and news programs are no different from those presented in stump speeches.

For a candidate, the main difference between television and the other media is the degree of public exposure he gets. He has to be more consistent before the television audience, both in speech and appearance. With newspapers, magazines, or radio, the audience is not liable to be so vast, and a candidate can get away with certain inconsistencies. But under the microscopic eye of the television camera which projects his image into millions of living rooms at the same time, he can not change his presentation or alter his program to suit a particular audience. Thus the candidate is more apt to talk in generalities before the TV camera. He must concentrate on those broad ideas that appeal to the greatest number of voters.

While television has shaped the candidate's style, it has also given the public a picture of the candidate never possible before. Informing the public is only one part of the input process. Once information has been absorbed by the public, it will be reshaped by the political attitudes that have already been molded by the family, education, and occupation. The next step is to transmit the people's will to the government.

Review questions

1. What is the function of mass media with regard to the political system?
2. Which of the mass media enjoys the largest audience today? Which one has declined in comparison?

Chapter Review

Terms you should know

dilution of information	Gallup Poll	party loyalty
editorialize	issue familiarity	political attitude
equal time	managed news	public opinion
Federal Communications Act of 1934	mass media	voting patterns

Questions about this chapter

1. Why is public opinion usually narrow in scope?
2. How is the family a force for political stability?
3. If a presidential candidate appealed only to people with college educations, would his chances of victory be good or poor? Why?
4. How does the 1960 presidential election illustrate religious voting patterns?
5. Why might magazines that reach selective audiences have greater political influence than magazines with mass appeal?
6. What is the difference in the audiences of a newspaper and a magazine? Which audience is likely to be more politically active?
7. How does the "equal time" rule affect television coverage of presidential elections?

Thought and discussion questions

1. Of the following, which do you think is the major influence in the formation of political attitudes: the family, education, religion, ethnic background, or mass media? Support your choice.
2. Do you think the government should ever release deceptive information to the mass media? Why? If so, under what conditions?
3. In 1969, Vice President Agnew charged that the news media, particularly television, were not providing a balanced analysis of the news. How do you feel about establishing a supervisory body to regulate the mass media?
4. If the mass media in the United States were nationalized, how do you think this would affect election news? What advantages are there to a government-owned television network similar to the BBC in Great Britain? What disadvantages are there?

Class projects

1. Make up a questionnaire to determine the basic political attitudes of the students in your school. From your results, determine what qualifications a candidate would most likely need to win a school election. Would your parents and those of your colleagues answer these questions in the same way? What would your parents' candidate be like? Are either of these model candidates similar to any contemporary politician representing your area?
2. National news magazines try to be impartial in their reports of the news. Sometimes they fail. Compare the treatment of specific political issues in different news magazines, such as *Time, U.S. News and World Report,* and *Newsweek.* What similarities and differences exist in the content of these articles?
3. What are the major communications media in your community? Which of these played the greatest role in a recent municipal election? How?

Case Study: A presidential-election survey

The social scientist uses surveys as a means of gathering samples of facts, figures, and opinions. Based on the data he collects, he can advance new theories in his field.

Realizing the importance of the surveying technique and how it has become an integral part of the social sciences, the University of Michigan established the Survey Research Center as a division of the Institute for Social Research. The Center was created to provide a well-trained staff for conducting surveys on economic and social problems and to provide graduate training in all the phases of survey methodology. The Center has been studying presidential elections since 1948.

As late as the 1950's, the most effective agent in determining a person's political attitudes was the family. "My parents are Democrats (or Republicans)" was often the only reason given by a voter when asked how he chose his party affiliation. But all this is changing. Some of these changes are shown by the questions adapted from the Survey Research Center's questionnaires included in this case study.

On a separate sheet of paper, answer all the questions from the "Pre-Election" and "Post-Election" surveys produced by the Center. While you do this, keep in mind the rationale behind each question and what the survey hopes to disclose by it.

1968 PRE-ELECTION STUDY

SURVEY RESEARCH CENTER
INSTITUTE FOR SOCIAL RESEARCH
THE UNIVERSITY OF MICHIGAN
ANN ARBOR, MICHIGAN 48106

1. Generally speaking, would you say that *you personally* care a good deal which party wins presidential elections, or that you don't care very much which party wins?
   —Care   —Don't care

2. Which of these statements would you agree with:
   —White people have a right to keep blacks out of their neighborhoods if they want to; or

---

Questions from the Survey Research Center's "1968 Pre-Election Study" have been reprinted with permission of The Survey Research Center, Institute for Social Research, the University of Michigan, Ann Arbor, Michigan.

—Blacks have a right to live wherever they can afford to, just like anybody else.
—Don't know; depends; can't decide (Go to Q. 3)
Do you feel strongly about your position on this question or not too strongly?
—Strongly —Not too strongly

3. In general, how many of the blacks in this area would you say are in favor of desegregation—*all* of them, *most* of them, *about half, less than half* of them, or *none* of them?
   —All —Most —About half —Less than half —None —No blacks in area

4. How about white people in this area? How many would you say are in favor of strict segregation of the races—*all* of them, *most* of them, *about half, less than half* of them, or *none* of them?
   —All —Most —About half —Less than half —None —No whites in area

5. What about you? Are you in favor of desegregation, strict segregation, or something in between? —Desegregation —Segregation —In between

6. (a) Is the neighborhood you now live in:
   (b) Is the grade school nearest you:
   (c) Is the junior high school nearest you:
   (d) Is your school:
   (e) Are the people who shop and trade where you do:
   (f) Are your friends:

   —————— All white
   —————— Mostly white
   —————— About half and half
   —————— Mostly black

   —————— All black
   —————— Don't know

7. As you have been growing up, has your father been very much interested in politics, somewhat interested, or doesn't he pay much attention to it? —Very interested —Somewhat interested —Not much attention

8. Does he think of himself mostly as a *Democrat,* as a *Republican,* or what?
   —Democrat —Republican —Other (specify) _____

9. Now how about your mother? As you have been growing up, has she been interested in politics, somewhat interested, or doesn't she pay much attention to it? —Very interested —Somewhat interested —Not much attention

10. Does she think of herself mostly as a *Democrat,* as a *Republican,* or what?
    —Democrat —Republican —Other (specify) _____

11. Some people don't pay much attention to the political campaigns. How about you; would you say that you have been very much interested, somewhat interested, or not much interested in following the political campaigns so far this year? —Very much interested —Somewhat interested —Not much interested

12. Would you say that most public officials care quite a lot about what people like you think, or that they don't care much at all? —Care —Don't care

13. Would you say that voting is the only way that people like you can have any say

about the way the government runs things, or that there are lots of ways that you can have a say?   —Voting only way   —Lots of ways

14. Would you say that politics and government are so complicated that people like you can't really understand what's going on, or that you can understand what's going on pretty well?   —Can't understand   —Can understand

15. Would you say that people like you have quite a lot of say about what the government does, or that you don't have much say at all?   —Have a lot of say   —Don't have much say

16. There's been some talk these days about different social classes. Most people say they belong either to the *middle class* or to the *working class*. Do you ever think of yourself as belonging in one of these classes?

    —Yes (Go to Q. 16a)   —No (Go to Q. 16b)   —Don't know (Go to Q. 16b)

16a. Which one?
(Record below)

16b. If you had to make a choice, would you call yourself middle class or working class? (Record below)

—Middle class (Go to Q. 16c)

—Working class (Go to Q. 16e)

16c. Would you say that you are about average middle class, or that you are in the upper part of the middle class?   —Average middle —Upper middle

16e. Would you say that you are about average working class, or that you are in the upper part of the working class?   —Average working —Upper working

(Go to Q. 16d)

(Go to Q. 16f)

16d. Would you say you feel *pretty close* to middle class people, or that you don't feel much closer to them than to people in other classes?   —Close —Not closer

16f. Would you say you feel *pretty close* to working class people, or that you don't feel much closer to them than to people in other classes?   —Close —Not closer

17. What would you say your family is: —Middle class or   —Working class?

18. Are you: —Protestant   —Roman Catholic   —Jewish or   —Other (specify) _____

19. Would you say you go to church *regularly, often, seldom* or *never?*
    —Regularly   —Often   —Seldom   —Never

20. There are many groups in America that try to get the government or the American people to see things more their way. We would like to get your feelings toward

some of these groups. We call [this] a "feeling thermometer" because it measures your feelings towards groups. Here's how it works. If you don't know too much about a group, or don't feel particularly warm or cold toward them, then you should place them in the middle, at the 50 degree mark. If you have a warm feeling toward a group or feel favorably toward it, you would give it a score somewhere between 50° and 100° depending on how warm your feeling is toward the group. On the other hand, if you don't feel very favorably toward some of these groups—if there are some you don't care for too much—then you would place them somewhere between 0° and 50°.

	Rating			*Rating*
a. Big Business	---		k. Vietnam war protesters	---
b. Liberals	---		l. Labor Unions	---
c. Southerners	---		m. Lawyers	---
d. Catholics	---		n. Republicans	---
e. Policemen	---		o. School teachers	---
f. College students	---		p. Protestants	---
g. Democrats	---		q. Blacks	---
h. The Military	---		r. Conservatives	---
i. Jews	---		s. City and county officials	---
j. Whites	---			

21. What kind of work does your father do for a living? _____

22. Were you brought up mostly on a farm, in a town, in a small city, or in a large city?
—Farm —Town —Small city —Large city

1968 POST-ELECTION STUDY

SURVEY RESEARCH CENTER
INSTITUTE FOR SOCIAL RESEARCH
THE UNIVERSITY OF MICHIGAN
ANN ARBOR, MICHIGAN 48106

1. Would you say that you and your family are *better off* or *worse off* financially than you were a *year ago?* —Better now —Same —Worse now —Uncertain
1a. Why is that? _____

Questions from the Survey Research Center's "1968 Post-Election Study" have been reprinted with permission of The Survey Research Center, Institute for Social Research, the University of Michigan, Ann Arbor, Michigan.

2. Is your family making as much money now as they were a *year ago,* or more, or less? —More now   —About the same   —Less now

3. Now looking ahead—do you think that a *year from now* your family will be *better off* financially, or *worse off,* or just about the same as now?   —Better   —Same   —Worse —Uncertain

4. Would you say that *at the present time* business conditions are better, or worse, than they were a *year ago?*   —Better now   —About the same   —Worse now

5. And how about a *year from now,* do you expect that in the country as a whole business conditions will be better or worse than they are *at present,* or just about the same?   —Better a year from now   —About the same   —Worse a year from now

6. Did you pay much attention to recent election campaigns? Take newspapers for instance—did you read about the campaigns in any newspaper?
   —Yes   —No (Go to Q. 7)   —Don't know (Go to Q. 7)
   6a. How much did you read newspaper articles about the elections—*regularly, often,* from *time to time,* or just *once in a great while?*   —Regularly   —Often —Time to time   —Once in a great while
   6b. What paper did you read most? _____
   6c. Would you say that this newspaper took sides either for or against one of the major political parties, or that it did not take sides?   —Yes, took sides for —Yes, took sides against   —No, didn't take sides (Go to Q. 7)
   6d. Who was the newspaper (for/against)? _____

7. How about radio—did you listen to any programs about the campaigns on the radio?
   —Yes   —No (Go to Q. 8)   —Don't know (Go to Q. 8)
   7a. How many programs about the campaign did you listen to on the radio—*a good many, several,* or *just one or two?*   —Good many   —Several   —Just one or two
   7b. Would you say that the radio reporting you heard took sides either for or against one of the candidates or parties, or that it did not take sides?
   —Yes, took sides for   —Yes, took sides against   —No, didn't take sides (Go to Q. 8)   —Don't know (Go to Q. 8)
   7c. Who was the radio reporting (for/against)? _____

8. How about magazines—did you read about the campaigns in any magazines?
   —Yes   —No (Go to Q. 9)   —Don't know (Go to Q. 9)
   8a. How many magazine articles about the campaigns would you say you read—*a good many, several,* or *just one or two?*   —Good many   —Several   —Just one or two
   8b. Do you read about politics pretty regularly in any magazines?   —Yes —No (Go to Q. 9)
   8c. What ones are they? _____
   8d. Would you say that any magazine (specify) _____
   took sides either for or against one of the parties, or that it did not take sides?

—Yes, took sides for
—Yes, took sides against   —No, didn't take sides (Go to Q. 9)
—Don't know (Go to Q. 9)

9. How about television—did you watch any programs about the campaigns on television?
—Yes   —No (Go to Q. 10)   —Don't know (Go to Q. 10)

9a. How many television programs about the campaigns would you say you watched —*a good many, several,* or *just one or two?*   —Good many   —Several   —Just one or two

9b. Would you say that the television reporting you watched took sides either for or against one of the candidates or parties, or that it did not take sides?
—Yes, took sides for
—Yes, took sides against   —No, didn't take sides (Go to Q. 10)
—Don't know (Go to Q. 10)

9c. Who was the television reporting (for/against)? _____

9d. When you say television took sides (for/against) (Answer to Q. 9c), do you mean national television or local television?
—National television   —Local television   —Both   —Don't know

10. Of all these ways of following the campaign, which one would you say you got the most information from—newspapers, radio, television, or magazines?   —Newspapers —Radio   —Television   —Magazines   —None of these

11. During the campaign, did you talk to any people and try to show them why they should vote for one of the parties or candidates?   —Yes   —No

12. Did you do any other work for one of the parties or candidates?   —Yes   —No

13. Did you wear a campaign button or put a campaign sticker on your car?   —Yes   —No

14. Do you belong to any political club or organizations?   —Yes   —No

15. You know that the parties try to talk to as many people as they can to get them to vote for their candidates. Did anybody from either of the two major parties call you up or come around and talk to you during the campaign?   —Yes   —No

16. During this last year, were you or any member of your family *asked* to give money or buy tickets to help pay the campaign expenses of a political party or candidate?
—Yes   —No   —Don't know

17. Have you ever written to any public officials giving them your opinion about something that should be done?   —Yes   —No, never

18. Have you ever written a letter to the editor of a newspaper or magazine giving any political opinions?   —Yes   —No, never

19. Some people seem to follow what's going on in government and public affairs most of the time, whether there's an election going on or not. Others aren't that interested. Would you say you follow what's going on in government and public affairs:

—Most of the time   —Some of the time   —Only now and then   —Hardly at all?

We would also like to ask you about the types of government and public affairs you follow.

19a. First, how about international and world affairs; do you pay a great deal of attention, some attention, or not much attention to international affairs?
—Great deal   —Some   —Not much   —Don't know

19b. What about national affairs; do you pay a great deal, some, or not much attention to national affairs?   —Great deal   —Some   —Not much   —Don't know

19c. And how about state affairs; do you pay a great deal, some, or not much attention to state affairs?   —Great deal   —Some   —Not much   —Don't know

19d. Finally, what about local affairs; do you pay a great deal, some, or not much attention to local affairs?   —Great deal   —Some   —Not much   —Don't know

We would also like to know about some of the things that happen in your own community; particularly with regard to education and school affairs.

20. People differ in how interested they are in what their district school boards do. How about you—would you rate your interest in what your school board is doing as:
—Very high   —Moderately high   —Moderately low or   —Very low?

21. How often does the school board take a stand that you disagree with? Would you say this happens often, sometimes, rarely, or never?   —Often   —Sometimes   —Rarely   —Never

22. In your opinion what is the most important problem facing education in this school district? _____
_____
_____

23. How do you think this problem should be handled? _____
_____
_____

24. Recently teachers in many parts of the country have been demanding a greater voice in the determination of school policies. Do you think that teachers in this district should have a greater voice in major decisions?   —Yes   —No (Go to Q. 25)
—Don't know (Go to Q. 25)
24a. In what ways? _____
_____
_____

25. Do you think teachers should feel free to go on strike to secure higher salaries and other benefits, or is this something they should not feel free to do?
—Should feel free to   —Should not feel free to   —Don't know

26. Do you feel that the federal government has too much or too little control over local education, or haven't you thought about it? —Too much —Too little —About right —Haven't thought about it

27. What about your state government? Is the control it has over local education too much or too little, or haven't you thought about it? —Too much —Too little —About right —Haven't thought about it

28. Some people think it is all right for the public schools to start each day with a prayer. Others feel that religion does not belong in the public schools but should be taken care of by the family and the church. Have you been interested enough in this to favor one side over the other? —Yes —No —Don't know

    28a. Which do you think: —Schools should be allowed to start each day with a prayer or —Religion does not belong in the schools?

End questions

1. What was the purpose of each survey? Can you determine what the surveys are trying to prove?
2. What questions would you have added to more completely measure your class's behavior? How important are these surveys to anyone who wants to study electoral behavior-patterns in America? Why have surveys become a tool of research for the social scientist?
3. From these surveys, list all the forces that you can detect at work in determining political behavior and attitude formation. After compiling the results in your class, which of these forces would you say is the most important influence on the attitudes of your classmates? Has the influence of the family been replaced by other factors?

CHAPTER 8

The Organization and Functions of American Political Parties

The primary role of the political party is to bridge the gap between the people and their government. In a democracy, the performance of this role means that the party should transmit public opinion to government and aid in transforming that opinion into government policy, usually in the form of legislation.

Edmund Burke defined a political party as "a body of men united for promoting by their joint endeavors the national interest, upon some particular principle in which they are all agreed." This definition is that of an idealistic school of thought which holds that parties must operate in the national interest and not according to individual or local demands.

Max Weber, the German sociologist and political economist of the late nineteenth century, was less idealistic when he defined a party. Interpreted by Robert Michels, Weber described a party as

"a spontaneous society of propaganda and of agitation seeking to acquire power, . . . for the realization either of objective aims or of personal advantages, or of both. Consequently, the general orientation of the political party, whether in its personal or impersonal aspect is that of machtstreben [striving for power]."[1]

Weber's definition is much more cynical than Burke's. Weber recognized that political parties may be used either for high moral ends or merely for personal gain.

Whether political parties are idealistic or not, their principal objective is gaining and maintaining political power. Practically, then, *political parties* are groups of people who unite for the purpose of achieving a general political objective. They do this by organizing to elect officials who will carry out their demands.

Because political parties are fundamentally spokesmen for the people, no democratic government can function without them. In Great Britain, for example, the development of democracy in the nineteenth century was closely associated with the rise of political parties. Democracy expands as more people gain the right to vote, and the political party serves as a vehicle by which people strengthen this right. As the liaison between people and government, political parties provide voters with an opportunity to make known their choices of policy. It should not, however, be thought that the political party is unique to democracies. Even totalitarian states have parties. Voters may vote for handpicked officials, but the party still puts candidates on the ballot.

Nature of the American Party System

Just as there are contrasting ideas about the nature of political parties, there are

[1]*Robert Michels,* First Lectures in Political Sociology, *trans. Alfred de Grazia (Minneapolis: Univ. of Minnesota Press, 1949), p. 134.*

◄ Is the two-party system in the United States an effective vehicle for conveying the demands of the people to government? What action can the voters take when the parties do not respond to their needs?

many different types of parties. Some are based on strict ideologies or philosophical principles, others are more loosely defined and organized only for practical purposes of gaining specific objectives.

Contrast with European parties. American parties are usually far less disciplined than their British counterparts, and they are far less ideological than parties in Europe. Although British parties arrive at their programs through political compromise, once the compromise is accepted, the party ranks close behind the decision. Political parties in America also depend on compromise to establish programs, but their members are not obligated to support these programs.

Many European parties adhere to narrow ideological interests based on some "Absolute Truth." The Socialist parties, for example, that developed in Italy, France, Sweden, and other European nations prior to World War II, accepted rigid programs based on ideological doctrines. These parties do not change their programs for practical reasons if such changes mean a divergence from ideology. American parties, however, do not cling to any overruling philosophy, nor do they strive to encompass all areas of life to promote a dogmatic ideology. Instead, American parties, speaking for large conglomerations of people, support loosely defined principles and strive for ends that are not always clearly stated. These characteristics were evident early in the development of the parties in America.

Early American concern about parties. While no formal organization of political parties existed in eighteenth-century America, an informal system did operate. A passage from the diary of John Adams reveals that by 1793, the concept of political organization was already part of the American political tradition.

"This day I learned that the Caucus Club meets at certain times in the garret of Tom Dawes, the Adjutant of the Boston Regiment. He has a large house, and he has a movable partition in his garret, which he takes down, and the whole club meets in one room. There they smoke tobacco till you cannot see from one end of the room to the other. There they drink flip, I suppose, and there they choose a moderator who puts questions to the vote regularly; and selectmen, assessors, collectors, firewards, and representatives are regularly chosen before they are chosen in the town."[2]

Some traces of this informal system can still be seen today. In many cities, Cincinnati for instance, parties are prohibited by law from participating in city elections. In cases like these, certain groups, such as civic organizations or groups of influential citizens behind the scenes, function as if they were parties. These "informal parties" recruit and endorse candidates whose names are then placed on ballots by means of non-partisan nominating procedures.

The constitutional context of parties. Initially, American democracy was to be a system of indirect participation. State legislators would choose Senators for Congress, and electors chosen by each state according to its own formula were to select the "best man" for President.

Thus provision for political parties was not included in the original constitutional framework, because in an indirect election parties would not be needed to select the candidates or to convince the voters of who deserved election. The public was voting indirectly through the representatives in the state legislatures and through the electoral college. Despite this, political parties did develop and they became a vital feature of the American constitutional system.

America's two-party system. In a few respects, the United States is closer to France than to Great Britain where most American social and political traditions originated. Strong and diverse economic, regional, and social interests exist within the French community as they do in the

[2]Cited in V. O. Key, Jr., *Politics, Parties, and Pressure Groups,* 3rd ed. (New York: T. Y. Crowell Co., 1952), pp. 217–218.

United States. With the institution of the republic following the revolution in 1789, a *multi-party* system developed in France to represent each of these various and diverse interests.

The United States, on the other hand, has only two major political parties. This development can be attributed to three major factors: (1) the election system, (2) the centralizing influence of the Presidency, and (3) the general division of interests into two camps. This does not mean, though, that multiple interests are not represented politically. It means that American parties must be broader in scope than the French parties to include the diverse interests within the electorate.

■ *The election system.* Whether a nation's political-party structure consists of two parties or many parties will depend, in part, on the election system. Election systems are usually based either on the *single-member district* or on *proportional representation.* Whatever form the election system takes, the political parties must be able to get candidates elected and must be organized so that they function well in this most crucial test.

□ *Single-member district.* Under a single-member-district system, no matter what size an election district is, whether it be a congressional district, a state, or the nation, it is represented by only one individual—a Representative, Senator, or President. This is the method used in the United States.

To win an election in a single-member district, a candidate needs a mere *plurality,* or just more votes than any other candidate, to be elected. For example, if *A, B,* and *C* are running for office and out of 1,000 votes cast, *A* has 450 ballots, *B* has 300, and *C* has 250, *A* wins because he has a plurality. He does not need a majority, or more than half the votes, to win.

A candidate for Representative, Senator, or President (except in rare instances) needs only a plurality of votes to win. But in a single-member district, only one candidate is elected. There is only one President for the entire nation, only one Senator at a time up for election from a state, and only one Representative from a congressional district. Thus, there is a tendency for some groups within a district to form coalitions, or to combine forces, so that together they may elect that official. This tightens the entire political organization. As more coalitions are formed there are fewer parties.

This is not to suggest that the single-member-district system always produces only two parties. There have been some exceptions. But the single-member district does in fact produce a favorable situation for the development of two opposing parties rather than many parties.

□ *Proportional representation.* Unlike the election systems based on single-member districts, with the proportional-representation method a district may elect several representatives in a single election. Such a system is used in France and in a few American cities for local elections.

Under such a system, legislative seats for each district are divided according to the percentage of total votes given to each political party. For example, in the "Baywater" district there are twenty delegates to be elected to a local council. The Blue party wins 40 percent of the vote and gets eight of the twenty seats; the White Party wins 30 percent of the vote and it gets six seats; the Green party wins 25 percent of the vote and gets five seats; and the Red party gets 5 percent of the vote, or one seat. Such an election procedure encourages a multi-party system because all parties have a chance to gain some representation.

Coalitions of diverse interests and parties occur, not before but after an election,

"Oh, Washington himself is all right. It's the men around him like
Jefferson and Adams and . . ."

(Coalitions of interests from almost opposing factions may even be reflected in the President's Cabinet.)

when policies are formulated. For exam- ple, once on the council, the Green party members have to form a coalition with the White party or the Blue party to enact specific legislation. By joining forces, the Green and White parties can control the council even if the Blue party and the Red party, which are at the extremes of the political poles, decide to forget their ideo- logical differences and vote together on a proposal.

■ *The effect of the Presidency.* A second important reason for the evolution of the two-party system in the United States is the centralizing influence of the office of the Presidency. To elect a presidential candidate, the political party tries to band together as many different groups as it can. This requires a vast coalition of inter- ests throughout the country. Those interests that oppose the groups in one party flock to the opposing party. The nation, which is the single-member district that elects the President, thus splits into two major parties. The objective of both parties is to win a simple majority of the nation's total electoral college vote. (See also Chapter 6, pages 139–142.)

The Presidency is such an important office that it is a catalyst for coalition between interests that would normally be at loggerheads. It has succeeded, for example, in unifying southern conservatives and northern liberals in the Democratic party. The Republicans, composed of eastern moderates and midwestern and western conservatives, also seem able to close ranks behind a presidential selection.

■ *Division of interests.* A third explanation for the two-party system in the United States is that there tends to be a polarization of interests on any problem. Some people will be for one solution and some people will be against it. Thus, a pro and a con will always exist. Different sets of interests in conflict with each other normally gravitate to opposite political parties. Even prior to the adoption of the Constitution in 1787, there was a natural polarization of the country into two camps along economic and political lines.

After 1787, there was a division over the nature of constitutional government itself, and it formed the basis for the Federalist and the Antifederalist parties. A similar division also developed between the agricultural interests and the mercantile and financial groups. By the end of Washington's administration in 1796, agricultural interests were represented largely by Jefferson's Democratic-Republicans, who also desired a weaker federal government. Financial and commercial interests, on the other hand, were represented by Hamilton's Federalists who advocated a powerful central government.

With the passage of years, these initial divisions assumed new forms. The Civil War established new patterns and, at the same time, reinforced some old divisions. Added to the original industrial-agricultural division, there developed an emotional division of hatred between North and South that flared up in the Civil War. As a reaction to the northern Republican victory, the South became the bastion of the Democratic party. Even today traces of the sharp conflict between Democrats and Republicans can be attributed to this regional division.

In the twentieth century, the division of political and economic interests has continued. With the growth of urban areas, the old agricultural-industrial division has been replaced more and more by a division along labor-management lines. Labor unions ordinarily support the Democratic party which formerly was rooted in the rural agricultural sections, especially in the South. And business interests tend to support the Republicans.

Of course each party attracts some followers who would normally be categorized as belonging to the opposing party. Thus some businessmen are Democrats, and some labor-union members vote Republican. Issues of a local nature often cause individuals to abandon their usual party loyalties to support the candidate of another party who promises solutions of the immediate problem. A working man who agrees generally with the Democratic party's position may vote for a "safety in the streets" Republican conservative. Nevertheless, the overall division of interests does seem to contribute to the maintenance of the two-party system.

■ *Geographic distribution of party strength.* During the last century in the United States, the economic and political differences between the two parties have been complicated by an uneven geographical distribution of party strength. Until recently, the Democratic South was counterbalanced by heavily Republican areas in New England and certain parts of the Midwest. Curiously enough, these *one-party regions* allow the minority party, even in a landslide election, to retain some representation in Congress.

The two-party system would not function so well if political strength were evenly distributed geographically over the whole nation. It might then be possible for one party to receive 51 percent of the vote and capture all of the representatives in government, legislative as well as executive. The party obtaining 49 percent of the popular vote would have no representation at all. This has happened in certain state elections. But in the national election, there are a sufficient number of dedicated Democratic or Republican areas which, despite the issues, will return traditional party choices to the legislature.

In the United States, these divisive political, economic, and geographic influences are weak, while the spirit of compromise is strong. The country does not have strong political divisions based on principle and ideology. Consequently, a variety of interests are able to work together within the framework of just two political parties.

Third party dilemma. Any nation's political-party system mirrors the division of interests within the country itself. If there are fairly clear-cut divisions along definite lines, the party system will tend to represent these. A simple division of interests tends to produce a two-party system as it does in the United States. On the other hand, a multiplicity of sharp differences often leads to a multi-party system.

Occasionally, the division of interests does not have the flexibility to contain a certain faction's desires. This is when the third-party becomes active. In the United States, this phenomenon has occurred frequently. Henry A. Wallace ran for President in 1948 on the ticket of the Progres-

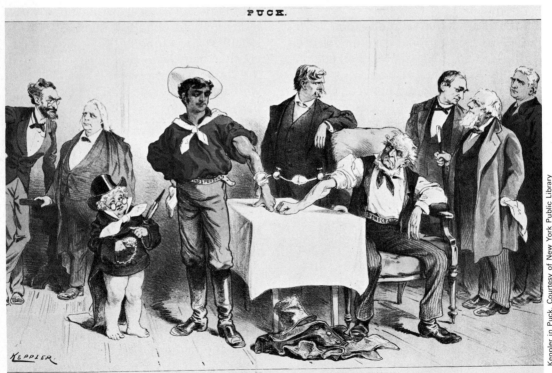

PUCK.

THE TRANSFUSION OF BLOOD.—MAY THE OPERATION PROVE A SUCCESS!

(Independent Republicans deserted their party's candidate Blaine in 1884 for the Democratic entry Cleveland.)

sive party, a group of dissident liberals who could not agree with the policies of the regular Democratic candidate, Harry S. Truman. The same year, a States' Rights candidate, J. Strom Thurmond, also polled over a million votes. Again in 1968, a number of right-wing and segregationist voters flocked to the banner of the American Independent Party and its candidate, George C. Wallace.

A third party identifies a set of demands that is otherwise ignored by the two major parties. The third party forces the major parties to take some demands into consideration. And this is where they have succeeded. While they have not won any major elections, third parties have induced the major parties to adopt third-party policies as part of their own platforms in order to win later elections.

It might be said that third parties tend to "punish" a major party that has been unresponsive to the third party's interests. Theodore Roosevelt's "Bull Moose" party in 1912 took enough votes from the Republicans to "punish" them for not taking the "Bull Moose" antitrust view into account. Roosevelt wanted some federal regulation of big business. Roosevelt split the Republican vote and Democrat Woodrow Wilson won the election. Eventually, Wilson adopted some of the Roosevelt proposals. He supported a bill to prohibit unfair trade practices and established the Federal Trade Commission (FTC) to enforce measures aimed at preventing monopolistic maneuvers.

Review questions

1. How has the single-member district encouraged the development of the two-party system?
2. Explain the effect of the Presidency on the two-party system.

American Party Organization

The two principal American political parties are "umbrella" parties, containing widely divergent groups. Virtually everyone is welcome under the umbrella. To maintain themselves, the two parties have to represent a large variety of interests. Party programs must reflect many points of view, and therefore must be expressed in very broad, general terms. Party organizations from the national committees down to local wards or electoral districts, reflect this effort to take into the party structure as many elements of society as is possible.

Obviously the nature of party organization mirrors the composition of the electorate. Clear-cut organization and issues can not arise in the party unless they prevail in the electorate. The framework for this type of party organization is so loose that virtually every holder of an elected office, whether he calls himself a Republican or Democrat, is an individual independent of the central party organization. Even within a state there are factions within party organizations, and elected officials often reflect these factions rather than a unified party organization. The Senators and Representatives from the same state and the same party sometimes disagree sharply. Actually, a Republican from California may have more in common with a Republican from New Jersey than with another Republican in California.

The effect of federalism. The federal structure has contributed to the form of political party organization in America. By accepting federalism and developing within the federal structure, the states were able to solidify their own power. The outcome was separate and often powerful state governments. When the political parties were established within this federal framework, it was only natural that state power be reflected in party organizations.

Today, the national party apparatus is composed of state parties, serving the needs of state government first. States have elected offices to be filled, and the state party organizations try to fill these offices before they tackle the subject of national candidates. Instead of the state parties depending on the national organization, it is the national organization that relies on political support from state and local party leaders. Presidential candidates must have substantial support in state and local party organizations to get nominated in the first place. To win an election, a presidential candidate also needs concentrated support from the state and local party organizations.

Members of Congress must also depend on state party organizations. Each Senator or Representative relies on the support of the party organization in the state or congressional district he or she represents. This lack of reliance on a dominant national party organization has led to some fragmentation or splintering of the parties within Congress itself.

Party leadership. In most organizations, including political parties, power tends to reside in a few leaders. This is because most organizations are cumbersome and can be effectively administered only by a capable minority. But in American political parties, there is no consistent party leadership on the national level. When a party's candidate becomes President, the White House is the natural focal point of party leadership. But the "out-party," the party that has lost in the presidential campaign, has no such focal point of national leadership. Without such leadership, the out-party tends to split into its various factions. As a result, there is no cohesiveness of party program.

The only place in the American political system where an effective party leadership might exist is within the subgroups that make up the national organizations. State parties tend to have some leadership control, and in certain areas of the country this is maintained by particular families, individuals, and groups for long periods of time. A group of party leaders that become firmly entrenched in controlling a local or state party organization is often referred to as a "machine." A good illustration of such a machine was the Byrd family which, until recently, dominated the Democratic party in Virginia. Numerous city party organizations have also been termed "machines"—Jim Curley of Boston and Frank Hague of Jersey City were leaders of two of the most famous of these.

Formal and informal party organization. In spite of their loose formation and lack of national leadership, American political parties do conform to a definite formal pattern in their structure. Each party is composed of the following:

(1) a national committee, with a national chairman who heads the party;
(2) national congressional and senatorial campaign committees, chosen independently of the national committee;
(3) state committees;
(4) county and city committees; and
(5) sometimes ward committees including precinct and block captains.

Alongside this formal organization which suggests a chain of command from national to local committees, there is an informal organization which is often at sharp variance with the formal party leadership. The informal organization is composed of influential party members such as "party bosses," the Senate's "inner-

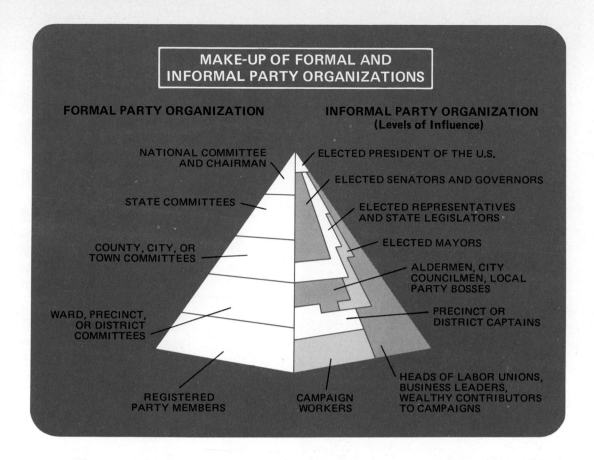

MAKE-UP OF FORMAL AND INFORMAL PARTY ORGANIZATIONS

FORMAL PARTY ORGANIZATION

- NATIONAL COMMITTEE AND CHAIRMAN
- STATE COMMITTEES
- COUNTY, CITY, OR TOWN COMMITTEES
- WARD, PRECINCT, OR DISTRICT COMMITTEES
- REGISTERED PARTY MEMBERS

INFORMAL PARTY ORGANIZATION
(Levels of Influence)

- ELECTED PRESIDENT OF THE U.S.
- ELECTED SENATORS AND GOVERNORS
- ELECTED REPRESENTATIVES AND STATE LEGISLATORS
- ELECTED MAYORS
- ALDERMEN, CITY COUNCILMEN, LOCAL PARTY BOSSES
- PRECINCT OR DISTRICT CAPTAINS
- CAMPAIGN WORKERS
- HEADS OF LABOR UNIONS, BUSINESS LEADERS, WEALTHY CONTRIBUTORS TO CAMPAIGNS

club" (a clique of Senators who control party politics in the Senate), and congressional party leaders. These people often carry great weight in political party affairs. Such individuals are recognized as party leaders even though they hold no position of importance in the formal party hierarchy.

A loose, undefined party organization generally results in a diffusion of power within the party. At the national level, informal power is always exercised by the President in his own political party. The opposition party must find its national leaders among political figures who are well known to the public nationwide, such as Senators, state governors, or sometimes writers and university teachers. In Con-

gress, power in both parties resides in the hands of senior members who may be the chairmen of important committees. The presidential and congressional sources of influence do not show up on the party-organization charts. Moreover, at the state and local levels, party organizations are virtually self-governing, and respond to local sources of informal power.

Review questions

1. To be nominated, is it more important for a presidential candidate to have substantial support from his national party organization or from the state and local party organizations? Why?
2. Who are the formal and informal leaders of the "out-party"?

DIFFERENCES OF POLICY PREFERENCES OF PARTY LEADERS AND FOLLOWERS

Percentage which favors decrease / Percentage which favors keep as is / Percentage which favors increase

ISSUE		DEMOCRATIC Leaders favor % decrease	DEMOCRATIC Leaders favor % keep as is	DEMOCRATIC Leaders favor % increase	DEMOCRATIC Followers favor % decrease	DEMOCRATIC Followers favor % keep as is	DEMOCRATIC Followers favor % increase	REPUBLICAN Leaders favor % decrease	REPUBLICAN Leaders favor % keep as is	REPUBLICAN Leaders favor % increase	REPUBLICAN Followers favor % decrease	REPUBLICAN Followers favor % keep as is	REPUBLICAN Followers favor % increase
PUBLIC OWNERSHIP	Public ownership of natural resources	19	25	56	15	50	35	52	35	13	20	49	31
	Public control of atomic energy	7	20	73	7	28	64	15	40	45	10	30	60
GOVERNMENT REGULATION OF ECONOMY	Level of farm price supports	29	29	43	28	33	39	67	26	7	40	37	23
	Government regulation of business	39	41	20	33	48	19	84	15	1	46	47	7
	Regulation of public utilities	6	35	59	11	50	39	18	64	18	12	62	26
	Regulation of trade unions	12	28	60	9	44	47	5	9	86	11	31	58
EGALITARIAN AND HUMAN WELFARE	Federal aid to education	13	20	66	5	20	75	43	35	22	8	27	65
	Slum clearance and public housing	6	16	78	6	14	80	22	38	40	8	19	73
	Social security benefits	4	36	60	3	28	69	13	64	23	4	39	57
	Minimum wages	5	45	50	3	38	59	12	72	16	5	52	44
	Enforcement of integration	27	29	44	27	31	42	32	43	25	24	35	41
TAX POLICY	Tax on large incomes	23	50	27	14	39	47	38	57	5	21	44	35
	Tax on business	38	49	13	24	51	25	71	28	1	33	51	16
	Tax on middle incomes	50	47	3	49	46	5	64	35	1	44	53	3
	Tax on small incomes	79	20	1	78	20	2	65	32	3	70	28	2
FOREIGN POLICY	Reliance on United Nations	18	33	49	17	48	35	35	41	24	19	47	34
	American participation in military alliances	17	41	42	14	47	39	26	51	23	15	53	32
	Foreign Aid	51	31	18	31	59	10	62	30	8	57	33	10
	Defense spending	34	45	21	16	33	51	33	53	14	15	39	46

Source: Herbert McClosky, Paul J. Hoffman, and Rosemary O'Hara, "Issue Conflict and Consensus Among Party Leaders and Followers," *American Political Science Review,* Vol. 54 (Menasha, Wisc.: The American Political Science Assoc., June 1960), pp. 406–427.

Party Objectives and Public Opinion

Do American political parties, with their lack of organizational unity, perform as they should in a democracy? Do they effectively transmit public demands to the government? Are the two major parties so all-encompassing that they can not be distinguished one from the other? Is it possible that there is more agreement between similar groups within opposing parties than there is within the parties themselves? If the parties have no identifying ideology, how do they fulfill their important functions of formulating and presenting issues to the electorate and of implementing party programs? Do the attitudes of the party leaders agree with those of other people who identify themselves as followers of the party? By comparing the attitudes of party leaders and followers regarding the various areas of public policy, it can be determined if the political parties are really reflecting the public's attitudes and how much of this opinion is being passed on to the government.

A contrast of party attitudes. Regardless of the fact that the major American parties are decentralized in organization and seemingly weak in ideology, there are still recognizable differences between them. These differences show up in general surveys of the leaders and followers of the two parties. In general, the public issues that cause the greatest disagreement between the parties are those that relate to whether there should be more or less government involvement in such areas as agriculture, business regulation, and welfare programs.

■ *Attitudes of party leaders.* Studies have been made which show definite differences between Democrats and Republicans regarding various issues of policy. The chart on the preceding page shows the findings of a survey of party leaders and followers that was compiled by political scientists Herbert McClosky, Paul Hoffman, and Rosemary O'Hara. This study indicates that in fact the leaderships of the two political parties are not identical in their attitudes toward general principles and issues. Both groups tend to agree more closely on foreign policy than in any other area and disagree more markedly with regard to governmental regulation of the economy and tax policy.

The survey also showed that the leaders of the two parties tend to fit the images that are often ascribed to them. Democratic leaders, who often come from the ranks of labor unions, ethnic minorities, or university professors and other intellectuals, demonstrated a consistent belief in the need for welfare programs. They also regarded a strong, effective government as a positive instrument of public policy. Republican leaders, who are generally drawn from the ranks of managers, proprietors, and persons of higher economic and social status, adhered to the principles of individualism and laissez-faire economy, advocating a reduced role for the government in most areas.

■ *Attitudes of party followers.* In spite of the policy differences between Democratic and Republican party leaders, there is much less evidence of such division between their respective followers. Generally, party followers do agree that there should be increased government involvement in the area of human welfare. A substantial majority in both parties apparently support increased federal aid to education. Nevertheless, there are still basic differences in the attitudes of party followers toward government regulation of the economy—for example, on the level of farm price supports and on regulation of trade unions. However, these distinctions are not nearly so great as those between the leaderships of the two parties.

It is easy, of course, to see that leaders of a party may have to take more definite stands on one side of an issue or the other to formulate policy programs that are in opposition to the other party's program. Since party leaders still have to present their programs to the followers prior to election, the followers have an opportunity to reject or accept these programs. The party followers can modify any really extreme stand of the leaders by rejecting those leaders who support that extreme stand. The followers can also influence the party's programs. If they agree with a pro-gram, they support it with their votes. If they do not agree, they can switch parties or vote for another party's candidates. The party that has the most popular program among the voters will supposedly get control of the government.

Review questions

1. Are the party leaders or the party followers more likely to be definite in their policy objectives?
2. On which areas of policy is there the greatest disagreement between the Democratic and Republican leaderships? On which policy areas are the two parties in more agreement?

The Role of Parties in Government

Political parties have several very essential jobs to perform within the government even after they have decided what their general policy goals are going to be. The most important of these jobs is to get their program pushed through and enacted as government policy. They also provide opposition to proposals they and their followers do not like. They educate the public with respect to political issues. And they supply candidates for office.

Limits on party policy-making. Party leaders may be in complete agreement about pushing a certain legislative measure. Yet, no matter how unified they may be in their support of a program, there are obstacles which may prevent them from getting it enacted. First, the leaders can not always depend on their followers' support while a policy is being debated. The constitutional separation of powers also hinders any single party from controlling the entire government structure. The President may be from one party and the majority in Congress, from another. Although a party may get a program through the

(Sometimes the positions held by factions within a political party provide almost ridiculous contradictions.)

legislature, the program may be vetoed by a President from the opposition party.

■ *Divisions within parties.* Party loyalties are often split, too, over certain party proposals. Even when the same party controls both the White House and the Capitol, there may be splits within the party over some legislation. Some party leaders and followers will support the President while others support the Congress. Thus, although the party may be considered the primary means of making demands on the government, often its power is fragmented when it comes to making policy.

At several times in the nation's history, a party in the government has attained enough cohesion to implement dramatic new government policies. The New Deal was an illustration of this. Most of the Democratic party as well as some Republicans got behind President Franklin D. Roosevelt to enact a domestic policy designed to solve the dilemmas of economic depression. Another example of strong party leadership resulting in cooperation among Democrats within the executive and the legislative branches was during the early days of President Lyndon Johnson's administration. The Democratic party acted in unison to enact major domestic programs such as Medicare, increased aid to education, and anti-poverty programs.

■ *Other limits on party policy-making.*

There are other barriers to the control of policy-making by the parties. As instruments of public policy, the parties are limited by:

(1) the size of both national and state governments;

(2) the complexity of public issues;

(3) the power of interest groups;

(4) the internal domination of Congress by committee chairmen who often do not represent the party as a whole; and

(5) the role of administrative agencies in policy formulation.

While programs of political parties tend to reflect public sentiments, these sentiments are usually only general viewpoints that must be transformed into the more concrete terms of governmental policy. In the process of becoming policy, such a program somehow becomes diluted by all of the above factors. It is gradually removed from the people as a whole and falls more and more into the hands of specialists. Interest groups may take up the battle, for example. Then congressional committees hold hearings and debate the program among themselves. Finally an administrative agency is given the authority to administer the program. The best recourse left to the people if they want it changed is to express their dissatisfaction at the ballot box.

Other functions of parties. Whether or not parties successfully implement policy,

AND SO, TODAY IN THE FIELD OF CIVIL RIGHTS. WE TRADITIONALLY RECOGNIZE THE NEGROES' RIGHT TO PROTEST WHILE BEING TRADITIONALLY OPPOSED TO LEGISLATIVE CONCESSIONS WON BY PUBLIC DEMAND.

THEN SIR, YOUR ADVICE WOULD BE –

CONCILIATION. RESPONSIBLE MODERATES FROM BOTH SIDES SHOULD MEET AND MEET AND MEET UNTIL THEY NAIL DOWN FIRM PROPOSALS ON WHICH ALL MEN OF GOOD WILL CAN UNANIMOUSLY AGREE.

BUT, SIR, WON'T THAT TAKE **YEARS**?

I CAN WAIT.

© 1963 Jules Feiffer

195

they do perform other functions vital to the political system. Even when they are not directly concerned with the course of particular public policies, parties do serve a definite purpose.

■ *Reconciliation of interests.* First, the fact that there are only two major parties demonstrates the ability of these parties to reconcile highly diversified interests within society. The parties have organized the politics of a vast continent and have expressed, in relatively meaningful terms, the population's divergent points of view.

The parties provide the channels of reconciliation and compromise by binding the different political interests together for the purpose of gaining the political rewards of office, power, and prestige. In doing this, they have prevented the fabric of the democracy from being torn apart by the opposing interests within the community.

■ *The loyal opposition.* In a democracy, one key function that the party system must perform is that of providing "loyal opposition" to the party in power. This consists of criticizing the program of the party in power without advocating a radical change in the system—that is, without taking over the government by force (*coup d'état*), or by initiating revolution.

The party in power should be subject to criticism by various members of the opposition on an almost continuing basis. Unfortunately, such criticism tends to be sporadic because the opposition will criticize only when it feels strongly about a matter. Sometimes criticism is initiated for reasons other than party interest or the merits of an issue. The motivation in some cases may be personal advancement or publicity rather than party interest. A Senator may criticize the President's labor policy not because his party feels strongly about it but because through such opposi-

tion he may further his own career by getting union backing and campaign support for his next election.

Despite this self-interested side of party criticism, it is a valuable contribution of the party system. In the United States, the opposition is constantly testing, debating, and challenging the party in power.

■ *Supply of candidates for office.* Political parties also supply the personnel needed to fill the elected offices of government at all levels—national, state, and local. The parties are, in effect, government personnel agencies, providing the candidates from among whom the electorate can select the people to do the job of governing. Naturally, government could not continue if such a supply of candidates were not available.

In addition, parties channel personnel into appointive offices. Frequently, Senators, officials in the President's administration, and other party leaders will suggest people for posts as ambassadors or judges. This permits each political party to have an additional, but indirect, voice in the making of public policy. By making suggestions for appointments, political leaders try to choose men who agree with their policies and at the same time are suited for the job.

■ *Political socialization.* Through public debating, campaigning for candidates, and formulating policy proposals, the political parties aid in the general political socialization of the public. They help to educate the public on political issues, always operating within the party framework. With the help of television coverage and other mass media, national party conventions and the presidential campaigns bring the major problems confronting government home to the people and help them to make more informed judgments. The political party is directly responsible for initiating most of this informative material.

Evaluation of America's two-party system. The American party system has been much maligned by some political scientists for a long time. These critics of the system contend that it is weak and generally ineffective, that leadership is not strong and deliberate, that there is not enough difference between the parties, and that the parties do not accurately reflect public sentiment on policy issues. These criticisms are healthy, but sometimes exaggerated.

Political parties should be judged first in terms of the characteristics of the system in which they function. If American parties are evaluated in these terms, they perform very well indeed.

The American political system is characterized by pluralism and fragmentation of public interest and of the governmental policy-making structure. It is not realistic to expect the party structure in such a system to be unified. Considering the nature of the system in which they operate, American parties are more cohesive and effective than might be expected. Criticisms of American political parties are really nothing more than criticisms of the whole American political scene.

Reform of the party system. Even though the American political party is adequate enough for the system in which it operates, there probably is room for reform. Suggestions have been made to produce a more vigorous and disciplined national party-system. As yet, none of these reforms has been pursued energetically largely because they would require basic changes in the Constitution and might even upset the present separation-of-powers system.

■ *Coinciding terms of office.* First, the election terms for the House of Representatives, the Senate, and the President might be made to coincide. As a minimum, Representative terms could be increased from two years to four years, and the terms of Senators could be reduced from six to four years. With this arrangement, a President and Congress of the same party might be elected at the same time and for a long enough period to carry out a party program. At the same time, credit for the success or failure of the program could be fixed on the particular party in power, without passing on the rewards or reproach to a succeeding party administration.

Meshing of election periods might, on the other hand, produce serious problems as well. Even if the terms of office for the President and the Congress were made to coincide, there still would be no guarantee that the White House would be occupied by the same party that provided the majority in Congress. Nor could it be assured that the House of Representatives would be controlled by the same party as the Senate. The net result of having the terms of the executive and legislators coincide might be

Reprinted by permission of New York Post

CHIPPING AT THE BASE

(Because of the oncoming war in 1940, the divisions of interests between the two parties became less distinct.)

197

a stalemate in government for longer periods than is the case with staggered terms of office. Or it might allow one party to get so entrenched, that the "opposition" would never be able to replace it.

■ *Repeating terms of the President.* Another feasible constitutional reform that would strengthen party government would be repeal of the Twenty-second Amendment. This amendment, which limits any President to two terms, tends to diminish the President's authority during his second term of office. By prohibiting a third term of office, the Twenty-second Amendment reduces the President's potential for party leadership, and decreases the meaningfulness of party responsibility at the national level. Toward the end of a President's second term, interest shifts from the incumbent to the personalities and programs of potential candidates who may take his place.

Although the American party system has its imperfections and pitfalls, it has managed over the years to perform its duty of funneling public opinion into government. Even without the support of the Framers of the Constitution, the political parties have been able to develop and have become an important wheel in the machinery of government. They are a practical answer to the necessity for selecting candidates and for providing an outlet for dissent.

Review questions

1. What non-policy-making roles do political parties play?
2. Explain the importance of "loyal opposition" in a democratic government.

Chapter Review

Terms you should know

division of interests	machine	party leaders
formal party organization	multi-party system	plurality
informal party organization	out-party	political party
inner club	party bosses	proportional representation
loyal opposition	party followers	single-member district

Questions about this chapter

1. Explain how divisions of interest within the United States have been reflected in the make-up of American political parties. Make reference to specific historical and political events.
2. What major factor contributes to the "looseness" of American party organization?
3. Explain how federalism and the separation of powers affected the development of political parties.
4. State and explain the various factors that caused a two-party system to evolve in the United States?
5. What is the typical characterization of a Republican leader; a Democratic leader? Are these characterizations as true for the electorate as they are for the leaders?
6. Why is it difficult for American political parties to implement their policies? How can parties get around these barriers? Does this difficulty in getting policies implemented mean public opinion is seldom taken into account when policies are legislated? Explain.

Thought and discussion questions

1. Is it possible to have a disciplined party system and at the same time retain a high degree of democratic discussion in decision-making? Explain.

2. What are the advantages and disadvantages of the "umbrella" type of party which characterizes the American party system? Discuss the advantages and disadvantages of other types of parties. Evaluate both types in terms of their practicality and their idealism.

3. After the Civil War, political parties went through a period of realignment. Democrats became Republicans, Republicans became Democrats. At what other times in the country's history have party loyalties shifted? Compare these situations to what is happening today and try to decide whether this is a new period of party realignment.

4. Evaluate the suggestions for party reform that have been proposed by political scientists. Consider: (a) their real necessity, (b) their practicality, (c) their potential effect on the political system.

Class projects

1. Examine the formal party organizations in your local community. Are there any informal organizations present? Does the formal or informal organization exert more influence in the community? Is this situation advantageous to the general populace?

2. Check today's newspaper for indications of policy differences between the two major parties. Make a list of these differences. How real are these differences? Do they support your image of each party?

3. Make a chart of the political trends in your community since World War II, showing the percentages of votes received by the major parties in various elections. Is there any similarity between these local trends and national trends? Explain.

Case Study: How a third party affects the vote

The voter in a presidential election is sometimes influenced more by the personalities of the candidates than by party commitments. Often, candidates for other offices are elected by "riding in on the coattails" of a popular presidential candidate. But this did not happen in the 1968 presidential election. Analysis of the returns reveals that voting habits were broken in this election. A Republican was elected to the Presidency while the Democrats carried both Houses. Yet, this analysis does not tell us why traditional voting patterns were broken. A major reason was the intrusion of a third party—George Wallace's American Independent Party—into the traditional two-party framework.

As you read this case study, which examines the unusual aspects of the 1968 election, consider the following:

1. How did the 1968 vote demonstrate a shift away from the traditional two-party system?

2. Why did the American Independent Party and George Wallace generate so much excitement among some people?
3. Since the third-party phenomenon has become more successful in recent elections, does this signal the end of the two-party system?

How We Voted—and Why

Despite early predictions that the Wallace candidacy would mainly attract conservative Republican voters, it now seems clear that Mr. Wallace drew a large proportion of his votes from people who would ordinarily have voted Democratic. These Democrats voting for Wallace were not given the opportunity to support his American Independent Party ticket at the Congressional level; there were no candidates. Apparently most of these voters, having made their protest at the Presidential level, then dropped back to their accustomed support of the Democratic ticket, including the candidates for Congress.

. . . Nixon not only has the problem of a Democratic Congress; he also comes to national leadership as the choice of a minority of the electorate. Not since the election of Woodrow Wilson in 1912 has a President been elected with so small a proportion of the total vote. It is a wry fact that in losing to John F. Kennedy in 1960 Nixon received a considerably higher proportion of the popular vote than he did in winning against Hubert Humphrey. . . . He can neither command the loyalty of the majority party in the Congress nor draw strength from a mandate of the electorate. . . .

The contribution of George Wallace to all this can hardly be overestimated. His 13 percent of the national vote is the largest a third party has achieved since Theodore Roosevelt undertook to defeat Wilson and Taft in 1912. . . . Precinct data indicate that outside the South he drew most heavily from areas which would ordinarily be expected to vote Democratic. . . . The Wallace votes came much more commonly from Democrats and self-styled independents than they did from Republicans. . . .

It is . . . likely that the vote for Wallace was in the main a protest and a renunciation of the Democratic Administration, and that a large part of it would have gone to Nixon if Wallace had not been on the ballot. It became evident . . . that the Johnson Administration had built up a formidable stockpile of resentment and ill will within the electorate, and that 1968 was not a propitious year to inherit the Democratic nomination.

. . . Of course no one can say how many of the Wallace supporters would have found Nixon a satisfactory choice if Wallace had not been available. The strongest indication of where those votes would have gone comes from preliminary survey data which make it possible to compare the political attitudes of those respondents who were intending to vote for Humphrey, Nixon or Wallace. On questions of welfare legislation, Medicare, aid to education and guaranteed employment, Humphrey supporters were far more favorable than either Nixon or Wallace people, who did not differ greatly from each other. The Wallace supporters were very critical of the nation's foreign policies and very hawkish on Vietnam; in both respects they resembled Nixon supporters more than those favoring Humphrey. On questions of racial integration and civil rights, Humphrey supporters were clearly more favorable than Nixon people and the Wallaceites were by some distance the least favorable. In all these respects those intending to vote for Wallace stood much closer to Nixon supporters than to those favoring Humphrey. More than a third of them reported that they had voted for Goldwater in 1964. Would they have seen Humphrey as being closer to their point of view if they had had to choose between him and Nixon? It seems hardly plausible. George Wallace attracted the votes of a great many people who were out of sympathy with the Democratic Administration and all

This excerpt from "How We Voted and Why" by Angus Campbell, The Nation, November 25, 1968, is reprinted with permission of The Nation. Copyright © 1968 by The Nation Associates, Inc.

its works, and had he not been there to receive them, Nixon would almost certainly have been the principal beneficiary.

... The total turn-out at the polls appears to have been about 72 million. This means that somewhat less than 60 percent of the adult population exercised their franchise, the lowest turn-out record in a Presidential election since the phenomenally low one in 1948. ... There was a good deal of bitter talk on the college campuses and in some of the liberal magazines about the irrelevance of the Humphrey-Nixon choice. In the end this alienation and apathy did not have as depressing an effect on the vote as it had earlier threatened, and it is likely that the swing toward Humphrey, which the polls recorded during the last few days of the campaign, was made up largely of disgruntled Democrats who finally decided it was better to support their party's ticket than not to vote at all.

... In the immediate aftermath of the Chicago imbroglio* many unhappy Democrats were insisting that the convention system would have to go, to be replaced presumably by some system of national primaries. It would require an act of Congress to impose such a system on the states, and it does not seem likely that the new Congress will have much enthusiasm for any such revision of established practice. ...

There have also been a number of apocalyptic [prophetic] statements regarding the future of the two-party system and its failure to present meaningful alternatives to the electorate. The fact is that more than 9 million people voted for an alternative to the two major parties in this election. The various left-wing candidates for the Presidency drew few votes, and little promise exists of a serious party development to the Left of the Democrats. The potential at the other extreme seems far more real and George Wallace's 9 million supporters may well be the advance guard of a full-blown right-wing party.

The extraordinary difficulty of establishing a third party in the United States is best attested by the fact that for the past hundred years it has not happened. The problem of building an organization of true believers that extends down to the precinct level is overwhelming, especially when the organization cannot provide any immediate political rewards. Perhaps if Wallace undertakes to build on the impressive showing he made in this election he may be able to fashion the party apparatus and the mass following necessary for the continuing development of his party. Certainly there have been repeated demonstrations over the past twenty years that a fraction of the electorate is prepared to break away from the two-party pattern to support a right-wing candidate.

There is great respect in this country for the durability of the institutions of our party system and the power of the two established parties; it would thus be foolish to imagine that they will yield readily to pressure for change. But the Wallace vote this year was the most serious departure from a straight two-party vote we have seen in more than fifty years. Was this due to the particular genius of George Wallace? Was it a reflection of the out-of-jointness of this particular time? Did it reveal a growing alienation among people who feel the country is changing too fast? One cannot say at this point what precisely the Wallace vote meant, but it has shown beyond question that the two old parties are vulnerable to attack from the Right.

*In the summer of 1968, the Democratic national convention held in Chicago was the scene of serious clashes between police and young dissidents and protestors angered by the continuation of the Vietnam war.

End questions

1. If George Wallace had not been on the ballot in all 50 states, Hubert Humphrey would have easily won the election. What do you think about this statement?

2. How did the American electorate show their displeasure with the leader of the Democratic party? Who profited most from this displeasure?

3. Did the 1968 election returns of your state follow the trends in the national election? If there were differences, why did they exist?

Case Study: How you choose a party

According to Chapter 8, studies made by the Survey Research Center indicate that "in spite of the policy differences between Democratic and Republican party leaders, there is much less evidence of such division between their respective followers." Would a study of your own classmates reveal a similar conclusion? Some of your classmates probably identify with a particular political party; others may not. Why not find out where they stand and where you stand politically? When you compile the answers given by your classmates to this survey, you should be able to determine which party your classmates identify with.

The questions in the survey have been extracted from the Survey Research Center's "1968 Pre-Election Study." When you have completed the questionnaire, compile the results from the entire class. You will then be able to see how followers of different parties think about public issues.

1968 PRE-ELECTION STUDY

SURVEY RESEARCH CENTER
INSTITUTE FOR SOCIAL RESEARCH
THE UNIVERSITY OF MICHIGAN
ANN ARBOR, MICHIGAN 48106

1. Generally speaking, would you say that *you personally* care a good deal which party wins presidential elections, or that you don't care very much which party wins? —Care —Don't care

2. Is there anything in particular that you like about the Democratic party? —— If so, what?

3. Is there anything in particular that you don't like about the Democratic party? —— If so, what?

4. Is there anything in particular that you like about the Republican party? —— If so, what?

Questions from the Survey Research Center's "1968 Pre-Election Study" have been reprinted with permission of The Survey Research Center, Institute for Social Research, the University of Michigan, Ann Arbor, Michigan.

5. Is there anything in particular that you don't like about the Republican party? ——
If so, what?

_____

6. As you well know, the government faces many serious problems in this country and
in other parts of the world. What do you personally feel are the most important
problems the government in Washington should try to take care of? (list five)

_____

Some people have different ideas about the sorts of things the government in
Washington should or should not be doing. Following are some general statements
that you may agree or disagree with. Indicate your choice in each case.

7. "Some people think the government in Washington should help towns and cities
provide education for grade and high school children; others think this should be
handled by the local communities." Have you been interested enough in this to favor
one side over the other?   —Yes   —No (Go to Q. 7b)

   7a.   Which are you in favor of: —Getting help from the government in Washington   —Handling it at the state and local level?

   7b.   Which party do you think is more likely to want the government to help local
communities provide education for children, the _Democrats,_ the _Republicans,_
or wouldn't there be any difference between them on this?   —Democrats
—Republicans   —No difference   —Don't know

8. "Some people are afraid the government in Washington is getting too powerful for
the good of the country and the individual person. Others feel that the government
in Washington is not getting too strong for the good of the country." Have you
been interested enough in this to favor one side over the other?
—Yes   —No (Go to Q. 8b)

   8a.   What is your feeling, do you think: —The government is getting too powerful
or do you think   —the government is not getting too strong?

   8b.   Which party do you think is more likely to favor a stronger government in
Washington or wouldn't there be any difference between them on this?
—Democrats   —Republicans   —No difference   —Don't know

9. "Some say the government in Washington ought to help people get doctors and
hospital care at low cost; others say the government should not get into this." Have
you been interested enough in this to favor one side over the other?
—Yes   —No (Go to Q. 9b)

   9a.   What is your position? Should the government in Washington: —Help people
get doctors and hospital care at low cost or   —Stay out of this?

   9b.   Which party do you think is more likely to want the government to help in
getting doctors and medical care at low cost?   —Democrats   —Republicans
—No difference   —Don't know

10. "In general, some people feel that the government in Washington should see to it that every person has a job and a good standard of living. Others think the government should just let each person get ahead on his own." Have you been interested enough in this to favor one side over the other? —Yes —No (Go to Q. 10b)

10a. Do you think that the government: —Should see to it that every person has a job and a good standard of living or —Should it let each person get ahead on his own?

10b. Which party do you think is more likely to favor the government seeing to it that each person has a job and a good standard of living? —Democrats —Republicans —No difference —Don't know

11. Do you think it will make any difference in how you and your family get along financially whether the Republicans or Democrats win the election? ——(If yes) Why is that? _____

_____

_____

12. "Some people feel that if blacks are not getting fair treatment in jobs the government in Washington ought to see to it that they do. Others feel that this is not the federal government's business." Have you had enough interest in this question to favor one side over the other?
—Yes —No (Go to Q. 12b)

12a. How do you feel? Should the government in Washington:
—See to it that blacks get fair treatment in jobs or
—Leave these matters to the states and local communities?

12b. Which party do you think is more likely to want the government to see to it that blacks get fair treatment in jobs? —Democrats —Republicans —No difference —Don't know

13. "Some people say that the government in Washington should see to it that white and black children are allowed to go to the same schools. Others claim that this is not the government's business." Have you been concerned enough about this question to favor one side over the other?
—Yes —No (Go to Q. 13b)

13a. Do you think the government in Washington should:
—See to it that white and black children go to the same schools
—Stay out of this area as it is not its business?

13b. Which party do you think is more likely to want the government to see to it that white and black children go to the same schools?
—Democrats —Republicans —No difference —Don't know

14. "As you may know, Congress passed a bill that says that blacks should have the right to go to any hotel or restaurant they can afford, just like anybody else. Some people feel that this is something the government in Washington should support. Others feel that the government should stay out of this matter." Have you been interested enough in this to favor one side over another? —Yes —No (Go to Q. 14b)

14a. Should the government support the right of blacks:
—To go to any hotel or restaurant they can afford *or should it*
—Stay out of this matter?
14b. Which party do you think is more likely to favor the government supporting the right of blacks to go to any hotel or restaurant?
—Democrats —Republicans —No difference —Don't know

We now come to a few questions about our dealings with other countries.

15. "Some people say that we should give aid to other countries if they need help, while others think each country should make its own way as best it can." Have you been interested enough in this to favor one side over the other?
—Yes —No (Go to Q. 15b)
15a. Which opinion is most like yours? Should we: —Give aid to other countries *or should* —Each country make its own way?
15b. Which party do you think is more likely to give aid to other countries, the Democrats, the Republicans, or wouldn't there be any difference between them on this? —Democrats —Republicans —No difference —Don't know

16. "Some people think it is all right for our government to sit down and talk to the leaders of the Communist countries and try to settle our differences, while others think we should refuse to have anything to do with them." Have you been interested enough in this to favor one side over the other? —Yes —No (Go to Q. 16b)
16a. What do you think? Should we: —Try to discuss and settle our differences *or* —Refuse to have anything to do with the leaders of Communist countries?
16b. Which party do you think is more likely to sit down and talk with the leaders of Communist countries? —Democrats —Republicans —No difference —Don't know

17. "Some people say that our farmers and businessmen should be able to do business with Communist countries as long as the goods are not used for military purposes; others say that our government should not allow Americans to trade with the Communist countries." Have you been interested enough to favor one side over the other? —Yes —No (Go to Q. 17b)
17a. How do you feel? Should farmers and businessmen be:
—Allowed to do business with Communist countries *or should they be*
—Forbidden to do business with Communist countries?
17b. Which party do you think is more likely to allow farmers and businessmen to trade with Communist countries? —Democrats —Republicans —No difference —Don't know

18. Which of these would you say you are *most* concerned about: —Vietnam, —Cuba, *or* —Communist China? Which are you *least* concerned about: —Vietnam, —Cuba, *or* —Communist China?

19. Would you say that in the past year or so the United States has done pretty well in dealing with foreign countries, or would you say that we haven't been doing as well

as we should?   —Pretty well   —Not well   —Well in some ways; not in others
What do you have in mind? _____

_____

20. Would you say that in the past year or so our position in the world has become
stronger, less strong, or has it stayed about the same?   —Stronger   —Less strong
—About the same
What do you have in mind? _____

_____

21. Generally speaking, do you usually think of yourself as a *Republican,* a *Democrat,*
an *Independent,* or what? (Record below)

_____

—Republican	—Democrat
21a. Would you call yourself a *strong* Republican or a *not very strong* Republican? —Strong —Not very strong	**21c.** Would you call yourself a *strong* Democrat or a *not very strong* Democrat? —Strong —Not very strong
21b. Was there ever a time when you thought of yourself as a Democrat rather than a Republican —Yes —No, never	**21d.** Was there ever a time when you thought of yourself as Republican rather than a Democrat? —Yes —No, never

—Independent   —No preference   —Other

21e. Do you think of yourself as closer to the *Republican* or to the *Democratic*
party? (Record below)

—Republican	—Neither	—Democratic
21f. Was there ever a time when you thought of yourself as closer to the Democratic party instead of the Republican party? —Yes —No, never	**21g.** Was there ever a time when you thought of yourself as a Democrat or as a Republican? (Which party was that?) —Yes, Democrat —Yes, Republican —No, never	**21h.** Was there ever a time when you thought of yourself as closer to the Republican party instead of the Democratic party? —Yes —No, never

End questions

1. According to your compilation of the answers given by your classmates to this survey, can you determine if your colleagues tend to support more or less government involvement in domestic issues? In which party would you place people who favored more government involvement in domestic issues? How about integration of the schools? And medical care? And education? And relations with Communist nations?

2. Do the political leaders in your community reflect the opinions of their followers? Compare the opinions of your classmates with the statements of local politicians, your Representative in Congress, and your state Senators, which you have read or heard through the mass media. Do Democratic politicians agree on issues with your classmates who identify themselves as Democrats? Do Republican leaders agree with your classmates who identify themselves as Republicans? In principle, how far apart or how close are your classmates to the leaders of the party that they identify with?

CHAPTER 9
Nominations, Campaigns, and Elections

CANDIDATE'S GAME

START

1. OHIO · MISSOURI · FLORIDA · NEW YO[RK] · ALASKA — Party delegates too many half votes, runs out of invitations. *GO TO JAIL!*

5. Each delegate nominates his very own *Favorite Son*. *LOSE ONE TURN*

4. Overburdened party platform collapses! *GO TO HOSPITAL*

3. SNAFU CIGARETTES — "Friends, workers, folks out there in TV land, our party will lead the country to a new prosperity, a new..." Keynote speech is read from notes on a cigarette pack. TV coverage canceled. *PAY $100 FINE*

2. *HACK HACK COUGH COUGH* — Delegate passes out in smoke-filled room *GO BACK TO START*

6. No candidate nominated after **104** ballots. Convention is recessed. *ROLL DICE AGAIN*

7. figurehead — Party members rally behind who misses rally. *PAY $5 FINE*

8. Presidential nominee chooses TV star for running-mate. *ADVANCE TO WHITE HOUSE*

9. Candidate loses speec[h] for fund-raising dinn[er] *FORFEIT BANKROLL*

10. Candidates show "different fronts" on TV.

14. Election ends in a tie. *GO BACK TO START*

13. VOTE SAM SUPERCHIEF FOR PRESIDENT! Union newspaper runs full page ads at no charge to candidate. *COLLECT $50*

12. Pay $355 for hand lotion and mouthwash.

11. Candidate runs out of hot dogs at Boy Scout jamboree. Lose votes of 250 scoutmasters.

SMILE! Pay $65. for makeup

Charles Johnson has been nominated by the Charter party to run for city councilman this fall. How was "Chuck" selected as a candidate for the position? What credentials does he have that qualify him for the office? And now that he has been chosen, what forces will shape his electoral campaign? Who will decide what principles and demands he will advocate—in other words, what his *platform* will be?

Selection of Candidates

Whether a political system is democratic or totalitarian, nothing is more important to its continuation than the selection of candidates for office, because some of these candidates will eventually run the government. Government policies can not be generated by themselves. Someone must guide demands through the conversion structure until they finally emerge as policy. This duty falls to the elected officials. The nominations, campaigns, and elections of candidates are input mechanisms which supply officials for the government's policy-making activities. With tens of thousands of political offices available—from city councilmen to the Chief Executive—these mechanisms are vital to both the input and conversion processes of our political system.

The nominating procedure. Early in the Republic's history, there was no provision for the nomination, or selection, of candidates to run for office. But then, it was not the intention of the Framers that political parties would form a central core of the election system. A nominating procedure was even further from their thoughts. The Constitution now provides for the election of Senators and Representatives by the people, but it does not outline how candidates are to be chosen. The election of the President is stipulated in the paragraphs on the electoral college, but there is no mention in the Constitution of nominating procedures for the Presidency. These procedures have, instead, evolved over the years along with the evolution of political parties and the gradual democratization of the political system.

In a democracy, the nominating process must involve the people. If the selection of candidates were left entirely to political-party elites, the most fundamental principle of democracy—popular participation—would be denied. The political parties could then become tyrannical, ignoring the wishes of the party followers and the general public.

On the other hand, if everyone took part in all the steps of candidate nomination, the process would be too unwieldy. The political parties would collapse from the sheer number of people who wanted to express their individual opinions. Therefore, the party leaderships have had to provide a responsible mechanism for candidate selection that takes into consideration their followers' wishes.

Caucuses, conventions, and primaries. Prior to the 1830's, all party candidates were chosen by small groups of party leaders, called *caucuses*. Presidential candidates were nominated by caucuses of influential party members in Congress, whereas congressional candidates were selected by similar caucuses in state legislatures. Because it was too exclusive, this

What parallels and contrasts are there between the serious business of nominations, campaigns, and elections of candidates for the offices of government and the moves of competing players on a board game?

method was felt to be undemocratic. By 1832, all major-party candidates for the Presidency were nominated by national *conventions,* or meetings of party members. The state parties also developed convention systems for nominating candidates for Congress and state-wide offices. Gradually the convention systems, as well, were taken over by local party bosses and the elites of the political parties within the states. As a result, conventions for the selection of congressional and state offices have been largely replaced by *primary* elections. However, conventions are still held on a national scale for the nomination of presidential candidates and are also widely used on the state level for the selection of party delegates to the national conventions.

Party primaries have grown in popularity as the convention system has declined. The primaries allow the "rank and file" members of a political party to vote more directly for the candidates they wish to support in an election. First held in New York and California in 1866, primaries quickly took on one of two forms: (1) direct selection of candidates by party members, or (2) selection of candidates indirectly by party members who chose delegates to nominating conventions. The *direct primary* soon became the selection device most recommended by reform groups throughout the country to circumvent the "smoke-filled rooms", or private gatherings of the party elite, where candidates were traditionally selected.

By the turn of the century, two-thirds of the states had passed primary laws, and by 1927 almost all states held state-wide primaries for the selection of candidates for federal and many state offices. In 1968, forty-four states selected both senatorial and congressional candidates by holding direct primary elections. The six exceptions to this rule included Indiana, where

Senators are nominated by conventions while Representatives are selected through the primaries; Virginia, where Senators are selected in primaries and Representatives may be chosen by either convention or primary; Delaware, where both Senators and Representatives are nominated by conventions; Connecticut and Utah, where each party first chooses a slate of candidates at a party convention, and final nominations are made through primaries; and New York, where Senators are endorsed by party committees, and both Senators and Representatives may be chosen in a primary.

Within each state, the parties may also vary in their methods of nominating candidates for Congress. In South Carolina, Virginia, and Alabama, for example, the Republican party uses conventions exclusively—reflecting the lack of Republican voter strength in those states. Between 1956 and 1964, an increase of Republican-party strength resulted in a shift from the convention to the primary method by Republican parties in Arkansas, Georgia, and Texas.

In several states where primaries are held, parties also hold conventions to endorse candidates who are subsequently submitted to the party members in the primary. Convention endorsement, however, does not necessarily guarantee a candidate's nomination. Party members may reject the convention's preference in the primary. An illustration of this point was the contest in 1962 between Massachusetts Attorney General Edward T. McCormack and Edward Kennedy for a Senate seat. Kennedy challenged the party's convention endorsement of McCormack, and easily acquired the Democratic nomination by winning the primary. Kennedy then went on to capture the Senate post.

Control over nominating procedures. Since the election process is such an integral part of democracy, as well as a key means of providing "inputs" for the political system, the procedures that parties use to nominate candidates can not be determined solely by the parties themselves. Thus, nominating procedures as well as the qualifications for voters in primaries are generally regulated by state laws.

The endorsement of candidates by conventions held prior to primaries, however, is generally left to the discretion of the parties. In Colorado and Massachusetts, the holding of conventions to endorse candidates is required by law. But in every other state where nominating conventions are held, they are conducted according to the rules set up by the parties.

■ *Types of primaries.* While state conventions are largely the responsibility of the parties, only state laws can determine what type of primary will be conducted within the state. In general there are two types of primaries—open or closed.

In *closed primaries*—the most frequently accepted—voters have to declare they are members of a party to vote for that party's candidates. Closed primaries are the most effective method of allowing party members to choose their party's candidates. In *open primaries,* any registered voter, whether a party member or not, may vote in a party's primary. In recent years, Alaska, Michigan, Minnesota, Montana, North Dakota, Utah, Vermont, Washington, and Wisconsin have utilized the open primary method. A refinement of the open primary, known as the "jungle" primary, is used in Alaska and Washington. A voter may choose any party's candidate for any office and does not even have to confine himself to the party slate. The results of such a primary may indicate the popularity of a candidate, but they also distort the party's real strength in the state.

The significance of primary results are

A Charlie McCarthy Act

Courtesy of *Columbus Dispatch*

(As this cartoon shows, a President can exercise some influence in the selection of candidates by his party.)

also distorted when the voters of a party are allowed to vote for a nominee in another party whom they have no intention of supporting in the final election. Voters can even sabotage an opposition party by voting for a candidate who would be unlikely to receive the votes of that party's members in later elections. Until 1959, California allowed a *cross-filing* system which confused primary results even further. Since nominees could be placed on the ballots of either party, Republicans could thus win a Democratic primary, and vice versa.

Review questions

1. Why was a system for nominating congressional and presidential candidates not written into the Constitution?
2. Explain the different types of primaries. Why has the closed primary become the most popular way to select candidates?

211

National Nominating Conventions

Political party nominating conventions in the United States have been so colorful and disorganized in the past that one European observer has called the convention a "colossal travesty of popular institutions," and the platform a "collection of hollow, vague phrases."[1] While the conventions may not be august assemblages, they do perform a vital function in the political system—naming candidates to run for the offices of President and Vice President.

The national nominating conventions were developed to fill a serious gap in the constitutional structure. Originally, it was anticipated that the electoral-college procedure would suffice for selecting a President. Ideally, electors in each state would assemble, debate, and deliberate solemnly and judiciously to arrive at their selection for President. The early development of political parties, however, required a broader nominating process that included all elements within a party.

At first, the congressional party caucuses acted as nominating bodies. For a time, the caucuses worked because members of Congress really were the most important party leaders from each state. A congressional-caucus decision about who was to run for President was sufficiently representative of a party's outside interests. But when the Federalists lost control of Congress in 1804, those Federalists remaining in Congress no longer represented the party as a whole. A new method had to be devised to select candidates with support outside the Congress as well as within it; otherwise, defeat at the polls was certain.

[1] Moisei Ostrogorski, Democracy and the Organization of Political Parties, abridged by Seymour M. Lipset (New York: Anchor Books, 1964).

In 1808, Federalist party leaders met secretly in New York in the first American "nominating convention" and selected candidates for the Presidency and Vice Presidency. By 1831, the popular base of the existing parties had expanded so that the rank-and-file party members wanted more voice in the selection of candidates. Before the 1832 election, all three political parties—the National Republican, Anti-Mason, and Democratic—held full-fledged national presidential nominating conventions, which enabled many party followers to participate in the selection of a presidential candidate.

Allocation of delegates. Naturally, the national presidential nominating conventions would be too cumbersome if all party members attended. Therefore, some means of allocating the number of delegates from the various states, as well as methods of selecting the delegates, had to be devised.

The formulas by which the parties allocate convention delegates change from time to time. Determined by the national leadership of each party, the formulas are based on the strength of the party within the respective states. Those states that show the strongest party affiliation have the highest number of delegates.

During the twentieth century, the Democratic party has had less difficulty than the Republican in arriving at a formula for allocating delegates, because its strength has been more evenly distributed among the states. Traditionally the Republican party has been weak in the "Solid South" where the votes have almost always gone to the Democratic party. If the Republicans had allocated convention delegates to each state according to the number of Representatives or Senators from that state, this would have allowed southern states to send delegates who would be unable to deliver votes in the final election. The Republicans, therefore, devised a formula to reward those regions, states, and districts that had supported previous Republican candidates.

In 1968, for example, there were 1,333 delegates at the Republican presidential nominating convention. These delegates had been allocated to the states in the following manner.

Each state party was automatically entitled to send four *delegates-at-large*— that is, delegates who represented the state party as a whole. Two additional delegates-at-large were also allotted for each Republican Representative from the state. In addition, if the state's electoral votes in the 1964 presidential election had gone to the Republican candidate, or if the state had elected a Republican Senator or governor since 1964, the state was entitled to a bonus of six more delegates. Each state was also allotted one additional delegate for each congressional district where voters had cast at least 2,000 votes for the Republican presidential candidate in 1964 or for a Republican congressional candidate in 1966, and one additional delegate for each congressional district that had cast a minimum of 10,000 such votes. Under this system, Republican states were rewarded with bonus delegates and heavily Democratic states were punished.

With the splitting of the "Solid South" in 1964 and the delivery of more votes to the Republican candidate, the Democratic party also began to feel that some bonus system would be necessary to reflect party strength throughout the country. Thus, the Democratic formula of 1968 provided for bonus votes.

Each state was allotted three convention votes for each elector from that state in the electoral college. One additional convention vote was earned by the state for every hundred thousand popular votes that had been cast in the state in 1964 for the Democratic presidential candidate, Lyndon B. Johnson. A bonus of 10 votes was given to each state that had cast its entire electoral vote for the Democratic hopeful in 1964. Finally, each state and territory has a national committeeman and committeewoman, both of whom are entitled to one vote. The system resulted in 2,622 convention votes, to be cast by 2,989 delegates including 110 members of the national committee. The discrepancy between the numbers of votes and delegates is accounted for by the fact that states are apportioned fewer votes than delegates.

Selection of delegates. Once the number of delegates to the national convention has been allotted to each state, then the candidates have to be chosen. National convention delegates are selected either by presidential-preference primaries, by district or state party conventions, or by the party's state committee.

■ *Presidential-preference primaries.* Once employed extensively, presidential primaries are now used by only sixteen states and the District of Columbia. Where such primaries are held, each state has developed its own primary system. In some primaries, voters elect delegates to the national party conventions who have indicated preference for a particular candidate; in others, the voters merely express their preference for one or another presidential candidate, and the delegates are not pledged to abide by the voters' indicated preference. In some states, only some of the national convention delegates are chosen in the primaries and the rest are selected at state party conventions. In Alabama, New York, and the District of Columbia, neither the presidential candidates' names nor the preferences of the delegates are listed on the primary ballot;

the voter must know which candidate the delegate supports. In Maryland and Indiana, voters express a presidential preference; but a state convention then elects delegates in accordance with the choice expressed in the primary.

In the few states where delegates are pledged to follow the voters' choice, they must honor their pledges on the first convention ballot only. Many of these pledges are to "favorite sons," candidates popular in their home states only, who have little or no chance of capturing the national nomination. Haphazard as it may seem, the presidential primary does have one advantage—it involves party followers in the selection of candidates.

"Yeah, but who's for you guys besides the people?"

(A convention delegate may shrewdly examine a candidate's potential support before he commits his vote.)

■ *State party conventions and committees.* Used by the majority of states for choosing delegates to the national convention, state conventions held by the parties do not permit as much direct involvement of party followers. These conventions consist of the party leaders from cities, counties, and the state, who then select delegates to the national convention, usually by oral or roll-call votes. The preferences of party followers may be taken into consideration or not, according to the feelings of the convention delegates.

State party committees select delegates in only five states. This method confines the selection process even further to those few people who belong to the party committee for that state. In Arkansas, Georgia, and Rhode Island, the Democratic party uses this method for all delegates. In some states though, state party committees select only the delegates-at-large. This is the case in New York for the Democrats, and in Pennsylvania for both Democrats and Republicans.

Conventions in operation. Even before a nominating convention meets, the choice of a site is considered of prime importance. Usually the party's national committee selects a city in a region of the country that it expects will support its candidate in the final election. With the advent of national television coverage, a site has become less important. In the pre-1952 period, though, residents in the area where a convention was held felt a greater sense of identification with the proceedings than those outside that region.

■ *The keynote address.* Once the delegates are selected and the site chosen, the convention meets and various party rituals are performed. Roll calls are read, welcoming speeches are made, and temporary officers including a chairman of the convention are chosen. The keynote address, or opening speech, is the first important event to take place. It is given by the temporary chairman. In the past, keynote addresses have been designed to stir up enthusiasm and to rally the delegates behind the party banner for victory in the November election. Excerpts from keynote addresses of past conventions illustrate the general tone that has been taken. In the midst of the Great Depression in 1932, Senator Alben Barkley introduced the Democratic convention with an emotional attack on the Republican administration:

"No, my countrymen, there is nothing wrong with this Republic except that it has been mismanaged, exploited, and demoralized for more than a decade by a statesmanship incapable even now in the midst of its fearful havoc of understanding the extent of its own mischief."

Even during the grave times of war in 1944, Oklahoma's Governor Walter Kerr, in delivering the Democratic keynote address, went to extraordinary lengths to inspire enthusiasm for the party in office:

Table 9:1

Method of Selecting Delegates to National Conventions

Primary Method

Alabama (D)	Indiana (R)	New York	Oregon
California	Massachusetts	(D—for district delegates)	Pennsylvania
District of Columbia	Nebraska	(R—also use conventions)	South Dakota
Florida	New Hampshire	Ohio	West Virginia
Illinois	New Jersey		Wisconsin
(District delegates)			

Convention Method

Alabama (R)	Illinois	Minnesota	Oklahoma
Alaska	(delegates-at-large)	Mississippi	Rhode Island (R)
Arizona	Indiana	Missouri	South Carolina
Arkansas (R)	Iowa	Montana	Tennessee
Colorado	Kansas	Nevada	Texas
Connecticut	Kentucky	New Mexico	Utah
Delaware	Louisiana	New York	Vermont
Georgia (R)	Maine	(R—also use primary)	Virginia
Hawaii	Maryland	North Carolina	Washington
Idaho	Michigan	North Dakota	Wyoming

State Committee Method

Arkansas (D)	New York	Pennsylvania	Rhode Island (D)
Georgia (D)	(D—delegates-at-large)	(D & R—delegates-at-large)	

(D)-*Democrats*
(R)-*Republicans*

Source: Congressional Quarterly Almanac, 1969. (*Washington, D.C.: Congressional Quarterly Service, Inc., 1969*), pp. 1313 and 1339.

"Our aim is complete and speedy victory. Our goal is a just and abiding peace. Our promise to our world at peace is responsibility and cooperation. . . . To give these modern Bourbons, these Republican leaders, control of the nation for the next four years would bring about the certain return of 1932."

The keynote addresses of recent years have been equally flamboyant in their praise of the party before which they are delivered, and in their denunciation of the opposition. It is difficult to imagine a broad cross section of Americans watching televised broadcasts of such addresses, unless they felt a strong sense of identification with the party. Actually, television coverage of the conventions may change the style of future keynote addresses. Instead of being directed to loyal party followers,

they may become more sober attempts to marshal broad support for a party throughout the country.

■ *Party platform.* Another convention ritual is the composing of a *platform*—a statement of principles and objectives—that the party intends to strive for if its candidate is elected. The policy objectives included in the platform are called "planks" and express the demands of the various interest groups contained within the party. Two members from each state are placed on the platform committee which has several informal meetings to hear the views of various interest groups before the final draft is written. Ordinarily, party leaders and, especially, the President and his advisors if the party is in power, have great influence on planks in the platform.

Much careful attention is given to the formulation of the platform, for it must

Oliphant in *The Denver Post*

(As in 1968, parties sometimes have difficulty placing the planks of all factions within their platforms.)

represent the party to the people during the campaign. The platform is often vague, so that it will appeal to a wide selection of voters.

■ *The nominations.* After the keynote address has been delivered and the party's platform developed, the nominating process begins. First, there are nominating speeches which heap praise on the various hopeful candidates presented to the convention. When all the nominating speeches have ended, the balloting begins. As the roll call of states is made, the chairman of that state's delegation stands and gives the vote of the state's delegates orally.

■ *The ballots.* Sometimes, early political maneuvering enables a strong candidate with a large following to win the nomination on the first ballot or roll-call vote. On the other hand, 103 ballots were taken over nine days in 1924 before a Democratic candidate received the nomination. In recent decades, most Democratic candidates have been nominated on the first ballot. Exceptions have been Franklin D. Roosevelt, who won the nomination of 1932 after four ballots, and Adlai Stevenson, who was nominated in 1952 on the third ballot. The one-ballot tradition has applied generally for the Republicans as well, although in 1948 it took Thomas E. Dewey three ballots to secure the nomination; and in 1940, the nomination of Wendell Willkie required six ballots.

■ *Selection of a vice-presidential candidate.* Once the presidential candidate has been selected, a running-mate, or vice-presidential candidate, must be chosen. Ordinarily, the presidential candidate merely chooses someone from another region of the country, or from another political faction within the party, who he feels will strengthen the ticket. Often the presidential candidate names a person who has proved to be a worthy opponent within the party, and who can guarantee substantial support at the ballot box. The presidential nominee's choice is rarely questioned and the approval of the convention delegates is usually unanimous.

The functions of conventions. Originally conventions were developed to provide rank-and-file party members with an opportunity to participate in the selection of candidates. The national conventions have lost some of this function to the presidential primaries. Primary choices, however, are rarely those of the conventions. Even at the conventions the official choice of the delegates may be directed by strong pressure from a small number of party leaders. For the party in office, it may be the President himself who has the greatest influence on the convention choice; for the out-party, the pressures for the convention choice may come from a number of influential sources, such as the state political leaders, governors, or Senators and Representatives.

Nevertheless, the national conventions are important in maintaining the two-party system. By permitting various interest groups within a party to take part in selecting a candidate, a convention provides the party's divisive elements with an opportunity for coming together, solving their differences, and rallying behind one acceptable figurehead. Party differences are reconciled through the adoption of planks in the platform, the choice of the presidential candidate's running-mate, and patronage promises. Thus, the national conventions discourage the development of third parties which might otherwise grow out of dissident groups within a major party. In parties as fragmented as those in the United States, compromise at national conventions is instrumental in preserving the two-party system.

Party conventions have always been important political ceremonies. They whet the interest of prospective voters in the forthcoming election and inspire party followers. With the advent of television, the electorate has been able to observe the conventions closely; and this has placed the burden on party and convention leaders to put on a good show.

Review questions
1. What is the purpose of the keynote address at a party convention? If the keynote speech were eliminated, would this affect the convention?
2. How do national conventions reinforce the two-party system?

Political Campaigning

Campaigning during presidential elections begins with the close of the conventions and grows in volume and intensity until the crescendo is reached just before the November election. Campaigning in the United States is a big business. The development of mass media, especially television, has profoundly reshaped the nature of political campaigning, whether it is for an office as high as the Presidency or for local level offices. Moreover, professional public-relations techniques have injected a new dimension into campaigning.

Campaigns and the mass media. With the increasing use of air travel as well as public-relations techniques and mass media for campaigning, candidates are able to reach much larger audiences than in the past. Today, a candidate may reach literally millions of voters within twenty-four hours. He can appear on a nationally televised debate in California one day, make a speech in Kansas that same evening in time for reports in the morning papers, and talk to a crowd in Boston the next morning as thousands listen by radio.

In an ideal democracy, the electorate would make its choices by debating the pros and cons of alternative policy proposals made by the various parties. In a modern democratic state, however, ideal conditions do not always exist. The electorate must base its choices, not on the merits of concrete proposals, but rather on the personalities of the candidates and on their vaguely worded statements concerning issues. The appearance of candidates on nationwide television has probably increased the significance of a candidate's personality in the minds of the voters. At the same time, television coverage may encourage candidates to obscure their own views so as to present favorable fronts to different audiences.

Campaigns and public relations. A public-relations man once commented that as far as he was concerned, the only difference between a politician and a can of peas was that one spoke and the other did not. He was suggesting that political candidates could be advertised and "sold" in the electoral arena in the same manner as a can of peas in the supermarket. Maybe the commenter has exaggerated his own importance. Yet, professional public-relations advisers are becoming part of the accepted political picture as they are in most other phases of American business. The public-relations agent, by writing articles for publication, by carefully overseeing the speech-writing activity, by scheduling television appearances and so forth, tries to create an image of his candidate-client that will be most appealing to the voters.

With the election of 1952, the use of public-relations techniques began to appear in political campaigning. This development coincided with the introduction of television as a medium for campaigning purposes. In 1952, both parties hired public-relations advisers.

■ *Campaign goals.* The central objective of the professionally run campaign is to present the personality of the candidate and to concentrate on issues in a manner most likely to win votes. Actually, the vote-getting objective of modern campaigns is no different from the campaign objective of an earlier day.

Modern appeals to the voter differ from the earlier versions only in that they are based on more advanced research into what makes people behave in certain ways. Studies show that people are more apt to react to things involving their feelings than to things about which they are completely objective. Because public-relations and advertising agencies want to guide people into coming to certain conclusions, they present their messages so as to appeal to what people feel rather than to what they think. This is equally true whether they want to sell toothpaste or to win an election.

Before the New York City mayoralty election in 1969, the primary campaign of Robert F. Wagner illustrated the use of professional techniques to appeal to the emotions of voters. During the campaign, television audiences were exposed to spot commercials in which the candidate appeared and suggested that people not come to the polls after dark. By appealing to peoples' fear of crime, Wagner was implying that if he was elected, he would make the streets safe at night.

Campaign expenditures. Political campaigns today are characterized not only by the extensive use of public relations and advertising techniques but also by the large expenditures made for these two items, as well as for the rest of the campaign hoopla. There are campaign costs

GHOST TO GHOST NETWORK

Courtesy of Walt Kelly. Copyright © 1960 Walt Kelly.

(Is it possible for a candidate's image to be entirely molded by public-relations techniques in a campaign?)

for office rents, billboards, telephones, electricity, pamphlets, auto rentals, contributions to a local volunteer firemen's ball, hot dogs at the Boy Scout Jamboree, and a thousand other items.

Any reasonable estimate of the costs incurred during the 1968 campaign for presidential, congressional, and local offices would probably exceed $250 million. The actual figure is difficult to ascertain. Reported expenditures are not necessarily equal to actual expenditures.

Under the Corrupt Practices Act of 1925, Senators must report campaign costs and contributions to the Secretary of the Senate; similar reports of campaigns for the Presidency and the House must be made to the Clerk of the House of Representatives by the national party committees or by individuals. Still there are a number of loopholes in the Act. In 1968 the television and radio campaigns alone involved reported expenditures of about $50 million.

219

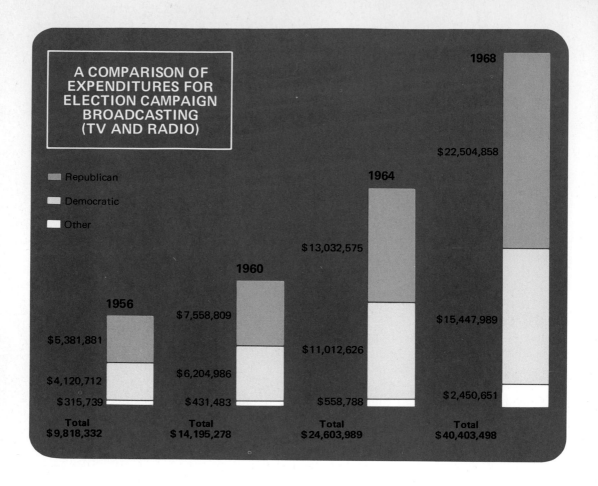

A COMPARISON OF
EXPENDITURES FOR
ELECTION CAMPAIGN
BROADCASTING
(TV AND RADIO)

■ Republican
□ Democratic
□ Other

1956
$5,381,881
$4,120,712
$315,739
Total
$9,818,332

1960
$7,558,809
$6,204,986
$431,483
Total
$14,195,278

1964
$13,032,575
$11,012,626
$558,788
Total
$24,603,989

1968
$22,504,858
$15,447,989
$2,450,651
Total
$40,403,498

But another $10 million was spent in primary campaigns, none of which had to be reported because the Act does not cover primary elections. Candidates avoid reporting certain sums by stating that funds have been spent in their behalf but without their knowledge. Corporations and unions both contribute indirectly by lending office equipment or the time of their employees to register voters, or by campaigning in "house organs" and union newspapers. These contributions also go unreported.

The need for vast sums of money to run campaigns raises the question of the influence of contributors on party programs. Dinners honoring the candidates at $1,000 a plate are not uncommon. The President's Club, an innovation of John Kennedy, usually earned for its $1,000-a-year members personal privileges including visits with the President. In 1964 more than 40 percent of the contributions to the Democratic presidential campaign were in lump sums over $10,000. With political parties relying so extensively on contributions of such magnitude, it is natural to assume that they might be influenced somewhat by their larger contributors.

Fund raisers who have been particularly adept at winning contributions for a candidate have also been suspected of having certain privileges and influences over the candidate. These suspicions may or may not be true. Certainly all fund raisers and contributors do not enjoy the favors meted out by a successful campaigner.

It is conceivable, of course, that a politician could be "bought" by a big campaign contributor but this would only happen rarely, and the cases reported have been few. Possibly, more rigid legislation should be enacted to restrict any obligation that a candidate might have to a contributor. But strict laws by themselves will not lessen the necessity for campaign expenditures. As in the past, tremendous demands will continue to be placed on politicians who want to get messages to large audiences by means of mass communications.

Effect of the ballot. Political campaigning has also been influenced by the type of ballot used in the election. Two types of ballot are used in the United States—the *single-choice* and the *multiple-choice* ballot. The states decide which form of ballot they prefer. Both types are marked in secret by the voters. The votes are then placed in ballot boxes or are tabulated by voting machines.

■ *Single-choice ballots.* On a single-choice ballot, each party's candidates for various offices are listed in a column, or party "ticket." Thus, the voter has the option, if he desires, of voting for all of the party's candidates from President to local city councilman by simply marking one spot on the ballot, usually under the party's symbol.

■ *Multiple-choice ballots.* Multiple-choice ballots require more effort from the voter. Each candidate is listed on the ballot with other candidates for the same office. Although each candidate's party is indicated, the voter must search for this information; and he votes for each office separately. This form of ballot is more flexible but is often thought to be more confusing. On the other hand, it makes it easier for the voter to switch from one party to another as he votes.

Whether the ballot is single- or multiple-choice, the party must gear its campaign to take this into account. Where the single-choice ballot is used, the campaigner will try to identify more closely with the party. Because a strong candidate will sometimes pull the rest of the slate or ticket with him, the party is going to concentrate the campaign on popular candidates. Where a multiple-choice ballot is used, each candidate must stand on his own campaign and impress the voters with his own abilities. The voter, in this case, is more likely to vote on familiarity with the names and deeds of candidates than solely for the party.

Review questions

1. How are professional public-relations firms being used by candidates seeking public office?
2. How does the type of ballot affect the way a campaign is run?

Types of Elections

Once the voter is in the voting booth, the campaign is over and the election has begun. It is the election process that gives real meaning to democracy, because it is through the election that people can express their political hopes and dissatisfac- tions to government. Without the opportunity to choose among different alternatives, however, such expressions by the people have little meaning and democracy can not function. It is the element of choice in elections that makes the difference between democracy on one hand and an authoritarian form of government on the other. There is certainly more meaning to a multi-party choice, as in the elections of France, the United States, or Japan, than there is in the one-party ballots of the Soviet Union or Spain.

Essentially, the results of elections reflect popular attitudes toward governmental policies, personalities, and parties. Changes in the electorate's attitudes will produce changes in the outcomes of elections.

Every election is different from every other election. For example, the Democratic-party landslide in the 1932 presidential election was profoundly different from the Democratic party's victory in 1960, when John Kennedy squeaked into the White House with less than a one percent margin over his opponent in the popular vote. The issues were different, the electorate was different, and the resultant elections were different.

Classification of elections. Members of the Survey Research Center at the University of Michigan, as well as the late V.O. Key, Jr., the political scientist, developed a classification of elections that is useful in analyzing how the electoral system works and what the long-range results are. These researchers feel that presidential elections not only have the immediate effect of electing a President for the next four years, but also show trends and indicate radical changes in the electorate's thinking about politics in general. On the basis of such indications, researchers have divided elections into four categories: maintaining elections, critical or realigning elections, deviating elections, and reinstating elections.

■ *Maintaining elections.* The type of election that occurs most frequently is the *maintaining* election. This is an election in which the electorate, voting according to previously established voting patterns, re-tains the party already in power. In other words, the balance of the parties in government remains about the same as it was before the election.

Most American elections fall into this category, thus producing a pattern of political continuity. A series of maintaining elections over a few decades would indicate a lack of any drastic changes within the electorate and government. Accepting the status quo, most voters go along with the political party in power.

There were several eras of maintaining elections--one immediately following the Civil War, one at the turn of this century, and another during the 1920's—during which Republican control was virtually uninterrupted. Similarly, after 1932, the Democratic victories of 1936, 1940, 1944, and 1948 can all be categorized as maintaining elections.

■ *Critical or realigning elections.* When voters diverge from their ordinary partisan loyalties, elections become more crucial. This is true whether the party in office retains its power or not. *Critical* elections are those where there are lasting shifts in the fundamental political thinking of a large portion of the voting public.

By examining a few trend-setting districts in New England, V. O. Key, Jr., concluded that the elections of 1896 and 1928 were critical because new permanent partisan alignments were formed. In these years, the voting in sample New England districts was indicative of what was going to happen in the rest of the country in subsequent elections.

In 1896, there was a decided shift of New England voters, dissatisfied with the Democratic President, Grover Cleveland, to the Republican William McKinley. This shift, which became nationwide, solidified behind a succession of Republican Presidents that lasted until 1912 and was broken only by Woodrow Wilson's two terms.

Although most people think only of the 1932 election as critical because it changed the party in power, regrouping of party alignments had actually begun to take place in New England by 1928. Working-class and urban voters had switched to the Democratic party four years before the first Roosevelt campaign.

■ *Deviating elections.* Unlike a critical election, a *deviating* election is one in which temporary shifts take place in the electorate as a result of temporary issues, and not as a result of a fundamental change in political thinking. A deviating election is most likely to occur when a popular figure is running for the Presidency.

The Survey Research Center's team has established that the Eisenhower victories of 1952 and 1956 were in the deviating category. The personality of Eisenhower was a powerful factor in swaying voters to vote for the Republican candidate. In addition, the voters were dissatisfied with the Democratic party's performance during the second Truman administration. The issue of corruption in the federal government was raised, and the Korean War had become increasingly unpopular. Eisenhower's promise to end the hostilities won him many votes.

All of these issues, it should be noted, were temporary. No permanent political realignment was established. This was evidenced by the fact that while the President was a Republican, Congress returned to the control of a Democratic majority in 1954 after Eisenhower's first two years in office. The voters did not change their basic partisan loyalties in the state or congressional elections.

■ *Reinstating elections.* A *reinstating* election occurs when the electorate returns to normal voting patterns. Reinstating elections take place after deviating elections when the temporary forces that caused the

transitory shift in partisan loyalty are no longer operative.

The election of 1960 can be classified as a reinstating election. Even Kennedy's loss of a large number of votes because of his Catholicism did not keep the electorate from "reinstating" the Democrats after the Eisenhower years. The Survey Research Center team concluded that

"the eight-year Eisenhower period ended with no basic change in the proportions of the public who identify themselves as Republican, Democrat, or Independent. If there had been an opportunity in 1952 for the Republican Party to rewin the majority status it held prior to 1932, it failed to capitalize on it. The Democratic Party remained the majority party, and in the 1960 election returned to the Presidency."

The Survey Research Center has estimated that the Democratic majority within the electorate approximates 53 to 54 percent. As long as this majority is maintained, reinstating and maintaining elections probably will continue to return the Democratic party to control of the government. Richard Nixon's victory in 1968 substantiates this fact, for while he won the Presidency, he failed to carry many Republican candidates into the Congress.

Evaluation of elections. Elections are essential both to maintain the stability of the democratic process and to permit some change within the system. Elections do not, however, transmit an itemized list of popular demands to the governmental decision-makers. They merely determine whom the people want to represent or govern them. It is the representatives who effect the real change in policy.

Thus, an election is just an indicator of how the electorate feels about past performance. If the voters are in accord with what the government is doing, things do not change. At crucial times in history,

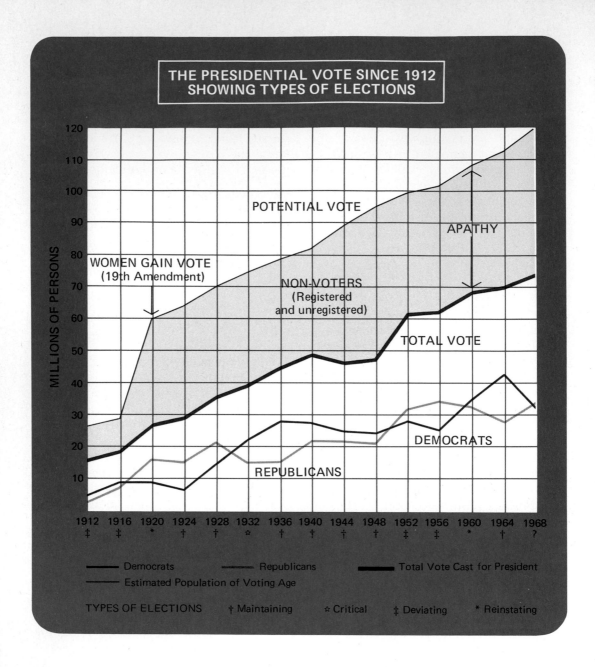

THE PRESIDENTIAL VOTE SINCE 1912
SHOWING TYPES OF ELECTIONS

MILLIONS OF PERSONS

POTENTIAL VOTE

APATHY

WOMEN GAIN VOTE
(19th Amendment)

NON-VOTERS
(Registered
and unregistered)

TOTAL VOTE

DEMOCRATS

REPUBLICANS

1912 1916 1920 1924 1928 1932 1936 1940 1944 1948 1952 1956 1960 1964 1968
‡   ‡   *   †   †   ☆   †   †   †   †   ‡   ‡   *   †   ?

—— Democrats   —— Republicans   —— Total Vote Cast for President
—— Estimated Population of Voting Age

TYPES OF ELECTIONS   † Maintaining   ☆ Critical   ‡ Deviating   * Reinstating

though, critical elections have acted as safety valves for the voters' anger. Such elections have allowed the voters to express their disenchantment by replacing the party in power and keeping it out of power for periods of time.

Review questions
1. Why are elections so meaningful to a democracy?
2. What fundamental attitude about the government is indicated by a critical election? by a maintaining election?

224

Chapter Review

Terms you should know

caucus	direct primary	open primary
closed primary	keynote address	party platform
critical election	maintaining election	party ticket
cross-filing	mixed primary	presidential-preference primary
delegate-at-large	multiple-choice ballot	reinstating election
deviating election	nominating convention	single-choice ballot

Questions about this chapter

1. Contrast the primary system with the convention system for the selection of candidates. Which system is more democratic?
2. How does the electoral-college system affect the selection of delegates to the presidential nominating conventions?
3. Are national political conventions fulfilling their major purpose? Why are they "important political ceremonies"?
4. How is the election process an input of the American political system?
5. "Changes in the attitudes of the electorate will produce basic changes in the outcomes of elections." Explain this statement.

Thought and discussion questions

1. Is it possible for a candidate to lose an election but run a successful campaign? How does this happen? Cite a few examples since 1945.
2. "Only a rich man can win an election." Do you agree? Why has money become a key element in campaigning?
3. What type of party realignment do you envision taking place in America? Would such a change result in a "critical" election on the national level? During what previous historical periods have critical elections taken place? What elements in the political climate bring about such elections?
4. If a national primary system replaced the present national nominating conventions for selecting presidential candidates, how would this change affect local and state political organizations? Would such a move democratize the political process? Explain.
5. Study the diagram on page 224. Which types of election are the most prevalent? Why? Which are the least prevalent? Why? Why is the election of 1968 not identified as maintaining, critical, deviating, or reinstating? How do you think it will eventually be classified? Where on the graph should the potential vote line and percentage of apathy be for the election of 1972?

Class projects

1. From the list on page 215, determine how the parties in your state select delegates to the national presidential nominating conventions. Does the method used in your state affect the organization of the political parties within your state? How? What must a potential candidate do to get the delegates who support him selected? Does past history prove your answer?

2. You are in charge of raising campaign funds for the Representative from your congressional district in the next election. What percent of the budget would you allocate for (a) television, (b) radio, (c) newspaper advertisements, (d) billboards, (e) speaking engagements, (f) meetings with students, and (g) miscellaneous? What criteria did you use to make your distribution of funds?

Case Study: Television and a presidential campaign

Television is now being used extensively in presidential election campaigns. Use of this electronic medium is an easy way to reach millions of Americans. No longer does a candidate for public office have to rely on the newspapers or magazines; he can televise his personality right into the living room. But he must be very conscious of the image he projects. The printed word is excellent for transmitting ideas, policies, and opinions that require concentration and should be reread. The television camera records more spontaneous reactions and will register the candidate's warmth, charm, and polish. On the other hand, it also immediately magnifies any faults in a candidate's image and transmits them to the public before there can be any attempt by his campaign workers or the television staff to correct them, if they are not pre-taped.

Any candidate who wishes to use television to his advantage must also compete with established TV personalities, image for image. Like the TV star, the candidate must appeal to his viewing public. The American viewer is accustomed to the warmth of Merv Griffin and the wit of Johnny Carson, and consciously or not, he will compare a candidate's performance to theirs. The candidate, then, is in a popularity race with his opponent. He would like to believe that his TV performance is better than his opponent's, and that he presents the best image of a President for the country.

Of utmost importance in television campaigning is the ability to project sincerity. The candidate must work hard at being convincing. In his book *The Selling of the President,* Joe McGinniss describes the significance of television in Richard Nixon's 1968 presidential campaign. It is the story about developing a new image for a man who had already experienced the impact of TV on the American electorate.

As you read this selection, look for possible answers to the following questions:
1. What is the importance of political image-making?
2. Why did Richard Nixon discard his 1960 image and develop a new one for 1968?
3. What was Nixon's personal opinion on the relationship between image and getting votes?
4. How important is the Semantic Differential Test in evolving an image? What does it show?

Packaging the President:
The New Political Values

by JOE McGINNISS

Advertising, in many ways, is a con game. . . . Human beings do not need new automobiles every third year; a color television set brings little enrichment of the human experience, a higher or lower hemline no expansion of consciousness, no increase in the capacity to love.

It is not surprising then, that politicians and advertising men should have discovered one another, once they recognized that the citizen did not so much vote for a candidate as make a psychological purchase of him.

The voter, as reluctant to face political reality as any other kind, was hardly an unwilling victim. "The deeper problems connected with advertising," Daniel Boorstin has written in *The Image,* "come less from the unscrupulousness of our 'deceivers' than from our pleasure in being deceived. . . ."

With the coming of television, and the knowledge of how it could be used to seduce voters, the old political values disappeared. "In all countries," Marshall McLuhan writes, "the party system has folded. . . . Policies and issues are useless for election purposes. . . . The shaping of a candidate's integral image has taken the place of discussing conflicting points of view."

Americans have never quite digested television. The mystique which should fade grows stronger. We make celebrities not only of the men who cause events but of the men who read reports of them aloud. . . .

Television seems particularly useful to the politician who can be charming but lacks ideas. . . . Newspapermen write not about people but policies; the paragraphs can be slid around like blocks. Everyone is colored gray. Columnists—and commentators . . . —concentrate on ideology. They do not care what a man sounds like; only how he thinks. . . .

The TV candidate, then, is measured not against his predecessors—not against a standard of performance established by two centuries of democracy —but against Mike Douglas. How well does he handle himself? Does he mumble, does he twitch, does he make me laugh? Do I feel warm inside? . . .

We forgave, followed and accepted [John Kennedy] because we liked the way he looked. And he had a pretty wife.

Then came Lyndon Johnson. . . . He might have survived the sniping of the displaced intellectuals, had he only been able to charm. But no one taught him how. . . .

"The success of any TV performer depends on his achieving a low-pressure style of presentation," McLuhan has written. The harder a man tries, the better he must hide it. Television demands gentle wit, irony, understatement. . . . The TV politician cannot make a speech; he must engage in intimate conversation. He must never press. He should request, not demand.

Warmth and sincerity are desirable but must be handled with care.

Into this milieu came Richard Nixon: cold and aloof. . . .

His enemies had him on two counts: his personality, and the convictions—or lack of such—which lay behind it. They worked him over heavily on both. But Nixon survived. . . .

He nearly became President in 1960, and that year it would not have been by default. He failed because he was too few of the things a President had to be—and because he had no press to lie for him and did not know how to use television to lie about himself.

It was just Nixon and John Kennedy, and they sat down together in a television studio and a little red light began to glow and Richard Nixon was finished. Television would be blamed, but for all the wrong reasons. . . .

The content of the programs made little difference. What mattered was the image the viewers received, though few observers at the time caught the point.

McLuhan read Theodore White's *The Making of the President 1960* and was appalled at the section on the debates. "White offers statistics on the number of sets on in American homes and the number of hours of daily use of these sets, but not one clue as to the nature of the TV image or its effects on candidates or viewers. White considers the 'content' of the debates and the deportment of the debaters, but it never occurs to him to ask why TV would inevitably be a disaster for a sharp, intense image like Nixon's and a boon for the blurry, shaggy texture of Kennedy." In McLuhan's opinion, "Without TV, Nixon had it made."

In 1968 America still saw him as the 1960 Nixon. If he were to come at the people again, as candidate, it would have to be as something new; not this discarded figure from their past.

He spoke to men who thought him mellowed. They detected growth, a new stability, a sense of direction that had been lacking. He would return with fresh perspective. . . .

His problem was how to let the nation know. . . .

Television was the only answer. . . . His television would have to be controlled. He would need experts. They would have to find the proper settings for him, or if they could not be found, manufacture them. These would have to be men of keen judgment and flawless taste. He would need men of dignity. Who believed in him and shared his vision. . . .

Nixon gathered about himself a group of young men attuned to the political uses of television. The key man was Harry Treleaven, a [former] vice president of J. Walter Thompson [an advertising agency]. . . .

Frank Shakespeare, formerly of CBS and . . . head of USIA [at the time], was another of Nixon's television campaign advisers. One night during the campaign he talked optimistically about Nixon's election:

"Let me say this. Without television, Richard Nixon would not have a chance. He would not have a prayer of being elected because the press would not let him get through to the people. But because he is so good on television he will get through despite the press. The press doesn't matter anymore.

"We're going to carry New York State, for instance, despite the *Times* and the *Post*. The age of the columnist is over. Television reaches so many more people. You can see it in our attitude toward print advertising. It's used only as a supplement. TV is carrying our campaign. And Nixon loves it. He's overjoyed that he no longer has to depend on the press."

Another addition to the Nixon staff was Charley Garment, brother of Leonard Garment, now a Presidential adviser, who was a partner in the Nixon law firm and a campaign planner. Charley Garment . . . had been producer of the *Monitor* show on NBC radio.

It was about this time that the results of the Semantic Differential Test came in. Treleaven and Garment and Shakespeare went into the big meeting room at Fuller & Smith & Ross [advertising agency] and watched John Maddox . . . explain what all of it meant.

"The semantic differential is the most sensitive instrument known to modern marketing research," he said. Then he pointed to a big chart on a slide screen on the wall. Running down the chart were 26 pairs of adjectives or phrases such as weak-strong, wishy-washy-firm, stuffed shirt-sense of humor, tense-relaxed, stingy-generous, and on like that. The bad description, like wishy-washy or stingy, was on the left side of the chart, the good one on the right.

John Maddox explained that he had gone all through the country asking people to evaluate the Presidential candidates on the scale of one through seven, and also asking them to evaluate the qualities an ideal President would have. If they thought Humphrey, for instance, was very generous, they would give him a seven on the stingy-generous line; if they thought he was not much of either, they would give him a three or a four. Maddox had plotted what he called the Ideal President Curve, which was the line connecting the points that represented the average rating in each category as applied to the ideal. Then Maddox plotted curves for Nixon, Humphrey, and Wallace. The gaps between the Nixon line and the Ideal line represented the personality traits that Nixon should try to improve. It was considered especially important, Maddox said, that Nixon close the "Personality Gap" between himself and Humphrey.

"It is of substantial significance, we believe," Maddox wrote later in a report, "that the widest gap of all is the 'cold-warm.' We believe it highly probable that if the real personal warmth of Mr. Nixon could be more adequately exposed, it would release a flood of other inhibitions about him—and make him more tangible as a person to large numbers of Humphrey leaners." . . .

The idea was, even if Nixon would not start to act warmer, Harry Treleaven could produce commercials that would make him seem so.

But now, in September, the campaign was starting to drift out of Harry Treleaven's control. Nixon had never liked the idea of advertising men's giving him an image, and now that he had the image, he wanted to get rid of the men. As Shakespeare had feared, Nixon's old friends had pushed their way back to his side. . . .

They told him he did not need television. That if he only would play it safe, wiggle his fingers, say "sock it to 'em" at every stop and use law and order six times in each speech, there was no way he could lose. . . .

Six months earlier, Nixon had said, "We're going to build this whole campaign around television. You fellows just tell me what you want me to do and I'll do it." Now he was grumbling about a one-hour taping session once a week. . . .

The problem was that Richard Nixon really was the 1950's. Richard Nixon did not trust television. He refused to look at himself, even on a newscast. He refused to use a TelePrompTer, no matter how long his speech. . . .

He would not debate. He would not go on the question shows. He said "sock it to 'em" everywhere he went and balloons were sent into the sky in a restrained and organized way. He wanted no part of the campus. . . .

"Everybody has the jitters," Harry Treleaven said. "They all feel a change. They haven't a single damn figure to prove it but they can feel the undecided vote going to Humphrey."

In search of new perspective, I paid a visit to Arie Kopelman, who had been supervisor of the Hubert Humphrey account for Doyle Dane Bernbach, the advertising agency, until Doyle Dane Bernbach had been dismissed.

"A candidate can't be too smooth," Arie Kopelman said. "There have to be some rough edges that cling to the surface of the country and find their way into the nooks and crannies. If a communications effort is too smooth it becomes just that—a communications *effort* on the candidate's behalf rather than a projection of the candidate himself.

"Nixon is hiding behind his communications effort. Humphrey, because he doesn't have one, is out front."

Meanwhile, the new advertising men who worked for Hubert Humphrey had produced a half-hour film called *The Mind Changer*. . . . It showed Hubert Humphrey and Edmund Muskie crawling down a bowling alley in their shirt sleeves. It showed Humphrey wearing . . . a fisherman's hat and getting his lines snarled. . . .

It was the most effective single piece of advertising of the campaign.

It showed Hubert Humphrey as a person. It began with the assumption that of course he had faults as a politician and of course he had made a lot of mistakes, but it said again and again that Hubert Humphrey, at least, is a person. Here he is, sweating, laughing, crying, out in the open air. The contrast with Nixon was obvious. . . .

We were close to the end of this painful and difficult year and the urge was powerful to reach out to a man who cared. *The Mind Changer* matched Hubert Humphrey's heart against Richard Nixon's skills, and the heart seemed by far the more appealing. . . .

The Mind Changer did not look it, but it was a work of genius, simply because it worked. It did not call attention to itself. One did not turn it off saying, "My, what an interesting commercial," . . .

[After Nixon's victory, Harry Treleaven remembered what Nixon had said during the primary campaign about this whole business of image.] "People are much less impressed with image arguments than are columnists, commentators, and pollsters," he said. "And I for one rejected the advice of the public relations experts who say that I've got to sit by the hour and watch myself. The American people may not like my face, but they're going to listen to what I have to say."

Harry Treleaven smiled.

"I don't know why I enjoy that," he said, "but I do."

End questions

1. Is the age of the columnist over? Has TV replaced all other media for campaigning?
2. How did American political campaigns change with the advent of radio and TV? Compare Franklin Roosevelt's use of radio during cam-

paigns with Richard Nixon's use of television. Did both media have the same effect on their audiences?

3. It is not what the candidate is but how he can be made to appear that will get him elected. How do you feel about this new postulate in politics? Can the voter be educated to ignore the candidate's personality and just consider the issues?

4. What do you imagine was the influence of TV on the most recent elections in your community? Does the type of community have anything to do with the impact that TV may have on it?

CHAPTER 10

*The Nature of
Interest Groups and
Their Demands*

"**P**ilots Back CAB's Request for New Airport." "Farmers Like Administration's Soil Bank Plan." "Teachers Threaten Strike Unless Raise is OK'd." As these headlines illustrate, pilots, farmers, and teachers, like most people, often make demands on or support the actions of their government. And they do it frequently through the spokesmen of their particular interest groups.

An interest group is composed of people who share a common concern about public policies which affect them directly. This does not mean, however, that all members of a particular interest group always agree on all policy objectives.

In a pluralistic democracy, pressure or interest groups, like political parties, are vehicles that citizens use to express their wants and complaints to government. Both political parties and interest groups employ similar methods—propaganda and public relations—to influence public opinion. But unlike political parties, interest groups do not supply candidates for political office. Furthermore, the concerns of individual interest groups are narrower and more specialized than those of political parties. Interest group policy preferences are usually expressed directly to the decision-makers in the form of specific information and special demands.

Interest-Group Demands on Policy-Making Subsystems

The importance of interest groups in the American political system can be ascribed to several factors. First, within the political system, the many policy-making conversion structures—at local, state, and national levels—provide numerous access points through which interest groups can make demands on decision-makers. Second, because of the constitutional limitations to political-party control of government, interest groups have been encouraged to play an important role in the policy-making process. Third, the lack of agreement within political parties has often left a demand-making vacuum that has been filled by influential interest groups.

Major categories of interest groups. Interest groups can be divided into two major categories—*private* interest groups and *public,* or governmental, interest groups.

Groups in both categories try to influence the policies and decisions made by various governmental conversion structures to obtain the results they desire.

■ *Private interest groups.* There are private interest groups outside of government that represent almost every facet of society—economic, religious, professional, and so forth. Private interest groups place pressure on all the branches of national government—the legislature, the President, administrative agencies, and the courts.

The judiciary and the bureaucracy are particularly accessible to direct influence from private interest groups. For example, interest groups can bring cases directly to the courts or can make complaints directly to the administrative agencies. Because of their highly specialized functions, administrative agencies tend to rely on the support of those interest-group constituents who maintain close relationships with the agencies. Since the President and Congress have broader electoral constituencies which support them, the private pressure

Why are pressure groups organized and how do they try to achieve their objectives? What functions do such groups perform in a democratic political system that can not be met by other groups and organizations?

233

groups find it harder to influence the decisions of these two branches.

■ *Public interest groups.* The second major category of interest groups is found within the government itself. Agencies, departments, congressional subcommittees, or executive offices of government sometimes act as public interest groups when they have an interest in policies being promoted by other governmental conversion structures. In the area of antitrust policy, for example, the antitrust division of the Justice Department tends to have a strong viewpoint opposing business mergers. It therefore acts as an interest group in trying to influence decisions of the Interstate Commerce Commission (ICC), which must approve such mergers. The Defense Department also may act as an interest group when it tries to influence the proposals of the Senate Armed Services Committee.

Public interest groups often reflect the views of the groups that they regulate. The ICC, for example, tends to support mergers in accordance with its general policy to promote growth in the industries, such as the railroads, under its jurisdiction. Each administrative agency similarly reflects the attitudes of those groups from which it receives most of its political support. The constant contact between agencies and private interest groups, as they trade specialized information, tends to produce a common outlook.

In addition to administrative agencies, other segments of the government also reflect the views of the private interests they affect directly. For an example, the Senate Armed Services Committee may be very interested in seeing a bill passed to increase defense spending or to have appropriations set aside to build a new type of submarine or airplane. Some of the Senators on the committee may come from areas where defense contracts will benefit the local economy and give jobs to more workers.

The President himself, recognizing that his support comes from one segment of the population more than another, may use his power to influence measures that will benefit those people who support him. For example, he may get a large amount of support from labor-union members, and thus favor legislation that will allow unions certain advantages in their negotiations with private companies. Or he may feel that his political strength lies with urban voters. So he will in turn support those measures, such as more public-housing and mass-transit funds, that benefit people living in the cities.

Interaction of interest groups. Because the structures of government and the various segments of American life have become so interrelated, both public and private interest groups find that the special policies they advocate affect the public as a whole. For example, the demands of labor groups for better wages have led to

Courtesy of Ed Valtman

"I have a feeling I'm being shadowed."

(The President can not make an important decision without considering interest-group support.)

minimum wage standards which in turn affect the profits of business and the prices paid by consumers. Farmers' demands for higher price supports also affect the consumers. Consumer groups which demand more regulation of the drug industry or safer automobiles may at the same time deplore the higher prices charged by manufacturers to compensate for more research or new safety devices.

Often, the demands of any one of these groups will produce responses from several other groups which are affected by the demands. The construction of federal highways produces various responses from several groups—construction companies and labor unions, local governments, farmers whose fields are requisitioned, conservationists who want to preserve a picturesque site, and industrialists who want to speed their products to markets.

Economic interest groups. Despite the overall complexity of the American economy, private interest groups can be divided into three major groups, corresponding to the general divisions of the economy—business, labor, and agriculture. The interests of private groups in each economic sector are in turn reflected in the demands of those public groups which regulate or support them. Thus, for each area of the economy, both public and private interest groups act to achieve the same goals.

■ *Business groups.* The business community includes people who make their livings in profit-making enterprises in such industries as manufacturing, insurance, banking, and so forth. Business is represented by several private pressure-group organizations including the National Association of Manufacturers, the Chamber of Commerce of the United States, and the National Small Business Association. All of these are supported by the Department of Commerce, a primary public interest group for business.

Although the interests of a particular industry may be served by one government department, frequently groups within the industry deal with different government agencies. For example, while the interests of the transportation industry are served by the Department of Transportation, the industry includes specialized interests—such as railroads, airlines, and trucking—which are in competition with each other in a limited number of activities. The Interstate Commerce Commission (ICC) has exclusive jurisdiction over the railroads and also deals with the truckers, while the airlines are regulated by the Civil Aeronautics Board (CAB) and the Federal Aviation Agency (FAA). Each of these governmental agencies, responding to the pressures from its particular constituency, will often independently determine rates, mergers, and other policies that affect all segments of the transportation field.

When several railroads are given the nod by the ICC to merge, the airlines may not be especially concerned. Similarly, the railroads may not be interested in whether the CAB approves an increase or decrease in passenger air fares. The railroads, desiring to drop their passenger service and to concentrate on carrying freight, would probably welcome a decrease in passenger air fares, which would make it impractical for people to take the train. But this type of disinterest does not always prevail. For example, since the airlines and the railroads do compete with each other as freight carriers, any rate policy in this area by the ICC or the CAB might be of great concern to the competing interest.

At the same time that agency policies influence business activities, interests within the business community also affect agency policies. The influence of business on policy-making is accomplished primarily by pressure groups that have direct access to administrative agencies with which they trade specialized information. Subtler business pressures are applied to politicians and legislators when interest groups contribute to political campaigns, or give publicity to government officials.

■ *Labor groups.* During the first third of the twentieth century, America experienced the rise of a powerful labor movement. As the conflict developed between the interests of labor and management before and during the New Deal era of the 1930's, labor succeeded in securing governmental agencies to represent its interests. There had been a separate Cabinet-level Department of Labor since 1913; and in 1935 the National Labor Relations Board (NLRB), an independent agency, was established to handle disputes between business and labor. Both the Labor Department and the NLRB were responsive to the demands of labor groups such as the American Federation of Labor (AFL), the Congress of Industrial Organizations (CIO), the Teamsters Union, and other unions. At first, the NLRB favored the interests of labor groups over those of business groups in cases of unfair labor practices and union representation. The Taft-Hartley Act of 1947 attempted to restore a balance between labor and business. It has been only recently, however, that the NLRB has ceased to rely so strongly on labor groups for political support and has begun to render decisions that reflect the influence of business as well as labor.

The major labor organization in the United States is the AFL-CIO. It includes two giant unions that merged in 1955: the AFL, a federation of unions organized according to trades or crafts, such as plumbers, carpenters, or bricklayers; and the CIO, a federation of unions organized by industry, such as the steelworkers or the automobile workers. Today, the combined membership of this one large syndicate is approximately some 16 million workers. The list of affiliated unions is extensive, and each has a membership list totaling from 100,000 to 200,000 workers. Altogether these affiliated unions represent almost all the craft, trade, and industrial workers in the nation. Outside of the AFL-CIO, there is only one other large labor organization—the International Brotherhood of Teamsters, which claims a total membership in all its units of about 1.5 million.

As labor-union membership grew, it was feared that labor groups would be able to gain control over the electoral process by dictating how their members should vote. Since union members represent 10 percent of the total population, they, together with their families and other sympathizers, could become a significant political force. They could even form a separate political party, or gain control of an existing one. So far, control of the election system has never been realized, though, because the interests of union members are as diverse as those of other groups in society.

■ *Agricultural groups.* There are also special interests groups, both public and private, which represent the agricultural segment of the economy. These groups correspond to the various farm commodities produced, such as dairy or meat products, grain, cotton, tobacco, peanuts, and so forth. Most of the demands made by these groups are funneled through the mammoth Department of Agriculture.

In the private sphere there are three major farm organizations that exercise great influence over farm legislation in Congress and thus help shape the policies of the Department of Agriculture. The American Farm Bureau Federation, the most important of the three, was founded in 1920 and now contains over 1.5 million farm families as its members. It is particularly strong in the Midwest. The National

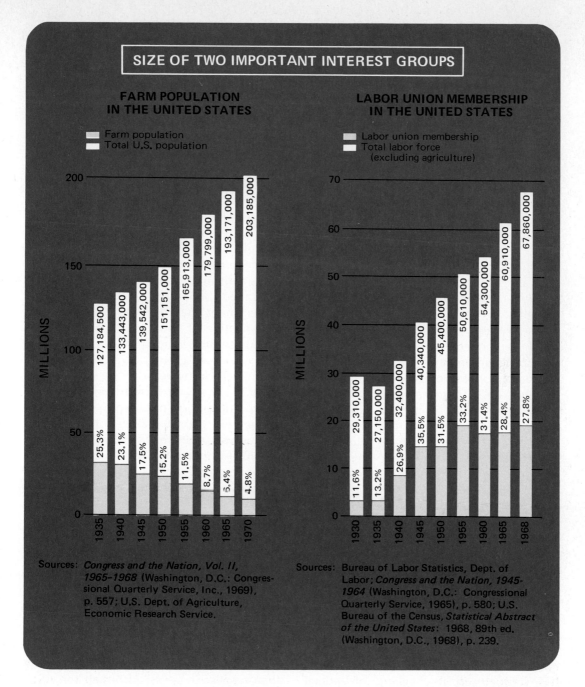

SIZE OF TWO IMPORTANT INTEREST GROUPS

FARM POPULATION IN THE UNITED STATES

- Farm population
- Total U.S. population

MILLIONS

Year	Total U.S. population	Farm population %
1935	127,184,500	25.3%
1940	133,443,000	23.1%
1945	139,542,000	17.5%
1950	151,151,000	15.2%
1955	165,913,000	11.5%
1960	179,799,000	8.7%
1965	193,171,000	5.4%
1970	203,185,000	4.8%

Sources: *Congress and the Nation, Vol. II, 1965–1968* (Washington, D.C.: Congressional Quarterly Service, Inc., 1969), p. 557; U.S. Dept. of Agriculture, Economic Research Service.

LABOR UNION MEMBERSHIP IN THE UNITED STATES

- Labor union membership
- Total labor force (excluding agriculture)

MILLIONS

Year	Total labor force	Union membership %
1930	29,310,000	11.6%
1935	27,150,000	13.2%
1940	32,400,000	26.9%
1945	40,340,000	35.5%
1950	45,400,000	31.5%
1955	50,610,000	33.2%
1960	54,300,000	31.4%
1965	60,910,000	28.4%
1968	67,860,000	27.8%

Sources: Bureau of Labor Statistics, Dept. of Labor; *Congress and the Nation, 1945–1964* (Washington, D.C.: Congressional Quarterly Service, 1965), p. 580; U.S. Bureau of the Census, *Statistical Abstract of the United States*: 1968, 89th ed. (Washington, D.C., 1968), p. 239.

Grange, founded in 1867, lists about 860,000 dues-paying members. It is strong in New England, the Northwest, and Ohio. The National Farmers Union was founded in 1902 and numbers about 250,000 farm families. It is influential in the Plains states and in the Great Lakes region.

In addition to these three large farm

organizations, the agricultural community includes special groups interested in particular commodities. These groups include the National Milk Producers Federation which represents dairy-farmer cooperatives and federations, the National Livestock Feeders Association, the American Meat Institute, the National Wool Growers Association, and others. On the government level, the demands of these groups are focused on the House Agricultural Committee, which is divided into commodity subcommittees. Representatives on each of these subcommittees are generally from districts where the particular commodity is farmed extensively. Thus, they are primarily interested in supporting legislation which will benefit their constituents.

All of these private groups, large and small, are concerned about federal agricultural programs relating to their particular commodity areas and special interests. As in the areas of business and labor, the scope and complexity of federal agricultural legislation is truly staggering. It involves farm price supports, acreage allotments, land diversion, soil conservation, and other programs. Such legislation is of great concern, not only to the agricultural community in this country, but also to other countries which import farm produce or depend on United States agricultural surplus to avoid mass famine.

Because of the pluralism within the agricultural community, there are some basic disagreements among the major farm pressure groups about public-policy goals. The Farm Bureau Federation favors a reduction in the role of the federal government, while the National Farmers Union has stepped up its backing of federal price-support and commodity-control programs. The interests of the small specialized groups are highly varied, too, and often come into conflict, although there

is a general effort among them to secure federal protection for all commodity areas.

Political, professional, and special interest groups. Most pressure groups are "political" in the sense that they strive to advance their own interests via the governmental process. On another level, there are special groups that are based entirely on advancing a particular political philosophy. These groups, such as the Americans for Democratic Action (ADA) or the John Birch Society, are organized solely to represent certain groups whose policy goals are not represented by the large political parties. The National Association for the Advancement of Colored People (NAACP), the American Civil Liberties Union (ACLU), and the Committee for Constitutional Government may also be placed in the classification of "political" groups.

Representing various shades of political opinion, these groups do have access to the decision-makers in governmental agencies. They put forward general policy viewpoints but do not identify themselves completely with any one political party. They most often make demands on and provide supports for special branches of the government. Particularly notable in this regard are the activities of the NAACP and the ACLU with respect to the courts. These groups have encouraged the judiciary to advance civil liberties and civil rights and, in turn, have applauded favorable decisions of the Supreme Court.

Professional groups also play a considerable role in the development of public policy. The American Medical Association (AMA), the American Bar Association (ABA), and the National Education Association (NEA) have influenced legislation affecting their respective fields. Although the AMA could not defeat Medicare legislation in 1965, it was able to shape various proposals relating to it. Undoubtedly, the AMA's continuing interaction with government officials who enforce Medicare will affect future public policy. The ABA affects policy development in all branches of the government, but most particularly within the judiciary and in the Department of Justice. Primarily, the ABA has been concerned with the education of lawyers, the methods of selecting judges, and clarification of laws. The NEA has been working to improve conditions for teachers by demanding more federal funds for education as well as high standards of qualification. Most of its lobbying activity is directed at the national level of government.

Some special interest groups such as those that represent veterans have man-aged to work through several government agencies to obtain their objectives. They have secured several advantages ranging from financial bonuses to civil service preference. Major veterans' lobbies include the American Legion, the Veterans of Foreign Wars, and the Disabled Veterans. Through the Veterans Administration, a government agency, veterans receive over $5 billion in benefits each year.

Review questions

1. What are the differences between private and public interest groups?
2. How is the agricultural segment of the economy a pluralistic one?

Characteristics of Interest Groups

For a lobby (another term for a pressure group) to be effective, it must be fairly well organized so that the goals desired by the membership can be related to the policy-making structures in the government. Any pressure group must solve the problem of setting goals that will really represent the views of the people it claims as members. Once the general goals of a pressure group are determined, then its leaders must decide which of the techniques available is best for getting the results it wants.

Pressure-group organization. Despite the variety of pressure groups and their interests, they all do have some common organizational characteristics. Most pressure groups include: (1) elite members who lead the organizations and formulate the policies and tactics to be used; (2) the lobbyists who work for these elites and bring policy demands to the attention of either the people or government; and (3) the members who provide the basis and

reason for the establishment of the interest group in the first place.

■ *Reasons for joining a pressure group.* People do not necessarily belong to an interest group because they agree with its political objectives. It is true that members of some interest groups, such as the Daughters of the American Revolution (DAR) or the NAACP, do join because they agree with the particular philosophy or general goals of the group. But members of other groups, particularly those which represent economic and professional interests, often join because of more practical or financial considerations. For example, a carpenter may find that he has to join the United Brotherhood of Carpenters and Joiners of America to get a construction job on a building site in his home city. A policeman may find that by joining the Policemen's Benevolent Association, he adds his voice to those of others striving for the same benefits; and a teacher will discover that by joining the

NEA, he acquires group support. In any case, in none of these instances does the member have to accept the group's political goals.

■ *Differences between elites and members.* Just as there are significant gaps between the attitudes of political-party leaders and followers, similar divisions exist between the leaders and members of pressure groups. Sometimes the leadership of a pressure group can not even get support for those policies that clearly seem to be in the group's interest.

For example, since 1947 union leadership has been very much in favor of repealing the Taft-Hartley Act. The Act limits the power of the unions somewhat by outlawing the "closed shop" (an industrial plant where a person had to be a union member before he could be hired), and provides for "cooling-off" periods between the time that a strike is threatened and its occurrence. A survey of union and nonunion workers taken in 1952, however, revealed that while union members favored repeal more often than nonunion workers, the majority of union members either did not favor repeal or had no opinion at all on the issue. In fact, the highest percentages of both union and nonunion workers had no opinion. The data from this survey can be seen in Table 10:1.

About 40 percent of the union members, both blue-collar and white-collar, registered no opinion on the Taft-Hartley issue; and another 20 percent felt the Act should be changed but had no opinion about the nature of the changes needed. Such data indicate that leadership attitudes and intensive group propaganda do not necessarily have an impact on the political opinions of members.

■ *Overlapping memberships.* The limited impact of organized interest groups on their members is due, in part, to overlapping group memberships of some individuals. An individual who is a member of one interest group may have many concerns and will thus belong to several other groups as well. For example, a member of a labor union or professional organization may also belong to a conservationist group, an athletic association, or a political club—all of which compete for his loyalty and support. Add to this the influence of family,

Table 10:1
Union and Nonunion Opinion on Taft-Hartley Issue

Opinion	White-Collar		Blue-Collar	
	Union	Nonunion	Union	Nonunion
Repeal or change to prolabor	23%	12%	29%	10%
Leave as is or change to promanagement	20	20	12	9
Change, no attitude how	22	25	18	9
No opinion	35	43	41	72

Source: Survey Research Center, University of Michigan, 1952.

friends, neighbors, and other informal groups on political attitudes, and it becomes almost impossible for any one interest group to win the complete adherence of all its members to its political goals.

■ *An example of conflicting loyalties.* The goals of different interest groups do not always coincide. Therefore, a person is bound to develop conflicting loyalties for the various groups to which he belongs.

For more than a decade, sharp differences of opinion have been expressed by the American Medical Association (AMA) and the Veterans Administration (VA) over the issues of socialized medicine, health insurance, and particularly the free medical care provided for veterans by the VA. Yet, doctors who work for the Veterans Administration are at the same time members of the AMA. As members of two groups that are diametrically opposed on important issues of public policy, these doctors are pulled in several directions at once. They are confronted with the dilemma of deciding whether to go along with the AMA or to support the Veterans Administration.

Although there is no conclusive evidence on this question, there are indications that VA doctors oppose the AMA on these conflicting issues. It is only natural that a doctor's first loyalty is going to be with the group that employs him. Thus, the VA has more direct influence on the views of its doctor-employees than the AMA does on its VA members. The VA doctor may have only indirect contact with the political pronouncements of the AMA through the Association's professional journal, or through television and other news media.

No interest group can claim that all of its members are completely behind any one policy objective. Overlapping group memberships and conflicting loyalties

From *Straight Herblock* (Simon & Schuster, 1964)

"UH—PERHAPS WE SHOULD HAVE A CONSULTATION."

(It is not uncommon for members of the same interest group to take conflicting stands over a policy goal.)

toward such groups do prevent a pressure group from becoming too powerful.

The mechanics of putting on pressure. Because interest groups are often fragmented by differences between leaders and members, overlapping memberships, and conflicting loyalties, it would seem that the interest groups might have little real influence on government policy-making. Actually, though, some groups are quite powerful, not only because of their lobbying activities, but also because they do command the attention of certain segments of the population by means of their lobbying, public relations, and electioneering methods. Pressure-group activity, then, is a two-way street. Group leaders engage in making demands known to the government, and they gain support from the general public as well as their own members for the policies they are advocating.

■ *Objectives of lobbying.* Although lobbyists are drawn from many professions, the most effective lobbyists are former members of Congress whose access to former colleagues guarantees at least that their cause will be given a hearing. Naturally, the techniques used by lobbyists are highly varied, depending on the individuals and the public-policy issues at stake.

No matter who they are, or how they operate, lobbyists have two principal goals: (1) to influence legislation, and (2) to gain entry into administrative agencies so as to acquire information about how policies affect supporters. Probably the most important function of the lobbyist today is that of obtaining information about matters pertaining to his group's interests. In turn, the lobbyist supplies information to government officials.

■ *Public relations.* Much pressure-group activity today is directed at developing a favorable public image of the institutions the groups represent, in the hope that this may have some influence on the policy-making process. Public-relations techniques are, thus, a primary tool of the interest groups.

Articles may be written for the newspapers showing how a particular industry is joining in the fight against pollution. Or posters in subways and buses may inform the riders of how the International Ladies Garment Workers Union has carried on the fight for better working conditions, and why people should look for the union label before they purchase clothes.

In addition, public-relations techniques are sometimes used by pressure groups to win public support for their viewpoint on an important issue. There may be a concerted effort by a labor union, for example, to educate the public as to why the union favors a countermeasure to the Taft-Hartley Act.

If the pressure-group expenditures for advertising on television, in magazines, newspapers, and other media were totaled, the amount would be staggering. It is estimated that millions of dollars were spent in advertising by the AMA to defeat compulsory health insurance when it was proposed by the Truman administration in the late 1940's.

■ *Electioneering.* A third method used by pressure groups to influence the public and get policy goals accepted by the government is to help elect people to public office. The elected official, it is hoped, will in turn support the objectives of the pressure group. A pressure group, thus, may help a sympathetic candidate's election by contributing to his campaign, or by entering directly into the campaign with its own public-relations staff. It may also try to influence the platform committee of a party about a plank that will benefit the pressure group.

Administrative lobbying and propaganda. Technically, lobbying is a function of private interest groups, but administrative agencies themselves perform a similar function within the government. Essentially, administrative agencies are "interest groups" with definite policy goals they would like to see achieved. To suggest that agencies are involved in lobbying activities raises many eyebrows. Still, the agencies often become major spokesmen for specific policies. As experts in their particular fields, agency representatives are called before congressional committees and consulted in other ways. In addition, their viewpoints are far more likely to be heeded by members of Congress than those put forward by lobbyists of private pressure groups.

Because of their access to Congress, administrative agencies have an inside track on the formulation of legislation. Since they are staffed by specialists who have continuous contact with the subject matter under their jurisdiction, the administrative agencies are often asked to submit ideas about legislation. The passage of legislation without the approval of dominant administrative agencies is virtually impossible today.

Like private pressure groups, agencies employ many public-relations techniques to press their viewpoints in Congress. While an agency can not set up a "publicity department," which would be in violation of congressional statutes, many administrative agencies do have extensive public-relations staffs. As an example, the Defense Department maintains a "liaison staff" of approximately 150 officers to "advise" congressmen on military matters. Another major function of such a staff is to provide the news media with press releases that are favorable to the particular agency. Therefore, an important part of the staff's activities is to maintain good relations with the press. This activity increases in proportion to the administrative agency's strength and its involvement in the process of policy-making.

Review questions

1. What factors tend to split the members of an interest group from their leadership?
2. Describe the techniques used by interest groups to achieve their policy goals.

Interest Groups in a Democracy

Despite their use of the "hard sell" approach through lobbying and public-relations techniques, the pressure groups and their spokesmen in the government do serve a vital function in the overall panorama of a democratic state. Collectively, they are the voice of a large segment of the nation's people.

On the other hand, some people feel that to keep pressure groups within democratic boundaries, they must not be allowed to gain so much power that they could direct the policy-making process entirely. For this reason, controls over lobbying activities have been a concern of government since early in the twentieth century.

Role of interest groups in a democracy. Undoubtedly, the development of interest groups, both private and public, has altered the mechanics of the constitutional system. Government can no longer be limited only through such constitutional devices as the separation of powers and the checks-and-balances mechanism. Government today is large and complex; and many demands for policy that formerly came directly into the legislative arena from the people now filter in by way of the interest groups.

In some cases, it probably appears that interest-group activity does not conform to what would be expected in a constitutional democracy. Occasionally, the leaders of interest groups develop policies that do not conform to the attitudes of the members. Perhaps even more significantly, the elites may make decisions about which memberships have no opinions at all.

If interest groups do not always reflect the opinions of their members, does this mean that interest groups do not function democratically? Can interest-group participation in the governmental process be

From *The Herblock Gallery* (Simon & Schuster, 1968)

"THERE'S GETTING TO BE A LOT OF DANGEROUS TALK ABOUT THE PUBLIC INTEREST."

(Interest groups naturally fear confrontation with any broad consensus that would oppose their goals.)

called popular participation? Democracy does not *demand* the participation of the entire electorate, nor is everyone required to have opinions on all matters of public policy. On the contrary, the democratic process should permit people to participate in any area they feel concerned about. Interest groups provide a means by which informed and politically active members and other interested citizens can participate in the political process.

The power of interest groups. The fact that there are conflicts between pressure groups over goals would indicate that no single interest group could ever dominate the entire government. Still, interest groups do operate in coalitions, thereby increasing their strength. In each of the government's policy-making spheres—defense, budget, transportation, agriculture, securities regulation, labor, health, education, welfare, natural resources, urban housing, etc.—there are coalitions of interest groups that are extremely powerful.

In addition, the general fragmentation of the policy-making process between legislative, executive, and administrative branches, plus the increasing delegation of legislative and judicial power to the administrative agencies, means that final decision-making power often rests with a few people who could easily be swayed by strong coalitions of interest groups. If such groups can gain control of the policy-making apparatus through the administrative agencies, how is the interest of the general public protected?

Formal controls over lobbies. Nothing has occupied American legislators and political commentators more than the power and actions of lobbies. As with other segments of the democratic society, interest groups are limited legally so that they do not gain too much power. Because of the vast amounts of money spent by pressure groups each year on lobbying and public-relations activities, the government has taken measures to limit these activities to some extent. Such limitation has seemed necessary for several reasons. On one hand, it has been felt that lobbies, acting in the name of groups of people and being financed by these people, must be prevented not only from exerting excessive and improper pressure on the government but also from acting against the interests of their own memberships.

In addition, lobbies are often pictured as evil influences on government because, in the past, the activities of lobbyists have ranged from furnishing propaganda to influence the legislative process, to outright bribery, fraud, deceit, and chicanery.

Therefore, some disclosure of the use of funds for lobbying and other activities has seemed necessary.

■ *Early attempts to control pressure-group activities.* Since the start of the twentieth century, Congress has tried to set up legislative restrictions on some interest-group activities. Early attempts at such legislation were directed at eliminating the pressures exerted both on political parties and on individual members of Congress. In 1907 Congress passed a law prohibiting corporations from making political campaign contributions in federal elections. A statute passed in 1909 made it a crime to attempt to bribe a member of Congress as well as to accept such a bribe.

Later, attempts were made to legislate controls on expenditures rather than to eliminate lobbying activities. In 1919 the Internal Revenue Service held that lobbying expenditures were not deductible from federal income taxes by businesses or individuals. The Corrupt Practices Act of 1925 required political candidates to report campaign receipts and expenditures, so that it would be easier to determine who paid for their campaigns. But loopholes in the law have prevented full disclosure.

There were also numerous statutes enacted to regulate corporation and labor-union contributions to political parties. In 1943 the War Labor Disputes Act barred political campaign contributions by labor unions in federal elections for the duration of the World War II emergency. In addition to these statutes, Congress has passed a number of bills designated to halt the use of federal funds by administrative agencies for public-relations purposes, thereby prohibiting the agencies from pressuring Congress.

An attempt was made to control lobbyist activities in 1936 when the House passed a registration bill for lobbyists, but it was never enacted into law. It was not until after World War II that such a measure was finally passed.

■ *The Federal Regulation of Lobbying Act of 1946.* At the war's end, Congress engaged in an extensive investigation of legislative procedures. The purpose was to re-tailor the legislature to meet the needs of an increasingly complex society. The extent of lobbying was also included in these investigations. As a result of congressional hearings, a section of the Legislative Reorganization Act of 1946 dealt with the regulation of lobbying. The major provisions of this Act required lobbyists to register with the Clerk of the House of Representatives and the Secretary of the Senate, divulging their names, addresses, and employers, and to submit quarterly reports of income and expenditures.

The penalty for violation of the registration requirements was set at either a fine of not more than $5,000, or imprisonment for not more than twelve months, or both. Moreover, any person convicted of violating the Act was prohibited for a period of three years from attempting to influence directly or indirectly the passage or defeat of any proposed legislation before Congress. Violation of this section carried either a fine of not more than $10,000, imprisonment for not more than five years, or both fine and imprisonment.

■ *Constitutionality of the "Lobbying Act."* The Lobbying Act of 1946 was challenged before the Supreme Court in 1954. Two years after the bill was enacted, the government had charged several individuals for supposed violations of the registration and reporting sections of the Act. A lower federal court ruled in 1953 that the lobbying law was vague and unconstitutional on the grounds that it violated the "due process of law" clause of the Fifth Amendment. Moreover, the lower court found that the registration, reporting, and penalty provisions of the Lobbying Act abused

First Amendment freedoms of speech, assembly, and the right to petition government for a redress of grievances.

In *United States v. Harriss,* the Supreme Court, in a 5-to-3 decision, upheld the constitutionality of the Lobbying Act, stating that the Congress

"wants only to know who is being hired, who is putting up the money, and how. . . . Under these circumstances, we believe that Congress, at least within the bounds of the Act as we have construed it, is not constitutionally forbidden to require the disclosure of lobbying activities. To do so would be to deny Congress in large measure the power of self-protection."[1]

At the same time, the Court gave a narrow interpretation of the Act. Chief Justice Warren made it clear that the Act applied only to *direct* lobbying. Direct lobbying was defined as including those activities dealing with legislation pending before Congress, and to contributions which "in substantial part" are used to influence such legislation.

Vigorous dissents were registered to the opinion of the Court in the *Harriss* case by three Court justices. Justice Robert H. Jackson contended that the Court had gone too far and was, in effect, "rewriting" the act. He felt that an act of Congress could not be rewritten by the Court in order to be upheld, and he opted for returning the Act to Congress for restudy. Justices William O. Douglas and Hugo L. Black claimed that if the Act were construed as originally intended by Congress, it would be unconstitutional because virtually anyone could be ensnared in a violation. Black and Douglas further contended that even as "rewritten," the Act was unconstitutional.

■ *Registrants under the Act.* The 1954

[1] United States v. Harriss, *347 U.S. 612 (1954).*

Supreme Court decision did little to clarify the provisions of the Lobbying Act of 1946. Today there is a great deal of ambiguity about who is supposed to register. The exact meaning of a "direct" attempt to affect legislation before Congress is still undetermined.

For example, in 1966 the National Association of Home Builders registered a lobbyist in Washington who also had a number of other responsibilites. When asked to identify the particular legislation before Congress that interested him, the lobbyist answered, "I am interested in all legislation affecting the home-building industry and its members." What part of his compensation was devoted to directly influencing legislation before Congress? He

Copyright © 1962 *The Chicago Sun-Times.* Reproduced by courtesy of Wil-Jo Associates, Inc. and Bill Mauldin.

"Thanks, sport – and here's a little something for you."

(Such abuses by some lobbies have resulted in congressional legislation to curb pressure-group activities.)

could not say, and observed that "my annual rate of total compensation is to be $35,000, of which quarterly reports will detail the amount which might be considered to be allocable to legislative interests." He could not relate his expenses in any greater detail.

Since lobbyists are required to report only those sums that are billed to legislation actually before the Congress, total amounts expended by them are difficult to determine. The money spent to influence administrative agencies or in general propaganda is not reported.

Informal protection of public interest. There are some informal mechanisms which also protect the public interest against the excessive demands made by certain interest groups. One such mechanism is community response. For example, a government proposal to eliminate a recreation area, because of demands by business groups who want to develop it, will provoke people into organizing a group to protect the area. Thus, the interests of one group have prompted the organization of a new group for the purpose of counteraction.

In summation, although their interests may be narrow in scope and their methods of operation may be less than forthright, pressure groups do serve a very vital function in our democracy. They do provide a voice for those the many special interests that can not be represented by the broadly based political parties. And they are much more effective than an individual would be acting alone. Pressure groups contribute substantially to the inputs of the governmental system.

Review questions

1. How do interest groups contribute to the democratic system of government?
2. How is the influence of interest groups limited?

Chapter Review

Terms you should know

conflicting loyalties	Lobbying Act of 1946	public interest group
direct lobbying	National Labor Relations Board	registered lobbyist
interest-group elite	overlapping membership	*United States v. Harriss*
lobbying	private interest group	

Questions about this chapter

1. How has the separation-of-powers concept provided for the growth of interest groups, both public and private?
2. How are interest groups similar to political parties? How are they different? Describe how they serve as an input function in the political system.
3. What is the significance of an intra-group rivalry such as that between the American Medical Association and the Veterans Administration? How does this rivalry contradict Madison's fear of control by factions?
4. What is the principal activity of a lobbyist?
5. How do pressure groups influence and promote public policy? How might they affect an election, for example?
6. Why is a good public image so vital to a pressure group?

Thought and discussion questions

1. How do conflicting loyalties within a pressure group check that group's effectiveness? How does this account for the increase in the coalition of pressure groups to attain their objectives?
2. Are interest groups an integral part of the democratic system? Would you say that they are important to the policy-making process? What effect would the absence of interest groups have on a democracy? If they were forbidden, what would this indicate about the condition of the democracy?
3. Could an interest group work against the national interest? Should the activities of interest groups be controlled—for example, as they are by the Lobbying Act of 1946? Are there any interest groups that you feel presently threaten the public interest?

Class projects

1. Try to determine which pressure groups are active in your community. Activities of such organizations as the Chamber of Commerce, the parent-teacher organization, the women's clubs, the service clubs (Rotarian, Kiwanis, Elk), and labor and agricultural groups should be researched through the local paper. Identify the spokesmen for these groups. Can you tell which groups have had the most success in influencing local government decisions? As a result of your research, do you think that membership in a pressure group provides for grass-roots participation in democracy?
2. Find out from the state legislature (Secretary of State) the names of the registered lobbyists in your state, and the regulations governing their activities. Under what conditions must a lobbyist register? How do state regulations compare with federal ones in this respect?

Case Study: A pressure group shows its muscle

The National Rifle Association (NRA) is the most powerful pressure group opposing firearms-control legislation. Founded in 1871 by a group of National Guard officers, its original purpose was to improve members' marksmanship. A little less than a century later, the NRA claimed over 900,000 members and had a budget of more than $5 million. The bulk of this money is spent on the publication of the Association's magazine, *The American Rifleman*.

The NRA has never registered as a lobby, claiming that its functions are primarily educational. But the organization is unparalleled in its efficiency and in its use of propaganda methods. It is actively engaged in distributing copies of proposed legislation to its members, encouraging them to write letters to their congressional representatives, and maintaining complete files of federal, state, and local laws that in some way effect firearms control.

The following excerpts from the *Congressional Quarterly Almanac* illustrate the effectiveness of the NRA in suppressing federal legislation aimed at controlling firearms.

As you read, answer the following:
1. What kind of pressures have built up in the United States for gun-control laws? Describe the catalysts for these pressures.
2. Why is the NRA so strongly opposed to any gun-control legislation? How successful have the techniques employed by the NRA been?
3. Judging from this study, how vulnerable is Congress to the demands of pressure groups?

King's Murder, Riots Spark Demands for Gun Controls

[April 12, 1968]

A single bullet from a sniper's gun at 6:05 p.m. April 4 in Memphis, Tenn., killed the Rev. Dr. Martin Luther King, Jr. The world at once was stunned and horrified.

People were shocked, however, because of the magnitude of the dead man—an apostle of nonviolence and a Moses to black Americans—not because another American had become the victim of hate, and of a bullet.

Assassinations with guns have become part of the American epic. Dr. King, like all civil rights leaders, leading politicians and other controversial figures, lived in fear of it. Four American Presidents are among the dead.

Dr. King's murder, and the ensuing riots, sparked another round of demands for stricter laws controlling firearms in the United States....

A similar outcry followed the assassination of President Kennedy on Nov. 22, 1963. But thanks to an incredible amount of grass-roots pressure from the nation's gun lovers, much of it drummed up by the National Rifle Assn. (NRA), Congress did not act.

In the wake of Dr. King's murder, however, the Senate Judiciary Committee approved, by a 9-7 vote, a gun-control amendment to the Administration's anticrime bill. ... It was the first time since 1938 that firearms legislation had been approved by a Congressional Committee. ...

Every year since 1965, President Johnson has asked Congress for a tough gun-control law. "Congress must stop the trade in mail-order murder," he said in his 1968 State of the Union Message. Attorney General Ramsey Clark pleaded with Congress during 1967 testimony before a Senate Subcommittee: "How long will it take a people deeply concerned about crime in their midst to move to control the principal weapon of the criminal: guns? ...

BACKGROUND

Interest in strengthening federal laws governing interstate traffic in firearms grew out of a study initiated in March 1961 by the Senate Judiciary Subcommittee on Juvenile Delinquency, headed by Sen. Thomas J. Dodd (D Conn.). The study showed that existing federal and state laws did not restrain mail-order sales of firearms to juveniles and to felons, narcotic addicts and other "undesirables." The study also took notice of a vast increase since 1955 in the number of foreign military-surplus weapons of all varieties—rifles, handguns and even bazookas and antitank guns—that were being imported into the United States. These weapons were easily obtained at low prices from mail-order houses.

Possession of and traffic in firearms in the

These excerpts from "Lobbying Activities," and "Floor Action," Congressional Quarterly Almanac 1968 (April 12, 1968; June 7, 1968; June 14, 1968; October 18, 1968) are reprinted by permission of the Congressional Quarterly. Copyright © 1968 by Congressional Quarterly, Inc.

United States is governed by federal postal, licensing and tax law, state laws and local ordinances. The strict gun-control bills that have been introduced in Congress since 1963 have been based on the Federal Government's authority to regulate interstate commerce. . . .

1963–64 Action

In 1963 Sen. Dodd introduced a bill (S 1975) to restrict the mail-order sale of hand guns. It prohibited interstate firearms sales to persons under 18 and required a person (other than a licensed dealer) wishing to purchase a gun in interstate commerce to provide a sworn affidavit that he was not violating federal, state or local law in receiving the weapon. The affidavit was required to list the principal local law enforcement officer, and the dealer was obliged to provide the officer with a copy of the affidavit and a description of the weapon, including serial number. . . .

Following the assassination Nov. 22, 1963, of President Kennedy with a mail-order, military-surplus rifle, Dodd amended S 1975 to cover rifles and shotguns as well as handguns. Eighteen bills of varying stringency were introduced in the House in 1963. . . .

The National Rifle Assn. helped draft the original provisions of S 1975. But the NRA never told its members this. The September 1963 issue of *The American Rifleman* accurately described the provisions of S 1975 as introduced, but there was no mention of NRA support or opposition. . . .

The January 1964 issue of *The Rifleman* told readers that the Dodd bill was "based on irrational emotionalism" and listed the members of the Commerce Committee so NRA members could write letters. In its first four issues of 1964, *The Rifleman* devoted more than 30 columns to firearms legislation, never telling its members of the NRA support during testimony.

At the outset of the hearings, Members reported receiving mail in the ratio of eight to one in favor of the bill. But the tide changed during and after the hearings, with an onslaught of letters against the bill. Hostile correspondents accused Dodd of hasty action and some letters warned that the bill was part of a Communist plot to disarm America. . . .

It was noted, however, that the NRA's legislative and public affairs division, according to the Association's 1963 annual report, spent $144,459 in that year "to inform its members about proposed anti-gun laws" so they could be "alert" to "act quickly and decisively, in a well organized manner, to defeat such threats" to the right of "loyal Americans" to "keep and bear arms." The spending figure was nearly double the amount spent by the legislative and public affairs division in each of the two preceding years. . . .

The Commerce Committee Aug. 11, without a roll-call vote, decided to defer action on S 1975. Dodd called the Committee action "an avoidance of the issue" and an indication that "the gun runners are more powerful than the American people, who I believe want this law." . . . And he threatened an investigation "to identify and expose the activities of the powerful lobbyists who have successfully stopped gun legislation from being passed in every Congress." . . .

1965 Action

. . . On March 8, in his first message to Congress on crime, President Johnson proposed strict gun-control legislation. . . . Mr. Johnson said a "significant factor" in the rise of violent crime in the United States was "the ease with which any person can acquire firearms." . . .

NRA Pressure. On April 9, 1965, the NRA sent a letter to its more than 700,000 members urging them to write their Congressmen to oppose S 1592 [the Administration bill]. The letter said the bill could lead to elimination of "the private ownership of all guns" and would give the Secretary of the Treasury "unlimited power to surround all sales of guns by dealers with arbitrary and burdensome regulations." The letter warned NRA members that "if the battle is lost, it will be your loss, and that of all who follow."

By any accounting, the letter was replete with distortions of the fact. NRA members were told that "anyone engaged in the manufacture of ammunition would be required to have a $1,000 manufacturer's license." In fact, the license fee was set at $500. Furthermore, the letter stated, "Apparently this (license fee) would apply to a club engaged in reloading for its members." It was not clear how the NRA determined that reloading constituted manufacturing of ammunition.

Another paragraph stated: "If you transported your rifle or shotgun to another state, for a lawful purpose, such as hunting, you would have to comply with such burdensome restrictions and red tape as might be required by the regulations." In fact, there were no restrictions in the bill against carrying guns in interstate commerce for a lawful purpose (except for a felon or a fugitive from justice), and there would have been no reason for the Secretary of the Treasury to impose regulations which had nothing to do with administering the legislation.

The letter also stated: "A dealer could not sell to a nonresident of his state." In fact, the bill only prohibited selling handguns to out-of-state residents. Shotguns and rifles could be purchased freely anywhere.

During Senate hearings, Dodd went through the NRA letter paragraph by paragraph and pointed out items he called "patently untrue." Dodd asked NRA officials to correct the record with a new mailing. NRA President Harlon B. Carter told Dodd he felt "a keen sense of responsibility" and would consider sending another letter.

No new letter was sent. In the December 1965 issue of *The American Rifleman.* Orth, the NRA executive vice president, thanked members for the "response to my April letter. Probably no issue before the 1st Session of the 89th Congress drew the volume of mail that poured into the nation's lawmakers in opposition to S 1592. . . . That these letters were effective in preventing the passage of S 1592 is beyond question." . . .

1966 Action

The Juvenile Delinquency Subcommittee March 22, 1966, approved S 1592, heavily amended, by a 6–3 vote and sent it to the full Judiciary Committee.

The full Committee showed little sign of acting through most of the summer. Then, on Aug. 1, Charles J. Whitman stood atop a tower on the University of Texas campus and fired shots at passersby. Before Whitman could be killed by police, he had killed 16 persons and wounded 30 others.

President Johnson Aug. 2 renewed the call . . . and urged the Judiciary Committee to reinstate the ban on the mail-order sale of rifles and shotguns. . . .

On Aug. 25, Sen. Roman L. Hruska (R Neb.) introduced a bill . . . which was limited to a prohibition on the interstate shipment of pistols to persons less than 21.

The Judiciary Committee rejected S 1592, the Administration bill, and instead, on Sept. 22, ordered the Hruska bill reported. The bill was not actually reported until Oct. 19, . . . three days before the 89th Congress adjourned and too late for further action.

1967 Action

In 1967, firearms legislation was approved by subcommittees of both the House and Senate Judiciary Committees, but it never reached the floor of either chamber.

President Johnson stepped up his advocacy of strict gun-control measures, and the President's blue-ribbon Commission on Law Enforcement and Administration of Justice recommended in its Feb. 18 report far stricter legislation than even the Administration had suggested. . . .

In another development, FBI Director J. Edgar Hoover Sept. 1 released an open letter to law enforcement officers urging action to ban mailorder firearms sales, to control interstate shipment of firearms and to require and enforce local registration of weapons.

. . . Dodd Jan. 11, 1967, introduced a bill . . . which was identical to S 1592 as amended by the Subcommittee in 1966. . . .

. . . Pressure intensified in 1967 both for and against legislation.

The National Rifle Assn. Feb. 20 mailed a letter to all members urging them to write Members of Congress to oppose the Administration bill. . . .

Many of the NRA's appeals were emotional and took the form of attacks on persons who supported strong gun laws. . . .

Nine of the monthly editorials in *The American Rifleman* concerned gun-control legislation. The editorial in the November issue defined the "opposition" to the NRA position as either "do-gooders," "politicians," "fanatics" or "extremists determined to destroy what we know and treasure as the American way of life."

"All of these people," the editorial continued, "would like to bury our guns. Some of them would like to bury us, also."

Finally, the editorial described the "enormous propaganda campaign against gun ownership" and asked, "What can be done about it?"

Then it answered its own question: "Help the NRA grow. Time and again, the NRA has proven itself exactly what it is acclaimed for being: foremost guardian of the American tradition and constitutional right of citizens to keep and bear arms. The stronger we make the NRA, the less chance there is that we shall someday lose the right of firearms ownership."

There was no way to judge how many letters, phone calls and petitions this campaign generated. One Congressional aide closely connected with gun-control legislation estimated in 1967 that "hundreds of thousands of letters (opposing gun-control legislation) were received on the Hill." . . .

President Johnson, in both his State of the Union and crime messages, urged Congress in 1968 to stop the trade in "mail-order murder." . . .

❀ ❀ ❀ ❀

House Sends Omnibus Crime Control Bill to President; Final Action Follows Death of Robert Kennedy

[June 7, 1968]

The House June 6, by a 368–17 roll-call vote, cleared for the President's signature the Omnibus Crime Control and Safe Streets Act of 1968. . . .

Final action came the day of the death of Sen. Robert F. Kennedy (D N.Y.). Kennedy died early in the morning in Los Angeles from a bullet wound in the head. He had been shot 25 hours earlier at the conclusion of a celebration following his victory in the California Presidential primary. . . .

❀ ❀ ❀ ❀

Pressure Mounts on Congress for Tough Gun Controls

[June 14, 1968]

Following the assassination of Sen. Robert F. Kennedy (D N.Y.) with a .22 caliber pistol, massive pressure mounted for Congress to enact strict gun-control legislation. . . .

Several times during the week after Kennedy was shot, President Johnson publicly pleaded with Congress to pass a law banning the mail-order and out-of-state sale of rifles, shotguns and ammunition. . . .

Members of Congress were flooded with letters, telegrams and telephone calls urging support for a strong gun law, and some Members who had opposed such a law in the past announced they had shifted their position.

The National Rifle Assn. . . . , champion of the fight against strict firearms regulations, was picketed daily. A Washington-based organization called the Council for a Responsible Firearms Policy began circulating a petition calling for support of the President's proposals and seeking registration of all firearms. . . .

Congressional Mail. Most observers believed that Congress in the past had failed to enact strong firearms legislation, despite the fact that nationwide polls showed strong support for such a law, because of the heavy mail against gun controls. Much of this mail apparently had been instigated by the NRA. But a large proportion of it was spontaneous, reflecting the fact that many gun owners felt strongly that their possession of weapons should not be regulated.

In the week after the Kennedy assassination, however, the tide turned markedly. Tens of thousands of letters poured into Congress from all over the country, nearly all of it favoring stronger regulations. . . .

NRA officials continued to oppose stricter gun laws. Franklin L. Orth, executive vice president of the 900,000-member organization, said there was "no law now in existence or proposed that could have prevented" Kennedy's assassination. . . .

Gun Controls Extended to Long Guns, Ammunition

[October 18, 1968]

Congress Oct. 10 completed action on a major Administration-requested gun control bill (HR 17735). The measure strengthened and extended to long guns and to ammunition the restrictions that had been placed on handguns by the Omnibus Crime Control and Safe Streets Act . . . which the President signed June 19. It not only banned most interstate shipment of long guns to individuals, but also prohibited individuals . . . from buying guns except in their own states.

Together with the handgun provisions of the Omnibus Crime bill, HR 17735 made 1968 the most important year for gun control legislation since 1938. In that year, Congress enacted the Federal Firearms Act, regulating interstate commerce in all types of firearms by requiring licenses for manufacturers, dealers and importers. Except for banning firearms sales to criminals, the 1938 law did not apply strong federal regulations to transactions between dealers and individuals. . . .

Although HR 17735 did not include provisions for licensing of gun owners and registration of firearms—which President Johnson had requested June 24—it was nonetheless a stronger measure than had been considered possible at the beginning of the year. Opposi-

tion to rifle and shotgun controls had seemed insurmountable early in the session when on May 16 the Senate, led by Southern and Western members, rejected by a 29–53 roll-call vote a long-gun control measure proposed as an amendment to the Omnibus Crime Bill by Edward M. Kennedy (D Mass.).

But a wave of public support for controls arose in the aftermath of the assassination of Sen. Robert F. Kennedy on June 5. Like his brother, the late President, Robert Kennedy was killed with a gun. And Robert Kennedy's assassination followed by just two months the fatal shooting of Dr. Martin Luther King Jr., the best-known leader of the civil rights movement in the United States.

A subsequent mass-mail lobbying effort directed at Congress by the National Rifle Assn. . . . eroded some of the newly created support for stronger restrictions (notably that for licensing and registration), but HR 17735 passed the House July 24, and with strengthening amendments, passed the Senate Sept. 18.

Effective Date. Provisions of HR 17735 were to take effect Dec. 16, 1968, with the exception that the restriction on imports of firearms and ammunition were to take effect on the date of the enactment of the bill.

End questions

1. Why was the mail-order sale of guns one of the most controversial sections of the firearms proposal?
2. The increasing use of firearms in crime has made stronger gun control necessary. Do you agree with this statement? Why or why not?
3. In your opinion, how can the crime rate be reduced in your community? Is the cause of crime the weapon, or the person using it? Explain.
4. Is the National Rifle Association an effective pressure group? Is it achieving its goals? What lobbying methods is it using?

Supplementary Reading

BUCKLEY, WILLIAM F., JR. *The Unmaking of a Mayor.* New York: Viking, 1966. This book presents a delightful and unpredictable adventure into the politics of New York City. It generates insights into what the substance of a political campaign in a big city should and should not be about.

BURNS, JAMES MacGREGOR. *The Deadlock of Democracy.* Englewood Cliffs, N.J.: Prentice-Hall, 1963. (Also in paper.) Because of the fragmentation in America's political parties, Burns believes it is more appropriate to view the American party system as a four-party rather than a two-party system. He also raises the question of whether ideological parties are vital to the preservation of a republic.

DAVID, PAUL T.; GOLDMAN, RICHARD C.; and BAIN, RALPH M. *The Politics of National Party Conventions.* 2nd ed. New York: Vintage, 1963. Paperbound. How do the major parties nominate presidential candidates? What factors influence the choices of voters? These are the two fundamental questions explored in this book.

FROST, DAVID. *The Presidential Debate, 1968.* New York: Stein & Day, 1968. Frost has done thorough research into the background of the candidates seeking election in 1968—their speeches, writings, and personal records are all dissected. Frost's interviews elicit the basic personal and political philosophy of each aspirant.

HENNESSY, BERNARD C. *Public Opinion.* Belmont, Calif.: Wadsworth, 1965. This book is a summary of the available scientific methods used to determine "vox populi"—what the public really wants. With the increasing importance of public opinion in determining public policy, this book is essential to understanding politics.

HOLTZMAN, ABRAHAM. *Interest Groups and Lobbying.* New York: Macmillan, 1966. (Also in paper.) This is a concise handbook on the interaction of legislative actors and lobbyists. Mr. Holtzman has interviewed legislators, staff members, "executive lobbyists," and lobbyists for a number of private groups. By comparing lobbying activities in America and other countries, the author shows how lobbying activities are affected by certain characteristics of a political system.

LAZARSFELD, PAUL; BERELSON, BERNARD; and GAUDET, HAZEL. *The People's Choice.* New York: Columbia Univ. Press, 1948. (Also in paper.) This is a classic study which concentrates on one particular election in an attempt to find out why people vote as they do. A more recent study on voting behavior has been done by Angus Campbell, Philip E. Converse, Warren E. Miller, and Donald E. Stokes, in *The American Voter,* abridged edition (New York: John Wiley & Sons, 1964; paperbound).

MARTIN, RALPH G. *Ballots and Bandwagons.* Chicago: Rand McNally, 1964. The excitement and behind-the-scenes details of five national party conventions are described in this volume.

SEASHOLES, BRADBURY. *Voting, Interest Groups, and Parties.* Glenview, Ill.: Scott, Foresman, 1966. (Also in paper.) Primary attention is given in this volume to three major avenues of mass participation in a democracy—voting, working as members of interest groups, and joining in party-related activity. Readings have been included.

VIDAL, GORE. *The Best Man.* Boston: Little, Brown, 1960. (Also in paper.) Originally seen on Broadway, this play's theme is timeless: "Who is the best man to rule?" The locale is a convention, where we learn why individuals choose to run. Vidal suggests that the best man is the one who combines idealism with practicality.

"The President announces Vietnam troop withdrawal"; "Congress passes a draft-lottery bill"; "The Supreme Court orders desegregation of public schools"; "Interstate Commerce Commission permits railroad to abandon passenger service." These headlines illustrate the structures of the national government in action. Behind the headlines, various political forces have been vying for positions to advance their particular interests. Their demands and support are reflected in the government decisions.

Each branch of the national government—the Presidency, Congress, the Supreme Court, and the bureaucracy—acts as a conversion mechanism within its own policy subsystem. Each receives demands and support from particular sets of interests, and converts these inputs into policy outputs. Rarely, however, can one branch alone determine public policy. The system of shared functions ensures that some cooperation is almost always necessary.

The Constitution's simple formula—whereby Congress would make the law and the President would execute it—has been altered and complicated by the course of events since 1789 when Washington took office. Today, the President and the bureaucracy are primary sources of legislative proposals enacted by Congress. The Supreme Court, too, has become more prominent in government than was foreseen by the Framers.

The change in the relative power of the three branches has challenged traditional standards of constitutional responsibility. For example, since World War II, the congressional power to declare war has been replaced by "police actions" initiated by the President in Korea, Lebanon, the Dominican Republic, Vietnam, and Cambodia. Many commentators and some congressmen feel that Capitol Hill has become too subservient to the White House and that Congress must regain the initiative.

The system devised in 1787 will undoubtedly continue to face challenges in the future. But will the fragmented mechanism of government remain adequate for the needs of a highly technological, complex, and interdependent society? The solutions to many questions of public policy, such as protection of the environment, may require more coordination between the branches of government.

UNIT FOUR
The Conversion Structures of the National Government

CHAPTER 11

*The Congress:
Its Framework,
Members,
and Supporters*

Whatever form the Founding Fathers may have intended for Congress, the responsibilities of the institution have changed considerably in the past two hundred years. The basic framework is still there, but the functions of Congress and of its members have been gradually altered. Like other governmental structures, Congress is constantly being reshaped by the changing forces to which it responds.

As a conversion structure of the larger national political system, Congress receives special demands and supports. When the character of these inputs changes, the character of the legislative structure and functions must also change. Ultimately, the changes in inputs and in structure alter the nature of congressional outputs as well. To understand how these changes have been made and what they mean today, it is necessary to look at what the Framers established in the first place.

Constitutional Background

Under the Constitution, Congress alone was to exercise the legislative authority, while the President and the Supreme Court exercised executive and judicial authority respectively. This formula embodied the concept of parliamentary supremacy—so carefully nurtured in the Anglo-American political tradition—that the legislature was to be the most powerful institution of the government.

The legislature alone was to represent the interests of the people. Therefore, it alone was explicitly granted extensive powers, including the power to tax, regulate commerce, declare war, and appropriate money for the military services, which made it the dominant branch. Yet, because these powers were so carefully enumerated, they also limited Congress so that it could not abuse its authority at the expense of the other branches.

The bicameral framework. As intended by the Framers, the House was to be the forum of popular representatives, dealing with matters of local concern; while the Senate was to be the forum of state governments, concerned with matters of wider national interest. Therefore, the bicameral structure was deliberately designed so that the functions and tone of each house would reflect the focus of its particular responsibilities.

■ *Members and functions.* The original constitutional formula for selecting members of Congress and the particular functions designated to each house were based on the constituency and purpose that each house was to serve. Thus, the Framers provided that members of the House of Representatives would be elected directly by the people every two years. Frequent elections of Representatives, it was felt, would ensure that these legislators would always be responsive to the constituents of their local districts.

While the popular election of Senators was eventually guaranteed by ratification of the Seventeenth Amendment, the Constitution as originally written left the selection of Senators to the state legislatures. This seemed to be a logical arrangement in 1787, when it was assumed that the primary responsibility of the upper house would be to represent the interests of the states as sovereign entities.

◀ What responsibilities besides enacting legislation are members of the Senate and the House of Representatives expected to take on when they are elected by their constituents as delegates to Congress?

Hans Richter. Copyright © 1967 Saturday Review, Inc.

"Did you ever have one of those days when you didn't know whether to advise or consent?"

(The Senate has the authority to give "advice and consent" on treaties and presidential appointments.)

Although all appropriations bills have to be approved by both houses, the lower house—because it alone was to represent the people—was given the authority to originate money bills, which would be funded through taxes paid by the people. In addition, the House was also granted the power to impeach high government officials. The Senate, on the other hand, was given exclusive authority to approve treaties, to confirm certain presidential appointments, and to conduct trials of officials who had been impeached.

■ *The character of the two houses.* When they designed the bicameral legislature, the Framers expected that the two houses would check each other. It was thought that the older members of the Senate would act with wisdom and moderation, offsetting the more enthusiastic approach to legislation that might come from the popularly elected House. As stated in *The Federalist,* No. 62, "the nature of the senatorial trust, which, requiring greater extent of information and stability of character, requires at the same time that the senator should have reached a period of life most likely to supply these advantages."

Thus, the Framers provided that Senators should be at least thirty years old, as opposed to Representatives, who could be elected at the age of twenty-five. Senators had to be citizens for at least nine years, a longer period of time than the seven years required for Representatives. Furthermore, by providing Senators with six-year terms, by leaving their selection to the state legislatures, and by requiring that only one third of the Senate could be chosen every second year, the Framers intended to isolate the Senate from direct popular control and from being swayed by popular pressures. Thus, any rash or unreasonable legislation proposed by the lower house in response to popular whim would be modified or rejected by the more conservative upper house.

Today, on the contrary, the Senate is often regarded as less conservative than the lower house in its approach to legislation. For example, civil rights legislation usually has been passed more quickly by the Senate than by the House. This may be due, in part, to the fact that Senators do not have to answer as frequently as Representatives to their electoral constituents, who might resist legislative change.

Size of the legislature. The Constitution provides that each state shall have two Senators; the number of Representatives allotted to each state depends on the size of its population, with each state having at least one Representative. The Framers assumed that each house would be small enough for all members to participate directly in the enactment of legislation.

The author of *The Federalist,* No. 58, warned that under no circumstances should the size of the House of Representatives be indiscriminately increased, because "in all legislative assemblies, the greater the number composing them may be, the fewer will be the men who will in fact direct their proceedings." Little did the author of *The Federalist,* No. 58, realize that by 1970, the United States would be populated by over 200 million persons, and that the nation would span the North American continent and include noncontiguous states—Alaska and Hawaii.

During the early years of the Republic, the House and Senate were small bodies compared to their present size. The first Senate, which had 26 members, was not much larger than legislative committees are today. Each state subsequently admitted to the Union added two more Senators to the upper house so that, today, there are 100 Senators representing the fifty states.

The Constitution provides that a census is to be taken every ten years in order that the number of Representatives can be properly apportioned. The House of Representatives in the first session of Congress was allotted 65 members. For more than a century, as Congress reapportioned Representatives after each census, the membership of the lower house grew as the population of the country increased. By 1810, the total number of seats had risen to 186; and a century later, in 1910, 435 Representatives sat in the House.

It was determined after 1920 that the House would grow to such large proportions that it would become more and more difficult to conduct debate. In 1929 a reapportionment act was passed that fixed the number of Representatives permanently at 435. While the permanent number of Representatives has remained the same since 1929, the number of citizens represented by each member has increased. Thus, in 1970, each Representative spoke for about 460,000 people.

Officers of Congress. The Framers were aware that certain presiding officers would be needed by the Congress to direct the legislative proceedings. Article I of the Constitution provides that "the House of Representatives shall choose their Speaker and other officers. . . ." It follows this statement several paragraphs later by stipulating that the Vice President of the United States is to be president of the Senate and that the members of the Senate "shall choose their other officers, and also a President *pro tempore,* in the absence of the Vice President, or when he shall exercise the office of President of the United States." As the political parties grew in importance, these posts became the rewards of the dominant party in each house of the legislature.

From *The Herblock Gallery* (Simon & Schuster, 1968)

"NONSENSE—I HAVE A FIRM GRIP ON THE REINS."

(The age of House Speaker John McCormack, who retired in 1970 at 79, irked younger congressmen.)

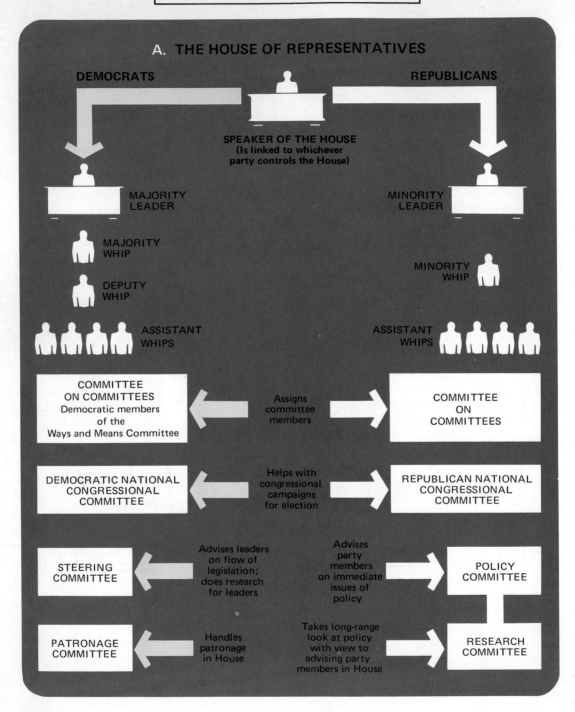

A. THE HOUSE OF REPRESENTATIVES

DEMOCRATS

REPUBLICANS

SPEAKER OF THE HOUSE
(Is linked to whichever
party controls the House)

MAJORITY
LEADER

MINORITY
LEADER

MAJORITY
WHIP

DEPUTY
WHIP

MINORITY
WHIP

ASSISTANT
WHIPS

ASSISTANT
WHIPS

COMMITTEE
ON COMMITTEES
Democratic members
of the
Ways and Means Committee

Assigns
committee
members

COMMITTEE
ON
COMMITTEES

DEMOCRATIC NATIONAL
CONGRESSIONAL
COMMITTEE

Helps with
congressional
campaigns
for election

REPUBLICAN NATIONAL
CONGRESSIONAL
COMMITTEE

STEERING
COMMITTEE

Advises leaders
on flow of
legislation;
does research
for leaders

Advises
party
members
on immediate
issues of
policy

POLICY
COMMITTEE

PATRONAGE
COMMITTEE

Handles
patronage
in House

Takes long-range
look at policy
with view to
advising party
members in House

RESEARCH
COMMITTEE

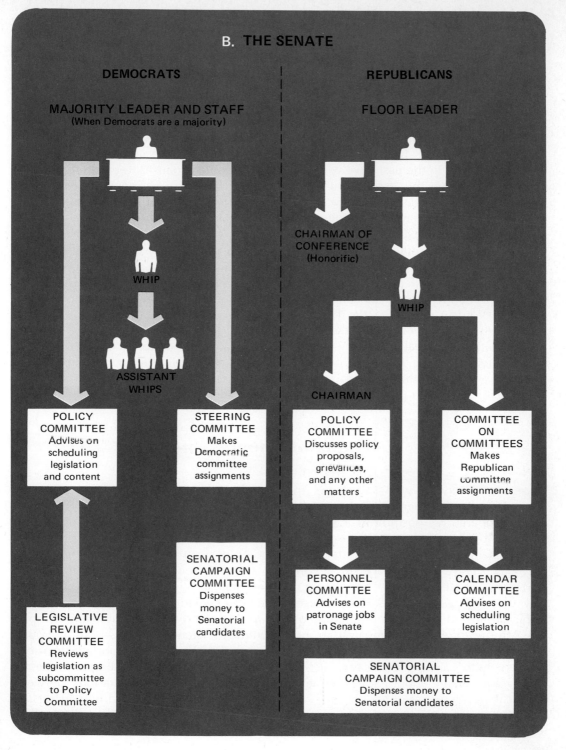

B. THE SENATE

DEMOCRATS

REPUBLICANS

MAJORITY LEADER AND STAFF
(When Democrats are a majority)

FLOOR LEADER

CHAIRMAN OF
CONFERENCE
(Honorific)

WHIP

ASSISTANT
WHIPS

WHIP

CHAIRMAN

POLICY
COMMITTEE
Advises on
scheduling
legislation
and content

STEERING
COMMITTEE
Makes
Democratic
committee
assignments

POLICY
COMMITTEE
Discusses policy
proposals,
grievances,
and any other
matters

COMMITTEE
ON
COMMITTEES
Makes
Republican
committee
assignments

SENATORIAL
CAMPAIGN
COMMITTEE
Dispenses
money to
Senatorial
candidates

PERSONNEL
COMMITTEE
Advises on
patronage jobs
in Senate

CALENDAR
COMMITTEE
Advises on
scheduling
legislation

LEGISLATIVE
REVIEW
COMMITTEE
Reviews
legislation as
subcommittee
to Policy
Committee

SENATORIAL
CAMPAIGN COMMITTEE
Dispenses money to
Senatorial candidates

■ *Speaker of the House.* A very influential individual, the Speaker of the House directs the business on the floor during meetings. He recognizes members who wish to speak and he appoints members to select and special committees. Moreover, since the Speaker is now selected by the majority party in the House, he is also able to use his position to encourage the passage of his party's political programs.

Some Speakers in the past have wielded much power. From the 1820's until 1850, Henry Clay was able to engineer compromises that held North and South together. More recently, Sam Rayburn enjoyed great prestige in the same office.

■ *President of the Senate.* The Vice President serves as president of the Senate, but he is not a member of the Senate and can only vote in case of a tie. He also does not have any control over the order of recognition for speaking on the Senate floor. Thus, the Vice President can not direct the business of the Senate to achieve support for his party's program.

■ *The president pro tempore.* Whenever the Vice President is unable to attend Senate meetings, a president *pro tempore* takes over as the presiding officer. Like the Speaker of the House, the president *pro tempore* of the Senate is elected by the members, and the majority party invariably controls this position.

■ *Other party leaders.* In both the House and the Senate, the majority and minority parties hold caucuses to elect officers who direct the party's programs, plan the party's strategy, and keep all party members informed about bills coming up for vote. The majority and minority floor leaders in each house are assisted by majority and minority *party whips* who act as the liaisons between the party leaders and the party members in that house.

Review questions

1. What basic differences between the two houses did the Framers incorporate in the bicameral legislature?
2. Is Congress still evolving? Explain.

Functions of Congressmen

During an interview with CBS News in June 1967, the late Senator Robert Kennedy compared his position as a Senator with his previous jobs in the executive branch. Somewhat ruefully he noted that the Senate was not the place for action. But then, Senator Kennedy had been in very demanding situations as an adviser to his brother in the White House and as the Attorney General. Compared to his prior jobs, the Congress must indeed have seemed dull. It spends more time deliberating and talking about issues than acting on them.

Freshmen Representatives and Senators usually arrive in Washington full of optimism and even idealism about how they are going to help the country. They soon find that they are in the center of a whirlpool, and do not know where they are going or what they can accomplish.

Congress today is composed of 435 Representatives and 100 Senators. This is a rather unwieldy body, yet it is expected to work efficiently in a disunited and complex political system. Congress is so large and fragmented that most important decisions are made in congressional committees or through informal consultations between members of Congress and bureaucrats.

Congress is the principal lawmaking body in the country, and congressmen in both chambers are referred to as "lawmakers" or "legislators." Naturally, members of Congress themselves consider the lawmaking function their primary responsibility. But as representatives of the people and as lawmakers in a complex political system, congressmen must respond to many constituent demands and perform many functions that are only indirectly related or even unrelated to making laws.

As representatives. As elected representatives of the people, congressmen are expected to make laws that reflect the will of the people who elect them. Therefore, congressmen strive to please their constituents with respect to their legislative actions. But constituent demands only rarely relate to legislation that is being contemplated or debated by Congress. Since congressmen consider thousands of public policies, the general public can not be expected to know which action is being talked about at any given time. Occasionally, of course, an issue of national concern precipitates constituent response at the right time, but these incidents are rare.

A congressman's working relationship with his constituents and, thus, his ability to represent their views are clearly limited by the type of demands that his constituents make. Congressional constitutents are more alert and active on some issues of public policy than on others. Urban voters, for example, usually have stronger views on such issues as housing and welfare than agricultural constituents, who are more interested in farm support programs.

■ *Voter apathy.* Nevertheless, there are few instances when members of Congress are actually guided in their decisions by the electorate. On the whole the public is likely to be apathetic. There is no evidence to support the traditional view that members of Congress win or lose elections according to how well they carry out the opinions of the majority of their constituents on policy questions.

The findings of two political scientists, in interviews with voters prior to congressional elections, indicate the apathy of the electorate in choosing their representatives in Congress. The study revealed that "less than one in five said they had read or heard something about these candidates, and well over half conceded they had read or heard nothing about either." Moreover, in most districts

"... what the voters 'knew' was confined to diffusive evaluative judgments about the candidate: 'He's a good man,' 'He understands the problems,' and so forth. Of detailed information about policy stands, not more than a chemical trace was found. Among the comments about the candidates ... less than two percent had to do with stands in our three policy domains [Social Welfare, Foreign Involvement, Civil Rights]; indeed, only about three comments in every hundred had to do with legislative issues of any description."[1]

Since the voters do not express their opinions on issues when they elect their representatives, how can members of Congress know which legislation to support? There is only one answer. Congressmen must exercise independent judgment and decide for themselves what the interests of their constituents are.

■ *Influence of opinion leaders.* Although most voters are apathetic, there are certain individuals and groups—opinion leaders of a community—who do express their views to congressmen and who rally others to their particular causes. Thus, while legislators may not be influenced by the ordinary apathetic voter, they are often the

[1] Warren E. Miller and Donald E. Stokes, "Constituency Influence in Congress," American Political Science Review, Vol. 57, No. 1 (1963), p. 53.

object of considerable pressure from these smaller segments of their constituencies.

When they respond to the views that are expressed, most lawmakers assume that the wishes of the general electorate are being carried out. This assumption has been refuted by the scholars who conducted the study described on the preceding page.

"The communications most Congressmen have with their districts inevitably put them in touch with organized groups and with individuals who are relatively well informed about politics. The Representative knows his constituents mostly from dealing with people who do write letters, who will attend meetings, who have an interest in his legislative stand. As a result, his sample of contacts with a constituency of several hundred thousand people is heavily biased: even the contacts he apparently makes at random are likely to be with people who grossly over-represent the degree of political information and interest in the constituency as a whole."[2]

Thus, while lawmakers must rely on their own judgments to determine the public's interests, their judgments often reflect the opinions of only a small minority of their constituents.

■ *Party identification.* Despite his relative freedom in deciding what legislation to support, a congressman has to be careful not to oppose completely the view of his political party. In a sense, the legislator chooses his policy position even before he goes to Congress—when he identifies with a particular party. While he may be able to diverge at many points from the positions of his party leaders in Congress or in the White House, he can not completely transfer his allegiance without losing the confidence of the electorate and the support of his party.

[2] Ibid, pp. 54–55.

For example, if a Representative from a heavily Democratic district suddenly started to vote for most of the Republican programs in Congress, there is no doubt that he would be defeated in his campaign for reelection. The electorate ordinarily votes solely on the basis of party identifications and could easily be persuaded to support a more loyal party candidate. Furthermore, party leaders could withhold their support, and influential party members might withhold contributions, which would be crucial for a successful campaign.

Confronted with an apathetic electorate on one hand and the pressures from opinion leaders and party leaders on the other, many congressmen shy away from taking stands on controversial issues. They may even prefer, instead, to support congressional procedures that permit the *pigeonholing,* or filing away, of controversial legislation.

As buffers between government and people. Given the scope and nature of present-day governmental activity, some agent must act for the people in their

Yardley—Courtesy of *Baltimore Sun*

"I love to sample these grass roots."

(The opinion samplings that lawmakers receive tend to come from only small segments of their constituencies.)

day-to-day affairs with government. Congress is the ideal choice for this task. Legislators are close to the people and should understand their concerns and problems. To whatever extent the viewpoints of legislators influence the choices of voters, the ability of congressmen to service the requests of their constituents is at least of equal importance. Congressmen can not afford to ignore these requests. Their "public images" are determined as much by their handling of these non-legislative functions as by their prowess in the legislative arena.

The relationship between a congressman and his individual constituents is often based primarily on his representation of them in counteractions to adverse decisions by administrative agencies. The grievances of constituents usually involve complaints or challenges to measures taken by administrators as a result of legislation already passed. For example, a group of suburbanites may challenge the Defense Department's construction of a missile site close to a residential area. In handling such grievances of their constituents against the government, congressmen have earned the designation by some cynics of "errand boys."

In addition to handling such grievances, congressmen provide constituents with information about governmental action that may have little if anything to do with Congress. Because of the size of government today, members of Congress actually spend far more time in this non-legislative work than in committee work and other activities related to legislation. Some lawmakers claim that these matters consume almost 90 percent or more of their time.

■ *Casework.* Members of Congress refer to the bulk of their workload pertaining to administrative action as *casework.* As a convenience to legislators, many administrative departments maintain liaison groups within the House of Representatives for the sole purpose of answering congressional inquiries about decisions the agencies have made. For example, congressmen receive so many inquiries about actions of the military regarding servicemen and their families that the Pentagon maintains a special office in the House Office Building to deal with these matters.

The Department of Agriculture has estimated that in 1962 and 1963, it spent about 31,000 man-hours answering requests relating to congressional casework. In this regard, the Department received 13,477 letters and 43,201 telephone calls. During the same period, the Treasury Department liaison staff received close to 22,000 requests for congressional information, and the Post Office Department handled about 30,000 requests. This list could be expanded at length. Obviously the volume of representative business handled by Congress that is unrelated to pending or proposed legislation is very great indeed.

■ *An "ombudsman" office.* Proposals have been made to establish an office of "ombudsman," a separate unit of the bureaucracy acting as an agent of Congress to perform the "representative" functions and relieve congressmen of this responsibility. The term "ombudsman," meaning "agent," comes from Swedish. Originally tried in Europe, the idea of the ombudsman office to handle citizen complaints against government agencies has become more and more intriguing to American legislators. In 1967 Hawaii set up the first such office in the United States, and the idea has been proposed since in a number of other states.

Any such office, to be effective, must be independent of the bureaucracy as a whole and a true agent of congressional intent. Although there would be problems of overlapping jurisdiction and conflicting policy, there is little doubt that an ombudsman would facilitate the handling of constituent grievances.

As investigators. In addition to personal grievances expressed to individual congressmen, major appeals to Congress as a whole often occur after an unpopular administrative decision has been made. Here larger interests are at stake. The Food and Drug Administration (FDA), for example, may have ordered the removal of a potentially dangerous drug from the market. Both the pharmaceutical corporations which have done extensive research on the drug and the users who have been relieved by it will demand to know why it has been removed.

When congressmen receive an unusually high number of complaints about a given governmental action, or when a civil wrong or the improper administration of government policy is brought to their attention, congressmen often react by calling for investigations. Such in-depth studies of particular problems are most often conducted by congressional subcommittees. Through such investigations, congressmen publicize major issues of public policy, and thus help to inform and interest the public as well as the other branches of the government.

Beside helping to mold public opinion, congressional investigations increase the public's acceptance of future legislative and administrative changes. For example, widely publicized investigations of crime, labor racketeering, monopoly practices by manufacturers, and so on, may build public sympathy for government policies relating to such problems. In addition, the investigations provide congressmen with information on which to base new legislation. In turn, information and insights gained by Congress are employed by the President, the administrative agencies, and even the judiciary when they make decisions.

From *Straight Herblock* (Simon & Schuster, 1964)

CIGARETTE BOX

(The Surgeon General's 1964 report on "Smoking and Health" led to widely publicized hearings in Congress.)

As researchers. The congressional-committee system is one means of coping with the specialized knowledge needed to make or reshape laws. But the subjects handled by these special committees are often so broad that committee members—with their many other responsibilities—can not hope to match the knowledge of the administrators who deal with the same subjects every day.

Thus, when confronted with these special matters, congressmen must get their information from those who have it—primarily from the administrative agencies and their clientele groups. The views of legislators on policy matters are formed by the kinds of information supplied by these outside groups.

■ *The congressional staff.* Congressmen, however, are not wholly dependent on the administrative agencies for their information. Their own staffs also supply them with information necessary for legislation. The Legislative Reorganization Act of 1946 increased the staffs of congressmen and congressional committees so that legislators would no longer have to depend on the administrative agencies for all their research.

However, the congressional staff members must rely to a considerable extent on outside sources of information anyway. Because the operating agencies of government are the most available repositories of specialized information, congressmen and their staffs still rely on these agencies and on private interest groups for a considerable amount of the information they need.

■ *Institutional staff aids.* Apart from the staffs of the individual congressmen and committees, there are other institutions that aid Congress with research, such as the Library of Congress and its Legislative Reference Service. The Library of Congress contains nearly all books and periodicals published in the United States, as well as many publications printed in foreign countries. It also has available historical items including personal papers, opera librettos, play manuscripts, motion pictures, and prints. The Legislative Reference Service answers congressional requests for information of all kinds. These queries may or may not relate to legislation. Over 30 percent of all congressional requests to the Legislative Reference Service come originally from constituents. Congressmen simply transfer these constituent requests to the Service for an answer.

As speakers, correspondents, and guides. Congressmen must spend a great deal of time performing other non-legislative jobs for the citizens whom they represent. These duties, added to their functions in dealing with a vast bureaucracy, make the congressman's job seem endless.

Congressmen are present at groundbreaking ceremonies, college and high school commencements and parades; they appear on local television programs and attend meetings of all types in their home districts. Congressmen may make policy speeches on some of these occasions, but more often they simply attend because their constituents expect it of them.

A considerable amount of time is spent by congressmen and their staff aides on maintaining some direct contact with individual constituents. In addition to general mailings which inform all constituents of a congressman's activities, letters of a more personal nature often must be written. Sometimes these letters explain legislation, but in most cases they are written to congratulate new mothers, to extend holiday greetings, or to offer sympathy to bereaved constituents. Even if the majority of these letters are composed by aides, a congressman still has to establish the general tone of this correspondence, keep abreast of how extensive it is, and know what subjects are being discussed.

When constituents visit the capital, congressmen act as hosts and arrange tours of Washington. They also must respond to constituent requests for jobs and appoint sons of their constituents to the service academies at West Point, Annapolis, and Colorado Springs. And they make suggestions for administrative and other executive appointments as well.

Review questions

1. Describe the relationship between a congressman and his electoral constituency.
2. What do you consider to be the most important function of a congressman? Explain.

Other Sources of Demands on Congress

The electorate is not the only group that makes demands on the congressional structure through congressmen. Members of Congress must also respond to the President, the administrative branch, and to private pressure groups.

The President. Probably the most important and concentrated source of demands on Congress in matters of major public policy is the President. "The President's program" of legislation is outlined every year in his State of the Union message and in subsequent budgetary proposals and special messages. Many proposals that come from the President also reflect administrative demands. In any case, administrative requests for legislation must be formally channeled through the White House via the Office of Management and Budget. Table 11:1 shows the number of presidential proposals submitted to and approved by Congress, 1954–1970.

Table 11:1

Presidential Proposals to Congress, 1954–1970

President	Year	Proposals		Party Strength				Approval Score
		Submitted	Approved	House		Senate		
				Dem.	Rep.	Dem.	Rep.	
Eisenhower (Republican)	1954	232	150	213	221*	47	48*	64.7%
	1955	207	96	232	203	48	47*	46.3%
	1956	225	103	232	203	48	47*	45.7%
	1957	206	76	232	201	49	47	36.9%
	1958	234	110	232	201	49	47	47.0%
	1959	228	93	283	154	66	34	40.8%
	1960	183	56	283	154	66	34	30.6%
Kennedy (Democrat)	1961	355	172	263	174	65	35	48.4%
	1962	298	133	263	174	65	35	44.6%
	1963	401	109	258	176	67	33	27.2%
Johnson (Democrat)	1964	217	125	258	176	67	33	57.6%
	1965	469	323	295	140	68	32	68.9%
	1966	371	207	295	140	68	32	55.8%
	1967	431	205	248	187	64	36	48.0%
	1968	414	231	248	187	64	36	56.0%
Nixon (Republican)	1969	171	55	243	192	58	42	32.0%
	1970	210	97	243	192	58	42	46.0%

*Plus one Independent Representative or Senator
Sources: Congress and the Nation, Vol. II; Congressional Quarterly 1969, Vol. 25 and Congressional Quarterly 1970, Vol. 26.

"Another one of those bipartisan state funerals."

(A President needs great political skill to get legislators from both parties to support his proposals.)

An examination of Table 11:1 reveals that there are great variations in presidential success in getting legislative proposals from the White House passed by Congress. Both the President's political skill and the relative strength of his party in Congress play a significant part. When the President faces an opposition majority in Congress, his legislative proposals usually have more trouble getting through Congress than when that body is dominated by his own party. This point is illustrated by the Eisenhower years.

During 1954, there was a slim majority of Republicans in Congress and almost 65 percent of President Eisenhower's legislative proposals were passed. But after the congressional elections in November of that year, both houses of Congress shifted to slim Democrat majorities. During the remainder of Eisenhower's terms, the strength of the Democratic party increased in Congress with each succeeding congressional election. By 1960, Eisenhower was successful in gaining congressional approval for only 30 percent of his legislative requests.

On the other hand, presidential success with the legislature is not always assured when the President and the majority in Congress are from the same party. Table 11:1 also shows that from 1961 to 1963, President Kennedy had only moderate success with Congress even though the Democratic party had a majority in both houses of the legislature during this period. By contrast, President Johnson's record in 1965 was extraordinary. Compared to both Eisenhower and Kennedy, he was able to get his proposals passed by Congress with relative ease during all the years of his administration.

While an average of about 285 legislative proposals are issued from the White House yearly, only approximately 25 to 50 of these are of major significance to large segments of the population. Table 11:2 lists the major demands received from the President during an active session—the 89th Congress (1966)—and indicates which

269

Table 11:2

Major Presidential Demands on Congress in 1966

Passed by Congress	Rejected or Delayed by Congress
1. Department of Transportation	1. Civil Rights
2. Truth-in-Packaging	2. Repeal of 14(b) (Taft-Hartley Act)
3. Demonstration cities	3. Unemployment Insurance amendments
4. Rent-supplements funds	4. D.C. Home Rule
5. Teacher Corps funds	5. Truth-in-Lending
6. Asian Development Bank	6. Election reforms
7. Water pollution control	7. Four-year term for House members
8. Food for Peace	8. East-West trade
9. Anti-inflation tax package	9. Firearms control
10. Narcotics rehabilitation	10. International Health
11. Child safety	11. Hospital modernization
12. Vietnam supplemental funds	12. Rural Community Development
13. Foreign aid extension	13. Electoral College reforms
14. Traffic safety	14. Consolidated federal correctional system
15. Highway safety	15. National Wild Rivers System
16. Reorganization Plan No. 1—Community Relations Service	16. Transportation-user charges
17. Reorganization Plan No. 2—Water Pollution Control Administration	17. Stockpile-disposal bills
18. Reorganization Plan No. 3—Public Health Service	

Source: Congressional Quarterly Weekly Report *December 2, 1966, p. 2926.*

of these demands were passed or rejected by Congress.

The President is a leader in the legislative process for a number of reasons. He is leader of his political party and responsible for its program. The cohesiveness of his office allows him to initiate proposals without delay. And he has at his command a vast range of information which flows into his office from the bureaucracy. This highly expert information provides a vehicle through which the administrative agencies are able to make their demands on Congress.

Administrative agencies. When Congress formulates legislation on a particular matter, it tends to rely substantially on the experience of those who deal directly with the area concerned rather than on its own sources of data. The staff of the Library of Congress can only reply to factual questions. It can not advise legislators on general questions of policy, such as: What changes should be made in the weapons system to properly balance offensive and defensive capabilities? What changes should be made in the securities laws to protect the public against fraud and unnecessary stock-market fluctuations? What kind of fiscal policy will promote employment, reduce inflation, and spur expansion of the economy? What type of labor legislation is needed to reduce employer-employee conflict? Should agricultural supports be expanded or modified in any way? Information relevant to such questions is generally in the hands of the administrative agencies and the private pressure groups concerned, and they pass it on to legislators.

Besides obtaining information from administrators, congressmen depend on the agencies for an honest appraisal of what is in the public interest. After all, one of the primary reasons that Congress creates an agency is to deal with the public's needs and interests in a particular subject area.

There is a common bond of purpose between Congress and the administrative branch. Many administrative agencies, particularly the independent regulatory commissions, are considered agents of Congress. Among other things, they are supposed to recommend legislation to Congress when there is a need for it. It is highly unlikely that any regulatory legislation will pass Congress without the approval of the agency that has jurisdiction over the subject matter. Congress may veto legislative proposals from the commissions, but it rarely supports regulatory legislation that has not been cleared by the commission concerned.

■ *Liaison between Congress and the bureaucracy.* The exchange of information between Congress and the bureaucracy takes place on several levels. Formal channels via the Executive Office are used for official communications. Through these channels, the position of the administration currently in power is made known to the Congress. The President's Office of Management and Budget (OMB), acting as the chief clearing house for legislative proposals from administrative agencies, seeks to bring these administrative demands into line with presidential policy.

Budgetary proposals coming from the bureaucracy also must be approved by the OMB. If the OMB approves such a proposal without any major changes, it is evident to the Congress that the President agrees with the purpose and performance of the agency initiating the proposal. Official communications of this sort from the executive branch reflect the policy stand of the party in the White House.

■ *Informal channels.* Often, however, it is through informal channels of communication with the bureaucracy that Congress acquires the most revealing information on legislative matters. While political appointees who support the administration are heard at such formal occasions as committee hearings, career civil servants may not have the same opportunity to make their views heard. And Congress is interested in the opinions of both.

In their informal contacts with congressmen—by telephone, at parties, luncheons, and the like—subordinate administrative officials may express opinions on legislation or even provide aid on the actual drafting of bills. Even though the President may wish to prevent such informal contacts, it is almost impossible for him to do so.

Still, members of Congress who oppose a presidential program that is being supported with vigor will find it more difficult to acquire information from the bureaucracy. Some administrators will defend presidential policy, whether they personally like it or not. For example, congressmen have found it hard to get information from the armed forces even when the military has opposed the policies of the President and the Secretary of Defense. Military men are usually reluctant to testify in open committee hearings, where their views and plans may be aired before the public. In any case, whatever feelings the military chiefs have regarding defense policy are sometimes conveyed through informal channels.

Generals and admirals, of course, have a status that most bureaucrats below the Cabinet level do not possess. They can sometimes act without fear of losing their positions, whereas civilian bureaucrats can not. Subordinate administrators have to be careful when they supply Congress with information that opposes a program of the President or contradicts the views of their department or agency heads.

Pressure groups. The lobbyist plays an important role, too, in making demands on congressmen and supplying information to them. The amount of attention a legislator pays to the views of a particular interest group is often based on the influence a pressure group might have in his future elections. If a congressman feels a certain group is strong in his constituency, he may be more attentive to its wishes.

Many pressure groups—especially the larger ones such as the Farm Bureau Federation, the AFL-CIO, and the National Association of Manufacturers—maintain research staffs that are available to mem-

bers of Congress. Lawmakers can call on such organizations to provide information regarding legislative proposals. Congressional use of such facilities is by no means universal, and many congressmen rely only slightly, if at all, on information supplied by private pressure groups. This would seem to indicate that these groups do not have a profound impact on Congress.

Sometimes private pressure groups influence congressional committees and individual members of Congress indirectly through the administrative agencies. Private groups are important supporters of such agencies, and some of their demands are transferred to Congress by the agencies through legislative proposals. In this way, agencies may support the cause of private interest groups. The Defense Department, for example, wins benefits for the armaments industry when it obtains money from Congress for weapons.

Review questions

1. How effective is the President in getting his proposals through Congress?
2. Why does Congress have to rely on administrative agencies?

Chapter Review

Terms you should know

casework	Office of Management	party whips
"errand boys"	and Budget	pigeonholing
Legislative Reference Service	ombudsman office	president *pro tempore*
Library of Congress	opinion leaders	Speaker of the House

Questions about this chapter

1. How does Congress act as a conversion structure in the national political system?
2. Why did the Constitution originally provide for the popular election of Representatives, but not Senators? When this procedure was changed, what effect did it have on the political behavior of Senators and subsequently on the Congress?
3. What non-legislative duties do members of Congress have? Why are these important?

4. What might the effect of an ombudsman office be on the workload and functions of a congressman?
5. What are the sources of information that a congressman must rely on to determine what legislation is most necessary? With whom does a congressman communicate in order to determine his course of political action?
6. Why is the President a leader in proposing legislation? What tools for drawing up legislation does the executive branch of the government have that are not always available to an individual congressman?
7. What are the formal and informal channels of communication between Congress and the bureaucracy?
8. How do private pressure groups influence Congress, both directly and indirectly?

Thought and discussion questions

1. Do you think there is still justification for a bicameral legislature in the United States? If you had to reorganize Congress into a unicameral legislature, how would you go about it?
2. Discuss the immediate and long-range effects voter apathy may have on our democratic system. How might extensive voter apathy be avoided in the United States?
3. Some citizens believe a Representative should represent the views of his district, while others believe he should serve the interests of the nation as a whole. Still others think he should legislate according to his conscience. What do you think is the proper role of a congressman? Which role does your Representative play?

Class projects

1. Write to the Representative from your district, and ask him how he voted on recent laws passed by Congress. What is his position on current issues and government policies? Perhaps he has a newsletter which explains his actions. Do his positions agree with the interests of your community? Can you determine which interest groups are influencing him?
2. The establishment of offices of ombudsman is gaining support on both the national and state levels of government. Have there been any proposals made in your state for such an office? Write to your state legislature for information. Do you feel that such an agency is needed? Why or why not?

Case Study: Congressmen contact their constituents

The personal letters which Senators and Representatives write to their constituents often reveal personality traits and distinctions that are not evident in their other official communiqués, such as newsletters and questionnaires.

Former Senator Stephen M. Young of Ohio liked to answer personally some of the mail he received, and his writing style and clarity of thought were the envy of other legislators. He had the audacity to answer in kind when someone from home wrote him an insulting letter.

In response to a letter to the editor about him which appeared in the Columbus (Ohio) *Dispatch,* he wrote this letter to his critic. (It is reprinted with former Senator Young's permission.)

"Dear Sir: Reading the Columbus *Dispatch* it was startling to observe on the editorial page a silly and utterly false letter evidently written by some stupid crack-brain who was afraid to sign his name and used your name.

"Feeling you would like to protect your own good name, else that lying jerk might again be guilty of writing a letter which if published would be to your utter discredit, I send for your information this false, and in fact, idiotic statement attributed to you."

Although few legislators would risk alienating voters in a manner such as Senator Young's, nevertheless, publicity is vital to all members of Congress. Legislators want their names to be household words so their constituents will reelect them. Both the content of newsletters and the responses requested in questionnaires sent by members of the House of Representatives to their constituents reveal a great deal about each Representative and his or her constituency.

While reading the following sample newsletters, try to answer these questions:
1. What is the purpose of each newsletter?
2. Should all members of Congress be obliged to send their constituents newsletters informing them of legislative progress?

11TH DISTRICT MASSACHUSETTS
COMMITTEE ON WAYS AND MEANS
NOT PRINTED AT GOVERNMENT EXPENSE

Congressman
James A. Burke
Reports from Washington

INTERIM REPORT

July 6, 1970

Dear Friend:

As your Congressman, I am happy to submit this Interim Report to you on matters which I hope you will find to be of interest. . . .

Following is a partial list of Federal funds which have entered your area to date:

7/3 A grant from the Department of Health, Education & Welfare to St. Coletta's School in the amount of $263,504 for the construction of a new Day Care Facility. . . .

4/28 The award of a contract in the amount of $269,296 from the U.S. Soil Conservation Service of the Department of Agriculture for the construction of the Harland Site of the Pine Tree Brook Watershed Project in Milton for Watershed and Flood Protection. . . .

3/6 A contract from the General Services Administration to the Randy Manufacturing Company in Randolph for footwear and special process clothing which could amount to as much as $163,000 if federal agencies buy according to presently indicated requirements. . . .

July 13, 1970

* * * *

6/12 Approval of a contract by the Department of Housing and Urban Development to the City of Quincy Housing Authority under the Turnkey Concept of the Low Rent Public Housing Program in the amount of $5,083,681 for housing for the elderly.

6/1 Reservation of $4,422,166 by the Department of Housing & Urban Development for the Salisbury Grove Urban Renewal Project in Brockton. A planning advance of $404,556 was also issued this date.

5/28 A grant to the South Shore Community Action Council for a Summer Headstart Program from the Department of Health, Education & Welfare in the amount of $35,656 to serve all of Plymouth County.

5/26 A grant from the Department of Housing and Urban Development to the City of Boston in the amount of $49,978 for Historic Preservation Planning activities. . . .

4/20 A grant from the Office of Economic Opportunity for Self-Help, Inc. of Brockton in the amount of $93,427 for Program Administration, Neighborhood Centers, Community Organization, Manpower Program, Housing Services, Mental Health Care and Economic Development. . . .

4/4 A grant from the National Science Foundation to Eastern Nazarene College in Quincy in the amount of $18,358 for supplemental training for secondary school teachers in the fields of science and mathematics. . . .

3/27 From the Veterans Administration to the Brockton V.A. Hospital an additional $59,492 for the balance of the fiscal year through June 30.

3/17 The Defense Supply Agency awarded a contract to Raytheon Corporation in Quincy in the amount of $247,232 for electronic supplies.

3/12 A grant from the Office of Economic Opportunity to the South Shore Community Action Council in the amount of $111,195 to serve Plymouth and Norfolk Counties to benefit low income residents. . . .

1/27 A grant from the Department of Health, Education & Welfare to the City of Boston in the amount of $1,964,313 to improve the quality and availability of diagnosis, treatment and care for the more than 7 million people living in Massachusetts, New Hampshire and Rhode Island, especially in the areas of heart disease, cancer, stroke and related diseases. . . .

1/22 A contract from the Department of Labor, Manpower Administration, to the City of Boston to train 56 jobless in various skills in the amount of $152,537 for between 9-35 weeks of on-the-job training.

1/13 A grant from the Department of Housing and Urban Development to the City of Boston in the amount of $176,841 for an Urban Beautification Program. . . .

At this time, I would like to invite any young man between the ages of 17-21 who is interested in attending the U.S. Air Force Academy, Military Academy, Naval Academy or Merchant Marine Academy to contact me here in Washington no later than September 15, 1970 in order to receive an application form and information necessary to participate in the Civil Service Designation Examination next Fall.

It is a pleasure to make this report to you and if there is ever any matter of a Federal nature in which you are interested or should you have any difficulty involving the Federal Government, please do not hesitate to contact me. I am always happy to receive your thoughts and be of assistance whenever possible. Remember, my office is always open to you by mail, phone or in person.

With continued kindest regards, I remain,

Sincerely,

James A. Burke

JAMES A. BURKE
Member of Congress

1. What is Burke telling his constituents in his newsletter? What does he hope to accomplish with this type of newsletter?
2. Judging from the financial allocations, how would you describe the constituency served by Burke?
3. Comment on Burke's invitation to young men interested in applying to one of the armed services academies.

Washington Newsletter of
Congressman Michael J. Harrington
6th District, Massachusetts
Washington Office: 1205 Longworth
Building, Washington, D.C. 20515

Vol. 1, No. 1   February 28, 1970
Not printed at Government expense

Harrington Reports

It has now been almost four months since I was elected as your Congressman and I welcome the opportunity to share my experience with you through this newsletter. . . .

For someone who is characteristically a "yes" or "no" type of person, I have found that the past four months have not yielded quite as easily as I might have expected to such direct packaging.

The job is complicated. The issues are complex and unlimited. And the federal government—Congress included—is every bit as large, as unstructured, and as unresponsive as it has been unflatteringly described by its critics.

But before I get into an assessment of my position and views, let me first extend my deep gratitude to the citizens of the Sixth District for their help, for their encouragement, and for their patience as I falteringly set up an office midstream in the Congressional session. . . .

Reluctantly, I find that my somewhat negative assessment of Congress as an effective force in national affairs has been confirmed.

The structure of Congress with its dependency on seniority robs the Congress of fresh perspective, insulates the Congress of relevancy in its actions. Seniority is now the basis for Congressional operation. Committee chairmen who exercise great power through their control of legislation, which authorizes and funds federal agencies, are selected on the basis of the number of years they have served on their particular committees. To gain power in Congress one has only to be reelected and remain on the same committee; rural Congressmen from "safe" districts reach the pinnacle and inevitably their control has worked to the disadvantage of urban areas. More importantly, the constitutional purpose of electing one house every two years so that it might continually stay close to the views of the electorate is patently thwarted by the internal reliance upon seniority.

I believe, however, that change is possible and I will join with other Congressmen working toward this goal. The rules by which Congress operates are not sacrosanct; they were different before and they can be different again.

From another point of view, I have found inaccurate my preelection assessment concerning the role Congress plays as an instrument of service within the Congressional district.

The reality of the demands of the districts have been made clear to me, and I stand corrected. I have learned of the meaningful role that a Congressman must play in bridging the gap between private citizens and the giant mechanism of federal government. I accept that role. There's no doubt . . . that the Congressman and his staff serve as district ombudsmen, as the ear to which any citizen—regardless of party—should turn when his affairs get muddled or misinterpreted in the vast and impersonal federal government. . . .

In sum, this has been a beginning. Not altogether good. Not altogether bad. I hope. In the four months in office I believe we have begun to master some of the mechanics of the job: I know what the different bells mean, I know how to reach the appropriate Congressional liaison personnel to cope with problems which constituents may have, and I know now what the proper channel for filing legislation is. What remains to be defined more clearly is my role in terms of national affairs—in an age when national affairs are immensely intriguing and complex. I certainly will welcome your comments in this regard. . . .

Here's a list of [some of] the legislation which I have sponsored or co-sponsored:
- A bill to establish a commission on marijuana to study its use and laws now existing.
- A bill adding $25 million for re-

search in drug abuse. . . .
- A bill to continue programs in OEO pending authorized funding.
- A bill to lower interest rates to help housing and small business.
- A bill to require the federal government to purchase vehicles equipped with anti-pollution devices when possible.
- A bill to provide increased Social Security benefits. . . .
- A bill to allow class action for acts in defraud of consumers.
- A bill to create a marine resources conservation and development fund.
- A bill to establish a drug testing and evaluation center.
- A bill to provide aid to the U.S. fishing industry.
- A bill to revise the immigration and naturalization act, giving admittance to U.S. on a first-come, first-serve basis. . . .
- A resolution proposing a Constitutional amendment for women's equal rights.
- A call for designation of the 1970's as "The Environmental Decade."
- A bill to expand the Merchant Marine fleet by building 30 ships per year for 10 years.
- A resolution calling for face to face negotiations between Israel and Arab states. . . .
- A bill to provide supplemental funds for urban renewal, model cities, rent supplement and low income homeownership and rental housing assistance programs.
- A bill establishing an institute to coordinate information on juvenile delinquents and to train workers in the field.
- A bill to establish education programs relating to environmental quality. . . .

1. What type of constituency does Mr. Harrington represent? To which groups would this newsletter appeal?
2. How does Mr. Harrington feel about his new job?
3. Why does this letter go to such lengths to show what bills Mr. Harrington has sponsored or co-sponsored?

CONGRESSMAN'S REPORT

May 20, 1970
Vol. IX, No. 1

MORRIS K. UDALL · *2d District of Arizona*
House Office Building, Washington, D.C. 20515

The Environment—What YOU Can Do

It was my good fortune to attend Earth Week gatherings in Arizona, Ohio, Massachusetts, Michigan and Washington State. I spoke to and listened to hundreds of people of all ages drawn together for a common cause: to clean up the mess.

But no speeches or discussions ever cleaned up a river. Therefore, I'm happy to report, letters are coming in from Arizona and elsewhere asking: What can I *do*? That's a key question. Although politicians and scientists have extremely important roles to play, and although new laws and more dollars are needed, these aren't the whole answer. Government can't do the job by itself. What ordinary people do or don't do is even more important, particularly since their support is essential to any meaningful crackdowns by our local, state and national governments.

As I traveled around the country I heard many suggestions which I'd like to share with you. I'll follow these with some personal observations.

INDIVIDUAL ACTION—DAILY LIFE

Even if you are not, and don't intend to be, part of the solution, you are part of the problem.

You and I, in our daily lives, can develop habits which can chip away at "the mess." And during our lifetimes we can make personal decisions which can have a great effect on this planet's environment. Here are some of the suggestions which are emerging.

► Demand from Detroit 60 instead of 360 horsepower. When you trade cars, buy one which consumes less fuel. Since automobiles are the No. 1 air polluter, start at the top in the cleanup campaign. Instead of spending money for model changes, Detroit ought to be producing more efficient automobiles.

► Since you have to drive some of the time, keep your engine tuned, your anti-pollution equipment operating. . . .

► Walk, ride a bike or use public transportation, if available. Support creation or extension of public transit.

► Since production of power for homes and businesses creates pollution, turn off unnecessary lights and equipment. . . .

► Do your best to conserve on water use. . . .

► Cut down on the amount of water you use for a bath or shower. . . .

► Don't over-water your lawn and plantings. . . .

► If you must use pesticides and/or herbicides, use as little as possible. DDT is particularly harmful to the environment. . . .

► Don't dispose of pesticides through the sewer system.

► Keep and use a litter bag in your car and keep your yard picked up. If you are an apartment renter, demand that management keep the surroundings clean.

► Use detergents, shampoos, toothpastes, etc., which do the least damage to you and to water supplies. . . .

▶ Use white rather than colored facial tissues. Dyes used in manufacture can contribute to stream pollution.

▶ Avoid buying products with unnecessary extra packaging which creates both a disposal problem and demands extra tree cutting. Shampoos, for example, shouldn't need an extra outer container.

▶ Return leaves, lawn clippings, etc. to the soil. . . .

▶ Don't play your own TV, radio, record player or musical instrument amplifier too loud. Noise is a pollutant too.

▶ If you are in a position of responsibility with a business or an agency, try to deal with suppliers who have an environment conscience.

▶ Lastly, encourage smaller families. . . .

A STEP FURTHER

Having set your own house in order, you are now ready to start going after others. But bear in mind that the pollution monster has grown among us and was recently unseen except for a few whose counsel over the past decades has largely been ignored. If you are going to convert someone else, it's recommended you try first with a smile and a "please."

Carry your concern into the establishments with which you deal. Tell your grocery store manager you'd appreciate a cleaner parking lot, some natural landscaping, prominent display of quality, natural foodstuffs and returnable bottles. If he's doing a good job, tell him so. . . .

Learn the identities of your area's worst polluters. Whether they are private or public institutions, find out the name of the top executive of each and write him a personal letter expressing your strong concern. (Maybe you can do something to help him.)

Make it a point to attend hearings of governmental anti-pollution groups and local governing bodies to educate yourself and to take a stand on the side of pollution abatement.

Good letters to newspapers are published and widely read; try your hand for a better environment.

GROUP ACTION

You may already belong to some group organized for a civic, business, professional or social purpose. Or your own efforts and interest in protecting the environment may lead you into a group organized expressly to fight pollution. In the latter, concentrate on learning facts and developing strong, responsible stands. In the former, stir interest and persuade your group to undertake specific projects dealing with the environment.

Some suggestions:

• Take your group through the local sewage treatment plant and learn if it is top-notch.

• Invite speakers from anti-pollution agencies.

• Probe the adequacy of such things as community waste disposal, planning for open spaces, ordinances for car, truck and motorcycle mufflers.

• Press for billboard and sign control ordinances. . . .

• Stage anti-litter drives.

• Find out if your community is taking advantage of all possible federal and state programs. . . .

• Put on contests and make awards to progressive business firms.

• If your group is really interested in improving the environment, it ought to take a stand for necessary expenditures, including bond issues. Demand that your air monitoring and enforcement agencies, the water treatment plant, the sanitation department, etc., be adequately staffed, trained and paid.

- As part of the group's education process, talk to developers, utilities, private and university scientists, architects, planners, physicians, recreation specialists, lawyers, and other experts in fields in which you'll necessarily need knowledge.

WHEN THE CHIPS ARE DOWN

If you are really determined to force reform in the way man treats his environment, you have to be prepared for some unpleasant confrontations. They can't always be avoided. No matter what facts you and your groups present, no matter how strong your logic, you will not always be able to win over the opposition. For selfish economic reasons your opposition may elect to fight you—to foot-drag, threaten or end-run.

Be sure you are right and present your case to the media, civic groups, churches and politicians. You may even end up in court as a plaintiff or even a defendant.

Above all, set yourself for a long struggle. Our oceans, lakes, streams, air, soils and quiet were not spoiled overnight. . . .

We are learning fast what we *can* do. We don't know yet if we will *do* what we can. I have hope, though, encouraged by a Tucson second grade girl who wrote me:

"Please help America stay clean. I pick up trash too. Every time when I have a candy and I have the candy wrapper I throw it in the garbage can."

Let's you and I do likewise.

Morris K. Udall

1. How does this newsletter differ from the others presented in this case study? Which newsletter is the most informative, the most relevant to the constituency, the most timeless in content?
2. From reading this newsletter could you tell what type of constituency Mr. Udall represents? Explain.

The questionnaire is an extremely popular means of measuring constituent reaction to current issues and problems. It also allows the Representative to get a closer look at what his constituents want. Although many voters do not answer the questionnaires, those who take the time feel that perhaps their Representative does listen to the people who elected him; and that maybe their opinions do count.

After reading the following excerpts from three questionnaires, answer these questions:

1. Compare the two questionnaires from California. Can you determine the political make-up of the two constituencies by the type of questions and the responses? How do they differ?
2. Which questions are found in all three questionnaires? Why?
3. Can you determine each Representative's political party from his questionnaire and the responses of his constituents?
4. Would you answer a questionnaire if your congressman sent you one? Why or why not?

WILLIAM S. MAILLIARD
SIXTH DISTRICT
CALIFORNIA

COMMITTEES:
FOREIGN AFFAIRS
MERCHANT MARINE FISHERIES

Congress of the United States

House of Representatatives

Washington, D.C. 20515

APRIL, 1969

Approximately 15% of those to whom I sent my 1969 questionnaire responded. The results are tabulated below.

1. In the area of firearms control, do you favor:

     a. Federal gun registration? 35%
     b. State gun registration? 19%
     c. Federal gun owner licensing? 21%
     d. State gun owner licensing? 21%
     Declined to answer 4%

2. ....

3. When it becomes possible to reduce the cost of the U.S. military commitment in Southeast Asia, should the surplus funds be used primarily to:

     a. Reduce taxes? 43%
     b. Reduce the National Debt? 16%
     c. Expand domestic programs? 34%
     d. Strengthen our defenses against nuclear attack? 5%
     Declined to answer 2%

4. In urban areas, should surplus government lands be made available primarily for:

     a. Open space and recreation? 56%
     b. Construction of schools, colleges, hospitals? 18%
     c. Low-cost public housing? 18%
     d. Sale to private land developers? 7%
     Declined to answer 1%

5. The 91st Congress will be considering proposed changes in the method of nominating and electing the President and Vice President. Of the major proposals, would you favor:

REPORT
From Congress

by CRAIG HOSMER
REPRESENTATIVE IN CONGRESS - CALIFORNIA

Dear Friends—

Many thanks to all who helped make the 32nd District Poll a huge success. The results are [in this report.]

32ND DISTRICT 1970 POLL

	YES	NO
1. Do you approve Pres. Nixon's handling of the Vietnam War?	72%	28%
2. Should we stop sending men to the moon?	50%	50%

3. When the Vietnam War ends, the money saved should go first to (check one):

—domestic programs	48%
—up-grading military defenses	13%
—tax relief	39%

	YES	NO			YES	NO

4. Do you favor President Nixon's plan for Federal government to assume some welfare expenses of states and cities   70%   30%

5. Should we elect the President by direct popular vote? . . .   83%   17%

6. Should welfare be replaced for many by a Federally financed minimum family income plan?   46%   54%

7. What are the two most important issues facing the country today? . . . VIETNAM AND CRIME

Congressional Record

PROCEEDINGS AND DEBATES OF THE 91 CONGRESS, FIRST SESSION

WASHINGTON, TUESDAY, DECEMBER 23, 1969

House of Representatives

CULVER REPORTS RESULTS OF FIFTH ANNUAL SECOND DISTRICT QUESTIONNAIRE

Mr. CULVER [Representative from the Second District, Iowa.] Mr. Speaker, again this year, I have prepared a questionnaire on the issues before this Congress and the Nation. . . . I am pleased to report that the response to this fifth annual questionnaire has been the largest one we have ever received. More than 18,000 forms have been returned to date, and they are still arriving in the mail.

So that we could report the results of this survey to the House before adjournment, we have tabulated the first 12,672 returns. . . . I include those tabulations at this point in the RECORD.

1. *The National Budget.* Present inflationary pressures require restraint in federal spending. If you were required to make the choice as to where the budget should be cut, which areas would you select?

	Percent
Defense	55.1
International affairs	30.2
Space	47.3
Agriculture	12.2
Natural resources	2.3
Commerce, Transportation	11.3
Community development	11.7
Education and manpower	6.8
Social security	10.4
Health and welfare	13.3
Veterans benefits	6.2
General government	7.3

2. *Vietnam.* Which one of the following do you consider to be the most preferable course in Vietnam at the present time?

Percent

Immediate withdrawal of all combat forces, while continuing economic and social assistance and maintaining military advisers 14.1

Continued phased withdrawal of American combat forces as South Vietnamese army assumes more responsibility for conducting the war 57.7

Complete immediate removal of any American presence in Vietnam 13.6

Resumption of full scale attacks on the North with any necessary increase in American men and material 9.8

No response 4.8

3. *Foreign Commitments.* Would you favor a Congressional resolution requiring the President to obtain approval of Congress before United States troops are committed to fight in foreign countries?

Percent

Yes 73.7
No 15.7
Undecided 6.5
No response 4.0

4. *National Security.* Which one of the following do you feel poses the most immediate and serious threat to the security of the United States?

Percent

Foreign Communist aggression 17.8
Instability in the developing nations of Asia, Africa, and Latin America 4.9
Radicals in this country 46.0
Unmet domestic human needs which give rise to internal tensions 26.8
No response 4.4

5. *Campus Disorders.* Who do you feel should have the primary responsibility for controlling campus unrest and disciplining students who disrupt the functions of the university?

Percent

The college or university itself . 71.6
Local law enforcement officials 15.5
The Federal Government 9.0
No response 3.9

6. *Social Security.* Do you favor legislation which would provide an automatic cost-of-living increase for social security recipients?

Percent

Favor 70.5
Oppose 16.6
Undecided 10.2
No response 2.6

7. *Consumers.* Would you favor legislation establishing a separate federal agency, either as a full Cabinet-level department or as a statutory office, to consolidate and direct current consumer programs and serve as a spokesman for consumer interests?

Percent

Favor 43.2
Oppose 28.1
Undecided 22.3
No response 6.4

8. *Agriculture.* The present farm program will expire in 1970, and various proposals are now under consideration by the Congress. Which one of the following do you feel would best meet the needs of Iowa farmers and a generally stable agricultural economy?

Percent

Continuation of present programs, based on voluntary annual acreage diversion and price supports for individual commodities, with changes and additions which experience has proven necessary .. 35.7

Shift from present annual acreage control and direct payments to general long-term land retirement, emphasizing whole farm retirements 10.4

No farm program 19.7
Undecided 26.6
No response 7.6

Exactly how are the interests and demands of voters and pressure groups transformed into laws? What obstacles must legislative proposals hurdle before they are enacted into statutes?

The complicated procedure by which proposals are first introduced in either house of Congress, then referred to committee for debate, re-debated by the entire chamber, and finally voted on is time-consuming and full of procedural pitfalls. And that's only half of the process. The whole cycle is repeated in the other house before a bill is sent to the President for his signature. It is no wonder that members of Congress and their constituents become impatient with this slow and cumbersome procedure.

First Steps in the Lawmaking Process

Like the other conversion structures of the government, Congress deals with demands and makes policy. The first step in this process is to determine the nature and urgency of inputs coming from the electorate, the Presidency, the administrative branch, and private pressure groups into the congressional structure. The next step is to put the congressional apparatus into action that will transform the demands into outputs, or laws.

Introduction of bills or resolutions. Proposals introduced and enacted by Congress may take the form of either bills or resolutions. *Bills* are proposed laws and fall into two principal categories—public bills and private bills. *Public bills* deal with matters that apply to everyone, such as voting rights, appropriations for education, or reform of government agencies. *Private bills,* on the other hand, refer only to certain named individuals. Many private bills concern foreign citizens who are requesting dispensation from regular immigration requirements; others concern individual citizens who are suing the federal government but can not do so without

Why do bills introduced in Congress take such a long time to become law? Are the results any better because of the obstacles and procedures encountered by bills before they are finally sent to the White House?

the consent of Congress because of the common-law doctrine of sovereign immunity. (See also Chapter 6, page 131.) Bills on most matters may originate in either house, but must be approved by both houses before being signed into law.

Most *resolutions* are passed by either house alone and do not have the effect of law. They ordinarily deal just with the business of the chamber in which they originate. For example, either house may pass resolutions to change its rules or to express messages of a personal nature, such as congratulations or condolences, to other members of Congress.

In addition, there are two types of resolutions that are passed jointly by both houses. *Joint resolutions* have the effect of law and are signed by the President. Usually they concern matters requiring immediate action, such as the approval of a diplomatic move taken by the President. *Concurrent resolutions* do not have the form of law and do not require the President's signature. Normally they consist of changes in rules that concern both chambers, or of ceremonial statements, such as messages to other nations.

Procedures for the introduction of bills and resolutions differ slightly in the House and Senate. In the House, a member may introduce a bill or resolution simply by handing it to the Clerk of the House or by dropping it into the box (the "hopper") at the Clerk's desk. In the Senate, though, a member must be present, gain recognition from the officer in charge, and announce his proposal orally before the other members of the chamber.

In recent years the number of bills and resolutions introduced in both houses has been extraordinary. However, the number of both public and private bills passed is sharply below the number introduced. In a typical two-year session of Congress, slightly more than 1,000 bills are passed. One-third of these are private; the other two-thirds are public. Of the approximately 700 public bills passed, 500 come from proposals made originally by the

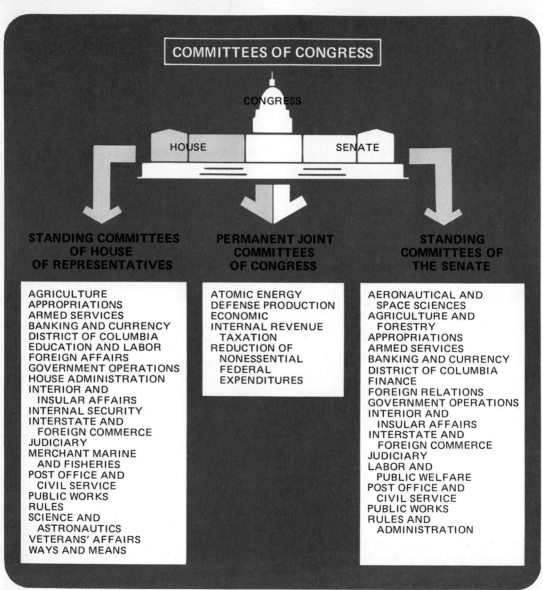

COMMITTEES OF CONGRESS

CONGRESS

HOUSE   SENATE

STANDING COMMITTEES OF HOUSE OF REPRESENTATIVES

AGRICULTURE
APPROPRIATIONS
ARMED SERVICES
BANKING AND CURRENCY
DISTRICT OF COLUMBIA
EDUCATION AND LABOR
FOREIGN AFFAIRS
GOVERNMENT OPERATIONS
HOUSE ADMINISTRATION
INTERIOR AND
   INSULAR AFFAIRS
INTERNAL SECURITY
INTERSTATE AND
   FOREIGN COMMERCE
JUDICIARY
MERCHANT MARINE
   AND FISHERIES
POST OFFICE AND
   CIVIL SERVICE
PUBLIC WORKS
RULES
SCIENCE AND
   ASTRONAUTICS
VETERANS' AFFAIRS
WAYS AND MEANS

PERMANENT JOINT COMMITTEES OF CONGRESS

ATOMIC ENERGY
DEFENSE PRODUCTION
ECONOMIC
INTERNAL REVENUE
   TAXATION
REDUCTION OF
   NONESSENTIAL
   FEDERAL
   EXPENDITURES

STANDING COMMITTEES OF THE SENATE

AERONAUTICAL AND
   SPACE SCIENCES
AGRICULTURE AND
   FORESTRY
APPROPRIATIONS
ARMED SERVICES
BANKING AND CURRENCY
DISTRICT OF COLUMBIA
FINANCE
FOREIGN RELATIONS
GOVERNMENT OPERATIONS
INTERIOR AND
   INSULAR AFFAIRS
INTERSTATE AND
   FOREIGN COMMERCE
JUDICIARY
LABOR AND
   PUBLIC WELFARE
POST OFFICE AND
   CIVIL SERVICE
PUBLIC WORKS
RULES AND
   ADMINISTRATION

President and the administrative branch.

One reason for the difference between the number of legislative proposals introduced and the number passed is that many proposals made in one house are duplicated by similar proposals in the other. Furthermore, many bills introduced do not receive strong support from powerful members—such as party leaders or committee members—or even from the congressmen who introduce them. (Congressmen often introduce measures to please constituents even though they have no intention of working for passage.)

Referral of bills to committees. It would be impossible for all members of Congress to consider all the proposals introduced at every session. Thus, a system of committees has been developed in each house to cope with the volume of legislation.

■ *Types of committees.* After a bill is introduced, it is given a number, prefixed by "HR" in the House or "S" in the Senate, and gets its "first reading"—often by title only. It is then referred by the Speaker of the House or the president *pro tempore* of the Senate to the appropriate *standing committee*—a permanent committee that continues its work from one session of Congress to the other. There are twenty standing committees in the House and sixteen in the Senate. In each house there are standing committees for all major subject areas, such as agriculture, foreign affairs, public works, labor, and government operations.

In addition to these standing committees, *select committees* are set up by each house to handle temporary problems. Members of these committees are appointed by the Speaker of the House or the Senate's president *pro tempore.* Examples of select committees which have been set up by the Senate in recent years include a committee to study poverty in America (Senate Select Committee on Nutrition and Human Needs) and a committee on congressional ethics (Senate Select Committee on Standards and Conduct). Many of the select committees which are established to investigate special problems eventually become permanent or are replaced by standing committees. For example, in 1945 the House members voted to change the status of a special committee that had been set up in 1938 into the permanent, or standing, Committee on Un-American Activities. More recently, the House in 1967 created a standing Committee on Standards of Official Conduct to devise a code of ethics for House members; this committee replaced the select committee set up for a similar purpose the previous year.

Besides the committee organization within each house, there are also committees that are made up of members from both houses of Congress. *Joint committees* are set up to study special matters of concern to both houses. So far, despite the volumes of proposals that are duplicated in the two houses, only a few joint committees have been created; the Joint Committee on Atomic Energy and the Joint Committee on Legislative Reorganization are two recent ones. Members of both houses are also appointed to *conference committees* to develop compromise versions of bills when both houses have passed substantially different versions.

■ *Work within committees and subcommittees.* Once a bill has been sent to a committee, it is placed on the committee's calendar. Many bills are pigeonholed, or disregarded, right away because they are considered nonessential. If a bill is considered important enough for consideration, the committee chairman determines whether it will be studied by the full committee or a special subcommittee.

The committee or subcommittee studying a bill may hold *hearings* to which interested government officials, private citizens, and pressure-group spokesmen may be invited to express opinions on the measure. Some hearings are open to the public, while others, known as *executive sessions,* are not. For some bills, both open and closed hearings are held. In addition to hearings, committee members sometimes make "field trips" to a particular region to study a problem firsthand.

Once committee findings or subcommittee reports on a bill have been studied, the full committee must vote on whether to "report" the bill to the chamber floor. The committee may vote to report the bill with a favorable or unfavorable recommendation or with amendments added.

Or it may pigeonhole the bill at this point, or even substitute a completely new one—a "clean bill"—for the original one. Once a bill has been reported out of committee, it is placed on a schedule, or *calendar,* for action by the entire chamber.

■ *Committee members and chairmen.* Many observers of the American political system have concluded that the committees form the backbone of the legislative system. As early as 1885, Woodrow Wilson, in his book *Congressional Government,* noted that the real power in the House of Representatives resided in the committees and, particularly, in their chairmen. Wilson likened the chairmen to feudal barons who conducted the affairs of their

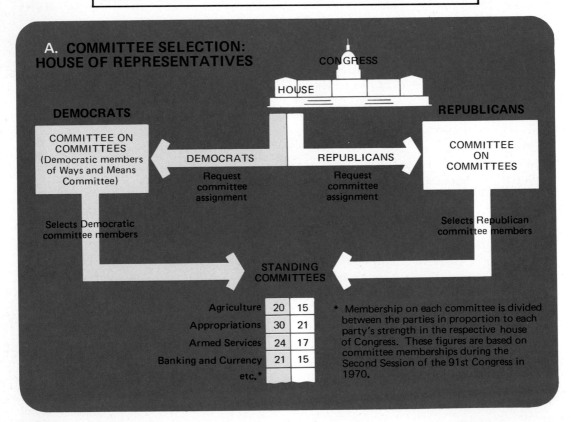

SELECTION OF COMMITTEE MEMBERS IN CONGRESS

A. COMMITTEE SELECTION: HOUSE OF REPRESENTATIVES

CONGRESS

HOUSE

DEMOCRATS

COMMITTEE ON COMMITTEES (Democratic members of Ways and Means Committee)

DEMOCRATS
Request committee assignment

Selects Democratic committee members

REPUBLICANS

COMMITTEE ON COMMITTEES

REPUBLICANS
Request committee assignment

Selects Republican committee members

STANDING COMMITTEES

Agriculture	20	15
Appropriations	30	21
Armed Services	24	17
Banking and Currency	21	15
etc.*		

* Membership on each committee is divided between the parties in proportion to each party's strength in the respective house of Congress. These figures are based on committee memberships during the Second Session of the 91st Congress in 1970.

own territories in complete independence of each other and of any higher governing authority. As Wilson pointed out:

"The chairmen of the standing committees do not constitute a cooperative body like a ministry. They do not consult and concur . . . there is no thought of acting in concert, each committee goes its own way at its own pace."[1]

For every standing committee, the Democratic and Republican parties are allotted the same percentage of committee members as they have of the total membership in that house. Committee members are selected in a variety of ways,

[1]*Woodrow Wilson, Congressional Government, (New York: Meridian Books, Inc., 1958), pp. 58–59.*

by party leaders or by party Committees on Committees in each chamber. Generally, senior members are given their choice of committees. Ordinarily, when members of Congress are assigned to committees, some attempt is made to match the talents, expertise, and constituency interests of the member with the subject dealt with by the committee. If dairy products and tobacco are important to a legislator's constituents, for example, he may be assigned to the subcommittees dealing with those commodities.

By congressional tradition, committee chairmanships are determined solely by means of the "seniority rule." According to this tradition, the senior majority-party member of each committee becomes chairman automatically. The seniority rule

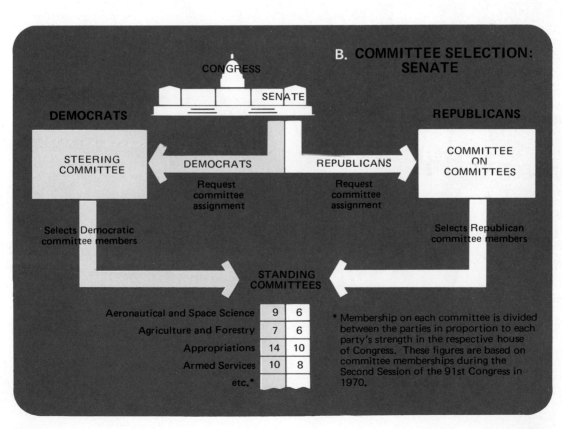

B. COMMITTEE SELECTION: SENATE

CONGRESS
SENATE

DEMOCRATS — STEERING COMMITTEE

REPUBLICANS — COMMITTEE ON COMMITTEES

DEMOCRATS — Request committee assignment

REPUBLICANS — Request committee assignment

Selects Democratic committee members

Selects Republican committee members

STANDING COMMITTEES

Aeronautical and Space Science	9	6
Agriculture and Forestry	7	6
Appropriations	14	10
Armed Services	10	8
etc.*		

* Membership on each committee is divided between the parties in proportion to each party's strength in the respective house of Congress. These figures are based on committee memberships during the Second Session of the 91st Congress in 1970.

'They can't hear us'

(The seniority system tends to isolate congressional committee chairmen from exposure to "new ideas.")

probably avoids much petty squabbling among members of Congress over the control of the committees and gives the committees a sense of continuity. On the other hand, this procedure has been criticized because it retains in power older members of Congress who tend to be conservative and keeps younger, perhaps more aggressive members from heading committees.

■ *Power of committee chairmen.* The committee system is largely controlled by individual chairmen. Generally, it is the chairmen who determine the order in which bills will be considered by their committees and the frequency of committee meetings. In addition, they decide who will be recognized to speak during such meetings. The chairmen also establish subcommittees and determine how committee funds are to be expended.

Committees whose activities receive wide attention are usually identified in the minds of the public with the names of their chairmen. During the early 1950's, for example, when the Permanent Investigations Subcommittee of the Senate Committee on Government Operations conducted its investigations into "subversive" activities, public attention was focused on the subcommittee's chairman—Senator Joseph R. McCarthy of Wisconsin. The "McCarthy Committee" became notorious for its freewheeling and arbitrary operations, which frequently impinged on the rights of individuals, both within and outside the government. Later in the same decade, the nationally televised investigation into labor racketeering, conducted by a select committee in the Senate, earned a wide reputation for the committee chairman, Senator John L. McClellan of Arkansas. More recently, Senator J. William Fulbright, also of Arkansas, Chairman of the Senate Foreign Relations Committee, was in the spotlight when his committee held hearings on policy in Vietnam.

The power of committee chairmen has often been questioned by critics of Congress. In the past it has been relatively easy for a committee chairman to pigeonhole bills by simply refusing to hold hearings or by failing to report them out of committee. This overriding power has been somewhat diminished by the Legislative Reorganization Act of 1946. The Act stipulates that committees must set regular meeting days, hold public hearings whenever possible, and keep records of any actions or votes taken. It was hoped that if these rules were followed, some of the backlog of proposals in the committees would be eased. Nevertheless, in spite of the reforms, committee chairmen still exert considerable influence.

Review questions

1. Describe the different kinds of bills and resolutions that can be introduced in the House and Senate.
2. Explain the different types of congressional committees. Why are the congressional committees essential to the functioning of Congress?

From Committee to Floor Action in the House

Once a bill is reported out of committee in either house, it is listed on a calendar or schedule in the order that it will be considered by the entire chamber. The process by which a bill goes from committee to calendar to "floor action" (debate and voting) in the House of Representatives is more flexible than in the

Senate, where the procedure is more routine. But it presents more obstacles.

House calendars. Public bills dealing with appropriations and revenue are placed on the *Union Calendar* (which is the abbreviated name for the Calendar of the Committee of the Whole House on the State of the Union), while nonrevenue public bills are placed on the *House Calendar.* All private bills are listed on the *Private Calendar.* In addition, to speed House action on a noncontroversial public bill from the Union or House calendars that requires little debate before passage, a House member may request that the bill be placed on the *Consent Calendar.* A fifth calendar, the *Discharge Calendar,* schedules petitions to force, or discharge, bills out of committees.

Without major objections from any member, public bills on the Consent Calendar and private bills can be passed quickly and sent on to the Senate. Bills on the Consent Calendar are "called," or considered, by the floor on the first and third Mondays of each month. Ordinarily, a *quorum,* or a minimum, of 218 Representatives must be present in the House before a vote can be taken on a bill. However, bills on the Consent Calendar can be passed by a quorum of 100 members acting as a committee for the entire House. Should a bill on the Consent Calendar meet an objection the first time it is considered, it is held over until the next time the Consent Calendar is called. If a minimum of three members object to the bill on the second call, the bill is considered controversial and is sent back to the Union or House Calendar. It can not reappear on the Consent Calendar during that session.

Bills on the Private Calendar are called on the first Tuesday of each month, and on the third Tuesday of any month if the Speaker decides it is necessary. Approval of a bill on this calendar in effect requires unanimous consent, because only two objectors are needed to have a bill sent back to a committee (usually the Judiciary Committee) for further consideration.

The Rules Committee. Before they reach the floor, most bills must pass the hurdle of a second committee, the *Rules Committee,* which determines how the bill will be handled in House debate. The Rules Committee provides essentially another screening action that a bill must go through before it reaches the floor. Public bills on the Consent Calendar and private bills automatically bypass the Rules Committee. A number of other bills, such as District of Columbia bills and certain categories of bills from several specific committees, also automatically bypass the Rules Committee.[2] Other bills may bypass the committee if considered under a "suspension of the rules."

The Rules Committee decides which standing rule of procedure will apply to a particular bill. Ordinarily there are two types of rules, the *closed rule* and the *open rule.* The closed rule allows only members of the sponsoring committee to make amendments to a bill. The open rule permits amendments from the floor. In most cases, rules limiting debate time are also made. If no such rule is made, each member is allowed one hour of debate.

When the chairman of a committee reporting a bill wants to speed action on it, he may request a special rule from

[2] *These include general appropriations bills from the Appropriations Committee, revenue bills from the Ways and Means Committee, bills governing public lands and admission of new states from the Interior and Insular Affairs Committee, bills governing rivers and harbors from the Public Works Committee, pension bills from the Veteran's Affairs Committee, rules relating to the administration of the chamber from the House Administration Committee, and bills governing procedure and the order of business from the Rules Committee.*

From *Straight Herblock* (Simon & Schuster, 1964)

"THIS IS WHAT YOU MIGHT CALL DEFENSE IN DEPTH."

(The Rules Committee has been traditionally regarded as a major barrier to the passage of legislation.)

the Rules Committee to consider the bill out of order, to limit debate, or to declare that certain sections or none of the bill's sections may be amended. Those who oppose a special rule for one reason or another usually label it a "gag rule."

In the past, members of the House Rules Committee have been able to effectively block legislation they disapproved of. Because membership on the committee is so desirable and because of the seniority system, it is usually the older, more conservative Representatives who win places on the committee. As recently as 1961, bills providing for federal aid to education were pigeonholed by the conservative members of the Rules Committee and thus withheld from House consideration.

Civil rights legislation was similarly delayed. Often bills that were reported out of the Rules Committee had been modified to conform to the views of the conservative committee membership.

■ *Curbing the Rules Committee.* The control of the Rules Committee over the fate of legislation has long been a source of frustration to House members eager for legislative action. During this century, attempts have often been made to reduce the committee's power.

Until 1910, the Speaker of the House was automatically Chairman of the Rules Committee. In effect, this meant that one man could dominate the House by combining the power of the Speakership with control over the Rules Committee. Abuses inevitably occurred.

In 1903, Joseph G. "Uncle Joe" Cannon, an "Old Guard" Republican, became Speaker of the House. Over the next few years, Cannon used his power to prevent the passage of progressive legislation. Finally in 1910, there was a peaceful revolt in the House and a resolution was passed which thereafter excluded any Speaker from membership on the Rules Committee. The resolution also provided that members of the Rules Committee would be elected by the entire House.

Freeing the Rules Committee from the Speaker's domination, however, did not prevent conservative minorities from controlling the committee. By the time of the New Deal, the Rules Committee was again firmly controlled by a coalition of Democratic and Republican conservatives. A number of progressive New Deal measures in such areas as fair labor practices and social security met with stiff opposition from this coalition.

As the Rules Committee continued to thwart passage of legislation, new attempts were made to curb its powers. During Harry Truman's last term in office, the

Rules Committee bottled up bills that provided for universal military training, amendments to social security, civil rights, and other legislation. A twenty-one-day rule was adopted in 1949, which provided that if the Rules Committee held a bill for twenty-one days, the chairman of the committee originally reporting the bill could ask for House action on it. The twenty-one-day rule was abolished in 1951 when conservatives regained a majority in the House. Again, a conservative coalition on the Rules Committee began to thwart legislation counter to its views.

Liberals in the House continued to press for reform. When John F. Kennedy won the Presidency in 1960, it became evident that the Rules Committee would have to be revamped if any of his progressive proposals were to pass the House. On January 31, 1961, the House, led by the Democratic Speaker, Sam Rayburn, voted 217 to 212 to liberalize the committee by adding three new members, two Democrats and one Republican. This placed the conservative coalition into a minority on the committee. Conservatives on the Rules Committee took another setback in 1965 when the twenty-one-day rule was restored, but they have since managed to have the controversial rule abolished again.

■ *Bypassing the Rules Committee.* In recent years the Rules Committee has not delayed the consideration of important legislation, but its potential power to do so remains. If a bill does not belong in a category which automatically bypasses the Rules Committee, and if its advocates are unwilling to wait for its scheduling through the regular calendar, it may be forced out of the Rules Committee in one of three ways: by suspension of the rules, by a discharge motion, or on Calendar Wednesday.

To *suspend the rules,* a member has to be recognized by the Speaker and ask that the rules be ignored so that a particular bill can be considered. If two-thirds of those members present agree to suspend the rules, debate is limited to forty minutes, and the bill is brought to a vote. No amendments, however, are allowed to be attached to a bill brought to the floor under a suspension of the rules.

A *discharge petition* requires approval of a majority of the House. This is difficult to obtain. From 1909 to 1964, only 22 discharge petitions out of over 800 filed placed bills on the Discharge Calendar. Only two of these bills—the Fair Labor Standards bill of 1938 and the Federal Pay Raise bill of 1960—passed both the House and the Senate to become law after being wrested from the Rules Committee by formal discharge.

The *Calendar Wednesday* method of bypassing the Rules Committee is also difficult to use. Under this procedure, on two Wednesdays of each month, committee chairmen can place bills that have been reported from their committees on the calendar for consideration that day. If the bill is passed on the Wednesday it is called, it becomes law without going through the Rules Committee.

The Calendar Wednesday method has not been used successfully in recent years. The difficulty with the method is that opponents of a bill can easily use delaying tactics to prevent the bill's passage on the day it is considered. There is also a time limit of two hours on debate for each bill.

Because of the difficulty in using these various methods to bypass the Rules Committee, the committee still has considerable control over the passage of legislation. Yet there has been no serious attempt by the members of the House to abolish the committee because it does play a role necessary to the House procedure. It does screen out the unwanted, unsupported, and nonessential bills. And Representatives can use the committee as a "whipping boy." That is, they can publicly blame the committee for killing those bills that they privately wanted to die.

Debate in the House. When a bill finally reaches the floor of the House, it must be read for a second time, debated, and voted on. Many bills, which are of little concern to the majority of the members, create no opposition and are dealt with quickly. Bills which are more important, such as tax measures and appropriations bills, are considered by the House acting in a *Committee of the Whole*. At the request of a House member, other bills can be brought before a Committee of the Whole as well. There are two kinds of Committees of the Whole; private bills are handled by the Committee of the Whole House, and public bills by the Committee of the Whole House on the State of the Union. In any case, the House serves as a committee of itself; the Speaker steps down, and the House itself is not officially in session.

Debate under a Committee of the Whole is freer. A quorum of only 100 members, instead of the normal 218, is required for doing business. Each member opposing or supporting amendments to a bill under discussion is given five minutes to participate in debate. Once debate is concluded, the Speaker calls the House back into regular session to vote.

Voting procedures in the House. After a bill has been debated, the House must vote, first on whether to add various amendments, and finally on the bill itself.

There are four types of voting procedures in the House: (1) the *voice* vote—when members merely answer "yea" or "nay" in unison; (2) the *roll-call* vote—when members are asked to voice their votes individually; (3) the *standing* vote—when members in favor or against a measure stand and are counted; and (4) the *teller* vote—when members file by a teller or "counter" of their own party to have their votes recorded.

After the proposed amendments to a bill have been voted on, a motion may be made to recommit the bill to committee. If the motion is carried, the bill, in effect, has been "killed." If the motion to recommit is not carried, the bill is read for a third time and the final vote is taken.

Once a bill is passed by either house of Congress, it becomes officially an "act." An act passed first by the House of Representatives has reached the halfway point; it is then sent on for consideration by the Senate.

Review questions

1. On which calendar in the House would the following bills be placed after being reported out of committee?
   (a) a bill for an excise tax on telephone usage;
   (b) a proposal to nationalize the railroads;
   (c) a proposal to allow a foreign citizen to immigrate even though the immigration quota has been filled.
2. Why was the twenty-one-day rule adopted by the House in 1949?

To Floor Action in the Senate

Owing to its smaller size and the longer terms of its members, the Senate is able to operate less formally than the House although its procedure is essentially the same. A bill is introduced, given a reading and a number, and referred to the appropriate committee for study and consideration. However, there is no Rules Committee in the Senate to stall legislation as there is in the House. The majority-party leader directs the order of business within a flexible set of rules of procedure.

There are only two Senate calendars. All bills reported from committees go onto the *Calendar of General Orders;* presidential nominations and treaties go onto an *Executive Calendar.* Bills are scheduled for floor action by a majority vote of the Senate or by the majority party's policy committee in consultation with the minority leader.

Bypassing Senate committees. When Senate committees delay action on legislation, there are a number of devices which can be used to get bills onto the floor quickly. Some of these circumventing methods are the discharge rule, the "rider," suspension of the rules, and the special procedures for House-passed bills.

■ *The discharge rule.* Under the *discharge rule,* a Senator may introduce a motion to discharge a bill or resolution from committee. Such a motion can be passed by a majority vote on the legislative day after it has been introduced.

While this procedure seems very simple, the discharge rule is almost impossible to invoke successfully. Senators opposed to a discharge motion can easily prevent its introduction by speaking on the floor during the morning hours—when such motions must be introduced according to the rules of the Senate. Moreover, the majority leader, or even a small group of influential Senators who oppose the motion, can prevent the recognition of a Senator who wishes to call a discharge motion introduced the previous day. Only fourteen discharge motions have been made in the history of the Senate, and only six of these have passed. Only one of the passed motions resulted in a law! This one exception

was a totally noncontroversial bill which permitted the federal government to make a medal for a State of Florida celebration in 1964.

■ *Non-germane amendments.* In addition to the discharge rule, Senators can use *non-germane amendments* to side-step committees. Under this procedure, a proposal which is stalled in committee may be attached in the form of an amendment, or *rider,* to an unrelated bill which *has* been reported to the floor from committee. The use of non-germane amendments is not permitted in the House, but is allowed in the Senate except in the case of general appropriations bills. Of course, without support from a majority of Senators, such amendments do not have a chance of passage. Even a strong minority can usually succeed in tabling, or stalling, such a rider.

In 1960 proposed civil rights legislation was being held up in committees of both houses of Congress. Senate Majority Leader Lyndon B. Johnson attempted to get such legislation attached as a rider to a bill that provided for aid to a Missouri school district. In 1964 Senator Everett Dirksen tried to attach to a foreign aid bill a non-germane amendment that would have delayed the implementation of a Supreme Court decision requiring that both houses of state legislatures be apportioned on the basis of population. While neither of these attempts was successful, both examples reveal the potential importance of non-germane amendments.

■ *Suspension of the rules.* Another way to bypass Senate committees is through a *suspension of the rules.* Through this method, a procedure normally prohibited under Senate rules can be used if a simple majority of Senators vote to suspend the applicable rule. For example, suspension of the rules is required before a non-germane amendment can be attached to a general appropriations bill, and before the amount of appropriations on such a bill can be increased. Regular Senate rules prohibit both of these procedures. Suspension of the rules is more easily accomplished in the Senate than in the House, where two-thirds of the members must approve it.

■ *House-passed bills.* There is also a special Senate procedure by which House-passed bills can go directly to the Senate calendar for a floor vote without having to go through committee. This procedure is normally used to circumvent a committee that is dominated by a minority group unrepresentative of the Senate as a whole.

During the late 1950's and early 1960's, for example, when civil rights legislation was being supported vigorously by many groups, the Senate Judiciary Committee was chairmaned by Senator James Eastland of Mississippi. Senator Eastland represented a small minority in the Senate that wanted to block civil rights legislation at any cost. By use of the special procedure for House-passed bills, however, the civil rights bills of 1957 and 1964 succeeded in coming to the Senate floor without committee action.

The filibuster. Unlike the House, debate in the Senate is not subject to rules and not limited to any time period. Senate tradition permits unlimited debate on floor motions, unless two-thirds of the Senate agrees to close debate. This factor gives Senators their most powerful delaying tactic, the *filibuster.*

Employed after a bill is on the floor and open to debate, the objective of a filibuster is to "talk a bill to death" in order to gain concessions or even withdrawal of the bill. Senators using this tactic talk for hours on topics that may or may not be relevant to the subject of debate. During a filibuster, some Senators even read old issues

Fermin Martin in *The Houston Chronicle*

(Some Senators feel that attempts to halt filibusters threaten the Senate's privilege of unlimited debate.)

of the Congressional Quarterly or the daily newspapers to keep the filibuster going. A filibuster continues as long as interested Senators have the collective energy to go on. When one Senator tires, he yields the floor to one of his colleagues who has agreed to keep on with the debate. Senator Strom Thurmond of South Carolina holds the individual record for a filibuster. He talked for over twenty-four hours to halt the passage of a civil rights bill in 1957.

Filibusters can be stopped by using the *cloture* rule (Senate Rule 22). One-sixth of the Senate (sixteen members) must initiate cloture action by petitioning the Senate to close the debate. The vote to limit debate by the cloture rule is automatically taken two days after the petition is submitted. Two-thirds of the Senators present must approve it. After the petition goes into effect, no Senator may speak for more than one hour on the bill being considered. In a few days the bill must come up for a vote.

While filibusters have been used most frequently by conservative minorities to stall the legislative process, they have also served the liberals in the Senate as well. In 1962 a group of nine liberal Senators, led by Senator Wayne Morse of Oregon, tried to halt the communications-satellite bill. They felt the bill gave too much power to a private company—the American Telephone and Telegraph—that was using some federal funds to develop a communications-satellite system. The Senate ended the filibuster by invoking cloture—one of the few times since 1917 that the cloture rule has been employed successfully. Regardless of who uses the filibuster, whether they be liberals or conservatives, the tactic does slow down the legislative process in the Senate.

The Senate establishment. Besides the procedural delaying tactics used by the Senate, there is a rather informal group of Senators who themselves act as a bulwark against speedy progress. This group is often referred to as "the establishment." In recent years, this term has come to signify the group in a society which is entrenched in positions of authority and thus able to wield significant power. Usually it takes time to acquire such power, so the older, more conservative members of the Senate are ordinarily tagged with the label "establishment," or "inner club" as one political scientist has termed it. This group is influential because it is composed of the Senate leaders, chairmen of committees, and leaders in the party caucuses.

To become part of the Senate establishment, a Senator usually is a senior member, although not all the senior members of the Senate belong to the inner club. A member of the inner club must also be a "Senate type." This means he should respect the sanctity of the Senate institution and advocate continuance of the procedures and traditions—such as the fili-

buster—that give power to the inner club. Thus, it is a Senator's personality combined with his acute sense of politics—rather than the area of the country he represents, his seniority, financial backing, or family position—that determines whether he is a member of the Senate establishment.

In 1963 Senator Joseph S. Clark of Pennsylvania rose on the floor of the Senate and openly attacked the Senate establishment. To do so publicly was, to say the least, novel.

Calling the establishment the "antithesis of democracy," Clark criticized the inner club for not being responsive to the programs developed by the party caucuses in Congress and by the President as well.

From *Straight Herblock* (Simon & Schuster, 1964)

"What does he think this is—a legislative body?"

(Any try at reforming procedures in Congress is sure to be opposed by those benefiting from the status quo.)

Senator Clark also claimed that freshman Senators were rewarded or punished with committee assignments on the basis of their attitudes toward the establishment. Those who supported Senate customs and procedures which enhanced the establishment's power received more important committee assignments than those who favored substantial changes in Senate rules.

In the 88th Congress (1963–1964), there was, in fact, a definite relationship between the committee assignments of Democratic Senators and the views of these Senators on the cloture rule. Of the twenty-two non-freshman Democratic Senators who submitted bids for new committee assignments, eight were opposed to changing Rule 22 and thus changing the filibuster procedure, while fourteen favored such a change. Six of the eight Senators who upheld the filibuster were given new assignments, while only five of the fourteen who wanted to see Rule 22 changed got new assignments. And only one Senator from the latter group, Senate Majority Leader Mike Mansfield, was assigned to the committee of his first choice.

Adjusting House-Senate differences. Once the debate on a bill has been terminated in the Senate, voting on the bill is scheduled. It is a much simpler procedure in the Senate than it is in the House. All of the methods used in the House, except the teller vote, are also employed in the Senate.

But this may not be the end of the procedure for passage of a bill. If the bill has originated in the Senate, it must next go to the lower house for consideration. If the measure has passed both houses, there may still be problems to iron out. Because each house of Congress has its own constituencies, procedures, and organization, the policy outputs of the two houses often differ. A bill passed first by one chamber may be substantially altered when it is finally passed by the other. Since these House-Senate differences must be resolved before a bill can be sent on to the White House for signature, some compromise between the two versions of a bill must be made.

Most often, such differences are resolved when the chamber initiating a bill simply accepts the second chamber's amended version. The House, for example, may pass an appropriations bill and send it to the Senate, where amendments are made. The bill is then returned to the House which by majority vote may agree to accept the amended version of its original bill. Similarly, a bill first passed by the Senate may eventually be returned and accepted with House amendments. House-Senate differences are adjusted in this way on approximately 90 percent of all public and private bills passed. The version of a bill passed by the second house is usually the one that is finally accepted.

On controversial bills, where House and Senate versions differ greatly, a *conference committee* made up of members of both chambers is usually appointed. All conference committees are bipartisan, but the majority party of each house is given a majority on that house's committee delegation. Conferees are appointed by the Speaker of the House and by the president *pro tempore* of the Senate, and are almost always senior members of the House and Senate committees that dealt with the bill originally. Technically, the conferees are also supposed to have demonstrated support for the bill on which they are conferring, but this practice is not always followed.

The rules of both houses of Congress limit the agenda of the conference committees to specific matters of disagreement between the two houses. Thus, the conference committees are prohibited from writing entirely new legislation. Conference committees nevertheless exercise a great deal of discretion within these boundaries.

Once the conference committee has reached a compromise, a report is sent to the two chambers for their approval or rejection. If the bill is accepted in its final version, it is signed by the Speaker of the House and the president *pro tempore* of the Senate. Finally, it is sent to the White House for the President's signature or his veto.

Review questions

1. What is a non-germane amendment? What other devices can be used in the Senate to bring "stalled" legislation to the floor?
2. How are differences between House and Senate versions of a bill resolved?

Future Trends in the Congress

In the final analysis, the success of the legislature in a modern democracy depends on how well it performs the law-making function. The Framers thought they had set up a very effective instrument for this purpose—"the Congress." But Congress has gradually taken on a somewhat passive character. It is far more capable of stalling or changing proposals that come from the outside than it is in generating new legislation internally. In addition, laws passed by Congress are often vague. This is indicative of the unwillingness of Congress to cope with the conflicting demands of the many groups in its constituency. As a solution, some legislative authority is delegated to administrative agencies and to the Presidency. Quite understandably, support has been growing for reforms which would make Congress more efficient and more responsive to legislative needs.

Nevertheless, Congress has never given up its power to make laws. It is still the principal debating arena for legislation. And it is one of the most powerful legislative bodies in the world, for it can and often does use its authority under the Constitution to turn down presidential and administrative requests for legislative action. It is a rare session of Congress that sees more than 50 percent of the President's legislative recommendations passed. In countries with parliamentary governments and a disciplined two-party system, such as Great Britain, the parliament is nothing more than a rubber stamp for the Cabinet. The Congress of the United States is anything but a rubber stamp!

Results of fragmentation. The Framers divided Congress into two houses, partly because they hoped that such "fragmentation" would always provide an internal check on legislative power. The subsequent delegation and dispersal of power to the many standing committees and subcommittees expanded this initial division of interest. The lack of disciplined political parties and the highly specialized, complex nature of policy-making made the committee system the only practical arrangement in which Congress could operate. Now Congress is hard pressed to take any positive action, because it has to arrive at agreements on so many levels.

Sometimes this fragmentation of Congress results in negative rather than positive outputs. It is relatively easy, for example, to produce vague legislation or to pigeonhole legislation in the numerous standing committees of the House and the Senate. This is true especially if there is no substantial majority support behind a proposal or if a large minority is opposed to it.

Because Congress operates largely through committees, it is almost impossible to speak of Congress as a whole. It does not act as a unit. Objectively speaking, then, there is no collective congressional intent; there is only the intent of many individuals and groups within Congress.

On those occasions when there is a high degree of unanimity at governmental and private levels, Congress can, however, take very vigorous and meaningful action. The passage of the Revenue Act of 1964, calling for substantial tax reductions, took less than a year to pass from the White House through Congress and back to the President for his signature.

Congressional reform. The seniority system of Congress and the domination of both chambers by certain regional elites have also been changed by recent political developments. Throughout the twentieth century, for example, the southern bloc of Senators had prevented the passage of any important civil rights legislation. In 1964, however, a civil rights act was passed which extended the authority of the federal government to protect voting rights and to bring about desegregation of public schools. To accomplish this, cloture was successfully invoked for the first time in history on a civil rights bill, and thus terminated a determined filibuster by southern Senators.

As American society becomes more intradependent and mass communications draw the nation together, it will become increasingly difficult for Congress to ignore national concerns. Pressure will continue to be put on Congress to de-emphasize regional interests and to eliminate the seniority rule, which gives disproportionate power to entrenched conservatives in both major political parties.

■ *Congressional procedures.* The pressure for reform may even result in a change in congressional procedures. The targets of reform are those procedures that appear to slow down and distort the legislative process, making it incapable of dealing with critical problems. The House requirement, for example, that almost every important bill must go to the Rules Committee is seen by some reformers as a legislative bottleneck. Reformers are similarly critical of the Senate filibuster, which hampers efficient lawmaking. The secrecy of House committee operations and of the votes of House committee members on

HAUNTED HOUSE

Copyright © 1970 by Herblock in *The Washington Post*

(Some critics feel that congressional reform is badly needed in order to revitalize the democratic process.)

legislative proposals has also been under attack by legislators pressing for reform.

A possible means of ending the seniority rule would be to have committee chairmen selected by the leaders of the majority parties in both the House and the Senate. This would increase party responsibility and make it more possible for the President, through his own party leaders, to have tighter control over Congress.

Aside from altering congressional procedures, another proposed congressional reform would extend the terms of the House members from two to four years so that they would coincide with the term of the President. Some Representatives would most probably ride into the House on the "coattails" of the presidential candidate. This would contribute to legislative efficiency by eliminating some troublesome policy differences which arise between Congress and the White House. Many reformers also seek to make Congress more efficient by granting more staff aids to congressmen, by creating an ombudsman office to help congressmen handle constituent grievances, and by encouraging specialization within committees to help match the expertise of the bureaucracy and private pressure groups.

■ *Ethics.* Congressional ethics are another target of reformers. "Unethical" congressional behavior, it has been charged, ranges from putting relatives on the congressional payroll as staff aids (a common practice) and taking unnecessary junkets abroad, to *conflicts of interest.* Charges of conflict of interest arise when legislators have investments in firms and industries that are regulated by the government or subject to federal legislation. A Representative on the Ways and Means Committee, for example, might have investments in the oil industry and could thus benefit from the "depletion allowance" clause

in the tax laws. This clause allows the industry to deduct a percentage of the money it spends on oil exploration from federal income taxes. Such a legislator has a vested interest in keeping the tax law as it is, even when good arguments might be made that it should be changed.

Two committees—the Senate Select Committee on Standards and Conduct and the House Committee on Standards of Official Conduct—were set up in recent years to recommend codes of ethics to be approved by chamber members. However, members of Congress generally have been reluctant to impose enforceable restrictions on their own conduct. The only methods authorized so far to deal with congressional ethics problems have been the public disclosure of congressional payrolls and the registration of lobbyists. Both of these requirements focus publicity on unusual contacts and "unethical" practices. The requirements for public disclosure are very limited, however, and attempts to have members of Congress publicize their private financial interests have failed. Nevertheless, many legislators do voluntarily disclose their investments.

A powerful and vital legislature is a key component of any constitutional democracy. Congress must be capable of acting swiftly, deliberately, and responsibly to meet the urgent problems facing our society. In the future, Congress will undoubtedly find that internal reforms will help it to continue playing a central role in our political system.

Review questions

1. What congressional procedures and practices have been most criticized as being in need of reform?
2. A congressman who owns stock in a tire company supports a bill to lower taxes on imported rubber. What offense might he be accused of?

Chapter Review

Terms you should know

Questions about this chapter

1. Describe the different types of congressional committees and the function of each. When does the House of Representatives itself act as a committee?
2. President Wilson likened the chairmen of congressional committees to feudal barons. Explain why. What are the sources of the chairmen's power?
3. What reforms have been made to try to change the conservative make-up of the House Rules Committee?
4. "Calendar Wednesday is the only means of successfully bypassing the Rules Committee." Comment on the validity of this statement. What other devices can be used to bring a bill to the House floor if the Rules Committee refuses or prolongs scheduling of a bill?
5. What are the characteristic attitudes of the "Senate establishment"?
6. Is Congress more fragmented than the Framers intended? Explain. What result has congressional fragmentation had on lawmaking?
7. When is a bill on the Consent Calendar reclassified as "controversial"? What procedure follows this reclassification?
8. How many members usually constitute a quorum in the House? Under what circumstances can fewer members be present to pass a bill?

Thought and discussion questions

1. In what way is the Senate establishment the "antithesis of democracy" as Senator Clark claimed? Give a counter-argument justifying the existence of such a group in a democratic government. Discuss also whether or not other aspects of Congress are "democratic": (a) the filibuster, (b) power of committee chairmen, (c) seniority rule.
2. Evaluate the present legislative system in terms of Congress being able to respond quickly to crises. Discuss what reforms might make Congress more efficient.
3. Explain what you believe the "ethical behavior" of a congressman should be. Whose interests should concern him most?

Class projects

1. Analyze the present composition of the House Rules Committee as to (a) the ages, (b) home districts (locale, economic background, ethnic and racial make-up of constituencies), and (c) other occupations or business interests of the members and chairman. (You will find a list of the current Rules Committee members in the Congressional Quarterly Weekly Report. For more information, write to the clerk of the

Rules Committee.) What does your analysis tell you about the problems that may arise on this committee?

2. There have been many successful and unsuccessful Senate filibusters. Research several of them to find out what common factors they may have had with regard to (a) the Senators who participated in the filibuster, (b) the legislation they were obstructing or supporting. Would the nation be better served if the filibuster were eliminated? Explain your answer.

Case Study: A time when Congress is "Congress"

Congressional policy-making is played out behind drawn curtains; only a handful of citizens watch the show, and they are usually in the wings of either the House of Representatives or the Senate. The two chambers meet separately except when rare joint sessions are called. Yet, to get the total picture of how Congress operates, it is not enough to sit in the wings of either house; one should also observe a joint congressional conference at work. At such conferences, select members of both houses meet to iron out their differences and put finishing touches on legislation. Compromise is difficult to achieve, due to personal conflicts and the loyalty of each conferee to his respective chamber.

This article points out the importance of the "conferees" of Congress and the key role they play in the legislative process.

As you read, think about the following questions:
1. What is the major function of the "Committee of Conference"?
2. How does a legislator get to be a member of a conference? Is this the fairest way? Explain.
3. Under what conditions do the conferees work?

Those Powerful 'Conferees' of Congress

By ARLEN J. LARGE

WASHINGTON—According to an old Capitol Hill wheeze, a flustered lady tourist once approached a U.S. Capitol guide and said: "I've seen the House, and I've seen the Senate, but where do I find Congress?"
. . . If the lady had poked into some of the closed rooms along the Capitol's corridors, chances are she would have found the kind of "Congress" she was looking for.

In these rooms meet the mysterious and powerful "conferees," senior members of the House and Senate whose job is to put the final touches on almost every important bill passed. Here, more than at any other stage of the legislative process, is the quintessential Congress. . . .

This kind of swapping and bluffing and conniving—done in secret—can touch the lives of every citizen, and not always for the best. But in a bicameral legislature with houses of equal power, there's really no alternative. A major reason for having two houses is to get diversity. After one house passes a bill, the other will—in theory—improve upon it with amendments reflecting second thoughts and new facts. Then the whole thing must be brought back together again, and that's the responsibility of the 10 or 15 members of the "Committee of Conference."

Completing One's Education

. . . It's a pity the puzzled lady tourist couldn't be allowed inside the odd-shaped room on the Capitol's first floor where conferees were meeting . . . on the cigaret advertising bill. One exchange, as reported by somebody who was there, illustrates nicely the poker-table atmosphere in which the nation's laws are made.

Under discussion was the health warning on the cigaret pack. The House version of the bill attributed the warning of dangers from lung cancer and other diseases to the surgeon general; the Senate didn't attribute its warning to anybody. The House conferees were determined to hang the responsibility on the surgeon general, not on Congress. Rep. Harley Staggers of West Virginia, chairman of the House Commerce Committee, and a 21-year veteran in Congress, read out a proposed compromise text: "Warning: The Surgeon General Has Determined That Cigaret Smoking Is Dangerous to Your Health."

"Agreed?" said Mr. Staggers, all business and ready to get on to the next item.

"Tentatively agreed," said Sen. Norris Cotton of New Hampshire, laden with 15 years' seniority. "I want to see what we'll be getting in return." The Senate, in the end, got plenty.

There's no set rule on how many conferees there should be, but 15 is a common number. In case a disagreement must be settled by a vote, the question isn't put to the entire group. The eight Senators, for example, would vote among themselves on whether to accept a House provision, while the seven House conferees just watch. But veterans of many conferences say an impressive number of decisions are reached by a sort of rolling consensus, without formal votes. Rep. Wilbur Mills of Arkansas, who often heads conferences on tax legislation, is renowned for guiding the discussion to an "everybody agreed?" conclusion.

Seniority the Answer

How do you get to be a conferee? Generally, the seniority system will do it for you, if you keep getting elected. Conferees usually are selected from the most senior members of the House and Senate committees that originally considered the bills. This, in turn, means that key conference decisions often rest in the hands of conservative Southerners.

In theory, each chamber's conferees must fight to the bitter end to preserve their version of a bill, even if they personally disagree with it. In practice, conferees sometimes can't wait to sell their colleagues out.

Three years ago, the House approved a bill saying Congressional districts in a state would meet the Supreme Court's one-man, one-vote test if there were not more than a 30% population difference between the biggest and smallest. The 30% rule would apply to the 1968 and 1970 elections. The Senate voted for a tougher 10% test promoted by Sens. Edward Kennedy of Massachusetts and Howard Baker of Tennessee.

But five of the six Senate conferees, picked from the conservative seniors on the Judiciary Committee, had voted against the Kennedy-Baker test on the floor, and quickly abandoned it in conference. The full conference group recommended no numerical test for the 1968 and 1970 elections. However, both houses of Congress must agree on a conference bill before it can be sent to the President, and the House asked the conferees to try again. But the Senate rejected the second bill, and the effort was permanently scuttled.

The system also can put conferences into the hands of liberals, and then the conservatives lose. Recently, members of the liberal-dominated Senate and House Labor committees—an unusually swollen conference of 12 Senators and 24 Representatives—were in charge of settling differences over a bill extending Federal school aid. The biggest problem was a Senate amendment requiring uniform enforcement of desegregation rules, North and South. Sponsored by John Stennis of Mississippi, the amendment had put the Senate through an unusual emotional wringer before passing, 56 to 36.

Haggle, Haggle

A decisive roll-call vote like that was, in theory, supposed to put iron in the will of the Senate conferees. It apparently did, for a while, though only four of the 12 Senators had voted with the majority. The House conferees, described as adamantly opposed to any Stennis-type amendment, opened with a demand for total deletion, but the Senators refused. When Rep. Albert Quie of Minnesota then proposed language changes that would have nullified the amendment, the Senators turned him down twice. There was more haggling, and then Rep. William Ford of Michigan proposed inserting other words that, according to Sen. Stennis, ruined the amendment. At that point the Senate conferees caved in, and this week they persuaded the Senate to accept defeat.

For both lawmakers and Capitol Hill reporters trying to follow the progress of legislation, the conference stage and its aftermath can produce considerable confusion. The final conference version of a bill sometimes isn't available in writing, and everyone must use a "report" worded in impenetrable legislative code.

One would think it would be easy to tell when Congress has finally passed a bill, but the post-conference paper-shuffling actually fooled the Congressional Record. . . . Conferees reached agreement March 12, [1970] on a bill setting liability rules for oil spills. The conference agreement was brought routinely to the Senate floor where it was approved, 80 to 0, without any discussion. Next morning's official Congressional Record reported the bill had been "cleared for President," although the House had not yet given its approval. It did so that afternoon, but not before the Record had scooped Congress.

End questions

1. Do joint conferences enhance the democratic procedure in Congress? Why or why not?

2. Does the conference stage of legislation have to be a confused one? Can you suggest a better method of finalizing legislation with both houses represented? Give reasons for your suggestion.

Case Study: A conference committee at work

Each bill passed by the legislature must pass through certain procedures; the conference committee is usually the last stage. It is in the conference committee that the differences between the House and Senate versions of a bill are reshaped by compromise and that the final legislative product is formed. The proceedings leading to the enactment of the Full Employment Act of 1946 demonstrate the importance of the conference committee, and how essential it is to the final passage of a bill.

The Full Employment Act of 1946 emerged out of conference as a composite product—with some elements of both the original bill passed by the Senate and the substitute bill passed by the House. The conference process cooled the personality conflicts and pressures that had been mounting for more than a year over the fate of this bill, S.380.

As you read this commentary on the Full Employment Act of 1946, keep in mind the following:
1. What was the effect of the Depression of 1929 on subsequent economic legislation?
2. Describe the catalyst for and the major purpose of the Full Employment Act.
3. Is there a relationship between war and unemployment? How did World War II influence the Congress in economic matters?
4. Why was a conference committee necessary in order for the Full Employment Act to reach the President?

Congress Makes a Law

THE IMPACT OF THE GREAT DEPRESSION

The economic disaster which started with the stock market crash of October, 1929, had a revolutionary impact on the minds of the American people. As year followed year and conditions of unemployment and insecurity became steadily worse, the great majority of Americans came to realize that something profound and terrifying had occurred. Insecurity and fear were ubiquitous. Louise V. Armstrong, writing of Chicago in 1932, notes, "One vivid, gruesome moment of those dark days we shall never forget. We saw a crowd of some fifty men fighting over a barrel of garbage which had been set outside the back door of a restaurant. American citizens fighting for scraps of food like animals."

The same could have been written of New York or Boston or Los Angeles or New Orleans. Farmers, whose conditions had been depressed since the early twenties, blockaded roads, overturned milk trucks, and sponsored "shot-gun auctions" on farms which had been taken over by foreclosure.

This condensation from Congress Makes a Law, by Stephen Kemp Bailey. New York: Columbia University Press, 1950. © by Columbia University Press, 1950. Condensation reprinted by permission from the publisher.

Unemployed veterans formed a bonus army and marched on Washington. . . .

Common to all this groping and intellectual and moral ferment was the awareness that whatever the theoretical causes or cures of depressions, the federal government was the only institution with sufficient power to do anything substantial—and at a practical level—about the economic collapse. The experience of the great depression forced the federal government to extend its functions and responsibilities. This change in public attitude about the legitimate sphere of federal activity in economic affairs, and the public's broadening conception of economic rights, were necessary prerequisites to, as well as products of, the New Deal of Franklin D. Roosevelt. Without this change there would have been no Full Employment Bill of 1945.

THE "DISMAL" THIRTIES

The relief and recovery programs of the thirties were remarkable in their scope and their vitality; remarkable also in their improvised and chaotic character. When it is remembered that the federal government was entering on uncharted seas, the improvisation and chaos is not surprising. . . .

. . . The enigma of unemployment was not solved at the end of that sorry decade. Eight to nine million jobless remained in 1939. It was the war which "cured" the unemployment problem. . . .

. . . The experience and the thinking of the thirties both at home and abroad provided the river of ideas which found their way into the Full Employment Bill [S.380]. . . . [I]n terms of social dynamics, probably the most important cause of the Full Employment Bill was the wartime memory of the public and of officials, alike, that the problem of unemployment had really never been solved in the days of peace. The fact that it had been solved by war only stimulated people to ask the question well posed by Lord Beveridge, "Unemployment has been practically abolished twice in the lives of most of us—in the last war and in this war. Why does war solve the problem of unemployment which is so unsolvable in peace?"

WARTIME FEARS ABOUT THE POSTWAR WORLD

Some indication of the sharpness of wartime memories about the depression of the thirties and of the wartime fears about the postwar world is reflected in a poll taken by *Fortune* early in the fall of 1944. In answer to the question, "Do you think the Federal Government should provide jobs for everyone able and willing to work, but who cannot get a job in private employment?" 67.7 percent said it should.

Perhaps an even more striking indication was the volume of postwar planning which mushroomed during the war years. On the question of how to maintain full employment in the postwar years, thousands of government officials, businessmen, labor leaders, farmers, journalists, planners, economists, and other interested citizens thought, wrote, and spoke. . . .

Rival or at least diverse concepts emerged. By and large, the business community believed as it had for generations that long-term full employment could be achieved by business initiative if only the government would follow policies aimed at promoting business confidence. . . .

Labor leaders in general saw a need for federal measures to protect the interests of labor as a basic condition of a full employment economy. They placed heavy emphasis upon such issues as higher minimum wages, a liberalized unemployment compensation program, fair employment practices, and the advance planning of public works. They also placed heavy emphasis upon cooperative planning on the part of government, business, agriculture, and labor.

Out of the minds of the thousands of government and private planners came suggestions and solutions which fell somewhere between the two poles of traditional *laissez faire* and comprehensive government controls over important parts of the economic system. . . .

The Full Employment Bill, as introduced, attempted to do four things: first, to establish once and for all the principle of the "right to work" and the federal government's obligation to assure employment opportunities for all those "able to work and seeking work"; second, to place responsibility on the President for seeing to it that the economy was purposively analyzed at regular intervals, and that the Congress was informed of economic trends and of the President's program to meet the challenge of those trends; third, in case the economic barometer read "stormy," to commit the federal government to undertake a series of measures to forestall serious economic difficulty —the measure of last resort being a program of federal spending and investment which was to be the final guarantor of full employment; and finally, to establish a mechanism in Congress which would facilitate legislative analysis and action, and fix legislative responsibility for the carrying out of a full employment policy.

The Full Employment Bill, then, was composed of (1) a statement of economic right and federal obligation, (2) an economic program, and (3) governmental mechanisms for the effectuation of that program. . . .

After the House of Representatives had passed its version of H.R.2202 [the Full Employment Bill] on December 14, 1945, the next step in the policy-making process was the appointment, in both Houses, of conference managers to whom was given the task of attempting to work out some compromise between the Senate-passed bill and the House substitute. . . .

PRE-CONFERENCE MANEUVERS

The Joint Conference Committee meetings began on January 22, 1946, just a year after the introduction of the Senate bill. Between December 14, 1945, and the Conference sessions, however, the issue of the fate of S.380 was by no means dormant. Immediately after the House vote, the liberal House sponsors [made] . . . a passionate plea for the Democratic Party chairman to put pressure on President Truman. The feeling of the sponsors was that Truman had let them down in the House struggle, that the party had lost popular prestige among its liberal supporters as a result, and that the only way the President could recoup his lost prestige would be for him to insist that the Conference Committee report out a strong and progressive full employment bill. . . .

As a result of . . . pressure, Truman on December 20, 1945, sent . . . letters . . . stating, ". . . no bill which provides substantially less than the Senate version can efficiently accomplish the purposes intended." On January 3, 1946, Truman followed this up with a radio speech in which he made a "blunt request for real full-employment legislation . . . urging voters to let their representatives know their sentiments." Finally in his Message to Congress of January 21, 1946, Truman restated his desire that "a satisfactory Full Employment Bill such as the Senate bill now in conference between the Senate and the House" be passed. The Message to Congress, which had been prepared in part by the Budget Bureau [now the Office of Management and Budget], had a number of references to the need for strong full-employment legislation, and altogether represented the strongest Presidential pressure for a liberal bill which came from the White House during the entire course of the struggle over S.380. . . .

Conference action began on January 22 and ended on February 2. The sessions were held in Senator Barkley's [Democrat, Kentucky and Senate Majority Leader] office in the Capitol, and were fairly well attended. . . .

The struggle in the conference was between Barkley and Cochran [Representative John J. Cochran—Democrat, Missouri] on the one hand, and Congressman Will Whittington [Democrat, Mississippi], author of the House bill, on the other. Bertram Gross, as Wagner's [Senator, New York] special representative, was present at every meeting. . . . A few minutes before each conference session, Gross buttonholed Barkley or Cochran or both, discussed with them the strategy of the day, gave them draft proposals—some purely for bargaining purposes—and in the case of Barkley, filled in the gaps in the busy Majority Leader's knowledge about the history and meaning of the various sections of the bill. . . .

Stalemate.—During the first two conference sessions, the possibility of any agreement between the House managers and the Senate managers seemed remote. Whittington outlined in detail the House objections to the Senate version of S.380, and made it quite clear that the House managers would not accept any compromise bill which contained the words "full employment" or "the right to work," or which suggested any government guarantee of employment, or which placed the ultimate emphasis upon federal spending. Barkley, for the Senate managers, on the other hand, issued a blast against the House substitute and reminded the conferees of the President's warning that only something close to the Senate version would be acceptable to him. Basing his remarks on an analysis of the House substitute prepared by Gross, Barkley outlined both the omissions and the "weaknesses" of each section of the House bill. Granted the adamant attitude of both sides, it was obvious that someone would have to retreat if the conference was to proceed.

The Struggle over the Declaration of Policy.—The deadlock was broken on the third and fourth days of the conference when Gross worked out for Barkley a series of alternative policy declarations, none of which contained the term "full employment," but all of which contained the phrase "conditions under which there will be afforded useful and remunerative employment opportunities, including self-employment, for all Americans who are willing to work and are seeking work." The nature of the first concession on the part of the Senate sponsors is important, for it illustrates the technique used by Gross all the way through the conference debate. If the House managers objected to a particular phrase, Gross went to a thesaurus and juggled words around until he hit on a verbal equivalent. The fact that both sides were ultimately satisfied with most of the compromises made during the conference struggle cannot be understood without an appreciation of this technique. The House managers believed that real Senate concessions were being made with every change in language; the Senate sponsors were satisfied that a rose by any other name smells as sweet.

Perhaps the crowning example of this battle of the thesauruses was the fate of the "spending" provisions. . . .

[One] provision had been attacked by almost every conservative spokesman, and it was one of the sections of the bill which the House managers in the conference insisted would have to come out. By the time the Conference Committee met, Gross and the leading Congressional sponsors of the bill had already come to the conclusion that special reliance on spending was both disadvantageous politically and naive programmatically. Although for bargaining purposes, they opposed Whittington's insistence that the spending provisions would have to come out, it is interesting to note that on January 18, three days *before* the conference, Gross had drafted a substitute policy statement which made no reference to government spending. What finally emerged in place of the spending clauses was a broad statement, part of which Gross had lifted from President Roosevelt's declaration of war against Germany in 1941:

Sec. 2. The Congress hereby declares that it is the continuing policy and responsibility of the Federal Government to use all practicable means . . . *to coordinate and utilize all its plans, functions, and resources* for the purpose of maintaining conditions. . . . [Emphasis supplied.]

Since part of the "resources" of the federal government are its instrumentalities for spending and investment, and since the phrase finally accepted read "all . . . resources," the Senate sponsors felt, not without reason, that the conference phraseology was stronger than that in the original bill or in the Senate version. The House managers felt equally certain that dropping any specific mention of federal spending was a victory for their side. Conceivably they were both right.

The debate on the opening declaration of policy consumed the better part of five conference sessions. . . . "Full employment" had been a point of contention from the very beginning of the bill's long history. Almost impossible of unambiguous definition, the phrase had been challenged . . . in the Senate, and had been completely deleted from the House substitute. . . . At long last, Senator [Charles] Tobey [Republican, New Hampshire] came through with "maximum" to replace "full," and everyone seemed satisfied. Tobey was also responsible for adding the phrase "and the general welfare" after "free competitive enterprise" in the statement of the government's obligation to "foster and promote.". . .

The Final Agreement.—Once agreement had been reached on the Declaration of Policy, the rest of the discussion went rapidly. The section dealing with the Economic Report of the President was a condensation and clarification of the House substitute on this issue. Written by Gross . . . this revised section was adopted with almost no opposition.

The provisions for the Council of Economic Advisers as outlined in the House substitute were taken over almost intact. . . . The big issue, of course, was the relationship of the Council to the President and to Congress. The Senate managers insisted that any provision which in any way served to make ambiguous the relation of the Council to the President would be unacceptable. The House bill, it will be remembered, carried the statement, "The President is requested to make available to the Joint Committee on the Economic Report, if it desires, the various studies, reports, and recommendations of the Council which have been submitted to the President." The Senate managers forced the House managers to delete this section. . . .

With the general sanction of all concerned, the membership on the proposed Joint Committee on the Economic Report was cut to seven representatives from each House. . . .

A rapid survey of the work of the conference gives no real indication of the human side of the proceedings. Major credit for keeping the discussion moving must go to Senator Alben Barkley. Whenever discussions became tense and acrimonious, Barkley, as chairman, relieved the tension with a joke or a gentle whim. He performed . . . the function of the "master broker"—

the classic job of the statesman-politician: the discovery of areas of agreement. This was not always easy in the Full Employment conference. Ideological conflicts were mixed up with personality conflicts. Senator Taylor [Democrat, Idaho] was angry with Senator Taft [Republican, Ohio] when the latter dismissed the old-age pension provisions of the Senate bill as "window dressing"; Senator Tobey took such a personal dislike to Representative Carter Manasco [Democrat, Alabama] that he had to force himself to sit in the same room with him; on the rare occasions when Clare Hoffman [Republican Representative, Michigan] appeared, tempers rose noticeably; Whittington had to exercise considerable tact in getting Manasco to agree to a number of the compromises.

But on February 2, 1946, the job was done. The long legislative battle was all but completed. . . .

HOUSE AND SENATE APPROVAL

On February 6, 1946, the House listened to a number of schools of opinion about the meaning and value of the Employment Act of 1946. . . .

On one thing almost everyone was agreed: that the question of Presidential appointments to the Council was of vital importance. The conservatives wanted men "of business ability." The liberals wanted men who were "wholeheartedly devoted to the principles of the bill."

The Employment Act of 1946 was finally passed in the House by a vote of 320 to 84. . . . Two days later, on February 8, . . . the conference bill went through the Senate without opposition. It was signed by President Truman and became law on February 20, 1946. . . .

. . . The real question posed by the story of S.380 is what it suggests about the Congressional formulation of important social and economic policies in the . . . twentieth century.

Certainly one generalization is that the process is almost unbelievably complex. Legislative policy-making appears to be the result of a confluence of factors streaming from an almost endless number of tributaries: national experience, the contributions of social theorists, the clash of powerful economic interests, the quality of Presidential leadership, other institutional and personal ambitions and administrative arrangements in the Executive Branch, the initiative, effort, and ambitions of individual legislators and their governmental and non-governmental staffs, the policy commitments of political parties, and the predominant culture symbols in the minds both of leaders and followers in the Congress.

Most of these forces appear to be involved at every important stage in the policy-making process, and they act only within the most general limits of popular concern about a specific issue.

End questions

1. Why should every conference committee have a Gross and a Barkley? How effective were they in their respective roles?
2. Why did public attitudes change from restricting the government from interfering in the economy to a more permissive one?
3. Why is it difficult to reach agreements in conference committees?
4. Why is the House generally more "conservative" than the Senate with regard to federal spending? How is this illustrated with the Full Employment Act?

The American Presidency is unique, both as an office and as an institution. Unlike a king or prime minister, the American President must perform the two functions of Chief of State and Chief Executive at the same time. Moreover, he is directly responsible to all the people. Although attempts have been made by other nations to copy the office of the United States President, none of them have completely succeeded. This is because the nature of the American Presidency is derived from the traditions, history, and complexities that are peculiar to the United States. Still, there have been some instances when a foreign copy has come relatively close to the American model. France, Mexico, and Chile all have presidential structures now that combine some ceremonial duties with executive functions.

The Evolution of the Presidency

In the nearly two centuries of its existence as a conversion structure in the national political system, the American Presidency has become more and more powerful. Like other American political institutions, the organization of the executive branch has undergone major changes since the office of the President was established by the Framers of the Constitution. While in the past the Presidency was one of the weaker parts of the national system, today in certain respects it may be the strongest.

As the social, economic, and political climate of the nation has changed, the personal role of the President in government and the organization of the executive branch have been greatly expanded. Each occupant of the White House has construed the role of the President in his own way. While most have not altered the strength of the Presidency at all, a few have been adept at expanding the vaguely worded constitutional powers so as to assume more leadership in the legislative and other policy-making spheres. At the same time, Congress has had to provide the Chief Executive with an increasingly vast administrative structure to assist him in his expanded role.

Constitutional powers. There is little in the Constitution for anyone to have predicted in 1789 the extent to which the Presidency would expand its powers. Essentially, the document gives the President only two, very general, powers. Article II states first, that "the executive power shall be vested in a President" and second, that "the President shall be Commander in Chief of the Army and Navy of the United States, and of the militia. . . ." Aside from explaining that the President "shall take care that the laws be faithfully executed," and that "he may require the opinion, in writing, of the principal officer in each of the executive departments," the Constitution does not specify how the "executive power" is to be exercised.

Article II specifies only a few powers that belong solely to the President. Some require the "advice and consent of the Senate," including the powers to make treaties, and to "appoint ambassadors, other public ministers and consuls, judges of the Supreme Court and all other officers of the United States whose appointments are not . . . otherwise provided for [in the Constitution]." It would appear that the

How can one person, the President, be expected to cope with all the problems and responsibilities of his office? Should he be able to wear all of these hats or should some of them be assigned to other officials?

Framers were extremely reluctant to give the President too much power aside from commanding the military services, and they carefully limited his powers by requiring the approval of the Senate.

Besides these powers, the President has several duties stipulated in Article II. He presents "State of the Union" messages to Congress and recommends legislation. He can also convene either or both houses of Congress on "extraordinary occasions." In addition, he can "receive ambassadors and other public ministers," see that laws are "faithfully executed," and "commission all officers of the United States."

The strengthening factors. Over the years, the role of the President has greatly expanded, in spite of the scant number of constitutional guidelines for exercising the office. The Framers, of course, could not foresee all the changes that would take place in the role of the executive. They did, however, consciously provide the

Don Hesse in *The St. Louis Globe-Democrat*

(If executive powers strain the "original concept" too much, a constitutional change may be needed.)

office with certain strengths that have enabled the extent of its power to increase.

■ *One-man office.* First, the Framers rejected the idea of a plural executive and gave the executive powers to one man alone. The combination of the executive's singular office and his authority, which is independent of Congress, makes it possible for the President to act with far greater efficiency and dispatch than any other branch of the national government. This is especially obvious when the President wishes to have a particular policy carried out. The President's ability to make certain decisions alone—as in matters of setting tariff quotas and international trade negotiations—gives him an edge over the legislature in introducing policy as well as in putting policy into action.

■ *Fixed four-year term.* Second, because the President's term is fixed at four years, a holder of the office does not have to court popular and legislative support for every decision he makes in order to stay in office. This differs from a parliamentary system in which the chief executive does not have a fixed term but must rely on the legislature's periodic votes of confidence for his programs to stay in power. In the United States, a President can take an action that is unpopular in the short run, without any immediate risk to his position. He can be voted out of office by the electorate only at the end of his four-year term. Thus, the fixed term has been an important factor in permitting the power of the Presidency to expand.

■ *Separate constituency.* Third, although the President is somewhat limited by the functions he must share with the other branches, his independent authority and separate constituency have provided a base from which the power of the office could expand. By granting the powers of executive and Commander in Chief to the President exclusively, the Constitution protects the office against encroachment by the other branches—particularly the legislature. By setting up the electoral college system, the Constitution gave the President a constituency completely free from the control of the legislature. Because the electoral college has necessarily become more and more responsive to political parties and the democratized electorate, the President has been able to broaden his power as his electoral constituency has widened.

□ *Growth of political parties.* The Founding Fathers envisioned the electoral college as a means of insulating the President and presidential hopefuls, not only from the control of the legislature, but also from direct participation in popular politics. The electors from each state were to be appointed according to the rules set up by the state legislatures. It was assumed that the members of the electoral college would be the more responsible people from their respective states, and that they would select the most able and respected man for President without making prior commitments to particular candidates. The man they selected for the office would, in turn, be detached from partisan influences and would fulfill his duties in the best interests of the nation.

All of this was changed by the growth of the political parties. During the early 1800's, as political parties began to be important in the selection of presidential candidates, the electors became less independent. (Today electors are little more than puppets controlled by the parties.) Each political party nominated first the candidates for President and Vice President and then the candidates for the electoral college who were committed to elect the party's presidential choice.

As a result, potential presidential candidates and Presidents seeking reelection were identified with the political parties.

They had to satisfy these partisan groups in order to win nominations and the majority of the electoral college votes. At a later time, the political party of the successful candidate provided the man in office with a strong base of support.

□ *Democratization of the election process.* Another means of adding strength to the Presidency was the democratization of the procedures for nominating presidential candidates and for electing presidential electors. The shift of the party nominating process from congressional caucuses to national conventions permitted greater participation by the party's rank-and-file members. But this shift has not been completely successful. Although party nominating conventions reflect a broader base of party opinion than caucuses did, they are still controlled to some extent by cliques of influential politicans. The struggle to make conventions more responsive to party followers' opinions is still going on.

In addition, the popular election of presidential electors and the gradual democratization of the electorate itself have broadened the President's constituency. As suffrage has ceased to be the prerogative of property-holders and has been extended to blacks, women, and others, the President has acquired an even greater base of support which has strengthened the office considerably.

□ *Leader of the party.* With the increased strength of national political parties, the President and the opposition's presidential candidate became the most influential people in their respective parties. Obviously, the presidential candidates are vote-getters, and their parties are naturally going to support them and their programs. As leader of his party, the successful presidential candidate also controls, to some degree, his party's members in Congress. Once he is President, he should be able to depend on their support, in most cases, for any legislation he deems to be essential.

Today, the President also lends his image to the party he represents. The image of a party that is conveyed to the people is strongly shaped by the particular style of the White House occupant. The image of a President as a midwestern military hero such as Dwight D. Eisenhower, as a sophisticated easterner such as John F. Kennedy, or as a homey southwesterner such as Lyndon B. Johnson has considerable appeal to certain groups of the electorate. Each President lends his own personality to the office, and each organizes the office to suit himself. People within his party or outside of it identify with his particular style and consequently support him and his program.

■ *Vagueness of constitutional language.* Lastly, the language of Article II has encouraged the growth of the President's power. Unlike Article I which carefully enumerates, and thus limits, the powers of Congress, Article II does not specify what duties the "executive power" or the power of the "Commander in Chief" are to include. These powers, therefore, have been broadly interpreted to permit the President's role to expand. While there are other constitutional factors that have contributed to the strengthening of the Presidency, the expansion of presidential power can be assigned in part to the lack of conciseness and detail in the language of Article II.

Review questions

1. What powers were specifically given to the President in Article II of the Constitution?
2. How has the separate constituency of the President been a vital factor in the "evolution" of the office?

The President's Duties and Responsibilities

As the office of the Presidency has been steadily strengthened, the functions and responsibilities of the President have also been increased and reshaped by the demands of the times. Thus, the President has acquired a number of duties in addition to those originally assigned to him by the Constitution. In performing all of these functions, whether assigned or acquired, the President makes decisions and establishes policies, which constitute the outputs of the presidential subsystem. The executive branch as a conversion structure has been shaped as much by the outputs expected of it as by the many demands made on it.

Chief of State. In some countries, such as Germany, the United Kingdom, India, and Japan, the burdensome ceremonial functions are carried out by the president or the monarch acting as Chief of State, while the prime minister handles the duties of the executive. In the United States, both of these important functions fall to the President. The Constitution makes no provision for an independent Chief of State, and the President acquired the responsibility by default. Nevertheless, the ceremonial functions do add to his political strength. As the symbol of the American nation, he attracts a great deal of support from both within and outside the nation.

In his capacity as ceremonial chief, the President receives foreign ambassadors, presides over state dinners, sponsors the arts, and meets with representatives of such national groups as the Boy Scouts of

America and the Urban League. He lights the national Christmas tree, proclaims national holidays, and throws out the first ball to open the baseball season. Moreover, he sponsors numerous charity drives, buys the first Christmas seals, supports cancer research, and so forth.

As head of state, the President also signs all bills, treaties, and many appointments. The signing of bills and executive communications can occupy an hour or more of his time every day.

Essentially, when the President acts as head of state, he represents all the American people. The ceremonial functions of the nation must be performed with tact and finesse. They are very vital to any nation, because a breach of standard diplomatic protocol will be noticed by other nations and may affect international relations on a wide scale.

The role of the Chief of State is one of the few aspects of the Presidency that has not become rigid in its conduct. Each occupant of the White House has a certain amount of latitude to add his own personal touch to the performance of his ceremonial functions. The informal hospitable style of Lyndon Johnson, who invited visiting foreign dignitaries to his Texas ranch, was replaced by the more formal style of Richard Nixon in the early 1970's.

Commander in Chief. Article II, Section 2, of the Constitution provides that the President "shall be Commander in Chief of the Army and Navy of the United States, and of the militia of the several states, when called into the actual service of the United States." The growth of this presidential responsibility is one of the most remarkable developments in the office since the framing of the Constitution.

The President was originally given the responsibility of Commander in Chief for two primary reasons. First, it was clearly necessary to place this power in the branch of government that could act with the greatest cohesion and dispatch. Second, it was prudent to place the military under civilian control to keep the potential strength of the military within bounds. Otherwise, the control of the government might fall into the hands of a powerful military clique.

Likewise, to prevent the President from abusing his privileges as the commander of the armed forces, the Framers balanced this presidential power by giving Congress some major responsibilities with respect to the military. Congress has the power to declare war, to raise and support armies, and generally to maintain a military establishment. As seen by the Framers, the President's duty was to direct the organization that Congress created. Military action would be taken only after agreement had been reached by the House of Representatives and the Senate.

The role of Congress, however, in determining military actions has declined in importance in recent years as the President has gained more capability to direct military actions in undeclared wars, as in Korea and Vietnam. It would have been unthinkable to the Founding Fathers to give one man the power to declare war, just as it would be unthinkable today. Yet, the Commander in Chief clause has been interpreted so as to grant the President considerable power to act in case of conflict.

The significance of this presidential power was illustrated by the actions of Harry S. Truman in Korea. President Truman, acting on his own initiative, sent troops to Korea in 1950 after the North Koreans invaded South Korea. Congress never declared war nor did it participate in the initial decision to involve American troops.

■ *The Cuban missile crisis.* The ability of

the President to take quick and effective action in his role as Commander in Chief was dramatized in 1962. President John Kennedy had to react fast when he learned that the Soviet Union had begun to install missiles in Cuba, only ninety miles from the United States mainland. He, himself, had to review the possible consequences of any direct or indirect actions the United States might take. There was no time to call Congress or to consult congressional leaders. Such consultation would not have been fruitful because Congress lacked the necessary military and diplomatic information to give intelligent counsel. To catch the Soviet Union off guard and enable the United States to seize the initiative, the decision to blockade Cuba and isolate the island had to be made with utmost speed and in complete secrecy. At few times since World War II had a President been confronted with a more delicate situation than the Cuban crisis.

■ *Limits on presidential initiative.* In exercising his power as Commander in Chief, the President is not a completely free agent. He is limited, first, by the information and counsel of his advisers. He must also think of the political consequences of any action he takes, with respect to both international and domestic reactions. On the other hand, nothing in the Constitution prescribes what he should do.

Just as the Cuban crisis illustrated the weight of his responsibility, it also showed how limited the executive is in the choices he can make. The probable responses of the Soviet Union had to be carefully calculated, as well as the effect any decision would have on the United States and the rest of the world.

■ *The Vietnam conflict.* Almost all deci-

"How can I put it in a face-saving way?"

© *Punch*, London

(The President must weigh foreign against domestic needs even when he makes decisions as Commander in Chief.)

sions pertaining to United States commitments in Indochina during recent decades have been made by the President. Actually, the Congress followed a hands-off policy in Vietnam, leaving the conduct of the "war" entirely to the President. In August 1964, in response to a reported attack by the North Vietnamese on United States ships in the Gulf of Tonkin, Congress passed a resolution. In effect, this statement gave the President carte blanche to deal with the Vietnamese situation.

Not since World War II has the burden of the Commander in Chief been as great as during the Vietnam conflict. The Cuban crisis reached a rapid climax, but the Vietnam "war" has demanded the constant attention of two Presidents. The obstacles confronted by both Presidents Johnson and Nixon in attempts at peace negotiations and the continuation of this prolonged conflict prompted increasing criticism by those opposing the war. This is an instance when the President's mantle as Commander in Chief has been less than comfortable.

Leader of foreign affairs. The President's role as leader of foreign affairs is a natural complement to his roles as ceremonial Chief of State and Commander in Chief. In fact, all three of these roles merge at many points. Presidents often travel abroad. When they do, they represent the American people and act as major figures in the development of American foreign policy. The stature of the Presidency helps the occupant of the White House to deal with foreign nations, for they know that the President speaks with authority and with power.

Major foreign policy decisions are made by the President. This responsibility has been derived from his constitutional powers (1) to make treaties; (2) to nominate ambassadors, ministers, and consuls; (3) to receive foreign ambassadors; (4) to

report to Congress on the state of the union; and (5) to command the military forces.

How much the President becomes personally involved in the conduct of foreign policy depends on the nature of the man as well as on the times. During a major emergency, decisions will obviously require his personal attention. In most cases, though, the President can delegate his authority to subordinate officials. He relies heavily on the advice of the Secretary of State, the Secretary of Defense, and other officials directly engaged in the nation's foreign policy. This delegation of responsibility in foreign affairs results in increased authority for the President's administrators. Yet, although the State Department, the Defense Department—and the more than forty administrative agencies that participate in the foreign policy arena—play important roles, it is the President who makes the final decisions and directs the steps that the country takes in foreign policy.

■ *Shared functions of the Senate. The Federalist* carefully points out that there is a need for continuity as well as for speed and wisdom in the conduct of foreign policy. The Presidency, unified under one man, is the branch most able to meet these criteria. But to check the possibility of too rash a move by a President, the Constitution also gave certain foreign policy responsibilities to the Senate. The Framers felt that the older, supposedly wiser, Senators, with their longer terms in office, would offer more stability to the conduct of foreign affairs than the Representatives. Therefore, it is the Senators who must approve presidential appointments of ambassadors and ministers, and who must ratify treaties.

The major constitutional limitation on the President's power in the conduct of foreign affairs is that he needs the consent of two-thirds of the Senate for approval of a treaty. Although for years the Senate has not turned down a major treaty supported by the President, it did veto the treaty that provided for United States entry into the League of Nations in 1920. Today, if there is even the possibility of such a senatorial veto, the President will negotiate an *executive agreement,* an arrangement that is outside the framework of a formal treaty and does not require Senate approval. The executive agreement is not mentioned in the Constitution, and has only been accepted in usage. The Supreme Court, however, has declared that the executive agreement is "implied" in the President's treaty-making power.

Although the Constitution recognized an important role for the Senate in foreign relations, the dominance of the President was established very early. George Washington's neutrality proclamation, issued in 1793 during a war between France and Britain, established a precedent in foreign affairs that was carried on until the twentieth century. Jefferson's deal with France in 1803 for the Louisiana Territory was another example of presidential freedom in the conduct of foreign affairs. James Monroe's assertion of the "Monroe Doctrine" in 1823—which warned the governments of Europe against further colonization or political intervention in the Western Hemisphere—established another precedent, still in force.

The increasing involvement of the United States in foreign affairs during the twentieth century has resulted in an even greater assumption of authority by the President. Given the power by Congress to grant aid to any nation whose defense was vital to the United States, President Franklin Roosevelt was able to promise lend-lease credit of $1 billion to Soviet Russia, nearly six months before the United States entry into World War II. Gradually, Presidents have expanded this authority to aid and defend other nations against incursions, even ideological ones. The Truman Doctrine, granting aid to countries in Europe for the containment of communism, and Eisenhower's extension of this doctrine to the Middle East are two examples. Most recently, American involvement in Southeast Asia has been brought about through the President's power to use the armed forces when he feels the interests of the United States are at stake.

■ *The role of Congress and the Court.* However, because of its important role in domestic matters, Congress as a whole often acts as a negative check on the President in foreign policy matters. Congress can, for example, cut foreign aid

Courtesy of Hugh Haynie, *The Courier-Journal.*
© 1970 Los Angeles Times Syndicate.

"But, pray! What prompts you to question my divine power . . . huh, knave?"

(In foreign policy matters, Congress has some powers but the President's dominance is rarely questioned.)

appropriations. Or it can legislate tariffs and import quotas to protect American industries and thus affect the ability of the President to conduct diplomatic affairs with certain nations. Actually, Congress has little opportunity to make positive contributions to foreign policy, because it lacks the diplomatic channels and access to information available to the President.

The courts have generally supported the President's leadership in conducting foreign affairs. As Justice George Sutherland pointed out in his opinion in the *Curtiss-Wright* case:

"In this vast external realm [foreign affairs] with its important, complicated, delicate and manifold problems, the President alone has the power to speak or listen as a representative of the nation. He makes treaties with the advice and consent of the Senate; but he alone negotiates. Into the field of negotiation the Senate cannot intrude; and Congress itself is powerless to invade it."[1]

Chief Executive. The role of the President as Chief Executive is clearly one of his most fundamental powers. Article II bestows on the President some authority over the bureaucracy by providing that he shall "take care that the laws be faithfully executed." To accomplish this task, he is given the right to "require the opinion, in writing, of the principal officer in each of the executive departments, upon any subject relating to the duties of their respective offices."

Alexander Hamilton, in *The Federalist,* No. 72, recognized this duty of the President as leader of the bureaucracy. He argued that since the President would appoint those people who would be essentially responsible for carrying out his

[1] United States v. Curtiss-Wright Export Corp., *299 U.S. 304 (1936).*

functions, they should be considered his assistants and "subject to this superintendence." Coupled with Article II, Hamilton's argument has been used to support the theory that the Framers intended the President to be leader of the bureaucracy. In line with this concept, the Report of the President's Committee on Administrative Management in 1937 recommended that the number of presidential aides be increased so that he could better deal with the bureaucracy. This report held not only that it is the constitutional responsibility of the President to be the leader of the executive branch, but also that efficiency and democracy require him to operate in this capacity. The establishment of the Executive Office of the President, was a direct result of this report. (See Chapter 14, pages 341–344.)

The views of the President's Committee in 1937 were echoed by the Hoover Commissions in 1949 and 1955. These two reports stated that there should be a direct line of command from the top to the bottom and from the bottom to the top within the federal bureaucracy, with the President as the leader. Later reports, such as the Landis Report on Regulatory Agencies to the President Elect in 1960, emphasized the importance of giving the President the tools for coping effectively with his responsibilities as Chief Executive.

The increasing size of the bureaucracy has made the Chief Executive's job more and more complex. At the same time, the bureaucracy has been able to function with less and less supervision. Still, there is little doubt that the President is usually held responsible for what the bureaucracy does.

Legislative leader. The role of the President as chief legislator stems from several constitutional sources. First, the Constitution has given him the authority to recommend legislation to Congress. Second, he is required to inform Congress about the "state of the union" from time to time. In the annual "State of the Union" message, the President often suggests projects or proposals for legislation.

In addition to these constitutional provisions, there are other factors from which the President derives his role as "legislator." As the head of his party, he helps shape platforms and policies which are recommended for congressional action. Furthermore, in his role as leader of the bureaucracy, he naturally becomes the spokesman for legislative proposals coming from the administrative agencies. In turn, administrative agencies may draw up proposals for legislation at the President's request.

Whenever the President involves himself in legislative activities, his position as leader of the bureaucracy enables him to be highly effective. He can call upon the resources—the information and technological "know-how"—of the bureaucracy to aid him in the development of particular programs. He can also direct agencies, if they come under his authority, to take action that will have the effect of legislation. For example, President Kennedy directed the administrative agencies to write nondiscrimination clauses into all government contracts when federal funds were involved. In effect, this was a legislative mandate. It accomplished something that Congress had been unable to do.

Party leader. Obviously, when he takes office, the President has already won the leadership of his political party. He has shaped the party platform, emphasized campaign issues that he felt were important, and generally determined the nature and organization of the party.

But a strong President must continue to be an effective politician throughout his years in the White House. He must maintain a strong position in his party in order to influence the legislature and to maintain the support of the community as a whole. A President who does not pay attention to his duties as party leader will find himself isolated and unable to start the programs he feels are important.

Strong Presidents are invariably strong party leaders. This is illustrated by the administrations of several Presidents in the last few decades. Franklin Roosevelt gave a new and vigorous image to the Democratic party in 1933. Throughout his years in office, Roosevelt held a firm hand on the helm of the Democratic party. His strength in his party helped him to get New Deal legislation enacted.

Dwight Eisenhower, on the other hand, was less willing to bend to all of the wishes of the Republican party leaders during his terms in office. In keeping himself somewhat aloof from party politics, Eisenhower probably limited his chances to get legislation through Congress.

President John Kennedy, a Democrat, followed in the footsteps of Eisenhower. Although his New Frontier policies were admired by many Democratic leaders, he was unable to get control of his party; and this hampered his ability to get proposals passed by either house of Congress. Lyndon Johnson's term in office was another story. Even before Congress had a chance to examine the Great Society program, Johnson included it in the platform of the Democratic party in the campaign of 1964. By doing this, he gained a party commitment to his policies which many Democratic congressmen felt they had to uphold after the election.

Limits on presidential power. At the same time that presidential duties may add to the stature and prestige of the office, they may also mark the limits of its power. In each of his many roles, the President responds to a particular constituency. Included among his constituents are the general electorate, private interest groups, congressmen, administrative agencies, foreign nations, and many others. Because the President relies on the support of each group, the interest of each one will limit his activities in all areas of his responsibility. For example, as leader of his political party, the President may increase his power in Congress and in the community generally. At the same time, he is somewhat limited by party considerations when he exercises his other responsibilities. When acting as Chief Executive or as Chief Legislator, the appointments he makes and the programs he proposes will have to conform somewhat to the interests of his political party. Similarly, he will be limited by the interests of the bureaucracy and private interest groups when responding to the demands of party leaders.

Thus, while the President can use his constituency groups to gain necessary political support, he must be careful when making policies and decisions not to go beyond what they consider appropriate. Before making decisions, he must weigh what his constituents' reactions will be.

In describing the limitations of the Presidency, Theodore C. Sorensen, an adviser to President Kennedy, noted: "No President is free to go as far or as fast as his advisers, his politics, and his perspective may direct him." According to Sorensen, presidential decisions must be workable, enforceable, and possible without violating constitutional or statutory law; the President is limited by money, as well as "manpower, time, credibility, patronage, and all the other tools at his command."[2]

[2] *Theodore C. Sorensen,* Decision-Making in the White House *(New York: Columbia Univ. Press, 1963), pp. 22–23.*

A PRESIDENTIAL CONJUROR.

Keppler in *Puck*

(One way to increase party support is to hand out favors as President Chester A. Arthur is shown doing here.)

Review questions

1. Why were the duties of Commander in Chief of the armed forces given to the President rather than to Congress or to a military officer?

2. In which of his roles does the President function when he:
   (a) vetoes a bill,
   (b) requests a report from an administrative agency,
   (c) negotiates a treaty?

Chapter Review

Terms you should know

advice and consent	executive agreement	Hoover Commissions
Chief Executive	executive power	presidential constituencies
Chief of State	fixed term	State of the Union message
Commander in Chief	Gulf of Tonkin resolution	Truman Doctrine

Questions about this chapter

1. What characteristics of the American Presidency make it unique?
2. Explain how each of the following provided a base on which the strength of the President could expand: (a) independent authority, (b) singular power, (c) separate constituency, (d) fixed four-year term.
3. What was the original purpose for having the President elected through an electoral-college system? How did the development of political parties affect this system?
4. How is the President's power strengthened by his role as party leader?
5. How has the balance between the President and Congress changed regarding control over the military? What considerations limit the President's power as Commander in Chief?
6. Describe the President's duties as Chief of State. What advantages and disadvantages would there be to having another person perform these duties?
7. What Senate responsibility is a major check on the President's power to conduct foreign affairs? How else can Congress limit this power?
8. What two arguments support presidential control of the bureaucracy?
9. Why is the President held responsible for most foreign policy decisions?
10. How is the President limited by his various roles and constituencies?

Thought and discussion questions

1. What developments have contributed to the increased strength of the President? Discuss whether this increase in the President's power has created an imbalance between the executive and legislative branches of government.
2. It has been said that "strong Presidents are invariably strong party leaders." Referring to Table 11:1 (Chapter 11, page 268), explain what this statement means. In a democratic society, should a President have to be a strong party leader to be a strong President?
3. Congress gave Franklin D. Roosevelt the power to grant aid to "any nation whose defense was vital to the United States." How did later Presidents expand this power?

Discuss the advantages and disadvantages of the President's power to call out troops in a crisis.

4. Discuss what Theodore Sorensen meant when he said, "No President is free to go as far or as fast as his advisers, his politics, and his perspective may direct him." Does this indicate that the system of checks and balances actually limits the President?

Class project

Check the back issues of your local newspaper, or of a weekly periodical such as *Time* or *Newsweek,* for articles about the President's activities in the last six months. From each of these news articles, identify the various roles that the President is performing: Chief of State, Commander in Chief, leader of foreign affairs, Chief Executive, legislative leader, or party leader. In which of these roles is the President most active? Which does he seem to perform best?

Case Study: Should the President overshadow Congress?

From the beginning of the American Republic, the relationship between the executive and legislative branches has been strained—especially over the power to declare war. Even though the Constitution reserves this power for the Congress, increasingly Presidents have taken it upon themselves, as Commanders in Chief, to send troops into combat. Presidents have even indirectly involved the United States in hostilities, leaving Congress with no alternative but to formally declare war, or to appropriate funds for its conduct.

The Founding Fathers conceived of the legislative branch as a countervailing force to the executive. But in foreign affairs, it seems that the Chief Executive often acts on his own. Has the Presidency assumed too much power? Should the balance of power be restored?

The polarization of the American people over the Vietnam conflict gave such questions special import. Eric Goldman, in the following article, discusses the struggle between the executive and legislative branches and tries to determine who actually has the authority to make decisions that lead to military involvement.

While reading the excerpt, consider the following:
1. What are the origins of the presidential-congressional conflict? Why did the Founding Fathers give the power to declare war to Congress and not to the President?
2. Why is Theodore Roosevelt often called "the first modern President"?
3. What circumstances can make a President decide to lead the nation into war?
4. How have regional pacts and joint resolutions affected presidential and congressional power?

THE PRESIDENT, THE PEOPLE,

The Constitution of the United States declares in the plainest possible English: "The Congress shall have Power . . . To declare War." Yet in the last twenty years Americans have fought two major wars—in Korea and in Vietnam—without a congressional declaration of war. . . .

Naturally, many Americans opposed to the Vietnam war are crying outrage. Many others, for or against the war or somewhere in between, ask a worried question: What has happened to the traditional constitutional procedure whereby the President leads in international affairs but Congress has a potent check on him when the decision involves life and death for the nation's young men and sweeping consequences for the whole country? Is there no way to bring foreign policy back under greater popular control, by restoring the congressional role or through some other technique?

. . . [I]n actuality the answers [to these questions] are entangled in complex considerations of just what the Founding Fathers did and did not write into the Constitution. . . .

The wise and hardheaded men who assembled in 1787 to write a constitution for the United States were members of a generation that had just fought a bitter war against the British executive, King George III. They were sick of battles and their devastation and intensely concerned to circumscribe any decision for war. . . . [A half century later], Representative Abraham Lincoln wrote in 1848 that the Constitutional Convention gave the warmaking power to Congress because "kings had always been involving and impoverishing their people in wars, pretending generally, if not always, that the good of the people was the object. . . ."

So the Congress, not the President, was to decide war or peace. . . . The Founding Fathers made one man who was on the scene, the President, Commander in Chief of the Army and Navy. The wording of the first draft of the Constitution gave Congress the exclusive power to "make" war. On the floor of the convention, "make" was changed to "declare," assigning the President the right to use the Army and Navy in order to meet specific emergencies while retaining for the House and Senate the power to decide full-scale war.

. . . The Founding Fathers may have made the President the Commander in Chief, but they gave Congress the power of the purse in determining the size and nature of the armed forces. Until late in the convention, the right to make treaties was vested in the Senate alone. But there were obvious advantages in having one man initiate treaties, receive foreign ambassadors, name and instruct American ambassadors. The Chief Executive would do these things, although he was to appoint ambassadors only with the approval of a Senate majority and make treaties with the "Advice and Consent" of two thirds of the Senate.

In foreign affairs, as in all areas, the Founding Fathers were notably spare in laying down specific dictates and in the language that they used to write the provisions. Yet they said enough to make it clear that they envisaged a foreign policy system in which the President would lead, but in collaboration with Congress, especially the Senate, and in which the Chief Executive would be subject to continuing scrutiny and formidable restraints whenever his activities touched that most serious aspect of foreign affairs, general war.

. . . Inevitably, Presidents tended to feel that they had superior information and were acting only after mature consideration of the matter; congressmen were interfering out of impulse, ignorance, politics, or a yen to encroach on White House prerogatives. Inevitably, congressmen, considering themselves sound in judgment and closer to the popular will, tended to believe that Chief Executives were trying, . . . to create situations in which [as one Senator

AND THE POWER TO MAKE WAR

has declared] "advices and consents [would be] ravished, in a degree, from us."

Before many decades it also became clear that while Congress might have the war power, a determined Chief Executive could put the House and the Senate in a position where they had little alternative except to vote war. The Democratic President elected in 1844, the unsmiling, tenacious James K. Polk, believed it was manifest destiny for America to expand. Texas had been formally annexed, but Mexico still considered it a rebellious province, and border disputes continued; California lay a luscious plum ready for the plucking from Mexico. President Polk kept trying to maneuver Mexico into acceptance of his ambitions, while he built a fervid public opinion behind expansionism. Finally the President ordered General Zachary Taylor into territory claimed by Mexico, and Mexican troops attacked American cavalry. . . .

Half a century later the obverse of the coin was showing. Of all wars the United States has fought, none has come to be considered more pointless and reprehensible than the Spanish-American War, and that venture was the doing of Congress, driven on by public opinion. During the 1890's a rebellion in the Spanish colony of Cuba, brutally combatted by the Madrid government, caught up a mounting jingo sentiment in the United States. . . .

When Congress roared through a resolution recognizing the "belligerency" of the Cuban rebels, President Cleveland denounced the move as an intrusion on the powers of the Chief Executive and privately remarked that if Congress declared war, he as Commander in Chief would refuse to mobilize the Army. . . . Finally, the President capitulated. He planned to run for re-election; besides, he was scarcely deaf to voices like that of the senator who thundered to Assistant Secretary of State William R. Day, "Day, by———, don't your President know where the war-declaring power is lodged? Tell him by———,

that if he doesn't do something, Congress will exercise the power." . . .

A war of territorial seizure maneuvered through by a determined President, an ugly war forced by public opinion and Congress . . . more and more instances of acrid White House-Congress clashes in foreign affairs—during the late eighteenth and nineteenth centuries the constitutional system was hardly functioning with glowing results in international matters. Yet the wars or quasi-wars did not pile up long casualty lists; they did not slash through everyday living. The most disruptive conflict, the Civil War, was removed by its very nature from the usual questions of constitutional responsibility. Whatever the underlying reality the Mexican-American War was fought under an authorization overwhelmingly granted by Congress. . . .

President Theodore Roosevelt has often been called "the first modern President," and he was that in many ways. . . . No man to turn away from power, [he] . . . [drove] deep into the American system the doctrine that the Chief Executive is—to use his phrase—"the steward" of the nation, endowed under the Constitution with vast "inherent powers" to act in behalf of what he considers the good of the country.

Action accompanied doctrine. . . . In 1903 T.R. saw to it that Panamanian rebels set up an independent state covering the desired canal zone, and the new nation, to no one's surprise, gave him what he wanted. ("I took the Canal Zone," said President Theodore Roosevelt, "and let Congress debate.") Did T.R. arrive at the conclusion during the Russo-Japanese War of 1904–05 that the security of the United States was best served by a Japanese victory? In entire secrecy he informed Tokyo that, if needed, America would act as an ally, which could have proved a commitment for war. In 1907 T.R. ordered the entire American fleet on a razzle-dazzle trip around the world, loosing all kinds of diplomatic reverberations.

329

. . . Yet this first modern President was . . . anticipating in a serious way the modern presidential trend. Stirred on by changed conditions, he was moving through that broad arch erected by the Founding Fathers— between, on the one side, the clear power of the Chief Executive to lead in foreign affairs and to command the armed forces and, on the other side, the powers of Congress to do certain specific things.

As the twentieth century progressed and the enmeshments of the world grew tighter and more troublesome. . . . The President felt full blast the forces of modernity, which came crashing daily into his office. As the leader of the whole nation, he was heavily influenced by considerations of collective security, the moral position of the United States before international opinion, and the problems that tied in with the stability of the country's economy. Of course members of Congress knew these same concerns, but they were also subject to local, more inward-looking pressures. . . . More and more, Presidents viewed Congress as the adversary and thought in terms of skirting around it or, if necessary, ignoring it.

This occurred at critical points on the road toward American participation in both World Wars I and II. During the European phase of World War I, Germany climaxed three years of friction with the United States by announcing unrestricted submarine warfare. . . . In February, 1917, President Wilson asked Congress for authority to arm merchantmen, an act that could scarcely fail to lead to war. The debate was stormy, and in the upper house eleven senators filibustered the measure to death. Thereupon the President announced that "a little group of willful men had rendered the great government of the United States helpless and contemptible" and ordered the merchantmen armed anyhow. War was declared in April.

After the eruption of [World War II] in 1939 President Franklin Roosevelt was convinced that for the good of the United States it belonged at the side of the antifascist powers. Yet he faced tremendous anti-intervention sentiment, . . . amply reflected in Congress. . . . Under the circumstances, F.D.R. undertook an extraordinary series of executive actions, which sought to hem in Japan economically and to help the nations fighting Nazi Germany. . . .

By the time America was fighting in World War II, it was manifest that President Roosevelt had made war and was continuing to conduct foreign policy with only a defensive concern for congressional opinion. Plenty of angry comment was made about this, yet still the warmaking power did not become a major national issue. In the case of both World Wars I and II, a semblance of congressional authority was preserved by the ultimate declaration of war voted by the House and Senate. Of more significance, the two wars were generally accepted by the public; they were led by widely popular Chief Executives; and if they brought serious problems to the society, they did not seem to tear it apart.

In June, 1950, President Harry Truman . . . learned of the invasion of South Korea by North Korea. . . . This was plain aggression, the President told himself; aggression unchecked during the 1930's had led to World War II; he was not going to be party to another such tragedy. The next morning the reports were grim: South Korea appeared about to collapse. That night Harry Truman ordered American armed forces into the Korean fighting. Then the United Nations Security Council, on motion of the United States representative, "recommended" assistance to South Korea, and the President summoned congressional leaders, as he put it, "so that I might inform them on the events and decisions of the past few days.". . . At no time did President Truman ask congressional authority for the war.

. . . The simple fact was that the traditional concept of a President leading in foreign policy and then, if necessary, going to Congress for a declaration of war had become obsolete. Historically, war meant that a nation, using whatever weapons seemed feasible, attempted to conquer another country or to beat it into submission. In an era of Cold War, and after the development of nuclear weapons, armed conflicts were taking a different form. Small Communist nations, unofficially backed by large ones, were probing remote areas. The United States was replying not by war in the conventional sense but by what was being called "limited war"—limited in the use of weapons . . . and limited in objective.

. . . Over the decades, by laws and even more by precedents, a declaration of war had come to confer on the President sweeping powers over the entire national life, particularly in the sensitive area of economic affairs.

Fighting a limited war, President Truman wanted to limit its home effects, and the opposition to them which could be aroused. . . .

. . . Public opinion, which at first strongly favored the Korean intervention, swung against it and to an extent that had not occurred during any previous conflict; by 1951 the Gallup poll reported a majority believing that the whole intervention was a mistake and favoring prompt withdrawal. Opposition leaders in Congress now were storming against "Truman's War," that "unconstitutional" war; and this time the attacks were building a feeling that something was definitely wrong with the warmaking procedures of the United States.

After the Korean War, and as part of the mounting American concern over Communist expansionism, the United States stepped up negotiations with other nations for regional defense pacts. These agreements were impeccably constitutional; they were treaties, negotiated by the executive branch, then debated in the Senate and approved by a two-thirds vote. Yet they contained clauses that could be construed to give Presidents further leverage in foreign affairs. A typical pact was SEATO, negotiated in 1954 by the Eisenhower Secretary of State, John Foster Dulles. It bound the United States, in the event of "armed aggression" by a Communist nation in Southeast Asia, to "act to meet the common danger in accordance with its constitutional processes" and, in the case of other types of threats in the area, to "consult" on the measures to be adopted—whatever a President might take all that to mean, in whatever specific circumstances he found himself.

Simultaneously, an old procedure—a joint House-Senate congressional resolution concerning international affairs—was gathering fresh meaning. . . . Presidents who contemplated moves that might result in war or quasi-war sought some form of mandate from the House and the Senate. They also wanted to gather bipartisan support behind their action or projected action and behind their general policy . . . they sought to present a united front to warn off Communist or Communist-allied nations from adventurous plans.

. . . The joint resolutions varied in a number of ways. But they were alike in their general pattern of giving congressional approval to a specific action or contemplated action of the Chief Executive and to his broadly stated policy for a particular troubled area of the world.

During the presidential campaign of 1964, the celebrated shots were fired in the Gulf of Tonkin by North Vietnamese gunboats against an American destroyer. . . .

President Johnson ordered a harsh retaliatory bombing of North Vietnamese patrol-boat bases. Then he summoned congressional leaders and told them he thought a joint resolution, like the Formosa and Middle East and Cuban resolutions, should be put through Congress swiftly. The document reached the House and Senate the next morning. It approved the bombing; spoke of America's "obligations" under SEATO to defend South Vietnam; declared that the United States was "prepared, as the President determines, to take all necessary steps, including the use of armed force," to assist any SEATO nation "in defense of its freedom"; and provided that the resolution remain in force until the Chief Executive declared it no longer necessary or the Congress repealed it by majority votes.

. . . How many congressmen wanted to vote No on such a proposition, especially three months before an election? The debate on the Tonkin Resolution in the House took just forty minutes, and the tally was 416–0. The Senate, after only eight hours of discussion. approved 88–2.

. . . More than the Korean War, Vietnam distorted American society at a time when it was still less able to stand further dislocation. And as a large part of public opinion and of Congress turned against the involvement, the cries once again went up, against "Johnson's war," that "unconstitutional horror." But this time there was a difference.

. . . When the subject of his authority for the war came up [Johnson] would pull out the slip containing the Tonkin Resolution and read from it. . . . [T]he problem treated in the Tonkin Resolution turned into a major war, and L.B.J. exploited the document fully, privately and publicly. . . .

. . . The nub of the situation is the power of the Chief Executive as Commander in Chief and those general or "inherent powers" that have come to cluster about the office of the Presidency. Is there really a way to restrict the powers of the Commander in Chief without possibly doing more harm than good in an era when one man's swiftly pressing the button may be necessary for some degree of national survival, or his prompt decision to use non-nuclear armed forces could be essential to achieving a purpose generally agreed upon by the country? Do the words exist that could inhibit "inherent powers" without simultaneously harassing the President, or blocking him, in taking actions that are widely considered necessary? Is this not particularly true in a period when his office is the one instrumentality that can make decisive moves in behalf of the national interest, whether that interest be expressed in domestic or foreign affairs . . . ?

Apart from the difficulty of controlling the President by new language, there is a still more troublesome question—whether, in fact, the Congress and "the people" are less likely than a Chief Executive to get the country into an unwise war. There is not only the glaring instance of the Spanish-American war; other examples, most notably the War of 1812, give pause. Then a rampant faction in Congress—a group with dreams of conquering Canada, who brought the phrase "war hawks" into the American language—helped mightily in pushing the United States into a conflict that was a credit neither to the good sense nor the conscience of the nation. Similarly, in the early, frightened Cold War days, President Truman was worried, and justly so, about a considerable congressional bloc that was restless to take on Russia.

Yet whatever must be said about the dangers or difficulties of restricting the presidential power to make war, the fact remains that something is decidedly wrong with the process. . . . It *is* a travesty of democracy to have so vital a decision so completely in the hands of one man. As Benjamin Franklin observed during the Constitutional Convention, the nation can never be sure "what sort" of human being will end up in the White House; some might be overly ambitious or "fond of war." The country can also never be certain—no matter how able and peaceminded the Chief Executive—that he will not be led into an unfortunate decision by his dogmas or his limitations. . . .

Ideally, what is needed is the creation in modern terms of a system something like the one envisaged by the Founding Fathers, in which the President would have his powers as Commander in Chief and would lead in foreign policy while being guided and checked to some degree by Congress. Toward that end, no good purpose is served by continuing the practice of congressional joint resolutions in international affairs. Either the resolution must say so little that it does not significantly present a bipartisan front to the enemy, or it must be so sweeping that it hands the Chief Executive a blank check.

. . . For this purpose it is essential to note that in every instance when the United States has gone through all the prescribed constitutional forms, with the President recommending war and the Congress "declaring" it, the House and the Senate have never really "declared war." Five consecutive times, from the War of 1812 through World War II, what Congress actually did was to recognize an existing state of war, allegedly caused by other nations. This was not simply the result of the natural desire to make the enemy appear the cause of the fighting. More important, it reflected the facts that by the time Congress considered a declaration of war, a long train of actions had made combat involvement inevitable or next to inevitable and that, in most instances, the actions had been taken by the White House.

The problem of increasing the participation of Congress in foreign policy . . . involves less the matter of a declaration of war than a continuing role for the legislative branch in the decisions that lead to large-scale military intervention. . . .

The slow and intricate process of building a realistic base for congressional participation in international affairs—will the American people press for it? A natural aftermath of war is the urge to forget about its horrors, including the way that the country got into them. Yet Vietnam has been a shock to millions and to groups containing many influential figures, and certainly the foreseeable trend of events will keep ever present the possibility of large-scale United States combat involvement. Perhaps the present high feelings about Vietnam will carry over sufficiently to create a congressional stance that will give the American people some degree of responsible surveillance over the disposition abroad of their lives, their fortunes, and their sacred honor.

End questions

1. What parallels exist between the Korean War and the Vietnam conflict? Where do the similarities end?
2. What is the solution recommended by Goldman for restoring the balance of power between the executive and the legislative branches? Does Goldman feel the problem of correcting the imbalance between the President and the Congress is solvable?
3. How do you feel about Goldman's thesis? Do you think the President has been usurping congressional power? Can you find any articles other than this one, to support your opinion?

CHAPTER 14
Presidential Policy-Making

"The President Supports Recommendations of Special Panel on American Indians"; "Chief Executive Proposes New Excise Tax"; "The White House Lowers Tariffs"; "United States Signs Fishing-Rights Treaty." These headlines are announcing outputs of the presidential conversion structure. When the President makes recommendations to an executive department, sets fiscal policy for congressional approval, or initiates measures that affect international trade, he has performed one of his many roles to arrive at a policy-output. What factors influence the policies he makes? What advisory and administrative apparatus does he utilize within the presidential conversion structure? How is the continuity of this structure preserved when there is a change of Presidents?

Inputs for the Presidency

Although the many roles of the President have been formally shaped by the Constitution, congressional legislation, and court decisions, his real performance is molded informally by his various constituencies as well as by his personal political goals. To a great extent, the President depends on the support of constituencies outside of government to ensure his own reelection and the election of legislators who will favor his programs. In addition, the President depends on support from within the government itself if he is to accomplish his programs while in office.

To maintain the support he needs, the President must respond to the demands of his many constituencies. While setting policy, he must listen to and weigh the advice, opinions, and needs of all of them. The demands as well as the support of these constituencies constitute the inputs of the presidential policy-making subsystem. Obviously, the President needs an enormous amount of political skill to cope with all of these demands.

Non-governmental constituencies. Outside of government there are several constituencies whose demands must be considered by the President. These include the general electorate, private pressure groups, and his own political party.

■ *Electorate demands.* A President who may run again for office, like any presidential candidate, must be responsive to those segments of the electorate whose support is crucial to his election. Each candidate can count on his own party to deliver a certain number of electoral votes. For example, most Republican candidates are fairly certain that they will get the votes of the wheat-belt states of Kansas, Nebraska, North and South Dakota. Until recently, the southern states of Alabama, Arkansas, Georgia, South Carolina, Mississippi, and Louisiana were known as the "Solid South" because their electoral votes always went into the Democratic column.

But these few sure states are not enough to win a plurality in a presidential election. Urban and industrial states—such as Pennsylvania, New York, California, Michigan, and Illinois—cast the greatest numbers of electoral votes. The presidential candidate who can swing these states will very likely win an election.

If one analyzes the presidential elections in the twentieth century, there have been few variations from this rule. For the most part, it is the urban states that determine

The many roles of the presidential office are concentrated in one elected official. What are the informal mechanisms and institutional devices that allow the President to work as an effective conversion structure?

the results of a presidential election. The largely rural, southern states, for example, may control Congress through the Democratic party as a result of seniority rules (see Chapter 12), but they are not usually a deciding factor in presidential elections. The electoral votes of the "Solid South" have swung the election for a Democratic President only once in this century. That was in 1916 when Woodrow Wilson triumphed over Charles Evans Hughes with a margin of twenty-three electoral votes.

To retain the urban support he needs, the President must answer some of the demands made on him by urban dwellers. These include demands for improved mass transportation, welfare programs, better housing, and more recently, the cleanup of environmental (air and water) pollution. No President can ignore the numerous policy areas that have such a profound impact on the voters who reside in the nation's larger cities.

The Democratic party has tended in the past to respond more to the demands of lower-income voters who live in such large numbers in the metropolitan areas. Democratic Presidents have ordinarily encouraged legislation to combat unemployment, uphold collective bargaining, increase federal aid to education, and institute Medicare. On the Republican side, the major sources of electoral strength have been found in middle and high-income areas of large and medium-sized cities, and in suburban and rural areas. Republican Presidents have tended to respond to demands for fiscal responsibility, balancing of the budget, tax cuts, and less governmental control of business.

Most recently, presidential candidates from both parties have had to pay stricter attention to demands for civil rights as voters in urban areas have expressed increasingly strong feelings on the issue. The urban electorate, made up of many minority groups, tends to be far more involved in the question than the rural segment of the country.

In addition, some minority groups in large cities, especially those composed of naturalized or first-generation Americans, tend to be more interested in international matters than the rest of the electorate. This interest will, of course, be brought to the attention of the President whenever he has to deal with some aspect of international affairs.

It is true that between presidential elections, there are few instances when the general electorate—whether urban or rural—expresses its demands or support of the President. Most voters do not express themselves and remain within the "silent majority." While the President pays close attention to public opinion polls to learn what the electorate is thinking, he usually interprets the silence of this large group as support for his activities.

The electorate, however, can and does reaffirm or retract its support of the President indirectly through the election of other government officials. This becomes most apparent during congressional election years when voters may express dissatisfaction with the President by electing legislators who oppose him. Another device the electorate can use to influence the President is the presidential primary. The significance of this device was illustrated by the New Hampshire primary in 1968 when President Lyndon Johnson received fewer votes than Senator Eugene McCarthy who had campaigned vigorously against the President's Vietnam policy. Thus, in spite of the general apathy or silence of the electorate, no President can completely ignore this important constituency when he formulates policy during his term in office.

■ *Private interest groups.* The demands of private interest groups influence the outputs of the Presidency as well. The ability of private groups to influence presidential decision-making depends, in part, on the President himself. He will, of course, be influenced by an interest group if its goals fit into his own program. If he is advocating a policy of controlling air and water pollution, for example, then he is almost sure to accept the support, be accessible to, and agree with the demands of conservation groups.

The extent to which a President responds to such demands depends on several factors, including the importance of the particular group's support. Labor-union or business-community leaders may be sources of campaign contributions, and may also have some influence over large segments of the voting population. The pronouncements of some groups on presidential policies may also contribute to the President's public image. A statement by the National Education Association favoring the President's education program could boost his appeal among people who are interested in education. Sometimes the support of an interest group is even necessary to the implementation of presidential policy. Some farm groups support the White House by accepting farm policy and helping to execute it.

The ability of an interest group to reach the President also determines the extent of its influence over him. There are some cases when the President meets directly with pressure-group spokesmen. Such meetings are sometimes arranged at the request of the groups wishing to express their demands; others may be called by the President himself if he is trying to acquire support for a program. Black leaders, for example, may have face-to-face discussions with the President over civil-rights policies, or business leaders may request an invitation to the White House to talk about trade policies.

Fallout From SST

Courtesy of Hugh Haynie, *The Courier-Journal.*
© *1970 Los Angeles Times Syndicate.*

"But, but . . . . . this stupid thing's supposed to be faster than sound!"

(In 1971, public feeling turned from apparent support for the President on the SST to outright opposition.)

Most pressure-group demands which do reach the President, however, come to him indirectly through Congress, the courts, and administrative departments and agencies. Demands of certain business groups, for example, may be directed to the Department of Commerce, which in turn submits them as proposals to the President. These demands may then be incorporated into the President's economic policy.

At the same time, pressure groups which have easy access to the courts, to certain congressmen, or to the administrative

'EVER TRIED HANDLING A TEMPERAMENTAL MULE?'

BALKY—

RUNS AWAY→

AND CAN BE JUST PLAIN ORNERY

Cartoon by Parish. Copyright © 1957, Chicago Tribune

(In 1959–1960, President Eisenhower had problems trying to influence a balky, opposition-party Congress.)

agencies are even able to limit the President's power. In 1969 Robert Finch, the Secretary of Health, Education, and Welfare, submitted to the President the name of Dr. John H. Knowles to be appointed as an Under Secretary for HEW. After strong opposition to the appointment was voiced by the American Medical Association and its sympathizers in Congress,

President Nixon decided not to make the appointment.

Groups which have neither direct nor indirect access to the President find it more difficult to influence his policy. They may express their demands by flooding the White House with letters or by holding demonstrations. The effect of these demands depends largely on the President himself and on the strength and influence of competing groups.

■ *Political-party demands.* The President needs and gets strength from his position as the leader of his party, but to keep political control he must occasionally be the servant of his party and responsive to its demands. The President often finds he must respond to the demands of political-party members on both the national and state levels to whom he owes favors. Such political obligations affect the President's authority to appoint public officials of all kinds from his Cabinet members to district court judges.

The President, in turn, receives general support from his own party as it functions outside of Congress. Party support is instrumental first, in securing his election; and once he is elected, the party continues to support him by upholding his policies, and by trying to get legislators elected who will also support him.

Governmental constituencies. There are numerous governmental constituencies that are important to a President if he is to put his policies into action. He must be responsive to the demands of congressmen, administrative agencies, and the courts as well as to the demands of governments abroad.

■ *Congressional forces.* The President depends on the support of Congress in a number of ways. It is the members of Congress who provide or withhold support for the President by accepting or rejecting his legislative proposals, by legislating the extension or restriction of his activities, and by accepting or rejecting his government appointees. The extent to which individual congressmen support the President is determined partly by how much they depend on him politically and partly by the constituencies which they represent.

In a presidential election year, members of the President's party and even some of the opposition party's members, will fall into line behind the President if he and his programs are popular. They do this to reap the reward of his popularity. Some very popular Presidents, like President Eisenhower, pull many congressional candidates into office on their "coattails." Even at other times, legislators who run for reelection will support the President, or fail to do so, if such an attitude will appeal to the voters.

If the constituents of a congressman are similar in outlook to the constituents of the President, the congressman will tend to support the President's programs. President Lyndon Johnson easily received congressional support from legislators representing large urban areas for such programs as Medicare.

On the other hand, if a congressman's constituency is largely opposed to the President's program, the congressman will be inclined to counter the President whenever he can. Johnson was not supported by legislators representing conservative constituents, whether they were from rural, small town, or urban districts.

Congressmen often express their demands of the President when they participate in committee hearings or floor debates. The type of congressional pressure that can be brought to bear on the President is illustrated whenever a presidential program, or any part of it, becomes unpopular with a sizeable segment of the Congress. The actions taken by Vietnam "doves" in Congress are examples. These actions have included hearings of the Senate Foreign Relations Committee, led by Senator William Fulbright. Critics of the Vietnam policy have used these hearings to urge both the Johnson and Nixon administrations to take more vigorous peace initiatives. In another example, the Senate in 1970 approved a measure, proposed by Senators Frank Church of Idaho and John Cooper of Kentucky, limiting the President's use of funds for military operations in Cambodia. Such congressional demands are, no doubt, taken as seriously if not more so by a President than are peace demonstrations in the streets.

■ *Administrative forces.* Administrative agencies are also a vital source of demands and supports for the presidential subsystem. Agencies provide inputs as they participate in making and implementing presidential decisions. Although many agencies jealously guard their independence, a large part of the administrative branch seeks to work through the White House.

Administrative agencies relate to the President in different ways. While some, such as the major executive departments, have Secretaries appointed by him, such agencies are not necessarily controlled from the White House. Franklin Roosevelt once quipped, "When I woke up this morning the first thing I saw was a headline in the *New York Times* to the effect that our Navy was going to spend two billion dollars on a shipbuilding program. Here I am, the Commander in Chief of the Navy having to read about that for the first time in the Press."

Although the President can not control such agencies, neither can he escape from their influence over him. The President does provide general guidelines for the agencies' policy-making activities; but, at the same time, he depends to a great extent on the information which he receives from them when making his decisions. When setting up welfare policies, for example, he can not ignore the demands which come from the Department of Health, Education, and Welfare.

The independent regulatory agencies depend even less on the President. It is usually only on the financial level that they make demands of the President. Since the making of the budget is within the President's realm, he must answer some of these demands for funds if he is to maintain the support of agencies for his programs. (For more information about the relationship between the independent agencies and the President, see Chapters 15 and 16.)

Down To Size!

Courtesy of The McClatchy Newspapers

(Interpretation of presidential powers by the Supreme Court can weaken the executive as well as support it.)

■ *Judicial forces.* In addition to congressional and administrative forces, the judicial branch, through court decisions, makes demands on and provides support for the President. For example, the Supreme Court decision in *Brown v. Board of Education* and subsequent federal court orders for school desegregation created demands on the President to uphold desegregation policies. Both Presidents Eisenhower and Kennedy responded to these demands by using federal troops to prevent the governors of Arkansas and Mississippi from defying the court orders.

Sometimes the courts will even prohibit executive action, although this is rare. One of the most notable examples of judicial prohibition is the *Steel Seizure* case of 1952. The courts stopped President Truman from seizing the steel mills for governmental needs during the Korean conflict, despite his claim of authority for such action as the Commander in Chief and Chief Executive. Congress had established certain procedures for such cases and the President had ignored them.

The courts also provide support for the President by upholding certain presidential actions. In a number of Supreme Court decisions, such as *United States v. Curtis-Wright Corporation* (1936) and *United States v. Pink* (1942), the validity of foreign policy decisions made by the President were defended against challenge (See Chapter 5, pp. 112–114).

■ *Foreign nations.* Still another constituency of the President is made up of the many foreign nations whose military and economic interests must be considered when he formulates foreign policy or takes diplomatic and military action in the foreign arena. No President in the twentieth century can afford to ignore these international forces, whether they be the warring nations of the Middle East, the peoples struggling for independence in

Africa, the developing countries of Latin America, or the conflicting communist and anti-communist forces in Asia.

Presidential words and actions in such areas as civil rights or military and economic policy all have a real impact on the image of the country as seen from abroad. The President, as the representative of the nation as a whole, tries to maintain this image in a good light. Foreign nations, on the other hand, support the President and his power by entering into alliances, agreeing on tariffs, and cooperating in other negotiations.

Review questions

1. Why are Presidents and presidential candidates especially concerned with problems of states such as Pennsylvania, California, and New York?
2. What are the different components of the "non-governmental" and "governmental" constituencies of the President?

The Contemporary Structure of the Presidency

Obviously, it would be impossible for any one man or even a small staff directed by one individual to handle all of the demands, duties, and responsibilities with which the President is expected to deal. The structure of the Presidency has expanded considerably since the early days of the office. Under the first President, the structure included only four Cabinet officials—the Secretaries of State, Treasury, and War, and an Attorney General. Today, the President is surrounded by a vast organization of people, in addition to the members of his Cabinet, who give him advice and information so that he can come to proper conclusions and take necessary action.

The Executive Office of the President. At the summit of this hierarchy of presidential aides and agencies is the Executive Office of the President, which is composed of bureaus, offices, and councils to help the President perform his duties. An institutionalized extension of the White House the Executive Office was created by executive order in 1939 on the recommendation of the President's Committee on Administrative Management. The need for the office was a direct result of the increased presidential responsibilities during the New Deal period. Existing solely for presidential needs, the Executive Office can be expanded or contracted as new agencies are added and old ones dropped. Originally, the Office consisted of six agencies. Subsequent reorganizations have changed the composition of this original Executive Office, so that presently there are ten agencies.

Today, the Executive Office of the President employs about 1,500 staff members. Its agencies are supposed to collect information, plan programs, and generally assist the President much as congressional staff aides help members of Congress.

■ *The White House Office.* The staff for the White House is chosen by the President directly. It includes most of the President's clerical staff and his top personal advisers. Experts are selected to answer questions on military and defense strategy, economic policy, foreign policy, domestic policy, urban affairs, science and technology, and other subjects with which the President might wish to become familiar. Moreover, the White House staff acts as the liaison between the President and Congress, the heads of executive departments and agencies, the press and other information media, and private groups.

Members of the staff are in personal contact with the President on a daily basis, giving them far greater access to the center of power than any other people in the bureaucracy. The significance and influence of the White House staff is easily illustrated by the publicity that key members receive. During the Kennedy and Johnson years, for example, such names as McGeorge Bundy, Walt Rostow, Theodore Sorensen, Pierre Salinger, and Arthur Schlesinger, Jr. became widely known. Under President Nixon, men such as Daniel Moynihan, John Ehrlichman, Ronald Ziegler, and Henry Kissinger have earned national reputations.

■ *The Office of Management and Budget.* Probably the single most important segment of the Executive Office is the Office of Management and Budget (OMB). Originated by President Richard Nixon in his reorganization of the Executive Office in 1970, OMB couples the functions of the old Bureau of the Budget (BOB) with the duty of establishing priorities for presidential policies.

Until 1970, the Budget Bureau was essentially a clearing house for the budgets and legislative proposals made by all the other administrative agencies, both administrative departments and independent regulatory agencies. Administrative proposals were submitted to Congress only after the Bureau's approval. Frequently there were clashes between the head of the Budget Bureau and the Cabinet heads of the various departments. The Bureau was run by civil servants, unresponsive and sometimes unsympathetic to the departments' problems. At the same time, the overlapping responsibilities of many departments resulted in the inefficient duplication of some activities by administrative agencies.

Besides taking over the functions of the former Budget Bureau, the OMB is also responsible for overseeing the execution and management of all government programs. According to President Nixon, the establishment of the OMB was an attempt to bring "real business management" into the executive branch. As a major part of its management function, the OMB is expected to set priorities for the implementation of government programs and to bring such programs in line with presidential policy.

With the creation of the OMB, President Nixon also set up a *Domestic Affairs Council* to replace three other bodies: the Urban Affairs Council, the Rural Affairs Council, and the Cabinet Committee on Environment. The Domestic Affairs Council is now responsible for coordinating the programs of several agencies. For example, if programs for environmental control are being advocated by the Departments of Transportation, Interior, and HEW, the Domestic Affairs Council will coordinate the various programs before proposals are submitted to Congress.

■ *The Council of Economic Advisers.* The Council of Economic Advisers is composed of three economists appointed by the President with the Senate's approval. It is one of the agencies designated by Congress to keep a constant watch on the economy. Under the terms of the Employment Act of 1946 which defined its functions, the Council analyzes the national economy with a view to maintaining an adequate growth rate as well as economic stability. Each year the Council issues an Economic Report that is the basis for the President's recommendations to Congress on economic matters. The establishment and continued operation of the Council indicates the general American acceptance of the belief that the economy can and

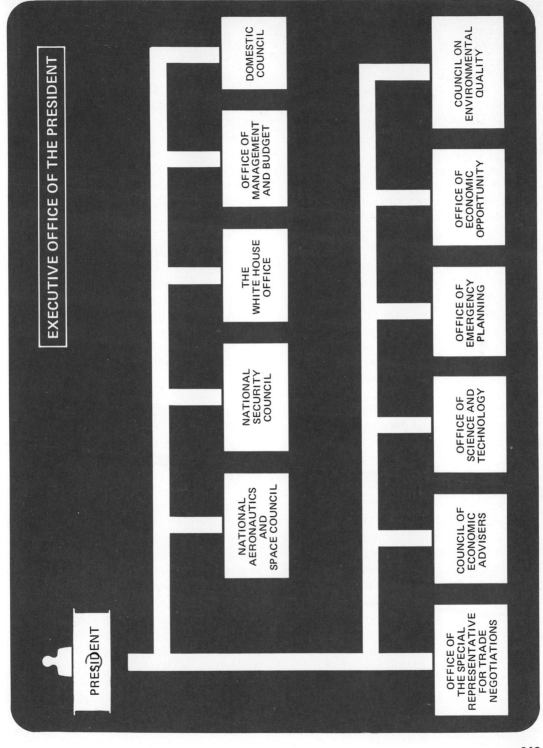

EXECUTIVE OFFICE OF THE PRESIDENT

PRESIDENT

NATIONAL AERONAUTICS AND SPACE COUNCIL

NATIONAL SECURITY COUNCIL

THE WHITE HOUSE OFFICE

OFFICE OF MANAGEMENT AND BUDGET

DOMESTIC COUNCIL

OFFICE OF THE SPECIAL REPRESENTATIVE FOR TRADE NEGOTIATIONS

COUNCIL OF ECONOMIC ADVISERS

OFFICE OF SCIENCE AND TECHNOLOGY

OFFICE OF EMERGENCY PLANNING

OFFICE OF ECONOMIC OPPORTUNITY

COUNCIL ON ENVIRONMENTAL QUALITY

should be stabilized through timely government action.

■ *The National Security Council.* First organized in 1947 under the terms of the National Security Act, the National Security Council (NSC) is made up of the President, the Vice President, the Secretary of State, the Secretary of Defense, and the Director of the Office of Emergency Planning. Generally, its members also include the President's close advisers. The Chairman of the Joint Chiefs of Staff and other officials may participate in Council meetings by invitation of the President.

The primary functions of the NSC are to advise the President on matters of concern to the security of the nation and to coordinate the actions of government departments and agencies with respect to these matters. The Central Intelligence Agency (CIA) also comes under the jurisdiction of the NSC. Responsible for intelligence activities such as espionage and other undercover work, the CIA is more than an advisory agency. Occasionally the CIA is even responsible for political activities abroad that are not publicly recognized by the government.

■ *The Office of Emergency Planning.* The largest planning agency within the Executive Office, the Office of Emergency Planning (OEP), is one of the least known by the general public. Its responsibilities include advising the President on or planning for emergency preparedness in many areas. These areas include manpower, industrial capacity, communications, transportation, the civil defense, and government operations in cases of disaster—whether from military or non-military causes. In line with responsibilities for military preparedness, the Director of the OEP is involved in planning the fallout-shelter program, the stockpiling of strategic materials, and for possible rehabilitation. In the non-military field, the OEP coordinates federal assistance to states and localities after such natural disasters as earthquakes, floods, or hurricanes.

■ *The Office of Economic Opportunity.* Set up in 1964, the Office of Economic Opportunity (OEO) was established to "eliminate the paradox of poverty in the midst of plenty," and to oversee the implementation of federal anti-poverty programs. While operation of the Job Corps has been under the OEO itself, the operation of other related programs, such as Community Action, Adult Education, Rural Poverty, and Vista (Volunteers in Service to America), has been delegated by the OEO to the Department of Labor.

Aside from the CIA, the OEO, unlike other agencies of the Executive Office, is an operating agency—that is, it plays an active part in the administration of policies besides coordinating them and advising the President.

■ *Other components of the Executive Office.* Several specialized offices have been added to the Executive Office to aid the President with particular problems. In 1958, the *National Aeronautics and Space Council* was set up to help the President plan space programs. In 1962, the *Office of Science and Technology* was established to assist the President in the development and coordination of policies that concern matters of science and technology. Since this office's inception, closer ties have been made between the scientific and engineering communities within and outside of government. The *Office of the Special Representative for Trade Negotiations* was established in 1963 to advise the President on trade agreements, tariffs, and other matters relating to international trade.

The Cabinet. The Cabinet is an informal group of government administrators who also serve the President in an advisory capacity. Not mentioned in the Constitution, the Cabinet was first formed as a four-member staff by George Washington in 1789 and gradually grew to a thirteen-member body by 1967. All but one of the present twelve members are heads of major administrative departments of the federal government; these include the Attorney General and the Secretaries of State; Treasury; Defense; Interior; Agriculture; Commerce; Labor; Health, Education, and Welfare; Housing and Urban Development; and Transportation. The United States Representative to the United Nations also has Cabinet status, although he does not head a major department. Over the years, as Congress has increased or consolidated the administrative departments, the size of the Cabinet has changed accordingly. Most recently, Congress voted in 1970 to reorganize the Post Office Department as an independent government agency, thus removing the office of Postmaster General from the Cabinet.

The President selects the members of the Cabinet and the Senate confirms his choices. A number of deliberations must be made by the President before making a Cabinet nomination. He considers the opinions of important political-party leaders within Congress and in the states. The interests of private groups that come under the jurisdiction of the departments concerned also affect presidential nominations. The availability of capable candidates is another important limitation on the President's choice. In selecting his Cabinet, the President must strike a balance among all these considerations. When he retires from office, the Cabinet members also tender their resignations. In a few cases, Cabinet members have served under two Presidents. Many members of Kennedy's Cabinet, for example, also served Lyndon Johnson.

Cabinet members aid the President in many ways. If they perform outstandingly in their jobs, they do enhance the public prestige of the President. As his chief lieutenants in the bureaucracy, they provide the President with assistance and advice on matters of general policy affecting their departments. They help to represent him before Congress, where they often give long hours of testimony in defense of "administration" positions on controversial matters of public policy. During 1966 and 1967, Dean Rusk for example, spent many grueling hours defending President Johnson's position on Vietnam before the Senate Foreign Relations Committee.

Although the President and his Cabinet are usually thought of as a "team," the Cabinet members often act independently on matters concerning their own departments. The President can not completely control the Cabinet, because each member is responsible not only to the President but also to the people and groups who provide support for his department. According to a contemporary political scientist, Richard C. Fenno, the position of Cabinet members presents a paradox. In order for a Cabinet member to enhance the image of the President, he should develop his own public image and should build up his own influence within his department, sources of support within the legislature, and a following within his political party. But as a Cabinet member grows in stature, he may find that while he is contributing to the prestige of the President's administration, he is also operating semi-independently—outside of the President's direct influence. This usually happens when he responds to political demands that do not originate at the White House. A Secretary of Agriculture, for example, may respond to constituents of his own department and advocate higher price supports for farmers while the President may be opposed to the same policy.

THE PERFECT CABINET

(While a malleable Cabinet of straw men might be desirable, it could actually damage the President's image.)

Of course, when a Cabinet member becomes too independent he will be replaced or asked to resign. The pluralism underlying the American democratic system is displayed on all levels, even here in the relationship between the President and his Cabinet.

Review questions

1. Describe an "operating" unit within the Executive Office. Why is it different from the other units?
2. How does the Cabinet differ from the agencies within the Executive Office?

Special Problems: Succession, Disability, Transition

Despite the complicated structure of the executive branch today, its key element is still only one man—the President. If he is suddenly incapacitated or dies in office, who takes his place? The Framers were aware that some provision for such a contingency was needed. Therefore, in writing Article II of the Constitution, they provided that in the case of the "death, resignation, or inability" of the President to discharge the duties of his office, he would be succeeded by the Vice President. But suppose both the President and the Vice President become incapacitated during a single, four-year term? The Constitution also authorizes Congress to enact a law providing for succession to the office if both the President and the Vice President are incapable of performing the presidential duties.

Because of the expansion of both the President's functions and the executive structure since 1789, the process of transferring the office of the President from one person to another has become increasingly difficult. The inadequacy of congressional statutes providing for presidential succession and disability have been only partially overcome by the ratification of a constitutional amendment. Moreover, the burdens of the office continue to complicate even the natural transition of the Presidency through the election process every four years.

Presidential succession. The crucial problem of presidential succession was most recently spotlighted by the assassination of President John F. Kennedy on November 22, 1963. There have been a total of eight Presidents who have died or been killed in office.[1]

Since 1789, Congress has passed three different succession laws. The first, passed in 1792, provided that the president *pro tempore* of the Senate and then the Speaker of the House would succeed to the Presidency after the Vice President. Under this law, these congressional leaders were to be merely "Acting Presidents" and not fully empowered under the conditions of the Constitution. If both President and Vice President became incapacitated during the first two years and seven months of a term, Congress was to call for another presidential election. This succession law was never used.

The growth in size and importance of the

Cabinet and of the entire executive branch during the nineteenth century dictated the need for a new succession law. A second act, passed in 1886, provided that the line of succession to the Presidency after the Vice President would run from the Secretary of State to the Secretary of the Treasury and on through the list of Cabinet officers in the order of each department's year of origin. No provision was made for a special election, and no man could assume the Presidency unless he met the constitutional qualifications of age, citizenship, and residence.

■ *The Succession Act of 1947.* Congress passed another succession law again in 1947 at the request of President Truman. At the time, there was no Vice President and President Truman felt it was undemocratic for him—with his power to choose the Secretary of State—to name his own successor. Since the Speaker of the House and the temporary presiding president of the Senate are elected officers, it seemed to Truman that they were the most natural choices to succeed the President.

Following Truman's suggestions, the Succession Act of 1947 provided that the Speaker of the House and then the president *pro tempore* of the Senate would succeed to the Presidency after the Vice President. The Members of the Cabinet would then follow in the order of their departments' seniority in the government.

■ *Problems with the 1947 Act.* The assassination of President Kennedy displayed the weakness of the 1947 Act. The Speaker of the House in 1963 was John McCormack, then 71 years of age, and the president *pro tempore* of the Senate was Carl Hayden, then 86. The country was thus faced with the prospect of a rather aged President if anything happened to Lyndon Johnson. For a man to reach a position as the head of the House or the Senate, he must have been reelected over a period of

---

[1] *William Henry Harrison, Zachary Taylor, Warren G. Harding, and Franklin D. Roosevelt died in office; Abraham Lincoln, James Garfield, William McKinley, and John F. Kennedy were assassinated.*

many years. Both of these positions would undoubtedly continue to be held by senior members of Congress who might be unable to survive the rigors of the Presidency if they succeeded to the office. Furthermore, their succession would not necessarily be more democratic than the succession of appointed government officials. Although the Speaker and the president *pro tempore* are chosen by their elected congressional colleagues, they are not representatives of the nation as a whole, but only of the one district or state from which they are elected. Moreover, they are likely to be from "safe" districts, where the electorate is not changing.

■ *The Twenty-fifth Amendment.* For the present, the problem of presidential succession has been resolved by the Twenty-fifth Amendment to the Constitution. Ratified in 1967, this amendment provides that "whenever there is a vacancy in the office of the Vice President, the President shall nominate a Vice President who shall take office upon confirmation by a majority vote of both houses of Congress." Presumably, if the Vice President either dies in office or replaces the President, this procedure would ensure that there would almost always be another Vice President who could succeed to the Presidency.

So far, the new solution to the problem of presidential succession has not been tried. Its supporters feel that since presidential candidates ordinarily choose their own running mates at nominating conventions, this procedure for filling a vice-presidential vacancy is in keeping with established tradition.

Presidential disability. Presidential succession becomes an issue not only when a President dies but also when he is disabled. Over the years, the problem of presidential disability has been as crucial as the problems resulting from the death or assassination of a President. The serious-

ness of presidential disability has been illustrated most dramatically in the twentieth century during the administrations of Woodrow Wilson and Dwight D. Eisenhower.

Wilson became incapacitated in the fall of 1919. He was partially paralyzed and totally unable to cope with the responsibilities of the Presidency. Wilson's paralysis was not immediately conveyed to the American public. In fact, an attempt was made to maintain the appearance of vitality in the White House. The possibility of his resignation was discussed but rejected. At the suggestion of the doctors, Mrs. Wilson herself handled presidential business. No one was given access to the President without first going through Mrs. Wilson. The country survived this crisis, but the question remained. Can a nation that relies so heavily on the Presidency endure for long when the holder of the office is actually incapable of performing his duties?

The problem was raised again during the administration of President Eisenhower, who was disabled on several occasions— by a heart attack in 1955, an ileitis attack in 1956, and a stroke in 1957. The first two illnesses partially disabled the President for almost six months. After Eisenhower's heart attack, presidential assistant Sherman Adams performed most of the necessary functions for the President. Although a delegation of power to the Vice President was hinted at, it never occurred. Vice President Nixon was placed in a difficult situation. There was no legal arrangement or political precedent to serve him as a guide. Under such circumstances, any attempt by the Vice President to assume presidential duties while a President was living would be interpreted as something akin to a *coup d'état* (a change of government by force).

■ *Remedies for disability.* Death is final

Cartoon by Dong. Courtesy of Minneapolis Star Tribune

"The law of succession."

THE PRESIDENT IS INCAPACITATED AND CAN'T BE DISTURBED

Alexander in The Philadelphia Bulletin

"In which case, who'd be in charge?"

(Prior to passage of the Twenty-fifth Amendment, presidential succession was a common cartoon subject.)

and easily recognizable. On the other hand, disability in many cases is almost impossible to define. Was President Eisenhower *sufficiently* disabled to require the Vice President to take over? Who should determine when a President is disabled? Who should determine when the President is sufficiently recovered to resume his duties? These are subtle questions, and it is almost impossible to reach any general agreement on the answers.

After 1957, Presidents Eisenhower, Kennedy, and Johnson made informal arrangements with their Vice Presidents to provide for future presidential disability. According to these arrangements, the President himself would determine if he was disabled and would tell the Vice President when to assume his presidential functions; if the President was too disabled to communicate, the Vice President would have to assume the duties of office on his own authority after he had consulted others. But these arrangements left the solution of presidential disability to informal personal agreements reached between two men. Some constitutional or statutory authority was necessary for the Vice President to rely on to determine when he should take the reins of government.

■ *The constitutional solution.* With the ratification of the Twenty-fifth Amendment, a definite procedure by which the Vice President can assume the duties of a

349

disabled President has been established. Either the President himself or the Vice President together with "a majority of either the principal officers of the executive departments or of such other body as Congress may provide" can submit a written declaration to the Speaker of the House and Senate president *pro tempore* stating that the President is unable to perform the functions of his office. In either case, the Vice President would immediately become acting President. By granting the Vice President and others the authority to inform Congress of presidential disability, this amendment should provide for the possibility of a President being totally disabled or unconscious.

The Twenty-fifth Amendment also includes a procedure by which a formerly disabled President can resume the duties of his office. He can transmit a written declaration to the Speaker and president *pro tempore* that he is no longer disabled. If the Vice President and a majority of the principal executive officers, however, believe that the President is still unable to perform his functions, they can submit a counter declaration to Congress. It is then up to Congress to decide within twenty-one days, and by two-thirds majority of both houses, whether the Vice President should continue as Acting President or the President can resume his responsibilities.

Transferral of office. The problems of transferring the office of the Presidency arise both when the President unexpectedly dies or is disabled and when there is an expected transferral of power after a presidential election. In each case, there are certain problems which are peculiar to that situation.

■ *Vice President to President.* When he begins his term of office, a President must decide to what extent he wants to involve the Vice President in his administration. Usually, Vice Presidents have been kept in the dark about presidential objectives, policies, and procedures. Until Franklin D. Roosevelt was President, Vice Presidents did not even sit in on Cabinet meetings. Yet, although Harry Truman participated in Cabinet meetings as Vice President, he was not informed about vital matters of foreign policy and the war then going on. He did not even know about the development of the atomic bomb until he assumed office after Roosevelt's death.

In addition to the problem of having limited information, a Vice President who assumes the Presidency after the death of a President in office has the chore of deciding whether he wants to keep all the Cabinet members and top administrative officials in their posts. In most instances, he replaces the former President's personal advisers relatively quickly. Cabinet members, though, may remain in their posts for lengthier periods. When Lyndon Johnson assumed the Presidency on John Kennedy's assassination, all of the Cabinet members stayed at the heads of their departments, and only the Attorney General and the Secretary of Commerce were replaced before the beginning of Johnson's second administration. In any case, the transition from one man to another as head of the executive branch is bound to cause some disruptions in the administrative operation of the government.

■ *A newly elected President.* Unlike the members of Congress who may be reelected over long periods of time, the President is absolutely sure that he will turn his office over to someone else, after either four or eight years. The transition of executive power from a President to a President-elect is a completely different situation from that created by disability or succession. There is no decision to be made as to who will succeed the President, or as to how the successor will be chosen.

To ensure the smooth transferral of his

office without disrupting the operation of the executive branch, a White House occupant sometimes keeps all his potential successors informed on major issues of foreign and domestic policy, even before a presidential election. Remembering the difficulty he had had when he assumed office in 1945 after Roosevelt's death, President Truman invited both presidential candidates to the White House in 1952 to inform them about world problems. Although he declined Truman's invitation, Eisenhower himself as President continued the practice for the Democratic candidate in 1956 and for both candidates in 1960. Of course, transferring the Presidency from a member of one political party to a member of another presents more difficulties than when the office is passed between members of the same party.

From the time of his election in November until his inauguration on January 20th, the President-elect must bide his time. He operates under the shadow of a lame-duck administration which can still initiate some policies counter to his own goals.

Naturally, a certain period of time is needed to make the transfer from the old to the new administration. Ideally, the outgoing administration should make every effort to ease the transition by consulting with the President-elect to reveal current problems and by refraining from the adoption of programs that would be embarrassing to the new administration. The position of a new President is never easy. If he is from the opposition party, he probably does not want to be identified with the outgoing administration. Therefore, he may withdraw from any serious attempts at consultation lest he be "tainted" by such association.

"I'D LIKE YOU TO MEET YOUR CONGRESS..."

(In 1968 the new Republican President, Richard Nixon, could expect little help from a Democratic Congress.)

351

1. What changes in the executive branch led to the enactment of the succession law of 1886? Why was this law replaced in 1947?

2. How has the Twenty-fifth Amendment resolved the problem of presidential succession? By what procedure in the amendment could a formerly disabled President resume his duties?

The Future of the Presidency

Despite the many problems that confront the executive branch today, none appears to be so pressing that a basic change in the system is required. In any event such an alteration would be impossible without major upheavals in the political system as a whole.

Presidential weaknesses and strengths. Any observer of the President notices the signs of aging, strain, and fatigue that the person in office suffers. The responsibilities of the job are awesome. Even with a staff of highly competent assistants, the President is still held responsible for most major decisions—some of which may determine the fate of mankind. In time of crisis, the President often stands alone, separated from all but his closest advisers. And in spite of all his power, he is restricted in his actions by many pressures.

The effectiveness of the President's leadership is checked by several factors. First, the separation of powers in the Constitution inhibits his access to congressional centers of power. He can not always make Congress accept the legislation he wants passed. Second, the size and complexity of the federal bureaucracy also acts as a check on presidential action. The many specialized administrative agencies are often very independent of him in their operation. And third, the undisciplined and fragmented party system in the United States places a check on presidential leadership. If he alienates enough of the various groups supporting the party banner, he will lose support of the party. At such times, the party leaders go around the President and deal directly with Congress or the administrative agencies.

Sometimes, the President overcomes these limitations and draws his strength directly from his electoral constituency. Abraham Lincoln resisted the pressures of "radical" Republicans in Congress and went ahead with his plans for "reconstruction." Woodrow Wilson almost succeeded in winning approval of the League of Nations by taking the proposal to the people. Franklin Roosevelt withstood judicial and congressional attacks and took his plan for the New Deal directly to the people in his "fireside chats." President Nixon has appealed to the "silent majority" for support in his Vietnam policies.

However, because of the limitations of the office, its most important responsibilities and duties are best accomplished by a President who can coordinate the efforts of the bureaucracy and channel information to others—in Congress, the administrative agencies, and the courts—who have the power of decision-making. The President is caught up in the same fragmentation of the political system as other structures of government.

Popular expectations. So far, the Presidency has fulfilled the expectations of the people regarding executive responsibilities. That the American people are satisfied with the institution is alone a measure of its success. As the voice of the people and the head of the nation, the Presidency has also become a symbol of democratic leadership.

At the present time, proposals for changes in the American presidential system are few. The Presidency is and probably will remain a highly personal institution, dominated by one person. The success of the office will continue to depend largely on the political abilities of the various people who occupy it.

Review questions

1. Explain how each of the following may limit the President's leadership:
   (a) Congress,
   (b) the bureaucracy,
   (c) his political party.
2. When might a President appeal to his electoral constituency for support of a program? Which Presidents have done this?

Chapter Review

Terms you should know

Cabinet	"fireside chats"	succession
CIA	NSC	Twenty-fifth
"coattail" candidates	OEP	Amendment
coup d'état	"silent majority"	"wheat-belt"
Domestic Affairs Council	"Solid South"	states

Questions about this chapter

1. What problems of the urban electorate have affected the platforms and programs of presidential candidates? Why?
2. What must the President do while he is in office to maintain the support of his political party? How does this make him a "servant" of his party?
3. In what way can the President's congressional constituency bring pressure on him? Give specific examples.
4. Explain the significance for the Presidency of the Supreme Court decisions in : (a) *Brown v. Board of Education,* (b) *United States v. Pink,* (c) the *Steel Seizure* case.
5. Which agencies within the Executive Office perform the following functions: (a) acts as a liaison between the President and the Congress, other agencies, the press, etc.; (b) oversees the execution and management of all administrative programs; (c) coordinates domestic programs; (d) advises the President on the national economy; (e) works "to eliminate poverty in the midst of plenty."
7. Why is it important for Cabinet members to build up their own public images and the following of supporters? How does this create a paradox in their relationship with the President?
8. What attempts have been made by some Presidents to ensure the smooth transferral of their office?

Thought and discussion questions

1. Discuss whether or not the channels of communication between the President and the electorate are adequate during non-election years. How can the electorate express

its approval or disapproval of the President at these times? Comment on the assumption that the silence of the electorate means tacit approval of the President.

2. What social trends do you see developing today that might result in either new Cabinet offices or new administrative agencies?

3. Why do you think Vice Presidents have not been informed on crucial issues? Should there be laws to insure that Vice Presidents will always be informed on such matters? What problems might result if such provisions were made?

Class projects

1. Refer to newspapers and news magazines of the last year and make a list of presidential outputs—appointments, bills signed or vetoed, military actions, treaties negotiated, etc. Try to determine which presidential constituencies may have influenced each presidential action or decision.

2. Make a study of the people who have held Cabinet posts in recent presidential administrations. In this study consider such questions as the following: (a) What occupations did these people hold before their appointments? (b) Did any of them play a role in the presidential election and how could such a role be of significance to their present positions? (c) Have any of these people supported programs or policies contrary to those of the President? If so, what was the result?

Case Study: A presidential transition

On January 20, 1953, President Harry S. Truman and President-elect Dwight D. Eisenhower emerged from the Capitol and proceeded to the inaugural platform where the President-elect repeated the oath of office and was invested with the authority of the Presidency. Presidential authority had been legally transferred from one administration to another. At the same time, the continuity of the system had been maintained.

For some time, both before and after election day, the President and the President-elect had been preparing for this change in power. Because a new President must redefine policies in the light of the new adminstration, presidential transition is often a period of uncertainty and change. This case study, taken from a volume by Laurin L. Henry entitled *Presidential Transitions,* provides a close look at the principal figures and problems surrounding the presidential changeover in 1953.

While reading this case study, keep the following questions in mind:

1. How was Eisenhower affected by Truman's telegram and the words "if you still intend to go to Korea"?

2. How did Truman and his staff get ready for the changeover?

3. How did the personalities of Eisenhower and Truman affect the transition period?

4. Which general policy areas are affected most by a presidential transition?

REPUBLICAN RESTORATION

About two o'clock in the morning of November 5, 1952, General Dwight D. Eisenhower addressed a jubilant crowd in the ballroom of the Hotel Commodore in New York City:

> May I ask your attention one moment. I am not certain, my friends, whether or not you have read or heard the telegram that Mr. Stevenson just sent me. It reads:
> "The people have made their choice and I congratulate you. That you may be the servant and guardian of peace and make the dale of trouble a door of hope is my earnest prayer. Best wishes. Adlai Stevenson"
>
> Just as I came down to the ballroom I replied . . . as follows:
> "I thank you for your courteous and generous message. Recognizing the intensity of the difficulties that lie ahead, it is clearly necessary that men and women of goodwill of both parties forget the political strife through which we have passed and devote ourselves to the single purpose of a better future. This I believe they will do." Signed with my name.
> Now my friends, it is trite to say that this is a day of dedication rather than of triumph. . . .[1]

As he stepped down from the platform the Secret Service detail closed in around the President-elect.

Out in Springfield, Illinois, reporters asked Stevenson how he felt. Stevenson quoted Lincoln's comment on a lost election: "He said he felt like a little boy who had stubbed his toe in the dark. He said he was too old to cry but it hurt too much to laugh."[2] . . .

While the congratulations and acknowledgements were being exchanged, President Harry S. Truman was already asleep on the train carrying him back to Washington from Independence, Missouri. The early returns had told him enough. But the President was up early the next morning to begin a job he had thought about a great deal in the past few months. From Martinsburg, West Virginia, he dispatched a telegram to President-elect Eisenhower:

> Congratulations on your overwhelming victory. The 1954 budget must be presented to the Congress before January 15th. All the preliminary figures have been made up. You should have a representative meet with the Director of the Bureau of the Budget immediately. The Independence will be at your disposal if you still desire to go to Korea.
>
> Harry S. Truman

On this sharp note, the change of administrations was under way.[3] [Eisenhower had campaigned on the promise of ending the war in Korea.]

. . . Later that morning, [November 5, 1952] President Truman's blunt telegram was received at the Commodore. Eisenhower, already angry at Tru-

----

[1] New York Times (Nov. 6, 1952).
[2] Ibid.
[3] Harry S. Truman, Memoirs, Vol. 2 (1956), pp. 504-05, © 1956, Time, Inc.

This condensation from Presidential Transitions, *by Laurin L. Henry, is reprinted with permission of The Brookings Institution. © 1960 by The Brookings Institution.*

man's campaign tactics, was further infuriated by his dig "if you still intend to go to Korea." However, he responded promptly, in a contrasting tone that could hardly escape notice:

> I deeply appreciate your courteous and generous telegram. I shall try to make arrangements within the next two or three days to have a personal representative to sit with the Director of the Budget. I am most appreciative of your offer of the use of the Independence but assure you that any suitable transport plane that one of the services could make available will be satisfactory for my planned trip to Korea. With your permission I shall give the Secretary of Defense the earliest possible notice of my proposed date of departure.
>
> Dwight D. Eisenhower[4]. . . .

TOWARD AN ORDERLY TRANSITION

President Truman's post-election telegram opening the question of transition arrangements with President-elect Eisenhower was unexpectedly prompt and abrupt in tone, but the act itself caused no great surprise in Washington officialdom. Actually, the approach to the President-elect had been planned months in advance as part of a general policy of the administration for dealing with its successor. While there had been no scheduled change of Presidents since 1933, several lines of thought and experience in the intervening years had led to an awareness of the transition problem in some governmental circles and gave at least partial guidance to action.

As a legacy of the New Deal and World War II, the Truman administration commanded the services of a large number of able and experienced officials in the upper reaches of the federal departments and agencies. Many of these officials, both civil servants and political appointees, regarded themselves as professional managers of government; they had strong loyalties to their respective agencies and to the executive branch as a whole, regardless of whatever personal commitments they might have to the political fortune or specific policies of the Truman administration. In such circles there had long lurked the realization that transferring political control of an organization as large and complex as the government had become would some day be a challenging task. . . .

A second body of experience in the background of the Truman-Eisenhower transition was the long effort of the war [World War II] and postwar years to maintain national unity and a bipartisan approach to defense and foreign policy. . . .

A third important factor in 1952 was the attitude of President Truman. Vivid in Truman's memory was his own experience in 1945 when he had been thrust suddenly into the Presidency, required to make vital decisions

[4] New York Times, *(Nov. 6, 1952.)*

promptly, and found it extremely difficult to acquire the necessary background information. . . . Despite his intense partisanship, he was determined to give a fair start to his successor, whoever he might be, and to rectify what he later called the ". . . omission in our political tradition that a retiring President did not make it his business to facilitate the transfer of the government to his successor."[5]

PREPARATIONS IN 1948

The experience of the immediately preceding presidential campaign also provided important background for the transition of 1952–53. During the Truman-Dewey contest of 1948, in a show of unity on foreign policy, the State Department had briefed John Foster Dulles (. . . serving as Dewey's adviser) on the administration's plans with respect to the Soviet blockade of Berlin. This led to a Dewey statement supporting the administration on that subject. A little later, Dulles was included in the official delegation to a United Nations General Assembly in Paris. With the approval of General George C. Marshall, who was then Secretary of State, Dulles had informal talks with some of the European foreign ministers in order to assure them of Dewey's constructive intentions.[6] . . .

Governor Dewey, confident of winning the election, apparently made more specific plans to take over the government than any previous presidential candidate. His counsel, Charles D. Breitel, assembled the elements of a legislative program. It was rumored that cabinet members had not only been selected but were shopping for houses in Washington prior to election. Dewey staff members and advisers moved in and out of Washington during the campaign. They talked openly with Republican members of Congress and other Dewey supporters; they also talked discreetly with officials of the administration who were concerned about the transition problem. . . .

While the interest of some of his subordinates in these arrangements did not escape President Truman's notice, he made no official recognition. Doing so would have detracted from the air of complete confidence he was maintaining in the face of what seemed overwhelming odds against his re-election. Afterward there was a good deal of chuckling in Washington over Dewey's abortive preparations, but as 1952 approached, the experience of the transition that never occurred appeared in retrospect as useful and relevant.

EARLY PLANNING IN 1952

If it were necessary to identify a single point in time at which the 1952–53 transition began, the date would have to be March 29, 1952. On that evening President Truman, speaking at a Jefferson-Jackson Day dinner in Washington, departed from his script and ended the widespread speculation about his intentions by announcing firmly that he would not be a candidate for another term. No matter how the conventions and the campaign turned out, there would be a new President in the White House in less than a year! . . .

In the White House and several other strategic points in the government,

[5] *Harry S. Truman, Memoirs, Vol. 2 (1956), p. 508.*
[6] *John Robinson Beal, John Foster Dulles (1957), p. 104.*

both political and career officials began to consider the specific problems of turnover and the appropriate course of conduct for an outgoing administration. One locus of such thinking was the Budget Bureau, which had been enlarged and transformed during the Roosevelt and Truman years and was now staffed by experienced professionals who regarded themselves as reliable custodians of the President's—any President's—interests. Within a few days after Truman's announcement, staff papers on transition, most of them apparently unsolicited but written with confidence that such activity would be favorably regarded from topside, were circulating in the bureau. Some of these papers reviewed the historical record of relationships between Presidents and Presidents-elect. Others wrestled with the question of who should be responsible for the budget and other presidential messages; the 1948 study of the law on these points was brought up-to-date. One division of the bureau began planning the materials that would be needed to brief a new President and his associates on the budget system and the current budget, the functions of the Executive Office of the President, and major organizational problems of the government.[7]

A second source of serious thinking on the problems of transition was the policy planning staff in the office of the Secretary of State. Pursuant to this group's broad mandate to exercise forethought about matters vital to the nation's international interests, one of its members was assigned shortly after Truman's withdrawal announcement to study the problem of relations between outgoing and incoming regimes and ways to maintain continuity and stability in foreign policy. Several weeks later a lengthy document was completed, approved by the Secretary, and forwarded to the White House where Truman read it appreciatively. The paper contained both a review of historical experience and an analysis of problems immediately ahead. . . . Note was taken of the backgrounds of the leading potential candidates and how each might approach the question of foreign policy continuity. It was recommended that in the interest of responsible conduct during the campaign and the subsequent transitional period, both candidates should be briefed and kept currently informed on defense and foreign affairs. After the election, the flow of information to the victor should be stepped up, and his representatives should be taken into the most important agencies. It was pointed out that in certain types of situations, the President should make special efforts to give the President-elect full background on what he was doing, and might even in special cases invite his concurrence in decisions; however, the President must be prepared to bear full responsibility for the duration of his term. This document apparently coincided with President Truman's thinking and served as an important policy guide during the subsequent months.

THE BRIEFING BUNGLE

. . . In August, soon after the Democratic convention, President Truman invited Governor Stevenson to confer with him at the White House. Instead of extending a similar invitation directly to Eisenhower, he told General Omar N. Bradley, Chairman of the Joint Chiefs of Staff, to get in touch with

[7] Budget Bureau memorandum, Arnold Miles to William Finan. "Development of Briefing Materials for New President," May 6, 1952.

the Republican candidate and offer him a general briefing, plus regular intelligence reports during the campaign. . . .

Stevenson arrived at the White House shortly after noon on August 12 and was ushered into the cabinet room for a briefing session. General Bradley and General Walter Bedell Smith, Director of the Central Intelligence Agency, apparently did most of the talking, although an impressive array of officials . . . and the heads of all the units of the Executive Office of the President, also attended. Despite the presence of all this talent, the session was reported to have lasted less than half an hour. After the briefing, Stevenson had luncheon with the President and the cabinet. Later he had a private talk with the President. . . .

Meanwhile General Bradley had not carried out his assignment to communicate with Eisenhower. Apparently not realizing that it was urgent, he was waiting until he could see Eisenhower personally; the latter was then in the west but coming east in a few days.

. . . The evening of the Truman-Stevenson conference, Eisenhower made a public declaration that the event showed how Truman had handpicked and intended to dominate his political heir. Eisenhower charged an attempt to use the prestige of the White House to gather votes for the Democratic candidate. He particularly criticized the President for having Generals Bradley and Smith participate, since it implied "a decision to involve responsible nonpolitical officers of our Government . . . into a political campaign in which they have no part." Various Eisenhower supporters made similar criticisms.

The next day Truman tried to recover the fumble by extending a direct invitation to Eisenhower to come to Washington. . . .

Eisenhower declined the invitation. . . .

Truman then tried to soften the impression that his invitation to Eisenhower had been made belated . . . by stating in his press conference that arrangements for Eisenhower to be briefed had been made much earlier. Eisenhower headquarters promptly denied it. After several hours of confusion, General Bradley issued a statement taking responsibility for failing to carry out this assignment.[8]

. . . This put President Truman in a little better light, but he remained angry at Eisenhower's rebuff. On August 16 he dispatched one of his famous handwritten letters:

Dear Ike:

I am sorry if I caused you any embarrassment.

What I've always had in mind was and is a continuing foreign policy. You know that it is a fact because you had a part in outlining it.

Partisan politics should stop at the boundaries of the United States. I'm extremely sorry that you have allowed a bunch of screwballs to come between us.

You have made a bad mistake, and I'm hoping that it won't injure this great Republic.

There has never been one like it and I want to see it continue regardless of the man who occupies the most important position in the history of the world.

May God guide you and give you light.

From a man who has always been your friend and who always intended to be!

Sincerely,
Harry S. Truman[9]

[8] Washington Post (Aug. 15, 1952.)

[9] Apparently Mr. Truman made a copy of his handwritten letter, because he quotes it in full in his Memoirs, Vol. 2, p. 513.

Eisenhower responded three days later with a note expressing his appreciation of Mr. Truman's intention but reiterating his reasons for declining the White House invitation.

This apparently was the last communication between Truman and Eisenhower until after the election, although both Eisenhower and Stevenson received regular CIA reports. . . .

PREPARATIONS DURING THE CAMPAIGN

As the campaign wore on, discussion of and preparation for the inevitable transition continued in Washington. Only a few days after the briefing controversy, Secretary of Defense Robert A. Lovett, a Republican who had served Democratic Presidents in several posts, devoted most of his press conference to . . . the importance of an orderly change of civilian leaders of the incredibly complex military establishment. With the Korean War going on, a smooth transfer was needed now far more than it had been in 1948. . . .

The Budget Bureau made active preparations. The bulk of the staff carried on the usual autumn task of reviewing departmental estimates, assembling preliminary budget figures, and sharpening the issues for top-level decisions in November and December prior to submission in January. For the benefit of the next administration, the bureau's management experts prepared documents on the current administrative problems and proposals for reorganization in each major agency. Its legislative reference office, a clearinghouse on presidential policy, summarized the legislative recommendations Truman had made to Congress and what action, if any, had been taken on each, thus providing a ready guide to the status of the major policy issues of the preceding years. . . . As election day approached, a final step was to draft a letter that the President might send after election, inviting the winner to send a representative to the Budget Bureau.

ESTABLISHING CONTACT

The morning after election found President Truman disappointed at the outcome but prepared to face the future and follow through with the plans that had been laid. . . . As his train rolled into Washington, he emphasized to his staff his determination to set an example of statesmanship, to do what he could to achieve national unity and continuity of policy in foreign affairs, and to ease the transition and assist General Eisenhower in every possible way. Apparently there also had been some forethought on this matter in the Eisenhower group because, as already noted, the President-elect responded almost immediately and agreed to appoint a budget representative.

An Invitation Accepted.

After receiving Eisenhower's message and conferring with his Secretary of State and close adviser, Dean Acheson, Truman sent a . . . message to the President-elect:

> . . . I know you will agree with me that there ought to be an orderly transfer of the business of the executive branch of the government to the new administration, particularly in view

of the international dangers and problems that confront this country and the whole free world. I invite you, therefore, to meet with me in the White House at your early convenience to discuss the problem of this transition period, so that it may be clear to all the world that this nation is united in its struggle for freedom and peace.[10]

That afternoon Truman issued a public statement indicating acceptance of the election results as the will of the people and asking the nation to join him in supporting the President-elect. He announced that he had invited General Eisenhower to send a representative to consult with the Bureau of the Budget but made it clear that he would submit the budget himself as required by law. There would be cooperation on other aspects of the transition if the President-elect wished it. Referring to the many problems of foreign affairs to which there was "no quick and easy solution," Truman announced that he was inviting Eisenhower to the White House in order to discuss the problem of the transition in person with his successor. . . .[11]

Clarifying Roles

Truman's language up to this point had implied that Eisenhower's representatives might somehow participate in interim decisions on foreign and budget policy. Eisenhower now thought it necessary to insert a note of caution. In a note on November 7 he told Truman: "In your letter you use the word 'authoritative' by which I take it you mean that my representative be able accurately to reflect my views. This he will be able to do, but quite naturally this will likewise be the limit of his authority since I myself can have none under current conditions."[12] . . .

. . . "President-elect Eisenhower gave notice yesterday that . . . he would not participate in any government decisions before taking office. . . ." The written statement released by Press Secretary Hagerty emphasized that Eisenhower would have no authority until he had taken the oath of office. The men being sent to confer with the administration would have no authority except to represent his personal views. Their chief function would be to obtain information, and they "would not and could not be bound in any way on foreign or fiscal policy." . . . [13]

The Black Books

In preparation for the White House meeting, Truman had important security information put directly into Eisenhower's hands. . . . The contents included the basic NSC [National Security Council] policy papers, country-by-country summaries of United States policies and programs abroad, intel-

---

[10] *Truman, Memoirs, Vol. 2, p. 505.*

[11] Ibid., pp. 505–06.

[12] Ibid., p. 509. *It might be noted that in the* Memoirs *this message is quoted just prior to Truman's message saying: "We are evidently thinking along the same lines. . . ." However, the wording of these exchanges suggests that Truman had not yet received Eisenhower's message qualifying the role the representatives would play.*

[13] Washington Post (*Nov. 9, 1952*).

ligence estimates on the world's danger spots, and plans to be followed in the event of communist attack or other emergencies in various locations. About this time the Atomic Energy Commission also gave the President-elect a secret briefing. The AEC had news indeed. Only a few days earlier, in tests at Eniwetok atoll in the Pacific, there had been a successful explosion of "Mike," a thermo-nuclear device, forerunner of the hydrogen bomb.[14]

PRESIDENT AND PRESIDENT-ELECT

Arriving at the Washington airport on November 18, Eisenhower's party was escorted into the city over the roundabout parade route. Large crowds, including the government workers Truman had ordered released from their jobs for the occasion, greeted him enthusiastically.

. . . First on the program was a private talk between Truman and Eisenhower. Truman, according to his recollections, told the General that his purpose in inviting him was to emphasize the sincerity of his desire to be cooperative in the national interest and to reassure other countries about the stability of American foreign policy. . . .

After the Meeting

. . . The Truman-Eisenhower meeting seemed to have achieved its essential purpose of suggesting American solidarity and establishing a framework for cooperation. Nevertheless, Truman had been left disturbed by Eisenhower's lack of responsiveness, the "frozen grimness" he displayed. An uneasy feeling that all was not well spread through the administration. Eisenhower's own view of the meeting has never been recorded, but the reporters agreed that he was stiff and unusually serious as he left the White House.[15]

There also were suggestions that more than partisanship and personal dislike of Truman was affecting the President-elect. Speaking informally to an audience of CIA employees a few days later, Truman remarked what an advantage it was for Eisenhower to have the CIA, the NSC, and all the briefings; there had been no such help when *he* took over the Presidency in 1945. Even so, reported Truman with grim satisfaction, Eisenhower had been "rather appalled at all that the President needs to know."[16]

Columnist Tom Stokes put it more eloquently:

It is possible, even likely, that Gen. Eisenhower really did not have a full awareness of the awesome responsibility imposed upon him . . . until the hour he spent in the White House. . . . At least the President-elect seemed to observers to be a different and changed man when he came from the conference with President Truman. . . . His face wore a grim and startled look as he confronted the horde of newspapermen. . . . The infectious grin of campaign days was missing. . . . When he had arrived at the White House an hour earlier he had put on a smile for the photographers. . . . Then he had come fresh from the cheers of the throngs gathered along the Capital's streets to welcome him, a familiar re-echo of the crowds which had greeted him everywhere all over the country in his triumphant campaign. But, only an hour later, the

[14] H. D. Smyth, Acting Chairman of AEC, letter to the President, Jan. 8, 1953 (*From the files of Charles S. Murphy, Harry S. Truman Library*).

[15] Washington Post (*Nov. 19, 1952*); New York Times (*Nov. 19, 1952*).

[16] Ibid. (*Nov. 22, 1952*).

prison doors of the White House had become very real to him, and for the first time we may imagine. Now, suddenly, as a result of what he had heard behind the closed doors in the cabinet room, . . . all the millions he had seen on his campaign . . . had become his charges, his responsibility. . . . He had faced the man who had had this stewardship for nearly seven and a half years. . . . The Nation's Chief Executive who sat at the head of the table had once, himself, been an awe-stricken and grim-faced man. It was that late afternoon back in April, 1945. . . . Symbolically, Gen. Eisenhower had reached the same hour; for the shadow of his coming responsibility fell upon him in the same surroundings, abruptly. Long ago and far away now must have seemed the cheering multitude of the campaign, and the golf course at Augusta. Ga. . . . This was it—from now on. This White House.[17]

[17]Thomas L. Stokes, "Eisenhower Grim After Meeting." Washington Evening Star (Nov. 19, 1952).

End questions

1. What is the significance of the date March 29, 1952 in the political career of Harry Truman? Compare this date with another similar one in the career of a more recent President.
2. Under what types of situations should the President give a full briefing to the President-elect? Do you think the President-elect should be informed of what is happening at all times? Explain.
3. What is the relationship between presidential transition periods and stability in government?
4. How does the American form of democracy provide for turnovers of party leadership and transition in administration? Do you think this is a good practice? Why is policy continuity and government responsiveness to a new political leader so important in a democracy?

CHAPTER 15
The Bureaucracy: Why and How It Developed

The bureaucracy of the federal government is composed of the administrative units or agencies that carry out and enforce the policy outputs of Congress and the Presidency. Within the bureaucracy itself, each department or agency operates as part of its own particular subsystem which has components similar to other subsystems.

Generally it is assumed that the bureaucracy is "neutral" politically—that it plays no role in making policy and that the direction of its activities is determined solely by Congress or the President. It is also assumed that if the actions or decisions of the bureaucracy are unjust, they can easily be overturned by the courts.

Nothing could be further from the truth. As the bureaucracy's responsibilities have become more fundamental to the operation of the government, it has become increasingly independent of other branches. Only occasionally does this so-called fourth branch answer to Capitol Hill or to the White House, and even less frequently is it subject to review by the courts. In fact, the bureaucracy has considerable influence on the other three branches and does, in many cases, play a significant role in making government policy.

Constitutional Context

Despite the importance of the federal bureaucracy today, the Framers gave so little thought to this necessity of government that they included very few specifications in the Constitution for government administration. They merely provided a mechanism by which an administrative structure could be created. After listing the powers of Congress, Article I, Section 8 of the Constitution states that the legislative body can "make all laws which shall be necessary and proper for carrying into execution" the enumerated powers. It is this clause, along with the enumerated powers, which has been used to justify the legislature's creation of the administrative departments and agencies. The bureaucracy, then, is largely an extension of congressional authority.

Attempts to make the bureaucracy fit into the tripartite system of government have still not satisfied some political observers. As the bureaucracy has grown and become increasingly autonomous, it has been difficult to determine how the power of this administrative branch of government should be controlled.

Control of the bureaucracy. The Constitution was not specific about who was to control the bureaucracy of the new Republic. As a result, both the President and Congress have been in a continuous contest to direct the bureaucracy.

■ *Arguments for presidential control.* The intentions of the Framers as well as the language of the Constitution are cited by those who believe that the President should control the bureaucracy. In *The Federalist*, No. 72, Alexander Hamilton regarded administration as little more than "executive detail," and he thought the President should have the sole responsibility for administrative personnel:

"The persons . . . to whose immediate management, the different [administrative] matters are committed ought to be con-

What does the President or the Congress gain in winning the "tug of war" for control of the bureaucracy? How has the Constitution affected the development, structure, and responsibilities of the "fourth branch"?

sidered as the assistants or deputies of the chief magistrate, and on this account, they ought to derive their offices from his appointment, at least from his nomination, and ought to be subject to his superintendence."

Like Hamilton, most of the Framers assumed that the President, as "chief magistrate," would supervise the individuals who would carry out the mandates of Congress. They did not make it clear, however, just where the mandates of Congress ended, or where presidential interpretation and execution of these mandates began.

Although the Constitution is vague about the powers the President can exercise over the bureaucracy, it does, without qualification, grant him the executive power, and Article II gives him the responsibility to "take care that laws be faithfully executed." The thrust of Article II, then, is in the direction of recognizing the President as the head of the government's administrative branch. Since the Constitution does not give the President the tools to control the bureaucracy, those who, like Hamilton, have supported presidential supremacy in this sphere have encouraged Congress to delegate more authority to him for this purpose.

Whatever the Framers' intentions may have been, the fact is that the system they constructed did permit the organization of a bureaucracy which could function independently of the President. Since the *creation* of the bureaucracy is the responsibility of Congress—which by nature competes with the President for power—Congress has retained control over some elements of the bureaucracy instead of giving control entirely to the President.
■ *Congress' Powers over the bureaucracy.* The constitutional powers of Congress over the bureaucracy are considerably greater than those of the President. First,

Congress has virtually complete authority (should it decide to exercise it) to arrange administrative processes and determine where responsibilities shall be placed. Since Congress has the power to create or terminate an agency, it also can determine how each agency shall operate. Every administrative unit—whether an executive department such as the Department of Transportation or a specialized operation such as the Tennessee Valley Authority—is created by an act of Congress. It is Congress which decides whether an agency is to be part of the executive branch or outside of it; and it is Congress which may or may not decide to let the President exercise various types of controls. Congress has used this power to create many independent agencies which are in varying ways beyond presidential interference.

Second, not only can Congress formally set up administrative agencies independent of the President and determine their functions and jurisdiction, but it can also maintain an agency's independence in several ways. The legislature can pass laws that grant additional authority to existing agencies for implementing new programs. On some occasions, Congress has refused to accept presidential proposals to reorganize agencies under tighter executive control. An agency which has such congressional support does not need to heed the wishes of the President.

The legislative branch can also interfere with presidential appointments to the bureaucracy. Cabinet members who head executive departments, for instance, are appointed by the President but can not take office without "the consent of the Senate." Congress may, of course, grant the President power to appoint officers to any new agencies it creates, but it may set the conditions for such appointments and for the removal of administrative officers by the President as well.

366

Congress also grants appropriations and is thus potentially able to exercise a great deal of power over its administrative arm. Increasingly, however, it is the President who has the initial, as well as the final, say over the nature of the budget for the various administrative agencies. Usually appropriations measures are first recommended to Congress by the President and, when passed as amended by Congress, are returned to the Chief Executive for his approval or veto.

Yet, while the President plays an important role in determining administrative budgets, it is still the function of Congress to enact the laws which provide the funds. And while it is usually difficult for Congress to muster the two-thirds majorities necessary to override a presidential veto, Congress does have the potential to counter the President in this way. The significance of this congressional power and its implications for administrative control were demonstrated as recently as 1970. Concerned with halting inflation, President Nixon in that year vetoed several appropriations bills that exceeded his budget recommendations. On two of these bills—those which provided funds for hospital construction and school assistance to be administered under HEW—Congress asserted its power and overturned the President's vetoes.

When the need for a larger bureaucracy developed after 1789, it was inevitable that Congress would resort to whatever constitutional powers it had to retain some control over the administrative structure. It has done so, in part, by creating many agencies in the bureaucracy which are independent of the executive branch, and in part, by exercising its various powers to influence the activities of all the agencies and departments it has created.

Structure of the bureaucracy. The federal bureaucracy developed in response to realistic requirements rather than according to any set formula. Because each administrative agency was created to meet specific problems, no two agencies are exactly alike. It is therefore impossible to classify the parts of the bureaucracy according to any definite arrangement of structures or functions.

It is possible, however, to identify the general forms which different agencies have taken. The lack of agreement over who should control the bureaucracy is evident in the present structure of the administrative branch. In keeping with Hamilton's argument for presidential supervision, many government functions are assigned to executive departments whose heads are directly responsible to the Chief Executive. The independent regulatory commissions, on the other hand, operate completely outside of presidential control even though he appoints the chairmen of most of these agencies and fills other vacancies whenever they occur. Between these two extremes are other *independent agencies* which function outside of the executive departments, but which may or may not be subject to the President's supervision—depending on how Congress has set them up. *Government corporations* comprise a fourth type of administrative unit; some of these operate as independent entities while others are within the jurisdiction of executive departments.

Just as the requirements and priorities of public policy are always changing, the form of administrative agency which performs a particular government function may be changed if there is sufficient need and demand. The history of the government's postal service illustrates this. Originally administered as a service outside of direct executive supervision, the postal system has been reorganized twice: first as an executive department in 1872 and again as an independent agency almost a century later. But, while the various subsystems of the bureaucracy are always potentially subject to reorganization, they generally take one of the forms described above.

Review questions
1. How is the creation of the bureaucracy justified by the Constitution?
2. How does the structure of the administrative branch reflect the lack of agreement as to who should control it?

The Development of Administrative Subsystems

The small size of the federal bureaucracy during the first century of the Republic corresponded to the widespread belief of that period that government activity should be limited—particularly in the country's economic life. During this period, the bureaucracy consisted primarily of executive departments. But by the end of the nineteenth century, major changes in the social and economic environment of the nation created new demands for government to take on more responsibilities. Since that time, the activities of government have increased in many spheres, and Congress has enlarged the federal bureaucracy—both under and outside of presidential supervision.

Executive departments. The original government bureaucracy consisted of three executive departments: the Departments of War, State, and the Treasury. The choice of these departments by the first Congress in 1789 reflected the concern with those matters that were of most crucial importance to the Republic at the time—defense, foreign (and some domestic) affairs, and national finances. The officers in charge of these departments were members of the Cabinet and were directly responsible to the President. Another Cabinet member— the Attorney General—was the adviser to the President on legal matters but did not head an executive department. A postal system was also established in 1792; but it did not become an executive department until late in the nineteenth century, although the Postmaster General was named a Cabinet member in 1829.

By the middle of the nineteenth century, only two executive departments—the Departments of the Navy (1798) and the Interior (1849)—had been added to the three established under George Washington's administration. All of the early executive departments were so small that the bureaucracy was easily subject to careful scrutiny by both Congress and the White House. It was only during this early period of the nation's history that the administrative branch was controlled primarily by the President.

■ *Later departments.* The bureaucracy remained small until the latter part of the nineteenth century when greater demands on government, brought on by territorial expansion and industrialization, increased the need for specialized policy-making. When it created the Justice Department under the Attorney General in 1870 and made the postal system an executive department in 1882, Congress merely reaffirmed the importance of matters which had long been of government concern. But the establishment of other new departments in the years that followed indicated a definite shift in the federal government's attention to issues which were entirely new.

The changing economy in the late nineteenth century encouraged various eco-

| James G. Blaine, | William Windom, | James A. Garfield, | Samuel J. Kirkwood, | William H. Hunt, | Robert T. Lincoln, | Wayne MacVeagh, | Thomas L. James, |
| *Secretary of State* | *Secretary of the Treasury* | *President* | *Secretary of the Interior* | *Secretary of the Navy* | *Secretary of War* | *Attorney General* | *Postmaster General* |

PRESIDENT GARFIELD AND HIS CABINET

(In 1881, the federal bureaucracy still consisted mainly of executive departments supervised by the President.)

nomic groups to demand that government look after their interests. In response to this new concern for the nation's economic life, the Department of Agriculture—which had been created under a Commissioner in 1862—was given executive-department status in 1889. The Department of Commerce and Labor, established in 1903, was split into two separate departments in 1913. Today, the Departments of Agriculture, Commerce, and Labor are engaged in research, information distribution, and other activities which help to promote the well-being of the economic groups for which they were set up.

Following the New Deal period of the 1930's, the government's concern with an even broader range of national problems led to the creation of still other executive departments to coordinate policy in many areas. After World War II, several attempts to reorganize and consolidate the military services resulted in the creation of the Department of Defense in 1949. The Departments of the Army (formerly the Department of War), Navy, and Air Force were all placed within the Defense Department. In 1953, a number of government agencies which dealt with problems of general welfare were combined under a single executive Department of Health, Education, and Welfare. During the 1960's the increasing concern of the government with the need for improvements in urban development and nationwide transportation led to the shifting of a number of agencies from other departments to two new executive departments: the Department of Housing and Urban Development (1965) and the Department of Transportation (1966).

■ *Department organization.* Like other structures of the government, each executive department operates as part of a sub-

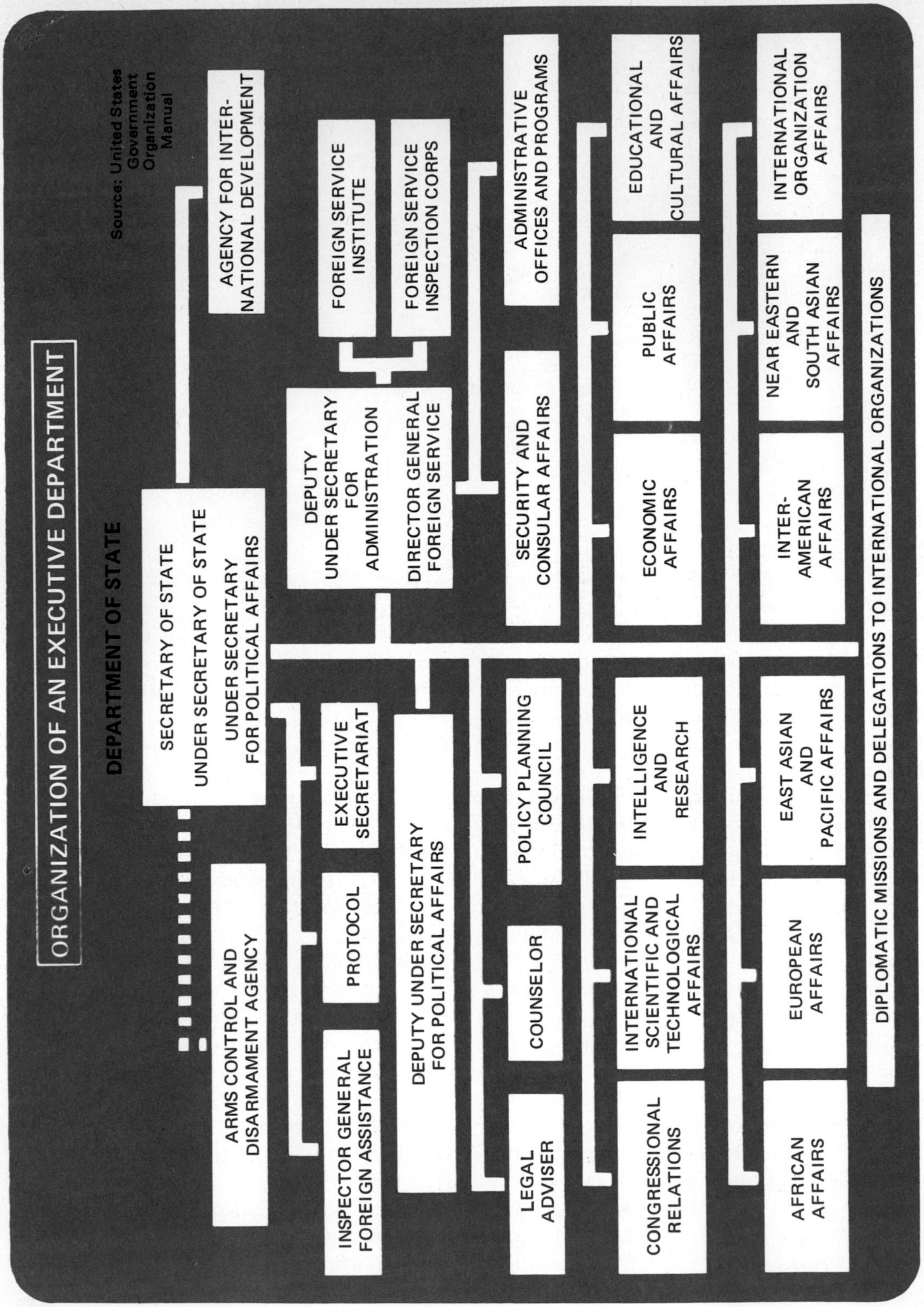

ORGANIZATION OF AN EXECUTIVE DEPARTMENT

DEPARTMENT OF STATE

Source: United States Government Organization Manual

SECRETARY OF STATE

UNDER SECRETARY OF STATE

UNDER SECRETARY FOR POLITICAL AFFAIRS

ARMS CONTROL AND DISARMAMENT AGENCY

AGENCY FOR INTER-NATIONAL DEVELOPMENT

DEPUTY UNDER SECRETARY FOR ADMINISTRATION

DIRECTOR GENERAL FOREIGN SERVICE

FOREIGN SERVICE INSTITUTE

FOREIGN SERVICE INSPECTION CORPS

SECURITY AND CONSULAR AFFAIRS

ADMINISTRATIVE OFFICES AND PROGRAMS

INSPECTOR GENERAL FOREIGN ASSISTANCE

PROTOCOL

EXECUTIVE SECRETARIAT

DEPUTY UNDER SECRETARY FOR POLITICAL AFFAIRS

COUNSELOR

POLICY PLANNING COUNCIL

ECONOMIC AFFAIRS

PUBLIC AFFAIRS

EDUCATIONAL AND CULTURAL AFFAIRS

LEGAL ADVISER

CONGRESSIONAL RELATIONS

INTERNATIONAL SCIENTIFIC AND TECHNOLOGICAL AFFAIRS

INTELLIGENCE AND RESEARCH

INTER-AMERICAN AFFAIRS

NEAR EASTERN AND SOUTH ASIAN AFFAIRS

INTERNATIONAL ORGANIZATION AFFAIRS

AFRICAN AFFAIRS

EUROPEAN AFFAIRS

EAST ASIAN AND PACIFIC AFFAIRS

DIPLOMATIC MISSIONS AND DELEGATIONS TO INTERNATIONAL ORGANIZATIONS

370

system—responding to the demands and support of its constituents in performing its particular functions. The internal organization of each department is far from simple, and each department is structured differently from every other. All executive departments are compartmentalized and fragmented into various types of units, so that each category of policy will get the specialized attention it requires.

In addition to the Cabinet-level Secretary who heads each executive department and is responsible to the President, there are numerous other officials—under secretaries, assistant secretaries, deputy assistant secretaries, bureau directors, and many others—who report directly or indirectly to the Secretary. Each of these officials is responsible for an office, bureau, regional area, or other division.

The hundreds of units and subunits within each executive department contribute to the complexity of government administration. Within the Department of Health, Education, and Welfare, for example, there are eight major divisions including the Public Health Service, the Office of Education, and the Food and Drug, Social Security, and Welfare Administrations. Each of these divisions, in turn, contains numerous specialized bureaus and offices, and has related regional offices throughout the country. The Office of Education alone contains at least five separate bureaus including the Bureau of Higher Education, the Bureau of Research, and others. In effect, all of the many administrative units within the departments of the executive branch operate as part of mini-subsystems which process the policies of government.

Independent regulatory commissions. Unlike executive departments which are directed by Secretaries responsible to the President, each federal regulatory commission is under the direction of a multi-member board of commissioners who function outside of executive supervision. Each commission is responsible for establishing regulations or standards which govern certain operations in the private sector of the economy. Because these regulations have the effect of law, the commissions are considered to be *quasi-legislative* bodies. In addition, the commissions can prosecute violators of any regulations they set and can conduct hearings and pass judgements in such cases, thus performing *quasi-judicial* functions.

The Interstate Commerce Commission (ICC), established in 1887, was the first independent regulatory commission and became a model for future agencies. Like the commissions which were established after it, the ICC was created to protect various economic groups against the inequitable policies of certain industries. The establishment of such federal commissions has been necessary to cope with problems of nationwide impact that could not be adequately handled by the individual states.

■ *The ICC as a prototype.* The immediate reason for organizing the ICC was political pressure from agrarian interests, primarily in the Midwest, to end abusive railroad practices. The farmers were particularly angered about high rates for the transportation of grain. Although state commissions were able to regulate railroads operating within the state boundaries, the Supreme Court held in 1886—in *Wabash, St. Louis, and Pacific Railway Co. v. Illinois*—that railroads conducting interstate commerce could not be regulated by state agencies.

The *Wabash* decision prompted the passage of the Act to Regulate Commerce—the enabling statute that created the ICC. The Act also gave the ICC jurisdiction over facilities that were engaged in transporting passengers or property "wholly by railroad and partly by water when both are used

(This Thomas Nast cartoon, "The Senatorial Round-House," which appeared in *Harper's Weekly,* portrayed defenders of the railroad interests in Congress not long before the ICC was created to regulate industry.)

under a common control, management, or arrangement for a continuous carriage or shipment." This gave the ICC the right to regulate the railroad industry.

In 1887 commission regulation, although not novel at the state level, was a new experiment at the national level. Thus, the experiences faced by the ICC provided precedents for later administrative development.

Although the ICC was at first under the partial direction of the Secretary of the Interior, by 1889 it had become independent in various ways from both the President and Congress. Later, it became somewhat independent from the courts as well.

Increasing independence is typical of the development of an independent regulatory commission. Although each commission is initially created as an independent entity, as political support from private groups increases, such agencies acquire even more power to prevent interference from other branches of the government.

■ *Reasons for an independent commission.* Although the immediate reasons for establishing the ICC are relatively easy to comprehend, the long-range political reasons for the agency's creation are more complex. Basically, the justification for regulation by all independent commissions is the same.

First, the ICC was organized because it could provide more expertise as a regulatory body for the railroads than Congress could. A commission of specialists could gain more expert knowledge about any particular subject or industry than a small handful of legislators, with their many responsibilities, could hope to attain.

Second, a permanent commission could provide more continuity in public policy than an elected body. Partially for this reason, ICC commissioners were originally appointed by the Senate for six-year terms. Later the terms were extended to seven years—five years longer than a Representative's term and one year longer than a Senator's. It was also expected that many commissioners would be reappointed when their terms expired, and this has happened frequently. Moreover, the agency's staff, which is a permanent force also provides continuity and stability to regulatory policy.

Third, an independent regulatory agency could combine the two functions—*legislative* and *judicial*—so necessary for effective regulation. At the time the ICC was created, it was not expected to exercise these two functions independently. Originally,

it was to act as an advisory body to both Congress and the judicial branch, with Congress enacting the policies that the Commission recommended and subsequently enforced.

It soon became evident that if the ICC could not exercise legislative and judicial power on an independent basis, it would never be effective. During the twentieth century, the ICC was greatly strengthened by several congressional acts providing it with more and more power to perform legislative and judicial functions. Over the years, Congress has given the ICC the authority to set rates on other types of carriers besides railroads, and even to set rates for intrastate transportation which competed with interstate carriers. The Transportation Act of 1958 extended the Commission's judicial authority by permitting it to approve or reject the application of a carrier to discontinue train or ferry service.

Fourth, as a broad-based impartial body, it was thought that the regulatory commission would be less inclined to succumb to pressure from private or governmental interests. Admittedly, the ICC at first was to be a partisan body representing nonrailroad interests such as the agrarian group. With the passage of time, the American Bar Association (ABA) and the legal profession, as well as other people connected with these groups, began to treat the agencies more as courts than as administrative authorities because agencies were settling cases. The ABA wanted to ensure that the exercise of the judicial function by these agencies would be as impartial as in the courts.

The debate over the real role of independent regulatory agencies has never been resolved. Today there is still some concern about whether an agency should favor the "public interest," or be an impartial adjudicator of the rights of private parties coming before it. The judicial pro-

373

From Herblock's *Special for Today* (Simon & Schuster, 1958)

"They Act As If They've Been Doped"

(The regulatory commissions are sometimes criticized for protecting private instead of public interests.)

cedure employed by the agencies is forced on them by law. Decisions must be based on the record made by the immediate parties involved. Yet, administrative procedure is only partially judicial. The agency heads do take into consideration, in addition to the results of initial judicial-type hearings, a wide range of factors in the decision-making process.

A fifth argument advanced in support of commission regulation was that national regulations were needed for national industries. Until the mid-nineteenth century, industry was inclined to be localized; but as the nation expanded so did the size of the various industries. The fact that such industries affected the life of the entire country was used to justify the creation of a federal regulatory body.

■ *Evolution of regulatory commissions.* The main changes that took place in the ICC after its creation illustrate the general direction other regulatory agencies have taken. Once a regulatory commission has dealt effectively with the problems it was originally created for, its primary function switches from regulation to general supervision.

The ICC, for example, was unable to solve satisfactorily the problem of regulating the railroad industry at first because it faced a hostile judiciary and a national atmosphere favorable to business interests. Even the pressures of agrarian interests which led to its creation did not bolster the ICC enough for it to bring the railroads into line.

In the early years of its existence, the ICC was prevented from doing anything significant without the approval of the courts. Faced with the likelihood of unfavorable ICC decisions, the railroads soon learned to rely on judicial review to protect their interests and paid little attention to the ICC. They even resorted to such devices as withholding evidence from the Commission, believing that if they brought new evidence to the attention of the judiciary on review, the courts would insist on a *de novo* (an entirely new) trial. In cases dealing with the ICC, the Supreme Court consistently interpreted the law and the Constitution to protect the sanctity of private property, and again and again refused to permit strong regulation of the railroads.

Reaction to continuing hostile judicial decisions finally led to the passage of the Hepburn Act (1906) which gave the ICC final rate-making power subject to judicial review only on complaint from the carriers. This placed the burden of proof on the carriers. If they wanted the judiciary to overturn an ICC decision, they had to disprove the legitimacy of an ICC decision before the courts.

After enactment of the Hepburn Act, the

Commission's authority was strengthened at various times to make it even more independent of the courts. By 1920, the ICC was beginning to assume real regulatory authority. At this point, however, a transformation began to take place in the ICC. It switched from being a punitive agency which regulated the railroads' in the public interest to being a promotional agency trying to maintain the railroads prosperity in the face of economic adversity.

■ *Swing to promotion.* As early as 1892, in a letter to railroad magnate Charles Perkins who had been critical of the ICC, Attorney General Richard S. Olney made an uncanny prediction for the trend that the ICC would take as it developed:

"The Commission, as its functions have now been limited by the courts, is, or can be made of great use to the railroads. It satisfies the popular clamor for a government supervision of railroads, at the same time that the supervision is almost entirely nominal. Further, the older such a Commission gets to be, the more inclined it will be found to be to take the business and railroad view of things. It thus becomes a sort of barrier between the railroad corporations and the people and a sort of protection against hasty and crude legislation hostile to railroad interests. . . ."[1]

As the ICC developed, it did, in fact, become a champion of railroad interests. Most regulatory commissions seem to follow the same pattern. Once the need to regulate the industry disappears, the political pressure that led to creation of the commission also fades away. The agency then has to cast about for new sources of support. Turning to the industry that it regulates is only natural.

The economic health of a regulated industry also may decline, necessitating some kind of promotional activity and possibly government subsidies to keep it alive. To answer such needs, an initially punitive commission turns to promoting the industry it was established to regulate.

■ *New regulatory commissions.* After the creation of the ICC, the number of regulatory commissions increased rapidly as a result of political and economic pressures. Changing technology and demands from various groups that their interests be protected against more powerful business enterprises expanded the need for regulation. Moreover, the development of the "welfare state" concept and the New Deal philosophy involved the government far more in the area of regulation than it had ever been before.

The Federal Reserve Board was organized in 1913 to head the Federal Reserve System and provide for national standards in the banking industry. The Federal Trade Commission (FTC) was created in 1915 to protect the free enterprise system against deceptive business practices and restraints of trade by business monopolies. Set up in 1920, the Federal Power Commission (FPC) —which regulates rates and other interstate matters of the electrical power and natural gas industries—was given independent regulatory authority in 1930. Initial steps were made in 1927 to regulate the communications industry by setting up the Federal Radio Commission. This agency was transformed into the Federal Communications Commission (FCC) in 1934.

During the New Deal period, there was a general burgeoning of administrative agencies. A new and more positive economic philosophy, decreeing that government should guide the national economy, had taken hold. The independent regulatory commissions set up during this period included the Securities and Exchange Com-

[1] *James Morton Smith and Paul L. Murphy, eds.,* Liberty and Justice, *(New York: Alfred A. Knopf, 1958), pp. 292–293.*

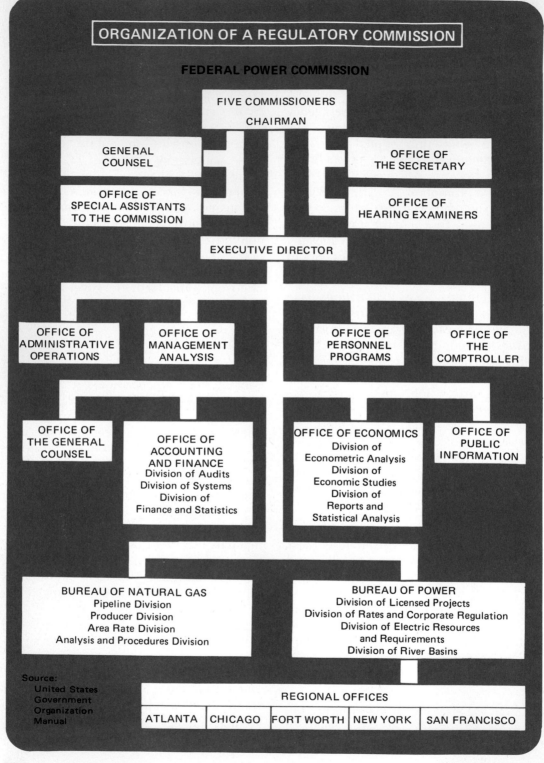

ORGANIZATION OF A REGULATORY COMMISSION

FEDERAL POWER COMMISSION

FIVE COMMISSIONERS
CHAIRMAN

GENERAL COUNSEL

OFFICE OF SPECIAL ASSISTANTS TO THE COMMISSION

OFFICE OF THE SECRETARY

OFFICE OF HEARING EXAMINERS

EXECUTIVE DIRECTOR

OFFICE OF ADMINISTRATIVE OPERATIONS

OFFICE OF MANAGEMENT ANALYSIS

OFFICE OF PERSONNEL PROGRAMS

OFFICE OF THE COMPTROLLER

OFFICE OF THE GENERAL COUNSEL

OFFICE OF ACCOUNTING AND FINANCE
Division of Audits
Division of Systems
Division of Finance and Statistics

OFFICE OF ECONOMICS
Division of Econometric Analysis
Division of Economic Studies
Division of Reports and Statistical Analysis

OFFICE OF PUBLIC INFORMATION

BUREAU OF NATURAL GAS
Pipeline Division
Producer Division
Area Rate Division
Analysis and Procedures Division

BUREAU OF POWER
Division of Licensed Projects
Division of Rates and Corporate Regulation
Division of Electric Resources and Requirements
Division of River Basins

REGIONAL OFFICES

| ATLANTA | CHICAGO | FORT WORTH | NEW YORK | SAN FRANCISCO |

Source:
United States Government Organization Manual

376

mission (SEC), created in 1934 to supervise the securities and financial markets; the National Labor Relations Board (NLRB), set up in 1935 to protect the rights of labor to organize and bargain collectively; and the Civil Aeronautics Board (CAB) established in 1938 to regulate the air transportation industry.

Many of the New Deal agencies were established as directed by the President with backing from various private interests. President Franklin D. Roosevelt acted as chief supporter for the expansion of the bureaucracy during the New Deal period. It was his ingenuity and power that often provided the balance of political support necessary for this purpose.

Other independent agencies. Like the regulatory commissions, the other independent agencies of the federal bureaucracy exist outside of the executive departments. However, they generally provide services or perform some administrative functions other than economic regulation.

The purposes of these agencies are diverse. Some, like the Farm Credit Administration and the Small Business Administration, perform services which benefit particular economic groups. Others, such as the General Services Administration and the Civil Service Commission, have special functions which benefit other government agencies and departments. There are also independent agencies that encourage development of the arts and sciences or that administer special government programs such as the National Aeronautics and Space Administration.

The organization and control of these agencies vary according to how Congress has set them up. Most of the officials in charge of administering them are appointed by the President with the advice and consent of the Senate. Some of the agencies are under the direction of multi-member boards or commissions, while others—such as the Veterans Administration—are under a single administrator directly responsible to the President.

Government corporations. A relatively new administrative device, the *government corporation* was virtually unknown before the New Deal era. Since the 1930's, and particularly during World War II and after, government corporations have increased in importance in the bureaucratic structure. Corporations were set up to accomplish relatively specific tasks, such as insuring and extending credit to banking facilities (Federal Home Loan Bank Board, Federal Deposit Insurance Corporation), or developing a regional public utility (Tennessee Valley Authority).

Initially, government corporations were given more freedom of action, especially with respect to the management of fiscal affairs, than regular departments and agencies. They were less accountable to Congress, could raise their own funds, and could function generally in ways similar to private business enterprises. In 1945, the Government Corporation Control Act made these corporations more accountable to Congress and the President. Still they preserved some of their previous independence.

Although there are only several dozen government corporations today, they cover many types of "businesses" and exercise functions vital to the community as a whole. While not officially a government corporation, the newly organized United States Postal Service is set up to be self-financing and, in this sense, to operate like a corporation.

Effects of federalism. One fundamental element of American government, federalism, has affected administrative organization and operation in a number of ways. Generally, federal-state cooperation is needed to execute national programs. The tremendous contrasts existing among the states in geography, economic wealth, and social make-up, almost necessitate a decentralization of many units of the federal bureaucracy to deal with various problems that arise on the state and local levels. Sometimes, it even happens that public policy cannot be implemented because of conflicting state authority and interests. When this occurs, federal incentives are usually employed to bring the states into line with national administrative policy. Thus, those states that are balking about constructing links of the interstate highway system may be induced to cooperate after a promise of national funds.

In sum, the effect of the constitutional system on the bureaucracy has been to fragment it. Lines of authority and control are blurred, organizational patterns are varied, and unity is absent. The Constitution has aided in fragmentation of the political decision-making apparatus generally. The bureaucracy is no exception.

Review questions

1. How does the increase in administrative agencies show (1) a changing attitude toward governmental regulation, and (2) concern for current problems?
2. Why is it necessary for independent regulatory agencies to exercise both legislative and judicial functions?

Chapter Review

Terms you should know

Act to Regulate Commerce	government corporation	quasi-legislative
de novo trial	Hepburn Act	quasi-judicial
executive department	independent regulatory commission	*Wabash* case

Questions about this chapter

1. Why might the Framers of the Constitution be surprised and concerned about the present fourth branch of government?
2. What powers does Congress possess that enable it to exercise a great amount of control over the bureaucracy? How does the Office of Management and Budget serve as a check on these congressional powers?
3. Compare the functions and structure of the various administrative units. Explain how independent regulatory commissions differ from (a) government corporations, (b) executive departments.
4. Since the late nineteenth century there has been a significant increase in the number of executive departments. What departments have been added? Why?
5. For what reasons was it necessary to give independent regulatory commissions the power to set standards for national commerce?
6. In what way did the economic conditions during the 1930's promote the creation of additional regulatory agencies? What role did President Roosevelt play in their development?
7. One characteristic of an independent regulatory commission is that it tends to develop from a "punitive" agency to a "promotional" one. Explain why this happened in the case of the ICC.

Thought and discussion questions

1. Do you think there are any administrative agencies that have outlived their usefulness? Considering the problems of the 1970's stemming from our urban-technological society, what type of agencies do you envision being established by Congress in the future?
2. It has been charged that the increase in the size and power of the federal bureaucracy, especially through the establishment of regulatory agencies and government corporations, is a dangerous threat to private enterprise. Comment.

Class projects

1. Refer to your local newspaper for the last year. Make a list of the national administrative agencies that have been active in your community. What kind of programs have they been involved in?
2. Examine news magazines for the past six-month period, and list the various activities of the eleven executive departments. A team of two or three students can be responsible for each department. Make a report to the class about your findings.

CHAPTER 16
Policy-Making Through the Bureaucracy

E ach administrative agency—whether it is an executive department, a regulatory commission, an independent agency, or a government corporation—performs certain functions that convert the demands and support of constituents into outputs. Each agency stands at both the beginning and end of the policy-making process. It makes demands on other policy-making structures and also carries out the policies that other conversion structures have made.

Depending on the kinds of demands it receives, an agency may perform several different kinds of functions. If it is authorized to set standards for implementing a policy, its outputs include *quasi-legislative* decisions. If it makes judgments about implementing policy in specific cases, it performs *quasi-judicial* functions. And if it gathers information, releases funds for a project, or implements policy-standards already established, it performs *executive* functions.

No matter what their functions are, administrators must consider all the interests and pressures—those of private groups and governmental agencies—that have come to bear during the policy's formulation. All too often, they find themselves sandwiched between the concerns of the private groups and those of the governmental branches. The administrator must try to satisfy both. Like other parts of the government, administrative agencies do not have complete independence and must operate within the framework of the political system.

Sources of Demands and Support for the Bureaucracy

Demands and support for any administrative agency come from both governmental and nongovernmental sources. Direct demands on an agency are made by other governmental conversion structures—the President, Congress, the courts, and other administrative agencies—usually in the form of policy outputs to be carried out by the agency. There are also demands and support that come directly from the private interest groups which are affected by the administrative agencies. These nongovernmental demands are the reactions of the private interest groups to policies which the agencies are putting into operation. The administrative agency concerned, in turn, acts as a conversion structure either by putting forth a modification of the policy in question or by making a new demand on the government structure which originated the policy.

Although the three original branches of the government do not control the agencies with an iron hand, they, along with private pressure groups, do place some important restraints on administrative action. Just as the President is limited in his decision-making role, for example, by the demands and supports within the presidential subsystem, administrative agencies have similar limitations. They can not consistently go against interests of the groups that are the reasons for their existence. Some agencies, especially the independent regulatory commissions, are virtually captives of the groups that they regulate. Whenever one of the commissions attempts stricter regulations, private interest groups exert pressure on the President, Congress, and the courts to curb administrative action.

In what respects are the responsibilities and functions of the federal administrative agencies similar to the responsibilities and functions of the other branches of the federal government?

The complexities of most issues and the need for both specialization and continuity in the formulation of policy have enhanced the authority and support of the bureaucracy. The agencies have won this support at the expense of the President, Congress, and the judiciary.

Presidential demands and support. Because the creation of an agency in the first place is usually the result of a presidential request, the President is the initial source of support for any agency established during his administration. It is the President who ordinarily asks Congress to establish an agency to oversee the regulation of a certain industry or to administer an area of government policy.

The President also acts as a general manager of the administrative agencies. All of the appropriations requests, legislative proposals, and reorganization recommendations concerning the administrative agencies are channeled through the Office of Management and Budget (OMB). The President is thus cognizant of the activities that concern the bureaucracy.

In addition, each President has certain goals which he hopes to achieve during his administration. These general policy intentions and aspirations are also funneled into the administrative agencies, and the agencies are expected to aid the President in attaining the goals of his programs. Some agencies, however, are more likely to be influenced by private groups than by the White House because these groups provide them with more intense, consistent, and informed support. The legal independence of some agencies may be such that the President can interfere only occasionally. Thus, before he can exert strong pressure on administrative officials to effect his policies, the President must consider the political forces within the general electorate, private organizations, and Congress that might rally to the defense of an agency or official opposed to his program. Usually the President tries to avoid such situations by appointing administrative officials who tend to agree with his policy objectives.

When the President finds that an agency under his supervision has become too independent, however, he does have recourse to a very effective action. He can alter the legislative and budgetary proposals which that administrative agency may initiate. Since the OMB must coordinate and approve the proposals of all agencies under presidential supervision, the President and the members of the OMB can bring the demands of these agencies into line with presidential policies before they are submitted to Congress.

The President and the Executive Office may even exert extraordinary influence on the bureaucracy in special circumstances. In times of crisis, the National Security Council which itself includes two top administrative officials—the Secretaries of State and Defense—may call for help from various parts of the bureaucracy to meet national security requirements. The Office of Emergency Planning can make special demands on the bureaucracy so that it can fulfill its responsibility to coordinate rescue efforts or civil defense operations in cases of national emergency.

■ *Evolution of agency independence.* For the most part, a new agency champions the causes of the President under whom it has been created, for he is the most logical and available source of immediate support. Later, however, as the agency develops independent sources of support, this new support may lead it into opposition with the President, especially if he is not the same person who proposed the agency's establishment. Sometimes it even happens that groups at first opposed to the agency later become important sources of support, as was the case with the railroads and the Interstate Commerce Commission.

SPEAK RIGHT INTO THE OLIVE, SIR...

"I'M CERTAINLY GLAD YOU ASKED THAT QUESTION—YES, J. EDGAR HOOVER ENJOYS MY ABSOLUTE AND COMPLETE CONFIDENCE . . ."

(The long tenure of J. Edgar Hoover as FBI director has strengthened the independence of that agency.)

■ *The merit system.* An important factor which limits the effect of presidential demands on the bureaucracy is the bureaucracy's own "merit system." Under this system, most jobs within the bureaucracy are granted on the basis of competence, not political affiliation. By removing federal employees from dependence on the President for their jobs, the bureaucracy has won a certain freedom that keeps the President from interfering with its work or from manipulating the administrative branch improperly.

Prior to the establishment of the Civil Service Commission in 1883, the selection of personnel for all administrative positions in government had been the reward, or "spoils," of the victorious presidential candidate and his party. The President gave jobs to his friends and supporters, and the staffs of various agencies changed every time the party represented by the occupant of the White House changed.

Demands for the creation of a civil service became particularly intense in 1881 after President James A. Garfield was assassinated by a man who had been turned down for a government job. Two years later Congress passed the Civil Service Act, also known as the Pendleton Act. This law set up the United States Civil Service Commission which fixes standards for recruitment of government employees, classifies personnel according to job categories, and oversees the competitive examinations given for various jobs. The establishment of the Commission eliminated the "spoils system" and gave continuity and permanence to most of the bureaucracy. Government staff members now stay in their jobs from one presidential administration to the next.

With the growth of the civil service, federal administrative employees—except for top-ranking policy-making officials such as Cabinet members—have gradually become members of the civil service. In 1968 there were nearly 3,000,000 federal employees. The greatest concentration—about 250,000 —of these employees lived in the District of Columbia and the neighboring counties in Maryland and Virginia. The remaining federal bureaucrats were scattered throughout the fifty states, and in those overseas areas where there are American military bases, or where economic aid programs are being carried out.

■ *The merit system in operation.* Through the Ramspeck Act of 1940, Congress has given the President the authority to extend the civil service to various government agencies. Some Presidents have extended the civil service before leaving office, and the power of the succeeding President has been limited as a result. This was illustrated when Dwight D. Eisenhower in 1952 became the first Republican President in twenty years. President Truman, at various times during his administration, had extended the civil service system to parts of the bureaucracy not previously covered by it. The Republicans favored the government's withdrawal from many activities in which Democratic administrations had involved it.

Eisenhower confronted the problem of trying to initiate new policies through a bureaucracy that was hostile to his proposals. He maintained that personnel changes alone would accomplish his goals, but the merit system prevented this. When he attempted to reduce the number of civil servants by dismissing those administrators he felt were disruptive to his program, the merit system enabled the bureaucracy to resist and to retain these people. The bureaucracy had defended its independence. The fact that this system protected many

policy-making officials raised questions in the minds of some, however, who felt the country had voted for a change and should have seen it implemented.

Congressional demands and support. The President's power over the bureaucracy is shared by Congress. Congress, acting on the basis of its enumerated and implied powers, establishes and maintains the agencies. Its authority to appropriate money is particularly important for maintaining the bureaucracy. In addition, just as Congress creates the agencies and determines how they operate, Congress can also alter the functions of an agency at any time by passing a law that increases or decreases the agency's independence and authority. This is probably the single most powerful stick it holds over the bureaucracy.

The administrative agencies maintain the support they need from Congress by providing Congress with information and by putting congressional policy into action. The major congressional demands on an agency come from the standing committees that determine the agency's policies and funds. Most administrative decisions are made in response to congressional committee hearings as well as to the demands of particularly powerful individual congressmen. Bills that eventually become law are formulated by these committees and are the basis of an agency's regulations and powers.

There are thirty-six standing committees —twenty in the House and sixteen in the Senate. (See the list on page 288.) In both the House and Senate there are Appropriations Committees which consider the bills funding all of the agencies. Each house also has individual subject-matter committees which investigate financial and other needs of the specific agencies. Consequently, an agency may find itself responsible to several committees. The Defense Department, for example, reports to the Armed Services

Committees as well as to the Appropriations Subcommittees on Defense, in both the House and the Senate.

The relationship between agencies and congressional committees is usually informal. Staff members are sometimes exchanged between the agencies and congressional committees, and in some cases there is continuous consultation between bureaucrats and congressional staffs. Committee chairmen who have been in office for some time usually develop informal working relationships with the administrators who report to their respective committees. Moreover, individual congressmen acting as spokesmen for their constituents raise a number of grievances before the agencies. In general, there is a great variety of ways that Congress contacts the bureaucratic officials and conducts its affairs with the administrative agencies.

Judicial demands and supports. The bureaucracy's primary legal responsibilities have been stipulated in congressional statutes. Agency action must take place within the boundaries of authority established by Congress. Moreover, agency procedures can not violate the basic constitutional safeguards found in the Bill of Rights.

By interpreting the laws under which the bureaucracy operates, the courts set limits on administrative authority. Upon review of an agency's decision, the courts may overrule the agency, denying that it acted according to the authority given it by Congress. Each time a court upholds or denies an agency's action, the agency is bound by this decision in similar cases in the future.

The courts themselves, however, are limited by the judicial process from acting against the bureaucracy. The courts can not initiate a case against an administrative agency, but must wait until such a case is presented by outside parties.

Demands and support of other administrative agencies. Administrative agencies also make demands on and provide support for each other—especially when they have related policy responsibilities. Several regulatory commissions—such as the Civil Aeronautics Board, Interstate Commerce Commission, and the Securities and Exchange Commission—have jurisdiction over mergers of industries under their supervision. Because the Antitrust Division of the Justice Department also has responsibility for enforcing the antitrust laws in all areas, it may challenge the decision of a regulatory commission if it feels that the commission is not upholding antitrust statutes. But the regulatory agencies do make the final judgment on a merger application unless, of course, judicial review through the courts is required.

In recent years the Justice Department

Cartoon by Zschiesche.
Reprinted by permission of King Features Syndicate.

"Pointing the way to school integration . . ."

(An agency must balance its independent action against guidelines imposed by the other branches of government.)

has attempted several times to defeat mergers pending before regulatory commissions. A notable case involved the merger application of the International Telephone and Telegraph Company and the American Broadcasting Company before the Federal Communications Commission (FCC). The Justice Department challenged the application before the FCC itself, thus delaying the merger. The parties involved eventually decided to withdraw their application.

Demands and support of private pressure groups. In addition to the demands and support it receives from other parts of the government, each administrative agency must also respond to the demands and support of private pressure groups. Private pressure groups actively support administrative independence because an independent agency is usually more accessible to them than one that is under presidential control.

Groups that fall under the jurisdiction of an administrative agency continuously make demands—both direct and indirect—for policies favorable to their own interests. *Direct* demands are expressed to administrators themselves by the spokesmen of interest groups. Such demands are made not only when the agencies implement policy but also when the administrators represent certain groups before other policy-making structures. Spokesmen for the oil industry, for example, may pressure the Federal Power Commission (FPC) to set favorable rates or to request certain rate policies through administrative proposals or at congressional hearings.

Pressure groups make demands on the bureaucracy *indirectly* whenever they bring pressure on other branches of government. When representatives of the armaments industries try to influence legislators or the President to adopt a particular weapons

Drawing by Wm. Hamilton; © 1968 The New Yorker Magazine, Inc.

"Just because you and I don't like the interest-rate ceilings, we don't go storming the Treasury Building, do we?"

(The accessibility of an agency to a particular group may determine how the group will express its demands.)

system, their demands indirectly affect the Defense Department and other agencies responsible for administering such programs. Companies in the oil industry may bring indirect pressure on the FPC by challenging a decision of the Commission in the courts. Also, pressure groups make indirect demands by attempting to influence public opinion.

No matter how pressure-group demands are channeled into the bureaucracy, administrators must give special attention to such demands. Because these groups are often powerful and possess specialized information needed for administrative decisions, the bureaucracy can not afford to ignore these important sources of support.

Review questions

1. What kinds of demands and support do federal agencies receive from other parts of the government?
2. How do private interest groups influence the activities of administrative agencies?

The Bureaucracy's Legislative Functions

It is a fundamental principle of republican government that laws are to be made by a legislature with members elected by the people. The delegation of legislative authority by an elected legislature to other parts of the government would seem contrary to this principle. Yet, as the activities of the American federal government have expanded, Congress has delegated substantial legislative authority to the bureaucracy, and the constitutionality of this process has been upheld by the Supreme Court.

The need for delegating legislative authority. It would seem contradictory that Congress should delegate its own authority to administrative agencies when it should be jealously guarding its prerogative to make laws. Yet in fact, Congress is unable to determine the content of legislation on numerous subjects because it does not have sufficient knowledge. And very often, congressmen leave the details out of legislation in order to avoid taking a positive stand on a controversial issue. For both reasons, Congress often passes laws so vague that the bureaucracy must fill in many of the details to make the legislation workable. The decisions which the agencies make in such instances are called *quasi-legislative* because, while they are not made through the regular law-making process, they are as enforceable as laws passed by Congress.

A perusal of congressional statutes would illustrate that extraordinary delegations of legislative authority have been granted to some administrative agencies and their various divisions. The regulatory commissions, for example, are given blanket au-

Drawing by Alan Dunn; © 1968 The New Yorker Magazine, Inc.

"Isn't it about time we issued some new guidelines for something?"

(For technical and political reasons, congressmen turn over many legislative functions to the bureaucracy.)

thority to make rules which are in the "public interest, convenience, and necessity." The commissions must determine what is in "the public interest" and act according to their own formulas whenever they implement new legislation.

Various divisions of the Department of Defense have also been given broad grants of authority. It is impossible for Congress to give concise guidelines to the military departments on all the technical details involved in maintaining adequate defense. Instead, Congress passes laws that state a general purpose with general guidelines, thus granting broad decision-making authority to those who have specialized military knowledge. For example, Congress may authorize the Secretary of the Army to:

"... procure materials and facilities necessary to maintain and support the Army, its military organizations, and their installations and supporting and auxiliary elements, including:

 (1) guided missiles;
 (2) modern standard items of equipment;
 (3) equipment to replace obsolete or unserviceable equipment;
 (4) necessary spare equipment, materials, and parts; and
 (5) such reserve supplies as is needed to enable the Army to perform its mission."[1]

On the basis of such a statute, the Secretary of the Army has considerable latitude for determining what missiles, equipment, and other supplies are "necessary to maintain and support" the army's operation.

In some instances, Congress does pass statutes with more specific standards for administrative guidance. But these standards tend to be procedural guidelines—that is, they prescribe the method to be used

by an agency for implementing a policy but not the details of what should be implemented.

Consent of the judiciary. Since the early nineteenth century, the Supreme Court has upheld the right of Congress to delegate some legislative power to the President and the bureaucracy. In a series of cases, the Court has developed the doctrine that Congress may delegate quasi-legislative authority to the agencies if, in making such delegations, it clearly states its intent. Furthermore, in stating its intent, Congress must establish the limitations of administrative authority.

■ *Establishing congressional intent.* The Court has realized that Congress can not make every specific decision to be executed by the bureaucracy and thus must delegate some of its authority as a practical necessity. Theoretically, in granting such authority to the President or to administrators, Congress merely permits others to do what it would do itself if it could. The Supreme Court has held, therefore, that Congress can delegate its authority to administrative agencies as long as it makes clear how it intends that authority to be used.

The concept of "congressional intent" has been important whenever a delegation of legislative power has been challenged in the courts. In 1922, for example, Congress passed a law permitting the President —after proper investigations by the United States Tariff Commission—to change tariffs when necessary to establish equal competition between the foreign and domestic producers of certain goods. The Constitution, however, grants Congress alone the power to set tariffs, and the law was challenged as an unconstitutional delegation of legislative power. Since the intent of Congress to permit equal competition between domestic and foreign producers was clearly stated in the law though, the Court upheld the Tariff Act, noting that "if Congress shall

[1] 10 U.S.C. 4531; 70A Stat. 253 (1956).

lay down by legislative act an intelligible principle to which the person or body authorized . . . is directed to conform, such legislative action is not a forbidden delegation of legislative power."[2]

■ *Limitations on the agencies.* While Congress can delegate legislative authority to administrative agencies, it can not empower agencies to do what would be unconstitutional for Congress itself to do. And just as the bureaucracy must conform to the limits of the Constitution when it exercises legislative functions, it can not perform such functions at all except as prescribed by specific laws of Congress.

When an administrative action is challenged, the courts must determine whether the administrative agency has acted according to standards set by Congress. A judicial determination that an agency has acted outside of its authority is known as a determination of *ultra vires* (beyond legal power) action. Yet, in order to establish that an *ultra vires* action has been committed, the courts must be able to refer to a statute which clearly indicates the limits of the agency's authority.

One of the few instances in which the Supreme Court has held a delegation of legislative authority to be unconstitutional involved the failure of Congress to set such limits. The decision concerned provisions of the National Industrial Recovery Act which Congress had passed in 1933 to deal with the economic depression. Under the Act, a National Recovery Administration (NRA) was set up to assist in the improvement of business and working conditions by enforcing "codes of fair competition." Under the Act, the codes were drawn up by representatives of various industries and became enforceable when approved by the President. The President was also authorized to impose codes on industries which failed to develop codes of their own.

When the Schechter Poultry Corporation of New York City was convicted by a federal court of violating the "Live Poultry Code," the case was appealed to the Supreme Court. The Court determined that the codes were unconstitutional because they set up regulations for intrastate businesses and thus went beyond the national government's legal power to regulate only interstate commerce. The Court argued further that the Act was an improper delegation of legislative power because it failed to prescribe limits on the President's authority.

Without such restrictions, the President could approve and disapprove codes completely at his own discretion and not according to any purpose intended by Congress. The Court's decision therefore narrowed its previous doctrine on the delegation of legislative power.

"We have repeatedly recognized the necessity of adapting legislation to complex conditions involving a host of details with which the national Legislature cannot deal directly. . . . [T]he Recovery Act . . . sets up no standards, aside from the statement of general aims of rehabilitation, correction and expansion. . . . In view of the scope of that broad declaration, and of the nature of the few restrictions that are imposed, the discretion of the President . . . is virtually unfettered. We think that the code-making authority thus conferred is an unconstitutional delegation of legislative power. . . ."[3]

■ *The Court's flexibility.* In the *Schechter* case, the Supreme Court refined the doctrine of delegating legislative authority by insisting that Congress define the limits of such a delegation to clarify its intent. Yet,

[2] *J. W. Hampton, Jr. & Co. v. United States,* 276 U.S. 394 (1928).

[3] *Schechter Poultry Corp. v. United States,* 295 U.S. 495 (1935).

even during the New Deal era, the Court cited other examples of vague delegations of legislative authority which were not declared unconstitutional. Since 1935, no congressional statutes have been declared to be in violation of the doctrine stated in the *Schechter* case and the Court has always been able to find some provisions within a statute to determine the proper limits for the agency being challenged.

This does not mean that Congress always includes clearly defined restrictions on agencies when it delegates legislative authority. It seems rather, for the most part, that the Court has been able to rationalize congressional delegations of authority according to the needs of government. Thus, during World War II, when Congress gave the Office of Price Administration almost complete discretion to set price ceilings and the head of executive departments discretion to collect "excess profits" from contractors, these delegations of power were upheld in two separate challenges before the Court.

With the help of the Court's flexibility, Congress has been able to grant broad decision-making powers to the bureaucracy. The indefinite language of congressional statutes enables administrators to use considerable discretion in interpreting the intent of Congress and in setting the standards which their agencies enforce. Thus, the Secretary of Transportation may be authorized to set "reasonable, practicable, and appropriate" safety standards for motor vehicles. No doubt, the Secretary of Transportation will have to interpret congressional intent in the light of pressures being exerted by the automobile industry. The Transportation Department—on the basis of its own determination of what is "reasonable, practicable, and appropriate" —will then issue standards that have the force of law.

Review questions

1. How do the administrative agencies get legislative authority from Congress? Why is this delegation of authority necessary?
2. Was the enforcement of the "Live Poultry Code" (at issue in the *Schechter* case) an example of an *ultra vires* action? Explain why or why not.

Judicial Functions of the Bureaucracy

Once an agency has set standards to implement government policy, that agency usually has the responsibility of ensuring that its standards are applied and enforced. But often, questions arise as to how such standards should be applied in specific situations. The decisions necessary to settle such matters are usually made, not by the courts, but by the agency concerned. Such decisions are *quasi-judicial* because, while they concern specific cases and controversies and are thus judicial in nature, they are determined outside of the formal judicial system.

Like legislative authority, the authority to make quasi-judicial decisions is delegated to the bureaucracy by Congress. The Constitution has placed the judicial power of the federal government in the Supreme Court and in whatever lower courts Congress chooses to create. The Supreme Court has interpreted this provision along with the implied powers of Congress to uphold the delegation of judicial authority to regulatory commissions and other agencies.

Limitations of the courts in agency cases. The need for giving judicial functions to the bureaucracy is partly due to the limitations of the formal judicial system. While questions concerning agency actions sometimes do reach the courts, basically the courts hear only cases and controversies that concern specific laws and treaties or the Constitution. Due to this restriction, the judiciary is an ineffective instrument for making judgments on quasi-lesiglative, administrative policy. The federal courts can not initiate cases to force compliance with public policy because Article III of the Constitution requires that decisions of the judiciary be limited to matters brought to it. In addition, the courts themselves have established rules that stop them from making decisions on broad public policy.

The administrative agencies, on the other hand, can affect public policy directly. Thus they can initiate cases which arise from their own rules and regulations and they can enforce the policy decisions which result from the cases they initiate.

Types of administrative judgments. Administrative agencies make different kinds of quasi-judicial decisions concerning private parties. Some administrative judgments are made to resolve controversies between private parties and an agency; other judgments are made to determine how agency policy and rules should be applied to particular individuals.

Controversies arise when an agency issues a complaint against a private party. Whenever the Internal Revenue Service (IRS) challenges a person's income tax return, for example, or the Department of the Interior charges a manufacturer with violating water-pollution-control standards, there is a controversy between the government and a specific individual or company. Usually, the same government agency involved in such a controversy also has the judicial authority to make a judgment settling the matter.

Agencies also make quasi-judicial decisions whenever they review applications

"SORRY, WALLY. LET'S SAY IT WAS EXPLOITATION FOR EXPLOITATION'S SAKE."

(The Interior Department plays a quasi-judicial role when it decides how to deal with a pollution offender.)

from individuals or companies to do certain things. If the Penn-Central Railroad, for example, applied to the ICC for permission to increase freight rates, the Commission's judgment on the matter would be a quasi-judicial decision. Similarly, the Veterans Administration makes a judicial-type decision whenever it determines if a particular applicant qualifies for certain benefits.

Administrative proceedings. Administrative agencies make judgments in two ways. They can come to judicial decisions informally or they can go through formal procedures. *Informal* proceedings are highly flexible and do not follow any set procedures while *formal hearings* follow many of the same procedures that are used by the courts. Almost all agencies conduct informal proceedings in an attempt to settle cases before they reach a formal stage of administrative decision.

The Internal Revenue Service affords a good example of how both informal and formal judgments are made. When the Service questions an individual's income tax payment, there is a controversy between the individual and the government; and a judgment must be made. A revenue agent first meets informally with the individual to settle the matter. When the taxpayer is found to have been in error on his payments, he usually agrees to settle the matter by making up the difference. When the IRS is found to have misjudged the taxpayer, the matter is normally dropped.

If the matter is not settled informally, however, it then goes through more formal procedures. The taxpayer becomes a defendant, must hire a lawyer, is confronted by a prosecutor, and will either be convicted or acquitted.

Formal hearings are usually far too time-consuming and expensive for both the agency and the individual involved. In addition, fear of governmental reprisal causes most individuals to settle informally. Informal settlements can be just as nerve-racking, however, because individuals and groups have to undergo the pressures of administrative investigation and prosecution.

Restrictions on agency actions. Administrative agencies do not have complete control over the judicial actions they take. Congressional statutes often require the agencies to hold hearings, report findings of fact, and base decisions on the records of proceedings. Moreover, since the courts have the power of judicial review over agency decisions, they do, at times, require the agencies to adhere to procedures that are considered fair to all the parties involved in the proceedings. Still, the agencies do have considerable independence in determining the judicial-type procedures

which they use. It is impossible for Congress, once it delegates judicial authority to the agencies, to exercise continuous supervision over their activities.

The broad judicial discretion of administrative agencies, however, has provoked some attempts to curb administrative power. For example, recommendations have been made in Congress that judicial review be expanded to permit the courts to examine agency decisions more closely. In addition, laws have been proposed requiring agencies to observe legal procedures similar to those used by courts of law. In 1946 Congress passed the Administrative Procedure Act to standardize the judicial-type proceedings in various agencies so that they would conform to court standards of due process of law. The Act also set up a separate class of hearing officers who listen to cases so that the same officer can not act as both prosecutor and judge on a single matter.

Executive functions. All of the functions performed by the bureaucracy, outside of the legislative and judicial functions, are "executive." The vast programs administered by such agencies as the Departments of Agriculture, Interior, and Defense are implemented largely through the exercise of executive functions—that is, those that do not involve general policy-making or the disposition of specific cases and controversies.

New trends in the federal bureaucracy. Because of the wide scope and complexity of the bureaucracy's activities, attempts are being made to modernize and streamline agency operations by using more sophisticated and technical methods similar to those used in business. *Systematic decision theory*—which includes systems analysis, operations research, and systematic budgetary theory—is being applied to executive functions as well as policy planning in government. It is hoped that these methods will make government operations more efficient and productive.

In addition, there has been a movement toward the basic reorganization of some administrative agencies. The postal service, for example, has been reorganized so that it can issue bonds to cover the costs of desperately needed modernization and operate along the lines of a government corporation.

A third trend may be developing toward greater consolidation of similar functions now performed by different agencies. In 1970 the President's Advisory Council on Executive Reorganization recommended a highly controversial plan to overhaul the entire system of regulatory commissions. Under this plan, several of the regulatory commissions would be combined into regulatory agencies under the direction of single administrators; judicial functions of all the commissions would be redelegated to a new Administrative Court.

Some observers praised the plan as a reform that would reduce the influence of select interest groups on regulatory agencies. Thus, the reform would be in the public interest. But the reluctance of Congress to place agencies under presidential control and the resistance of industries that benefit from commission independence promised to hinder the plan's execution.

Review questions

1. How does the judicial authority exercised by the administrative agencies differ from that of the courts?
2. What types of procedures do the administrative agencies use to arrive at judicial decisions? Give an example of each.

Chapter Review

Terms you should know

Administrative Procedure Act of 1946
civil service system
delegated power
executive functions

formal hearings
informal proceedings
merit system
Pendleton Act

Ramspeck Act
spoils system
ultra vires action

Questions about this chapter

1. In what form are governmental demands made on administrative agencies—nongovernmental demands?
2. Why is congressional support so important to an administrative agency?
3. How was the elimination of "the spoils system" supposed to curb the excesses of presidential power?
4. How did President Eisenhower's administration illustrate that the merit system can prevent changes in governmental policies?
5. Why are administrative agencies often responsible to more than one part of the Congress? Does this increase the power of Congress over these agencies? How?
6. On what basis can the courts limit the amount of authority an agency tries to exercise? How are the courts often prevented from exercising influence over an agency?
7. Why does the President sometimes have less influence over the bureaucracy than private interest groups? What recourse does a President have if an agency becomes too independent?

8. Explain the significance of the *Schechter Poultry Case* for the doctrine of delegating legislative authority.

9. What limitations has Congress put on the judicial authority of the administrative agencies? What suggestions have been made to further curb their judicial power?

Thought and discussion questions

1. The Constitution clearly grants legislative authority to Congress alone. Do you think the delegation of legislative authority by Congress is justifiable? In your answer, consider such aspects of the problem as necessity, effectiveness of limitations, both elected and non-elected bureaucrats, etc.

2. Interest groups make demands directly and indirectly on governmental agencies. How is this done? Can this be harmful to the nation's long-term interests? Is it beneficial? Explain.

Class project

1. Refer to Class project 1 in Chapter 15. After making a list of the federal administrative agencies active in your community, decide which of the programs and decisions these agencies have made are legislative and which are judicial. Are there some executive functions? Determine whether judicial decisions have been made through formal or informal procedures.

Case Study: Administrative policy-making

The bureaucracy is central to the policy-making process of most governments. In many cases, bureaucrats today make decisions that were formerly made by legislators, judges, and even the Chief Executive. Elected officials, in turn, must respond to initiatives and decisions of the bureaucracy.

The complex policy-making process of the bureaucracy becomes clear when a particular controversy involving a decision of an administrative agency is studied. One such controversy arose when the tobacco industry questioned the Federal Trade Commission's right to initiate a policy that required warning consumers of the dangers associated with cigarette smoking. An analysis of this problem taken from A. Lee Fritschler's book, *Smoking and Politics: Policymaking and the Federal Bureaucracy,* illustrates the internal procedures of one agency—The Federal Trade Commission—as well as the relations of that agency with Congress, the President, the courts, other administrative agencies, interest groups, and the general public.

As you read this case study, look for and think about the following:
1. Why have legislative bodies delegated authority to administrative agencies? Is this unconstitutional?
2. What procedural difficulty prompted the Federal Trade Commission to hold a hearing on the cigarette controversy?

3. How did Congress alter the work of the Federal Trade Commission? Why was this action within Congress' power?
4. Why did the Tobacco Institute want the cigarette bill moved from the jurisdiction of the Federal Trade Commission into the halls of Congress? What was the Institute's argument for such a move?

Development of Administrative Policy-Making Powers

The Federal Trade Commission's announcement of its intention to require a health warning [on cigarette packages in early 1964] was a reminder to everyone that [federal] agencies have the power to make policy. The cigarette interests were not pleased by the announcement, although they had every reason to expect it. They knew that Trade Commission policy-making would be different in both procedure and outcome from congressional policy-making, because agency personnel were much less sympathetic to the tobacco position than were congressmen. . . .

Congressional Delegation of Authority

The basis of the complaints of the cigarette interests rested in the clear language of Article I of the Constitution—"All legislative powers herein granted shall be vested in a Congress of the United States. . . ." There is nothing in other sections of the document to indicate that legislative or policy-making powers should reside in the bureaucracy. Yet the accumulation of policy powers in the legislature has never worked well, and from the beginning Congress has been obliged to find ways to share its powers. . . .

. . . Almost from the time the Constitution was adopted, Congress recognized that it could not effectively handle all of the complexities of policy-making. There are natural limitations on legislatures which make them incapable of acting as effective policy-makers under certain conditions.

These conditions arise when policy decisions involving complex and technical knowledge are called for. Congress does not have sufficient expertise or the necessary time to devote to the details of much modern policy-making. . . . Career experts in the bureaucracy are in a better position to devote continued attention to a particular problem and develop policy standards and guidelines than are members of Congress. If Congress were to enact all the specific rules and regulations necessary for the administration of programs, one of two equally undesirable results would occur: the rules would be too general to serve as effective guidelines for administrators, or they would be too rigid and inflexible and so would become useless in short order. In delegating policy-making powers to agencies, Congress relieves itself of the burden of detailed work and frees itself to devote time to issues of basic policy. . . .

This condensation from Smoking and Politics: Policymaking and the Federal Bureaucracy, *by A. Lee Fritschler is reprinted by permission of Appleton-Century-Crofts, Educational Division, Meredith Corporation. Copyright ©* 1969.

As the problems of society become more complex, Congress tends to rely increasingly on agencies for policy-making. American society has already reached a point where administrative agencies are producing more policy than the other two branches of the government combined. . . .

Although there are serious theoretical and practical obstacles to the delegation of policy-making authority, agencies have been operating under the umbrella of delegated authority for many years. In only two cases has the Supreme Court held congressional delegations to be unconstitutional.[1] Consequently, many claim there is little question about the ability and legality of Congress to delegate. . . . Nevertheless, this constitutional issue, as any other, is within the discretion of the Court. . . . The tobacco interests' strategy against the Commission's action was based in part on the hope that the FTC's mandate was an unconstitutional delegation. The position of the Tobacco Institute in regard to the FTC is summarized in the following words:

. . . in terms of policy and discretion, whatever substantive regulation may be believed to be necessary in this area of smoking and health, Congress alone should enact it.
. . . we respectfully submit that in these proposed Trade Regulation Rules the Commission is not exercising the authority conferred upon it by Congress in the Federal Trade Commission Act. It is plainly legislating.[2]

The tobacco interests must have recognized that their argument was, at the very least, risky, in view of what the Supreme Court had been saying for years about delegation. Their approach was nonetheless astute in more than one respect. Important segments of public opinion could be expected to rally to the cry that faceless administrators were performing a role which should be reserved to the elected representatives of the people. The powerful industrial and commercial communities could be expected to be sympathetic with that view. Furthermore, by arguing the delegation issue they were able to gain the attention of Congress and thus increase the possibility that the controversy would be transferred, eventually, from the Commission to Congress. . . .

When the Surgeon General's report appeared in 1964 [linking cigarette smoking with cancer, and other diseases] the Federal Trade Commission had had a substantial amount of experience with misleading advertising, including cigarette advertising. . . .

Yet even with this experience and the necessary legal authority, all was not well with the Federal Trade Commission and its regulation of cigarette advertising. Cigarette consumption was rising at a faster rate than ever. Policing advertisements had apparently not resulted in conveying to the public the health dangers involved in cigarette smoking. The Commission was coming around to the view that in the face of all the adverse health reports, it was cigarette advertising alone which accounted for the rise in sales. . . .

Ironically, the root of the Federal Trade Commission's problem was. . . . a procedural difficulty as much as anything else. The Commission was attempting to regulate cigarette advertising on a case-by-case basis. Each time the

[1] Panama Refining Company v. Ryan, 293 U.S. 388 (1935) and Schechter Poultry Corporation v. United States, 295 U.S. 495 (1935).

[2] From the statement on behalf of the Tobacco Institute, Inc., submitted to the Federal Trade Commission, p. 6 (mimeo.).

Commission ruled a particular advertisement deceptive, the industry came up with a variation which could squeak by under the rule of the previous case. This was proving to be an endless and fruitless process. The Commission needed to write general regulations for the whole industry; the case method, whether employed by an agency or by the courts, was proving to be too cumbersome a method of developing regulatory policy.

In 1963, the Commission moved to solve its problem by incorporating in its rules a procedure which could be used to write enforceable regulations for a whole category of industries. The Chairman of the Federal Trade Commission saw the adoption of rulemaking procedures as the only way to make the Commission an effective regulator. . . . This new procedure was set into motion one week after the Surgeon General released his report on smoking and health.

Procedures Used in Administrative Policy-Making

. . . Rulemaking is characterized by its general applicability. Rules formulated by agencies uniformly affect all within a given category, such as all cigarette producers. In contrast, adjudicatory actions are based on a specific case involving an individual, partnership. . . .

Federal Trade Commission's Experience with Cigarette Regulation

The limited effectiveness of the Commission's policy-making procedures are evident in its record on cigarette advertising regulation. The Commission has invoked its adjudicatory powers [powers used to perform judicial or courtlike activities] in cases involving cigarette producers [over] 25 times. . . . In dealing with an industry-wide problem such as deceptive cigarette advertising on a case-by-case basis the Federal Trade Commission found itself faced with problems not much different from those which the courts encountered when they attempted to make broad policies on a case-by-case basis. Discovery of the inadequacies of the case approach in the courts was one of the prime reasons for establishing the Commission in 1914. Ironically, nearly 50 years later, the Commission was attempting to act in a manner similar to that found ineffective by the courts.

The insufficiencies of the case approach stem from the fact that the judgment or order in each case applies only to the parties to the case. Others who might be engaged in the same deceptive act, or one closely related, are not immediately affected by the Commission's decision involving their less fortunate brethren. It is possible for those not named as a party to the case to continue the "illegal" practice until the Federal Trade Commission moves against them. This can take months or even years. Furthermore, only activities or practices complained of in the suit can be prohibited by the decision; slight variations from that practice even by the same parties must be dealt with by separate decisions.

. . . There was no way for the Commission to state authoritatively a general policy of what constituted deception in cigarette ads for all advertisers. . . . The Commission's action against cigarette producers only provided requirements about what *could not* be done, but not about what *must* be done. That is, the Federal Trade Commission could not require that a health warning appear on all packages through its adjudicatory procedures. The only way it could have approached this requirement would have been to ask the manufacturers to do this voluntarily or deal with the cigarette companies one at a time through cases which, in each instance, would have to prove that such a positive disclosure was necessary. . . .

Since it was impossible to fight the health inferences and subtleties in cigaette ads through adjudicatory procedures, the best way to eliminate deception, according to Federal Trade Commission, is to require that a positive health warning statement appear in each advertisement. Rulemaking authority was necessary before that requirement could be made. . . .

Federal Trade Commission Adopts Rulemaking Procedures

Some individuals outside the Federal Trade Commission also began to realize that without rulemaking powers the Commission could not hope to effectively warn the public of the health hazards of smoking. In April 1962, Senator [Maurine] Neuberger [Democrat, Oregon] wrote a letter to Paul Rand Dixon, the newly appointed chairman of the Federal Trade Commission, suggesting that any cigarette advertisement which failed to carry a health warning was inherently deceptive. She asked why the FTC could not adopt this position officially and subsequently require that all cigarette advertising carry a health warning. The answer to Senator Neuberger's inquiry was that the Commission had never adopted the necessary rulemaking procedures to do what she suggested. . . .

. . . Plans for the adoption of rulemaking procedures were already in the works when the chairman answered Senator Neuberger's letter. His response hinted openly that the only major obstacle to the adoption of the Neuberger suggestion was the gathering of substantial evidence establishing a direct relationship between smoking and ill-health. . . .

. . . The Trade Commission announced the adoption of general rulemaking procedures in June 1962. . . .

Although the adoption of rulemaking procedures was probably coincidental to the cigarette controversy, the Commission busied itself issuing trade regulation rules (the official name given the end product of the new rulemaking procedure) for uncontroversial products as if it might have been practicing for its cigarette rule. . . . The cigarette makers, who were . . . to be affected by a trade regulation rule, were determined to prove that the FTC had no authority to write such rules. Had they succeeded, they would have had a double victory: the cigarette rule would have been quashed, and the Commission would have remained a weakened watchdog of the public interest, confined to either its informal or its case method of regulation.

. . . Trade regulation rules give the FTC the capability of issuing formal rules or guides to govern the conduct of large categories of producers. And once the rules are issued, any violation of them could be used to initiate adjudicatory proceedings.

The commissioners themselves by majority vote decide whether or not to initiate rulemaking procedures. Citizens or groups may petition the Federal

Trade Commission to commence a proceeding but the Commission itself decides whether or not the petition should be acted upon. The proceeding on the cigarette labeling and advertising rule was initiated by the Commission. . . .

. . . Several months before the Surgeon General was to issue his report the Federal Trade Commission organized within its staff a special task force on cigarettes consisting of physicians, economists and attorneys. When the report was issued, the Commission was ready to move; within one week the Federal Trade Commission issued a notice that it planned to begin a rulemaking proceeding. . . .

In formal rulemaking, only some of the required adjudicatory procedures are employed; for example, hearings are conducted, a public record is kept and certain rules of evidence are followed. However, the most important difference between the formal and informal processes is that in the former a public hearing is required and in the latter, the decision as to whether or not to hold a hearing is left up to the agency. . . .

In all of its rulemaking the Federal Trade Commission has followed formal procedures. The commissioners never seriously considered adopting the cigarette labeling and advertising rule without holding a formal hearing because they sensed how controversial their proposal was. They knew that if they adopted the rule without hearings, the cigarette manufacturers could seize upon the secretiveness of their action to argue that the FTC is undemocratic, arbitrary and dangerous. . . .

The Federal Register

The first step taken was to give notice to interested parties. Although not required to, the Commission mailed a letter of its intentions to those it presumed would be interested. And, it released a news item to the press. Simultaneously, it placed a notice in the official publication of the executive branch, the *Federal Register,* an action required by the Administrative Procedure Act in all rulemaking activities. . . .

. . . The notice contained a draft of the proposed rule, an explanation of the legal authority upon which the action was to be taken, and the dates for hearings before the Commission. The public was also informed in the notice that they could file written data, views or arguments concerning the rule or the subject of the proceeding in general. . . .

. . . Copies of the cigarette notice were mailed to a large number of companies, associations and individuals who might conceivably have had some interest in the proceedings. Furthermore, shortly after the notice was placed in the *Register,* the Federal Trade Commission directly solicited statements from state and local health officers and associations, physicians, medical scientists, behavioral scientists, chemists, cigarette manufacturers and many others. . . .

When the hearings began, the commissioners were fortified with staff documents and prepared statements in much the same way a congressional committee is prepared for a hearing on proposed legislation. The draft of the rule had been widely circulated, perhaps even more widely circulated than proposed legislation might have been. Comments had been received from a sizeable cross-section of the public, and the commissioners were prepared to hear witnesses discuss the feasibility and wisdom of the proposed health warning for cigarette packages and advertising.

The Rulemaking Hearings

On March 16, 1964, the commissioners took their seats . . . to begin three consecutive days of hearings on the cigarette labeling and advertising rule. The proposed rule, which had been circulated well in advance of the hearing, contained three major sections. The first was the requirement that a health warning appear in all advertising and on cigarette packages. . . .

Another section of the rule attempted to reach the more subtle implications of cigarette advertising by banning "words, pictures, symbols, sounds, devices or demonstrations, or any combination thereof that would lead the public to believe cigarette smoking promotes good health or physical well-being." In addition, the draft rule prohibited the disclosure of tar and nicotine content in ads until the Commission established a uniform testing procedure. . . .

Witnesses

. . . The order of appearance of witnesses at a hearing is a clue as to how those conducting the hearings are disposed toward the issue involved. Sympathetic witnesses are scheduled during prime time, which is generally early in each day with the "prime" of the prime being early in the first day. These are the hours when interest is highest and the press is most alert to what is said. The whole tone of the hearings, at least in the public eye, can be governed by what happens first.

It was probably no accident that the Assistant Surgeon General of the Public Health Service was scheduled to appear first. He was followed by Senator Neuberger. Thus, the Federal Trade Commission began its hearings with two very strong statements in favor of their proposed rule. The third witness was from the Tobacco Institute and he was followed by two university research scientists who favored the proposed rule.

The second day of the hearings saw marketing experts, scientists, representatives of advertising and tobacco growers' associations testify. The third and final day was somewhat more unusual. It was politician's day at the Commission. Governors of the tobacco states or their representatives and four members of the North Carolina congressional delegation testified. The appearance of congressmen before an administrative agency is an interesting reversal of roles. It is not unusual for a member of Congress to intervene with agencies on behalf of a constituent, but it is unusual for members to testify at an agency hearing, especially when trying to prevent the agency from acting. The appearance of this large number of elected officials underscores the importance of agency policy-making activities. . . . Nevertheless, the commissioners understood that elected officials from the tobacco states really had no choice but to testify and vigorously protest a proposal such as this one which so directly affected their constituents. The congressmen present similarly knew that they were not going to change the commissioners' views simply by testifying against the proposed rule. Instead, they hoped with the cigarette manufacturers to have the issue transferred from the Commission to Congress. By the time the Federal Trade Commission announced that it was scheduling hearings, those who opposed the health warning requirement knew that congressional action would be one of the most effective ways, if not the only way, of halting the Commission's proposal.

Position of the Industry

. . . The attorney for the Tobacco Institute was faced with the task of developing the legal arguments necessary to show that the Commission was acting where it lacked the authority to do so. The major thrust of his argument was that if Congress had intended that the Commission formulate general rules under the Federal Trade Commission Act of 1914, they would have said so in the act itself. . . . The Tobacco Institute remained adamant in its position throughout the hearings, as was expected. Their opposition, although not well founded in prevailing opinions of the law, served to cast doubt on the Commission's authority and to make it clear that, should the Commission promulgate its proposed rule, there would be months of uncertainty as the issue was fought out in Congress, the courts, or both. . . .

Many of the arguments developed in testimony by the Tobacco Institute had been anticipated by the Commission. A lengthy document written by the Federal Trade Commission staff contained a detailed history of the smoking controversy including 24 pages of careful argument supporting the FTC's defense of its rulemaking authority. The arguments set forth in this document were used to answer the tobacco interests' position at the hearings. . . .

Promulgation of Rules

The official record remained "open" for two months after the Trade Commission's hearings so those who desired to add additional statements to the official record could do so. After the record was closed, the Commission issued its trade regulation rule on June 22, 1964. It was published in the *Federal Register* less than two weeks later. The Commission also published a small announcement of the rule and a summary statement of its background and purpose which was mailed to hundreds of people who had expressed some interest in this proceeding. . . .

The rule which the Commission adopted was nearly the same as the initial proposal with one interesting exception. In the promulgated rule the wording of the health warning was left up to the cigarette companies to determine. . . . The warning language which was eventually written into the congressional legislation and now appears on all packages is much weaker than the language the Commission had in its proposed rule.

Tobacco Interests Object to the Rule

The cigarette ruling was to have taken effect on January 1, 1965, about six months after the Federal Trade Commission published it in the *Register*.[3] In the period between the Commission's hearings and the first of January, the cigarette interests mobilized in earnest. Within a month after the conclusion of the hearings, the industry announced the creation of a voluntary code. . . . Creation of the voluntary code was intended to signify to Congress and the public that the industry was interested in regulating itself, and that the action of the Federal Trade Commission was an unnecessary obstacle to self-regulation. . . .

Congress reacted nearly as swiftly to the Federal Trade Commission's newly promulgated rule as the cigarette manufacturers did. After the announcement,

[3]The package warning label was required to appear on January 1, 1965 and the advertising warning six months later, July 1, 1965.

members introduced 31 bills in the House and 4 in the Senate. All of the Senate bills were intended to support the Federal Trade Commission and strengthen government regulatory powers over cigarette producers. . . . Congressional [House] reaction was overwhelmingly negative and it quickly became apparent from speeches on the floor and newspaper accounts that the Federal Trade Commission's action would not stand unchallenged. It is not unusual for bills to be introduced to reverse decisions of administrative agencies; however, most die without the formality of committee action. The cigarette interests had too much political muscle to allow the quiet death of the bills challenging the Federal Trade Commission. . . .

Judicial Review of Administrative Actions

. . . The cigarette manufacturers had the right to initiate a judicial proceeding to review the action of the Federal Trade Commission. Recourse to the courts is one of the protections provided an individual who believes that agency action interferes with his fundamental rights and liberties. The right to appeal an administrative decision to the courts is well established. The court is obliged to consider an appeal but it can dismiss it quickly if the charge clearly is without merit. . . .

While an appeal to the courts was being considered, lines in Congress were being drawn for the cigarette battle. The cigarette manufacturers had in the past been able to rely on Congress to kill any serious attempt by government agencies to interfere with their business. Now circumstances were different. The anti-smoking forces had the Surgeon General's report and a ruling by the Federal Trade Commission to bolster their position. Furthermore, a rather impressive number of senators and representatives had begun to associate themselves with the Commission's action. A prelude to the difficulties which the tobacco interests were to face had arisen unexpectedly shortly before the Federal Trade Commission hearings in the spring of 1964. An amendment was attached to a crop support bill in the Senate which would have abolished the tobacco support and acreage control programs. It was defeated, handily, by a vote of 63 to 26, but this frontal assault shook the tobacco men and the amendment took them by surprise. This was the first floor test of cigarette sentiment since the Surgeon General's report. It showed the tobacco lobbyists that they would have to work diligently to keep the sympathy they were accustomed to finding in Congress. To that end, the industry mobilized a very impressive lobbying team, a team which was at work well before the 89th Congress convened in January, 1965.

Congressional Power and Agency Policy-making

The [late Senator from Illinois] Everett McKinley Dirksen, once spoke lyrically of the exalted place of Congress in the governmental system. . . . He directed [his remarks] to Article One, Section Eight of the Constitution which says, "Congress shall have the *power*. . . ." Looking heavenward, the Senator said wistfully, "I *love* those words."

Among the implications of the Senator's comment is one which indicates that Congress has the strength to control the powers it delegates to administrative agencies. . . . But the hard facts of the modern policy process often shatter that dream.

Congressional Oversight

Article One, Section Eight has not been repealed and Congress does have the power to oversee the activities of administrative agencies. These agencies exist because Congress created them; they make policy because Congress delegates the authority for them to do so and appropriates funds for their continuing operation. Yet, Congress has considerable difficulty controlling in meaningful, constructive ways, the agencies it creates. . . .

Congressional oversight [supervision] of agency operations in nearly all cases is the responsibility of the committees or subcommittees within an agency's policy subsystem. Formal oversight can occur in annual appropriation hearings, hearings on proposed legislation or occasional investigations.[4] The quality of oversight varies from subsystem to subsystem; some agencies are subjected to detailed scrutiny of expenditures down to the number of new typewriters ordered; others receive more general and enlightened policy guidance. . . .

Federal Trade Commission's Oversight Struggle

In view of most congressional oversight, the actions of Congress against the Federal Trade Commission's cigarette rule were unusual. Unusual, in part, because Congress passed a bill designed to reduce in very specific terms a small portion of the Federal Trade Commission's power. Oversight legislation of this sort is often introduced by an irate member but it seldom is given even committee consideration. . . .

Open controversy between Congress and an agency is almost always avoided, an indication that those within a subsystem know each other's attitudes and positions fairly well before an agency tries something new. But the pressure exerted on the Federal Trade Commission by the health interests and the Surgeon General's report encouraged the Commission to take an action which was to invoke the full wrath of Congress. It appears that no one in the Commission bothered to check its cigarette rule with the appropriate members of Congress.

The resulting congressional reprimand of the Federal Trade Commission was unexpectedly severe in its intensity. It involved lengthy hearings in both houses of Congress on the substance and wisdom of the Federal Trade Commission action. Legislation was reported by the committees and adopted. This legislation specifically amended the Commission's rules and took away temporarily its powers over cigarette advertising. The Commission was prohibited from requiring or even considering the requirement of a health warning in cigarette advertising for at least three years. . . .

No Victory for Health

Congress was not acting alone when it moved against the Federal Trade Commission. It was assisted by the skills, rhetorical and organizational, of the

---

[4] See Joseph P. Harris, Congressional Control of Administration (Washington, D.C.: The Brookings Institution, 1964) for a description of the formal oversight functions of Congress.

Tobacco Institute and the allies recruited by the Institute. The lobbying effort mounted by this group was brilliantly conceived; it indicated that the cigarette manufacturers had the good sense to adapt their approach to the changing tides of public demand in the health field. . . . The Cigarette Labeling and Advertising Act subsequently passed by Congress in 1965 was more a victory for cigarettes than it was for health. . . .

In the face of mounting concern over cigarette smoking as a health hazard there was genius in the Cigarette Labeling and Advertising bill from the industry point of view. The bill contained just enough regulation to pass as a health measure; and while the bill required a health warning, it also contained provisions to dismantle an important part of the work of the Federal Trade Commission. Its most significant provision in these terms was the section which eliminated the Federal Trade Commission's rulemaking power in the cigarette advertising field.

The bill as originally introduced permanently banned such Federal Trade Commission action. When the bill was passed, Congress had reduced the length of the ban to three years or until July 1, 1969. Another important provision of the bill prohibited other federal agencies, for example, the Federal Communications Commission, from taking any action to require health warnings in advertising. State and local action was also blocked or preempted by congressional action. Foreclosing the possibility of state and local regulation was a major attraction of the bill for the cigarette manufacturers.

Despite the inclusion of these provisions, the bill was written in terms of protecting public health. The text of the act begins by declaring that it was the intention of Congress to establish a federal program to inform the public of the possible health hazards of smoking. . . . In a sense, this was the only significant provision of the bill for the health interests. The package labeling requirement was thought by most to be rather insignificant as long as no warning had to appear in advertising. . . .

The passage of the Cigarette Labeling and Advertising Act was a major victory for cigarette manufacturers and their allies. . . . Cigarette manufacturers needed some legislation from Congress or the much more onerous Federal Trade Commission rule would stand. . . .

The Cigarette Men Testify

The cigarette lobby's presentation before Congress was much different from the presentation they made at the Federal Trade Commission hearing. Before the congressional committees they covered all aspects of the argument: the Surgeon General's report, other studies on the health consequences of smoking, the importance of unfettered competition to the economy and the American creed, tobacco's contribution to the nation and the proper policy role of Congress vis-a-vis the states and administrative agencies. This full complement of arguments contrasted sharply with the limited legal argument presented at the Federal Trade Commission hearings.

Another significant difference in approach by the tobacco forces between the Federal Trade Commission and congressional hearings was the number of witnesses who appeared for cigarettes. At the Federal Trade Commission one lawyer represented the manufacturers. In Congress, dozens of witnesses from a variety of professional fields appeared. . . .

The passage of the Cigarette Labeling and Advertising Act marked the end of a well-organized campaign to move Congress to adopt an unusual oversight measure. The skills of the Tobacco Institute, enhanced by the sympathies of many members, helped to remove any doubts which might have existed in the Federal Trade Commission or elsewhere as to where ultimate policy-making authority resides. Congress is effective in disciplining errant agency policy-makers, particularly when those agencies challenge the interests of powerful economic groups. Although the lengths to which Congress went to discipline the Federal Trade Commission were unusual, it is not unusual for members to prevent similar agency actions through less stringent, more informal methods. . . .

Federal Trade Commission Rescinds Its Rule

The legislation marked the end of a turbulent excursion into congressional politics for the Federal Trade Commission. In the summer of 1965, the Commission settled down to its more normal routine and put to one side, at least temporarily, any plans for mounting a new rulemaking proceeding in the cigarette and health field until the ban against their doing so expired in the summer of 1969. . . .

Congress and the Bureaucracy: A Balance of Power?

. . . As the July 1, 1969 expiration date of the Cigarette Labeling Act of 1965 approached, the cigarette controversy emerged again. The Federal Communications Commission unexpectedly announced in February 1969, a proposed rule which would prohibit cigarette advertising on radio and television. [This ruling went into effect, January 1970.]

End questions

1. From this case study, can you see why there has been a rise of the administrative agency's power within the federal government? Explain.
2. Why is it impractical today for legislative bodies to write and enact all rules which govern society? What would be the results if legislative bodies attempted to do this?
3. How can administrative agencies be prevented from gaining too much legislative power?
4. Does the operation and organization of the federal bureaucracy reinforce representative government or remove the government further from the people? Do you think it would be possible today to have a democratic government without administrative agencies?

"**I**'m going to take you to court!" "You'll have to talk to my lawyer!" "He's been acquitted!" From these statements that one hears from time to time, it is obvious that the judicial system—made up of the courts at the local, state, and national level—is very important to American life.

The judicial system can be described in the same terms as other governmental subsystems. The judicial process is a cyclical one in which inputs, in the shape of specific cases and controversies, are converted by judges who review evidence and interpret the laws to produce outputs in the form of decisions and judgments.

Moreover, like any other decision-making process, judicial decision-making is exercised within a political framework. Thus, while the principal goal of the judicial system should be to arrive at objective and impartial interpretation of the law, the judges who make these decisions are influenced by their own beliefs, experiences, and political pressures. By establishing the federal judicial system as a separate branch of government, the Framers of the Constitution sought to minimize the extent to which judges could be swayed by these political pressures. The judicial system itself has developed a set of procedures that also serve as "neutralizing" factors in the process of making judicial decisions.

The Federal Court System

The concept of "a government based on laws not men" is an ideal deeply rooted in Western political tradition. Belief in this ideal is basic to democratic political systems and distinguishes them from totalitarian ones. Under a system based on laws, government can not wield power according to the whims of those who govern but only according to pre-established rules. Conflicts that arise between individuals or between an individual and the government also are resolved by applying pre-existing standards.

The Western tradition of government based on laws was established in ancient Greece and adopted by the Romans who had an extensive set of rules by which they governed their empire. In more modern times, the concept has been applied most successfully in Great Britain and its political offshoot, the United States.

The Framers inherited their concept of judicial organization along with their concept of law largely from Great Britain. The establishment of an independent judiciary had long been recognized as an essential part of any government based on law. Since the English constitution was based largely on unwritten or *common* law, there had developed in England an independent body of judges whose sole function was to determine what the laws were and how they should be applied when specific controversies arose. But even the existence of written rules does not, in itself, mean that government will always act within the limits of such rules or that the rules will be applied impartially to all individuals. The Framers realized that if a system of law was to be preserved, there had to be an independent judiciary authorized to interpret and apply the law in specific cases and controversies. This concept was embodied in the Constitution and is basic to the federal judicial system of the United States.

◀ Why are the proceedings that take place in the judicial arena referred to as the "adversary process"? What purpose do laws and standards of judicial procedure serve in the process of making impartial judicial decisions?

The judicial system in the Constitution.
The organization of the federal court system is derived from various provisions in the Constitution. First, the Framers made the national judiciary a separate branch of government because they recognized that the function to be performed by the courts was different from the functions of a legislature or an executive.

■ *The judicial function.* The nature of the judicial function of government sets it apart from legislative and executive functions. The legislative function involves *making* laws which usually pertain to the *general* community rather than to specific individuals. The exercise of judicial power, on the other hand, is concerned not with the general community but with specific parties and specific controversies. While a judicial decision in a specific case may set a *precedent*—a standard which becomes applicable to the entire community because it governs subsequent judicial decisions—the exercise of judicial power involves *interpreting* rather than making law.

It is true that in the American political system, judicial functions have been delegated to parts of the bureaucracy and that federal court decisions more and more have taken on the aspect of general government policies. In spite of this overlapping of government functions in practice, the Framers did understand the judicial function as distinct from other functions of government. They affirmed this distinction in Article III of the Constitution by assigning the "judicial power" specifically to the federal courts (Section 1) and by providing that judicial power should extend only to "cases" and "controversies" (Section 2).

■ *Federal court jurisdiction.* Any case or controversy that requires a judicial decision must be brought to the court that has the authority or *jurisdiction* to decide it. The jurisdiction of a particular court may be limited not only to a specific geographical location but also to cases and controversies that involve particular kinds of matters or parties.

Article III of the Constitution restricts the jurisdiction of the federal courts to cases and controversies that concern federal questions alone. Essentially, this means that the federal courts can hear only those cases that involve federal law or that would be beyond the authority of a state court. Cases that involve federal law are those "arising under [the] Constitution, the laws of the United States, and treaties." Also within federal court jurisdiction are cases affecting ambassadors and other public ministers, admiralty and maritime situations, controversies in which the United States itself is a party, and controversies between two or more individual states or between citizens of different states. (Article III, Section 2.) Other provisions for the

Courtesy of John Ruge.
Copyright © 1968 by Saturday Review, Inc.

"Has anybody seen my copy of the Constitution?"

(Knowledge of constitutional and statutory law is essential to any judge assigned to a federal court.)

jurisdiction of the federal courts are determined by Congress which is granted the power by Article III to create all federal courts other than the Supreme Court.

By limiting the jurisdiction of the federal courts to federal questions, Article III clearly separates the judicial branch from the judicial systems of the individual states. The organization and jurisdiction of state courts are determined within the states themselves; and cases and controversies that arise under the laws of a particular state must be settled by the courts of that state. Only when a case involves a conflict between a state law and a federal law does a state question become a matter for a federal court. In such instances, appeals are taken directly from the highest court of the state to the Supreme Court of the United States.

■ *Original and appellate jurisdiction.* Most court systems, both state and federal, include a hierarchy of courts, each of which has some degree of either original or appellate jurisdiction. A case is always decided first by a court which has *original* jurisdiction—that is, the authority to hear the case the first time a judicial decision is made. While most decisions of such courts are final, sometimes one of the parties to a case decides to challenge the original court's decision. The party can then "appeal" to a higher court which has *appellate* jurisdiction—the authority to review the decisions of a lower court. Article III of the Constitution specifies certain types of cases over which the Supreme Court always has original jurisdiction. The appellate jurisdiction of the Supreme Court and both the original and appellate jurisdictions of lower federal courts must be determined by Congress.

The courts of the federal judicial system are set up on three levels corresponding to levels of original and appellate jurisdiction. The *district courts* are trial courts which have been given original jurisdiction for most federal cases; the *courts of appeals* are intermediate appellate courts which may review district-court decisions; and the Supreme Court has final appellate jurisdiction for certain types of cases as assigned by laws of Congress.

While state court systems parallel the federal judicial system in some respects, the titles given to the various levels of state courts are not the same in every state. In California, for example, the highest state tribunal is called the supreme court; in New York State, the trial court of original jurisdiction is known as the supreme court while the highest court is the court of appeals.

■ *Civil and criminal* cases. Cases decided in the courts involve either civil or criminal law. *Civil* law includes those rules or standards that regulate the activities of private individuals with each other. *Criminal* law includes those laws that regulate the conduct of individuals toward the government and the rest of society. A law that regulates the making of contracts between individuals is an example of a civil law. Laws that prohibit people from selling dangerous drugs, inciting, riots, or conspiring to overthrow the government are examples of criminal law. There are two categories of criminal law: *felonies* which are serious crimes such as murder, arson, kidnapping, robbery, and forgery and which are punishable by death or long term imprisonment; and *misdemeanors* which are minor criminal offenses such as traffic violations, petty theft, or disorderly conduct and which are punishable by short jail terms or fines. At the federal level, Congress defines what are in fact criminal acts and determines the degree of punishment possible for such acts.

The nature of the parties and of judicial decisions differ for civil and criminal cases. Civil cases involve private individuals or groups. Usually one party to such a case—

409

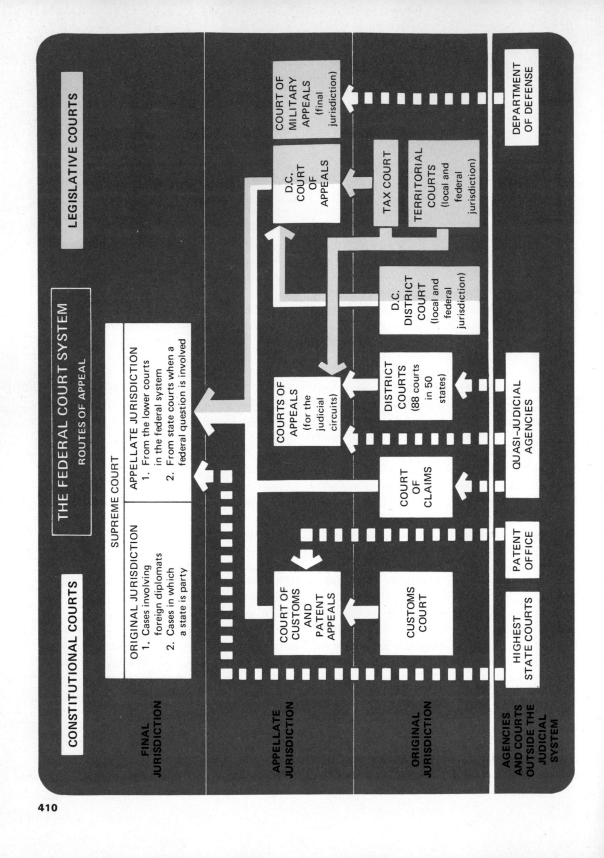

THE FEDERAL COURT SYSTEM
ROUTES OF APPEAL

CONSTITUTIONAL COURTS

LEGISLATIVE COURTS

FINAL JURISDICTION

SUPREME COURT

ORIGINAL JURISDICTION
1. Cases involving foreign diplomats
2. Cases in which a state is party

APPELLATE JURISDICTION
1. From the lower courts in the federal system
2. From state courts when a federal question is involved

APPELLATE JURISDICTION

COURTS OF APPEALS (for the judicial circuits)

COURT OF CUSTOMS AND PATENT APPEALS

D.C. COURT OF APPEALS

COURT OF MILITARY APPEALS (final jurisdiction)

ORIGINAL JURISDICTION

DISTRICT COURTS (88 courts in 50 states)

COURT OF CLAIMS

CUSTOMS COURT

D.C. DISTRICT COURT (local and federal jurisdiction)

TAX COURT

TERRITORIAL COURTS (local and federal jurisdiction)

AGENCIES AND COURTS OUTSIDE THE JUDICIAL SYSTEM

QUASI-JUDICIAL AGENCIES

PATENT OFFICE

HIGHEST STATE COURTS

DEPARTMENT OF DEFENSE

410

the *plaintiff*—files a complaint against a second party—the *defendant*—for redress of a personal grievance. The role of a court in a civil case is to determine if the grievance of the plaintiff is valid and if the defendant owes the plaintiff any *damages* such as monetary compensation.

In a criminal case, however, one of the parties is always the government acting as the *prosecutor* against a defendant who is accused of committing a criminal act. In such cases, the purpose of the judicial process is to determine first, if the defendant is guilty of the crime of which he is accused and second, what his punishment should be if he is guilty.

At the state level there may be separate courts that hear civil and criminal cases, but at the federal level all courts are involved in both areas of law. Although criminal cases must always be brought by a government, civil cases—even though they generally involve the redress of individual interest—may also be brought by the government. Specific acts, such as the Sherman Antitrust Act and statutes governing the Internal Revenue Service, provide that the agencies enforcing these statutes may bring either civil or criminal actions against individuals. For example, the Internal Revenue Service may seek civil damages from an individual for nonpayment of taxes, or it may seek imprisonment by bringing a criminal action. This is purely up to the agency involved.

While both civil and criminal cases are decided at all levels of the judicial system, the nature of the parties to any case and the laws involved determine whether a case is decided by a federal or state court. When both plaintiff and defendant to a civil case live in the same state or if a defendant is accused of violating a state law, such cases are heard in state trial courts. But when the plaintiff and defendant to a civil case are from two different states and the amount

of damages claimed by the plaintiff is more than $10,000, the plaintiff can file his complaint in a federal district court. The $10,000 limit for federal jurisdiction has been set by Congress. State and federal courts have *concurrent jurisdiction* in civil cases involving more than this amount. That is, parties to such cases can agree to go to either a state or federal trial court because Congress has given federal courts the authority to handle these cases concurrently with state laws. All cases involving a constitutional question, a federal law, or a United States treaty, whether civil or criminal in nature, go first to a federal district court.

Consider the case of Mr. Jones who hires Mr. Smith to build a ten-room summer cottage. Mr. Jones later discovers that the wiring and plumbing of his new house are defective. If Jones decides to sue Smith for $15,000 and both men live in the same state, Jones will file a complaint in his state's trial court. But if Jones lives in New York and Smith lives in Connecticut, the suit probably will be filed in a federal district court unless both parties agree to a trial in the state court of New York. Similar distinctions can be made for criminal cases. In most cases of robbery, the person accused of committing the crime is prosecuted by a state district attorney. But if a person is accused of robbing a federally insured bank, which is a federal crime, a federal attorney will prosecute the accused in a federal district court.

■ *Constitutional and legislative courts.* The federal court system embodies many courts throughout the United States which, except for the Supreme Court, have been established by Congress. The authority of Congress to create courts is derived from two parts of the Constitution. *Constitutional* courts are those created on the basis of Article III which grants judicial power to "such inferior courts as the Congress may

411

from time to time ordain and establish." Through the provision of Article I, which authorizes Congress to make whatever laws are necessary for carrying out its enumerated powers and the other powers of the federal government, Congress has established additional courts known as *legislative* courts. When Congress creates constitutional courts, its power to control the operations of such courts is limited by the provisions of Article III. In establishing courts under its powers in Article I, however, Congress has more discretion in determining the requirements for judges and the functions and jurisdiction of such courts.

Constitutional courts. Although it provided for a Supreme Court, Article III of the Constitution left the entire organization of the lower federal judiciary to Congress. Besides the Supreme Court, other courts—the courts of appeals, the district courts, and three other special courts—have been created as constitutional courts.

Once a court is designated as "constitutional" under Article III, there are certain areas in which Congress can not interfere. For example, Congress can not alter the provisions pertaining to tenure and salaries of judges which are stated in Article III:

"The judges, both of supreme and inferior courts, shall hold their offices during good behavior, and shall, at stated times, receive for their services a compensation which shall not be diminished during their continuance in office."

This section of Article III protects the judges of constitutional courts by making it almost impossible for Congress to remove a judge who has been appointed by the President with the advice and consent of the Senate.

Other limitations on Congress regarding constitutional courts are derived from the "case" and "controversy" stipulations of Article III. Because of these stipulations, Congress can not authorize the federal courts to interpret the law or make judgments when specific cases and controversies are not involved. For example, Congress can not authorize the courts to give *advisory opinions* to legislators or to the President about whether a bill under consideration is constitutional. Only after a law is passed and challenged by a specific party to a case can the federal courts render a judgment.

Another aspect of this limitation is that the federal courts can not be authorized to make *declaratory judgments* unless controversies exist. A declaratory judgment is a court statement as to what the rights of parties are under such legal arrangements as statutes, contracts, or wills. Unlike most judgments, declaratory judgments are issued not after a lawsuit is filed for damages, but as a preventive measure before damages occur. While its power over constitutional courts is thus restricted by Article III, Congress does have the power to determine the organization of these courts and most aspects of their jurisdiction as well.

■ *District courts.* The first Congress set up district courts as federal trial courts for various regions, and the number of district courts was expanded as the nation grew. There is at least one federal district court for each state, while some of the larger states have as many as four. Altogether, there are eighty-eight district courts for the fifty states. There is also a district court, established by Congress as a legislative court under Article I, for the District of Columbia. In 1933, however, the Supreme Court ruled that this District of Columbia court is both constitutional and legislative and that its judges are protected by the stipulations for office in Article III.

Each of the federal district courts has from one to twenty-four judges, depending on the workload of the particular court. As with all constitutional courts, the tenure of these judgeships is subject to the stipulations of Article III. Most district court cases are heard and decided by only one district judge, although Congress has provided that at least three judges be present to hear certain kinds of federal cases. These cases concern crimes against the United States, certain civil actions arising under the Constitution, statutes, and treaties (except where the Supreme Court has original jurisdiction), and certain cases involving citizens of different states, or citizens and aliens. Congress has also given the district courts the authority to review and enforce the decisions of certain administrative agencies.

Most district court decisions which are appealed are reviewed by a court of appeals. However, certain kinds of cases may be appealed directly to the Supreme Court.

■ *Courts of appeals.* Congress set up the courts of appeals in 1891 to relieve the Supreme Court from the need to review all cases that are appealed from the district courts. There are ten constitutional courts of appeals and each of the fifty states is assigned to one of the ten appellate *circuits* or areas of jurisdiction. The District of Columbia comprises an eleventh circuit and its court of appeals, like its district court, is both a legislative and a constitutional court.

Altogether there are eighty-eight appellate judges for the eleven circuits, with each court having from three to nine judges, depending on the amount of judicial activity within the circuit. For every case decided in a court of appeals, at least three judges preside at the hearings; but more judges may be present if there are more assigned to the court.

The courts of appeals have appellate jurisdiction only. They may hear cases on appeal from the district courts within their circuits and from various legislative courts. Congress has also provided for the appellate courts to review cases of certain administrative agencies which exercise judicial functions and, in some instances, has given the appellate courts authority to enforce administrative action by issuing appropriate judicial orders or *writs.*

■ *The Supreme Court.* The number of judges or *justices* on the Supreme Court is determined by Congress and has ranged at various times from five to ten. At the present time there are nine justices on the Court: eight associate justices and one Chief Justice. Each justice is appointed to the Court by the President, with the advice and consent of the Senate, and can not be removed except through impeachment and trial proceedings in Congress.

The Supreme Court devotes two weeks of each month to hearing arguments for various cases at sessions which are open to the public. For the remainder of each month, the justices confer on the cases that have come before them to arrive at their decisions. In addition, each justice is assigned to activities on at least one of the lower courts of appeals.

The Constitution gives the Supreme Court original jurisdiction in "all cases affecting ambassadors, other public ministers and consuls, and those in which a

"NO, I'M NOT GETTING TIRED, JUDGE HAYNSWORTH—ARE YOU?"

(A prospective justice's financial holdings can cost him Senate approval despite the President's support.)

413

state shall be party"; and Congress can not alter the Court's original jurisdiction. Such cases were given to the highest court in the land because it was considered appropriate that the judgments on such cases should represent the highest judicial authority. It would hardly be suitable for a state court, or even a lower federal court, to handle cases involving interstate controversy.

Very few cases of original jurisdiction reach the Supreme Court. In 1963, the Supreme Court had to resolve an interstate suit between Arizona and California concerning the amount of water from the Colorado River that could be used by California. Arizona sued California as well as Nevada, New Mexico, Utah, and the United States over the distribution of the Colorado River waters. Such a dispute, involving several states as well as the government of the United States, could not be tried in any court other than the Supreme Court. Cases of the magnitude of the interstate dispute over the Colorado River are rare. When they do arise though, the highest judicial authority must be invoked.

Most of the cases considered by the Supreme Court come to it through its appellate jurisdiction from lower federal and state courts. The appellate jurisdiction of the Supreme Court is limited in part by Article III, which authorizes Congress to make regulations concerning the Supreme Court's authority.

Congress has passed laws granting the parties in certain types of cases the right to appeal to the Supreme Court. In all other instances, cases reach the Court on appeal only if the members of the Court agree to hear them. Parties to such cases must first petition the Court to issue a *writ of certiorari* which is an order issued to a lower court to send the record of a case to the higher court for review. The Supreme Court issues such orders on a very small percentage of the petitions it receives, and only when it believes a case involves matters of far-reaching importance.

■ *Special constitutional courts.* During the 1950's, Congress changed the status of three of the most important legislative courts, and designated them to be constitutional. These are the Court of Claims, the Customs Court, and the Court of Customs and Patent Appeals which were originally established by Congress on the basis of its enumerated powers in Article I of the Constitution. The Court of Claims exercises nationwide original jurisdiction for cases that involve claims for compensation against the United States government. The Customs Court has original jurisdiction over cases involving tariff laws or other laws relating to imported merchandise. Most appeals from the Customs Court and all appeals from decisions of the Patent Office are made to the Court of Customs and Patent Appeals.

Although it is easy to distinguish legislative from constitutional courts in theory, it is more difficult in fact. This may readily be seen in the case of *Glidden Company v. Zdanok,* decided by the Supreme Court in 1962. At issue was the status of the Court of Claims and the Court of Customs and Patent Appeals. The Court of Appeals for the Second Circuit (New York and Vermont) had upheld a lower court decision in a dispute between the Glidden Company and its employees. The panel of judges that decided the case for the court of appeals included judges of the Court of Claims and the Court of Customs and Patent Appeals who had been assigned to the panel according to authorized procedure. The decision of the panel was appealed on the grounds that the "legislative" court judges who sat on the panel were not qualified to decide a case in a constitutional court.

In a confusing opinion, the Supreme

Court upheld the status of the disputed judges, and thereby declared the Court of Claims and the Court of Customs and Patent Appeals to be essentially "constitutional" courts. Justices Douglas and Black dissented, arguing that these courts performed functions and had status appropriate only to "legislative" courts, regardless of congressional enactments designating them as "constitutional" courts. Although the *Glidden* case did as much to confuse as to illuminate, it did illustrate that the problem of separating constitutional from legislative courts is not entirely one of definitions.

Legislative courts. The provisions in Article III that concern the judges and functions of constitutional courts do not apply to legislative courts. When Congress sets up legislative courts, it is free to establish whatever conditions it wants regarding lengths of service and compensation of judges. It can change these conditions at any time and for any reason by simply amending the law establishing the court. In addition, the functions of legislative courts are not limited to making decisions on concrete cases and controversies. Courts created by Congress under the authority of Article I may be assigned non-judicial functions and may engage in policy-making at the same time that they make judgments in specific cases and controversies. The Court of Military Appeals, for example, which reviews court-martial cases, can base its decisions on established military policy rather than on such judicial procedures and precedents that bind constitutional court decisions.

■ *District of Columbia courts.* The district and appellate courts of the District of Columbia were created by Congress through its constitutional power to govern the nation's capital. Established as legislative courts, the District of Columbia courts— unlike other district and appellate courts—

have jurisdiction over local as well as federal matters within the District and can perform certain non-judicial functions. As noted above, the Supreme Court has ruled that the courts of the District are at the same time both constitutional and legislative courts.

■ *Territorial courts.* The Constitution, in Article IV, grants Congress the authority to govern the territories of the United States. On the basis of this authority, district courts have been established in the territories of Puerto Rico, Guam, the Virgin Islands, and the Canal Zone. Like the constitutional district courts, the district court of Puerto Rico has jurisdiction for federal questions alone. The other territorial courts, however, also hear cases pertaining to local matters since there are no other court systems within these jurisdictions as there are within Puerto Rico and the states. A case decided in a territorial court may be appealed to the regular constitutional court of appeals to which the territorial court is assigned.

■ *The Tax Court.* The Tax Court of the United States is an independent agency which is often considered to be a legislative court because its functions are essentially judicial in nature. The Tax Court has jurisdiction over controversies involving taxpayers and the Internal Revenue Service. Sessions of the Tax Court are held at different places throughout the country for the convenience of parties to the controversies before the court. Some of the Tax Court's decisions are final while others are subject to review by the courts of appeals or the Supreme Court.

■ *Court of Military Appeals.* In 1950, Congress created the Court of Military Appeals as a court of final jurisdiction in court-martial convictions. This court operates as part of the Department of Defense, and its decisions can not be appealed to any other court.

Review of administrative decisions. The independent regulatory agencies, combined with other parts of the bureaucracy, also exercise a substantial amount of judicial power. (See Chapter 16, pages 390–392.) Ordinarily, organizational charts of the American judicial system show direct lines of appeal between administrative agencies and the federal courts.

While these routes of appeal exist, it is still extremely difficult to secure meaningful review of administrative judgments. The avenues of appeal are filled with obstacles and frequently closed entirely. Judicial review of administrative action is automatically limited because it is time-consuming and expensive. Moreover, the courts have exercised a great deal of self-restraint and have repeatedly refused to interfere with the administrative process, or to override the judgments of the bureaucrats.

More often than not, judicial-type decisions made by administrative agencies are final. The courts will intervene in some areas and review the decisions of certain agencies. Still, the development of administrative law and administrative adjudication has actually removed several areas of judicial power from the regular courts.

■ *The trend toward specialization.* As American society grows more complex and there is an increasing need for judicial expertise, the American judicial system is becoming more and more specialized. Federal and state courts of general jurisdiction already handle a broad spectrum of cases. The tendency even within the state and local court systems, however, is to create separate divisions or special courts to handle particular problems—traffic violations, small and large claims against other individuals, divorce, probate (wills, estates), equity courts, and so forth. On the federal level, administrative agencies act as such specialized courts when they judge cases arising within their particular jurisdictions.

This tendency toward a division of labor in judicial matters will undoubtedly increase in the future. One of the probable consequences of such specialization will be that appeals from one court to another will be less readily obtained. The decisions of specialized courts with particular capabilities will probably be accepted as final by the parties coming before them, as well as by any designated appellate body.

Review questions

1. Why did the Framers give the Supreme Court some original jurisdiction?
2. From what source does Congress derive its power to create each of the following courts: (a) Tax Court (b) territorial courts (c) courts of appeals.

Judicial Procedure

Regardless of which court has jurisdiction to resolve a particular matter, the basic judicial function of the court is always the same—to interpret the law and arrive at a fair decision for each particular case or controversy. The making of judicial decisions requires first that the judges be well-versed in the law. Second, there must be some procedure for examining all the facts pertinent to a case so that impartial judgments can be made.

Sources of judicial procedure. Probably more attention has been given to the development of logical and systematic procedures for the judicial process than for any other field of endeavor. The procedures of justice in the United States have evolved from the Constitution, the laws of Congress, and the decisions of the judicial system itself.

Many federal court procedures, especially in the area of criminal procedure, are established by the Bill of Rights. For example, the Sixth Amendment guarantees an accused person in a federal criminal prosecution the right to a speedy and public trial by an impartial jury, as well as the right "to be confronted with the witnesses against him," and "to have assistance of counsel for his defense." Many of these procedures have been extended to non-criminal cases as well, through legislation and court practice.

Congress establishes some judicial procedures not only when it creates various federal courts but also when it specifies how the courts should proceed if a case or controversy results from a particular statute. The Supreme Court has also played a significant role in setting precedents and making decisions that determine the procedures used by the lower federal courts. In addition, through its interpretation of the "due process" clause of the Fourteenth Amendment in specific cases, the Court has extended all of the protections of the Bill of Rights as well as many federal court procedures to the state court systems.

While the rules of judicial procedure are somewhat standard, there is room for some flexibility. The practical requirements for judging cases naturally cause a great many procedural variations. Different courts and different judges will apply procedures in accordance with the particular needs of the cases before them. Some judges favor formal procedures, while others adhere to informal techniques as much as possible.

Basic elements of judicial decision-making. While court procedures vary from case to case and from one judge to another, there are certain principles that are basic to all judicial proceedings. Whether in the criminal or civil realm, the nature of

From *Straight Herblock* (Simon & Schuster, 1964)

"YOU KNOW WHAT? THOSE GUYS ACT LIKE THEY REALLY BELIEVE THAT."

(Recent Supreme Court decisions, especially with regard to criminal law, have upheld the "equality" principle.)

the judicial procedure pits one party against another. This is the *adversary process*. From the outset, all parties to a case are presumed to be equal. Thus, the major elements of judicial decision-making are those that provide for the examination of all facts pertinent to both sides of a case so that fair decisions can be reached.

Both parties to a case, therefore, must be able to gather the necessary facts and to present them before impartial decision-makers. Judicial decisions, in turn, should be based only on the record of the facts presented, not on personal feelings or biases. In keeping with these requirements, all parties regardless of their individual financial status must be represented by counsel, or attorneys, who are supposed to know the maze of judicial procedures,

417

and who are able to present the facts of their clients' cases adequately.

■ *Notice of the proceeding.* The Sixth Amendment of the Bill of Rights stipulates that "in all criminal prosecutions" the accused has a right "to be informed of the nature and cause of the accusation." While this constitutional "right" of notice applies only to federal criminal cases, it is used in civil as well as criminal proceedings.

Parties involved in a dispute, must be informed of the nature of the proceeding so that they can present their cases accurately. A judicial proceeding conducted without adequate notice to the parties involved is similar to a tennis match in which one or both players are asked to play without getting in shape. The game will suffer as a consequence, and the best player may not emerge victorious.

■ *The hearing.* A fair settlement of a case requires that a hearing be held to bring out all the facts of the case. Such a hearing is open to all parties involved in a case and often to the public. This prevents decisions from being made secretly on the basis of personal friendships or biases. In this sense, the purpose of the hearing within the judicial process differs considerably from that of a legislative hearing.

An open judicial hearing, where sufficient notice has been given, provides each party with knowledge concerning (1) the nature of his adversary, and (2) who is to make the decision. It also provides each party with the opportunity (3) to present a record favorable to his point of view, and (4) to make use of certain procedures that may assist him in developing his case. Through standardized hearing procedures, all parties can be treated equally and fairly. Yet, as with the presentation of notices, a great deal of variety exists in the conduct of hearings. They can even be dispensed with if the parties to a case agree to an informal settlement.

■ *Decisions based on the record.* While the hearing is in progress, all proceedings are written down word for word by a stenographer. This is to insure that the final decision is based only on the evidence presented at the hearing. Whether the decision is made by a judge or jury, it is assumed that the decision is impartial because it is given only after the facts in the record have been considered and weighed carefully. Once the decision is reached, it too is written into the record.

This written record is of utmost importance when a case is appealed to a higher court. Whenever the Supreme Court or a court of appeals reviews a lower-court decision, the appellate court must produce a written decision based on the evidence from the original trial court record and any new evidence that is introduced.

Because judicial decisions are based on the record developed by the contending parties themselves, one might say that this process is more democratic than other forms of governmental decision-making. The manner in which they develop the record allows the parties to influence more directly the decisions made in their own cases. They have the opportunity to bring in all the evidence they can muster in their own favor to affect the final judgment.

■ *The right of appeal.* A final ingredient of judicial decision-making consists of the right of appeal. This right is very important because it will, in most cases, allow persons with different values, who view a given set of facts in another fashion, to be brought into the decision-making process. Thus, the parties are given every opportunity to present facts favorable to their own cases. By giving parties the right of appeal, a variety of personal judgments can be considered. This reduces the probability of bias to a minimum, and insofar as it is humanly possible, it permits an objective judgment of the facts to be made.

Courtesy of S. Harris and Saturday Review.
Copyright © 1967 by Saturday Review, Inc.

"It's nothing personal, Prescott. It's just that a higher court gets a kick out of overruling a lower court."

(Contrary to this cartoon comment, the higher court can not act on whim but must justify its decisions.)

Procedures in federal trial courts. The basic elements of judicial procedure are the same for civil and criminal cases that are settled in federal courts. However, civil cases are more apt to be settled informally or through simpler formal procedures than are criminal cases.

Of the more than 300,000 cases begun in federal district courts each year only a small proportion are criminal cases. Most criminal cases arise under state law and are therefore handled by state courts. Still, approximately 10 percent of the cases coming before the district courts are criminal in nature. The most common civil cases at the federal trial-court level include bankruptcy cases in which individuals file for bankruptcy under federal laws, and automobile damage cases involving citizens of different states when the amount in controversy exceeds $10,000. The largest portion of the work load of the district courts is composed of automobile damage suits between citizens of different states.

■ *Federal civil cases.* In most civil cases, because the government itself is not usually a party, the original charge is made by the *plaintiff* who brings suit against the *defendant* for the redress of grievances under civil law. The plaintiff, after filing the initial complaint, asks appropriate governmental authorities to serve a *summons* on the defendant. The summons constitutes the necessary notice of proceeding. It is signed by a judicial officer and includes the initial complaint with a requirement that the defendant appear in court.

If the defendant ignores the summons, a verdict may be rendered automatically against him, or he may be cited for *contempt of court.* A person who is in contempt of court has flouted the proper procedures of the court and can be punished by the court for interfering with the judicial process.

Once a civil case gets started, the attorneys representing the plaintiff and defendant may enter their *pleadings* in writing and exchange relevant information. At this stage, the defendant (or *respondent* as he is usually called in civil cases) is required to answer formally any charges that have been made against him in the pleadings of the plaintiff. Very often informal settlement of the case is made between the attorneys at this time. The case may be dismissed, or an informal agreement may be reached on the exchange of money, if that is at issue, and so on. But if agreement is not reached and the plaintiff insists, the case will be docketed or scheduled on the appropriate calendar of the court that has jurisdiction over the matter. Once docketed, further informal proceedings will take place in the nature of pre-trial conferences between the judge and the parties involved. These con-

419

Drawing by Richter; © 1968 The New Yorker Magazine, Inc.

"These steps are killing me. I say we settle out of court."

(A settlement out of court is usually based on expediency or a realization by one party that it can not win.)

ferences provide another opportunity for settlement before a formal trial.

Formal trials in civil cases do not always involve juries. If the case primarily involves interpretation of law, the judge alone will decide the matter after the presentation of arguments by the attorneys for both sides. But if there are facts to be determined, such as the extent of an injury in an automobile accident case, or whether a particular automobile manufacturer produced a faulty car, or a doctor actually engaged in malpractice, then a jury is necessary unless this right is waived by both parties to the dispute. When a jury is to make the decision in a case, both sides have the right to approve the selection of jury members. This enables each side to exclude from the jury anyone who may be prejudiced against him or who might contribute to an unfair jury decision.

During a trial the counsel for each side orally presents the facts relevant to the viewpoint of his client. Each attorney may also bring in witnesses and question them so as to bring out facts which will support his case. *Cross-examination* is a vital element in fair judicial procedure. It allows counsel for both the plaintiff and the defendant to question the witnesses for the other side and thus bring out facts hidden by the opposition that may be advantageous to their own cases.

Sometimes, at the request of either party to a case, the court will serve a prospective witness with a *subpoena*—a court order requiring the person to testify at the trial or to provide certain information relevant to the case. Failure to respond to a subpoena is considered to be in contempt of court.

Once the testimony of the parties is completed, the judge or jury must deliberate over the final decision. If there is a jury, the members of the jury are given instructions by the judge and then leave the courtroom to discuss the record of the case. In federal court cases, the decision of the jury must be unanimous.

Eventually, the jury reaches a decision either for or against the plaintiff. If the decision is in favor of the plaintiff, the jury must also agree on the amount of damages owed by the defendant. After the jury announces its verdict before the court, it is the responsibility of the court to record the decision and to see that it is carried out, unless the decision is to be appealed to a higher court.

■ *Criminal cases.* The first step in a criminal case is for the government to bring a charge against a particular defendant for violating a specific criminal statute. This charge is made by a legal representative of the federal government, either the Attorney General or one of the Deputy Attorneys General who serve throughout the country. After the defendant has been named, an arrest warrant is issued which enables the government to bring the defendant into custody.

□ *Pre-trial procedures.* Before a criminal case reaches trial, there is always a pre-trial process which begins once the defendant has been apprehended. These proceedings are very important to the ultimate fate of the defendant. In the first step of the pre-trial stage, the defendant is brought before a magistrate of the federal district court that has jurisdiction over the case.

The magistrate conducts a preliminary, informal pre-trial examination to determine whether the defendant shall be released or shall be held to answer for the crime of which he is accused. If the magistrate decides that there is sufficient evidence for the defendant to be held, he must determine whether the defendant shall be kept in custody or released on bail before the next step in the case takes place. In very unimportant cases, United States magistrates may actually try a case and render a verdict, which may include a sentence of short-term imprisonment.

After the preliminary investigation by the federal magistrate, the defendant may be held over for a grand jury investigation. Grand jury proceedings are actually part of the pre-trial process. The function of a grand jury, consisting of from twelve to twenty-three members, is to determine whether the evidence against a defendant is sufficient to hold him for trial. Grand jury proceedings take place when the defendant has been accused of a serious crime. These proceedings are in the interest of the defendant if the charge against him has been made on false or insufficient evidence. In such a case, they can save him from the tremendous cost and bad publicity of a public trial. At the federal level the charges in criminal cases are made so carefully that only about 10 percent of the defendants apprehended are released after preliminary hearings. At the state level approximately 50 percent are released in the pre-trial stage.

If the members of the grand jury determine that there is evidence against the defendant, they will formally *indict* or accuse him. Once a formal accusation is made, the defendant is *arraigned,* which means that the official charges against him in the indictment are read formally. The arraignment constitutes the notice given to the defendant of the nature of the charges in his case. It also indicates to his attorney the basis of the government's charges and the points that the defense will have to answer at the formal trial. After the arraignment, the defendant is given a chance to plead guilty or not guilty. Usually, if the guilty plea is entered, the judge will dispose of the case by reaching a verdict without a jury trial. If he pleads not guilty, the formal trial proceeds.

□ *Trial proceedings.* Before the formal trial, a number of informal meetings may occur between the attorneys involved and the judge. In these meetings, such procedural questions as whether the case might still be dismissed, or whether there should be a change of *venue* (the place of the trial and the court of jurisdiction), or a change in the pleadings, and so on are discussed. Once the trial begins, it is conducted by the judge with or without a jury. The right of the accused to a jury trial is guaranteed by the Constitution, but the defendant may prefer to *waive* or give up this right if he believes that a judge will render a more favorable decision. The prosecution and the judge must agree to the waiver of a jury trial.

The trial procedure in criminal cases, like that in civil cases, is adversary in nature. Both sides are presumed to be equal at the outset even though the government itself is a party. Evidence must be introduced by attorneys for both the prosecution and the defense, and neither party can introduce facts that are irrelevant to the specific case.

421

Before the jurists can reach a verdict, the judge must make clear to them the specific laws and corresponding punishments that are at issue. In its deliberations, the jury must then determine which, if any, of the charges against the defendant have been substantiated by the evidence presented at the trial. Although it is the jury that decides whether the accused is actually guilty or not, it is the trial judge who releases or sentences the defendant on the basis of the jury's verdict.

Obviously, if the verdict is "not guilty" the defendant is released. Otherwise, the judge determines what the punishment of the defendant should be in accordance with those laws that govern the charges upheld by the jury. If the defendant does not accept the verdict, he may appeal for review to the federal court of appeals that has jurisdiction over the case.

■ *Cases on appeal.* The review of a lower-court decision, whether by a court of appeals or by the Supreme Court, is made by the judges of the court without a jury. An appeal is initiated when the attorney for a party to a case submits a petition for review to the higher court. If the judges of the higher court decide to review the particular case, they issue a *writ of certiorari* to obtain the original record of the case from the lower court.

The appellate judges study not only the evidence presented at the trial court level but also the rulings and procedures followed by the lower-court judge. They also consider the precedents set by similar cases and listen to arguments of the opposing attorneys. After weighing all of these factors, the appellate court will issue a written opinion reversing or upholding the lower court's decision.

Decisions rendered by the courts of appeals or by the Supreme Court are not always unanimous. The written majority opinion of the court determines the out-come of the case, and carefully explains the laws and other factors which have led to the decision. But, also of significance are concurring and dissenting opinions. A *concurring* opinion is written by any of the judges on the appellate court who agrees with the court's final decision but who bases his decision on reasons not expressed by the majority opinion. A *dissenting* opinion may be submitted by one or more judges who disagree with the final decision reached by the majority. Concurring and dissenting opinions are important, because they may be referred to in later cases, and may influence subsequent court decisions.

Judicial theory and practice. When dealing with issues of law and the judicial process, it must be remembered, that the actual way things are done does not always conform with the formal content of law or the formal organization for making judgments. Theoretically, all citizens are entitled to their "day in court" provided a proper case and controversy exists. But the fact of the matter is that access to the courts is very limited.

Time and expense are basic obstacles to the proper conduct of the judicial process in both courts and administrative agencies. The main problem of the federal district courts, which now decide over one-quarter million cases each year, is time. Rarely is a case heard before at least six months have elapsed from the time that it was filed before the court. In many instances, it may take years before a matter is finally adjudicated. In addition, the process of hiring attorneys and of appealing cases is very costly and often discourages individuals from utilizing the judicial process even though they might benefit from the results.

Time and expense are not the only factors limiting the accessibility of the courts. Judicial procedure itself is one of the most important ingredients in shaping the role of the courts. The courts are restricted in their ability to protect rights and supervise government activity by their own procedure. They can exercise judicial review only if the proper conditions have been met.

Normally, the extensive use of informal procedure renders the administrative agencies more accessible than the courts. Agencies also have more flexible rules which allow them to initiate cases and settle matters through negotiations rather than through the time-consuming adversary process.

Review questions

1. Why is the pre-trial process important to a defendant? Explain this process.
2. Under what circumstances, in civil and criminal cases, may the right to a trial by jury be waived?

Chapter Review

Terms you should know

adversary process	criminal law	original jurisdiction
appellate jurisdiction	damages	plaintiff
arraignment	defendant	precedent
civil law	felony	prosecutor
concurrent jurisdiction	misdemeanor	*writ of certiorari*

Questions about this chapter

1. Explain the judicial function. Why was it logical for the Framers of the Constitution to make the judicial branch of government separate from the legislative and executive branches?
2. Determine which of the following cases would come under the jurisdiction of a federal court; a state court. If a federal court, which one?
   (a) A resident of Texas is seriously injured in an auto accident. He decides to sue the driver of the other car, a resident of Oklahoma, for $50,000.
   (b) A man is convicted of carrying weapons illegally across a state line.
   (c) An employee of a textile firm is charged with embezzlement of funds.
   (d) A state brings suit against the United States for passing a law that infringes on a power reserved to the state in the Constitution.
3. Refer to the diagram of the structure of the judicial system on page 410. Explain the function of each court.
4. What limitations are put on Congress when it creates constitutional courts? How does the congressional role differ when it sets up legislative courts?
5. List the general judicial procedures followed in civil and criminal cases. Why are these procedures followed? How may the handling of civil cases differ from that of criminal cases?
6. By what process does an appeal reach the Supreme Court? On what grounds may the Court refuse to review a case?
7. Defend this statement: *"Concurring* and *dissenting* opinions on a case may be more important than the majority decision."

8. What is the difference between a summons and a subpoena? If a person refuses to accept either of these, what offense is he guilty of?

Thought and discussion questions

1. How effective do you consider the judicial system? What practical problems limit its effectiveness? Do judicial procedures hinder or help? Cite particular examples from recent events that illustrate your point of view. What solutions can you propose for the problems facing the courts?

2. Explain why there is a trend toward greater specialization in the exercise of the judicial function. Considering the delegation of such functions to federal administrative agencies, discuss the advantages and disadvantages in this trend with regard to the (1) purpose and (2) effectiveness of our judicial system.

Class projects

1. Make a diagram of the court system of your state. (Information about the organization of the state's court system can be obtained from the Administrative Director of the Courts, or the Executive Secretary of the Judicial Department in most states, at the individual state capitols.) Contrast your diagram with the diagram of the federal court system on page 410.

2. Choose a case that has recently been decided by the Supreme Court. Trace the path of this case from the court where it was first heard to its final hearing in the Supreme Court. Were there dissenting and concurring opinions at lower court levels that may have contributed to a change in the verdict?

Case Study: The views of three judges

In spite of all the rigid procedures and precedents that are embodied in the judicial process, a judicial decision involves a large element of personal judgment. Judges themselves have admitted to exercising personal discretion in reaching their decisions. Judicial decisions then, like laws, are as fallible as the men who make them.

The drama of the actual courtroom is not predictable. Unlike a TV drama, the script can not be written in advance. The outcome is determined in each case by the parties to the case, by the attorneys who present the facts for their clients by the members of the jury who must reach a verdict, and by the judges who must interpret the laws.

At various stages in their careers as judges, three renowned Supreme Court justices—Oliver Wendell Holmes, Benjamin Cardozo, and Felix Frankfurter—described some of the human factors involved in the courtroom setting. The personal values and experiences of each of these men is reflected in the three essays that follow. After several years as a professor of law, Holmes concentrates mainly on the importance of the study of law and other disciplines needed by the lawyer. Cardozo discusses the process by which judges reach decisions and the direction law should take. Frankfurter emphasizes the qualities of character necessary for being a judge.

Yet all three speculate on the pressures and motivations that contribute to judicial decisions from a similar perspective.

As you read these excerpts, watch for the answers to the following questions:

1. How are Holmes', Cardozo's, and Frankfurter's views on the role of a judge similar? Where do they differ?
2. How does a judge decide a case? What factors should influence a judge most in helping him decide a case? How similar is his decision-making role to that of a legislator or administrator?
3. According to these writers, is there a difference between what is and what should be the purpose of law?

The Path of the Law

Oliver Wendell Holmes*

*[Justice, Massachusetts Supreme Judicial Court, 1882–99; Chief Justice, Massachusetts Supreme Judicial Court, 1899–1902; Associate Justice, U.S. Supreme Court, 1902–32.]

When we study law we are not studying a mystery but a well known profession. We are studying what we shall want in order to appear before judges, or to advise people in such a way as to keep them out of court. The reason why it is a profession, why people will pay lawyers to argue for them or to advise them, is that in societies like ours the command of the public force is intrusted to the judges in certain cases, and the whole power of the state will be put forth, if necessary, to carry out their judgments and decrees. People want to know under what circumstances and how far they will run the risk of coming against what is so much stronger than themselves, and hence it becomes a business to find out when this danger is to be feared. The object of our study, then, is prediction, the prediction of the incidence of the public force through the instrumentality of the courts.

The means of the study are a body of reports, of treatises, and of statutes, in this country and in England, extending back for six hundred years, and now increasing annually by hundreds. In these [historic] leaves are gathered the scattered prophecies of the past. . . . These are what properly have been called the oracles of the law. Far the most important and pretty nearly the whole meaning of every new effort of legal thought is to make these prophecies more precise, and to generalize them into a thoroughly connected system. . . . The primary rights and duties with which jurisprudence busies itself again are nothing but prophecies. One of the many evil effects of the confusion between legal and moral ideas, . . . is that theory is apt to get the cart before the horse, and to consider the right or the duty as something existing apart from and independent of the consequences of its breach. . . . But, . . . a legal duty so called is nothing but a prediction that if a man does or omits certain things he will be made to suffer in this or that way by judgment of the court:—and so of a legal right. . . .

The first thing for a business-like understanding of the matter is to under-

Condensed from "The Path of Law" by Oliver Wendell Holmes, Harvard Law Review, Vol. 10, p. 39 (1897).

stand its limits. . . . You can see very plainly that a bad man has as much reason as a good one for wishing to avoid an encounter with the public force, and therefore you can see the practical importance of the distinction between morality and law. A man who cares nothing for an ethical rule which is believed and practised by his neighbors is likely nevertheless to care a good deal to avoid being made to pay money, and will want to keep out of jail if he can.

. . . The law is the witness and external deposit of our moral life. Its history is the history of the moral development of the race. The practice of it, in spite of popular jests, tends to make good citizens and good men. When I emphasize the difference between law and morals I do so with reference to a single end, that of learning and understanding the law. . . .

. . . [T]hat distinction is of the first importance for the object which we are here to consider,—a right study and mastery of the law as a business with well understood limits, a body of dogma enclosed within definite lines. I have just shown the practical reason for saying so. If you want to know the law and nothing else, you must look at it as a bad man, who cares only for the material consequences which such knowledge enables him to predict, not as a good one, who finds his reasons for conduct, whether inside the law or outside of it, in the vaguer sanctions of conscience. . . . The prophecies of what the courts will do in fact, and nothing more pretentious, are what I mean by the law. . . .

. . . In every system there are . . . explanations and principles to be found. It is with regard to them that a . . . fallacy comes in, which I think it important to expose.

The fallacy to which I refer is the notion that the only force at work in the development of the law is logic. In the broadest sense, indeed that notion would be true. . . . The danger of which I speak is . . . the notion that a given system, ours, for instance, can be worked out like mathematics from some general axioms of conduct. This is the natural error of the schools, but it is not confined to them. I once heard a very eminent judge say that he never let a decision go until he was absolutely sure that it was right. . . .

This mode of thinking is entirely natural. The training of lawyers is a training of logic. The processes of analogy, discrimination, and deduction are those in which they are most at home. The language of judicial decision is mainly the language of logic. And the logical method and form flatter that longing for certainty. . . . But certainty generally is illusion. . . . Behind the logical form lies a judgment as to the relative worth and importance of competing legislative grounds, often an inarticulate and unconscious judgment, it is true, and yet the very root and nerve of the whole proceeding. You can give any conclusion a logical form. You always can imply a condition in a contract. But why do you imply it? It is because of some belief as to the practice of the community or of a class, or of some opinion as to policy, or, in short, because of some attitude of yours upon a matter not capable of exact . . . measurement, and therefore not capable of founding exact logical conclusions. . . . We do not realize how large a part of our law is open to reconsideration upon a slight change in the habit of the public mind. No concrete proposition is self-evident, no matter how ready we may be to accept it. . . .

I think that the judges themselves have failed adequately to recognize their duty of weighing considerations of social advantage. The duty is inevitable. . . . When socialism first began to be talked about, the comfortable classes of the community were a good deal frightened. I suspect that this fear has influenced judicial action both here and in England, yet it is certain that it is not a conscious factor in the decisions to which I refer. . . . I cannot but believe that if the training of lawyers led them habitually to consider more definitely and explicitly the social advantage on which the rule they lay down must be justified, they sometimes would hesitate where now they are confident, and see that really they were taking sides upon debatable and often burning questions.

So much for the fallacy of logical form. Now let us consider the present condition of the law as a subject for study, and the ideal toward which it tends. . . . The development of our law has gone on for nearly a thousand years, like the development of a plant, each generation taking the inevitable next step, mind, like matter, simply obeying a law of spontaneous growth. . . .

. . . Most of the things we do, we do for no better reason than that our fathers have done them or that our neighbors do them, and the same is true of a larger part than we suspect of what we think. . . . Still it is true that a body of law is more rational and more civilized when every rule it contains is referred articulately and definitely to an end which it subserves, and when the grounds for desiring that end are stated or are ready to be stated in words.

At present, in many cases, if we want to know why a rule of law has taken its particular shape, and more or less if we want to know why it exists at all, we go to tradition. . . . The rational study of law is still to a large extent the study of history. . . . It is a part of the rational study, because it is the first step toward . . . a deliberate reconsideration of the worth of those rules. When you get the dragon out of his cave on to the plain and in the daylight, you can count his teeth and claws, and see just what is his strength. But to get him out is only the first step. The next is either to kill him, or to tame him and make him a useful animal. For the rational study of the law the black-letter man may be the man of the present, but the man of the future is the man of statistics and the master of economics. It is revolting to have no better reason for a rule of law than that so it was laid down in the time of Henry IV. It is still more revolting if the grounds upon which it was laid down have vanished long since, and the rule simply persists from blind imitation of the past. . . .

. . . I look forward to a time when the part played by history in the explanation of dogma shall be very small, and instead of ingenious research we shall spend our energy on a study of the ends sought to be attained and the reasons for desiring them. As a step toward that ideal it seems to me that every lawyer ought to seek an understanding of economics. . . . We learn that for everything we have to give up something else, and we are taught to set the advantage we gain against the other advantage we lose, and to know what we are doing when we elect.

There is another study which sometimes is undervalued by the practical minded, for which I wish to say a good word. . . . I mean the study of what is called jurisprudence. Jurisprudence, as I look at it, is simply law in its most generalized part. Every effort to reduce a case to a rule is an effort of jurisprudence, although the name as used in English is confined to the broadest rules and most fundamental conceptions. One mark of a great lawyer is that he sees the application of the broadest rules. . . . Theory is the most important part of the dogma of the law, as the architect is the most important man who takes part in the building of a house. . . .

The Nature of the Judicial Process

*Benjamin N. Cardozo**

*[Judge, New York Court of Appeals, 1913–26; Chief Judge, New York Court of Appeals, 1926–32; Associate Justice, U.S. Supreme Court, 1932–39.]

The work of deciding cases goes on every day in hundreds of courts throughout the land. Any judge, one might suppose, would find it easy to describe the process which he had followed a thousand times and more. Nothing could be farther from the truth. Let some intelligent layman ask him to explain: he will not go very far before taking refuge in the excuse that the language of craftsmen is unintelligible to those untutored in the craft. . . . In moments of introspection . . . the troublesome problem will recur, and press for a solution. What is it that I do when I decide a case? To what sources of information do I appeal for guidance? In what proportions do I permit them to contribute to the result? In what proportions ought they to contribute? If a precedent is applicable, when do I refuse to follow it? If no precedent is applicable, how do I reach the rule that will make a precedent for the future? . . . Into that strange compound which is brewed daily in the cauldron of the courts, all these ingredients enter in varying proportions. I am not concerned to inquire whether judges ought to be allowed to brew such a compound at all. I take judge-made law as one of the existing realities of life. . . . The elements have not come together by chance. *Some* principle, however unavowed and inarticulate and subconscious, has regulated the infusion. It may not have been the same principle for all judges at any time, nor the same principle for any judge at all times. But a choice there has been . . . and the considerations and motives determining the choice, even if often obscure, do not utterly resist analysis. . . . There is in each of us a stream of tendency, whether you choose to call it philosophy or not, which gives coherence and direction to thought and action. Judges cannot escape that current any more than other mortals. All their lives, forces which they do not recognize and cannot name, have been tugging at them—inherited instincts, traditional beliefs, acquired convictions; and the resultant is an outlook on life, a conception of social needs . . . which, when reasons are nicely balanced, must determine where choices shall fall. In this mental background every problem finds its setting. We may try to see things as objectively as we please. None the less, we can never see them with any eyes except our own. . . .

We reach the land of mystery when constitution and statute are silent, and the judge must look to the common law for the rule that fits the case. . . . [H]ow does he set about his task?

The first thing he does is to compare the case before him with the precedents, whether stored in his mind or hidden in books. I do not mean that precedents are ultimate sources of the law. . . . Back of precedents are basic jural [legal] conceptions which are postulates of judicial reasoning, and farther back are the habits of life, the institutions of society, in which those conceptions have had their origin, and which, by a process of interaction, they have modified in turn. . . . Almost invariably, [the judge's] first step is to examine and compare [precedents]. If they are plain and to the point, there may be need of nothing more. . . . It is a process of search, comparison, and little more. Some judges seldom get beyond that process in any case. Their notion of their duty is to match the colors of the case at hand against the colors of many sample cases spread out upon their desk. The sample nearest in shade supplies the applicable rule. But, of course, no system of living law can be evolved by such a process, and no judge of a high court worthy of his office views the function of his place so narrowly. If that were all there were to our calling, there would be little of intellectual interest about it. The man who had the best card index of the cases would also be the wisest judge. It is when the colors do not match, when the references of the index fail, when there is no decisive precedent, that the serious business of the judge begins. He must then fashion Law for the litigants before him. In fashioning it for them, he will be fashioning it for others. . . .

The final cause of law is the welfare of society. The rule that misses its aim cannot permanently justify its existence. "Ethical considerations can no more be excluded from the administration of justice . . . than one can exclude the vital air from his room and live." Logic and history and custom have their place. We will shape the law to conform to them when we may; but only within bounds. The end which the law serves will dominate them all. . . . I do not mean, of course, that judges are commissioned to set aside existing rules at pleasure. . . . I mean that when they are called upon to say how far existing rules are to be extended or restricted, they must let the welfare of society fix the path, its direction and distance. . . .

My analysis of the judicial process comes then to this, and little more: logic, and history, and custom, and utility, and the accepted standards of right conduct, are the forces which singly or in combination shape the progress of the law. Which of these forces shall dominate in any case must depend largely upon the comparative importance or value of the social interests that will be thereby promoted or impaired. . . .

If you ask how [the judge] is to know when one interest outweighs another, I can only answer that he must get his knowledge just as the legislator gets it; from experience and study and reflection; in brief, from life itself. Here, indeed, is the point of contact between the legislator's work and his. The choice of methods, the appraisement of values, must in the end be guided by like considerations for the one as for the other. Each indeed is legislating within the limits of his competence. No doubt the limits of the judge are narrower. He legislates only between gaps. He fills the open spaces in the law. . . .

. . . [Yet] the judge, even when he is free, is still not wholly free. . . . He is to draw his inspiration from consecrated principles. He is not to yield to spasmodic sentiment. . . . He is to exercise a discretion informed by tradition, methodized by analogy, disciplined by system, and subordinated to "the primordial necessity of order in the social life." Wide enough in all conscience is the field of discretion that remains. . . .

Our survey of judicial methods teaches us, I think, the lesson that the whole subject matter of jurisprudence is more plastic, more malleable, the moulds less definitively cast. . . . So also the duty of a judge becomes itself a question of degree, and he is a useful judge or a poor one as he estimates the measure accurately or loosely. He must balance all his ingredients, his philosophy, his logic, his analogies, his history, his customs, his sense of right, and all the rest, and adding a little here and taking out a little there, must determine, as wisely as he can, which weight shall tip the scale. . . .

The Judicial Process and the Supreme Court

Felix Frankfurter

*[Associate Justice, U.S. Supreme Court, 1939–62.]

Judges are men, not disembodied spirits. Of course a judge is not free from preferences, or, if you will, biases. . . . He will be alert to detect that though a conclusion has logical form it in fact represents a choice of competing considerations of policy, one of which for the time has won the day.

. . . For judges, it is not merely a desirable capacity "to emancipate their purposes" from their private desires; it is their duty. . . . It is asked with sophomoric brightness, does a man cease to be himself when he becomes a Justice? Does he change his character by putting on a gown? No, he does not change his character. He brings his whole experience, his training, his outlook, his social, intellectual, and moral environment with him when he takes a seat on the supreme bench. . . .

. . . To assume that a lawyer who becomes a judge takes on the bench merely his views on social or economic questions leaves out of account . . . the scope and limits of a judge's authority. The outlook of a lawyer fit to be a Justice regarding the role of a judge cuts across all his personal preferences for this or that social arrangement. . . .

Need it be stated that true humility and its offspring, disinterestedness, are more indispensable for the work of the Supreme Court than for a judge's function on any other bench? . . .

. . . The answers that the Supreme Court is required to give are based on questions and on data that preclude automatic or even undoubting answers. If the materials on which judicial judgments must be based could be fed into a machine so as to produce ineluctable [inescapable] answers, if such were the nature of the problems that come before the Supreme Court, and such were the answers expected, we would have IBM machines doing the work instead of judges. . . .

The core of the difficulty is that there is hardly a question of any real difficulty before the Court that does not entail more than one so-called principle. Anybody can decide a question if only a single principle is in controversy. . . .

This contest between conflicting principles is not limited to law. In a recent discussion of two books on the conflict between the claims of literary individualism and dogma, I came across this profound observation: "But when, in any field of human observation, two truths appear in conflict it is wiser to assume that neither is exclusive, and that their contradiction, though it may be hard to bear, is part of the mystery of things." But judges cannot leave such contradiction between two conflicting "truths" as "part of the mystery of things." They have to adjudicate. If the conflict cannot be resolved, the task of the Court is to arrive at an accommodation of the contending claims. This is the core of the difficulties and misunderstandings about the judicial process. This, for any conscientious judge, is the agony of his duty.

End questions

1. Why does Holmes devote a large part of his discussion explaining the importance of studying law? In what sense does Holmes consider law as prophecy? Why does he equate the study of law with the study of history? By studying one field, can you learn about the other?

2. What does Cardozo mean when he says, "We may try to see things as objectively as we please. None the less, we can never see them with any eyes except our own"?

3. What qualities does Frankfurter consider most important for a Supreme Court justice? Does Cardozo's analysis of a judge's function support Frankfurter's viewpoint? Explain.

4. Cardozo comments on "the serious business of the judge" and Frankfurter refers to an aspect of decision-making which for a judge is "the agony of his duty." What are the judges talking about? Can you think of any actual or hypothetical court cases which might require such decisions? Do you think it is possible for a judge to be impartial and objective in resolving such cases?

When Chief Justice John Marshall declared that the Supreme Court had the power to review acts of Congress and that "it is emphatically the province and the duty of the Judicial Department to say what the law is," he set the stage for the involvement of the judiciary in the political realm. By saying what the law is, judges actively enter into public policy-making. Discussing this point, Harvard law school professor Paul Freund related the following:

"A generation or two ago it was thought rather daring to insist that Judges make the law. Old Jeremiah Smith, who began the teaching of law at Harvard after a career on the New Hampshire Supreme Court, properly deflated the issue. 'Do Judges make law?' he repeated. 'Of course they do. Made some myself.'"[1]

In many ways the courts affect public policy today more than ever before. Government itself has expanded, bringing about an increased role for the judiciary in both the interpretation of laws and their enforcement. *Adjudication,* the judging of specific cases and controversies, necessarily includes more and more questions of public policy as the number of cases relating to problems of government expands. As the courts become increasingly involved in the realm of policy-making, their decisions are subject to the same pressures that underlie the decisions of other conversion structures in the political system.

The Merging of Judicial Decisions and Policy-Making

It seems somewhat of a paradox that the exercise of the judicial function in specific cases and controversies between specific parties can also produce public policy. This paradox is explained, in part, by the fact that many specific cases involve the government as a party or concern government matters, from state and federal laws to actions of the President and the bureaucracy. In all cases, the federal judiciary is automatically brought into the policy-making process because in order to reach its decision it must interpret what the laws mean. In this merging of judicial decision-making and policy-making, no institution plays a more significant role than the Supreme Court.

The need to interpret law. Even if Chief Justice Marshall had not determined in 1803 that it was the duty of the judges "to say what the law is," the courts would still have had to assume this duty. One of the major reasons for judicial involvement in public policy-making is that law is usually vague. Ambiguous language, both in the Constitution and in congressional statutes, may be given as many different meanings as there are people who read it. When controversies arise under either the Constitution or the statutes, it is the judicial system, and particularly the Supreme Court, that must resolve such issues by deciding what the laws mean. Because the decision of the Court in any one case may set a precedent for other cases, judicial interpretations of law are generally applicable and thus set federal policy. This has been true since the establishment of the Supreme Court.

■ *Constitutional interpretation.* Nothing was more significant in developing the

How is it possible that the federal judicial system—which is responsible for interpreting laws impartially in specific cases and controversies—can make decisions that actually establish general public policy?

[1] *Paul H. Freund,* On Understanding the Supreme Court *(Boston: Little, Brown and Co., 1949), p. 3.*

framework of American government than the first dramatic interpretations of the Constitution by the Supreme Court in the early nineteenth century. Debates have always taken place about the intent of the Framers concerning such important constitutional provisions as the enumerated powers given to Congress under Article I, the executive powers of Article II, and the nature of the judicial functions delegated in Article III. At a very early stage in the nation's development, the Supreme Court had to resolve disputes over the meaning of the commerce clause (see Chapter 4, page 89), the supremacy clause (see Chapter 5, page 114), and other provisions relating to the powers of the national and state governments. Even today, conflicts still arise over the intent of the commerce clause. In addition, there has always been disagreement over the meaning of the Bill of Rights and other constitutional amendments.

Some of the most significant policy-making decisions of the Supreme Court in the last few decades have been based on its interpretations of the Constitution. Through a number of cases, the Court has expanded constitutional law regarding civil liberties and civil rights. (See also Chapter 19). While in the past the Court has exercised judicial self-restraint in these matters, today it tends to play a more positive role.

Much of the Court's intervention in the political process is due to its interpretations of the "due process of law" and "equal protection of the law" clauses of the Fourteenth Amendment. Through such interpretation, the high Court has developed guidelines governing state action in criminal proceedings, as well as state responsibilities with regard to First Amendment freedoms, public education, and legislative apportionment.

■ *Statutory interpretation.* Like the Consti-

"Can You See Me Now?"

From Herblock's *Special for Today* (Simon & Schuster, 1958)

(The Supreme Court has strengthened individual rights through its interpretations of the Bill of Rights.)

tution, statutes are stated in vague terms very often because of the inability of elected politicians to reach concrete agreements on policy needs. Just as the bureaucracy has to make policy when it decides how such laws are to be enforced, the courts also set policy when they interpret the meaning of these laws to reach judicial decisions.

The Supreme Court has sometimes been able to establish a new federal policy by interpreting a vague law of Congress to mean something substantially different from Congress' original intent. One instance of this was a 1937 Supreme Court decision in which the Court prohibited wiretapping on the basis of a provision in the Federal Communications Act of 1934; Congress had passed the Act to regulate radio broadcasting. (See also case study at end of this chapter.)

The scope of the judiciary's role in policy-making today can be seen by scanning the *dockets* (agendas) of cases being reviewed by the federal courts at the appellate level. They are almost entirely filled with questions of statutory interpretation. In cases involving the possible conflict of federal and state laws, the Supreme Court must often decide if state laws do or do not conform with the requirements set forth in federal statutes and the Constitution.

Judicial review. The power to exercise judicial review is one of the most important policy-making tools of the federal judicial system. The courts have exercised this power ever since it was defined by Chief Justice John Marshall in *Marbury v. Madison* (1803). In the *Marbury* case, the Supreme Court interpreted both the Constitution and a law of Congress and found that the two were in conflict. In deciding in favor of the Constitution over the statute, the Supreme Court established the basic principle behind judicial review as well as the authority of the courts to exercise it.

In the broadest sense, judicial review, includes the authority of the judiciary not only to determine whether government laws and actions are constitutional but also to void those which are not. The exercise of this power can be extended over executive and administrative actions as well as state and federal statutes. While the lower federal courts can wield the power of judicial review, most cases that involve constitutional questions eventually reach the Supreme Court.

■ *The intent of the Framers.* The power of judicial review is implied by the Constitution rather than stated. Over the years, there has been sometimes heated debate about whether the Framers of the Constitution intended to give this power to the Court. The most profound questions are raised when judicial review is exercised over legislative acts of Congress or of state legislatures. Such laws presumably reflect the will of the people as expressed through their elected representatives. Should the Supreme Court, a small group of men not elected by the people, be empowered to inflict its opinions on the rest of the country by applying constitutional "principles" that invalidate congressional and state legislative acts?

As with all attempts to assess the motives of the Framers of the Constitution, the search for conclusive opinions about placing the power of judicial review in the hands of the Supreme Court is doomed to failure. The argument today is really an academic one, and has been ever since John Marshall "found" the power of judicial review in the Constitution.

In *The Federalist,* No. 78 by Hamilton, however, there is evidence that at least one

THE PUBLIC WILL ULTIMATELY DECIDE THIS.

Rollin Kirby in *The New York Post,* 1936

(A dilemma of judicial review is whether the Constitution or Congress is the real guardian of the people.)

segment of the Founding Fathers intended that the courts would have some power of judicial review. In this paper, Hamilton stated that

"no legislative act . . . contrary to the Constitution, can be valid. . . . The interpretation of the laws is the proper and peculiar province of the courts. A constitution is, in fact, and must be regarded by the judges as a fundamental law. It therefore belongs to them [the judges] to ascertain its meaning, as well as the meaning of any particular act proceeding from the legislative body. If there should happen to be an irreconcilable variance between the two, that which has the superior obligation and validity . . . in other words, the Constitution ought to be preferred to the statute. . . ."

Hamilton defended this idea, not because he believed that the judicial branch should be superior to the legislative, but because "the power of the people is superior to both." According to Hamilton, the will of the people was represented in the Constitution and any statute contrary to their will should not stand.

Hamilton's argument, nevertheless, did support the idea of an independent judiciary with the power of judicial review over legislative acts contrary to the Constitution. His essay probably mirrored the thinking of an important segment of the leadership in 1787.

■ *The case of Marbury v. Madison.* The power of the Supreme Court to invalidate an act of Congress was defined by Chief Justice John Marshall's decision in *Marbury v. Madison* in 1803. At issue was a provision in the Judiciary Act passed by Congress in 1789. The Act extended the original jurisdiction of the Supreme Court by authorizing the Court to issue *writs of mandamus* (writs directing administrative officers to perform their duties) in cases involving public officers of the United States and private persons. This power was not conferred on the Court by the Constitution.

William Marbury had been appointed a justice of the peace by President John Adams under the Judiciary Act of 1801. This Act was passed by the Federalists in Congress shortly after Thomas Jefferson and the Republican party won the 1800 elections. The Act enabled Adams to load newly created judicial posts with Federalists before he took leave of the Presidency in March 1801.

Marbury was scheduled to receive one of the "midnight" appointments, but when Jefferson took office on March 4, Marbury's commission had not been delivered. Marbury filed a suit with the Supreme Court. He requested that the Court, under the powers of original jurisdiction granted by Congress in the 1789 Act, issue a writ of mandamus to force James Madison (Jefferson's Secretary of State) to deliver the commission.

In his decision, Marshall, a prominent Federalist, admitted that Marbury had a legal right to the commission and that mandamus was a proper remedy. The Chief Justice noted, however, that the Supreme Court could not exercise original jurisdiction beyond the limits specified by the Constitution. (See Article III, Sec. 2.) According to Marshall, then, the section of the 1789 Judiciary Act that granted the Court original jurisdiction to issue writs of mandamus to public officers was unconstitutional. Even though this provision was a legislative act of Congress, it had to be revoked.

Marshall noted in *Marbury v. Madison:*

"It is emphatically the province and the duty of the judicial department to say what the law is. . . . If two laws conflict with each other, the courts must decide on the

operation of each. . . . [T]he particular phraseology of the Constitution of the United States confirms and strengthens the principle . . . that a law repugnant to the Constitution is void; and that courts, as well as other departments, are bound by that instrument."[2]

■ *Implications of judicial review.* Since the concept was clarified by Marshall's decision, judicial review has become an essential ingredient of the American constitutional system and a fundamental power of the federal courts. The decisions made by the Supreme Court when it exercises this authority may be questioned, but the fact that the Court possesses this power can not be challenged.

While the Supreme Court uses considerable self-restraint in wielding the power of judicial review, the fact that it has that power has important implications for federal policy. The fate of many policies initiated by other branches may rest ultimately on whether or not they are considered constitutional by the high court in a specific case. The Civil Rights Act of 1964, for example, included fairly definite standards governing the rights of individuals to vote, to have access to public accommodations without discrimination, and generally to secure the equal protection of the laws. The Supreme Court had to clear up initial constitutional questions raised about the 1964 Act. When the constitutionality of the law was challenged, the Supreme Court found that Congress had the power to pass the Act under the commerce clause, that the law does not deprive individuals of liberty and property without due process of law nor take property without just compensation. The 1964 Civil Rights Act illustrates that even when Congress has passed a bill and the President has signed it into law, such law may be subject to judicial scrutiny before it can be accepted without question as government policy.

Enforcement of judicial policy. Once the judicial branch sets public policy, the problem of carrying out its policy decisions still remains. Sometimes the Supreme Court delegates part of this task to the lower federal courts. For example, after deciding that segregation in public schools was unconstitutional in the 1954 case of *Brown v. Board of Education,* the Supreme Court handed down a second decision the following year that provided guidelines for implementing the first decision. In the *Brown* decision of 1955, the Court delegated to the district courts in the states where the defendants resided the responsibility of issuing any orders and decrees necessary to desegregate the school systems in an orderly fashion. This delegation of responsibility did not give the lower courts the ability to enforce the Supreme Court's decision in all public school systems. In order for the desegregation policy to be applied to school districts not involved in the *Brown* decision, cases have to be brought to the lower federal courts for trials.

Enforcement of Supreme Court decisions may involve not only the lower courts but also the executive branch of government. After the Court's decisions in the cases of *Brown v. Board of Education,* the district courts became involved in new cases concerning the desegregation of public school systems. When desegregation orders from the lower courts were not followed voluntarily, the Chief Executive stepped in to enforce them.

In one such incident, Arkansas Governor Orval Faubus prevented black students from entering the Little Rock High School by assigning the Arkansas division of the National Guard to keep them out. President Eisenhower then called out federal

[2] *1 Cranch 137 (1803).*

437

troops and nationalized the Arkansas National Guard to enforce the federal court order to desegregate the high school.

In recent years, as Supreme Court determinations have increasingly provided for implementation of policies at lower judicial levels, the lower courts have become more deeply involved in settling political controversies and in shaping public policy. This development can be illustrated by considering the Supreme Court's pronouncement on legislative apportionment in 1962.

Traditionally, the apportionment of legislative representatives among the population was a matter left to each state. When population shifts took place within a state, state legislatures tended to maintain the old election districts. As a result, sparsely settled rural areas were often over-represented in both the state and the national legislatures, while densely inhabited urban areas did not have the representation proportionate to their populations. Thus, a smaller rural population often had more influence in the formulation of public policy than the larger urban populations.

For many years, attempts to challenge the state apportionment laws in the federal courts were unsuccessful because the federal courts refused to review the cases. When in the early 1960's such a suit was filed in a federal district court challenging the apportionment law of Tennessee, the district court dismissed the case saying it did not have jurisdiction to consider the matter. The Supreme Court, however, reversed the district court's decision in *Baker v. Carr* (1962), saying that matters of legislative reapportionment could properly be considered by the federal district courts on the basis of the "equal protection" clause of the Fourteenth Amendment. As a result of the landmark decision in *Baker v. Carr,* the District Court of Tennessee became involved in a matter that had far-reaching political implications and that required a determination of public policy. Other federal district courts were soon affected as well because many new cases were initiated that challenged the apportionment laws of other states.

In addition to enforcing decisions of the Supreme Court, the lower federal courts also play some role in the enforcement of congressional policies. Through the enactment of various laws, Congress has provided for the involvement of the courts in the enforcement processes of such administrative agencies as the National Labor Relations Board and the Federal Trade Commission. However, when the courts do become involved in such enforcement, it is the executive branch or the bureaucracy that initiates the enforcement proceedings. For example, if the FTC, under authority granted by Congress, seeks an injunction to halt what it considers to be an unfair trade practice, the agency must secure such an injunction through a district court. The court must then determine whether the request of the agency is proper before the injunction can be issued.

Apart from being directly involved in the policy enforcement activities of the bureaucracy, courts have general power of judicial review over administrative decisions. Although this power is strictly limited by congressional statute, administrative cases still comprise an important segment of the federal courts' work load. Rulings on antitrust problems, immigration matters, patent questions, and so forth, account for much of the judiciary's policy-making activity in the economic sphere.

Review questions

1. Explain how the powers of judicial interpretation and judicial review allow the courts to make policy.
2. Under what circumstances might the Chief Executive be called on to enforce a decision of the Supreme Court?

The Inputs of the Judicial Subsystem

Both the nature of the judicial function and the relative detachment of the federal judiciary from political pressures tend to limit the scope of inputs which enter the judicial subsystem. Since constitutional courts can only consider cases and controversies, individuals and groups must be parties involved in actual disputes to make direct demands on the courts. In order for such demands to result in judicial policy-making, the parties must contest definite statutes or interpretations of law. Because of the somewhat limited routes of access to judicial decision-makers, the most extensive and often the most effective sources of demands and support for the policy-making outputs of the judiciary come from the other branches of government.

Direct demands on the judiciary. It is more difficult to make direct demands on the judicial system than on other branches of government. The qualifications needed to vote are quite simple when compared with the requirements for making demands on the courts. To make a direct judicial demand, it is necessary first, that an actual case or controversy within the meaning of the law is involved; second, that the courts have jurisdiction under constitutional or statutory law to consider the case; third, that the parties requesting judicial action are "aggrieved" parties in the eyes of the law; and fourth, that the parties involved have the time to fight the case and the money to hire competent attorneys.

■ *Pressure-group demands.* The requirements for obtaining judicial action tend to limit the number and sources of demands on the courts. Generally, pressure groups are more apt to possess the time, money, and skill necessary for taking legal action than are individuals.

The types of groups that are involved in the judicial process include large corporations, labor unions, and farm groups as well as federal, state, and local governmental agencies, particularly law enforcement agencies. Some specialized groups such as the American Civil Liberties Union (ACLU) and the National Association for the Advancement of Colored People (NAACP) help individuals bring cases to court to obtain their rights through the judicial process. In the historic school desegregation case of *Brown v. Board of Education,* for example, the NAACP was largely responsible for assisting the plaintiffs in getting judicial action.

■ *The role of the legal profession.* The members of the legal profession provide the judiciary with another source of demands. Lawyers make demands directly when they argue cases before the courts. The legal profession may also influence the courts indirectly when its members write about important judicial decisions in legal journals or make their views on legal matters known to judges in other ways.

Trial lawyers make direct presentations to the courts in the form of written legal *briefs* as well as through oral arguments. These presentations may not determine the outcome of important cases affecting public policy which are argued before the Supreme Court, but at the lower court levels they do constitute a vital part of the record on which judicial decisions are based. A sloppy brief or poor oral presentation will not advance its cause, but a well-presented argument conducted by a persuasive attorney may sway opinion. Skillful criminal lawyers, for example, have often been able to keep their clients out of prison or from being sentenced to death. Attorneys can be equally effective in civil actions. Although no attorney is quite as

Courtesy of Ed Fisher.
Copyright © 1967, Saturday Review, Inc.

"Some of us are getting mighty sick of these masterful dissents of yours, Bodgsly!"

(A judge's well-reasoned dissent can have considerable impact on Supreme Court decisions in future cases.)

dramatic as Perry Mason, some do have "track records" almost as good.

The direct influence of the legal profession on the Supreme Court's major decisions, however, is inclined to be less spectacular. The Supreme Court justices must decide what is intended by constitutional or statutory law, what is needed to protect civil liberties and civil rights, and how to bring uniformity to federal law. In such matters the personal values of the Supreme Court justices are more important than the skill of attorneys presenting arguments before the Court. Since justices draw upon information from the social sciences such as political science, sociology, and psychology to reach an understanding of a case, attorneys arguing cases before the highest court sometimes introduce evidence related to these fields. In the *Brown v. Board of Education* case of 1954, the

Court considered evidence of the harmful psychological effects of segregation as a major reason for requiring integration of facilities. Thus, a judicial decision at the Supreme Court level is never based entirely on the record of a case produced by the parties or their attorneys, but is arrived at through a broader and theoretically more reflective method of decision-making.

■ *The Justice Department as a source of demands.* Direct demands also come to the judiciary from the Department of Justice. This executive department, under the supervision of the Attorney General, provides legal counsel for the national government on judicial matters. The Justice Department also has been given the responsibility of enforcing various federal laws by initiating cases in the courts. In addition, the Department aids the President and other executive departments and agencies in any matter that requires court action. Under the Taft-Hartley Act, for example, the President has the authority to delay a strike that he feels is against the national interest. In such an instance, the Justice Department may be asked to go before a federal district court in order to secure a court injunction against the union to halt the strike.

□ *The Solicitor General.* Within the Justice Department, the Solicitor General and his staff are responsible for arguing cases on behalf of the United States when the government is a party to a case at any level of the court system. The Solicitor General's office represents administrative agencies in the judicial process, and may also file amicus curiae briefs in all cases in which the government has an interest.

Since the government is a party to many cases, the Solicitor General is involved in one-half of the major cases and approximately one-third of all cases that reach the Supreme Court. With a few exceptions, no administrative agency can appeal a case from a lower federal court to the Supreme

Court without the approval of the Solicitor General. The Solicitor General's staff is also highly experienced in the judicial process and his opinion is given more weight than those of most private attorneys. This makes him a potent legal force in the federal courts.

The Solicitor General's office is subject to demands and supports, most of which come from the administrative agencies that make use of the office. The success of the Solicitor General before the courts depends not only on the special skills of his own office but also on the validity of the cases initiated by the administrative agencies.

□ *Antitrust Division.* Numerous other divisions within the Justice Department also create inputs for the judiciary. In contrast to the Solicitor General's office, the Antitrust Division of the Justice Department is essentially a separate administrative agency with specialized interests. A major activity of the division is that of filing suits against certain private parties to prevent mergers and business combinations that the agency considers to be restraints on trade in violation of antitrust laws.

□ *Tax Division.* The Tax Division of the Justice Department employs more than two hundred lawyers to represent the United States in both civil and criminal cases arising under internal revenue laws. The Tax Division acts as counsel for the Internal Revenue Service in all cases in federal and state courts, with the exception of the federal Tax Court. The Treasury Department also employs lawyers to plead cases for the Internal Revenue Service before the Tax Court.

□ *Other divisions.* There are several other divisions within the Justice Department that represent the government in various kinds of court actions. The Land and Natural Resources Division, with more than a hundred lawyers, handles claims relating to the more than 750 million acres of land belonging to the federal government. Also within the Department are the Internal Security Division and the Criminal Division which make direct demands on the courts by initiating certain kinds of prosecution proceedings.

The Civil Rights Division of the Justice Department handles cases arising under the various Civil Rights laws that Congress has passed in recent years. This Division can file suits against certain officials or private persons who interfere with the right of citizens to vote. The Civil Rights Division can also take similar legal action to enforce the regulations against racial discrimination in schools, hotels, and other public facilities covered by the Civil Rights laws.

■ *Effect of demands on outputs.* Cases that involve the government comprise most of the work load of the federal judiciary. About 60 percent of the cases argued before the Supreme Court have the government as a party or as an amicus curiae. The demands of the bureaucracy make up the largest single category of inputs for the courts.

The fact that government itself is the major source of direct demands made on the federal courts has had a profound effect on judicial outputs. Many recent cases that resulted in policy-making decisions on civil rights and voting rights would not have been taken to the courts without the government's participation. Requests by government agencies to appeal lower court decisions are often approved by the Solicitor General so that the Supreme Court can set important public policy even though the government itself might be overruled in such cases.

Sources of support for the judiciary. The judiciary, like other policy-making structures, must maintain support within the political system while it responds to demands. When the Supreme Court produces a major policy decision, for example, it must rely on the support of the lower courts as well as the President and the bureaucracy to implement the decisions. The federal courts, however, are far less dependent on public support than the other branches of government. As a result, the court system is able to maintain its position as an independent and impartial instrument of justice without having to cater to public approval or condemnation. Because it does need the support of other government structures, however, the Supreme Court can be accused at times of pulling in its horns to avoid confrontation with its elected partners—the legislature and executive.

■ *Limited effect of public opinion.* While it is sometime suggested that the output of the Supreme Court is affected by public opinion, no evidence has ever been obtained to support this supposition. Since the nature of public opinion is usually vague with respect to most public issues, it would be difficult to demonstrate that public opinion influences judicial policymaking. Furthermore, because Supreme Court justices and all other judges of constitutional courts are appointed for unlimited terms rather than elected, they do not have to depend on the support of the electorate or private interest groups to the same extent as the President or members of Congress.

The public does respond, however, after a major decision is made by the Supreme Court. Such public response comes, in great part, from those who strongly oppose the general trend of judicial decisions. There was such an outcry of opposition after the Court's 1954 decision in *Brown v. Board of Education.* A similar storm of protest was aroused by the Court's decision in 1962 that banned the recitation of prayers in public schools. (See page 445, this chapter.) While such public reactions do not and should not affect the Court's decisions, they do create pressures on the elected branches of government to counter the policies of the Court.

■ *Congressional control and support.* Because the Supreme Court is able to determine and even alter federal policy through its interpretations of law, it is not surprising that attempts are sometimes made to reverse or modify the Court's decisions. Generally, such attempts are unsuccessful. During Chief Justice Earl Warren's tenure from 1953 to 1969, the Court made many decisions that were sharp departures from precedent and that were opposed by a variety of groups. The reaction against

Legacy

Drawing by Obadiah; © 1968 The National Review

(Some critics said the Warren Court was so independent that it even disregarded constitutional principles.)

these decisions was most evident in Congress where many legislators tried to alter the Court's policies in response to constituent pressure.

In only a few of these instances was Congress able to modify the impact of the Court's decisions. Yet, because the legislative branch does have several methods by which it can control judicial outputs, its support is necessary to the Supreme Court and the rest of the judicial system.
□ *Control of appellate jurisdiction.* One method by which Congress can control the Supreme Court is through its power to determine the appellate jurisdiction of the Supreme Court and all lower federal courts. If Congress does not like the trend of judicial decisions in a particular policy area, it can simply pass a law limiting the ability of the judicial system to review cases arising in that field. This type of congressional control is particularly effective when it is used to limit judicial review over the decisions of administrative agencies.

During the 1950's, for example, the Supreme Court rendered several decisions curbing the authority of the Immigration and Naturalization Service over aliens and over the denial of passports. This raised the ire of a powerful Congressman from Pennsylvania, Francis E. Walter, who was not only chairman of the House Un-American Activities Committee but also a member of the House Judiciary Committee as well as chairman of its Immigration Subcommittee. Through a series of intricate parliamentary maneuvers, Walter succeeded in getting legislation passed that strictly limited the authority of the federal courts to review cases involving exclusion of aliens and other matters handled by the Immigration and Naturalization Service.

Such limitation of appellate jurisdiction does not prevent the Supreme Court from reviewing a case in which it finds a constitutional issue. In the long run, Congress has not exercised much control over the Supreme Court by using its constitutional authority to curb appellate jurisdiction. The Court can probably thank itself for this. Generally, the Court has been reluctant to construe highly controversial matters as constitutional issues. This exercise of judicial self-restraint by the Court on many issues has, on the whole, discouraged strong political opposition to the court.
□ *Control through legislation.* Apart from controlling the appellate jurisdiction of the Supreme Court, Congress can curb all levels of the judiciary by passing legislation with specific directions governing certain types of cases and controversies. Much of the business of the courts involves interpretation of legislation. Accordingly, vague statutes leave a great deal of discretion to the judges. Specific laws on the other hand, can severely limit the judges' power. Some statutes do contain clear directions to the courts regarding what they can or can not review. Because legislators do not often agree on specific language for the statutes they enact, judicial interpretation is rarely curbed in this manner; but the potential always exists.

If a storm of political opposition arises over a particular Supreme Court decision, Congress can pass new legislation altering that decision, as long as no overriding constitutional issues are at stake. An unusual example of a congressional attempt to reverse a series of Supreme Court decisions through legislation occurred in 1968 when the Omnibus Crime Control and Safe Streets Act was passed. During the preceding decade, the Warren Court had made a number of landmark decisions that vastly expanded the constitutional rights of defendants in criminal cases. Three of these decisions were particularly significant.

The first of these cases was *Mallory v.*

United States in 1957. The question at issue was whether a person arrested for a crime could be interrogated by police before he had been arraigned or charged by the court or before he had obtained legal counsel. The Supreme Court held that such action violated a statutory provision in the Federal Rules of Criminal Procedure which required that arraignments be made without "unnecessary delay." The Court also cited a previous judicial decision which specified that delay "must not be of a nature to give opportunity for the extraction of a confession."

In another controversial case, the Supreme Court interpreted the Fifth Amendment to define the rights of criminal suspects. In *Miranda v. Arizona* (1966), the Court held that prior to being interrogated, a suspect must be advised that anything he said could be used against him and that he could remain silent. He also had to be advised that he had the right to obtain a lawyer of his choice or have a court-appointed lawyer if he was too poor to pay a lawyer's fee. The Court said that these procedures were required by the Fifth Amendment provision that "no person . . . shall be compelled in any criminal case to be a witness against himself. . . ."

A third case allowed the Court to expand the rights of the accused further. In *United States v. Wade* (1967), the Court held that the Sixth Amendment "right to counsel" invalidated any identification from a police line-up that had been made in the absence of a lawyer for the defendant.

Although these decisions were based on both statutory and constitutional interpretation, they were essentially superseded by the Omnibus Crime Control Act of 1968. In this Act, Congress dealt with the *Mallory* decision by providing that police could hold a suspect for at least six hours, and in some cases even longer, before

Courtesy of Jon Kiegen and the *Saturday Review.*
Copyright © 1966, Saturday Review, Inc.

"No breakout for me—I'll just sit back and wait for the right Supreme Court ruling to come along."

(In recent decades, the Supreme Court has played a notable role in protecting the rights of the accused.)

arraignment and still obtain a confession that would be admissible in court. The Act also modified the decision in *Miranda v. Arizona* by stating that "voluntary" confessions could be admitted in evidence even if the defendant had not been warned of his constitutional rights. Finally, the Omnibus Crime Control Act negated the *Wade* decision by specifying that identification from a police line-up was admissible evidence at a trial despite the absence of a lawyer for the defendant at the line-up.

The constitutionality of these congressional provisions has yet to be tested before the Court. As with all statutes, there is always the possibility that the Supreme Court could nullify the provisions through its power of judicial review. The passage of the Act, however, illustrates how far Congress can go in resisting the Supreme Court if there is enough political opposition to the trend of judicial decisions.

□ *Constitutional amendment.* As a last resort Congress can try to change a Supreme Court decision by initiating a constitutional amendment. Should such an amendment be ratified by the necessary three-fourths of the states, the Court would be bound by the result.

In the last few decades, several attempts have been made in Congress to change judicial policies by adding amendments to the Constitution. During the 1950s, the so-called Bricker amendment was proposed as a way to reduce the President's constitutional authority to make treaties— an authority that had been expanded by Supreme Court decisions. The Bricker proposal, however, failed to pass Congress.

In more recent years, the late Senator Everett Dirksen of Illinois and others led another unsuccessful movement to alter Supreme Court decisions concerning legislative apportionment. They proposed constitutional amendments which would have provided that at least one house of a state legislature could be apportioned on a basis other than population.

During the 1960's, there was another attempt to amend the Constitution after the Supreme Court's decision in *Engel v. Vitale* (1962). The Court had held that a non-denominational prayer, which was required to be said aloud by all public school classes in New York State at the beginning of each school day, constituted a violation of the "establishment" clause of the First Amendment. In response to constituent pressure, constitutional amendments were proposed in both houses of Congress that would have altered the Constitution to permit prayers to be recited in schools. Although this attempt failed in both houses, the Senate proposal was rejected by only a narrow margin. Thus, while recent efforts to curb Supreme Court policies through constitutional amendments have been fruitless, there is always the possibility that such action might be successful.

■ *Court appointments.* Apart from congressional methods of changing judicial decisions through legislation and constitutional amendment, it is also possible for both the President and the Senate to alter the outputs of the Court through the appointment process. The Constitution has given the President the authority to appoint members of the federal judiciary with the advice and consent of the Senate. By selecting judges with certain political beliefs and values, the Chief Executive and the upper house of Congress can give some direction to judicial determinations.

The appointment of justices to the Supreme Court is sometimes regarded as the special preserve of the President. When a vacancy occurs on the Court, the President generally tries to influence the trend of future Court decisions by selecting a replacement who agrees with his administration's views. In 1969, for example, when there were two seats vacant on the Court, President Nixon nominated replacements who he believed would give a more moderate tone to Court policies than the appointees of his predecessors. In recent years, the Senate Judiciary Committee, which considers all presidential appointments to the federal courts, has also applied indirect pressure on the course of Supreme Court decisions by close questioning of new judicial appointees.

The natural friction between the legislative and executive branches can also surface over the matter of a Supreme Court appointment. This fact was demonstrated in recent years during both the Johnson and Nixon administrations. In the late 1960's, one presidential nomination for Chief Justice was withdrawn after strong Senate opposition, and two nominees for associate justice were rejected by votes of the Senate. In all three instances, there was strong pressure from the administration for approval of the appointments. Counterpressure from the Capitol was aroused, however, due to suggestions that either the financial interests or previous lower-court records of the appointees might conflict with their roles on the Supreme Court. In overriding these presidential appointments, the Senate demonstrated that it does have considerable control over the selection of those people who serve on the highest court.

It should be emphasized that judicial appointees do not always perform according to the original expectations of the President and the Senate. In 1953 when President Eisenhower appointed Earl Warren to be Chief Justice of the Supreme Court, the President was confident that his appointee would serve on the Court as a very moderate liberal. But as soon as Chief Justice Warren took on the judicial mantle, he helped initiate dramatic changes in judicial policy.

Another example of a turnabout in the predicted outcome of a judicial appointment was that of Justice Hugo Black, appointed to the Supreme Court by President Franklin D. Roosevelt in 1937. At the time, many observers felt that Black was a conservative although Roosevelt himself clearly did not agree. Once on the Supreme Court, Justice Black became a leading spokesman for liberal causes and provided particular support for the expansion of civil liberties

Cartoon by Wright in the *Miami News*

"When I hired Warren Burger he told me he'd never driven a bus in his life."

(President Nixon's Chief Justice appointee surprisingly upheld busing as a means of desegregating the schools.)

and civil rights. Throughout American history, it has been impossible to predict the tenor of judicial decisions by the type of men appointed to the bench.

A slightly different procedure is followed for making appointments to the lower federal courts. Such appointments, particularly at the district-court level, are determined by the tradition of "senatorial courtesy." This tradition requires that the senior Senator of the President's party from the state over which the federal court presides must first approve of the appointment. If the Senator is not granted this privilege, the entire Senate will extend the "courtesy" to that Senator of turning down any presidential appointment of which he does not approve. If there is no Senator from the President's party in a state where such an appointment must be made, the President consults with appropriate party leaders in that state.

Independence of the judicial subsystem. The Supreme Court, with its constitutional authority to review actions taken by all the other branches of the government, must play a very careful game. It can invalidate legislation passed by Congress or decisions of the President and the bureaucracy. This makes the Court potentially very vulnerable should it intrude on what the other branches feel to be their exclusive domains. If it did intrude too often, the Court might lose the support of coordinate governmental branches and actions might be taken to curtail its power.

■ *Fragmentation and restraint.* The Court has survived the turbulence of America's political history for two basic reasons. One factor that contributes to the Court's survival is the fragmentation of the American political system. The existence of separate constituencies for Congress, the President, and the many administrative agencies has made it difficult if not impossible for other branches of the government to get together to curb the power of the Supreme Court. The opposition of some groups to the policies of the Court is bound to be counteracted by the approval of other groups.

A second reason for the Court's continued strength is that the Court has exercised judicial self-restraint at critical times when intervention into the affairs of the other branches might have resulted in strong attacks on its authority. For example, the Court exercised self-restraint in the area of legislative apportionment until 1962, even though congressional and state legislative districts had been grossly malapportioned in terms of the one-man-one-vote criterion for decades. By the early 1960's, however, when the tremendous shift in population from rural to urban areas had become widely recognized and the public outcry loud enough, the Court was able to recommend the reapportionment of state legislatures according to the new alignment of the population.

■ *Current position of the Supreme Court.* The decades of the 1950's and 1960's were particularly active ones for the Supreme Court in terms of judicial policy-making. The Court's most significant contributions to federal policy were made through those decisions that extended constitutional law pertaining to individual rights and freedoms. In 1968 the Court retreated somewhat from the active position it had taken during the preceding decades. Some of the justices felt that the Court had sufficiently intruded into the political realm for the present.

In view of the mounting criticism of the Supreme Court's decisions, this shift from a very active to a less active role may be interpreted by some political observers as a strategic retreat by the Court. The fact is, however, that the Court has accomplished much of what it set out to do in the early 1950's. When the political climate of American society was right for change, the Court merely stole the ball away from the other branches of government and scored on the field of civil liberties and civil rights. The entire nation benefited. Today Americans live in a much freer society than existed even as recently as 1950. In large part, this expansion of freedom is due to the courageous stand taken by the Supreme Court to uphold the spirit of the Constitution.

Review questions

1. From what part of the political system does the federal judiciary receive the greatest number of demands?
2. Why are the legislative and executive branches the most important sources of support for the Supreme Court?

Chapter Review

Terms you should know

adjudication	legislative apportionment	Omnibus Crime
Baker v. Carr	legal briefs	Control Act
Bricker amendment	*Mallory v. United States*	"senatorial courtesy"
Justice Department	*Marbury v. Madison*	Solicitor General

Questions about this chapter

1. Explain the significance of the Supreme Court's 1937 interpretation of the Federal Communications Act of 1934.

2. What important precedent was established by Chief Justice Marshall in the case of *Marbury v. Madison* in 1803?
3. How did the Supreme Court defend the constitutionality of the 1964 Civil Rights Act?
4. What requirements make it difficult for individuals to make demands on the courts? How do groups such as the NAACP and the ACLU help to solve this problem?
5. What are the three major duties of the Justice Department? How do these duties lead the Justice Department to make demands on the courts?
6. What divisions of the Justice Department would be responsible for cases concerning the following: (a) evasion of federal taxes; (b) a merger between two competing companies; (c) a private claim against federal land; (d) a company's refusal to hire minority-group workers.
7. In what way can the Chief Executive influence the policies of the Supreme Court?
8. By what methods did Congress attempt to control Supreme Court policies with respect to (a) the rights of accused; (b) the right of the President to make treaties; (c) the rights of aliens?
9. How has the fragmentation of the American political system contributed to the maintenance of the Supreme Court's independence of the other branches of government? What other factor has also been important?

Thought and discussion questions

1. Since judicial review is not explicitly stated in the Constitution as a power of the Supreme Court, objections have been raised against the Supreme Court's exercise of it. What are these objections? Defend the Supreme Court's right to the power of judicial review. What was Hamilton's argument in *The Federalist*, No. 78?
2. Public opinion does not directly influence Supreme Court decisions. Do you think public opinion should or should not have a greater impact on the decisions of the Court? In your answer consider: (a) how public opinion can indirectly affect judicial decisions; (b) what the term "public opinion" really means; (c) why the Framers of the Constitution created the judiciary as a separate branch of government.
3. In 1970 President Nixon declared that he wanted a "strict constructionist" on the Supreme Court. Define "strict constructionist." (See Chapter 24, page 626.) Why do you think President Nixon wanted to appoint this kind of justice? Do you think such reasons are valid? Explain.
4. It has been proposed that a court higher than the Supreme Court be set up to review Supreme Court decisions. This court would be composed of justices from each of the state's highest courts. What is your opinion of the effect such a change would have on (a) our federal system, (b) the system of checks and balances, (c) judicial review.

Class projects

1. Find out the background of the Supreme Court justices appointed by the last three Presidents. Were any of the Presidents surprised or disappointed after their appointees became justices? Explain.
2. In the 1950's and 1960's, the Supreme Court made a number of far-reaching policy-making decisions. Among these were the decisions arrived at in the cases of *Baker v. Carr* and *Brown v. Board of Education*. Try to find evidence of how these decisions affected your community.

Case Study: The Supreme Court rules on wiretapping

Courts are an essential part of the policy-making process. Primarily, however, they are restricted to decision-making on questions of laws in specific cases. Narrow as this may seem, the courts still manage to be quite influential in setting national policy. The effect of the judiciary on policy can be illustrated by the history of wiretapping cases in which the courts have had to decide if evidence gathered by electronic apparatus was legally admissible in court.

In 1928, the Supreme Court made its first ruling on wiretapping in *Olmstead v. United States.* Before the case reached the Supreme Court though, it had to proceed through several steps that illustrate the complexity of the judicial process. The Court did make a decision nevertheless and a policy was established. Since the 1920's the Court has been challenged with similar cases, and the original ruling has been altered.

The case study which follows shows not only how the Supreme Court arrived at the actual policy decision, but also the complicated process involved in getting the highest Court to consider a question of policy. Refamiliarize yourself with the Fourth and Fifth Amendments to the Constitution. Then as you read, take notes on the following questions:

1. How are the Fourth and Fifth Amendments directly concerned with the constitutionality of using listening devices to apprehend criminals?
2. What techniques were used by the federal agents to apprehend the Olmstead gang? Were these techniques legal?
3. On what basis did the Supreme Court choose to review the trial of Olmstead, Finch, and associates?
4. What legal steps were taken by the parties in the *Olmstead* case to arrive at a final decision?

WIRETAPPING ON TRIAL:
A Case Study in the Judicial Process
by Walter F. Murphy

. . . The frustration and dedication of many honest prohibition agents probably made it inevitable that sooner or later some zealous officers would use wiretapping. And the dependence of bootleggers on the telephone made it very likely that the first wiretapping case would expose a sordid network of affluent businessmen, corrupt government officials, and petty criminals living off an unquenchable and illicit public thirst. . . .

This excerpt is adapted from Wiretapping on Trial: A Case Study in the Judicial Process, *by Walter F. Murphy, and is reprinted with permission of the publisher. Copyright, © 1965, by Random House, Inc.*

The Olmstead Gang

On the afternoon of October 13, 1924, federal Prohibition Agent Earl Corwin and two assistants watched a pair of known bootleggers drive out of a Seattle garage. The officers got into their car and whipped off in pursuit. . . .

. . . The agents took their prisoners back to the garage and went over the property with meticulous care. They found what their search warrant had specified they were looking for—illegal liquor, but only 30 cases. . . . When the boxes of contraband liquor were piled up, one of the bootleggers ventured a compliment: "You fellows will be getting the Big Boy himself one of these days, if you keep this up." When Corwin asked who was the "Big Boy," the bootlegger blandly replied: "Roy Olmstead, of course."

. . . Roy Olmstead ran the largest bootlegging operation in western Washington. . . . In 1920 he had been a lieutenant on the Seattle police force, but after pleading guilty to a charge of smuggling liquor he had been dismissed from his position. Once freed from official responsibilities, Olmstead was able to devote his full time to supplying the thirsty citizens of Seattle with liquid refreshment. With his connections in Seattle government, a small initial investment, and eleven partners . . . he was soon in charge of a prospering operation. . . .

For some months now [federal agents] . . . had been secretly tapping his telephone lines—at his home and at his office—and later the telephones of some of his associates. . . . His organization had some fifty employees—salesmen, telephone operators, watchmen, warehousemen, deliverymen, truck drivers, bookkeepers, a lawyer, and even an official fixer, though Olmstead himself remained on intimate terms with some of his old police colleagues. The liquor was brought from England to Vancouver in three small ocean-going freighters which Olmstead chartered. These ships would stay well outside of American territorial waters and would be met by one or more of Olmstead's three fast motorboats. The freighters, of course, could carry large quantities of whiskey, and each of the speedboats could haul over 700 cases.

Once ashore, the whiskey was stored at a ranch outside Seattle and at four distribution points (two garages, two paintshops) in town, and even occasionally at Olmstead's office. A small fleet of three trucks stood by to transport the liquor from the boats to the ranch or from the ranch to the distribution points. Deliveries to customers were made by four cars—one Cadillac and one Packard, plus two Fords for work in less affluent neighborhoods.

The list of customers was long and impressive. In addition to individuals, it included many of the better known hotels and restaurants in town, and even the local press club. The organization might move as many as 200 cases a day, and gross receipts usually ran between $150,000 and $200,000 a month, with a net profit of about $4,000 after expenses and protection had been paid. With his share of the proceeds Olmstead lived in the best section of town in a huge house which reporters were later to describe as "palatial." But he remained in most ways a humble, small business man. . . .

After a customer telephoned Olmstead's office and placed an order, the organization's man would call one of the distribution points and tell a driver to make the delivery. By crossing Olmstead's telephone wires, federal agents could cause him or his men to misdial. The telephone operator would then come onto the line and ask what number had been dialed. The agents could thus get the number—and indirectly the address—of the distribution points.

It was through this tapping process that the raids during the late summer and early fall of 1924 were carried out. An experienced gangster might have been alarmed at the success of the prohibition agents in spotting distribution points, but Olmstead was sure he was safe. After all, relations with the Seattle police were pleasant, if expensive. He was tipped off by a police lieutenant whenever local officials planned a raid, and telephone conversations indicated that the mayor himself was cooperating with the organization. . . .

At 9 o'clock on the evening of November 17, [1924] prohibition agents, armed with a search warrant, surrounded the Olmstead house. They quickly moved in, arresting Olmstead, his wife, and their guests. After a search of the premises uncovered no illegal liquor, the agents used Olmstead's telephone to call other members of his organization, asking them to come to the Olmstead house and bring some whiskey. In these conversations, one of the agents pretended to be Olmstead, and the officer's wife claimed to be Mrs. Olmstead. As the bootleggers arrived, they too were arrested and their liquor confiscated to be used in evidence against them. Sometime between 2:30 and 3:30 the next morning, after Olmstead's private papers had been found and seized (the warrant had stated that the thing sought was liquor, not papers, and a warrant gives lawful authority to seize only the objects specifically described), the whole group was taken to the U.S. district court and charged with violating the Volstead Act [the congressional statute enacted for enforcing the Eighteenth Amendment].

The next day, the Seattle newspapers carried banner headlines and front-page stories recounting the full story of the raid and arrests. . . . Before the afternoon papers were off the presses, however, Mr. and Mrs. Olmstead and most of their guests were back at their homes. Olmstead's lawyer, Jeremiah Finch, had gone to the federal courthouse and posted bail for them. Meanwhile, United States Attorney (the federal equivalent of a district attorney) Thomas P. Revelle, a former preacher who abhorred the use of intoxicating spirits, announced that he would convene a grand jury to consider the evidence against the Olmstead organization, but that because the evidence was so voluminous at least two weeks would be needed to put it into logical order for presentation.

On November 22, just five days after the Olmstead raid, prohibition agents raided the office of Jeremiah Finch. Again, although their warrant specified the items sought as certain bottles of illegal liquor, the agents seized only Finch's private papers—many of them correspondence with his client, Roy Olmstead. Before taking him to the courthouse and formally charging him with violating the Volstead Act, the officers thoughtfully gave Finch a receipt for his papers. . . .

. . . The wiretapping had been an official secret, but stories were now leaking out that the case against the Olmstead organization was built around evidence obtained through monitored telephone calls. When pressed by reporters, Revelle, the U.S. Attorney, admitted that he had heard such rumors but said he "understood" that federal officers had not engaged in wiretapping. . . .

On April 6, thirty-three of the defendants appeared in the United States District Court for the Western District of Washington and entered a plea in abatement. This is a technical motion by the defense which attacks not the merits of the opposing side's allegations, but the time or manner in which those allegations are made. Here the defendants asserted that the indictment was so defective that they could not be made to stand trial. . . .

First they asserted that the indictment had been based on wiretap evidence, and this sort of evidence was "incompetent, irrelevant, hearsay, and secondary testimony" because the persons who listened had merely scribbled longhand notes, which were later edited and typed by another person or persons and material added and subtracted. Thus the wiretap "evidence" presented to the grand jury was not a verbatim account supplied by the actual eavesdroppers but a doctored and unreliable second-hand version of what had been overheard.

Second, the defendants charged that a federal prohibition agent had pressured a member of the grand jury into voting for an indictment. . . .

Third, counsel argued that the searches of Olmstead's house and Finch's office were illegal in that agents had not shown the "probable cause" which the Constitution requires for the issuance of a search warrant. Moreover, when they had found no liquor, the agents had seized everything they thought might possibly help build a case—a "fishing expedition" in direct contravention of the Fourth Amendment's requirement that the place to be searched and the articles sought be specifically identified in the warrant.*

The U.S. Attorney, of course, opposed granting the plea and filed a motion "to strike," that is, to dismiss, the plea in abatement. U.S. District Judge Jeremiah Neterer took the arguments under consideration for two weeks, then granted the government's motion to strike. . . .

Undeterred by this initial defeat, the defendants in early May filed a demurrer to the indictment. A demurrer . . . is a plea that whether or not a defendant has committed the acts with which he is charged, these acts are insufficient to constitute an offense under law. . . .

Once again Judge Neterer ruled against the defendants. . . .

. . . Battered but still not beaten, the defendants returned to Judge Neterer twelve days later and asked that he order the government to file a "bill of particulars"—a detailed answer to questions relating to the specific offenses with which each defendant was charged—so that they might be better prepared to defend themselves at the trial. Defense counsel filed forty-two questions, but the judge ordered the government to answer only ten of them.

With these preliminaries taken care of, Mr. and Mrs. Olmstead, Finch, and most of the other defendants came to the court on May 25, 1925 and formally entered pleas of not guilty. . . .

Still the case was not yet ready to go to trial. During the summer, Olmstead and Finch requested the judge to quash, or nullify, the warrants federal officers had used to enter Olmstead's home and Finch's office. The defendants claimed that the warrants had been issued without "probable cause" and that the search of Finch's office and the seizure of papers relating to Olmstead's activities constituted an infringement of the Fourth Amendment as well as of the confidential nature of the attorney-client relationship. Second, the defendants asked that the property seized in these illegal searches be returned. In addition, Olmstead and Finch asked the judge to refuse to allow the government to use any evidence obtained through wiretapping, because wiretapping abridged the Fourth Amendment's protection of privacy and the Fifth Amendment's protection against self-incrimination. Moreover, insofar as conversations between Finch and Olmstead had been monitored, the wiretapping had interfered with the confidence of the attorney-client relationship.

On September 21, 1925, Judge Neterer issued his ruling, denying in part and granting in part the motions to quash. Neterer found that federal agents had shown probable cause and thus that the warrants had been properly issued. However, the warrants had specified the objects to be seized as bottles of illegal liquor. The agents, therefore, had had no authority to take Olmstead's papers, and these documents could not be used against him. Nor could Finch's papers be used against him. . . .

The judge then denied the motion to suppress wiretapping evidence:

> Wiretapping is not a national offense, nor made so by the statutes of the state of Washington [the judge was in error; wiretapping was a crime in

---

*The Fourth Amendment reads: "The right of the people to be secure in their persons, houses, papers, and effects, against unreasonable searches and seizures, shall not be violated, and no Warrants shall issue, but upon probable cause, supported by Oath or affirmation, and particularly describing the place to be searched, and the persons or things to be seized."

Washington]; even so, it would not violate any constitutional right of the defendants to receive the testimony. The conversation is not a property right. . . .

. . . [O]n the morning of January 19, 1926, exactly one year after the indictment had been returned and fourteen months after the raid on Olmstead's house, the clerk of the United States District Court for the Western District of Washington read the docket for the day: The United States of America versus Roy Olmstead, Elsie Olmstead, Jeremiah Finch, and numerous others. . . .

The Trial

. . . Essentially the defense attorneys made two points, and made them often and with increasing bitterness during the following weeks. First, they claimed that wiretapping violated the Fourth and Fifth Amendments to the Constitution. This much they had argued before the trial began, but now they added that wiretapping was illegal under state law in Washington. Thus, since the evidence was obtained in an unconstitutional and illegal manner, it could not be used in a federal court. As he had in the pretrial proceedings, Judge Neterer ruled against this objection each time it was raised.

The second defense objection related to the way in which the government witness presented the wiretap evidence. The eavesdroppers had jotted down cryptic longhand notes as they listened to telephone conversations and, shortly afterward, had dictated more coherent statements to Mrs. Clara Whitney [the wife of a federal Prohibition agent, William Whitney]. Mrs. Whitney transcribed these notes in shorthand and later typed them. Some months later, prohibition agents and the staff of the U.S. Attorney's office arranged the typewritten statements in a large black book of 775 pages. The original notes were then destroyed, and, Mr. Whitney admitted, the book itself was taken apart, rearranged, and rebound at least once.

Because there was no way anyone could test the veracity of Mrs. Whitney's shorthand notes and because the book had admittedly been edited, the defense argued that prosecution witnesses should not be allowed to use the book during their testimony at the trial. . . .

The judge recognized the importance of the use or non use of the book—the "Black Book," as the press quickly dubbed it—and allowed counsel for the defense and the government to argue the point for several hours. Then Neterer made his ruling: If an eavesdropper claimed an independent recollection of events about which he was testifying, he would be allowed to use the book to refresh his memory; but he would not be permitted to read from the book. . . .

A former prohibition agent was called and testified that he had been one of the eavesdroppers. He claimed, contrary to what the other eavesdroppers had said, that during the taps they had frequently been unable to recognize the voices and had later interpolated names when editing their notes. . . .

When the testimony had been concluded, counsel for each side made closing statements to the jury. Revelle claimed to have proved beyond a reasonable doubt that the defendants had conspired together to operate a bootlegging ring. Defense attorneys again attacked the credibility of prosecution witnesses and the use of wire-tapping. . . .

Judge Neterer then gave his instructions to the jury. . . . Next the judge summed up the evidence. . . .

It was 9:30 on Friday evening, February 19, 1926, when the judge completed his instructions. The jury then retired to consider the case in secret. . . . At

2:10 [the following] afternoon, the foreman opened the door of the jury room and called the marshal of the court over to inform him that a verdict had been reached. . . . Judge Neterer, his nerves worn thin by the incessant squabbling at the trial, was impatient to end this particular case and to move on to the other items on his steadily growing docket. As the judge took his seat, the bailiff called the roll of the jury, then asked: "Have you arrived at a verdict?"

"We have," the foreman replied and handed the bailiff a slip of paper. . . .

"We the jury," the bailiff [read], "in the above entitled case find the defendant Roy Olmstead" . . . "is guilty as charged."

The bailiff then read the verdicts for the other defendants. Finch and nineteen others were found guilty; Mrs. Olmstead and the rest, not guilty. . . .

Interviewed by reporters after the trial, the foreman of the jury stated that "the telephone conversations virtually were disregarded." . . .

Appeal

. . . Olmstead received two years at hard labor on each of the two counts on which he had been convicted, the sentences to run consecutively, plus an $8000 fine and all the costs of prosecution on the second count of the indictment. Finch received three years, an $8000 fine, and costs. The other defendants were given jail terms ranging from eighteen months to three years, with fines of from $500 to $6000.

The defendants then appealed to the Circuit Court of Appeals for the Ninth Circuit, and Neterer, as is customary in non-capital offenses, allowed them to post bond guaranteeing appearance if the appeal failed; the defendants thus retained their freedom until the appellate court could decide their case. By law every loser in a federal district court has the right to one review of his case by a higher court, provided he can give a legal reason which is not trivial or obviously dilatory. . . .

On appeal in a criminal case, the convicted party cannot ask the reviewing court to reweigh the evidence and to second-guess the jury. He can ask the court to do one or both of two things: (1) to review the rulings and instructions of the trial judge and decide whether in construing the law he made errors of sufficient seriousness to justify granting a new trial or perhaps even the dismissal of the indictment; (2) to examine the evidence only to the extent of deciding whether or not twelve honest men could reasonably have arrived at a verdict of guilty. Generally speaking, an appellate court will take up only those questions specifically brought to its attention by the appellant, and then only if the appellant had raised those same questions at the trial. . . .

The defendants—now the appellants—in the Olmstead case split into two different groups and appealed separately. Olmstead, Finch, and seven others brought one appeal; the remaining twelve brought a second action. The fundamental errors asserted by both groups, however, were pretty much the same: the pretrial motions should have been granted. Both groups repeated the earlier claims that the grand jury had considered improper and insufficient evidence and had been tampered with by a federal agent; the indictment had not accused the defendants of a criminal act; the trial judge should have ordered the full bill of particulars requested by the defendants; the search warrant should have been quashed; Finch and Olmstead should have had separate trials; and the trial judge should not have allowed the government to introduce evidence obtained through wiretapping. . . .

To hear the *Olmstead* appeal, William B. Gilbert, Senior Circuit Judge of the Ninth Circuit, [then Arizona, California, Idaho, Montana, Nevada, Oregon and Washington] appointed a three-judge panel composed of himself, Judge Frank H. Rudkin, and Judge Frank S. Dietrich. . . .

On May 9, 1927, after the briefs and reply briefs had been submitted and each side allowed oral argument, the Circuit Court of Appeals handed down its decisions. . . . By a vote of two to one the court affirmed all the convictions. Speaking for himself and Judge Dietrich, Gilbert filed an opinion that merely ticked off the points raised by the appellants as not well taken. Coming to the wiretapping issue, Gilbert stated that the prevailing rule was that evidence obtained by illegal means was not automatically inadmissible in court. Nor did the act of wiretapping itself constitute a violation of the Fourth Amendment's protection of privacy or the Fifth Amendment's protection against self-incrimination. . . .

In reply, Judge Rudkin wrote a respectful but sharply worded dissent. He began by noting that there was little doubt of the guilt of many of the defendants, but that this was not the issue before the court. The real issue was whether the defendants had received a fair trial free from serious legal error. And he found two major errors, one narrow, one broad. The trial judge had erred when he had allowed federal agents to use the Black Book while on the witness stand. . . . Moreover, Rudkin thought that the trial record showed that the witnesses had little if any independent recollection of events about which they were testifying. It was apparent, the judge said, "that the book and not the witnesses was speaking". . . .

It was on the broader issue, however, that Rudkin placed the main burden of his dissent. In general he agreed with the majority that how a witness obtained evidence was of no concern to a court, but the Supreme Court had established certain exceptions. The most important, and most relevant, was the *Weeks* rule, . . . laid down in the case of *Weeks v. United States* in 1914. This rule provided that evidence obtained in violation of constitutional commands could not be used in a *federal* court. . . .

The Supreme Court had announced this rule not as a matter of constitutional law, but as a principle to govern the administration of justice in federal courts. Thus the *Weeks* rule did not forbid state courts to consider unconstitutionally obtained evidence. But, Rudkin continued, since the Olmstead case had been tried in a federal court the *Weeks* rule had to be applied because wiretapping abridged rights protected by the Fourth and Fifth Amendments. The majority had contended that since the wiretapping activities of the prohibition agents had not caused them to trespass on Olmstead's property or to take any of his physical possessions, there had been no violation of his rights under the Fourth or Fifth Amendment. In rebuttal Rudkin pointed out that the chief purpose of these amendments "was not the protection of property, but the protection of the individual in his liberty and in the privacies of life." . . .

Rudkin's dissent probably stirred the hearts of civil libertarians. But his had been only one vote out of three, and on appellate courts. . . . unanimity is not required. The majority, however narrow, decides the case, and two of the three judges on the Circuit Court of Appeals had decided that Olmstead and his associates had been lawfully tried and convicted. Since the ferocity and futility of the federal government's war against liquor traffic made it foolish even to consider trying to secure a presidential pardon, there was only one more hope for the defendants: review by the . . . Supreme Court. . . .

Almost all cases presenting a question of federal statutory or constitutional law must thus come to the Court through the third avenue, a petition for a writ of certiorari. The decision to grant or deny the petition—and so to agree or refuse to hear the case—is completely within the discretion of the Court, and the justices rarely give reasons for their refusals to grant the writ. According to the Court's rules, petitions will be granted only where the case presents a question which is significant for general public policy in the United States, not merely because the issue is of importance to the individual litigants. The result of this procedure is to give the justices almost complete control over their docket. . . .

In their supporting briefs the defendants—now called "petitioners" since they were petitioning for certiorari—relied heavily on the language of Judge Rudkin's dissent, stressing the fact that wiretapping was a crime in the state of Washington, and arguing further that Judge Neterer should not have allowed prosecution witnesses to use the Black Book at the trial. These initial efforts were fruitless. On Monday, November 21, 1927 [the petition for the writ was denied].

The bad news hit Olmstead just when he had thought that the world was once again opening up for him. He had failed to appear for a second trial on a set of charges growing out of the same general evidence which had led to his conviction on the conspiracy counts. When later apprehended he had been forced to stand trial on these new charges, but on November 17, just four days before the Supreme Court had denied certiorari, the jury in the second case had acquitted him.

. . . At this point Olmstead decided to give up the fight and to start serving his sentence. He was taken to the federal penitentiary at McNeil Island, Washington.

Some of Olmstead's former colleagues, however, were still not willing to quit. Supreme Court rules then in effect provided that, within forty days of a decision, the losing party could apply for a rehearing, and two of the three groups of petitioners availed themselves of this opportunity. . . .

Because of the care with which each justice examines a case before voting on it, petitions for rehearing are rarely granted; and it came as no surprise when on January 3, 1928, the Court denied the rehearing request from the first group of petitioners. On January 9, however, government officials were shocked when the justices issued a new order:

> This Court now reconsiders all these three petitions for certiorari and grants the writs therein, limiting their consideration, however, to the question whether the use of evidence of private telephone conversations between the defendants and others, intercepted by means of wiretapping, is a violation of the 4th and 5th Amendments, and, therefore, not permissible in the Federal courts.

Thus the case had been narrowed to one issue—the constitutionality of wiretapping, and it was on this single point that counsel for both sides were ordered to focus their arguments. . . .

Meanwhile, Roy Olmstead was released from McNeil Island on bond, once more—temporarily—a free man. . . .

The Justices Deliberate

. . . [T]he Clerk of the Court set Monday, February 20, 1928, as the day for oral argument in *Olmstead v. United States.*

Essentially, petitioners reasserted their earlier arguments that wiretapping was a violation of the Fifth Amendment's protection against self-incrimination*

---

*The relevant part of the Fifth Amendment provides: "nor shall [any person] be compelled in any criminal case to be a witness against himself. . . ." For the Fourth Amendment, see above [page 452].

and the Fourth Amendment's [implied] protection of privacy. In addition, petitioners went beyond the expressed limits of the grant of certiorari and asserted that wiretapping was a crime in Washington and therefore under the *Weeks* rule should not be used in a federal court.

In reply the Department of Justice made three points. First, under the common law the way in which evidence was obtained had no bearing on its admissibility. The *Weeks* rule modified the common law only to the extent of excluding evidence obtained in violation of the Fourth Amendment. The issue of the criminality of wiretapping was thus irrelevant. Second, the Fourth Amendment protects against physical invasions of property. It had never been held to exclude evidence overheard by a person who was not trespassing. One cannot "search" or "seize" a conversation, and the Constitution forbade only unreasonable searches and seizures. If the Fourth Amendment were interpreted in its literal sense, Doherty [Special Assistant to the Attorney General] and Mitchell [Solicitor General] contended, "it does not seem possible to include within its meaning anything other than tangible personal property or extend it to include a telephone conversation or any intangible right of privacy. . . ." Third, the Department of Justice maintained that there was even less reason to find an invasion of Fifth Amendment rights. No one had coerced or induced Olmstead and the others to talk on the telephone. They had done so of their own free will, without fear of punishment or promise of reward.

Only one brief in the case met high professional standards. A group of telephone companies, including the Pacific Telephone and Telegraph Company, which serviced Seattle, asked and received permission to present a brief as *amicus curiae*. . . .

. . . [T]he companies asserted:

> The function of a telephone system in our modern economy is, so far as reasonably practicable, to enable any two persons at a distance to converse privately with each other as they might do if both were personally present in the privacy of the home or office of either one. . . . A third person who taps the lines violates the property rights of both persons then using the telephone. . . .

To bolster this last point, counsel cited a 1918 Supreme Court decision holding that International News Service had violated the property rights of the Associated Press in pirating news sent out over telegraph lines to other Associated Press agents. . . .

. . . On Saturday, February 25, 1928, the justices met for their weekly conference to discuss and vote on the cases just argued. At these conferences the Chief Justice presides. He usually opens the discussion on a particular case with a short summary of the facts and states his own views about the proper decision. Then, in order of seniority, each associate justice offers his views. When the Chief Justice feels that the discussion has played itself out or that the press of time forces the Court to move on, he calls for a vote. The justices vote in reverse order of seniority, the most recently appointed associate justice first, the Chief last.

These conferences are secret and no one except the justices is admitted to the room. . . . From copies of letters and memoranda in the [Chief Justice] Taft papers, however, it is possible to reconstruct the general outline of what went on at the *Olmstead* conference.

From his later opinion and his earlier statements warning against coddling criminals, it would be expected that Taft spoke in favor of affirming the convictions. He probably argued that wiretapping did not violate the Fourth Amendment because there was no invasion of property rights. Holmes, the senior associate justice, agreed reluctantly. He did not like wiretapping, but he thought it neither illegal nor unconstitutional. Van Devanter also agreed with the Chief. McReynolds was next and he probably said very few words—undoubtedly most of them caustic—but went along with the preceding justices.

It was Brandeis who put forth the first negative view. . . . He thought wiretapping was an invasion of the right to privacy, a right whose protection was the cardinal purpose of the Fourth Amendment. Moreover, wiretapping was certainly illegal in the state of Washington. Either at this point or somewhat later, Holmes interrupted and asked Brandeis why he had said wiretapping was illegal. Brandeis explained that it was a misdemeanor under Washington law. Holmes then stated that this fact changed his view. He did not believe that evidence obtained by crime could be used in a federal court.

Sutherland was the next senior judge. . . . Sutherland agreed with the Chief Justice on the merits of this case. Pierce Butler was next. Despite his close friendship with the Chief Justice, he had to register disagreement. For somewhat different reasons than those advanced by Brandeis, Butler felt that prohibition agents had violated the Constitution. Sanford then spoke and agreed with Taft. Last was Stone, the junior justice, and he came out in favor of the position Brandeis had stated.

When the voting was completed, the decision was five to four to affirm the conviction. The Chief Justice, if he votes with the majority, assigns the task of writing the opinion of the Court to himself or to one of the justices who voted with him. (If the Chief is in the minority, the senior associate justice in the majority assigns the opinion.) In making these assignments the Chief Justice has to weigh a number of factors: the workload of each justice, the peculiar expertise and taste of the individual members of the Court, and, of course, the substantive views of each potential writer. . . .

Taft was able to balance these considerations by assigning the *Olmstead* opinion to himself. . . .

. . . Depending on their inclinations and workload, the dissenters may agree to have one of their number prepare an opinion for the group, or each may decide to try his own hand. Alternatively, a justice may simply record his vote without offering an explanation. No matter which course the dissenters originally agree upon, no justice is obliged to put his name to an opinion that does not meet his full approval. This rule applies to the majority as well, and causes more difficult problems since, for an opinion to be labeled as that of the Court, at least five justices (or a majority of those sitting in a case) must sign it.

It was not until the last week in May that Taft had a draft of his opinion in condition to circulate. . . .

. . . Meanwhile, Brandeis had circulated a memorandum outlining the form his dissent would take, and to answer it Taft added a paragraph to his opinion stressing that the historical purpose of the Fourth Amendment was to protect physical property—homes, papers, and personal effects—and that the cases Brandeis cited were all to this effect.

In addition to matters of substance, Brandeis' draft had raised a serious problem of procedure for the Chief Justice. In spite of the limitation on the grant of certiorari to the constitutional question, Brandeis, as at conference, had reasoned that wiretapping evidence was also inadmissible because it had been obtained in violation of Washington law. . . .

Brandeis undertook the task of writing for the other dissenters and had a complete draft ready in the form of a memorandum a full two months ahead of Taft. Brandeis based his opinion on two independent grounds: (1) wiretapping violated the Fourth Amendment; and (2) it was a state crime. Holmes was unsure of the first ground, as he had been at conference, but agreed with the second. . . . Brandeis, seeing that their differences were major and not wishing to modify or conceal his own constitutional views, urged Holmes to publish his explanation as a separate dissent. Holmes at first thought he should not, but later gave in.

When Stone read Brandeis' opinion, he agreed to join in it, but with one reservation and one suggestion for an addition. . . . The addition Stone wanted was an explicit statement that it was equally wrong for federal officers to violate state law to obtain evidence as to violate the Constitution. . . .

. . . On the morning of June 2, 1928, the Chief wrote his brother: "We go for the last Conference of the Court . . . this morning, and we are going to have a divided Court on a very contested case. The decision may bring down, and probably will, the condemnation of idealists and others, but I am convinced that it is the law." . . .

The Justices Speak*

. . . Mr. Chief Justice TAFT delivered the opinion of the Court. . . .

It will be helpful to consider [a few] chief cases in this Court which bear upon the construction of these Amendments. . . .

. . . [P]erhaps the most important [case] is *Weeks v. United States* . . .— a conviction for using the mails to transmit coupons or tickets in a lottery enterprise. The defendant was arrested by a police officer without a warrant. After his arrest other police officers and the United States marshal went to his house, got the key from a neighbor, entered the defendant's room and searched it, and took possession of various papers and articles. Neither the marshal nor the police officers had a search warrant. . . . This court held that such taking of papers by an official of the United States, acting under color of his office, was in violation of the constitutional rights of the defendant, and . . . that by permitting their use upon the trial, the trial court erred. . . .

There is no room in the present case for applying the Fifth Amendment unless the Fourth Amendment was first violated. There was no evidence of compulsion to induce the defendants to talk over their many telephones. They were continually and voluntarily transacting business without knowledge of the interception. Our consideration must be confined to the Fourth Amendment.

The striking outcome of the *Weeks* case and those which followed it was the sweeping declaration that the Fourth Amendment, although not referring to or limiting the use of evidence in courts, really forbade its introduction if obtained by government officers through a violation of the Amendment. Theretofore many had supposed that under the ordinary common law rules, if the tendered evidence was pertinent, the method of obtaining it was unimportant. . . .

. . . The Fourth Amendment may have proper application to a sealed letter in the mail because of the constitutional provision for the Post Office Department and the relations between the Government and those who pay to secure protection of their sealed letters. . . . It is plainly within the words of the Amendment to say that the unlawful rifling by a government agent of a sealed letter is a search and seizure of the sender's papers or effects. The letter is a paper, an effect, and in the custody of a Government that forbids carriage except under its protection.

---

*The text . . . consists entirely of material drawn from the Supreme Court opinions in *Olmstead v. United States.*

The United States takes no such care of telegraph or telephone messages as of mailed sealed letters. The Amendment does not forbid what was done here. There was no searching. There was no seizure. The evidence was secured by the use of the sense of hearing and that only. There was no entry of the houses or offices of the defendants.

By the invention of the telephone, fifty years ago, and its application for the purpose of extending communications, one can talk with another at a far distant place. The language of the Amendment can not be extended and expanded to include telephone wires reaching to the whole world from the defendant's house or office. The intervening wires are not part of his house or office any more than are the highways along which they are stretched. . . .

Congress may of course protect the secrecy of telephone messages by making them, when intercepted, inadmissible in evidence in federal criminal trials, by direct legislation, and thus depart from the common law of evidence. But the courts may not adopt such a policy by attributing an enlarged and unusual meaning to the Fourth Amendment. The reasonable view is that one who installs in his house a telephone instrument with connecting wires intends to project his voice to those quite outside, and that the wires beyond his house and messages while passing over them are not within the protection of the Fourth Amendment. Here those who intercepted the projected voices were not in the house of either party to the conversation. . . .

While a Territory, the English common law prevailed in Washington and thus continued after her admission in 1889. The rules of evidence in criminal cases in courts of the United States sitting there, consequently are those of the common law. . . .

The common law rule is that the admissibility of evidence is not affected by the illegality of the means by which it was obtained. . . . The common law rule must apply in the case at bar.

Nor can we, without the sanction of congressional enactment, subscribe to the suggestion that the courts have a discretion to exclude evidence, the admission of which is not unconstitutional, because unethically secured. This would be at variance with the common law doctrine generally supported by authority. There is no case that sustains, nor any recognized text book that gives color to such a view. . . . Evidence secured by such means has always been received.

A standard which would forbid the reception of evidence if obtained by other than nice ethical conduct by government officials would make society suffer and give criminals greater immunity than has been known heretofore. In the absence of controlling legislation by Congress, those who realize the difficulties in bringing offenders to justice may well deem it wise that the exclusion of evidence should be confined to cases where rights under the Constitution would be violated by admitting it.

The statute of Washington, adopted in 1909, provides . . . that:

"Every person . . . who shall intercept, read or in any manner interrupt or delay the sending of a message over any telegraph or telephone line . . . shall be guilty of a misdemeanor."

This statute does not declare that evidence obtained by such interception shall be inadmissible, and by the common law, already referred to, it would not be. . . . Whether the State of Washington may prosecute and punish federal officers violating this law and those whose messages were intercepted may sue them civilly is not before us. . . .

The judgments of the Circuit Court of Appeals are affirmed. The mandates will go down forthwith under Rule 31.

Affirmed.

MR. JUSTICE HOLMES:

. . . I think, as MR. JUSTICE BRANDEIS says, that apart from the Constitution the Government ought not to use evidence obtained and only obtainable by a criminal act. . . . It is desirable that criminals should be detected, and to that end that all available evidence should be used. It also is desirable that the Government should not itself foster and pay for other crimes, when they are the means by which the evidence is to be obtained. If it pays its officers for having got evidence by crime I do not see why it may not as well pay them for getting it in the same way, and I can attach no importance to protestations of disapproval if it knowingly accepts and pays and announces that in future it will pay for the fruits. We have to choose, and for my part I think it a less evil that some criminals should escape than that the Government should play an ignoble part. . . .

MR. JUSTICE BRANDEIS, dissenting. . . .

. . . Protection against. . . invasion of "the sanctities of a man's home and the privacies of life" was provided in the Fourth and Fifth Amendments by specific language. . . . But "time works changes, brings into existence new conditions and purposes." Subtler and more far-reaching means of invading privacy have become available to the Government. Discovery and invention have made it possible for the Government, by means far more effective than stretching upon the rack, to obtain disclosure in court of what is whispered in the closet. . . .

. . . . The progress of science in furnishing the Government with means of espionage is not likely to stop with wiretapping. Ways may some day be developed by which the Government, without removing papers from secret drawers, can reproduce them in court, and by which it will be enabled to expose to a jury the most intimate occurrences of the home. Advances in the psychic and related sciences may bring means of exploring unexpressed beliefs, thoughts and emotions. . . . Can it be that the Constitution affords no protection against such invasions of individual security? . . .

. . . It is not the breaking of [a man's] doors, and the rummaging of his drawers, that constitutes the essence of the offence; but it is the invasion of his indefeasible [fundamental right] of personal security, personal liberty and private property, where that right has never been forfeited by his conviction of some public offence. . . . Breaking into a house and opening boxes and drawers are circumstances of aggravation; but any forcible and compulsory extortion of a man's own testimony or of his private papers to be used as evidence of a crime or to forfeit his goods, is within the condemnation of that judgment. In this regard the Fourth and Fifth Amendments run almost into each other."

. . . The mail is a public service, furnished by the Government. The telephone is a public service furnished by its authority. There is, in essence, no difference between the sealed letter and the private telephone message. As Judge Rudkin said below: "True the one is visible, the other invisible; the one is tangible, the other intangible; the one is sealed and the other unsealed, but these are distinctions without a difference." The evil incident to invasion of the privacy of the telephone is far greater than that involved in tampering with the mails. Whenever a telephone line is tapped, the privacy of the persons at both ends of the line is invaded and all conversations between them upon any subject, and although proper, confidential and privileged, may be overheard. Moreover, the tapping of one man's telephone line involves the tapping of the telephone of every other person whom he may call or who may call him. As a means of espionage, writs of assistance and general warrants are but puny instruments of tyranny and oppression when compared with wiretapping. . . .

. . . The makers of our Constitution undertook to secure conditions favorable to the pursuit of happiness. . . . They conferred, as against the Government, the right to be let alone—the most comprehensive of rights and the right most valued by civilized men. To protect that right, every unjustifiable intrusion by the Government upon the privacy of the individual, whatever the means employed, must be deemed a violation of the Fourth Amendment. And the use, as evidence in a criminal proceeding, of facts ascertained by such intrusion must be deemed a violation of the Fifth.

Applying to the Fourth and Fifth Amendments the established rule of construction, the defendants' objections to the evidence obtained by wiretapping must, in my opinion, be sustained. . . .

Independently of the constitutional question, I am of opinion that the judgment should be reversed. By the laws of Washington, wiretapping is a crime. . . . To prove its case, the Government was obliged to lay bare the crimes committed by its officers on its behalf. A federal court should not permit such a prosecution to continue. . . .

Will this Court by sustaining the judgment below sanction such conduct on the part of the Executive? The governing principle has long been settled. It is that a court will not redress a wrong when he who invokes its aid has unclean hands. . . .

MR. JUSTICE BUTLER, dissenting.

. . . The question at issue depends upon a just appreciation of the facts.

Telephones are used generally for transmission of messages concerning official, social, business and personal affairs including communications that are private and privileged—those between physician and patient, lawyer and client, parent and child, husband and wife. The contracts between telephone companies and users contemplate the private use of the facilities employed in the service. The communications belong to the parties between whom they pass. During their transmission the exclusive use of the wire belongs to the persons served by it. Wiretapping involves interference with the wire while being used. Tapping the wires and listening in by the officers literally constituted a search for evidence. . . .

When the facts in these cases are truly estimated, a fair application of that principle decides the constitutional question in favor of the petitioners. With great deference, I think they should be given a new trial.

MR. JUSTICE STONE, dissenting.

I concur in the opinions of MR. JUSTICE HOLMES and MR. JUSTICE BRANDEIS. . . .

Impact

After the Supreme Court's opinion was announced, Roy Olmstead surrendered to federal authorities in Seattle and was returned to the penitentiary at McNeil Island to serve the remainder of his four-year term. As far as the judicial process was concerned, the *Olmstead* case was now closed; the convicted defendants had become problems for the officials who administered the federal penal system. Olmstead himself was a model prisoner, served his full sentence, and returned to Seattle, where he became a respected member of the community. Some years later he received a full pardon from the President. The Mayor of Seattle was turned out of office at the next election.

End questions

1. Do you think the defendants in this case received a fair trial before Judge Neterer? Before the Circuit court? Before the Supreme Court? Olmstead was exonerated a few years after finishing his sentence. Find out why. Do you think justice was served in this case?
2. Under what circumstances is evidence inadmissible for presentation in the courtroom? How did Justices Taft and Brandeis differ on the "admissibility" of evidence?
3. On what grounds were Taft and Brandeis at loggerheads over the final Court decision? What does this difference tell you about judicial decision-making?

Supplementary Reading

ABRAHAM, HENRY J. *The Judicial Process: Introductory Analysis of the Courts of the United States, England, and France.* 2nd ed. New York: Oxford Univ. Press, 1968. Paperbound. This is a comparative study of courts and law providing a sound framework for understanding the judicial process. The book makes no attempt at being all-inclusive, but points out the basic similarities and differences of the three legal systems. A very useful reference for students who wish to discover how the judicial process affects human society.

ANDERSON, PATRICK. *The President's Men: White House Assistants from FDR through LBJ.* Garden City, N.Y.: Doubleday, 1968. Who are the President's men? What do they do? They are his personal aides, his communications men, his liaisons, and even his watchdogs, who all owe their jobs to the man in the White House. Mr. Anderson, who worked for Presidents Kennedy and Johnson, discusses their administrations along with FDR's, Truman's and Eisenhower's, presenting a firsthand picture of the men who work for the Executive.

BAYH, BIRCH. *One Heartbeat Away: Presidential Disability and Succession.* Indianapolis: Bobbs-Merrill, 1968. Told by a member of the Senate, this is the story of the passage of the Twenty-fifth Amendment which provides for presidential disability and succession. But Bayh goes even further and investigates the workings of Congress and its constitutional history.

BURNS, JAMES MACGREGOR. *Roosevelt: The Lion and the Fox.* New York: Harcourt, Brace, 1956. Paperbound edition by Harvest Books. Machiavelli, the Italian political philosopher, cautioned rulers that to be successful they should use both the courage of a lion and the cunning of a fox. By unfolding the story of FDR and his years as President, the author tries to discover to what extent Roosevelt had these qualities. This book blends biography with analysis, against a background of pressures and forces emanating from the White House.

GOODMAN, WALTER. *The Committee: The Extraordinary Career of the House Committee on Un-American Activities.* New York: Farrar, Strauss, and Giroux, 1968. Paperbound edition by Penguin Books. The House Un-American Activities Committee has been one of the most controversial committees ever established by the House. Why has this Committee been the subject of angry controversy for many years? For a scholarly look into the purpose of this committee, and the committee system in general, this book is a must.

JONES, CHARLES O. *Every Second Year: Congressional Behavior and the Two-Year Term.* Washington: Brookings Institute, 1967. Paperbound. In his 1966 State of the Union message, President Johnson called for a constitutional amendment to increase the term of office of a Congressman from two to four years, concurrent with that of the President. Professor Jones concisely and clearly discusses this reform measure, the growing power of the congressional reform movement, and why reform demands have met with stiff opposition.

LEACACOS, JOHN PETER. *Fires in the In-Basket: The ABC's of the State Department.* New York: World, 1968. This is an examination of the routines and methods of the State Department in handling everyday situations and crises. The author emphasizes the complexities and inherent problems existing within this area of government.

LEWIS, ANTHONY. *Gideon's Trumpet.* New York: Random House, 1964. This book, about the judicial process and the Supreme Court, tells the story of Clarence Gideon. Tried and convicted of burglary by a Florida court, Gideon petitioned the Supreme Court from his jail cell for a retrial, claiming that due to lack of funds he had been unable to engage legal counsel for his trial. The Court ruled for a second trial, in which he was acquitted. Lewis writes with wit and insight about a man's fight for freedom.

MOLLENHOFF, CLARK R. *The Pentagon: Politics, Profits, and Plunder.* New York: Putnam, 1967. Mr. Mollenhoff has written a book about the absolute power of the Defense Department. He outlines the organization, the dilemmas, and the battle for dollars. He then discusses the wheeling and dealing of officers and congressmen, indicating that the desire for power and profit is prevelant everywhere. This is a highly controversial and stimulating book.

TODD, ALDEN L. *Justice on Trial: The Case of Louis D. Brandeis.* New York: McGraw Hill, 1964. Paperbound edition by Univ. of Chicago Press. This is the story of the confirmation of Louis D. Brandeis to the Supreme Court in 1916. Up to that time, appointees to the highest bench had had little difficulty in getting confirmed by the United States Senate. But the actions of the Judiciary Committee in 1916 amounted to subjecting Brandeis to a "trial." Todd also analyzes the operations of checks and balances inherent in our system of government.

WARNER, W. LLOYD, and others. *The American Federal Executive.* New Haven: Yale Univ. Press, 1963. Paperbound. Who staffs the huge American bureaucracy? What type of people are they? This study of the social and personal backgrounds of more than a thousand of our civilian and military leaders tries to answer these two questions. The authors also explore the relationship between federal bureaucratic personnel and a representative democracy.

The reason for channeling demands to the conversion structures of a political system is, of course, to produce policy-outputs. By satisfying such demands and answering the needs of people within the system, outputs in turn create the support needed to preserve the system itself.

The outputs of America's political system fall into two very broad categories. First, there are policies that protect and expand the rights and freedoms of individual citizens. These outputs include judicial decisions that protect an individual's constitutional rights against government infringement and those laws that are passed and implemented to protect each person's opportunities to work, to get an education, or to vote. Second, there are policies that maintain the system by accomplishing the broader goals of society that could not be achieved individually. Some maintenance policies preserve the society against external and internal threats. Other maintenance policies are "developmental" because they are designed to respond both to change and to people's economic and social needs.

While it is useful to think of outputs in these neat categories, not every public policy can be placed exclusively under one label or the other. Certainly, the protection of one individual's rights also helps to maintain constitutional democracy for society as a whole. Similarly, national economic policies that guarantee the system's continued existence help to preserve the opportunity of an individual to work. Furthermore, there is a constant tug-of-war between outputs that protect individual rights and those that preserve the broader "public interest." Such conflict is illustrated by the fact that policies protecting a citizen's freedom of speech exist side by side with policies limiting the same citizen's right to speak when it might jeopardize the nation's defense.

All these government outputs cause some kind of reaction or feedback. Sometimes feedback consists of approval or support for a policy. Other feedback is negative and creates new demands. In either case, the ultimate effect of policy outputs is to initiate new inputs for the political system, and thus to reactivate the policy-making cycle.

UNIT FIVE

Outputs of the Political System

CHAPTER 19

Policies That Protect the Individual

For a democracy to be worthy of the name, it has to preserve the rights and freedoms of the individuals who constitute its very reason for existence. In the United States, these rights and freedoms cover a very broad area. They include the freedoms to speak, write, and worship as one pleases, the civil rights guaranteeing equal opportunities for education and employment, as well as such specific rights as the right of the accused to refuse to speak until he has received legal advice from his attorney. All of these individual freedoms and rights touch the very core of democracy.

Since the founding of the Republic, the idea of civil liberties—of limiting government interference with individual freedoms—has been fundamental in American political thinking. After their experiences under the Articles of Confederation, the states in 1789 were very concerned with limiting the national government so that it would neither overwhelm their own authority nor usurp the freedoms of their inhabitants. For this reason, most of the states insisted on adding the first ten amendments to the Constitution as a condition of ratification.

So strong has been this concept of civil liberties that even after the adoption of the Fourteenth Amendment, the constitutional guarantees of civil liberties continued to be interpreted so as to restrain the national government alone. Likewise, until the mid-twentieth century, the notion of government "restraint" continued to block the emergence of positive policies by which the national government could act to protect individual rights.

In this century, however, concern has steadily increased over the violations of minority rights by some states and by individuals. Demands for federal action have gradually gathered momentum and resulted in the coalition of pressure groups to secure a change in federal policies.

The most important conversion structure in setting national policy with respect to civil liberties and civil rights has been the Supreme Court. Because of this, the most effective demands for change have come from those groups, such as the American Civil Liberties Union (ACLU) and the National Association for the Advancement of Colored People (NAACP), that have taken specific cases to the courts. Through the efforts of such groups, the Supreme Court has reinterpreted the Fourteenth Amendment in a number of cases, extending the restraints of the Bill of Rights to state and local governments. The voting rights guaranteed by the Fifteenth Amendment also have been reinterpreted in the same way. The Court's reinterpretations of both of these amendments have enabled the federal government to play a more active role in protecting individual rights through the passage and enforcement of legislation.

The Nature of Civil Liberties and Civil Rights

While the terms civil liberties and civil

(If a citizen believes that his personal rights and freedoms are being threatened or denied by his state, a government official, or another individual, what can the person do to insure his rights will be protected?)

rights are often used interchangeably, it should be remembered that they identify two different concepts of a government's relationship to individual citizens. The concept of *civil liberties* is based on the idea that government must be *restrained*

Donald Reilly. Copyright © 1968, Saturday Review, Inc.

"I'm so proud of you—imagine having your hair defended by the American Civil Liberties Union!"

(Imposed standards of dress and hair length by public institutions have sometimes been challenged in court.)

from interfering with the freedom of individuals to do certain things. Thus, the First Amendment to the Constitution—which prohibits Congress from interfering with an individual's freedom to worship, to express himself through speech and press, to assemble, and to petition the government—is a guarantee of civil liberties. In the area of civil liberties, there is a restraining wall between government and the individual, protecting the individual's freedom of action against governmental encroachment.

The notion of *civil rights* on the other hand, assigns to government an active role as the *protector* of an individual's basic human rights against infringement by government or even by private individuals. The individual is entitled to certain rights, and government secures these rights for the individual. Laws that authorize government to use its power to guarantee an individual's right to equal job or educational opportunities are based on this notion of civil rights.

A crucial question immediately arises with respect to civil liberties and civil rights: Can government act to protect individual rights and at the same time be restrained from violating individual liberties? Understandably, the evolution of policies through the American political system, that pertain to individual liberties and rights, has been accompanied by continual debate over whether to limit or expand government activity.

Individual liberties and rights in the Constitution. The constitutional basis for any judicial determination of civil liberties and civil rights is found in the Bill of Rights and subsequent amendments, particularly the Fourteenth and Fifteenth Amendments. The Bill of Rights prohibits the national government from denying the people certain rights and freedoms; the Fourteenth Amendment, extends the same prohibitions to the states.

■ *Civil liberties in the Bill of Rights.* The most significant limitations on government in the first ten amendments have been those that prohibit the infringement of specific liberties and rights of individuals. Liberties such as the freedom of religion, of speech and press, of peaceful assembly, and the right to petition the government concerning one's grievances are considered basic to personal freedom. The First Amendment prohibits Congress from passing any law that interferes with these liberties.

Other important elements in the Bill of Rights guarantee certain legal procedures and protections to all citizens. These are *procedural rights* and are identified in the Fourth through Eighth Amendments. Procedural rights are given the most extensive treatment in the Bill of Rights and have been the subject of many cases before the courts. The Fourth Amendment protects people and their property against government "searches and seizures" without warrants affirming "probable cause." The Seventh Amendment guarantees a person the right of a jury trial in most civil cases. The Fifth and Sixth Amendments insure other important rights in criminal proceedings. The Fifth Amendment guarantees that no person shall be held for a capital crime without indictment by a grand jury, nor be compelled to act as a witness against himself (self-incrimination) in a criminal case. The Fifth Amendment also specifies that no person can be deprived of "life, liberty, or property, without due process of law." A person accused of a crime is guaranteed "the right to a speedy and public trial by an impartial jury" and to legal counsel and witnesses for defense by the Sixth Amendment. Excessive bails and fines, and cruel and unusual punishment are forbidden by the Eighth Amendment.

In addition to protecting and guaranteeing these liberties and rights, the Bill of Rights includes other guarantees against arbitrary actions of the federal government. The right of the states to keep militias, the right of people to "keep and bear arms," and the prohibition against the quartering of soldiers in private homes are all potential defenses against dictators or military rule.

While the adoption of the Bill of Rights made civil liberties an inviolable part of constitutional government, the imprecise language of some clauses has permitted variations in applying them in different situations. No one can dispute the right of a person to a trial by jury, established in the Sixth Amendment. There *can* be a difference of opinion, however, as to whether a trial is "speedy"; a jury, "impartial"; or a bail, "excessive." The meaning of these and other terms, such as "probable cause" and "due process of law," have had to be defined by the courts over the years, as cases have been brought before them.

■ *Civil liberties and rights in the Fourteenth Amendment.* By the end of the Civil War, it was apparent that the federal government had to extend the Bill of Rights so that former slaves would not be denied their civil liberties and other rights as citizens. Three amendments, known as the "Civil War Amendments," were added to the Constitution. The Thirteenth Amendment prohibits slavery. The Fifteenth Amendment guarantees to every citizen a political right—the right to vote.

The Fourteenth Amendment, however, is less clear-cut. It provides, first, that "all persons born or naturalized in the United States, and subject to the jurisdiction thereof, are citizens of the United States and of the state wherein they reside. No state shall make or enforce any law which

LePelley

"At least I'll be some company."

(The Supreme Court's reading of the Fourteenth Amendment has helped the blacks in their fight for equality.)

469

shall abridge the privileges or immunities of citizens of the United States." Second, the Fourteenth Amendment provides that no state may "deprive any person of life, liberty, or property, without due process of law." Finally, no state may "deny to any persons within its jurisdiction the equal protection of the laws." The amendment authorizes Congress to enforce its provisions by appropriate legislation.

Like the Bill of Rights, the Fourteenth Amendment has required clarification by the courts. Just what did the authors of the amendment mean by "privileges or immunities of citizens of the United States"? The meaning of "due process of law" is no clearer in the Fourteenth Amendment than it is in the Fifth. What exactly is "equal protection of the laws"?

The Supreme Court's interpretations of "due process of law" and "equal protection of the law" in the Fourteenth Amendment have been most important to the evolution of federal policies concerning civil liberties and civil rights. No precise meaning has been given to either clause. Both clauses, however, have been interpreted by the Court to negate state laws and government actions which it has considered unreasonable. The same holds true of the Court's definition of due process of law in the Fifth Amendment, which has been used to prevent what the Court considers unreasonable federal actions.

Like the outputs of other decision-making bodies, the interpretations of the Court have often changed with the prevailing attitudes and demands of the times. Since 1925, the Court has negated by means of the "due process" clause of the Fourteenth Amendment all state laws that abridged any civil liberties and rights guaranteed in the Bill of Rights. The "equal protection" clause of the Fourteenth Amendment has also been interpreted to broaden the obligations of state governments to protect the rights and opportunities of citizens for equal education, and equality in voting.

Constitutional dilemmas. Besides being subject to reinterpretation because of changing attitudes, judicial principles involving civil liberties and civil rights may often come into conflict with other constitutional requirements. In formulating its interpretations and decisions, the Supreme Court has had to determine the proper balance between conflicting principles.

■ *Individual rights versus community needs.* Because civil liberties and rights are fundamental to democracy, it is often assumed that personal freedoms can not be limited in such a system. When individuals, however, exercise their freedoms in ways that are harmful to other individuals or to the society as a whole, there is conflict between the rights of the individual and the needs of the community. The freedom of individuals, like the power of government, must have limits.

For example, the rights of all citizens to the freedoms of speech, press, and assembly are guaranteed by the First Amendment. Thus, people can organize themselves to achieve common purposes and can express personal opinions without these rights being abridged. However, freedom of assembly does not extend to people who meet for the purpose of conspiring to bomb a department store or for other purposes which are a threat to others. Freedom of the press does not prevent a newspaper from being sued when it prints libelous statements. And as Justice Oliver Wendell Holmes declared, "The most stringent protection of free speech would not protect a man falsely shouting 'Fire!' in a theatre and causing a panic." Thus, the freedoms of each individual, guaranteed by the Constitution, must be somewhat limited if

"24? TSK! TSK! HE'LL GET HIS WRIST SLAPPED FOR THAT!"

"HEY! I JUST KILLED 24 PEOPLE—AND YOU GOT THAT CONFESSION WITHOUT ADVISING ME OF MY RIGHTS!"

(The Supreme Court's insistence on protecting a suspect's rights has sometimes complicated law enforcement.)

public order and the rights of others are to be preserved.

There are times, however, when the boundaries between First Amendment rights and community rights are not clear-cut. This is particulary true when the exercise of free speech and press conflict with the taste and standards of the community. A novel which is considered to be a masterpiece in literary circles may be considered "obscene literature" by the general community. What is the meaning of "obscene"? What are community standards? How can the effects of such literature on the community be measured? Obviously, questions like these are not easily answered by the courts.

The procedural rights of suspected or accused criminals can also conflict with the welfare of the community. For example, the Constitution does protect people against "unreasonable searches and

seizures," against self-incrimination, and against being detained without a *writ of habeas corpus*—an order, issued by a court, to show cause for such detentions.

While recent court decisions have supported stringent adherence to these procedural rights, many law enforcement officials and others maintain that such protection of suspected criminals inhibits control of crime. They claim the safety of the community is thus threatened.

This conflict of individual and community interests has been at issue in recent years with respect to suspected drug pushers. The distribution of hard drugs has serious and harmful consequences for society. Yet such constitutional protections as the prohibition of "unreasonable searches and seizures" have often prevented officials from apprehending those who are suspected of distributing such drugs. Groups concerned with the preser-

471

vation of civil liberties argue that the denial of constitutional rights, even to suspected criminals, will lead to the infringement of the rights of law-abiding citizens as well. Groups concerned with the problem of crime believe that the need to protect society is more imperative than the need to protect the rights of suspected criminals. Such arguments must certainly be weighed and considered by the courts when constitutional questions are at stake.

The courts also have had to find the proper balance between community welfare and individual civil rights in regard to equal public education. Though the Supreme Court has declared that racial segregation in public schools denies "equal protection of the laws," it has had to give the lower courts discretion in determining the appropriate rate of desegregation necessary to preserve public order.

■ *Public versus private action.* Another distinct problem arises when private individuals violate individual rights. Except for the Thirteenth Amendment, all constitutional provisions concerning individual rights apply restrictions specifically to government; the Bill of Rights limits Congress and the Fourteenth Amendment applies specifically to the states. A crucial question that the courts have to answer is whether the "equal protection" clause can be extended to restrain individuals who violate civil liberties and rights.

Consider a situation in which a person is fired from his job by a nongovernmental employer for expressing a particular political point of view. Such an action would violate the right of that employee to freedom of speech. It would be difficult to challenge such a violation of a right in the courts, however, for government action is not involved.

Similarly, if a *public* school refuses to admit a student because of his race, this would violate the student's right to an equal education and would be a denial of "equal protection of the laws." If the student's civil right, however, is violated by a private school, can the government intercede to protect the individual?

Because of such constitutional questions, the definitions of individual rights and freedoms are never clear-cut. Each case involving such questions must be decided by the courts on the basis of different factors. The judges who make decisions must determine the meaning and limitations of individual rights in the Constitution and weigh these rights against other constitutional, moral, and social questions surrounding each specific case.

Review questions

1. Why did the states insist that the Bill of Rights be included in the Constitution?
2. Explain the difference between civil liberties and civil rights.

Nationalizing the Bill of Rights

Constitutional law is constantly changing because the Supreme Court's interpretations of the Constitution tend to reflect the changing attitudes of the national community. Such a change has taken place in the twentieth century with regard to civil liberties. The protection of personal freedoms, once thought to be exclusively

the duty of the states is now regarded as the national government's responsibility.

Early interpretations of the Bill of Rights. The Bill of Rights was added to the Constitution in 1791 to safeguard individual rights against encroachment by the national government. But the question of whether the provisions also applied to the states remained unsettled for more than forty years. When the question was finally brought before the Supreme Court in 1833, the Court determined that the Bill of Rights applied to the federal government alone. For almost a century thereafter, individuals had to rely on their own state governments to safeguard civil liberties against state infringements.

■ *Barron v. Baltimore.* The first decision on this question was handed down in 1833 by Chief Justice John Marshall. Barron was the owner of a wharf in Baltimore. The city of Baltimore had diverted several streams while paving streets. The diverted streams deposited dirt near Barron's wharf, making it too shallow for some boats. Barron claimed that his property was rendered useless and that he had thus been deprived of property without "compensation" in violation of the Fifth Amendment. Although the initial verdict of the state trial court was in Barron's favor, the decision was later reversed by the state court of appeals. Barron took his case to the Supreme Court.

The Supreme Court, however, decided that Barron's suit was not a federal matter and dismissed the case. In his opinion, the Chief Justice established that the Fifth Amendment pertained only to those cases brought against the national government. State and local governments could not be sued for violations of the Fifth Amendment: "Each state established a constitution for itself, and, in that constitution, provided such limitations and restrictions on the powers of its particular government as its judgment dictated." Marshall concluded that "These amendments [the Bill of Rights] demanded security against the apprehended encroachments of the general [national] government—not against those of the local governments."[1]

[1]7 *Peters* 243 (1833).

■ *The Fourteenth Amendment and the Slaughter-House Cases.* In keeping with the *Barron v. Baltimore* decision, individuals had to rely almost exclusively on their state constitutions or state legislation for protection of civil liberties and rights. But after the Civil War, with the adoption of the Fourteenth Amendment, parties to civil liberties cases began to invoke the amendment for protection of various freedoms against state encroachment. The first case argued under the Fourteenth Amendment concerned the constitutionality of a Louisiana law that created a slaughter-house monopoly and kept other companies from competing in that state. The independent butchers of New Orleans protested the statute on the grounds that it violated their "privileges and immunities," and their right to "due process of law" and "equal protection of the laws" guaranteed by the Fourteenth Amendment.

In the *Slaughter-House Cases* of 1873, the Supreme Court gave a very narrow interpretation to the Fourteenth Amendment so that it would not interfere with the laws of the states. The Court answered the plaintiff's first argument by distinguishing between United States citizenship and state citizenship:

"Not only may a man be a citizen of the United States without being a citizen of a state, but an important element is necessary to convert the former into the latter. He must reside within the state to make him a citizen of it, but it is only necessary that he should be born or naturalized in the United States to be a citizen of the Union."

On the basis of this distinction, the Court distinguished further between the privileges and immunities of the citizens of the United States and the privileges and immunities of the citizens of a state. Since the Fourteenth Amendment expressly prohibits only the violation of the "privileges and immunities of the citizens of the United States," the Court explained, it is in no way a limitation on the states and their jurisdiction over state citizenship. Thus the right to do business within a state—which was at issue in the *Slaughter-House Cases*—was a privilege of state citizenship and as such, was "left to the state governments for security and protection."[2]

The Court also dismissed the other arguments of the plaintiffs in the case. In the opinion of the Court, the Louisiana law did not violate due process of law. And finally the Court contended that since the "equal protection of the laws" clause of the Fourteenth Amendment had been written only to apply to emancipated blacks, it was not applicable to the parties in the *Slaughter-House Cases*.

The Supreme Court thus maintained essentially the same views regarding the Fourteenth Amendment that it had expounded earlier with respect to the Bill of Rights in *Barron v. Baltimore*. It left the responsibility for protecting individual liberties and rights almost entirely within the jurisdiction of the states and outside of the national government's constitutional powers. The Court's verdict in the *Slaughter-House Cases* reflected the dominant importance still given to the concept of state sovereignty in the late nineteenth century.

Extension of the Bill of Rights to the states. A gradual change in the Court's interpretations of civil liberties began in 1925. Since that time, as it has made decisions in specific cases and controversies, the Court has included more and more provisions of the Bill of Rights within the meaning of the "due process of law" clause in the Fourteenth Amendment. By 1970, these Court decisions provided a constitutional basis by which the national government could force the states to uphold all of the individual freedoms guaranteed by the Bill of Rights. This included not only the generalized freedoms in the First Amendment but also the procedural rights specified in the Fourth, Fifth, Sixth, Seventh, and Eighth Amendments.

■ *Including the Bill of Rights in "due process."* The first time that the Supreme Court included part of the Bill of Rights in its interpretation of the Fourteenth Amendment was in the historic case of *Gitlow v. New York* in 1925. Benjamin Gitlow had been convicted in New York, under the state's Criminal Anarchy Act, for distributing a publication that advocated the violent overthrow of government. Gitlow challenged the conviction on the grounds that the New York law violated his right to due process of law guaranteed by the Fourteenth Amendment.

The Supreme Court upheld the constitutionality of the New York law and Gitlow's conviction as well. However, the majority opinion handed down by the Court included a new definition of the meaning of the Fourteenth Amendment's "due process of law" clause. The Court said, "we may and do assume that freedom of speech and of the press—which are protected by the First Amendment from abridgment by Congress—are among the fundamental personal rights and 'liberties' protected by the due process clause of the Fourteenth Amendment from impairment by the states."[3]

This was the first time the Court formally recognized that the "due process" clause prevented a *state* from encroaching on the freedoms of speech and press guaranteed by the First Amendment. An important implication of the *Gitlow* decision was that the states as well as the federal government could be restrained from violating

---

[2] *16 Wallace 36 (1873).*

[3] *268 U.S. 652 (1925).*

other liberties guaranteed by the Constitution.

By nullifying a state law in a subsequent decision, the Court went a step further and gave the federal government a new role of *protecting* individual civil liberties against actual state violations. The first time that the Supreme Court declared a state law unconstitutional under the "due process" clause of the Fourteenth Amendment was in 1931 in *Near v. Minnesota*. The law in question, known as the Minnesota "gag law," permitted the suppression of newspapers which had published malicious, defamatory, or obscene materials. The law provided that injunctions on such publications could be lifted only if the publishers could first prove that they would print no such materials in the future.

While the Supreme Court's opinion noted that any publisher must take the consequences for issuing what is "improper,

BAD DENT IN BILL OF RIGHTS

Fitzpatrick in the St. Louis Post-Dispatch

(In the late 1940's, the Supreme Court still refused to make criminal procedural rights binding on the states.)

mischievous or illegal" after it was published, freedom of the press—which was guaranteed specifically by the First Amendment and through the "due process" clause of the Fourteenth Amendment extended to the states—meant "freedom from prior restraint." Thus a newspaper could not be sued for what it intended to publish. It could only be sued after the questionable material had appeared in print and was for sale. Therefore, the Minnesota law was declared to be an unconstitutional restraint of freedom of the press.

Once the Court had set a precedent for including civil liberties within the meaning of the "due process" clause, it was not long before all of the First Amendment provisions were "interpreted into" the Fourteenth Amendment. By 1947, the Court had decided through various cases that many of the rights in the Bill of Rights—including the freedoms of religion, petition, and assembly as well as the freedoms of speech and press—were all individual rights that could not be abridged by the states.

■ *Including procedural rights in "due process."* The interpretation of the "due process" clause to include the procedural rights of those accused of criminal acts has taken longer than the nationalization of First Amendment rights. This has been due, in part, to the reluctance of the Supreme Court to interfere with specific court procedures of the states. Since World War II, however, the Court has gradually defined the criminal procedural rights of the Bill of Rights into the meaning of the Fourteenth Amendment and has used such interpretations to limit certain procedures of the state courts.

In 1949, in the case of *Wolf v. Colorado*, the Court declared that the Fourth Amendment restriction against "unreasonable searches and seizures" was binding on the states through the Fourteenth Amendment. In the same decision, however, the Court

Courtesy of Handelsman and Saturday Review.
Copyright © 1967 by Saturday Review, Inc.

"If that click on the extension is you, Mother, remember that wiretap evidence is inadmissible."

(Legalizing the use of wiretaps has to be weighed against their potential threat to civil liberties.)

held that evidence gathered through such a procedure could be admitted to a state-court proceeding. Eleven years later, the Court decided that evidence acquired by state officials through any unreasonable searches and seizures could not be introduced against a defendant in a federal criminal trial. In 1961, in another decision, the same restriction was made applicable to state court trials.

During the 1960's, other constitutional procedural rights were made binding on state criminal proceedings. Among these were the Sixth Amendment guarantees of legal counsel and jury trials to all defendants in criminal prosecutions, and the Fifth Amendment guarantee against self-incrimination.

It is one of the ironies of America's pluralistic political system that while the Supreme Court has broadened the constitutional protection of individual procedural rights, Congress recently began to pass legislation that might increase the power of the federal government to curtail certain rights of suspected criminals. One example of such legislation is the Omnibus Crime Control and Safe Streets Act of 1968, which enlarged the federal government's authority to acquire evidence against suspected criminals through the use of wiretapping. In another crime-control law passed in 1970 for the District of Columbia, Congress included a controversial "no knock" provision. The "no knock" law permits federal officials, who have warrants showing "probable cause," to enter the premises of suspected criminals without warning to conduct searches and seizures. This law is intended to enable authorities to gather evidence against "pushers" of illegal drugs before such evidence can be destroyed.

Groups concerned with civil liberties may contend that the "no knock" provision is an invasion of the individual right to privacy—already defined into the meaning of "due process" by the Supreme Court. Whether the Supreme Court will consider the procedure to be an unconstitutional infringement of civil liberty remains to be tested by a specific case. The matter illustrates the ever-present need to find a proper balance between the rights and liberties of individuals and the welfare of the general community.

Religious freedom and the wall of separation. Unlike other civil liberties, the First Amendment restriction on government with respect to religion is twofold: "Congress shall make no law respecting the establishment of religion, or prohibiting the free exercise thereof. . . ." This means that Congress is prevented not only from interfering with an individual's freedom to worship according to his own beliefs but also from establishing an official religion of the state. The latter restriction was of particular concern to Americans in the eighteenth century. The diverse religious groups which had settled in America sought to prevent the kinds of persecution they had experienced abroad in countries with "established" religions.

In 1934, the First Amendment provisions on religion were nationalized when the Supreme Court included them within the meaning of the "due process" clause in the Fourteenth Amendment. As with other constitutional liberties, the exact meaning of this First Amendment restriction also has had to be interpreted by the Court. With respect to the "free exercise" of religion, Court decisions have generally involved defining the proper balance between individual and community rights. The issue of the "establishment" clause has been more complex. The precise meaning of "separation between church and state" is still open-ended and has been evolving as specific government activities concerning religion have been challenged through the judicial system.

■ The free exercise of religion. A person is free to worship as he pleases as long as the religious doctrines he upholds and the rituals that he practices do not result in injury to accepted community standards of public safety, morals, or health. In a specific case, the Supreme Court in 1879 upheld the conviction of a Mormon who had been practicing polygamy. The Court said that polygamy could be punished as a crime even though it was sanctioned by the Mormon religion. Religious freedom, like all freedoms, is not absolute.

In other cases, the Supreme Court has nullified various laws that it considered unconstitutional restraints on religious freedom. In 1943, for example, the court determined that a state could not tax the distribution of religious material by a religious group.

In the same year, overturning an earlier decision, the Court held that a state could not compel the members of a religious group to salute the flag when such an expression was contrary to the group's religious doctrines. In this instance, the Court noted that such a religious belief presented no "clear and present danger" to the interests of the state.

■ Separation of church and state. In defining the "establishment" clause of the First Amendment, the Supreme Court has held that there must be a wall of separation between church and state. That is, the government must not actively aid, support, or encourage any church or religious activity.

The majority of cases dealing with this issue have concerned the role of church and state with regard to education. The Court has had to decide whether or not certain government activity—such as the financing of transportation and textbooks for students in parochial schools, the use of public-school time and facilities for religious instruction, and the sanctioning of official prayers—constitutes government "establishment of religion."

In the case of Everson v. Board of Education (1947), the Supreme Court considered the issue regarding local governmental aid to Catholic parochial schools. The State of New Jersey had authorized local school boards to reimburse parents for bus transportation whether their children attended public or private schools. The New Jersey law was challenged by some taxpayers as a violation of the separation of church and state. In its opinion, the Court reasoned that New Jersey was not contributing money or supporting religious schools but was only providing a public service to all school children. In the words of Justice Hugo

Black, the law did "no more than provide a general program to help parents get their children, regardless of their religion, safely and expeditiously to and from accredited schools."[4]

In another case, however, the Court held that a board of education could not use tax-supported property for religious instruction. The case, *McCollum v. Board of Education* (1948), involved an Illinois program where students attended classes for religious instruction on public school property.

The distinction between what is considered an aid to religion and what is not was even more closely defined in the 1952 case of *Zorach v. Clausen*. This case established a precedent regarding the question of whether state or local governments could authorize public schools to give students time off for religious instruction. New York City had a program that released students to attend religious instruction outside the schools but during school hours. The students had to have parental permission, and the churches made reports to the schools of those who attended. In this decision, the Court retreated from its previous stand and held that the New York program did not violate the First Amendment. In the *McCollum* case, the Court said that the public school was actually used to promote religious instruction while in the *Zorach* case, it maintained that "the public schools do no more than accommodate their schedules to a program of outside religious instruction."[5]

The Supreme Court's most controversial decision regarding the religious question and the establishment clause was in *Engel v. Vitale* (1962). In this case it was held that the recitation of prayers in a public school clearly violated the First Amend-

[4] *330 U.S. 1 (1947).*
[5] *343 U.S. 306 (1952).*

From Herblock's *Straight Herblock* (Simon & Schuster, 1964)

"EVERY SCHOOLCHILD SHOULD BE MADE TO PRAY AGAINST GOVERNMENT INTERFERENCE WITH PRIVATE LIVES."

(There was much antagonism toward the Court after its decision forbidding prayers in the public schools.)

ment. New York State had adopted a program of daily classroom prayers that were not linked to any particular religion. The state's Board of Regents recommended that all the schools use them. The parents of ten students in New Hyde Park, New York challenged the Regents' prayer in the state court of appeals, which upheld the prayer as long as no student was compelled to join in the recitation. The Supreme Court, however, reversed this decision declaring that a "program of daily classroom invocation of God's blessing . . . is a religious activity." The Court concluded that the prayer program "officially establishes the religious beliefs embodied in the Regents' prayer," and that even though the prayer was "denominationally neutral" it still violated the establishment clause.[6]

The decision in the *Engel* case caused a furor. The Court was accused of "driving God out of the schools" and of "abolishing God." Some people have seen the Court's interpretation as interfering with the moral standards taught in the state educational systems. On the other hand, some laymen and religious leaders have found that the Court's stand is admirable because it upholds the doctrine of governmental neutrality with regard to religion.

Interpretation of the wall-of-separation doctrine is still somewhat ambiguous. Some decisions show a rigid use of the doctrine and others illustrate a liberal approach. The Supreme Court has held that a religious oath for office requiring an expressed belief in God is unconstitutional. Yet, it has held that Sunday closing laws are not unconstitutional, for even though they may once have had religious connotations, today they achieve secular goals such as providing a day of rest, amusement, and for families to be together.

The latest decisions of the Court suggest that it will continue to take a firm stand on the separation of church and state. Probably the most difficult problem it will have to face is whether extensive federal aid to education should be granted to religious and non-religious private schools. Token aid by state and local governments has been upheld. The Court, however, may not be able to rely on these decisions as a basis for solving the problem of federal aid to education on the national level.

Review questions

1. Cite the Supreme Court cases that were instrumental in the "nationalization" of the rights of the First Amendment.
2. What was the significance of the Supreme Court's rulings in the *Everson* and *McCollum* cases?

Policies on Civil Rights

Interpretations of the scope and meaning of civil rights have been evolving for the past several decades. The general trend of policy has been to follow an ever-widening definition of civil rights to include more and more areas considered necessary to human dignity. Along with civil liberties, civil rights have been expanded principally by means of outputs from the judiciary. Demands have been made by individuals and groups in the form of cases and controversies, and court decisions have determined government policy.

In order to make decisions regarding civil rights, the courts have had to hinge their decisions on constitutional principles.

The "equal protection" clause of the Fourteenth Amendment and the guarantee of voting rights in the Fifteenth Amendment, in addition to the "due process" clause of the Fourteenth Amendment, have provided vital constitutional supports to expanding civil rights.

Civil rights: a state matter. The significance of the Fourteenth Amendment on civil rights was first tested in the *Civil Rights Cases* in 1883. The amendment, which prohibits states from denying due process of law or equal protection of the laws, also authorizes Congress to enforce its provisions. In 1875 Congress had passed a Civil Rights Act, not unlike the private accommodations section of the 1963–64 Civil Rights bill. The 1875 act made it illegal for

[6] *370 U.S. 421 (1962).*

anyone to discriminate in private accommodations including inns, theaters, and places of public amusement. The congressional justification for passing the Civil Rights Act of 1875 had been the authority granted to Congress in the Fourteenth Amendment.

The Supreme Court, however, declared the Act unconstitutional. The prohibitions of the Fourteenth Amendment, the Court noted, were directed at the actions of state governments. Thus Congress was authorized to enforce the prohibitions against state laws and acts only, and not against *private* acts, which were entirely within state jurisdiction. In passing the law of 1875, Congress had gone beyond its constitutional authority in curbing private rather than state abuses.

Essentially, the Court was saying that within state jurisdictions, a right was a civil right only if it was declared to be so by the state. As a result of the *Civil Rights Cases,* Congress could not take positive action to curb violations of civil liberties and rights unless abridgment by the states had occurred. On the other hand, the states could sanction encroachments on individual rights and liberties by simply refusing to take any action at all.

"Separate but equal." Despite the Fourteenth Amendment provision that no state may "deny to any person within its jurisdiction the equal protection of the laws," racial segregation has been a fact of life in many parts of the United States. After the Reconstruction era, some states began to pass laws that required racial separation in public facilities including transportation and recreational facilities, residential areas, and public institutions such as schools. Though "separate," these facilities had to be "equal" in order to avoid violation of the Fourteenth Amendment's "equal protection" clause.

■ *Plessy v. Ferguson.* The separate-but-

equal doctrine was first stated by the Supreme Court in *Plessy v. Ferguson* (1896). A Louisiana statute required that all railroad companies "carrying passengers . . . in this state shall provide equal but separate accommodations for the white and colored races." The Supreme Court upheld the statute, saying that the Fourteenth Amendment could not possibly have been intended

". . . to abolish distinctions based upon color, or to enforce social, as distinguished from political, equality, or a commingling of the two races upon terms unsatisfactory to either. Laws permitting, and even requiring their separation in places where they are liable to be brought into contact do not necessarily imply the inferiority of either race to the other, and have been generally, if not universally, recognized as within the competency of the State legislatures in the exercise of their police power."[7]

Thus, state laws requiring the separation of the races, the Court said, were perfectly legal. The *Plessy* decision implied that social prejudices could not be overcome by legislation and that the Negro should not attempt to obtain equality by "commingling" with the white race. In its formal opinion, the Court considered that a state law had forced segregation in railroad cars, but that separate facilities were not "unequal" and, therefore, the state law did not violate the "equal protection" clause of the Fourteenth Amendment. The Court added that the Louisiana law was "reasonable" because it reflected the dominant interests and traditions of its citizens. In upholding the validity of separate but equal facilities in 1896, the Supreme Court itself merely reflected the customs and traditions of the time.

Yet, the prevailing mores did not prevent

[7] *163 U.S. 537 (1896).*

Justice John Marshall Harlan, a Kentuckian, from writing a vigorous and impassioned dissenting opinion. To Harlan, the "separate but equal" doctrine was a clear violation of constitutional rights. Accommodations that are supposedly "equal" are really not, and state segregation laws implied the inferiority of blacks. In Harlan's opinion:

"The destinies of the two races in this country are indissolubly linked together and the interests of both require that the common government of all shall not permit the seeds of race hate to be planted under the sanction of law. What can more certainly arouse race hate, what more certainly create and perpetuate a feeling of distrust between these races, than state enactments which in fact proceed on the ground that colored citizens are so inferior and degraded that they cannot be allowed to sit in public coaches occupied by white citizens?"[8]

Harlan's prophetic dissent was completely ignored for many years.

■ *Implications of "separate but equal."* It is, of course, impossible to speculate what the consequences would have been if the Supreme Court had handed down different decisions in the *Civil Rights Cases* and *Plessy v. Ferguson.* Since the nation was still recovering from the Civil War, it is quite possible that state segregation might have yielded. Racial separation had not yet become firmly entrenched by a century of tradition. To say this is not to overlook the difficulties that would have existed in overcoming the prevailing social attitudes. But it can not be said that the *Plessy* decision was the only decision possible in the late nineteenth century. The very fact that there was a vigorous dissent in the *Plessy* case indicates that another result might have been possible.

Following the decision in *Plessy v. Fer-*

[8] *163 U.S. 537 (1896) (dissenting opinion).*

guson, many states took advantage of the Court's approval of "separate but equal" and passed new laws providing for racial segregation. In the first decade of the twentieth century, the Court was extremely lenient and permitted state segregation of the races regardless of whether the facilities were in fact "equal." In one case it went so far as to say that a school district did not have to provide any high school at all for black children, even though it had one for whites.

The inequalities of state segregation that were pointed out by Justice Harlan in 1896 soon became evident, though, to an increasing number of people. As time passed, the Court became more and more insistent that the states provide "equal" facilities, at least in physical properties.

End of "separate but equal." By the time the Supreme Court held segregation of public education to be unconstitutional in 1954, precedents already had been established that weakened the "separate but equal" tradition. As early as 1938, the Court held, in *Missouri ex rel. Gaines v. Canada,* that the refusal of a state to admit an applicant to its state law school solely on the basis of the applicant's race was a denial of "equal protection of the laws." The state of Missouri had no separate law school for blacks and, in order to maintain racial segregation, had devised a plan whereby blacks would be granted tuition if they went out of state for their legal education. On the basis of this plan, Lloyd Gaines, a black citizen of Missouri, had been denied admission to the University of Missouri Law School. Gaines took his case to the Supreme Court. In its decision, the Supreme Court said that the Missouri plan did not release that state from its responsibility to provide equal educational facilities for blacks and whites within its borders. Gaines was thus "entitled to be admitted to the law school of the state university in the absence of other and proper provision for his legal training within the state."[9]

Ten years later, the Court reaffirmed its 1938 decision and held in *Sipuel v. University of Oklahoma* that a black student could not be denied admission to the University of Oklahoma Law School if whites were permitted to attend. And in *McLaurin v. Oklahoma State Regents* (1950), the Court decided that blacks attending the University of Oklahoma Law School had to be accorded the same and not just "equal" facilities to those of whites.

Relevant to the *Gaines, Sipuel,* and *McLaurin* cases, the states of Missouri and Oklahoma did not have separate law schools for blacks. Since the states had provided legal education for whites without making any provision whatsoever for blacks, the Court could justify its decision that such action was a denial of equal protection of the laws. But if the states made provisions for separate law schools for blacks, would not the Court then hold such action to be in conformity with the "separate but equal" doctrine?

■ *Sweatt v. Painter.* In an actual case, the Supreme Court decided that separate law schools could not in fact be equal. The decision, *Sweatt v. Painter* (1950), set the stage for the final blow to the "separate but equal" doctrine.

In 1946, at a time when no Texas law school admitted blacks, Sweatt applied for admission to the University of Texas Law School. Because his application was turned down on the grounds of his race, he appealed to a state court for a *writ of mandamus* which would compel university officials to admit him. As a result of a delay in state-court action, Texas gained six months in which to provide equal law school facilities for blacks. During the

[9] *305 U.S. 337 (1938).*

482

course of the appeal, a law school for blacks was opened in Texas. The state courts found that the new law school offered Sweatt the same "privileges, advantages, and opportunity for the study of law" as those given to white students.

Sweatt then took his case to the Supreme Court. The Court found that the facilities offered by Texas to blacks and whites were clearly unequal. In reaching a decision, the Court considered first whether the separate facilities in Texas for legal education were equal. It found that the new law school for blacks had no independent faculty or library. Four members of the University of Texas Law School faculty taught courses in both institutions. Although the library of the new school was supposed to have ten thousand volumes, virtually no books had arrived. There was no provision for a full-time librarian. As a result of these defects, the school had not been accredited. By comparison, the University of Texas Law School—with a student body of close to nine hundred, a library of over 65,000 volumes, a law review, moot court facilities, scholarship funds, an active alumni with access to numerous state legal positions, and full accreditation—was obviously superior. The Supreme Court found that the University of Texas Law School "may properly be considered one of the nation's ranking law schools." Most important the Court decided after its investigation that no separate schooling could ever be equal in legal education:

"Few students and no one who has practiced law would choose to study in [a] . . . vacuum, removed from the interplay of ideas and the exchange of views with which the law is concerned. The law school to which Texas is willing to admit petitioner [Sweatt] excludes from its student body members of the racial groups [whites] which number 85 percent of the popula-

tion of the state and include most of the lawyers, witnesses, jurors, judges and other officials with whom petitioner will inevitably be dealing when he becomes a member of the Texas bar. With such a substantial and significant segment of society excluded, we cannot conclude that the education offered petitioner is substantially equal to that which he would receive if admitted to the University of Texas Law School."[10]

■ *Brown v. Board of Education of Topeka.* In 1954, in one of the most far-reaching decisions in the history of the Supreme Court, the principle that separate was *not* equal was extended to all public education. The decision actually involved four separate cases in which black students were seeking admission to all-white public schools in the states of Kansas, South Carolina, Virginia, and Delaware. Because the four separate cases involved a single legal question, the Court determined that they should be heard and decided together.

The significance of the *Brown* case prompted the filing of amici curiae briefs by a number of groups interested in civil rights. (See also Chapter 2, page 37.) The cases on behalf of the students were argued by a legal team led by Thurgood Marshall of the NAACP.

The decision of the Court was unanimous. The Court found that the school districts in the case had separate schools of blacks and whites which were relatively equal with regard to "buildings, curricula, qualifications and salaries of teachers, and other 'tangible' factors." But tangible factors were not enough. The Court went on to say, "We must look instead to the effect of segregation itself on public education."

Education, the Court said, is the very keystone of individual success in all endeavors today. It is "a principal instrument in awakening the child to cultural values, in preparing him for later professional training and in helping him to adjust normally to this environment." Even though the tangible properties may be equal among segregated schools, this does not mean that they will have an equal impact on children. The Court concluded that "separate educational facilities are inherently unequal" and that such segregation "is a denial of the equal protection of the laws."[11]

Since the Court was aware that its decision would not be easily implemented, it refrained from dealing with implementation until the following year. In its 1955 decision, the Court said that desegregation

[11] *347 U.S. 483 (1954).*

Fitzpatrick in the St. Louis Post-Dispatch

CARRYING ON THE "SEPARATE BUT EQUAL" THEORY

("Separate but equal" Supreme Courts could only result in the inadequacy of one of the paired institutions.)

[10] *339 U.S. 629 (1950).*

was to be carried out with "all deliberate speed," but it permitted the district courts to determine the proper rate for desegregation. Because the Court took into account the impact its decision would have, it did not force immediate integration on states with a tradition of segregation. Consequently the rate of progress has been slow. By 1966, less than 10 percent of the black students in seventeen southern states, including the border states and the District of Columbia, were attending integrated classrooms. By 1970, all southern school districts had begun to end dual systems, but 85 percent of the black students were still attending schools which were predominately black. Nationwide, three out of every four black students attended schools where there were majorities of black students. Racial separation in public schools is as great if not greater in the North than in the South. The doctrine of equal education for all has been clearly established by the judiciary, but the courts alone can not enforce their decisions.

Civil rights legislation. Since the report of President Truman's Committee on Civil Rights in 1947, occupants of the White House have been urging Congress to pass various types of civil rights legislation. The 1954 decision of the Supreme Court provided additional impetus for Congress to take positive action. Finally, in 1957 Congress passed its first civil rights legislation in eighty-two years. Civil rights legislation passed since 1957 has dealt with the safeguarding of voting rights and federal protection against discrimination in public accommodations, jobs, and housing.

■ *Protecting the right to vote.* The 1957 civil rights legislation pertained to voting rights. Essentially, the Civil Rights Act of 1957 empowers the Civil Rights Commission to investigate any situation where the denial of suffrage because of race or color is suspected. Before 1957, a black who had

been denied his right to vote had to take his case into the courts. This was a costly and time-consuming procedure and few people took advantage of it. The 1957 Civil Rights Act gave the Attorney General of the United States the authority to file a suit against any state official who denied a person his right to vote.

Three years later, in 1960, Congress strengthened this legislation with another Civil Rights Act that gave the Justice Department the authorization to send voting referees to those areas where a "pattern or practice" of discrimination in voting had become evident. The voting referees were supposed to encourage the registration of black voters.

The Voting Rights Act of 1965 augmented the referee concept by barring all discriminatory "tests and devices" wherever less than 50 percent of the eligible voters had been registered in 1964. Examiners were appointed by the Justice Department to register qualified voters in these areas. (See also Chapter 6, page 147.)

The increase in civil rights legislation being put out by Congress culminated with the sweeping Civil Rights Act of 1964 which was the first major piece of civil rights legislation since Reconstruction. It was passed only after much debate and a lengthy Senate filibuster. The 1964 Act first fortified the voting rights acts of 1957 and 1960. The Act made it illegal for any local or state voter-registration procedure to be applied in a discriminatory way, and prohibited the voiding of registrations on the basis of minor errors on registration forms. The 1964 Act also required that all literacy tests be given in written form unless the Attorney General, in agreement with state and local authorities, allowed oral tests. The Act provided, further, that any person with a sixth-grade education had to be considered literate.

■ *Public accommodations.* The 1964 Act

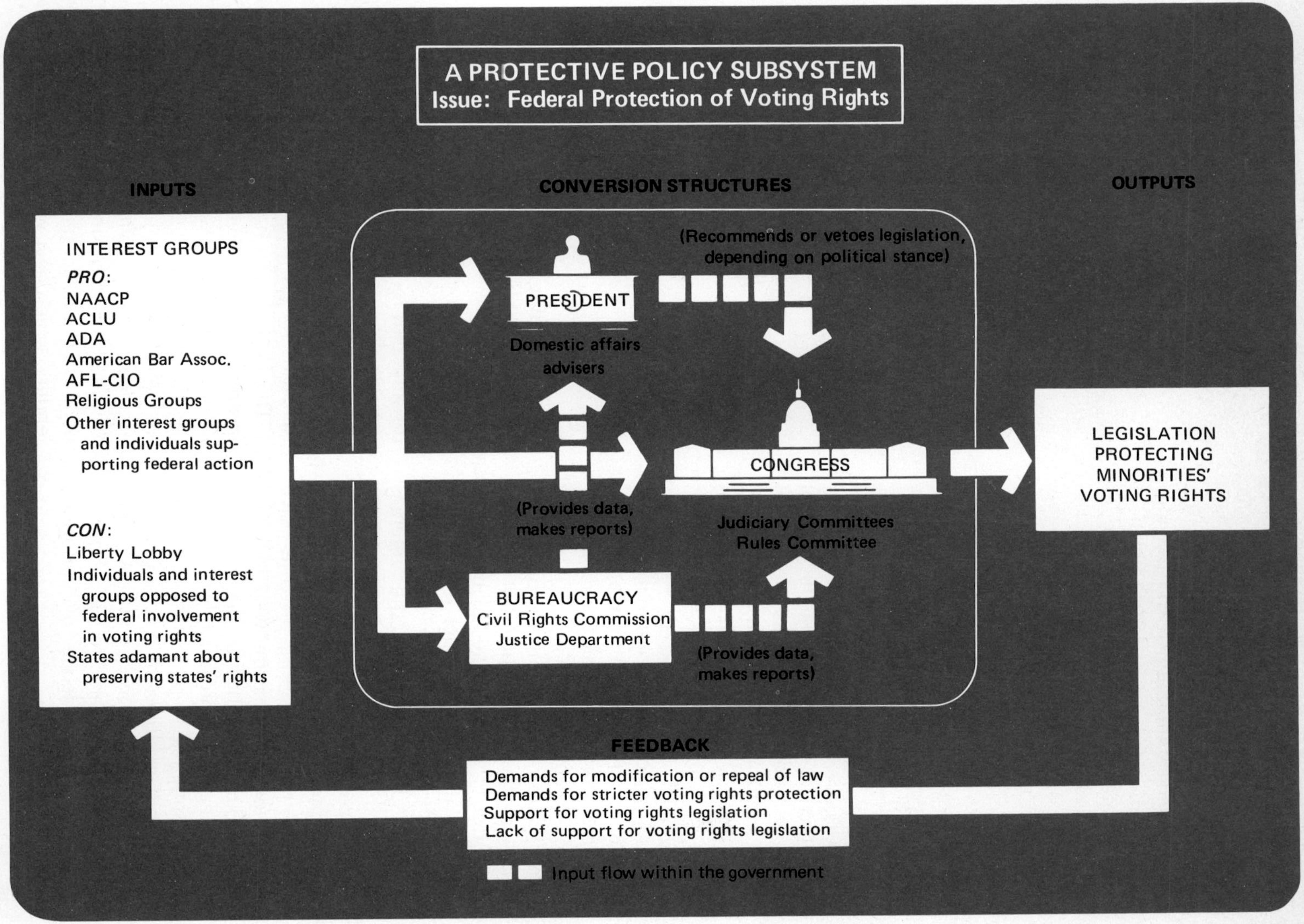

A PROTECTIVE POLICY SUBSYSTEM
Issue: Federal Protection of Voting Rights

INPUTS

CONVERSION STRUCTURES

OUTPUTS

INTEREST GROUPS

PRO:
NAACP
ACLU
ADA
American Bar Assoc.
AFL-CIO
Religious Groups
Other interest groups
and individuals sup-
porting federal action

CON:
Liberty Lobby
Individuals and interest
groups opposed to
federal involvement
in voting rights
States adamant about
preserving states' rights

PRESIDENT
Domestic affairs
advisers

(Recommends or vetoes legislation,
depending on political stance)

CONGRESS

Judiciary Committees
Rules Committee

(Provides data,
makes reports)

BUREAUCRACY
Civil Rights Commission
Justice Department

(Provides data,
makes reports)

LEGISLATION
PROTECTING
MINORITIES'
VOTING RIGHTS

FEEDBACK

Demands for modification or repeal of law
Demands for stricter voting rights protection
Support for voting rights legislation
Lack of support for voting rights legislation

■ ■ Input flow within the government

485

also established national criteria for ending discrimination in public accommodations. In setting up these standards, the 1964 legislation preempted any state laws or action supporting discrimination if the lodgings in question were used to house transient guests or interstate travelers, or if the goods sold or entertainment provided moved in interstate commerce. Under this provision, restaurants, movie houses, theaters, hotels, and other "public" establishments were directed to permit access to their facilities without regard to the race, color, or national origin of the customer. The scope of the 1964 Act also extended to nondiscrimination in federally assisted programs. It outlawed some discriminatory employment practices such as the classification of employees into a particular job because of race, or exclusion of such employees from labor unions, or discrimination against minorities in apprenticeship or job-training programs.

Policies of nondiscrimination in housing have emerged from both the executive and legislative branches. In 1962 President Kennedy signed an executive order forbidding discrimination in all housing built with federal assistance. This included not only public housing constructed with federal funds but also private homes when mortgages were guaranteed by the Federal Housing Administration or the Veterans Administration.

In 1966 President Lyndon Johnson began asking Congress to pass more extensive open-housing legislation. In the Civil Rights Act of 1968, measures were included by which discrimination in sale or rental became illegal for approximately 80 percent of all housing. The Department of Housing and Urban Development was authorized to investigate violations, and the Attorney General was empowered to sue whenever there was any evidence of continued discrimination.

Engelhardt in the St. Louis Post-Dispatch

"Back, I say—get back!"

(Many people consider the amassing of data by computer banks a real menace to their individual rights.)

A continuing struggle. National standards for civil liberties and rights have been achieved only after a long and difficult struggle. Only through the combined efforts of many groups and individuals has resistance to federal policies on individual rights been overcome. As a result, the three major conversion structures of the federal government have gradually responded to demands for positive action.

The bureaucracy has also played a role in strengthening the national committment to civil rights. For example, many administrative agencies have enacted regulations that give individuals equal opportunity for employment both within the federal government and in businesses, such as those of defense contractors and home-mortgage lenders, which deal with the government.

Most recently, labor unions have been encouraged to enlist new members from minority groups to win contracts on federally funded construction programs.

While progress has been made in civil rights, many major problems still remain. No governmental authority has asserted or precisely defined the rights of individuals before administrative agencies. These rights vary from agency to agency and from case to case in the same way that the application of the Bill of Rights used to vary within the states.

Despite the development of national standards, private discrimination and private encroachment on individual liberties still remain. The government can encourage people to conform to the spirit of the Bill of Rights and "equal protection" clause of the Fourteenth Amendment, but it can not force them to do so. Most likely, the question of what constitutes a private action and how it can be controlled will be one of continued importance in the immediate future.

Review questions

1. How did *Sweatt v. Painter* (1950) prepare the way for the destruction of the "separate but equal" doctrine?
2. What were the provisions of the 1964 Civil Rights Act? Why was it considered to be the "first major piece of civil rights legislation since Reconstruction"?

Chapter Review

Terms you should know

civil liberties

civil rights

government restraint

Near v. Minnesota

procedural rights

public accommodations

"separate but equal"

Slaughter-House Cases

state sovereignty

Questions about this chapter

1. Explain the origin and meaning of the concept of "government restraint." What problems were caused by the government's adherence to this policy?
2. Which is of greater significance in the determination of individual rights and liberties —the Bill of Rights or the Fourteenth Amendment? Explain.
3. What precedent was established by the Supreme Court's ruling in *Barron v. Baltimore* (1833)? How did the rulings of the Court in the cases of *Gitlow v. New York* (1925) and *Wolf v. Colorado* (1949) affect this precedent?
4. Justify this statement: "The freedom of individuals like the power of government, must have limits." Give specific examples that exhibit this statement.
5. Why has the Fourteenth Amendment needed clarification by the courts?
6. Why has the phrase "separation between church and state" been difficult to interpret? How have the cases of *Zorach v. Clausen* (1952) and *McCollum v. Board of Education* (1948) helped to clarify the issue?
7. On what constitutional principles has the Supreme Court based its decisions regarding civil rights? How has interpretation of these principles changed between the cases of *Plessy v. Ferguson* (1896) and *Brown v. Board of Education* (1954)?
8. What were the provisions of the Civil Rights Acts of 1964 and 1968? Has this legislation completely ended discrimination? Why or why not?

Thought and discussion questions

1. "Some people in the United States during the post-Civil War period believed in immediate equality for freed blacks." How is this statement evidenced by Justice Harlan's dissenting opinion in *Plessy v. Ferguson* (1896)? What other evidence is there to support this statement? Do you think the "traditions and mores" of the times upheld the majority opinion in the *Plessy v. Ferguson* case?

2. The civil rights of equal opportunity to education, housing, etc. are not explicitly stated in the Constitution; yet they have become a part of constitutional law. Discuss how this happened. In your opinion, have the courts been correct in defining these rights as constitutional law?

3. Discuss whether or not "the need to protect society is more imperative than the need to protect the rights of suspected criminals."

Class projects

1. Does your school have a constitution? If so, what rights are you guaranteed? What areas are left open to interpretation? Why? If you were writing a "student bill of rights," what would you include?

2. Try to find out what people think about the right to privacy. Make out a short questionnaire and send it to the following people: your local police chief or commissioner, district attorney, U.S. Congressman, and the local branch of the Civil Liberties Union. Include in this questionnaire such questions as (1) What is your opinion of the "no knock" provision of the crime-control law of 1970; (2) Do you consider it an invasion of the individual's right to privacy? Why or why not? On the basis of the answers received, formulate your own opinion of this provision and explain why this is your viewpoint.

Case Study: The fight for privacy

Modern technology and data-processing techniques are possibly endangering the constitutional rights guaranteed to American citizens. One cherished right, the "right to be let alone" as Supreme Court Justice Louis Brandeis once described it, has been the most threatened by the post-industrial age.

Few people realize the extent of the loss of personal privacy that has occurred in recent years due to technological progress. Apartment houses and office buildings are built with paper-thin walls. Hidden cameras watch while you shop. And banks, credit-card companies, and the Internal Revenue Service have files on almost every individual's income and financial status. It is even predicted that in the next few years, a computer may be programmed so that it can reveal the "private" lives of millions of Americans.

Of course, the computer itself does not invade privacy, but it has been used in ways that do. The huge volume of data that can be stored in a computer is remarkable. This, by itself, has encouraged and is used to justify the collection of many new kinds of information about individuals.

With the assassination of President Kennedy in 1963, the outbreak of urban riots in 1967 and 1968, the spread of campus violence, attacks on the police, and bombings, a great deal of rationalizing has been done to make routine of a new law enforcement concept—the keeping of records by police and military agencies on "persons of interest."

Consequently, with this build-up of information on individuals, there seems to be a need to develop certain rules for determining what information should be stored and who should be allowed access to it. Americans must also consider the broader implications of allowing information about themselves to accumulate so easily.

The use of the computer and electronic "listening devices" (wiretapping and bugging) has long been a subject of controversy in the newspapers, magazines, in the courts, and among politicians. The articles presented in this case study reveal the heated arguments about the right to privacy and the difficulty the government may have in arriving at a policy that satisfies all of the demands.

As you read these excerpts, watch for the answers to these questions:
1. What are the arguments for computerized dossiers in the area of law enforcement?
2. It has been alleged that most people reveal personal facts more readily today than ever before. If this is true, why has such a change occurred?
3. How might law-enforcement data banks endanger the Bill of Rights? Who are the targets of surveillance activity?
4. How can people guard their privacy from the encroachment of the computer?

TIME ESSAY

Personal Privacy v. the Print-Out

Political Scientist Alan F. Westin of Columbia University defines privacy as the right "to determine what information about ourselves we will share with others." . . . Some of this information, by right and necessity, [man] wants to keep to himself. Some of it he will share with his family and friends, some he will admit—often willingly, often reluctantly—to the impersonal organizations he must deal with in daily life. Westin argues that an attack on a man's ability to control what is known about him represents a basic assault on his humanity; to the extent that it is successful, it limits his freedom to be himself.

What makes the trespass on self possible is the fact that a man's life today is largely defined and described by written records, many of which remain potentially available to outsiders. Schools take careful note of his intelligence and keep a detailed record of his academic achievement. His doctors have files on his health; his psychiatrist, if he has one, takes notes on his inner turmoil, his secret fears. . . . Once he has ever served in the military or worked for a defense contractor, the Government knows a fair amount about his family and political associations. If he has moved recently, the storage companies have an inventory of his belongings. If he has ever been charged with a felony, the FBI probably has his fingerprints and often his photograph.

At present, much of this information is scattered over dozens of locations, divided among a host of different agencies. But what if, in the interests of national efficiency, the file keepers of the nation stored their separate masses of data in one gigantic computer bank? What if the recorded lives of millions of Americans were turned into an open book—or, more precisely, an open computer print-out, available to anyone who knows how to punch the proper keys? That, in fact, is what may happen in the next few years. [In 1966], a Budget Bureau task force recommended that the Federal Government establish a National Data Center for the common use of its many agencies. Under this plan, the Government's 3 billion "person-records" that have been compiled by such agencies as the IRS [Internal Revenue Service] and the FBI would be consolidated and computerized.

Although Congress so far has been cool to the federal data-bank idea, it has appropriated funds to help set up limited versions of it in several states. . . . The data-bank idea, moreover, has already been put into being by private business. The life insurance industry has cooperatively established a firm called the Medical Information Bureau, which operates from unlisted offices in five cities, and keeps files on 11 million people who have applied for life insurance. The files contain, among other things, information on the applicant's medical condition, travels, driving record, drinking habits, and even his extramarital affairs. The 2,200 credit-investigating firms that belong to Associated Credit Bureaus, Inc., together have (and trade) information on 100 million people who have applied for credit in department stores and elsewhere.

Age of Exhibitionism

Americans offer surprisingly little resistance to surrendering information about themselves. Giving up personal details is regarded by most people as a fair trade for convenience. Shoppers who like the idea of buying something with checkbooks and credit cards can hardly expect to keep their financial resources or their spending habits a total secret. Even Hollywood's ageless glamour girls have to trade a birth date (although not necessarily the real one) for a passport. And convenient or not, almost everyone acknowledges the right of the Government to know a lot about its citizens.

Nonetheless, experts in the field of privacy fear that the people have become much too indifferent about protecting personal facts that once were considered nobody's business. . . .

. . . One result is that it is becoming harder and harder for people to escape from the mistakes of their past, to move in search of a second chance. The creation of a national data bank could make it virtually impossible. Worse still is the danger of misinformation. An item of information wrongly added or omitted from tomorrow's total-recall data banks might ruin a reputation in minutes. Government and industrial prying into political opinions could produce a generation of cowed conformists.

Columbia's Westin believes that one vital way to save Americans from becoming the victims of their own records is to create laws protecting a man's "data being" just as carefully as present statutes guard his physical being. . . .

Surveillance of Citizens Stirs Debate

By BEN A. FRANKLIN
Special to the New York Times

The practice of collecting information n the personal activities of millions of americans, much of it computerized for uick access by government agencies, has ong been under attack . . . by a handful f critics in Congress led by Senator Sam Ervin Jr., Democrat of North Carolina.

Senator Ervin and other critics feel that ae growth of government surveillance and omputerized intelligence gathering on the ctivities, attitudes and life histories of illions of Americans seriously threatens onstitutionally protected liberties. Pro- nents say the data collection is justified / the requirement to prevent civil dis- ders and to properly protect public offi- als. . . .

In law enforcement, where computer- ed personal dossiers are having their eatest growth and controversy, a per- asive argument is being made that the ectronic processing of more and more telligence information on citizen activi- s serves the cause of justice not only by tching criminals but also by thwarting cial and political confrontations that ight lead to violence.

Resistance Expected

"If someone is out there plotting a riot a bombing," a Federal law enforcement icial says, "I think you will agree that is better for society if we know about and can act to head it off."

Critics of the Government's develop- nt of vast data-bank files expect to try entually to impose a counterbalancing tem of government regulation of com- er operations. But the resistance is pected to be strong. . . .

Counting other kinds of semiautomated ords—mechanical card indexes and ormation on microfilm, for example— Government, alone, already has vari- s kinds of sensitive information on ut 50 million people. The number and iety grows daily.

Jnknown to most, for instance, there now a national computer file in the Transportation Department containing, for police use, the names and offense records of all 2.6 million people in every state who ever had a driver's license suspended or revoked.

Under a law passed this year, the Justice Department is preparing to computerize and distribute nationally to the police and to prosecutors and courts the names of all persons charged anywhere with drug offenses. A drug user's past record no matter how slight, will become instantly available wherever he goes—by teletyped reports from the computer.

With Federal funds, the states also will be urged soon to pool in a vast permanent central computer file all of their arrest and conviction data on persons involved with the local police or brought to court for any reason.

This system would go far beyond the existing computer data bank of the Na- tional Crime Information Center, main- tained by the Federal Bureau of Investi- gation to store and instantly disseminate the names of criminal fugitives and stolen property. . . .

13,200 Names Recorded

To protect the President, for example, the Secret Service has begun a computer- ized intelligence watch on thousands of law abiding but militant critics of national policy. Among other things, the computer can suggest persons for special surveillance in nearly every city in the country when the President travels. Senator Ervin says that he, too, has criticized the President and accordingly may be on the Secret Service list.

The Justice Department's civil disturb- ance group, organized in 1969, to gauge civil disorder tensions by analyzing intel- ligence reports, has 13,200 names elec- tronically etched in its computer file of persons ever connected with riots or re- ported to have urged violence.

Some of this file-keeping activity is ac- cepted even by its critics on a case-by-case basis. A computer file of "malcontents" and the mentally disturbed that actually saves a President from an assassin's bullet, for example, would be hard to question if the data were handled with great privacy and discretion.

But there is no law now to prevent the massive exchange of information from one information system to others.

Many such cross-feeds of data already have occurred or are planned. The De- partment of Housing and Urban Develop- ment, for one, has told Senator Ervin that it is considering meshing its own files of private businessmen and building con- tractors whose reputations it questions with the 200,000 names in the Justice De- partment's computerized organized-crime file.

The judgment of one file—perhaps a mistaken judgment—can thus become a pervasive, governmentwide black mark; an indelible decision unknown to its subject and made and distributed without oppor- tunity for redress. It is this prospect that has stirred the sharpest reaction.

The Army has said that its intelligence branch had formerly conducted surveil- lance of civilian political activity believed to have a bearing on the Army's assign- ment to suppress any possible civil dis- orders in as many as 100 cities. Since last June 9, however, the official policy of the Army has been, officials have said, that the service no longer conducts any such sur- veillance.

'Protected Areas'

The Air Force and the Navy, for their part, justify their own separate intelligence gathering among civilian groups on the ground that in a civil disturbance they may have to give "logistical support" to the Army. . . .

"Prying into these protected areas of an individual's personality, life, habits, beliefs and legal activities," Senator Ervin has declared, "should be none of the business of government even in a good cause."

"This involves more than the currently popular notion of a so-called right to dis- sent," the Senator said recently in an- nouncing hearings on Government con- duct that he has called a "police-state" infringement of free expressions.

"Our system cannot survive if citizen participation is limited merely to register- ing disagreement with official policy. The policies themselves must be the product of the people's views. The protection and encouragement of such participation is a principal purpose of the First Amendment."

He noted that in response to questionnaires, the Civil Service Commission, alone has informed him that it keeps a total of more than 15 million names and index files and personnel dossiers dating back to 1939—10.2 million of them in a "security file" designed to provide "lead information relating to possible questions of suitability involving loyalty and subversive activity." . . .

Irrevocable Prejudice' Seen

A warning against unconstitutional abuses came recently from an important segment of the law-enforcement community. It was included in a 57-page report on the invasion of privacy and Bill of Rights dangers of law-enforcement data banks prepared for the Justice Department's $2.5 million "Project SEARCH."

The project is an experiment in computerizing the police and criminal records of 11 pilot states for national law-enforcement use. SEARCH is an acronym for System for Electronic Analysis and Retrieval of Criminal Histories. . . .

The report insists that only the strictest discretion, control over unauthorized dissemination and right of review of entries by included subjects can save a large interstate criminal-data system from abuses

that "might irrevocably prejudice the concept in the eyes of the general public."

The report makes as a fundamental recommendation for any national data system the requirement favored by Senator Ervin for citizen review of entries. "If a citizen believes that his records are inaccurate or misleadingly incomplete, he should be permitted reasonable opportunities to challenge them," it declares.

Insisting, too, on a strict requirement that the criminal data must be purged periodically of the names of persons who have demonstrated that they are not repeat offenders, the report declares that "society ought to encourage the rehabilitation of offenders by ignor[ing] relatively ancient wrongdoing." . . .

How Many Chinks in Your Privacy Wall?

By Robert P. Hey

Staff correspondent of The Christian Science Monitor

Washington

Jim S. is a friendly midwesterner who's good with figures—one of his company's really promising accountants. In nine years he's risen with abnormal speed through seniority-laden ranks.

But a month ago he nearly lost his job. His employer kept insisting that he buy U.S. savings bonds through payroll deductions—and he kept saying "No." He felt it was an invasion of privacy—whether he bought bonds was his business, not his employer's.

The concern he works for is a major government contractor. With the Vietnam war winding down, it foresees fewer contracts for all. It figures if it can boast to "Washington" that 100 percent of our employees buy government bonds," that just might help land some juicy contract.

Jim still can't quite believe what happened. This summer his supervisor asked him—and everyone else in the department—to buy bonds. Only Jim refused (citing high family expenses at the time).

Next the supervisor's supervisor tried. Then someone higher up the ladder pressured him. By this time Jim was more adamant than ever.

(Jim, incidentally, is no professional rebel. He can't stand long hair, hippies, or demonstrations. He voted for Mr. Nixon in '68; . . .)

Finally the chief accountant summoned him. (It was the first time in his nine years with the company that Jim had met him.)

When Jim entered the office, the boss erupted in a five-minute spiel on the virtues of government bonds; then mentioned that due to shortage of orders the company would have to let some accountants go. Finally he looked hard at Jim: "Now you *will* buy bonds, won't you?"

"When he said that," Jim recalls dourly, "I realized my job really depended on whether I joined that bond drive." He signed up—and has kicked himself ever since for capitulating.

Jim reflects wryly that "one of the supposed purposes of buying U.S. bonds is to protect freedom. I wonder whose?"

The incident has become nothing more to Jim than an annoying invasion of his privacy. But what if he'd stuck to his guns and been fired? On recommendations for future jobs, would his employer have given as reason for firing "refusal to buy U.S. bonds"—or would the company have trumped something up?

In any case, Jim's experience is but one illustration of the pervasiveness of invasions of Americans' privacy. Some of them can ruin lives—like psychological and lie-detector tests and the credit reports that occasionally victimize the innocent.

Privacy experts say that in addition to "no-knock" laws and wire taps . . . several areas bear watching. They include:

• Psychological testing—there's more industry in recent years, less in government. (But the latter could reemerge.)

• Sale of mailing lists—by government and private industry.

• Questionnaires from government— required census questionnaires; the voluntary ones sent out on behalf of other agencies—in which participation so often is assumed to be equally required.
• Administrating of drugs to some schoolchildren to calm them. The subject raised congressional hackles this year. Some observers said the potentials for abuse are frightening.
• Credit investigations—a problem which may be nearing solution. Congress this year passed a bill which gives consumers a chance to have their side of the story told in credit agency reports—and a legal comeback if agency negligence hurts them.

Coercion for "good causes"—as in the case already citied. There's much less in government, thanks to congressional publicity; an unknown amount remains in private industry. . . .

In recent years the federal government's investigation system has been changed to safeguard the right of privacy of anyone who applies for a government job. The questions asked do not range back so far in time, for instance. Routine questions about race and religion are out. And on the criminal front, the applicant now is only asked about convictions, not arrests.

But once a person becomes a government employee, as things now stand, he often feels—in the words of one—"disenfranchised. Once you're in the system, you discover that the best way to survive is not to make waves—which means not to bring up controversial ideas."

Last May [1970] some 250 State Department and AID employees signed form letters to Secretary of State William P. Rogers expressing respectful personal opposition to the Cambodian incursion.

Word was leaked to the press. Subsequently, some 50 of the foreign service officers who signed—mostly young—were called in to chat with Undersecretary of State for Administration U. Alexis Johnson. They were reminded they had a duty to support administration policy but that there would be no reprisals. Many present nevertheless felt they had been reprimanded and resented what they considered an implication of disloyalty.

Later Clark Mollenhoff, then a White House aide, requested the names of the letter signers, and got them from undisclosed sources within the department. (The White House subsequently denied any "dossiers" were being prepared on the signers.)

There is some concern among government employees that the signing in fact will be "remembered" by the government.

Important as this whole area is to many here in Washington, the public at large is more excited by privacy issues which touch them directly—such as sale of mailing lists and government questionnaires, specifically census . . . .

One of the most bizarre—and chilling—examples of potential privacy invasion concerns drug-research programs involving children judged overactive. A congressional hearing was held on the matter this fall. During it a government official estimated that from 150,000 to 200,000 children today are being treated in school with calming drugs.

. . . Research officials who were questioned denied that parents were coerced to have their children participate in such programs . . . .

Besides the issue of coercion, the hearing raised two serious questions:
• Do schools label pupils hyperactive who are merely exuberant—or bored with what the school is offering?
• What kind of credibility does an adult achieve when on the one hand he warns the child against the use of amphetamines and on the other encourages their use? . . .

The list of privacy invasions goes on. Sometimes it seems there isn't very much that can be done about it—at least, not by the average American. But specialists on the subject say individual action can be taken—and results obtained.

How You Can Fight Big Brother

By Robert P. Hey

Staff correspondent of The Christian Science Monitor

Washington

Prof. Allan M. was provoked—and disgusted. He sat right down and fired off a letter to Sen. Sam J. Ervin Jr.

He told the Senate's leading privacy exponent that he had sought a government grant from the National Science Foundation for a scientific research project he wanted to do. The application form the NSF sent included blanks for the usual data—purpose of research, expected result, and so on.

But then came this one: project director's social-security number. The form also asked for the social-security numbers of the director's four top aides.

The professor concluded that the NSF wanted the social-security numbers so its computer could communicate with somebody else's—either to take or give information about the five individuals. He didn't feel the government needed to know these numbers.

Professor M.'s letter prompted the North Carolina Democrat to ask Health, Education, and Welfare Secretary Elliot L. Richardson about the use of social-security numbers—were they being used too often, with potential dangers of privacy invasion?

(The grant for this scientific research would come from Secretary Richardson's department.)

In September Mr. Richardson wrote back that the government uses social-security numbers on its forms "as a means of clearly identifying individuals and avoiding the confusion and mistakes which can arise when a number of individuals have common or similar names." He spoke of severe restrictions on their use, to prevent any agency in most cases from "obtaining information from social security about an individual without his prior consent."

But Mr. Richardson did say he is concerned about possible abuses of individual privacy through misuse of social-security numbers. "Because of this concern," he reported, "the Social Security Administration is currently reviewing the policies governing the issuance, maintenance, and usage of the social-security number."

Too often when a person feels his privacy has been invaded he feels powerless. But Lawrence Speiser, director of the Washington office of the American Civil Liberties Union, points out that one person can effect change if only he knows whom to contact—as the professor did.

Automatic signing discouraged

"There's a wide range of actions individually he might take which at least will raise the issue with someone. For example, there are a lot of questions on government forms that most people sign automatically"—like the NSF form.

People shouldn't sign automatically, says Mr. Speiser. They should raise the specific privacy issue with someone—their senator, representative, the American Civil Liberties Union. If these persons take up this issue with the appropriate government agencies, they very well may get action.

"But it requires somebody to raise the question. It doesn't always require a lawsuit—just an inquiry."

Senator Ervin offers similar advice, though he isn't quite so optimistic about the chances of success:

"About all the individual can do is to call the attention of people" to the specific privacy invasion he is facing. "And also ask his senator and representative to do something about it."

Rep. Cornelius E. Gallagher, the primary privacy specialist in the House of Representatives, gives similar advice—write your elected representatives, including the President. Mr. Gallagher has an additional suggestion:

"I think the average guy has to, some-

where along the line say 'no' to all of the encroachments in his private life." He speaks specifically of the privacy invasions many industrial employees face from their employers—overly personal interviews, and in some cases the use of psychological testing, lie detectors, clandestine on-the-job surveillance.

The New Jersey Democrat comes down hard on unions on this issue: "I think that the unions are extremely lacking in any collective kind of approach to this problem . . . they all feel it. They all are aware of it. They all want to do something about it.

"But I haven't seen any big movement on the part of labor to become involved in this issue . . . ."

Some are flat-out pessimists about the possibility that anyone can take effective action to combat privacy invasions. One is Bernard Fensterwald Jr. During the '60's he was a staff counsel for former Sen. Ed Long's subcommittee, which exhaustively investigated wiretapping.

What can the individual do about privacy encroachments? "Adjust," says Mr. Fensterwald glumly. "Stay out of it and adjust. Look the other way. . . . I frankly think that privacy is dead and everybody better quit worrying about it."

But his view doesn't prevail among most privacy specialists. They have a host of suggestions for steps that should be taken to safeguard the rights of privacy, confidentiality, and due process for all Americans:

• Establish a new federal agency "to control federal data banks on behalf of the privacy and due-process rights of citizens." This proposal is strongly advocated by Senator Ervin, not normally a man who wants to add yet another federal agency.

• Set up commissions—with members representing many segments of society—to periodically review information that government and private computers and data banks are asking, collecting, storing, and dispersing. Some would give the commission power to write guidelines.

• Authorize a broadly based House of Representatives committee to delve thoroughly into the entire privacy issue—the needs of society, the choices that must be made between some of society's needs and individuals' requirements for privacy. Representative Gallagher advocates such a study to determine what the nation's "course shall be, and what laws may be necessary in order to protect our freedom. . . . We ought to look at the problem from every angle, and then determine where we want to go."

• Develop stronger presidential leader-

ship and more positive action from pres dential commissions . . . .

• Forbid the government from sellir mailing lists to anyone for any commerci purpose. This would prevent the gover ment from giving your name to third-cla mailers . . . .

• End the increasingly frequent quirement that people who fill out que tionnaires and surveys put their soc security numbers on the forms. Most p vacy specialists suspect that the only pu pose for this request is to enable vario governmental—and nongovernmental computers to exchange information whi ought to be confidential.

• Build more technical safeguards ir computers and computerized data ban to preserve the confidentiality of inform tion stored within them. In a recent iss of NAM Reports, put out by the Natio Association of Manufacturers, Robert Henderson mentioned some possibilit He is vice-president and general manag electronic data processing divisi Honeywell, Inc.

Safeguards on input and output

Said Mr. Henderson: "We can mak possible to limit those who are allowed put information into a system. We even have machines check data again given set of values and reject questiona information. In fact, all input could classified as it is received, ranging fr material of public record to top sec Sensitive information then could be coded during the input process.

"Similarly, there can be ingenious guards in the delivery of information. computer can require a password or swers to a series of questions before pr ing it. It could require several person be present, each possessing separate of a code. According to the passwo person possessed, the computer could access to a specific type of informa . . . It could be constructed to read ba and other forms of physical identi tion—or even compare the user's voic a 'voice print' stored within it."

More broadly, he also suggests:

• New legislation: "Perhaps the important new legal safeguard w provide a citizen with the ability to lenge in court the release of private about him without his consent."

Bill of rights for employees

Senator Ervin is pushing hard f more specific piece of legislation:

• A bill of rights for government ployees. Designed to prevent govern from invading the personal lives employees, it passed the Senate this Congress but did not get anywhere in the House. Senator Ervin intends to push again next year. One reason he will—government practices often are copied by defense contractors, later other industry.

In the past few years several steps have been taken toward coming to grips with parts of the privacy vs. society problem, among them:

• A 1968 federal law to bar private wiretapping and other electronic eavesdropping and to require a warrant for police wiretaps.

• A federal law to regulate credit bureaus.

• Increased attention to confidentiality in some computerized data banks. New York's identification and intelligence system for law enforcement is one frequently mentioned.

Despite these advances, privacy specialists are worried.

Representative Gallagher warns:

"I think the race is whether or not people will reassert themselves in time. Because the pendulum is being programmed out. The pendulum will not swing back [toward privacy] this time. Times have changed."

End questions

1. How might prying by the government and the military into an individual's political beliefs produce conformity? What is the place of dissent in a democracy?

2. Do you think the gathering of information by a computer infringes on the rights guaranteed in the Bill of Rights?

3. Why did Professor Allan M. refuse to give his social security number on an application for a National Science Foundation grant? Do you suppose Elliot Richardson's reply to Senator Ervin would satisfy Allan M?

4. How do you define "privacy"? Do you think this statement taken from one of the articles is true? "Privacy is dead, and everybody better quit worrying about it."

5. Has the federal government been responsive to citizens who feel their privacy has been invaded? Which of the policies for protecting privacy suggested in the article "How You Can Fight Big Brother" do you support? Why?

CHAPTER **20**

*Policies That Protect
And Maintain
the System*

Any political system, in order to survive, must be able to protect itself against the forces that threaten it. It must be ready to resist armed aggression and other conditions that challenge its stability from outside its borders. It must also be able to cope with threats from within that might destroy the structures of government and the public order. *Maintenance* policies answer both these conditions. They include those policies that a system develops to preserve itself against destructive forces.

In America's political system, these kinds of maintenance policies fall into two major categories. First, there are policies that preserve the nation's place within the world community and protect it from outside threats. These include the decisions that affect the political and economic relations of the United States with other nations and those that provide for military defense. Second, there are policies that protect the system against threats from within. These include not only policies designed to counter real menaces such as attempts to overthrow the government by force but also such policies as censorship which are undertaken in the belief that the moral standards of the community must be maintained.

Maintenance Against External Threats

The survival of any political system depends, at least in part, on how it responds to challenges from outside its own geographical boundaries. It must not only be prepared to defend itself against military attacks from abroad, but it must also conduct its political and economic affairs with other nations so as to protect its own national interests.

In the United States, the formulation of policies that maintain the political system against external threats is complicated by the pluralism within the system itself. As in all areas of government policy-making, policies that deal with foreign affairs and defense are affected by the natural competition between Congress and the President, the attempts by ethnic and economic interest groups to influence government decision-makers, and the need for democratic government to be responsive to public opinion. But unlike most policy questions, maintenance policies of this type are further complicated by events and conditions that exist outside the system. Throughout United States history, the development of policies with respect to international affairs has been a process of balancing the nation's own constantly changing interests and internal demands with the ever-present demands or dangers from without.

General trends in United States foreign policy. As soon as the United States declared its independence as a free nation, it had to start protecting its position in the world community. If the young agrarian nation was to survive, the government established by the people had to defend itself against foreign threats to its territorial integrity and to its political and economic stability.

The world community was much different in the late eighteenth century from what it is today. The European nations, whose mercantile economics were tied to colonies throughout the world, were

What kinds of policies must a political system develop to protect itself against internal and external forces that threaten to destroy it? How might such policies conflict with the other needs of a democratic system?

". . AND REMEMBER, YOU CAN ALWAYS DEPEND ON THEIR ARDENT SIDELINE SUPPORT!"

(Some American critics claim that Western Europe should be carrying its own weight in the NATO alliance.)

Kingdom, and the United States, the Southeast Asia Collective Defense Treaty promised protection for the Southeast Asian signatories against any aggression. The United States, however, added a statement to the treaty text qualifying its own understanding of the term "aggression" to mean *communist* aggression. In the event of non-communist aggression against a SEATO power, the United States reserved the right to consult its allies before taking any action. The protection of the treaty was later extended to South Vietnam, Cambodia, and Laos, even though they were not members of the pact.

During President Johnson's administration, Secretary of State Dean Rusk used the SEATO treaty as a basis for beginning an armed intervention in South Vietnam to counteract the infiltration of communist troops from North Vietnam. Those who

opposed the United States' action in Vietnam claimed that the SEATO treaty was not applicable to the Vietnam situation. They argued that, unlike NATO, the SEATO treaty does not require armed intervention but only mutual consultation and aid, and that Vietnam was not a clear-cut case of communist aggression, but a civil war or internal insurrection not covered by the SEATO treaty.

□ *CENTO.* United States participation in the Central Treaty Organization (CENTO) is different from the other alliances that make up the policy of containment. In this case, the United States only acts as an associate member. The original signatories were Turkey and Iraq in 1955. The United Kingdom, Pakistan, and Iran joined later the same year. Although Iraq withdrew from CENTO in 1959, the United States signed bilateral agreements with

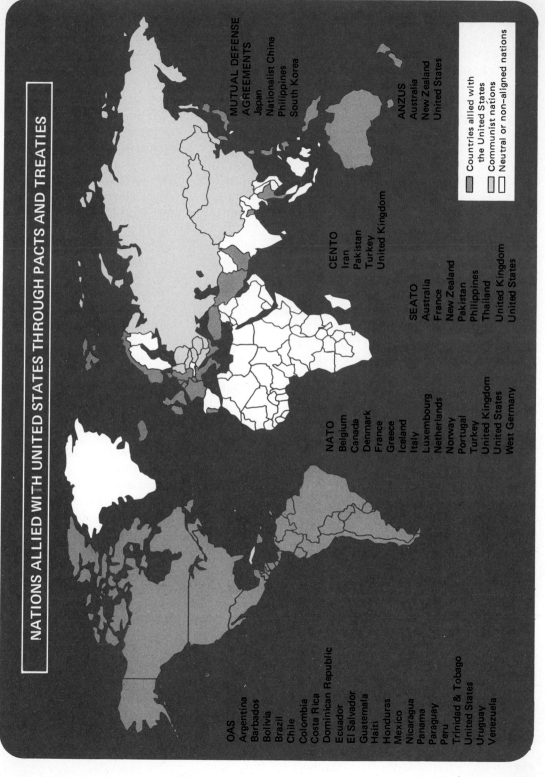

NATIONS ALLIED WITH UNITED STATES THROUGH PACTS AND TREATIES

OAS
Argentina
Barbados
Bolivia
Brazil
Chile
Colombia
Costa Rica
Dominican Republic
Ecuador
El Salvador
Guatemala
Haiti
Honduras
Mexico
Nicaragua
Panama
Paraguay
Peru
Trinidad & Tobago
United States
Uruguay
Venezuela

NATO
Belgium
Canada
Denmark
France
Greece
Iceland
Italy
Luxembourg
Netherlands
Norway
Portugal
Turkey
United Kingdom
United States
West Germany

SEATO
Australia
France
New Zealand
Pakistan
Philippines
Thailand
United Kingdom
United States

CENTO
Iran
Pakistan
Turkey
United Kingdom

MUTUAL DEFENSE
AGREEMENTS
Japan
Nationalist China
Philippines
South Korea

ANZUS
Australia
New Zealand
United States

Countries allied with
the United States
Communist nations
Neutral or non-aligned nations

501

Turkey, Iran, and Pakistan in that year which tied the United States closely to these CENTO signatories in case of communist aggression. Besides the bilateral agreements with CENTO nations, the United States has also signed mutual defense agreements with Nationalist China, South Korea, the Philippines, and Japan.

■ *Foreign aid.* In order for the United States' policy of containment to be effective, mutual defense arrangements by themselves are not enough. For this reason, the United States has helped to support its free-world allies by supplying them with substantial economic aid and technical assistance. The most notable program of American economic aid was the Marshall Plan instituted shortly after World War II to help in the rebuilding of war-torn countries of Western Europe and thus head off the threat of a communist takeover. Within four years of its beginning, more than 20 billion dollars worth of food, clothing, building supplies, machinery, and military equipment was supplied to the European nations by the United States. Additional millions of dollars were made available during the 1960's to Latin America, the Middle East, Africa, and Asia. The Agency for International Development (AID) within the State Department and the Peace Corps have both been in the forefront of the United States' foreign assistance program.

■ *Current trends.* For the present, the network of military alliances and treaties which the United States has joined, together with its programs of foreign aid, is still effective. But as World War II becomes an ever dimmer memory, there is a tendency for other nations to look less and less toward one of the two major ideological camps as a desirable champion in case of aggression. At the same time, the costly involvement of the United States in Vietnam has led many people to take a second look at the country's foreign commitments and to encourage other foreign nations to take more responsibility for their own defense.

Moreover, the communist world is not the solidly unified camp today that it was in 1950. Unsuccessful revolts have occurred in some communist nations, while China and Yugoslavia have successfully maintained their independence from the Soviet Union. In fact, the growing power of Communist China provided the impetus for the United States and the Soviet Union to consider mutual agreements on arms control and cooperation in space research. Increasingly, the United States is adjusting to the existence of different ideologies in the world community. This trend is illustrated by President Nixon's decision to seek better relations with Communist China that may lead to United States recognition of the Peking government.

Defense spending versus disarmament. The policy of containment would be ineffective without military defense to deter potential aggressors. The United States has had to support a large armed force both at home and abroad and to maintain the international balance of power by building weapons systems to match those of the communist nations. In 1969, there were about 3.5 million men and women on active duty in the armed forces of the United States. About a third of these were based at the approximately 100 overseas airfields, naval stations, and army posts scattered throughout the world. Most of these bases were in Europe, but others were spread from Greenland to Okinawa. In addition, nearly eight billion dollars were spent in 1969 on the research, development, testing, and evaluation of weapons systems.

The need for maintaining adequate defense to deter aggression poses many

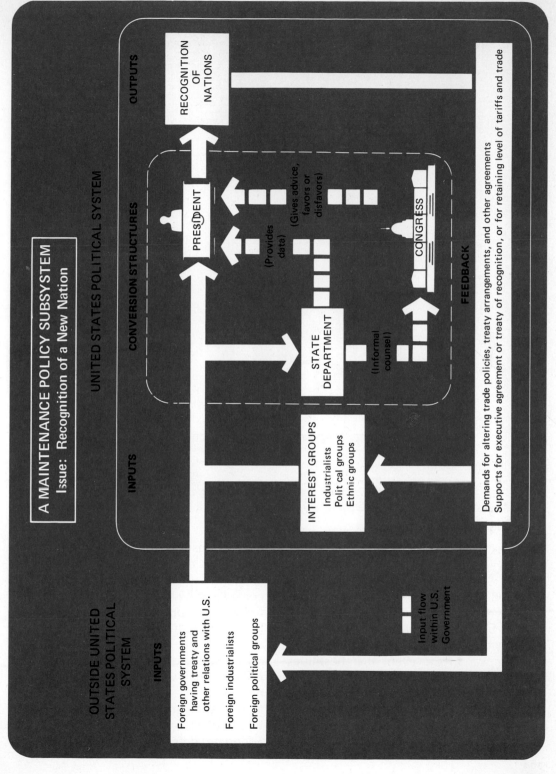

A MAINTENANCE POLICY SUBSYSTEM
Issue: Recognition of a New Nation

UNITED STATES POLITICAL SYSTEM

OUTSIDE UNITED STATES POLITICAL SYSTEM

INPUTS

Foreign governments having treaty and other relations with U.S.

Foreign industrialists

Foreign political groups

INPUTS

CONVERSION STRUCTURES

OUTPUTS

RECOGNITION OF NATIONS

PRESIDENT

(Provides data)

(Gives advice, favors or disfavors)

STATE DEPARTMENT

(Informal counsel)

CONGRESS

INTEREST GROUPS
Industrialists
Political groups
Ethnic groups

FEEDBACK

Demands for altering trade policies, treaty arrangements, and other agreements
Supports for executive agreement or treaty of recognition, or for retaining level of tariffs and trade

Input flow within U.S. Government

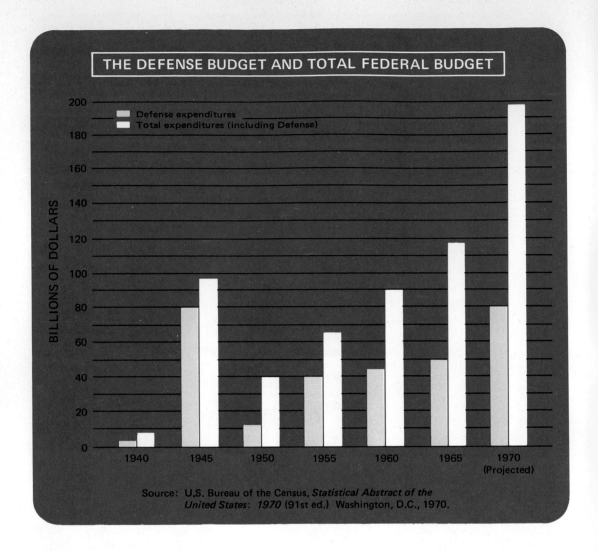

THE DEFENSE BUDGET AND TOTAL FEDERAL BUDGET

BILLIONS OF DOLLARS

☐ Defense expenditures
☐ Total expenditures (including Defense)

1940 1945 1950 1955 1960 1965 1970
(Projected)

Source: U.S. Bureau of the Census, *Statistical Abstract of the United States: 1970* (91st ed.) Washington, D.C., 1970.

complex questions for government policy-makers. For example, how much of the United States defense budget should be assigned to maintaining a balance of nuclear weapons with those of the communist bloc? How much should be spent on conventional weapons so as to avoid nuclear war in the event that hostilities do occur? And how much of the total federal budget can be poured into defense without sacrificing domestic needs?

Various points of view are put forth by numerous interest groups from the defense industries and labor groups to the supporters of federal assistance for health and education. All these opinions are considered by the many decision-makers—from legislators to the President to the bureaucrats in the Departments of State and Defense—who must answer to their own sources of support while producing policies that will effectively protect the nation.

■ *The ABM argument.* Since few people would disagree with the need to maintain adequate defense, Congress is generally willing to provide funds for defense programs. The difficulty in determining the proper defense policies, however, has been illustrated in recent years by the controversies over the building of the antiballistic missile (ABM) system. The original purpose of the ABM program was to place antiballistic missiles at strategic locations throughout the United States for use in case of a nuclear attack from Communist China. The strongest support for the ABM program came from the White House during both the Johnson and Nixon administrations. While Congress eventually voted to appropriate funds for limited production of the ABM's, it did so only after extensive hearings which were charged with heated debate in both houses.

Proponents of the ABM argued that the system would be necessary to deter a nuclear attack from Communist China. Others argued that it was also a necessary response to a missile build-up which was taking place in the Soviet Union. Another argument was advanced that the ABM would maintain jobs in the defense industries for workers who might otherwise be fired as a result of reductions in other defense programs.

The most heated opposition to the ABM proposal came from citizens living in areas that had been proposed as ABM sites. These groups feared that the program would only serve to provoke attack on the densely populated areas they were supposed to protect. Other opponents of the system argued that the ABM had not been sufficiently tested and might not be an effective deterrent. Some argued that the program would only provoke the Soviet Union into building more missiles or that it would destroy the chances for reaching international agreement on arms control. Still others thought that the unnecessary expense of such a program would be damaging to the national economy.

■ *Disarmament talks.* The ABM controversy demonstrated the complex issues that are involved in reaching decisions on defense policy. Such dilemmas are further complicated by the question of disarmament. As both the United States and the Soviet Union have developed and amassed nuclear weapons in the post-war period, the prospect of a nuclear confrontation has become ominous. Throughout the same period, the possibility of international arms control and disarmament has been a constant topic of international discussion. Both sides have recognized that nuclear war would be mutually destructive, but negotiations through the United Nations and other international meetings have resulted in only a few limited agreements.

In 1963, a number of nations signed a treaty agreeing to a ban on nuclear tests in space and under the seas. However, neither France nor Communist China, which were both in the process of developing their own nuclear armaments, agreed to sign the test-ban treaty. In 1969, the Senate of the United States ratified a Nuclear Nonproliferation Treaty which had been drawn up with sixty-one other nations including the Soviet Union. This treaty provided for a ban on the spread of nuclear weapons to any nations not already producing them.

Aside from specific treaties, other measures have been taken by the Soviet Union and the United States to provide for a "cooling off" of the arms race. In 1963 a system of direct communication between Washington and Moscow, known as the "hot line," was set up to prevent the sudden outbreak of a nuclear war. By the mid-1960's, both countries had also taken steps to reduce military spending. At the end of the decade, the two nations agreed to send representatives to Helsinki, Finland for strategic arms limitations talks

Gillam in Puck

OUR "INFANT INDUSTRY."
I think I am quite big enough to take care of myself !"

(Rapid industrial growth in the United States following the Civil War was encouraged by protective tariffs.)

(SALT) to discuss the possibilities of further arms-control measures.

Foreign trade policies. Apart from its mutual security and defense policies, the foreign trade policies of the United States are also fundamental to maintaining the welfare of the political system. In formulating policies which affect trade, the central question has usually been over setting or eliminating tariffs and quotas on products from abroad. Under a *protectionist* policy, high tariffs and restrictive quotas on imports are maintained to protect American industries from foreign competition. Under a policy of *free trade,* tariffs and quotas are made less restrictive or are eliminated to permit foreign and domestic producers to compete freely for foreign and domestic markets. As with other maintenance policies that protect America's position in the world community, decisions on foreign trade policies must balance the economic needs of the nation with the realities of the international political arena.

Since the 1930's, the shift in America's foreign policy from isolationism to international cooperation has been accompanied by a trend away from protectionism toward freer trade. As domestic goods become increasingly expensive to produce, however, consumers tend to buy more imported goods which are less expensive. If such conditions prove detrimental to American industries, there could be a return to more protectionist trade policies.

Protective tariffs and quotas are usually initiated as a result of pressure from those domestic industries that face stiff competition from foreign producers. Most recently, for example, the textile industry in the United States has been putting pressure on the President and Congress for protective tariffs or restrictive quotas on textiles from abroad—especially those from Japan. The costs of production in the United States and especially labor costs have driven up the prices of domestic textiles so high that foreign nations can produce cloth at much lower prices. The textile industries therefore favor tariffs on textile imports to bring these goods closer to the price of American goods.

Regardless of the special interests of particular industries, the government must look at foreign trade in a broader perspective. American industries also benefit from free trade. Since American industries export goods just as industries from other nations do, the nation is interested in keeping friendly relations with countries that buy American exports. If the United States put quotas or tariffs on textiles from Japan and Europe, these nations in turn could retaliate by placing high tariffs on other goods from the United States. Such action could force American producers out of foreign markets.

Thus, the government must constantly weigh the interests of different industries in determining trade policies. It must also consider other factors which concern the economy of the nation. It may have to consider the nation's *balance of payments*—that is, the balance of money leaving the country with the amount flowing in from abroad. If there is an excessive outflow of currency, it may be necessary to raise tariffs to prevent consumers from spending money on foreign goods. On the other hand, free trade may be a more appropriate solution because it would help maintain foreign markets and bring foreign money into the United States. In addition, the policy-makers must weigh the possibility of foreign retaliation for restrictive tariffs. Usually some compromise must be found between those who favor protective policies and those who favor free trade. Hopefully, the policy that results will be one that benefits the nation as a whole most and that also disturbs the

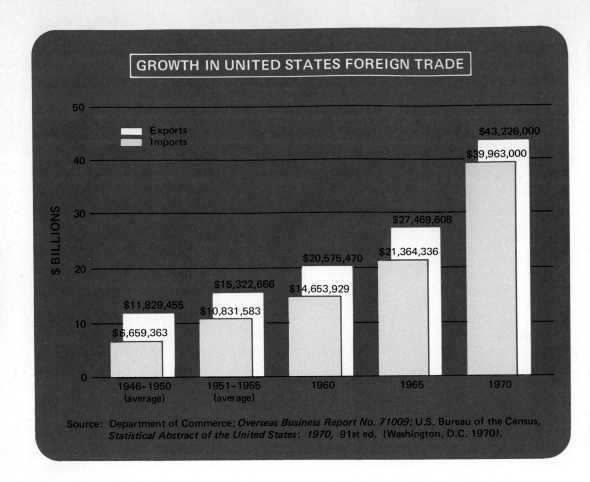

GROWTH IN UNITED STATES FOREIGN TRADE

Exports
Imports

$ BILLIONS

$11,829,455
$6,659,363

$15,322,666
$10,831,583

$20,575,470
$14,653,929

$27,469,608
$21,364,336

$43,226,000
$39,963,000

1946–1950
(average)

1951–1955
(average)

1960

1965

1970

Source: Department of Commerce; *Overseas Business Report No. 71009*; U.S. Bureau of the Census, *Statistical Abstract of the United States: 1970,* 91st ed. (Washington, D.C. 1970).

political system least.

Review questions

1. How does collective security con-tribute to the United States' contain-ment policy?

2. How do foreign trade policies main-tain America's political system?

Maintenance Against Internal Threats

If an enemy nation mobilized troops and missiles for an attack on United States territory, or if foreign industrialists con-spired to prevent Americans from export-ing goods to foreign markets, the United States would undoubtedly respond quick-ly by formulating policies to meet these external threats. Just as dangerous as these external menaces are the possibilities of coups d'état, revolutions, or riots that threaten the system from within. The obvious need for policies to curtail in-ternal threats, however, presents serious constitutional dilemmas.

A major dilemma confronting all democ-racies is the need to modify policies that protect civil liberties and civil rights when these civil freedoms are used or misused to attack the very foundations of the system itself. In the United States, for example, the First Amendment to the Constitution protects the citizen's freedoms of speech and press and the right to assemble peaceably. But at what point do verbal attacks on the government— through the exercise of these freedoms— become an actual threat to the system? At what point can the government abridge these freedoms if it believes the system is endangered?

The responsibility for drawing the constitutional line between individual freedoms and national security has rested primarily with the Supreme Court. The Court has often had to face this responsibility when the effects of congressional policies on internal security have been challenged by specific individuals in the courts.

Clear and present danger. The most rigid policies against internal threats are usually initiated during times of war. At such times, foreign powers could undermine the nation's fighting capability by encouraging espionage, sabotage, or the circulation of subversive propaganda. The people are usually primed, at wartime, to be suspicious of the enemy—looking for enemy agents even among loyal citizens— and ready to counteract any potential threat. At the same time, they are less likely to resist the sacrifices of their own individual freedoms when this would aid a war effort.

An example of this attitude occurred in the United States during the First World War. Even before the country joined its allies in the fighting, there was a great deal of pressure on Congress to pass legislation that would curtail certain activities by disloyal individuals. In June 1917, two months after the United States' entry into the war, the Espionage Act was passed. Under this Act, anyone circulating false statements that might interfere with military success, obstruct recruiting efforts, or encourage disloyalty in the armed forces was liable to punishment. To some individuals, this law seemed to be in direct conflict with the freedoms of speech and press protected by the First Amendment.

■ *The* Schenck *case.* The first opportunity the Supreme Court had to rule on the constitutionality of the Espionage Act came two years later in *Schenck v. United States* (1919). Schenck and his associates had circulated a pamphlet among draftees that was allegedly intended to cause insubordination and to obstruct recruitment.

The pamphlet argued that the draft violated the Thirteenth Amendment prohibition against involuntary servitude and suggested that it was a despotic, monstrous wrong against humanity committed in the interests of Wall Street. The pamphlet urged new recruits to assert their rights and to oppose the draft. Although this appeal was couched in rather strong language, for the most part the form of resistance suggested by the pamphlet was not violent. After Schenck was convicted in a federal district court for violating the Espionage Act, he appealed to the Supreme Court on the grounds that his First Amendment freedoms of speech and press had been unconstitutionally abridged.

The Supreme Court upheld Schenck's conviction. In delivering the majority opinion of the Court, Justice Oliver Wendell Holmes enunciated, for the first time, the "clear and present danger" test which has guided decisions in similar cases ever since. Said Holmes:

". . . in many places and in ordinary times the defendants in saying all that was said in the circular would have been within

their constitutional rights. But the character of every act depends upon the circumstances in which it is done . . . . the question in every case is whether the words used are used in such circumstances and are of such a nature as to create a clear and present danger *that they will bring about the substantive evils that Congress has a right to prevent. . . . When a nation is at war, many things that might be said in time of peace are such a hindrance to its effort that their utterance will not be endured so long as men fight, and that no court could regard them as protected by any constitutional right."* (Italics added.)[1]

Since the purpose and tendency of Schenck's act was to obstruct the recruiting effort, this alone constituted a violation of the Espionage Act of 1917 that could be upheld in wartime.

On the basis of the *Schenck* case, it became clear that the Supreme Court would limit the freedom of speech if such freedom resulted in a clear and present danger to the maintenance of national security. But just what constituted a "clear and present danger" was obviously a matter for further interpretation. The definition has varied from case to case depending upon the times and the circumstances.

■ *The Smith Act and the* Dennis *Case.* After the Supreme Court's decision in the *Schenck* case, many subsequent controversies were decided that further clarified the "clear and present danger" doctrine. One of the most famous of these decisions involved the constitutionality of the Smith Act which was passed in 1940 prior to United States' entrance into World War II. The Smith Act made it unlawful for any person "to knowingly or willfully advocate

. . . overthrowing or destroying any government in the United States by force or violence . . ." or to belong to any organization that so advocated. The Smith Act raised many serious questions concerning the freedoms of speech and press. The main issue was over the extent to which the government could properly curtail these basic freedoms in the interest of national security.

The issue was squarely faced in the case of *Dennis v. United States* which was decided by the Supreme Court in 1951. On the basis of provisions in the Smith Act, the eleven top leaders of the American Communist party had been indicted for conspiring to teach and advocate the overthrow of the government by force and violence. The initial trial was held in a federal district court in New York before a jury that brought in a verdict of guilty for all eleven party members. After the court of appeals affirmed the conviction, the defendants petitioned the Supreme Court for a review of the case. The Court granted the petition because the case raised several questions about the constitutionality of the Smith Act.

The authority of Congress to pass laws that would prevent the violent overthrow of the government was not questioned by the Court. But of primary constitutional importance to the Court was whether the Smith Act provision making it a crime to *advocate* violent overthrow of the government was an abridgement of freedom of speech.

In answering this question, the Court found a significant difference between *advocacy* of an illegal activity and the *discussion* of such ideas which was protected by the First-Amendment right to freedom of speech. Advocacy involved the *intent* to perform such activity while the discussion of ideas did not. Therefore, according to the Court, the Smith Act restriction on

[1] *249 U.S. 47 (1919).*

"advocacy" did not abridge freedom of speech:

"Congress did not intend to eradicate the free discussion of political theories, to destroy the traditional rights of Americans to discuss and evaluate ideas without fear of government sanction."

The Court reasoned that the restriction against "advocacy" in the Smith Act was directed against *intentions* to overthrow the government, which by their nature constitute "clear and present danger" to the system. Congress clearly had the authority to protect the government against intentions that constituted such danger.

The majority opinion of the Supreme Court further pointed out that the district-court judge at the original trial had made the distinction between advocacy and discussion very clear to the jury which had convicted the defendants in the *Dennis* case:

". . . the trial judge properly charged the jury that they could not convict if they found that petitioners did 'no more than pursue peaceful studies and discussions or teaching . . . in the realm of ideas.' "[2]

Although it is difficult to prove conclusively that any group intends to overthrow the government, there had been no doubt in the minds of the jury at the *Dennis* trial that the members of the American Communist party had had such an intention. The Supreme Court therefore upheld both the constitutionality of the Smith Act and the conviction in the *Dennis* case.

■ *The* Yates *case.* As a result of the decision in the *Dennis* case, the federal government proceeded to indict and convict close to 100 individuals who were connected with the Communist party. The

Justus in the Minneapolis Star.

More moderate people have begun to wonder if the investigators haven't been, at best, overenthusiastic . . .

(After the *Dennis* decision, the increase in convictions of communists heightened concern for civil liberties.)

reasoning behind these convictions was that the party was a conspiracy organized for the purpose of overthrowing the government, and anyone connected with the party obviously intended to be part of such a conspiracy.

In 1957, in *Yates v. the United States,* the Supreme Court overturned the conviction of fourteen Communist party members and further clarified the meaning of "advocacy" as it related to clear and present danger. The Court said that the advocacy of forcible overthrow of government as an abstract principle could not in itself be prohibited. Only if such a belief was extended to the actual "incitement to action" would clear and present danger be involved. To violate the Smith Act, the Court asserted,

[2] *341 U.S. 494 (1951).*

"those to whom advocacy is addressed must be urged to *do* something now or in the future, rather than merely to *believe* in something."[3] As a result of the *Yates* decision, belief in a doctrine such as communism—which advocates violent overthrow of government in principle—is protected by the First Amendment as long as no specific action for carrying out such a belief is contemplated.

The communist threat. The most consistent and continuous threat to the internal security of the United States' political system since the end of World War II has come from the Communist party. As a result, the government has been under pressure from a variety of groups to strengthen the security apparatus of the country. This pressure was most intense in the late 1940's as the Soviet Union increased its hold on Eastern Europe, and the Communists won mainland China from the Nationalists. It was increased in the early 1950's when the Communist North Koreans invaded South Korea.

■ *Investigations of enemy infiltration.* At the same time that the communist threat seemed to be threatening the community at large, the government was in the throes of searching out infiltrators within its own ranks. It was thought by many that the whole system was being menaced. President Truman responded to this concern by creating the first loyalty and security program in the federal government.

An executive order, signed by Truman in 1947, set up a Loyalty Review Board and required loyalty investigations of all federal employees and applicants for federal jobs. Federal employees were subject to dismissal if hearings revealed any activities or associations that suggested disloyalty.

The order specified that employees had the right to receive in writing any charges against them "stated as specifically and completely as . . . security considerations would permit," and the President issued other procedural guidelines for hearings to safeguard the rights of accused employees. Nevertheless, some civil servants claimed that they were being deprived of due process of law because the hearings did not follow all the usual judicial procedures and because they were not always informed of the nature of the accusations against them nor given the names of opposition witnesses. Obviously, the situation emphasized the conflict between the requirements of national security and individual rights and freedoms.

President Eisenhower later revoked the Truman executive order and established a new criterion for dismissing federal employees. Under the Eisenhower executive order, an employee could be dismissed if his employment was not "clearly consistent" with security interests. This standard made it easier to discharge employees. It was during this period that the phrase "security risk," referring to individuals who might present a security problem not only because of their political beliefs but also because of personal habits, came into vogue. A person who drank too much, for example, could be labeled a security risk because under the influence of alcohol he might disclose classified information.

It is not always easy to maintain the proper balance between the necessity to defend the government against those determined to destroy it and the need to protect the individual liberties of those employed by the same government. The administration of the loyalty program has usually been fair and cautious, so that only a few court cases have resulted. Such cases have dealt with procedures used in

[3] *354 U.S. 298 (1957).*

From Herblock's *Special for Today* (Simon & Schuster, 1958)

"Those Crazy Egghead Scientists—If You Didn't Hold 'Em Down They'd Want To Reach For The Moon"

(Some federal employees during the 1950's felt that the government's loyalty programs were oppressive.)

applying the loyalty standards, not with the standards themselves.

During the Truman and early Eisenhower administrations, Congress, too, was conducting investigations and considering legislation which would further counteract the threat of subversive activities. In 1948 the hearings conducted by the House Un-American Activities Committee (HUAC) drew wide public attention. In the most famous of the HUAC investigations, two admitted ex-Communists, Edith Bentley and Whittaker Chambers, accused a former high-ranking State Department official named Alger Hiss of being an ex-Communist party member. The committee's chief investigator for the Hiss Case was Richard Nixon, Republican Representative from California. The investigation aroused the public to the dangers of subversion and eventually led to the trial and conviction of Alger Hiss for perjury.

A month after Hiss was convicted in 1950, Senator Joseph McCarthy of Wisconsin took advantage of the political climate and claimed to have a list of 205 members of the Communist party who had infiltrated the State Department. McCarthy later reduced the number to 57. In response though, the Senate Foreign Relations Committee established a subcommittee to investigate the accusations. The subsequent investigations involved political figures, statesmen, and finally, in 1954, Army personnel. This last investigation brought countercharges from the Army. Although McCarthy and his aides were cleared of these charges, the Senate did later censure McCarthy, and the charges against Army personnel were dropped.

■ *The Internal Security Act of 1950.* Congress reacted to the continuation of internal pressure and foreign events by passing the Internal Security Act of 1950. Title I of this Act, known as the Subversive Activities Control Act, created a Subversive Activities Control Board. On the request of the Attorney General, the Board was authorized to issue an order declaring an organization a communist front and hence subversive.

Once an organization had been declared subversive, it was subject to some very rigid regulations. The organization had to register annually with the Attorney General, list the names of all members, and give a complete financial statement. Any mail sent by such an organization had to be labeled as communist propaganda on the envelope. No member of a subversive organization could hold federal office, secure a passport, or become an official or employee of a labor union. Finally, those associated with subversive organizations could not work in any defense plant listed by the Secretary of Defense.

The passage of the Communist Control Act of 1954 completed this legislative process by declaring the Communist party "a clear and present danger to the security of the United States" and "the agency of a foreign power." The party could not place its candidates on official election ballots. Under the provisions of the Smith Act of 1940, the Subversive Activities Control Act of 1950, and the Communist Control Act of 1954, stiff penalties can result from party membership. The Subversive Activities Control Board, however, has not gone beyond requiring the registration of Communist party members. The full penalties of the law have not been enforced.

■ *Other loyalty programs.* Loyalty and security programs have also been extended into the areas where federal funds are involved such as education and defense. Congress originally required loyalty oaths from students applying for scholarships supported by federal funds. This provision was repealed, although no member of a communist organization can legally apply for such funds. Defense contracts with weapons manufacturers also require that civilians who are employed on such projects be cleared for classified work.

The many limitations on federal employees with respect to loyalty and security exist also at the state and local levels of government. It is very difficult to measure the effect that the loyalty and security programs have had on federal and state employment. Very few employees have been dismissed for disloyalty, or because they were security risks. Undoubtedly, though, many talented people have been discouraged from trying to get federal employment because they were unwilling to sacrifice some of what they considered their basic freedoms. It is important for policy-makers, including members of Congress, the President, and the courts, to adopt programs that balance the security requirements of the government with the rights of the individual.

Review questions

1. Explain why the constitutionality of the Espionage Act of 1917 was called into question by the *Schenck* case.
2. How did the case of *Dennis v. United States* establish the difference between "advocacy" and "discussion"? Why was this distinction important? How did the *Yates* decision further clarify the meaning of "advocacy"?

Maintaining Public Order and Community Standards

Controversy is essential to the democratic process. It is vital that new ideas be introduced and tested through debate. The election of delegates to Congress, for example, would be inconceivable without the rounds of heated argument that the candidates engage in prior to the actual balloting. Recognizing the importance of open debate, the Framers made the freedoms of speech and press basic individual liberties in the Bill of Rights. These were

also the first freedoms to be nationalized by the Supreme Court's interpretation of "due process of law" in the Fourteenth Amendment.

Yet, this same Supreme Court has permitted limitations on the freedoms of speech and the press when the security of the nation seemed to take precedence. Moreover, there has also been a tendency to limit individual freedoms when it has been considered necessary to maintain public order and the standards of the general community.

Protection of public order. The maintenance of public peace and order is a requirement in any community so that people can go about their daily lives without fear of physical harm or the destruction and loss of their property. The need to maintain public order is a major reason for establishing government, and it remains one of government's major responsibilities.

■ *The guardians of public order.* In the United States, there is no single national police force. Many agencies, however, do maintain special agents to enforce particular laws. Both the Food and Drug Administration and the Public Health Service, for example, have inspectors who make sure that the regulations established by these agencies are followed. The Internal Revenue Service has agents who apprehend tax dodgers. Customs Bureau agents engage in activities to prevent the smuggling of goods into the country. The agents of the Bureau of Narcotics have an even tougher job of stopping illegal drug traffic. Enforcement officials in these and other federal agencies together make up a large force of agents who guard and preserve public order.

There are also two federal police agencies—the United States Secret Service and the Federal Bureau of Investigation (FBI). The United States Secret Service was created in 1860 within the Treasury Department to track down counterfeiters. Its concerns have been expanded to include detection of the forgeries of United States securities and other financial documents as well as foreign money. "T-men" or Treasury agents also protect the President and his family and maintain uniformed police units at the White House and the Treasury Department buildings.

Set up in 1908 within the Department of Justice, the FBI has responsibility for investigating violations of all federal laws not assigned to other agencies. There are about 170 types of felonies that the FBI can investigate. Among these are espionage, treason, kidnapping, extortion, bank robbery, thefts of government property, interstate transportation of stolen goods, fraud against the government, civil rights matters, and the assault or assassination of a President or federal officer.

Another force for protecting the public order is the National Guard. The Guard is an auxiliary force of the army and is made up of the militias of the separate states. While Congress provides for the organizing and arming of the National Guard, the governor of each state is the commander in chief of his state's militia and may call upon it to deal with riots or natural disasters such as floods and earthquakes. During wars and other national emergencies, the federal government may call the state militias into federal service; at such times, the National Guard comes under federal instead of state jurisdiction.

Apart from these national and quasi-national enforcement groups, the maintenance of public order is usually the responsibility of state and local agencies and officials. Exceptions to this practice occur when a problem is of such magnitude that it is necessary to call in the National Guard or federal agents.

■ *Public order versus individual freedoms.* A primary dilemma to be solved by those trying to maintain public order is how to do so without usurping individual freedoms. Ordinarily, when cases or controversies arise over this dilemma, the Supreme Court has upheld the limitation of speech and the press if there is a real danger that the public order will be disturbed. Laws that restrict speech and the press when a clear and present danger is

'I'm not going to marry either one of you'

(To preserve both civil liberties and public order, government has to avoid any course that is too extreme.)

not apparent, however, have been less clearly defined by the courts.

Two cases—*Terminiello v. Chicago* (1949) and *Feiner v. New York* (1951)—illustrate the two responses that the courts have used to answer this dilemma. In the *Terminiello* case, the Court decided in favor of maintaining the freedoms of speech and assembly, while the *Feiner* decision gave precedence to the maintenance of public order.

Terminiello was charged and found guilty of breaching the peace when he made an inflammatory, racist speech in Chicago that incited a protest crowd of about one thousand persons to riot. When the case reached the Supreme Court, it was decided that the local ordinance, as interpreted by the trial judge, was unconstitutional because it permitted undue abridgment of the freedom of speech. Justice William O. Douglas concluded the *Terminiello* opinion by stating that

"the function of free speech under our system of government is to invite dispute. It may indeed best serve its high purpose when it induces a condition of unrest, creates dissatisfaction with conditions as they are, and even stirs people to anger."[4]

Thus, the *Terminiello* decision held that freedom of speech had priority over the Chicago ordinance for maintaining public order.

Two years later, in the *Feiner* case, the Supreme Court made what appears to be an almost contrary opinion. Feiner had been arrested and convicted of disorderly conduct while addressing a meeting of about eighty persons on a street corner in Syracuse, New York. Two policeman who were witnesses to the incident testified that the crowd listening to Feiner had been "pushing, shoving, and milling around." As a result, the policemen, fearing that the situation would become uncontrollable, had urged Feiner to ask the crowd to disband. Feiner had been arrested when he refused to comply with this request. In this case, the Supreme Court upheld the conviction. The majority of the Court pointed out that when the speaker "passes the bounds of argument or persuasion and undertakes incitement to riot," the police must not be powerless to prevent public disorder.[5]

Although these two cases appear similar, there was an important distinction between the factors reviewed by the Supreme Court in producing the two decisions. In the *Terminiello* case, the appeal was based on the fact that the original trial judge had interpreted the Chicago ordinance so that it placed excessive limits on the freedom of speech. In the *Feiner* appeal, on the other hand, only an isolated police action was in question.

[4] *337 U.S. 1 (1949).*   [5] *340 U.S. 315 (1951).*

Although the two decisions were based on different questions, the *Feiner* decision established a precedent for upholding limitations on freedom of speech in public places when there was a "clear and present danger" that a riot would occur.

Maintenance of community standards. Virtually everybody in the country is exposed to some form of the mass media—newspapers, television, radio, magazines, or even motion pictures. A major television program can easily reach thirty to forty million people. Many magazines have circulations of several millions and probably are read by millions more. Radio programs and newspapers reach thousands and in some cases millions of people. Because these means of mass communication reach so many people, there has been concern over the effect of the media on the standards and moral fabric of the national community—particularly when the material disseminated is obscene or violent.

The principal means of controlling the mass media so that community standards are maintained has been through censorship. In most instances, stipulations for censoring material have been established by state legislatures or by the federal administrative agencies such as the Federal Communications Commission which has jurisdiction over the mass media of radio and television. As with other maintenance policies, the major question in dealing with the mass media is: At what point does the effort to censor material overstep the bounds of individual liberties and infringe on the freedoms of speech and press?

■ *Censorship of magazines and newspapers.* In a democracy where freedom of speech and press are so highly regarded that they are guaranteed in the Constitution, it is almost ironic to think that censorship exists at all. Nevertheless, it does. Although pre-publication censorship is forbidden (see *Near v. Minnesota,* page 475), the censorship of published material has been permissible when the moral standards of the community seem to be threatened. Obscene material is not protected, then, by the First Amendment. But what is "obscene" is often a matter of taste. This poses another basic question: If the community's moral standards are not stipulated in the Constitution, what *are* these standards, and who should decide what they are?

Ordinarily, it has been the responsibility of the states to establish the standards of their respective communities and to prosecute those who publish or sell materials that offend these standards. But the national government has also been able to control the circulation of certain materials through its regulation of imports and of the postal service. The Supreme Court, on the other hand, has provided a counterbalance to any overzealous government action which might infringe on basic freedoms in the name of upholding moral standards.

Through its decisions in recent years, the Supreme Court has adopted a three-part measure for determining if an item is "obscene." An item can be considered obscene (1) if it appeals to prurient, or lustful, interest, (2) if it offends community standards in relating representations of sexual matters, and (3) if it is devoid of any social value.

Additionally, the Court has defined who can purchase materials which fall into these categories. In *Butler v. Michigan* (1957), it was decided that adults can not be deprived of access to printed material which might be offensive to children. A later case, *Smith v. California* (1959), upset a lower court's decision which had convicted a bookseller of selling obscene material. The Supreme Court held that there could be no conviction unless it was first proved that the bookseller had sold the item with an intent to distribute obscene material. Since the bookseller could not be expected to be familiar with every item on his shelves, he had to be cleared of the charge.

When material is openly advertised and sold as obscene or pornographic, however, the Court is more rigid. In the case of *Ginzburg v. United States* (1966), the Court upheld the conviction of a New York publisher for mailing obscene material that had been advertised as such.

■ *Censorship of movies.* The film industry is a relatively recent development, and it has been only in the last few decades that the motion picture has attained status as a means of communication instead of just an entertainment medium. Since there were no provisions for motion pictures in the Constitution, the Supreme Court has had to decide whether freedoms guaranteed in the First Amendment can be applied to production of films as well as other media. If films were not so protected, they would be subject to the jurisdiction and censorship of both the states and the national government.

In one of the early motion picture cases, *Mutual Film Corporation v. Industrial Commission of Ohio* (1915), the Court held that films were not part of "the press of the country," but rather a form of entertainment. At issue was an Ohio statute that required the prior approval of a Board of Censors before a motion picture could be shown in the state. Motion pictures had to be "of a moral, educational, or amusing and harmless character" to be approved by the Ohio Board. In its opinion, the Supreme Court said that

"the exhibition of moving pictures is a business, pure and simple, originated and conducted for profit, like other spectacles, not to be regarded . . . as part of the press of the country, or as organs of public opinion." [6]

The Ohio statute, according to the Court therefore, did not violate the First Amendment. Following this ruling, many states and local communities established film-censorship procedures.

It was not until the *Miracle Case* in 1952, that this interpretation was challenged. "The Miracle," an Italian film, was initially licensed and shown in New York City. The plot of the movie involved a poor goatherd who was seduced by a stranger whom she later believed to be a saint. The film offended some people, and was attacked vigorously by the Roman Catholic Church.

From Herblock's *Straight Herblock* (Simon & Schuster, 1964)

"I ENJOYED CENSORING THE MOVIE SO MUCH, ONE OF THESE DAYS I'D LIKE TO CENSOR THE BOOK."

(The matter of censorship poses a problem as to *who* should decide what the community's standards are.)

[6] *236 U.S. 230 (1915).*

The outcry caused the New York Board of Regents, which was authorized to censor motion pictures under state law, to reconsider its original consent to showing the picture. The film was subsequently found to be "sacrilegious" under the terms of the New York censorship statute, which declared that a film could not be licensed if it "is obscene, indecent, immoral, inhuman, sacrilegious, or is of such character that its exhibition would tend to corrupt morals or incite to crime. . . ."

When the New York censorship board's decision was appealed, the Supreme Court held first that films were part of the press and entitled to protection under the First and Fourteenth Amendments. As such, the Court said, a film can not be banned by a state on the basis of a censor's conclusion that it is "sacrilegious." The Court claimed that this term is so vague that it would give overall power to the censor. Although the Court's decision in the *Miracle Case* did not consider whether movies could be banned under the other provisions of the New York law, the Court continued to upset New York bans on other films in later cases.

Despite all these censorship cases, it was not until 1961 that the Court considered whether a state's requirements for film censorship were constitutional. In 1961 in the case of *Times Film Corporation v. City of Chicago,* the Court held that a city ordinance that required the submission of films to a censor was not a violation of freedom of speech or the press. In a close five-to-four decision, the Court majority said that a municipality can protect its people against obscenity and that prior censorship in these cases can sometimes be justified.

The problem remains a very puzzling one. In recent years there has been a shift to a more flexible Court interpretation of community standards. This is no doubt due to the fact that community standards have become less rigid and there are, thus, fewer instances of censorship which seem to violate individual freedom.

■ *Censorship by the bureaucracy.* Although most censorship is carried out in accordance with state regulations, some federal administrative agencies also have censorship powers. Congress has granted them this power. Customs officials, for example, have been given authority to stop material they deem harmful to the public interest from entering the country. This authority has been couched in such vague terms that officials have a great deal of discretion. Not only may they ban what they consider obscene material, but they may also exclude foreign political propaganda.

Under the old postal system, the Postmaster General was given the authority to revoke the second class mailing privileges of publications he considered obscene, fraudulent, or subversive. On several occasions the courts had to curb the Postmaster's authority. When D. H. Lawrence's *Lady Chatterley's Lover* was first published in this country, the Post Office Department threatened to exclude it from the mails, but was finally prevented from doing so by the courts.

■ *Control of television and radio.* The Federal Communications Commission has been granted responsibility by Congress for regulating the radio and television industries. Within very broad limits, the FCC sets the standards that are to govern the industry. It can license television and radio stations and can revoke the license of a station that has committed a serious violation of the law. But the FCC must also heed the interests of the broadcasting industry which is one of the most powerful in the country. When the FCC threatens action that would affect the financial position of the industry, it is subjected to intense criticism from the networks. Naturally the networks have access

"...AND WHAT'S MORE, ME AN' MY CHEMISTS WILL SOON
ANNOUNCE A CIGARETTE SO LOW IN TARS AND
NICOTINE IT ACTUALLY *CURES* CANCER!"

(The dangers of smoking won out over tobacco-industry resistance when the FCC banned cigarette advertising.)

to members of Congress and officials in other branches of the government. Thus, while the FCC has broad authority for setting standards that affect the major broadcasting groups, its power is counterbalanced by the political influence of these groups. On the other hand, when the FCC applies sanctions against the less powerful broadcasters, its sanctions are less likely to be challenged.

The FCC is cautious in using its authority even against minor broadcasters. This was illustrated in 1963 when the Commission granted the applications of three noncommerical radio stations owned by the controversial Pacifica Foundation. Two of these stations were already in operation and had applied for renewal of their broadcasting licenses; the third station had applied for an initial license. The Pacifica

Foundation was subjected to strong attack at the time by individuals within the listening areas of its stations. The complaints charged, among other things, that the programing of the stations was provocative and often politically controversial. Moreover, it was alleged that the Pacifica Foundation had Communist party affiliations. Eventually, the complaints reached the FCC.

Compared to the major networks, the political power of the Pacifica Foundation was virtually nonexistent. For a time it looked as if the FCC might actually refuse to grant the applications of the Foundation stations. But after a thorough investigation of the issues, the Commission found that even though the programing was indeed provocative, highly controversial, and possibly offensive to some listeners, *"this does not mean that those offended have the right, through the Commission's licensing power, to rule such programing off the airways. Were this the case, only the wholly inoffensive, the bland, could gain access to the radio microphone or TV camera. No such drastic curtailment can be countenanced under the Constitution, the Communications Act, or the Commission's policy, which has consistently sought to insure the 'maintenance of radio and television as a medium of freedom of speech and freedom of expression for the people of the nation as a whole.'"* [7]

In this case the power of the FCC to refuse Pacifica Foundation its licenses was not used. The Commission upheld the principles of freedom of speech and press.

Private censorship. Ordinarily censorship, when it is used, is imposed by the government. Government censorship, though, can be counteracted by the courts when individual freedoms are unduly threatened. However, there is another kind of censorship that neither the government

nor the courts are capable of stopping—private censorship.

If a sponsor of a television program, for example, decides he no longer agrees with the message the program is communicating, he may withdraw his financial support and the program will be dropped. Or if a network itself decides that a program does not maintain the moral standards of the community, the contracts of the people working on the programs will not be renewed. For radio and television, the specter of private censorship is very real indeed, and the Constitution offers no redress against it.

As with all other policy decisions within the political system, maintenance policies must be reached through compromise. A balance must be established between the demands made to preserve public order and uphold community standards and the demands made to protect individual liberties. If this balance is not maintained, the result could be anarchy or dictatorship.

Review questions

1. How does the federal government maintain public order? How was this governmental function affected by the *Feiner* case?
2. What type of government policy has been formulated to maintain community standards? Why have such policies been challenged in the courts?

---

[7] In re—*applications of Pacifica Foundation, before the Federal Communications Commission, for the renewal of licenses KPFA-FM and KBFB (educational FM), at Berkeley, California, and Station WBAI-FM, New York; and for the initial license of Station KPFK (noncommercial educational FM), at Los Angeles, California, 1964.*

Chapter Review

Terms you should know

ANZUS	collective security	NATO
balance of payments	community standards	OAS
CENTO	containment policy	SEATO
clear and present danger	foreign aid	security risk
	HUAC	Smith Act

Questions about this chapter

1. How did President Truman define the concept of containment for American foreign policy? Is this policy still relevant today? Explain.
2. How is foreign aid an example of a "maintenance policy" in the national interest?
3. Why is it vital in a democracy that policy-makers balance the need for security with the necessity of protecting the rights of individuals?
4. How did the decision in *Yates v. United States* modify the Smith Act? If the Court had ruled differently in this case, what would have been the implications for free speech as guaranteed in the First Amendment?
5. What federal agencies are responsible for protecting public order and what are their duties?
6. How might censorship be an infringement on First Amendment liberties? Are there any situations in which you think censorship is permissible? Explain.
7. How might private censorship be more of a danger and threat to the freedom of speech and press than government censorship?

Thought and discussion questions

1. The Supreme Court first presented the test of "clear and present danger" in the *Schenck* case of 1919, but the meaning of this test has been reinterpreted several times in subsequent cases. Do you think Schenck's conviction would still have been upheld if it had been reviewed by the Supreme Court in 1957? In 1967? Why, or why not?
2. It has been charged that the Vietnam War "was not a clear-cut case of communist aggression, but a civil war or internal insurrection not covered by the SEATO treaty." Give reasons why you agree or disagree with this statement.
3. What limitations were put on the Communist party members by the Internal Security Act of 1950 and the Communist Control Act of 1954? Do you think such rulings are consistent with the Bill of Rights? Explain.
4. When several newspapers published a series of classified government documents on the Vietnam War in 1971, government attempts to halt publication of the series were overruled by the Supreme Court. What basic issues were in conflict in this case? In presenting their cases before the Court, what arguments do you think each side probably used? What precedents did the Court have for deciding the case? How would you have decided it if you had been on the Court? Why?

Class projects

1. Examine the literature (magazines, newspapers, and pamphlets) of such organizations as the Students for a Democratic Society (SDS), the Black Panther party, the John Birch Society, and the Minutemen. Do you think any of these groups are advocating the violent overthrow of the United States government? Select a judge and jury from your classmates, and argue the case for two of these organizations using the Supreme Court's decision in the *Yates* case as a precedent.
2. The maintenance of "community standards" is one of the government's responsibilities. Decide who sets such standards in your community. How is it done? What role can a private citizen play? Do you agree or disagree with the standards presently set? Why, or why not?

Case Study: One aspect of foreign policy

While it is important for a nation to unify itself behind a single cohesive foreign policy, such a goal may be difficult to achieve when there are conflicting points of view on what the policy should be. Some Americans believe that the most important objective of United States foreign policy should be to prevent communist domination of the world. Those who support this view often see the "Cold War" as a prelude to a third world war, and Vietnam as just one of the battlegrounds between the inevitable adversaries—the communists and the free world. To win this struggle, these Americans advocate the buildup of military defense systems.

Other Americans feel that the defeat of the communists should not be the primary goal of American foreign policy. They feel that if America is a nuclear giant commanding the air, sea, and land, this show of power will deter other nations from aggression. Military intervention, according to this view, should be pursued only when American interests are, or will become, directly involved.

Still other Americans argue that the military has allied itself with powerful industrialists and that together these two groups continue to shape policies that no longer reflect international realities. These Americans question the power of the military, the size of the military budget, and the military-industrial complex itself. America's ultimate battle, this argument contends, is not fighting communism, but learning to co-exist with communism. Treaties limiting arms are seen as a step in this direction.

The following case study is composed of statements representing these three viewpoints on American foreign policy. The first statement comes from a book by General Curtis E. LeMay, now retired from the United States Air Force. The second was written by John Kenneth Galbraith who is Professor of Economics at Harvard University and was formerly the United States Ambassador to India. The final article is by Hanson W. Baldwin, a former military editor and analyst for *The New York Times*. Each article reflects the particular experiences and perspective of its author.

As you read the opinions expressed in these statements, watch for answers to the following questions:

1. Which of these commentators says there is evidence that America has lost its military superiority? What criteria does he cite?
2. What should the priorities of a defense budget be? What is your reaction to the priorities mentioned by Baldwin?
3. What is the military-industrial complex? What arguments does Galbraith use to justify his claim that the military-industrial bureaucracy is in a position of tremendous power?
4. What changes have occurred that have led some people to question the power of the military? Should the military be brought under greater civilian control?

America Is In Danger

by General Curtis E. LeMay

AMERICA IS in danger.

The Soviet Union has been and is now eagerly pressing ahead to acquire a nuclear strategic superiority. Deterrence, *our total defense philosophy,* is not for them. They have already surpassed us in the total megaton yield of warheads. They have already deployed an anti-ballistic missile system and are rapidly improving and expanding it. It is even doubtful that we can now match them in the delivery capability of bombers: we know they lead us in numbers of strategic bombers.

At the same time we have permitted our general war capability to rust. We have scrapped one thousand B-47s without providing replacements. Our B-52s are also on the way out. Our Minuteman force has been reduced to a thousand missiles while our higher yield Titans are phasing out. Our Polaris submarine fleet is static at forty-one vessels. No anti-ballistic missile system has been put into service. We stand nakedly exposed to a first strike. Even our air defense system has been allowed to deteriorate. We have no space weaponry of any sort. Our survival depends almost exclusively on the effectiveness of Minuteman and Polaris. . . .

The equivocal manner in which we are waging the war in Southeast Asia is a direct result of the bankrupt nature of our deterrent philosophy. There is reason to believe that we have already lost our strategic military superiority. With such a rent in our nuclear umbrella it would be impossible to exert our real strength in a limited conflict. Our incessant appeals to negotiate are indications of a strategic, if not moral weakness in our cause.

Yes, America is in grave danger. If we have not already lost our military superiority we are well on the way to it. . . .

Let us now take a . . . look at the Vietnam situation. . . .

To begin with it is necessary to understand that Vietnam is part of a much larger and much longer war—a war between communism and the Free World.

This larger war was declared by the communists. It was declared by Marx and Engels before there was one communist country in the world. It was declared by Lenin. It was waged by Stalin. It has been pursued relentlessly by every communist leader. Communist conquest is the burning doctrine of Mao Tse-tung and Ho Chi Minh.

It is a war waged simultaneously on many fronts and in many forms. It is a cold war and a hot war, an economic war and a political war, a propaganda war and an ideological war. It is waged by the communists according to their own timetable and on battlefields of their own choosing. Although the war has many facets, it has but one objective: communist control of the entire world.

This is not my definition of their goal. It is the communists' definition. They have stated it over and over again in many different ways and they believe it. I believe it, too. . . .

While fighting a limited war with equally limited success in Southeast Asia,

This condensation from America Is In Danger, *by General Curtis E. LeMay, USAF (Ret.) with Major General Dale O. Smith, is reprinted with permission of Funk & Wagnalls, a Division of Reader's Digest Books, Inc. Copyright © 1968 by General Curtis E. LeMay and Major General Dale O. Smith.*

and while witnessing the rapid buildup of Soviet intercontinental nuclear forces, America languors with an illness of euphoria brought on by our leaders who have proclaimed an international détente [relaxation of tension] in the struggle against communism. This détente is unwarranted. It is not shared by our adversaries, who are frantically attempting to pass us in the nuclear weapons race. And they *are* passing us. . . .

We have come to that period in our history which John Foster Dulles [Secretary of State, 1953–1959] warned about in his book *War or Peace.* "If at any time in the near future," he wrote, "it seems like the danger of war has passed, that will be the period of greatest peril. Then we may be tempted to relax and get careless and disarm, materially and morally. By so doing, we should expose ourselves to a sudden attack, which is most likely to come at such a time."

The measures we must take to regain and maintain our military superiority are crystal clear. The very first step, of course, is to rid ourselves of those false prophets who have deceived us and who have guided us into the dangerous waters where we now find ourselves. They have been responsible for placing America in danger, and each day that they hold high office America comes closer and closer to oblivion.

The defense of our country has never been easy. But it has been worth any difficulty. And it is worth it today.

No hardship is too severe, no expense too much, and no life too dear to defend this America, the greatest country the world has ever known. . . .

How To Control
The Military

by John Kenneth Galbraith

What is now clear is that a drastic change is occurring in public attitudes toward the military and its industrial allies which will not for long be ignored by politicians who are sensitive to the public mood. And from this new political climate will come the chance for reasserting control.

The purpose of this pamphlet is to see the nature of the military power, assess its strengths and weaknesses, and suggest the guidelines for regaining control. . . .

. . . Although Americans are probably the world's least competent conspirators—partly because no other country so handsomely rewards in cash and notoriety the man who blows the whistle on those with whom he is conspiring—we have a strong instinct for so explaining that of which we disapprove. In the conspiratorial view, the military power is a collation of generals and conniving industrialists. The goal is mutual enrichment; they arrange elaborately to feather each other's nest. . . .

. . . The notion of a conspiracy to enrich and corrupt is gravely damaging to an understanding of the military power. . . . The reality is far less dramatic and far more difficult of solution. . . . The participants in these organizations are mostly honest men whose public and private behavior would withstand public scrutiny as well as most. . . .

. . . The organizations that comprise the military power are the Department of Defense embracing the four Armed Services, and especially their procurement branches. And the military power encompasses the specialized defense contractors—General Dynamics, McDonnell Douglas, Lockheed, or the defense firms of the agglomerates—of Ling-Temco-Vought or Litton Industries. . . . And it includes the defense divisions of primarily civilian firms such as General Electric or AT&T. It draws moral and valuable political support from the unions. Men serve these organizations in many, if not most, instances because they believe in what they are doing—because they have committed themselves to the bureaucratic truth. To find and scourge a few malefactors is to ignore this far more important commitment.

The military power is not confined to the Services and their contractors—what has come to be called the military-industrial complex. Associate membership is held by the intelligence agencies which assess Soviet (or Chinese) actions or intentions. These provide, more often by selection and bureaucratic belief than by any outright dishonesty, the justification for what the Services would like to have and what their contractors would like to supply. Associated also are Foreign Service Officers who provide a civilian or diplomatic gloss to the foreign policy positions which serve the military need. . . .

Also a part of the military power are the university scientists and those in such defense-oriented organizations as RAND, the Institute for Defense Analysis, and Hudson Institute who think professionally about weapons systems and the strategy of their use. And last, but by no means least, there is the dependable voice of the military in the Congress, most notably on the Armed Services and Appropriations Committees of the Senate and House of Representatives. These are the organizations which comprise the military power.

The men who comprise these organizations call each other on the phone, meet at committee hearings, serve together on teams or task-forces, work in neighboring offices in Washington or San Diego. They naturally make their decisions in accordance with their view of the world—the view of the bureaucracy of which they are a part. The problem is not conspiracy or corruption but unchecked rule. . . .

. . . Not long ago, Bernard Nossiter, the . . . economics reporter of the *Washington Post,* made the rounds of some of the major defense contractors to get their views of the post-Vietnam prospect. All, without exception, saw profitable tension and conflict. . . . [T]he head of Ling-Temco-Vought reported that "defense spending has to increase in our area because there has been a failure to initiate—if we are not going to be overtaken by the Soviets." . . . [O]ne of [the company's] vice-presidents was more outspoken. "We're going to increase defense budgets as long as [the Russians] are ahead of us." A study of the Electronics Industries Association, also dug up by Mr. Nossiter, . . . discounted the danger of arms control, decided that the "likelihood of limited war will increase," and concluded that "for the electronic firms, the outlook is good in spite [sic] of [the end of hostilities in] Vietnam."

From the foregoing beliefs, in turn, comes the decision on weapons and weapons systems and military policy generally. No one can tell where the action originates—whether the Services or the contractors initiate decisions on weapons—nor can the two be sharply distinguished. Much of the plant of the specialized defense contractors is owned by the government. Most of their working capital is supplied by the government. . . .

. . . In this kind of association some proposals will come across the table from the military. Some will come back from the captive contractors. . . .

We see here a truly remarkable reversal of the American political and economic system as outlined by the fathers and still portrayed to the young. That view supposes that ultimate authority—ultimate sovereignty—lies with the people. And this authority is assumed to be comprehensive. . . .

Here, however, we find the Armed Services, or the corporations that supply them, making the decisions and instructing the Congress and the public. The public accepts whatever is so decided and pays the bill. . . .

. . . How did this remarkable reversal in the oldest of constitutional arrangements come about? How, in particular, did it come about in a country that sets great store by individual and citizen rights and which traditionally has been suspicious of military, industrial, and bureaucratic power? . . .

Six things brought the military-industrial bureaucracy to its present position of power. To see these forces is also to be encouraged by the chance for escape.

First, there has been, as noted, the increasing bureaucratization of our life. In what . . . has [been] called the weapons culture, both economic and technological complexity are raised to the highest power. So, accordingly, is the scope and power of organization. So, accordingly, is the possibility of self-serving belief. . . .

Second in importance in bringing the military-industrial complex to power were the circumstances and images of foreign policy in the late forties, fifties, and early sixties. The Communist world, as noted, was viewed as a unified imperium mounting its claim to every part of the globe. The post-war pressure on eastern Europe and on Berlin, the Chinese Revolution, and the Korean War seemed powerful evidence in the case. And, after the surprisingly early explosion of the first Soviet atomic bomb, followed within a decade by the even more astonishing flight of the first Sputnik, it was easy to believe that the Communist world was not only politically more unified than the rest but technologically stronger as well.

The natural reaction was to delegate power and concentrate resources. The military Services and their industrial allies were given unprecedented authority—as much as in World War II—to match the Soviet technological initiative. And the effort of the nation's scientists (and other scholars) was concentrated in equally impressive fashion. . . .

This enfranchisement of the military power was in a very real sense the result of a democratic decision—it was a widely approved response to the seemingly fearsome forces that surrounded us. With time those who received this unprecedented grant of power came to regard it as a right. . . .

Third, secrecy confined knowledge of Soviet weapons and responding American action to those within the public and private bureaucracy. No one else had knowledge, hence no one else was thought qualified to speak. Senior members of the Armed Services, their industrial allies, the scientists, the members of the Armed Services Committees of the Congress were in; all others were out. It would be hard to imagine a more efficient arrangement for protecting the power of a bureaucracy. In the academic community and especially in Congress there was no small prestige in being a member of this club. . . .

Fourth, there was the disciplining effect of personal fear. A nation that was massively alarmed about the unified power of the Communist world was not tolerant of skeptics or those who questioned the only seemingly practical line of response. Numerous scientists, social scientists, and public officials had come reluctantly to accept the idea of the Communist threat. This history of reluctance could now involve the danger—real or imagined—that they might be suspected of past association with this all-embracing conspiracy. The late Senator Joseph R. McCarthy and others saw or sensed the opportunity for exploiting national and personal anxiety. The result was further and decisive pressure on anyone who seemed not to concur in the totality of the Communist threat. (McCarthy was broken only when he capriciously attacked the military power.) . . .

In 1961, in the last moments before leaving office, as all now know, President Eisenhower gave his famous warning: "In the councils of government we must guard against the acquisition of unwarranted influence, whether sought or unsought, by the military-industrial complex. The potential for the disastrous rise of misplaced power exists and will persist." This warning was to become by a wide margin the most quoted of all Eisenhower statements. . . .

Fifth, in the fifties and early sixties, the phrase "domestic priority" had not yet become a cliché. The civilian claim on Federal funds was not, or seemed not, to be overpowering. The great riots in the cities had not yet occurred. The appalling conditions in the urban core that were a cause were still unnoticed. Internal migration had long been under way but millions were yet to come from the rural into the urban slums. Poverty had not yet been placed on the national agenda, with the consequence that we would learn how much of it there is and how abysmal it is. And promises not having been made to end poverty, expectations had not been aroused. . . .

Military expenditures, although no one wished to say so, did sustain employment. Circumstances could not have been better designed, economically speaking, to allow the military a clear run.

Sixth and finally, in these years both liberal and conservative opposition to the military-industrial power were muted. . . .

. . . [F]or most, it was enough that the Communists—exponents of a yet more powerful state and against private property, too—were on the other side. One accepted a lesser danger to fight a greater one. . . . It became a tenet of a more extreme conservatism that civilians should never interfere with the military except to provide more money. Nor would there be any compromise with communism. It must be destroyed. . . .

By the early sixties the liberal position was beginning to change. From comparatively early in the Kennedy Administration—the Bay of Pigs was a major factor in this revelation—many saw that a stand would have to be made against policies urged by the military and its State Department allies. Military intervention in Cuba, military intervention in Laos, military intervention in Vietnam, an all-out fallout shelter program, unrestricted nuclear testing, all of which were urged, would be disastrous for the President as well as for the country and the world. . . .

. . . Suspicion of the military power in 1968 was the most important factor uniting the followers of Senators Kennedy, McCarthy, and McGovern. Along with the more specific and more important opposition to the Vietnam conflict, it helped to generate the opposition that persuaded Lyndon Johnson not to run. And the feeling that Vice-President Humphrey was not sufficiently firm on this issue—that he belonged politically to the generation of liberals that was tolerant of the military-industrial power—unquestionably diluted and weakened his support. Most likely it cost him the election.

To see the sources of the strength of the military-industrial complex in the fifties and sixties is to see its considerably greater vulnerability now. The Communist imperium, which once seemed so fearsome in its unity, has broken up into bitterly antagonistic blocs. Moscow and Peking barely keep the peace. Fear in Czechoslovakia, Yugoslavia, and Romania is not of the capitalist enemy but the great Communist friend. . . . The Soviets have had no more success than has capitalism in penetrating and organizing the backward countries of the world. Communist and capitalist jungles are indistinguishable. Men of independent mind recognize that after twenty years of aggressive military competition with the Soviets our security is not greater and almost certainly less than when the competition began. And although in the fifties it was fashionable to assert otherwise ("a dictator does not hesitate to sacrifice his people by the millions"), we now know that the Soviets are as aware of the totally catastrophic character of nuclear war as we are—and more so than our more articulate generals.

These changes plus the adverse reaction to Vietnam have cost the military power its monopoly of the scientific community. This, in turn, has damaged its claim to a monopoly of knowledge, including that which depends on security classification. . . .

Additionally, civilian priority has become one of the most evocative words in the language. Everywhere—for urban housing and services, sanitation, schools, police, urban transportation, clean air, potable water—the needs are huge and pressing. Because these needs are not being met the number of people who live in fear of an urban explosion may well be greater than those who are alarmed by the prospect of nuclear devastation. . . .

Certainly the day when military spending was a slightly embarassing alternative to unemployment is gone and, one imagines, forever.

With all of these changes has come a radical change in the political climate. . . . We have lived with the Communists on the same planet now for a half century. An increasing number are disposed to believe we *can* continue doing so. Communism seems somewhat less triumphant than twenty years ago. . . .

The anxiety which led to the great concentration of military and industrial power in the fifties having dissipated, the continued existence of that power has naturally become a political issue. . . .

Two other changes have altered the position of the military power. In the fifties the military establishment of the United States was still identified in the public mind with the great captains of World War II—with Eisenhower, Marshall, MacArthur, Bradley, King, Nimitz, Arnold. And many members of a slightly junior generation—Maxwell Taylor, James Gavin, Matthew Ridgway, Curtis LeMay—were in positions of power. Some of these soldiers might have done less well had they been forced to fight an elusive and highly motivated enemy in the jungle of Vietnam encumbered by the leisurely warriors of the ARVN [the South Vietnamese Army]. . . . The present military generation is intimately associated with the Vietnam misfortune. And its credibility has been deeply damaged by its fatal association with the bureaucratic truths of that war—with the long succession of defeats that became victories, the victories that became defeats, and brilliant actions that did not signify anything at all. . . .

Finally, all bureaucracy has a mortal weakness; it cannot respond effectively to attack. . . . The old slogans—we must resist world wide Communist aggression, we must not reward aggression, we must stand by our brave allies—were employed not only after repetition had robbed them of all meaning but after they had been made ludicrous by events. . . .

. . . As the military power comes under scrutiny it will be reduced to asserting that its critics are indifferent to Soviet or Chinese intentions, unacquainted with the most recent intelligence, militarily inexperienced, naive, or afraid to look nuclear destruction in the eye. Or it will be said that they are witting or unwitting tools of the Communist conspiracy. . . .

. . . In the years following World War II there was a spacious view of the American task in the world. We guarded the borders of the non-Communist world. We prevented subversion there and put down wars of liberation elsewhere. In pursuit of these aims we maintained alliances, deployed forces, provided military aid on every continent. This was the competition of the superpowers. We had no choice but to meet the challenge of that competition.

We have already found that the world so depicted does not exist. Superpowers there are, but superpowers cannot much affect the course of life within the countries they presume to see as on their side. . . . We have also found, as in the nearby case of Cuba, that a country can go Communist without any overpowering damage.

What we have not done is accommodate our military policy to this reality. Military aid, bases, conventional force levels, weapons requirements, still assume superpower omnipotence. (And the military power still projects this vision of our task.) Our foreign policy has, in fact, changed. It is the Pentagon that hasn't.

STRATEGY FOR TOMORROW

by Hanson W. Baldwin

The most difficult, the most expensive, the most vital and the greatest task of American strategy today is nuclear defense. Without it there is no defense, there can be no national security. With it there can be no perfect defense, no absolute security.

But this is not new to history; no fortress, no Maginot Line, no defensive system ever built has long remained impregnable; there is no absolute security—and there never will be—in the life of man.

This condensation from Strategy for Tomorrow, *by Hanson W. Baldwin, is reprinted with permission of Harper & Row. Copyright © 1970 by Hanson W. Baldwin.*

The implications of an enemy nuclear attack to the life of the nation are so staggering that nuclear defense must have absolute priority in any U.S. grand strategy. The defense of the continental United States is a categorical imperative. . . .

There are more ways than one to lose the world to Communism. Put in an oversimplified and extreme form, the strategy of nuclear parity or nuclear inferiority or of unilateral arms limitation is a strategy of defeat, not a strategy of national security.

Thus, any strategy for defense of the continental island and the Western Hemisphere—indeed, any world strategy—must start with a definite and clear-cut nuclear superiority to any potential enemy or combination of enemies—a superiority that is clearly discernible by the enemy. . . .

No administration can settle for less than this unless there is a global and policed arms-limitation agreement, subject to adequate verification and control. . . .

. . . [B]ut it is already evident that the U.S. legions, like the Roman legions of yesterday, are overextended. Conquest of the world, or its domination by U.S. power, is no longer a possibility, if it ever was, even in the short-lived era of our nuclear monopoly. We cannot now bend Russia and China to our will, eliminate them as threats to world peace, without unacceptable cost and damage to ourselves and to the world around us. World domination is not possible without world war—all-out war (the very development we are trying to avoid)—and even then the outcome would be sackcloth and ashes.

Nor can the United States continue indefinitely in the role of "world policeman"; the costs are too high. This is the service that Vietnam has done; it has exposed the high cost of universally applied containment to keep the peace; it has forced a reappraisal of our overseas commitments and our vital interests. It should be obvious, without argument, that the demands on the U.S. economy, the U.S. taxpayer and the U.S. Patience in the decades ahead are too great to support a global policy of intervention. . . .

In developing a global strategy, therefore, one must modify the desirable but pragmatically impossible goal of the "Never Again" school to "Never-Again-except-under-carefully-chosen-conditions-and-at-times-and-places-of-our-own-choosing-and-even-then-within-limits."

The problem is to choose the times and places and to set the limits [for military intervention]. The places must be where our vital, or highly important, interests are involved, or where there is a strong probability that they will become involved. . . .

Obviously the use of nuclear devices of any sort represents a last resort. Today even those in the Pentagon who hold that the atomic bomb—at least in its tactical version—is "just another weapon" agree that its employment postulates unknown dangers, and might invite response in kind. No one of responsibility advocates the use of any such weapons lightly. . . .

The formulation of a defense budget . . . is an intricate balancing act, which must, and does, start with some Presidential guidelines. The validity of these guidelines depends essentially upon the President himself and his manner of doing business. The input into the decision-making process from all sources—the utilization, or lack of utilization, of the State Department, the National Security Council, the Central Intelligence Agency and other agencies—and the thoroughness of the evaluation procedure strengthens or weakens the assessment of the risks. The Presidential procedure can, indeed, make the process simply an offhand gamble, or as rational a process as is possible. . . .

The clear priorities in any defense budget tomorrow must be: (1) unexcelled weaponry; (2) command of the air and of the oceans and of aerospace; (3) small, ready but modern and mobile ground forces, backed by an administrative structure and mobilization potential capable of providing sizable reserves. . . .

There will always be in any organization as big as the Department of Defense and the military services a certain amount of waste and inefficiency. Bigness and complexity—and both are an inevitable part of the armed services of tomorrow—involve an unavoidable degree of expense; this is, indeed, one agrument for a reversion, as far as possible, to the smaller, simpler, more elite services of the past, which were at once more manageable and had higher standards of duty, discipline and professionalism. But fundamentally force reductions mean reductions in total power; the old siren call of the politicians that billions can be saved by greater efficiency in the Defense Department simply is not true—millions, yes, but billions, no. We may reduce the budget by billions in the years ahead; if so, we will do it at the cost of total power. Every defense budget represents a calculated risk; we may increase the military risk (by cutting the budget) because the political risk has decreased, or the economic risk demands it, but we *must* squarely face these tradeoffs. It is the height of hypocrisy to claim that we can maintain the same defense posture for much less money. . . .

. . . We have allowed Moscow to overtake and surpass us in major elements of strategic power—numbers and size of land-based ICBM's, anti-ballistic missile systems, medium- and intermediate-range missiles, numbers of bombers. We still retain an equivocal lead in sea-based missiles, but it may be short-lived; the Russians launched an estimated 10 to 20 new submarines in 1969, the United States 5. By the end of 1970, Moscow will have a larger fleet of nuclear-powered submarines than the United States. By 1975, if present programs are maintained, the United States may well be in second place in sea-based missiles and in over-all nuclear striking power. Washington has already started a kind of unilateral arms-limitation program; for the first time in history major force reductions and cuts in the defense budget have been effected before a war was finished.

The limitation of armaments and some reduction of the costs and the tensions that arms races help to cause are highly desirable goals. But we may already have doomed our efforts; one cannot bargain successfully—or at least safely—from a position of actual or potential inferiority. Arms races are dangerous, but arms inferiority even more so; any agreement which would freeze the United States in an inferior position could well doom us to war or to loss of the things we hold dear. . . .

End questions

1. Are there any points of agreement between the authors of these articles? If so, what are they? On what points do they differ?
2. What does Baldwin mean when he says "there is no absolute security—and there never will be—in the life of man"? Do you agree with this statement? Why? How would LeMay and Galbraith respond to it?

3. Whom do you agree with most—LeMay, Baldwin, or Galbraith? Which course of action do you think American foreign policy is following? Is this good in your estimation? If you favor change, how would you go about it?

4. Do you think the primary goal of American foreign policy should be to combat communism? Explain why you answered this question as you did.

5. In your opinion, what circumstances would constitute an adequate reason for involving the United States in a military conflict? Compare your viewpoint with those of your classmates. What is the consensus of opinion in the class?

6. If you feel strongly about an aspect of American foreign policy, how would you go about trying to express your views? What organizations would you join? Which congressional leaders would you support?

CHAPTER 21

Policies That Respond to People's Needs

In addition to providing standards for protecting the rights of citizens and for resolving conflicts between individual members of society, government also pursues maintenance policies to achieve society's broader goals. Those maintenance policies by which the United States protects itself against potentially destructive threats were described in Chapter 20. There are other maintenance policies that the government formulates to meet economic and other needs of the general population. Maintenance policies of the second type may be referred to as *developmental* when they help to sustain and promote the continued well-being and advancement of particular groups and of the entire community.

Most such developmental policies are initiated to answer many different kinds of public and community needs: to alleviate and prevent economic insecurity and poverty; to improve health, education, housing, and the environment; to advance science and the arts. To assist in the achievement of such goals, government may adopt a variety of policies ranging from noninterference to regulation or direct financial assistance. Often, policies that originate as short-term responses to particular economic or social needs become permanent functions of government if the needs for them persist.

While developmental policies are usually undertaken in response to the demands of particular groups, they often provide benefits for the larger population at the same time. A policy formed to help a specific industry, for example, may also augment job prospects for the general labor force. Similarly, unemployment insurance is designed to help people who are out of work but it also contributes to the national economic stability by sustaining some of the spending capacity of that group.

The kinds of outputs formulated at any given time are determined by many factors. The social and economic conditions of the nation and the needs created by such conditions shape the demands people make and consequently the nature of policy output. As these conditions change, demands and policies change as well. Thus, developmental policies for the technological society of today are different from those produced in the agrarian era around 1800, or during the period of industrial expansion in the late nineteenth century.

These outputs are also determined by the ability of certain interest groups to make effective demands. Only recently, for example, have policies been devised which aim to eliminate poverty or protect consumers. This is due in large measure to the fact that spokesmen for the poor and for the average consumer have only recently become sufficiently organized to channel demands to decision-makers.

The Changing Economy

It is recognized by most people that government must play some role in the economic life of the nation. There have been, however, continual arguments over just how much government should intervene and what form such intervention should take. The actual results of such debate have been motivated more by the pressures operating within the political system than

Is there any group in society missing from this national table of plenty? If the bill of fare is not sumptuous enough to feed everyone, how can policy be changed so that those not presently feasting can be included?

by adherence to any one economic philosophy. As the structure of the economy has changed, the government's role in it has changed also, to answer those demands that seemed most in the public interest.

Early government control. There has been some government control of the economy since the earliest settlers stepped ashore in North America. In fact, the American colonies were settled and the United States was created in a period dominated by *mercantilism,* an economic system in which national governments expected to shape and control the economic order. The English mercantile system, under which the colonies were established, subjected all economic activity to regulation. Wages, prices, and conditions of employment were fixed, and unauthorized associations of either businessmen or laborers were forbidden by laws against conspiracy. Many American colonists bitterly resented some of these measures, notably those designed to prevent the growth of industry in America. On the other hand, some of the colonists, particularly the merchants, accepted and profited from regulations that gave them preferred status in the British market over the French and Spanish.

After they won their independence, the states retained some control of economic life within their borders. Every state had made some effort to fix food prices and prevent profiteering during the runaway inflation that accompanied the Revolutionary War. During and after the war, each state as well as the Congress of the Confederation issued and controlled the value of its own currency.

While the Constitution did give certain economic powers—such as the collecting of tariffs and the coinage of money—exclusively to the national government, it brought no change in basic attitudes toward the role of government in the economy. The states continued to regulate business, to grant monopolies, to subsidize and thereby maintain certain necessary industries such as saw mills, salt refineries, and iron works, and to regard these actions as natural governmental functions. Moreover, at the federal level, Alexander Hamilton, who was the Treasury Secretary under the first administration, believed completely in the right of the government to develop the national economy.

Hamilton thought that it was in the national interest to turn the United States from a nation of farmers and merchants into a self-sufficient commercial and industrial power. He therefore sought instruments of national economic policy that would achieve this end. First, he created a national credit structure. The key institution for this was the Bank of the United States, which regulated the currency, stimulated and controlled the rate of economic growth, induced foreign investment, and served as a depository for Treasury funds. Second, Hamilton persuaded the new national government to pay the debts of the Confederation and those debts that the individual states had incurred. By doing this he won the support of the commercial

"This business of taking from the rich and giving to the poor could easily become a political theory."

(Many factors besides political philosophy may determine the role a government plays in economic life.)

groups in the country for the new Republic. Third, he succeeded in instituting a protective tariff to protect infant American industries from foreign competition, and he urged the national government to establish and subsidize certain key manufactures and industries.

After 1795, the agrarian interests led by Thomas Jefferson adopted Hamilton as their pet devil. They claimed that Hamilton's program, particularly his bank, was an invasion of the powers reserved to the states. In short, they maintained that government did have power over the economy, but that such power should belong to the state governments and not the national government.

In the 1840's and 1850's there was a reaction against the intervention of government at all levels in the economic life of the country. Many people reacted bitterly against the evidence of widespread corruption and embezzlement of public funds in the construction of canals, roads, and railroads. This sentiment was soon reflected in legislation and state constitutional provisions forbidding the subsidization of private enterprise by the states.

The government's role in industrial expansion. The Civil War had an enormous impact on the American economy and the relations between government and economic life. First, the war gave a tremendous stimulus to industrialization in the North. In 1859, the year before the outbreak of the war, there were 1,311,000 wage earners producing products worth $1,900,000,000. Ten years later, there were more than 2,000,000 wage earners producing about $3,386,000,000-worth of goods. This indicates a substantial growth, even when it is considered that northern industries had to compensate for the almost total devastation of southern industries.

The half-century following the Civil War witnessed the rapid burgeoning of indus-

trial society in the United States. Throughout this period, economic wealth became concentrated among a few enterprising businessmen who dominated such industries as banking, oil, railroads, and steel. Waves of immigrants provided these growing industries with an ample supply of cheap labor. The powerful industrialists not only controlled their respective industries and the lives of people who worked for them, but they also had considerable influence on the government decision-makers. It was not surprising, then, that during most of this period, there was almost a total absence of government regulation of business. Still, government assistance to enterprise played an important role in economic development. Both national and state governments adopted policies to assist the development of the industries and to maintain them once they were established.

■ *The railroads.* The role of government in the industrial expansion is illustrated by the development of the railroads. Initially, the railroad companies had to acquire franchises from the state governments to build the lines. State and local governments granted millions of acres of land to the companies and also floated bonds to subsidize railroad construction. In Kansas, $175,000,000 was loaned in this fashion. The federal government also aided the building of some transcontinental railroads by providing loans and land grants. Such grants gave the railroads huge expanses of territory (in Minnesota, land grants were twice the size of Massachusetts) to develop and sell. With these grants, the companies were also awarded mineral rights as well as other indirect benefits.

Not only was government power employed in establishing the railroads, it also helped the companies maintain their power. In effect the railroads became private governments that drew on state and federal power to defend their sovereignty and their right to make and enforce decisions. By refusing to interfere with the companies, the government gave private decisions the status of public law. For example, if a railroad insisted that farmers store grain in railroad-owned silos and enforced the policy by refusing to load grain from other silos, the only authority that could intervene on behalf of the farmers was the state. If the state refused, which was generally the case, the railroad's policy became public policy.

Government power was also used to protect the companies more directly. The state authorities and later those of the federal government were often willing to defend the companies from their enemies. They imprisoned striking workers, penalized boycotting farmers, and in general invoked police power on behalf of railroads in crisis situations.

The railroads had full power, subject only to a few limitations in their franchises, to fix their freight and passenger rates. In 1873 it cost as much to ship a bushel of wheat from Minneapolis to Milwaukee as it did to transport it from Milwaukee to Liverpool, England. If the farmers opposed the rate, there was little they could do. If they banded together to boycott the railroad, the law soon apprehended them for conspiring to restrain trade. Similarly, if the railroad workers went on strike to protest low wages, the law of conspiracy would have been invoked against them.

When finally, in the 1870's and 1880's, irate farmers succeeded in getting state legislation passed regulating railroad abuses, they soon found themselves facing resistance from the Supreme Court. In the *Wabash* case (1886), the Court held that almost all state attempts to control the railroads were unconstitutional encroachments on the federal power to regulate interstate commerce. It was this decision that finally forced the Congress to take action. In the following year, Congress passed the Interstate Commerce Act, a milestone on the road to government regulation of industries. (See Chapter 15, page 371.)

■ *Liberty of contract.* Like the farmers, the workers who were employed in expanding industries sought state protection from the power of private companies. When they did succeed in getting state legislatures to enact regulations on their behalf, the workers came up against the same resistance by the courts as the farmers. The concept of "liberty of contract" was the legal principle the judiciary used to squash any actions of the state governments that were undertaken to provide protection for workers.

According to Article I, Section 10, of the Constitution, contracts are subject to regulation only when they affect the public safety, health, or welfare. Still, most private contracts, until the end of the nineteenth century, were subject to state regulations. During the 1880's, however, the courts began to include the concept of "liberty of contract" within the meaning of "due process of law." Since the Fourteenth Amendment extends the "due process" clause to the states, state legislatures could no longer interfere with the right of private parties to make agreements between themselves.

This new concept was applied specifically to labor contracts between workers and their employers. Some states had been trying to regulate the conditions of employment by passing minimum wage and hour laws. But under the new interpretation of due process, such laws were considered to violate the liberty of contract by which workers could sell their services on terms of their own choosing and employers could bargain for the cheapest

Keppler from *Puck,* Courtesy of the New-York Historical Society

The Modern Colossus of Railroads

(Railroad magnates Vanderbilt (center), Field (left), and Gould (right) were shown in 1879 holding the reins of the freight lines, thus keeping produce from market.)

labor. This interpretation usually worked to the advantage of the employer.

The Supreme Court upheld liberty of contract in the case of *Lochner v. New York* (1905). New York had passed a law specifying that no person could be "required or permitted to work in a . . . bakery or confectionery establishment more than sixty hours in any one week or more than ten hours in any one day . . . ." The majority of the Court in the *Lochner* decision considered the New York law to be a violation of the "right of contract between the employer and employees" which was protected by the Fourteenth Amendment.

In effect, the Supreme Court's decision crippled the growth of wage and hour legislation, checked the political ambitions of labor, and gave employers license to extort whatever conditions they could from their employees. The Supreme Court had reaffirmed government's role in protecting only the business community.

The New Deal. With the Depression of the 1930's and the election of Franklin D. Roosevelt to the Presidency, the pendulum began to swing in the opposite direction. Through the New Deal programs, government's intervention in economic life was extended to assist not just the business community but the population as a whole.

Still, the New Deal was as much pro-business as it was pro-labor or pro-farmer. The various agencies of the New Deal poured billions of dollars into economic recovery programs, and many sections of the economy reaped benefits. Government entered into the mortgage business, refinancing farms and homes to ease the responsibilities of banks and insurance companies. The Agricultural Adjustment Administration granted aid to farmers. The establishment of public works programs such as the Tennessee Valley Authority was an impetus for business to keep going, as well as a source of work and income to the unemployed.

Although it may seem that the New Deal was a calculated attempt on the part of government to enter into all aspects of the nation's economic life, it was not. In fact, the New Deal was merely a collection of economic experiments. In the long run, however, some of these so-called experiments—initially contrived to get the nation out of economic depression—became part of the permanent apparatus of government. Most important, as a result of the New Deal era, government's economic role turned from protecting just the business community to include the farmers, the workers, the unemployed, small businessmen, and other segments of the nation's economic life.

World War II and the post-war period. The outbreak of World War II and the ending of the Depression brought another change in national policy toward the economy. Even before the United States entered the war, factories had begun to increase production of war materiel. And as soon as the nation was involved in the actual fighting, its manpower was mobilized for the military services and for the factories. The government's intervention at this time was an effort to keep the fighting machine operating.

After the war, the economy continued to expand as Americans switched first to producing all those consumer items unobtainable during the war. Moreover, the advent of the Cold War and the military actions in Korea and Vietnam kept the manufacturers of war materiel in full operation. The economy began to boom, and it continued to expand as new markets opened in the rest of the world.

Government intervention in the economy as a result took a new twist. As labor unions became more powerful, the government was called on more frequently to act as an arbitrator between labor and business. The government also took on the role of protector in certain industries. As the number of passengers on intercity trains dropped and the railroads lost money trying to maintain these rail lines, the government stepped in to underwrite certain experiments in rail travel. At the same time, regulatory agencies took a more active role in regulating the railroads, airlines, and other industries, such as oil. An overabundance of farm products pushed prices down to levels that prevented farmers from making livable incomes.

The government was encouraged to intervene by providing subsidies for farm products priced too low, and by establishing soil banks which made it profitable for farmers not to plant acreage in surplus products. The government also aided scientific research projects financially, and cooperated with business on such endeavors as the development of a supersonic transport.

As in all periods of the nation's history, the government will continue through the last decades of the twentieth century to regulate the nation's economy in response to the demands made on it by the people. In the 1970's this will probably mean more help for the poor, more regulation of industries to prevent pollution and to clean up the environment, more health measures, and increased aid to education. The goals of economic policy will be to maintain economic stability and improve the quality of life for all Americans.

Editorial cartoon by Pat Oliphant. Copyright, *The Denver Post.* Reprinted with permission of Los Angeles Times Syndicate.

"IF YOU SET WATER STANDARDS SO HIGH, YOU MIGHT HINDER INDUSTRIAL DEVELOPMENT."—*WALTER J. HICKEL*

(Government has to balance the needs of the economy against the welfare and desires of all the people.)

Review questions

1. How has the role of government in American economic life changed since the eighteenth century?
2. Describe the government's policy concerning industry in the post-Civil War period. What factors contributed to the formulation of this policy output?

Special Groups and the Economy

It is difficult to single out any economic group that does not receive some special governmental services. There are, however, four major groups—labor, business, farmers, and war veterans—that have been the beneficiaries of most governmental economic policy.

Maintaining the welfare of labor. The federal government has two major programs of vital significance to the American worker. The first is directed at maintaining the economic security of workers. In this category fall such policies as social security, unemployment compensation, wage and hour legislation, child labor legislation, and so forth. The second major policy area is geared to maintaining the workers' right to organize and bargain collectively with their employers. In this category are all the laws and regulations that define the relationships between employees and employers and between labor unions and employers, as well as the machinery of collective bargaining.

■ *Keeping the worker secure.* When the Great Depression began in 1929, there was not a single state that had a program to combat unemployment. During the years that followed, the widespread poverty and the plight of millions of people out of work demonstrated that unemployment was not only a problem for the individual worker but that it also had devastating consequences for the entire society.

The first federal-state program for unemployment insurance was included in the Social Security Act passed by Congress in 1935. The Act provided for a federal payroll tax to be levied on employers of eight or more workers. But if a state set up an unemployment insurance program financed by similar payroll taxes, the Act provided that employers in that state would receive credit for the federal payroll tax. The 1935 Act made the enactment of state programs virtually mandatory, and unemployment insurance became available in all states by 1937. Today, every state in the Union has accepted the principle that unemployment is a government concern.

Since 1935 Congress has revised the federal-state unemployment insurance program to benefit many more workers than were covered in the original Act. Federally administered programs have also been enacted to protect railroad workers, veterans, and federal employees from the insecurity of unemployment. The federal-state programs, however, are frequently criticized in times of recession for being only a minimal answer to the problems of people out of work.

While many states have adopted similar standards for administering their programs, technically each state decides the amount of the payroll taxes it will collect, the amounts of the benefits it will pay, and the lengths of time for which jobless workers can receive benefits. Pressure from businessmen to keep the payroll taxes low, and the economic optimism generated during periods of full employment, tend to keep the states from increasing benefits.

During the 1950's and 1960's, attempts were made to standardize the benefits for all the states through congressional action. These attempts had the support of organized labor, but pressure from the business community and the persistence of a "states' rights" philosophy among many legislators prevented the enactment of national unemployment-insurance standards. In spite of weaknesses in the programs, however, they have alleviated to some extent the economic insecurity of unemployed workers and their families.

In the area of wage and hour legislation,

most federal law has been concerned with establishing standards of minimum wages and maximum hours. As early as 1840, the federal government had stipulated there should be a ten-hour day in the navy yards; and later in the nineteenth century, Congress set the working day for government employees, railroad workers, and sailors at eight hours. But it was not until 1938 that the Fair Labor Standards Act guaranteed most workers a minimum wage and a maximum number of hours in the work week. Since that time the government has periodically augmented the minimum wage per hour. Organized labor, however, has won contracts for wages much higher than the government minimum and for a lower number of work hours per week as well.

The employment of children as part of the work force was deplored by many people in the early years of the twentieth century. Wages for children were kept very low so that businessmen could keep prices of their goods lower than those of their competitors. This practice was resisted not only because of its effects on children but also because it limited the number of jobs available to adult workers. In 1916, Congress tried to stop the flow of goods produced by child labor in interstate commerce, but the Supreme Court considered the law as meddling with the powers of the states. Congress then tried to place a tax on such goods, but the Court again ruled the law unconstitutional. An attempt by Congress to amend the Constitution also failed. It was not until 1938 that the Supreme Court finally revised its definition of congressional power in interstate commerce. One year later, Congress was able to stop the flow of goods produced by child labor in interstate commerce, making it unprofitable for most businesses to continue employing children under sixteen.

■ *The workers' right to organize.* Despite labor's spectacular struggles against employers during the last half of the nineteenth century and the first few decades of the twentieth, very little was accomplished during those years toward guaranteeing the right of workers to organize labor unions. Although most of the states recognized trade unions, there was no national policy toward workers' organizations until the 1930's.

The machinery of the National Labor Relations Board (NLRB) is at the center of federal activity in labor-management relations. Established in 1935 as an independent regulatory commission, the NLRB has the task of supervising collective bargaining in those industries involved in interstate commerce.

The work of the Board is diverse and complex. Its task is not to guarantee the place of a union in a plant, but rather to see that fair practices are followed by both labor and management. When a union, for example, tries to organize the workers in a plant, its representatives first approach the organized workers and ask them to sign cards stating that they want this particular union to represent them. Often there is competition among several unions to represent the employees. If a third of the workers sign up for a union, that union requests the Board to hold an election in the plant where all employees will have the option of choosing the union they want. They can also vote to reject all union affiliation. If one union receives majority endorsement, it is designated as the bargaining agent of the employees in that plant, and the employer must thereafter negotiate with it on matters that concern workers. After a union has been operating for a year, the employer can ask the Board to hold a decertifying election at which the workers can reaffirm their choice of a union or end the union's claim to represent them.

The bulk of the Board's work, however,

is taken up with adjudicating so-called unfair practices—practices that destroy or interfere with the normal operation of collective bargaining or that violate the conditions of the contract between a union and an employer. If either union or management, for example, uses intimidating tactics in an election; if a union penalizes management by "wildcat strikes," after an owner has bargained in good faith; if the employer attempts to bargain with the workers behind the union's back; or if he discriminates against union members—these and many other similar actions constitute unfair practices. When the Board finds that there has been an unfair labor practice, it initiates administrative sanctions ("cease and desist" orders); if these are violated, it institutes proceedings in the federal courts to obtain enforcement. Employee strikes are generally condoned, but they are usually engaged in only as a last resort, after an honest attempt to settle an issue through collective bargaining has failed. Under the Taft-Hartley Act of 1947, the President may obtain an injunction for a "cooling-off period of eighty days to stop a strike endangering the welfare of the nation.

The political orientation of the NLRB changes as does any other government agency. In 1935 the unions were the underdogs and there was a strong pro-labor atmosphere in most political circles. As the power of unions has increased, however, their claims to special privileges have been regarded with more suspicion, and the mood of the Board has often reflected a more pro-management attitude. Still, there is no doubt that, since the 1930's, government policy with respect to labor has contributed to the acceptance of unions as legitimate institutions as well as to the development and maintenance of better working conditions for much of the labor force.

In the 1940's, observers of the American scene were predicting the development of a radical trade-union tradition

STEVENSON

"I see a long walkout, round-the-clock talks, mediation, binding arbitration, and return to work."

(Today, the round of procedures utilized to settle labor union grievances is fairly easy to predict.)

that would strongly oppose the capitalist system. This did not happen. Largely as a consequence of New Deal measures, the unions have been admitted instead to the club of legitimate American institutions. The union member has earned his rightful place in American society. His welfare is a constant source of concern to the government.

Aid to business. Throughout American history the government policy has aided business interests. Government has responded differently at different times to the requirements of keeping American commerce and business healthy. After the American Revolution, high protective tariffs on imports were used to encourage the development of industry in the new nation. The creation of banking systems, and adherence to the "liberty of contract" concept in the nineteenth century, were boons to business. On the other hand, by the end of the nineteenth century, when business had become too big, the government adopted antitrust policies and other devices designed to curb monopolies. The Federal Trade Commission was set up in 1914 to regulate the trade practices of businessmen and to prevent certain practices that it considered deceptive.

■ *The government as customer.* Today, the government aids and maintains business in a number of ways. The granting of contracts to private industries for defense production, for example, does much to bolster the business community as well as the rest of the economy.

At one time, the government produced weapons in its own arsenals. In fact, government naval shipyards built warships and United States arsenals turned out cannons and rifles. Today, however, the government turns the production of modern weapons over to private enterprise. The Navy and Air Force have transferred their missile production operations to civilian sub-

contractors—largely airplane and automobile manufacturers.

The use of private industry for arms development has resulted from the tremendous pressure put on Congress and the administration by business interests. Since the government spends billions of dollars each year for defense, it is one of the business community's most important customers.

■ *Fiscal and foreign trade policies.* Business often benefits also through the government's fiscal and foreign trade policies. The federal government raises money in various ways—through collecting income taxes, selling bonds, levying tariffs, and so forth. The government's fiscal policies are easy means of encouraging industrial expansion and maintaining American business at the same time.

"This Will Keep Out Foreign Salesmen"

From *Herblock's Special for Today* (Simon & Schuster, 1958)

(While tariffs keep foreign goods from competing with domestic goods, they also limit potential customers.)

For example, tax credits or "allowances" are extended to businessmen for plant depreciation, oil-well depletion, and other corporation costs. Protective tariffs and import quotas also help private businesses. A tariff is, in effect, a tax on foreign products imported into the country. This tax is designed to make lower-priced foreign goods more expensive in the American market and therefore less competitive with domestically produced goods. When the American consumer buys an imported cashmere sweater, approximately 50 percent of the price is tariff.

Other government policies are formulated to help maintain industry even though extra costs are passed on to consumers. The oil industry is a case in point. In the mid-1950's, when a crisis in the oil-producing Middle East resulted in the closing of the Suez Canal, there was a world-wide shortage of oil. American producers immediately and simultaneously increased their prices.

When the Suez Canal was reopened and Arabian oil returned to the European market, the demand for American oil dropped. Indeed, a surplus soon developed in the United States. Ordinarily, a surplus of oil distributed among a number of companies would lead to a price war, with maximum benefits to the happy motorist who can get five gallons for a dollar—or perhaps even five gallons and a quart of oil! Curiously, no such drop in prices occurred. Instead, the government intervened to cut down oil imports, thus terminating the surplus and maintaining the high domestic price.

The government reasoned that this intervention was in the interests of "national defense." If oil companies went out of business, they would also soon lose their capacity to refine crude oil. In a defense emergency the nation would surely need more crude oil. Therefore, oil companies could not be permitted to be forced out of business.

■ *Financial aid.* The national government has a policy of directly subsidizing or financing certain industries or corporations. For more than two decades, between 1932 and 1954, this function was handled largely by the Reconstruction Finance Corporation (RFC), which made loans to business. Many businesses, both large and small, were bailed out of near bankruptcy by the RFC during the Depression. The agency also financed needed expansion in certain industries during World War II. The RFC was subsequently replaced by the Small Business Administration. The construction industry has benefited from huge subsidies granted by other federal agencies to initiate housing renewal or slum-clearance projects. Most of these subsidies have come from the Federal Housing Administration.

It would be difficult to find a business in the United States that does not receive support in one form or another from the federal government. Even the periodicals that specialize in criticizing the government for being too liberal, or not liberal enough, are distributed through the mails at less than cost—which in effect amounts to a government subsidy.

Aid to the farmer. Until 1862, the national government did little in the way of interfering with or providing aid to the farmer. In that year, however, Congress passed several laws that indicated the government's interest in agriculture. First, it passed the Homestead Act, granting 160 acres of public land to any settler who claimed and stayed on such land for at least five years. Then, the Morrill Land Grant Act gave the states thousands of acres of public land for agricultural education. Congress also established the Department of Agriculture in 1862.

With the development of new farm machinery in subsequent years, agricultural production increased and the prices of farm products dropped. Many farms went bankrupt and there was a drift of farm labor to the cities. During the 1880's and 1890's, the farmers became increasingly militant about finding solutions to their problems. As a result, a number of independent political parties or groups emerged in the rural areas of the country—the Grange, the Farmers' Alliance, the Greenback party, and the Populists. But these organizations did not prove successful.

Around the turn of the century, farmers abandoned their attempts to form a third political party and began applying pressure on the national legislature. The "farm bloc" started to form in Congress. Gradually, a coalition of representatives in both major parties from different agricultural constituencies was organized. (By 1939, a congressional wit could observe that the Senate and House Agricultural Committees represented seven parties: tobacco, cotton, wheat, corn, peanuts, dairy products, and meat.)

The congressional farm bloc struggled throughout the 1920's to obtain federal assistance. After World War I, prices had dropped drastically, leading to a crisis for farmers. The principal effort to correct their plight was concentrated on creating Federal Farm Banks to subsidize crop-planting at low interest rates. Except for some tariff concessions, however, little else was achieved. Like the labor unionists, the farmers had to wait for the New Deal to obtain any substantial assistance from the federal government.

The first New Deal program to solve the farm problem was enacted in 1933. The Farm Bureau, the lobby that represents farmers to this day, had recently moved to Washington and was extremely instrumental in the drafting of the Agricultural Adjustment Act (AAA). The object of the Act was to force the prices of farm prod-

ucts up by reducing the supply of goods on the market. Administered by an Agricultural Adjustment Administration, the Act provided that farmers who agreed to limit their crop and livestock production would receive cash payments from the government. The cash payments were funded through a tax levied on processors of farm products, such as millers and meat packers.

After the Supreme Court declared the Agricultural Adjustment Act unconstitutional in 1936, Congress enacted a second AAA two years later—without the measures that had been objectionable to the Court. The second AAA was similar to the first but omitted the tax on processors. Federal assistance to agriculture is still based on the framework established by the AAA of 1938.

Essentially the system works like this: All the farmers who plant a certain crop participate in an annual referendum to decide whether the crop will be included in the government-control plan or be sold on the open market. While the agreement of two-thirds of the producers is necessary for the government-control plan to operate, producers generally vote 80 to 90 percent in favor of the government program.

Once this decision is made, the Production and Marketing Administration determines the total amount of the crop that will be needed for national consumption. This figure is then broken down by regions. Local committees, responsible to the Secretary of Agriculture, then allocate the amount of acreage to be planted by each farmer in the area. In return for agreeing not to plant more than his quota, each farmer receives a government guarantee of a minimum price per bushel. When his crop is harvested, the farmer has the alternative of selling it on the free market, if the price per bushel is higher than the government price, or of selling it to the government at the guaranteed price.

The impact of this system has been to maintain highly efficient producers and discourage the inefficient. The only limitation on the farmer is the amount of acreage he can plant, not his amount of production. Thus, the more bushels he can get from an acre, the better off he will be. This in turn has led to a great deal of crop research on hybrid, high-yield strains, and to a tremendous emphasis on mechanization. It has also led to bitter complaints from small farmers and their political lobby—the National Farmers Union. Small farmers contend that federal policy is driving the "family farmer" out of business and is nourishing "factories in the fields."

Federal policy has also led to huge annual farm surpluses that are difficult to dispose of. The surpluses belong to the federal government which, under the law, can not sell them in competition with its suppliers. Attempts to sell surpluses abroad at low prices have led to charges of "dumping" from foreign competitors. This has contributed to international tensions with such agricultural nations as Argentina, Australia, and Canada.

Many critics claim that the federal government has only provided an economic cushion for the big, efficient farmer. There are many federal benefits, though, that do assist the small farmer. Irrigation programs have been provided which limit the size of agricultural holdings in federally irrigated land. The Soil Conservation Service has encouraged farmers to improve nonproductive land by planting trees to prevent soil erosion. The Commodity Credit Corporation has made it easy for agricultural producers to borrow money. The Rural Electrification Administration has introduced electricity to most American farms. Special tax benefits, too, favor the establishment of farm cooperatives. Obviously, the federal government has underwritten the farmers' welfare.

Mergen in *The Atlanta Journal*

"Teacher's pet."

(Many farmers say that without price supports, they would not earn enough to make a living from farming.)

Aid to the veteran. Since the first American war, ex-servicemen have been a strong pressure group. They have been able to acquire federal pensions through legislation after every major conflict. Following the Civil War a veterans' lobby began to work in earnest for more than pensions, and the government was soon pressured into funding old soldiers' homes and hospitals.

The two large veteran pressure groups—the American Legion and the Veterans of Foreign Wars—that emerged from World War I took up the standard for the veterans. No sooner was the war over than Congress was besieged by representatives of the veterans demanding special consideration such as civil service preferment, bonuses, and hospital care for their clientele. The Veterans Administration became both an administrative spearhead of the veterans' lobby and a huge operating agency responsible for hospitals, cemeteries, pensions and other benefits. In 1936, the veterans' lobby scored its greatest triumph. It succeeded in getting Congress to override President Roosevelt's veto of a federal bonus for veterans.

After World War II, the veteran population was expanded by approximately 15 million newcomers, a significant proportion of the adult male population. The Veterans Administration, with its lobby supporters, rose to the challenge. The result was a number of new benefits for the ex-servicemen. Interested and eligible veterans received funds for education. The children of servicemen killed in action also became eligible for educational assistance. Those veterans who had difficulty finding civilian employment joined the "52–20 Club," receiving twenty dollars a week for 52 weeks to help them until they found jobs. Those wishing to purchase houses received help in obtaining mortgages and in meeting down payments. VA hospitals were established to treat veterans who returned from the war either physically or mentally ill.

In summary, those members of the population who have served in the armed forces comprise a special welfare club with membership extended to their families. Unlike laborers, farmers, or businessmen, this group is nonfunctional; it cuts across all occupations, all age levels, and all regions. The benefits that a serviceman receives from the government begin as soon as he is inducted into the military; they continue beyond the grave. The tradition of government assistance to servicemen and veterans has been extended by the Vietnam conflict. Today, the federal government dispenses more than $8 billion annually to an ever-increasing number of veterans and their families.

Review questions

1. What are three governmental policies that help to develop and maintain the position of the labor force?
2. Explain how each of the following is a government policy that aids business: (a) national defense program; (b) tax credits; (c) tariffs; (d) quotas; (e) subsidies.

"To Promote the General Welfare"

Despite the fact that the federal government has produced policies that benefit specific groups of people in the United States, there have always been some people who, for one reason or another, are not reached by any of these programs. While developmental policies have assisted laborers, farmers, businessmen, and veterans, other groups such as the poor, the elderly, the handicapped, and even students, have largely had to fend for themselves until fairly recently. The preamble to the Constitution clearly states that one of the major aims of the Framers in setting up the federal government was "to promote the general welfare." Yet, the national government has not always interpreted this to include the poverty-stricken or members of minority groups, who have not shared in the affluence enjoyed by others.

Nevertheless, these people were not completely ignored. Until the 1930's, state

ernment had t
It did so by pas
of 1935.

The Act of 19
problems at on
time was to pro
the elderly, and t
ernment's soluti
two channels—d
national governm
ance through the

The provisions
workers, for exam
of indirect federal
state administers i
insurance program
this chapter.) Like
grams, unemploym
stituted to solve an i
has become a perm
strument for mainta
fare of the populace

The programs estab
Act to assist the elde
viving children, and
the other hand, are a
by the national gov
these general insura
amassed from paymen
ers as well as emplo
Security Administration
ment of Health, Educa
Since 1935, the benefits
social security system ha
Today, these benefits in
sistance for the spouse
the dependents of a
death, for workers disabl
sickness, and for health i
to people over sixty-five.

Although these nationw
ance programs have tak
burden off the states, a
people are still not eligible
ance and depend on the
tance. In most instances t

(No matter what term is applied to the condition of the poor, government is expected to answer their needs.)

or loca
problem
capped
lums, p
tions w
governm
organiza
ades, ch
nomic c
more act
ment in

FUNDS
COME
FROM:

FUND
ADMINISTE

FUNDS ARE
USED FOR:

RETIREMEN
INCOME

BL

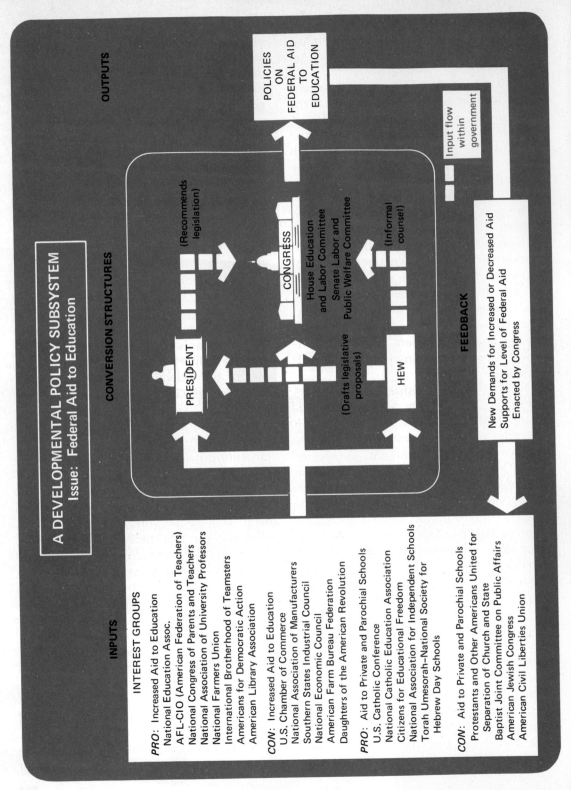

A DEVELOPMENTAL POLICY SUBSYSTEM
Issue: Federal Aid to Education

OUTPUTS

POLICIES ON FEDERAL AID TO EDUCATION

Input flow within government

CONVERSION STRUCTURES

(Recommends legislation)

PRESIDENT

CONGRESS

House Education and Labor Committee
Senate Labor and Public Welfare Committee

(Informal counsel)

(Drafts legislative proposals)

HEW

FEEDBACK

New Demands for Increased or Decreased Aid
Supports for Level of Federal Aid
Enacted by Congress

INPUTS

INTEREST GROUPS

PRO: Increased Aid to Education
National Education Assoc.
AFL-CIO (American Federation of Teachers)
National Congress of Parents and Teachers
National Association of University Professors
National Farmers Union
International Brotherhood of Teamsters
Americans for Democratic Action
American Library Association

CON: Increased Aid to Education
U.S. Chamber of Commerce
National Association of Manufacturers
Southern States Industrial Council
National Economic Council
American Farm Bureau Federation
Daughters of the American Revolution

PRO: Aid to Private and Parochial Schools
U.S. Catholic Conference
National Catholic Education Association
Citizens for Educational Freedom
National Association for Independent Schools
Torah Umesorah–National Society for
Hebrew Day Schools

CON: Aid to Private and Parochial Schools
Protestants and Other Americans United for
Separation of Church and State
Baptist Joint Committee on Public Affairs
American Jewish Congress
American Civil Liberties Union

the National Defense Education Act in 1958. Essentially, this Act provided loans to college students who were studying subjects such as science, engineering, mathematics, and foreign languages. Some money was also made available to secondary schools and for language laboratories and science equipment.

It was not until 1965, though, that a really comprehensive education bill was passed by Congress. The principal purpose of the Education Act of 1965 was to channel funds for education into poverty areas. Local officials were given the task of deciding where the funds were to be used. Federal funds were provided for the purchase of text and library books and other teaching aids, and for the establishment of "educational centers" as models for demonstrating experimental teaching methods. In the hope of curbing economic inflation in the late 1960's and early 1970's, however, the federal government began to reduce its spending for education programs. In spite of this, the government will probably remain committed to assisting the improvement of education and educational opportunities.

Health programs. The involvement of the federal government in improving the health of the general population has greatly expanded since the end of World War II. The initial thrust of this development was to provide federal funds for building medical facilities, for training medical personnel, and for supporting research efforts to find cures for diseases such as cancer and heart disease.

During the 1960's the emphasis of government health policies began to change. Of increasing concern to policy-makers was the fact that many people were unable to pay medical costs and were therefore neglecting their health. While labor unions and private insurance companies had instituted group insurance plans that cov-

ered the medical costs of workers and their families, there had been little or no coverage available for the elderly, the poor, the unemployed, and, in some cases, the self-employed.

As the cost of medical care has risen, there has been increased clamor for a program of national health insurance. The American Medical Association and some private insurance companies, on the other hand, have been trying to persuade the government not to initiate such a program. They argue that national health insurance will lead to socialized medicine which might tend to impersonalize the traditional doctor-patient relationships. However, the government has begun to undertake programs that directly assist some segments of the population in obtaining better health care.

Such a program, called Medicare, was first proposed in Congress in the early 1960's and was finally passed in 1965. This program provides national health insurance for people 65 years old or older. The Medicare program pays hospital and nursing-home bills for the elderly. It is administered as part of the social security system and is funded by taxes paid out of workers' wages.

Another program known as Medicaid was also instituted in 1965 to provide for the medical care of those needy people who are not eligible for Medicare. Federal funds were distributed among the states on the basis of the need within each state. Many states soon exhausted their funds. One reason for this was the rising cost of medical treatment. Another reason was that the states themselves decided who was eligible for Medicaid assistance and sometimes granted aid to people whose incomes were above the so-called poverty level. Although Congress revised the program in 1967 by setting eligibility standards, the costs of the program continued to increase. While Medicaid did provide some health-care assistance to the needy, rising costs continued to keep adequate health care beyond the reach of many people. The need to solve this problem became a major priority of the Nixon administration in the early 1970's.

■ *Product safety.* Throughout the twentieth century the government has taken on the responsibility of protecting the health of consumers against dangerous drugs and chemicals. By means of a series of laws the federal government tried to prevent the sale of dangerous, adulterated, and misbranded drugs, foods, and medical supplies.

The Biologics Control Act of 1902 forbade the interstate shipment of various antitoxins, serums, and other products, unless they were tested and licensed by the Public Health Service. The Food and Drug Act of 1906 prohibited the interstate shipment of adulterated and misbranded foods and drugs. The Meat Inspection Act of 1906 authorized the Department of Agriculture to inspect red-meat animals sold in interstate commerce and to control chemical additives to meat products. The Insecticide Act of 1910 authorized the federal government to take action against misbranded and dangerous poisons.

Today, almost every aspect of the food and drug industry comes under the scrutiny of the government. All drugs, for example, must be licensed by the Food and Drug Administration (FDA) to insure product effectiveness as well as product safety. A company that produces an ineffective drug misleads the consumers as much as one that produces dangerous drugs. In recent years, the FDA has ordered products off the market for both reasons.

The importance of the Food and Drug Administration was dramatically illustrated in the early 1960's when an FDA scientist, Dr. Frances Kelsey, delayed approval of the drug thalidomide, which was widely sold in Europe to pregnant women. The sale of the drug in Europe resulted in the birth of hundreds of tragically deformed children. The thalidomide incident and investigations into the drug industry generally resulted in greater restrictions on the marketing of drugs in the United States.

In recent years, controversy has arisen over the effects of pesticides. In 1969, HEW Secretary Robert Finch endorsed a report recommending that the use of DDT be eliminated in the United States by the end of 1971. Agreement was reached between the Departments of Agriculture, the Interior, and Health, Education, and Welfare, to impose limitations on the use and sale of DDT within the United States.

In the future, the federal government will undoubtedly tighten its laws to maintain product safety. In the early 1970's, a movement to strengthen the government's role in protecting consumer interests gained

Drawing by C. Rose; © 1969 The New Yorker Magazine, Inc.
"Beautiful, isn't it? Every last one of them a pharmaceutical banned by the Food and Drug Administration."

(The Food and Drug Administration has kept many dangerous drugs from being marketed to the unwary.)

wide support. President Nixon recommended the creation of a permanent office of consumer affairs in the White House and a new division in the Justice Department to represent consumers before regulatory agencies. He also recommended the establishment of federal court procedures that would allow consumers as a group to file suits for damages resulting from fraudulent or deceptive practices by manufacturers. Several congressmen have recommended the creation of a Cabinet-level department for consumer affairs that would consolidate all of the functions involving consumers, which are now carried out by more than forty agencies in the government.

Review questions

1. Why has it been necessary for the federal government to assume responsibility for the unemployed, the elderly, and the sick since the 1930's?
2. What groups of people were assisted by the National Defense Education Act of 1958 and the Education Act of 1965?

Developmental Issues of the 1970's

As the nation moved into the 1970's, national government policy-making began to focus on solving a number of difficult problems that were completely new or that had never been solved satisfactorily. Describing the federal government's new priorities for the 1970's, President Nixon noted in his 1971 budget message that

"about 41% of estimated outlays in the 1971 budget will be devoted to human resources—spending for education and manpower, health, income security, and veterans benefits and services. Spending for national defense, despite continued improvements in our military forces, will claim a smaller percentage of the budget than in any year since 1950. Although still comparatively small, other major programs of this Administration—pollution control, crime reduction, transportation, and housing—are planned to grow substantially in the years ahead."

As with all other policy solutions, the new governmental answers to the nation's problems are being sought in response to demands made by numerous groups. In some cases, the demands are being initiated because problems such as environmental pollution have only recently come to light. Other demands of the 1970's are and will continue to be feedback reactions to the government policies of previous decades. Such reactions will include new demands or nonsupport from those groups whose problems resulted from or have not been solved by existing policies. (See also Chapter 22, pages 586–588.)

Space exploration. During the 1960's there was a tremendous concentration of money and technology on exploration of space and, in particular, on the goal of landing an American on the moon before the decade's end. Because this program was so extensive and costly, only the national government could possibly fund it. At the height of the program, the National Aeronautics and Space Administration (NASA) was spending over four billion dollars a year.

In the wake of America's achievements in space exploration, many groups have reacted by demanding that some of the funds used for space projects be diverted to more urgent domestic needs. While the budget for the space program has been

Drawing by Garneke; © 1969 National Review,
150 East 35th St., New York, N.Y. 10016

"My regrets to the United States, the United Nations, the Soviet Union and all of human kind, but the Moon is mine."

(To some people, the benefits of sending Americans to the moon seem negligible compared to domestic needs.)

reduced as a result, President Nixon remained firmly committed to the program in his 1971 budget message:

"Man has ventured to the moon and returned—an awesome achievement.

In determining the proper pace for future space activities, we must carefully weigh the potential benefits of:
- *Scientific research by unmanned space craft.*
- *Continued exploration of the solar system, including manned exploration of the planets; and*
- *The application of space and aeronautics technology to the direct benefit of mankind.*

I have reviewed many exciting alternatives for the future. Consistent with other

national priorities, we shall seek to extend our capability in space—both manned and unmanned. . . . In our current efforts, we will continue to stress additional uses of space technology. Our actions will make it possible to begin plans for a manned expedition to Mars."

Obviously, space exploration will continue to be of primary interest to the government during the 1970's.

Income maintenance. The continuing poverty of certain groups in the population has become of paramount concern to the national government. The previous emphasis on aiding specific groups within the society is being broadened to include the notion that *every* American should have the minimum requirements needed to live. To insure that everyone will have at least a subsistence diet and a roof over his head, the development of some kind of income maintenance, or a guaranteed minimum income, is a major thrust for government policy today.

Early in his administration, President Nixon recommended the establishment of a new Family Assistance Program which would provide a minimum income to those people living at the poverty level, regardless of the reasons for their poverty. In order to collect payments, families would not have to go through the degrading experience of meeting "tests" set up by state welfare agencies to determine whether they are living "properly" and spending money "wisely." The only requirement would be that the family did not have an income sufficient for its minimum needs. The Family Assistance Program would also provide job-training opportunities and incentives for people to find work. Many legislators in both parties favored the Nixon plan. The initial controversy among legislators considering the proposal in congressional committee was over whether the plan should be adopted entirely or tried out first in a few experimental areas.

Other domestic programs. Domestic policies must compete with all other policies funded through the federal budget, and the largest part of any federal budget is still devoted to defense appropriations. Undoubtedly this situation will continue for some time in the future. While defense cutbacks are being made, these reductions are very small compared to the total spent for defense.

President Nixon's 1971 budget did indicate a shift from military and space programs to domestic programs, with concentration on control over the environment. Housing and transportation are two other areas of prime concern to the national government now, and this concern should continue throughout the 1970's.

▪ *Environment control.* New policies are being developed by the government to control pollution of water and air. These policies are a response to the demands of concerned conservationists, sportsmen, and other individuals who fear that uncontrolled processes of industrial production are poisoning the environment.

During late 1969 and early 1970, many environmental action groups sprang up throughout the country to save water, air, and land from contamination. Representatives of all factions within the political parties rallied to the cause. It is certain that the national government will be asked to spend more money and time in the 1970's developing policies that will keep the environment safe, and cleaning it up where it has already been tainted.

▪ *Housing.* The quality of housing in the United States continues to be a major problem. Indicative of the national government's concern for this problem was the establishment in 1965 of a Department of Housing and Urban Development at the Cabinet level. Since then, the national government has initiated several new programs to upgrade housing in both urban

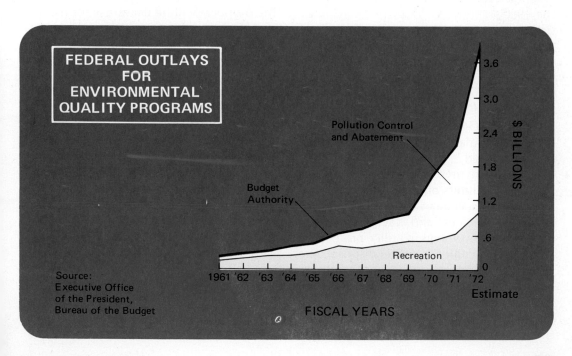

FEDERAL OUTLAYS FOR ENVIRONMENTAL QUALITY PROGRAMS

Pollution Control and Abatement

Budget Authority

Recreation

$ BILLIONS

1961 '62 '63 '64 '65 '66 '67 '68 '69 '70 '71 '72

Estimate

Source: Executive Office of the President, Bureau of the Budget

FISCAL YEARS

centers and rural areas. These programs provide for supplementing rents for low-income families, funding grants to low-income families to repair their homes, increasing grants for parks and playgrounds, authorizing housing loans, and so forth. (See also Chapter 23.)

■ *Transportation.* Programs now being supported by the national government in transportation include the development of sophisticated systems for air-traffic control and the improvement of urban mass-transit systems. The Department of Transportation, established in 1967 as a Cabinet-level agency, oversees most of these programs. It provides money for research in transportation and grants funds to states developing rapid-transit systems. Its budget also provides programs for modernization of the merchant marine and for the continuation of the interstate highway program. Highway safety has also become a primary concern of the government in the 1970's as death tolls on the nation's roads reached over 50,000 per year at the end of the 1960's.

Revenue sharing. For years the federal government has been providing funds to state and local governments to improve housing, transportation, and other conditions. Such assistance, however, has always been granted as part of specific programs, enacted by Congress, with federal standards and stipulations as to how such funds are to be used.

At the same time, many cities and states reached the limits of their own capacities to raise funds to meet the increasing costs of local services and facilities. Sorely needed improvements in police protection, sanitation facilities, sewage disposal, fire protection, and so forth, went largely ignored as a result. While state and local governments became more hard-pressed for cash to meet these needs, they were also reluctant to increase local taxes when citizens already contributed much revenue to the federal government. Thus, many governors and mayors began demanding the adoption of a revenue-sharing program that would enable federal income-tax revenues to be used for state and local purposes.

The adoption of revenue sharing became a top priority of the Nixon administration in the early 1970's. The enactment of the plan would permit the federal government to distribute its own revenues among the states according to their needs and in proportion to the tax contributions of each state. Congress would not stipulate how the money would be used, but would leave such decisions to the states and municipalities themselves.

The federal revenue-sharing program is a potential means of bailing out state and local governments. Moreover, this policy is particularly attractive at a time when many citizens feel that local needs and options should be primary considerations in policy-making. No doubt, some form of the proposal will be necessary for meeting the developmental needs of the 1970's.

There is no doubt that national priorities are shifting. The recent changes in political demands and the advances in technology will probably result in governmental policies that contrast sharply with policies of the past. But if the political system is to be maintained as the nation continues to grow, and if the government is expected to answer the demands made on it, this is the only possible course.

Review questions

1. In the 1970's, what demands for new developmental policies might result from governmental policies of previous decades?
2. Why have the cities and states emphasized the need for a policy of revenue sharing?

Chapter Review

Terms you should know

AAA	income maintenance	Medicare
farm bloc	liberty of contract	NASA
FDA	*Lochner v. New York*	NLRB
"52–20 Club"	Medicaid	Social Security Act

Questions about this chapter

1. Explain how two or three of the many specific developmental policies were created in order to meet a particular social or economic need and later became a permanent part of governmental institutions.
2. What was the significance of the Court's decision in the *Wabash case* and Congress's reaction to it?
3. "As the structure of the economy changed, the government's role in it has also changed to answer those demands which seemed to be most in the public interest." Explain the following policies and justify them in terms of the above statement: (a) mercantilism in the colonies, (b) Hamilton's economic policies, (c) New Deal programs, (d) post-World War II programs.
4. What prevented the development of a radical trade-union movement in the United States? How did government labor policies help maintain the political system?
5. How have lobbies for veterans created developmental and maintenance policy output?
6. Explain how the creation of the National Farmers Union exhibited a reaction to a specific developmental policy.
7. How was the Social Security Act of 1935 a policy that aided the general welfare both indirectly and directly?
8. Why did federal government health policies change in the 1960's? Which of these programs needs to be expanded?
9. What problems of previous welfare policies would the Family Assistance Program solve?

Thought and discussion questions

1. What would the adoption of revenue sharing do to the older concept of "states' rights" and the relationships among national, state, and local governments?
2. The Preamble to the Constitution states that a major aim of the government is "to promote the general welfare." How has this phrase been interpreted at different times in American history? What policies since the 1930's evidence a broad interpretaion? What policies might result in the future from a broader interpretation?
3. Explain the provisions of the proposed Family Assistance Program. What practical and theoretical arguments can be made for and against this kind of "income maintenance"?

Class projects

1. Check your local newspapers for five serious problems facing your community or city. Which of these problems would not have existed fifty years ago? Why? What developmental or maintenance policies might be created to rectify these problems?
2. Obtain a copy of your city's most recent budget. What proportion of it is devoted to social-welfare problems? How would federal revenue sharing affect that budget?

3. Examine the major domestic legislation of the New Deal (see Arthur Schlesinger's *The Politics of Upheaval*). Is there a need for a similar federal program today? What problems of the 1930's are still with us today?

Case Study: A policy for hunger in America?

National task forces—investigating committees that focus attention on social problems and recommend policies to solve them—are usually set up by the President or Congress as official governmental bodies. Only under rare conditions can a nongovernmental task force be highly effective in shaping public concern and affecting governmental policy. On some occasions, however, these nongovernmental committees do serve as mouthpieces, saying publicly for officials what they will not say, or—as this case study illustrates—providing politicians with a "handle" for promoting a public issue.

One such group formed by private citizens in hopes of prompting action on the part of the government was "The Citizens' Board of Inquiry into Hunger and Malnutrition in the United States." This group was established to investigate the scope of starvation and hunger in selected poverty areas throughout the United States, to examine the extent and quality of public and private programs under way to meet these needs, to suggest strategies to deal with the problem, and to make long-range recommendations for attacking the basic causes of hunger. It was an action-oriented investigation on the part of private citizens, one that successfully achieved its goals.

It has long been established that American farms and industries pour out torrents of goods and services that are the envy of people everywhere. Thus, it was a shock to millions of Americans to discover that starvation and malnutrition are no strangers to their land or that infant mortality rates in some communities are as high as those in underdeveloped nations in Asia, Africa, and South America.

This case study shows how the Citizens' Board of Inquiry was able to arouse sufficient public opinion sympathetic to its cause, acquire professional expertise and advice, and effect a commitment on the part of interested politicians, such as Senator Hollings, to bring about new governmental policy in response to people's needs.

As you read this study of a nongovernmental task force, watch for the following:
1. What are the effects of malnutrition on a child's growth?
2. Why did the problem of hunger and malnutrition go unnoticed for so long?
3. Why did the statistics revealed by the National Nutrition Survey shock many Americans?
4. How was the investigation into hunger carried out? What specific strategies were the most successful in arriving at the Board's goals?

THE REALITY OF AMERICAN HUNGER

by SEN. ERNEST F. HOLLINGS

Washington

Sen. Ernest F. Hollings, Democrat of South Carolina, has shown himself to be as deeply concerned as any man in the Congress about the continuing scandal and torment of hunger in this country. Accordingly, hearing early this month [April, 1971] that the Administration, after two years in office, was alerting itself to the problem, we wrote to Senator Hollings. We asked: What are the facts about hunger in the United States? Why has nothing been done about it? What are the present blocks to meeting the situation? What can and should be done? The accompanying article is his reply.

Our best resources have always been human. Progress is people. It is healthy bodies and sound minds contributing their best efforts to the wealth and well-being of the nation. But the sad fact is that today millions of Americans are not in a position to contribute that best effort. Millions of Americans are handicapped by hunger and malnutrition—their bodies weak and subject to disease, their minds crippled and performing at a level far below their original potential. . . .

. . . We have invented the tools to end hunger, to end starvation. And for most Americans, it has been done. Accordingly, we relax in the assumption that hunger is gone from this land—that, at worst, it concerns faraway places and faraway peoples. So confident have we in this country become that we no longer *mention* hunger on our list of national priorities.

The facts do not support our smugness. A surprisingly large number of Americans are still hungry and malnourished. Hunger is a reality for 15 million hard-core poor, and another 10 million stand in need of some food assistance. . . . The situation is the more cruel because it is unnecessary. Without harvesting another bushel of wheat or another ear of corn, this country could provide each of its 205 million citizens with a decent diet. . . . Hunger is costing the United States far more than would the most far-reaching of feeding programs. Think also of the billions of dollars funneled into fighting the side effects of malnutrition. The taxpayer foots the bill for medical care, hospitalization, truancy officers, crime fighting and all the rest. How much more effective it would be, and more economical, to eradicate hunger than to throw billions into a never-ending struggle against its painful symptoms. . . .

. . . We are only beginning to wake up to the reality of this curse. There were stirrings in the 1960's: some on-the-spot investigations, Senatorial inquiries, a White House conference, a television special or two. Yet follow-up action has been too little and too late. We don't need any more White House conferences. We *know* the facts—how malnutrition bends the body and warps the mind. What we need is action.

The facts I speak of are medical findings, not political revelations. They have been gathered by some of the country's most respected doctors and scientists, and it is impossible to ignore them any longer. The National Nutrition Survey was mandated by Congress, in an act passed in December 1967, to determine the extent of malnutrition and health-related problems among the population. That survey has been completed; all the data are in. The scientists who conducted the survey knew that malnutrition is indicated by three basic symptoms: growth retardation, lower serum and urinary excretion levels for various nutrients, and less efficient performance at work, in school or at other physical or mental tasks.

Of the 70,000 Americans covered by the national survey, most of course were poor. The design of the survey was to focus on low-income people because we know they stand the most risk of suffering from hunger and malnutrition. . . .

From 9 to 42 percent of those sampled around the nation had unacceptable levels of hemoglobin, which is an index of anemia. For comparison purposes, nutrition surveys conducted from 1965 through 1967 showed that hemoglobin deficiencies reached a high of 5 percent in Honduras. Anemia is caused largely by a deficiency of iron, which is supplied by

This article is condensed from "The Reality of American Hunger," by Senator Ernest F. Hollings, The Nation, April 26, 1971. Reprinted by permission of the publisher.

liver, green leafy vegetables, dried fruits, enriched cereals and cereal products, molasses and raisins. It results in weakness and fatigue, listlessness and inability to perform optimally with either mind or body.

Unacceptable levels of Vitamin A ranged from a low of 1 percent in California and New York to a high of 23 percent in the state of Washington. Vitamin A is essential for the formation of cells, particularly in the skin, as well as for normal vision. Its deficiency causes night blindness and in severe cases, permanent blindness. Vitamin A helps the body resist infection. It is found in whole milk and whole-milk products, dark green, leafy and yellow vegetables, and liver. The Vitamin A problem was most acute with children. . . .

Unacceptable levels of riboflavin exist in 30 percent of the population surveyed in South Carolina. That was the high, and the figures drop off to a low of 4 percent in New York. Riboflavin is essential for the utilization of protein and for other metabolic processes. It comes from dairy products, meats and green leafy vegetables, and the lack of it causes growth retardation, among other problems. Unacceptable levels of thiamine ranged from a high of 12 percent in West Virginia to a low of 4 percent in New York and Massachusetts. Thiamine affects physical growth, the function of the nervous system, and normal metabolism. A lack of it can cause growth retardation, edema and changes in the nervous system.

Advanced cases are identified as beriberi. Thiamine comes from liver, eggs, whole grain or enriched cereal, and lean meat. . . .

As many as one-third of the children from infancy to 6 years examined by the survey had already suffered growth retardation. That is about what one finds in problem areas in Africa, Asia and Latin America. Two methods were used to test for growth retardation: wrist bone X-ray and height and weight measurements for age. . . .

Those are merely some of the physical facts; equally critical is the effect of hunger upon mental capacity. The brain begins developing two weeks after conception, and the protein and nourishment it receives determine how it will grow. If the brain is denied protein during those critical months—in other words, if the mother is malnourished—the brain is stunted. It will never develop to its genetic potential. Medical studies indicate that protein deficiencies before birth and during the first few years of life can cost a child up to 20 percent of his intelligence. . . .

We are all responsible for the continued existence of hunger in America. Lack of awareness is no excuse. . . .

We have the means at hand to accomplish the eradication of hunger and malnutrition. Still, hunger persists. On one side is human want. On the other side stand the money and means to end hunger. We must build the bridge between them. . . .

HUNGER USA: THE PUBLIC PUSHES CONGRESS

by LARRY BROWN

Hunger has been discovered again in America. While millions of men, women, and children have always known its existence, Congress and the rest of the nation take notice only periodically. The most recent discovery began nearly three years ago, stimulated by a process of studies and exposés which led most recently to a White House Conference on Food, Nutrition, and Health last December [1969]. . . . That the issue is now on the public conscience

once again is apparent, but the process by which it got there is a fascinating account of action-oriented social scientists and professionals engaged in internal power politics at the national level. . . .

. . . One ad hoc group focusing on the issue of hunger, carried out an advocacy [giving verbal support to a cause] role with such success that it may serve as a model for social scientists who seek to alter government policy by coordi-

This article is condensed from "Hunger USA: The Public Pushes Congress," by Larry Brown, Journal of Health and Social Behavior, *Vol. II, No. 2, 1970. Reprinted by permission of the publisher. Copyright © 1970 by the American Sociological Association.*

nating academic expertise, public concern, and political commitment. . . .

This group, The Citizens' Board of Inquiry into Hunger and Malnutrition in the United States, was established by the Citizens' Crusade Against Poverty (CCAP), a private, anti-poverty organization supported by foundation money. CCAP Chairman [the late] Walter Reuther, President of the United Auto Workers, asked the Board of Inquiry to conduct an investigation into five areas . . . :

1. the scope of starvation and hunger in selected poverty areas throughout the country,
2. the extent of nutritional knowledge at medical schools and among medical practitioners, and within the United States Public Health Service,
3. the extent and quality of public and private programs now under way to meet these needs,
4. immediate strategy recommendations to deal with the problem, and
5. long-range recommendations to attack the basic causes of the problem.

The Board of Inquiry was instrumental in documenting hunger and the "politics" behind its continued existence; *Hunger USA,* the report issued by the Board, served a unique role in spurring America's most recent rediscovery of hunger. However, the focus of concern in this article is not the substantive issue of hunger, but the role of the Board, a group of academicians and professionals, in bringing the issue to national attention. . . .

BACKGROUND TO THE REPORT

The events in the process that prompted the establishment of the Citizens' Board of Inquiry to investigate hunger in America took place quite independently of one another, at least in a formal manner. In April, 1967, the Subcommittee on Employment, Manpower, and Poverty of the Committee on Labor and Public Welfare, United States Senate, toured Mississippi and reported that people were "slowly starving." Republican Senator George Murphy of California . . . accompanied Senators Joseph Clark, Robert Kennedy, and Jacob Javits to the Delta. He reported, "I didn't know that we were going to be dealing with the situation of starving people and starving youngsters." As expected, this revelation generated national attention and subsequent local denial. . . .

The following month—May, 1967—six physicians toured a six-county area of Mississippi to survey health and living conditions of black children in a pre-school program sponsored by the Friends of the Children of Mississippi (FCM). The issue of hunger flared up again when the doctors made their report, *Hungry Children.* . . . The topic remained in the national news, with implications that the doctors' harsh indictment of Mississippi was only an example (and not the worst one) of conditions that affect millions of Americans from counties in New York to Indian reservations in the West.

During these events, Richard Boone, then Director of CCAP, asked Robert Choate to look into the operation of government food programs. Working part-time for CCAP and part-time for the National Institute of Public Affairs, Choate compared a list compiled by the Office of Economic Opportunity (OEO), showing where the major poverty pockets existed, with a description of food program participation in those areas. Choate summarized his findings . . . : "We found a national scandal—a wide discrepancy between the highly touted food programs and their actual performance in behalf of the poor." So incensed was Choate by the maladministration of the food programs that he told Boone that the scandal invited cross-political involvement on Capitol Hill. Choate intended to involve both Republicans and Democrats in reviewing the Federal food programs. . . .

Two processes then preceded and influenced the creation of the Board of Inquiry: (1) the Mississippi situation, [and] . . . the physicians' report; and (2) the growing interest in the issue of hunger on the part of U.S. Senators, especially Kennedy and Javits, from their first Subcommittee tour to the presentation of Choate's findings. These two processes created a climate of concern on the part of public and private interests which would merge at some time in the future, with private concerns represented by the Board of Inquiry and public concern sponsored by the small coalition of Democrats and liberal Republicans. . . .

There was little structure to the formation and operation of the Board itself. . . . Although there was an effort to seek people who would provide divergence of input while publicly representing different professional interests, the actual process of choosing members was quite informal. . . .

Formed in July, 1967, the Board of Inquiry originally was to exist for only three to four months, but a major problem extended the time to the following April: Solid, factual information on hunger did not exist in a readily compilable form; [it] had to be dug out. . . .

STRATEGY

The Board of Inquiry was created because of a realization of the tremendous political forces to be dealt with. Hunger, the transcendent issue, cut across multiple jurisdictions. The strategy implicit in the structure and design of the Inquiry was to inform and shock the public, and thereby provoke the Congress to act. No one knew what would happen; the Board was trying to market information to generate a response. . . . The Board banked heavily on generating enough public furor to force Congress and the Administration to take action. . . .

. . . In early March, 1968, after the first draft of the Report had been completed, a handful of members had a meeting regarding a map, the Geographic Distribution of Hunger in the United States. . . . The decision to print this map as part of the Report was an important strategical move. The map and accom-

---

Table 1

Chronology of Reports and Events Regarding Hunger

Date	Event/Report
April, 1967	Senate Subcommittee (Clark, R. Kennedy, Javits, and Murphy) tours Mississippi and reports starvation.
May, 1967	Six physicians tour counties in Mississippi and find severe malnutrition and starvation, reported in *Hungry Children.*
July, 1967	Formation of a Citizens' Board of Inquiry into Hunger and Malnutrition in the United States.
March, 1968	Jean Fairfax's study of the School Lunch Program, *Their Daily Bread,* sponsored by a coalition of women's organizations.
April, 1968	Citizens' Board of Inquiry Report, *Hunger USA.*
May, 1968	CBS television documentary. "Hunger in America."
June, 1968	Poor People's Campaign, Washington, D.C. Leaders carry copies of *Hunger USA* to the White House.
Fall, 1968	Renewed Senate hearings, sponsored by McGovern.
October, 1968	Conference "To End Hunger in America" held in Washington, D.C. Formation of watch-dog body, National Council on Hunger and Malnutrition in the United States. Harvard nutritionist Dr. Jean Mayer elected Chairman.
January, 1969	U.S. Public Health survey reports widespread malnutrition and inadequate food programs.
May, 1969	Nixon appoints Dr. Mayer as Special Consultant.

panying tables carried specific political clout: They exposed the Congressmen who had hungry people in their own districts. . . .

After the July, 1967, hunger hearings of Senator Clark's Subcommittee, Senator Javits had warned Agriculture Secretary Freeman to start moving in this area, since the food programs were not feeding the poor. Senator Stennis of Mississippi was allegedly shocked by the talk of the liberals on the Subcommittee, and castigated them on the Senate floor. Responding to the physicians' report on Mississippi, he introduced a bill to feed the nation's hungry and provide medical care. This bill caught the liberals flatfooted: They had held hearings, talked and threatened, but only Stennis had taken action. . . . While Stennis had made it clear that he would accept no amendments to the bill, Choate suggested one—a nationwide study on hunger and malnutrition. With the amendment, the bill passed the Senate in eight days, and then was pigeonholed as expected. . . . Later, Robert Kennedy brought through the second half of the original bill, including the amendment.

As time neared for release of the Report, Choate's role changed. He knew of an impending CBS documentary on hunger and had heard of an analysis of the School Lunch Program due to be published in early spring. He began to anticipate the impact of the Report in conjunction with these other efforts. In January, 1968, he went to Senators McGovern, Mondale, and Hatfield and asked: "Do you realize there is a report coming out that is going to make you all look foolish? The scandal will be given great public airing, and if you plan corrective action now, it can quickly follow publication of these various exposés." Choate pushed them to have hearings on hunger following release of the Report. . . .

REACTIONS TO THE REPORT

Hunger USA received national news coverage, generated debate and interest at local levels, and prompted renewed Senate hearings. In retrospect, the Report came out at just the right time, in a sequence of related events, to receive wide national attention. At almost the same time *Hunger USA* was released, the study of the School Lunch Program, *Their Daily Bread,* sponsored by a coalition of women's groups, came out. . . .

Several factors seem to have created the national response to the CCAP-sponsored Report. A primary factor was that the Report provided a very comprehensive followup on a subject that had already been in the national news. The Clark-Kennedy Subcommittee had evoked public interest, which had been reinforced by the physicians' report. *Hunger USA,* as a study, revealed and documented the scope of the problem which the Senators had only brought to the surface; hunger was no longer a "Mississippi thing." Too, hearings held by the Board had created interest and concern in many local areas in various states; county and state officials anticipated the Report, and so did newsmen. Finally, certain Senators had a prior concern regarding hunger, and members of the Board, especially Choate, carried out a specific strategy of arousing more Congressional interest.

Two other factors served to reinforce the original impact of the Report. The Poor People's Campaign, led by Dr. Ralph Abernathy, went to the Capitol with copies of the Report in hand. Until the Report came out, the Poor People had no single, documented, nationally-visible issue to bring before the Congress. Now Abernathy and civil rights groups had one, and they would not let it die. But while *Hunger USA* gave Abernathy leverage in dealing with Congress, the CBS documentary "Hunger in America," produced a month after the Report, put the issue directly to the American people. The public saw the hardly bearable spectacle of hunger and death in different parts of the nation. . . .

By this time, a force of 34 Senators and 84 Congressmen was ready to sponsor hearings on hunger. The CBS program, coming at the later date, added to that momentum. In essence, then, Congress had to hold hearings, both because some politicians were committed to doing so and because public interest forced others to support them. . . .

Meanwhile as sentiment grew, adversaries stepped forward. . . . Mississippi Congressman Jamie Whitten, Chairman of the Agriculture Appropriations Subcommittee, put strong pressure on the Department to defend the programs that were not reaching the poor . . . Whitten had the power to apply [that] pressure forcefully; funds for the Department of Agriculture were given only through his kindness.

Pressure came from other sources too: A nutritionist in the Department of Health, Education and Welfare (HEW), conducting research on the incidence of hunger, did not study the situation in Mississippi, attributing this omission to "politics"; the medical profession's only response was that the issue needed more study; and Herbert Pollack (M.D.), of the Institute for Defense Analyses (IDA), issued a . . . paper condemning the Report for alleged errors and its impressionistic style. . . .

INTIMIDATION BY THE FBI

While these incidents amounted to inconsequential bickering, another did not: Representative Jamie Whitten sent out the FBI. Although the investigation by the FBI was only one of many reactions to the Report, it merits particular notice as an effort on the part of government officials to intimidate citizens concerned over so "non-controversial" an issue as hunger. But it was not the people who put out the Report who were investigated. . . . Rather, physicians, nurses, county officials, and the poor themselves—those who had taken part in Board of Inquiry hearings and the CBS documentary were the target of the agents. . . .

The FBI clearly aimed to discredit the Report, not to substantiate the facts. Bureau agents and Federal Communications Commission (FCC) investigators interrogated hospital personnel in San Antonio, where CBS had taken films of hungry children. One of the head nurses later told Harry Huge that the men "asked how the CBS program started, why it took place, who in the hospital cleared it, did CBS get proper credentials, who took the pictures, who was the cameraman, and did the television people 'behave themselves.' " In most instances, the agents would introduce themselves as being from the FCC or Appropriations Committee, but not from the FBI.

ROLE OF THE REPORT

Judging the significance of the Report is complicated because it was one of a series of studies and investigations into hunger and malnutrition: the Clark Subcommittee tour, the tour of the six doctors, the Report itself, the report on school lunch programs, the CBS documentary, renewed Senate hearings, the January, 1969, U.S. Public Health Service survey which found widespread malnutrition and inadequate government programs, and continued national press coverage.

Obviously the Report did not precede the most recent rediscovery of poverty and hunger in this country. But it appears to be the single most important element in generating the continuing interest in and awareness of hunger. Politically, it came at the right time, and it was produced by respectable, "non-controver-

sial" citizens. *Hunger USA* was the one document that gave "official" cognizance to the fact of hunger and malnutrition in this country. It, along with the documentary, raised some serious issues to which the Congress was forced to react. Public indignation was spurred by revealing the scandalous situation, documenting it, and criticizing the source of the failure to deal with it. The Report attacked a national problem with which a federal vehicle was supposedly dealing. Together, *Hunger USA* and "Hunger in America" precipitated most of the interest and action that followed, which it is quite likely that neither would have been sufficient to cause in itself.

But the report played several unique roles; it provided (1) a base for lobbying activity on Capitol Hill, (2) a platform from which the poor could speak out, and (3) a handle for sympathetic politicians. . . . Finally, *Hunger USA* enabled certain politicians to speak out on the issue. Though much general knowledge is available on poverty and malnutrition, a politician can hardly speak on isolated facts and hope to generate concern. The reason that none had criticized the Department of Agriculture Food Stamp or Commodities Program was that no one had had enough facts. With the Report however, Senators could point to the problem, systematically documented by nonpartisans, and demand action. Thus, the Report provided the basis for starting political processes.

The Report also played a unique role in educating the public, that is, in making people highly aware of the problem. . . .

A multiplicity of factors, then, both planned and unplanned, enhanced the impact of the Report. It is difficult to see how the Board of Inquiry could have done a better job of generating public interest, though two factors, finances and lack of planned follow-up, may have impeded an even greater impact. One key member of the Board considers it impossible to prevent criticism of such a controversial document [*Hunger USA*]. . . . He contends, however, that follow-up was not a problem, citing the interim meeting "To End Hunger in America," which led to the creation of the National Council on Hunger and Malnutrition in the United States. . . . the issue of hunger was catapulted into the public domain. . . .

THE ROLE OF PRIVATELY-SPONSORED INVESTIGATIONS

The Board of Inquiry, as a non-governmental body, had no legal authority that served to legitimize its investigation. It had to contain "respectable" people. While none of the members was nationally known, they were solid, reputable people of second-level stature. And, quite important, they represented various facets of American professional life: professor, attorney, doctor, minister. Thus, because legitimacy was built into the Board at the time of its formation, it did not need to develop a "gimmick" to sell itself. Additionally, contacts between certain members and the Congress served only to increase the likelihood that such a group would carry respected authority. . . .

But such factors, which enhance the effect of a non-governmental inquiry, have negative counterparts; there are certain requirements or conditions which such an inquiry must meet. First, the subject must be generally creditable (not a requirement for government reports) and potentially of high public interest. . . . Second, the information must be written in an interesting, journalistic manner, well-documented to explain the circumstances of the problem, how it came about, and the target for change. Third, and perhaps more important than anything except the subject itself, a non-governmental group must develop a constituency.

(The government already has one—itself.) Important people and groups must be briefed to generate response to the presentation. Fourth, there must be some access to information dissemination structures—the media. The last factor was the big gamble of the Board, the one variable over which it had the least control. Finally, there must be continued pressure, and a willingness to be rough with adversaries. . . . In short, a privately-promoted inquiry must seek to control as many of the foregoing variables or conditions as possible, for it cannot afford the luxury of dealing solely with the subject area and the political situation immediately related to it, as is often the case with government-sponsored task forces. . . .

CONCLUSION

Meeting the above requirements, the Board sought only to expose the problems and pinpoint responsibility for their resolution, while leaving particular details up to the government. In essence, then, the Inquiry was merely a "tool" used by private citizens to evoke action—to exhort the government to feed the hungry. . . .

EDITORIAL NOTE:

A policy subsystem on hunger and malnutrition in America is slowly evolving. The only tangible output of this subsystem is the food-stamp program. The political system does not always work as fast as many would like to see it work. The development of official policy is a slow process, as is revealed by this case study.

End questions

1. What does Senator Hollings imply by this statement: "Hunger is costing the United States more than would be the most far-reaching of feeding programs"?

2. Who has the ultimate responsibility, within the government, of eradicating hunger and malnutrition in the United States? Who should make this type of policy? Give reasons for your choice.

3. "Not many people go to bed hungry in this land of affluence, and if some did it is a result of their own laziness." What does this statement mean? Do you agree with it? Why or why not?

4. What, if anything, was unique about the role of the study performed by the Board of Inquiry? What accounted for the Board's success?

5. Why is a governmental task force generally more effective in evolving policy than a nongovernmental one?

CHAPTER 22

Feedback: Government Action and Political Reaction

The political process is constantly in flux. Once an accommodation is reached on an issue and a policy is made, that is not the end of the matter. Instead, as soon as a policy is established, it causes various changes in the system. As a result of a government policy to end job discrimination, for example, new jobs might open up for minority groups, new job-training programs might be instituted, employers might have to revamp personnel procedures, old employees might imagine a threat to their jobs, the federal courts might be swamped with new cases, and so forth. How would such changes affect the ability of the system to operate? Would they alter the amount of support for specific conversion structures or for the whole political system? How can the system adjust to new demands resulting from a policy's outcome?

The Feedback Process

No system can continue operating unless it is able to respond to changes that result from the outputs it produces. An aircraft that converts fuel into energy to stay aloft could not remain in flight indefinitely without replenishing the fuel it burns. But without various dials and computers in the cockpit to register the changes that take place in the plane's system as it flies, such crucial information would never be fed back to the pilot so that he would know when to land for refueling.

Political systems also require a feedback mechanism. In order for a political system to keep functioning, it must maintain a sufficient level of support to counterbalance any resistance or new demands that are made on it. Such vital support is maintained only if the system produces outputs that satisfy the demands of its members. Thus, information about the success or failure of policy outputs and about changes in the level of support must be channeled back to decision-makers. Otherwise, they would be unable to adjust future outputs to maintain or to replenish the support

necessary to keep the system operating.

The effect of outputs. The *feedback process*, then, is the process by which information about the effects of outputs flows back through the system so that adjustments can be made to keep support and demands in balance. Some political scientists describe this process as a series of related occurrences that begins as soon as an output is produced. If the federal government adopted a policy of limited medical insurance, for example, the feedback process would begin to work as soon as there was a congressional statute, an HEW regulation, or some distribution of benefits. In the first stage of the feedback process, the output would produce an effect: medical treatment might become available to people who formerly went without it; the benefits might prove to be inadequate; or a shortage of doctors and hospitals might be created.

Whatever the effect of the policy, it would result in an increase or decrease of support for the system. If the policy was successful, there would be new support from people and groups who were satisfied with it. If it proved to be inadequate or created new problems, there would be a decrease in support and new demands. In the next phase of the process, specific

Why is it necessary for the decision-makers of government to know whether their performance has been in harmony with the preferences of the people? How do the public's reactions to policy affect subsequent outputs?

"feedback" information would be communicated to decision-makers through normal political channels. Finally, the decision-makers would respond to these new inputs by continuing the established policy or by devising a new one. Through this feedback process, then, most government outputs ultimately engender new outputs.

A casual observer of the American political system might not find the elements of the feedback process as clearcut as they are in theory. Ideally, the political reactions to a specific output ought to reflect only the actual results of the policy. In fact, the same informal forces that operate in other phases of policy-making come into play in the feedback process. The complexity of these forces and of the many outputs producing feedback at a given time may make it difficult if not impossible to discern a logical pattern to the process at all.

One factor that complicates the feedback mechanism is that the results of specific policies are often difficult to determine. If Congress should reduce taxes to strengthen the economy, for example, it might be years before the desired effect became apparent. If changes in the economy did come about, it might be equally difficult to determine whether they were the result of the tax cut or of other outputs, such as spending for defense and welfare programs, or of non-governmental factors such as shifts in population. Furthermore, the *existence* of a government output may foster support for the system whether it produces the intended effect or not. The very fact that Congress reduced taxes might produce support from many happy, tax-paying constituents even if the measure had no concrete or positive effect on the condition of the economy.

Another difficulty in assessing the feedback process is the factor of political apathy. While political reactions to an

Drawing by Handelsman; © 1969 The New Yorker Magazine, Inc.

(Political apathy is more difficult to measure than are the quite vocal responses of some groups in the system.)

output may be stronger from those who oppose it than from those who support it, the failure of citizens to vote or to join in other political activities may still give political observers and policy-makers a distorted idea of the actual support or discontent resulting from a specific policy. The expressions of new demands and support that are forthcoming, on the other hand, may reflect not only the concrete effects of an output but political attitudes, party loyalties, the relative strength of pressure groups, and other conditions that affect inputs generally. And finally, the ability of decision-makers to respond to feedback is tempered by the same conflicts and procedural hurdles that normally operate in the congressional, executive, bureaucratic, or judicial conversion structures.

Balancing demands and support. The pluralistic political system in the United States comprises many hundreds of subsystems that are constantly producing a

570

vast number of outputs—each of which generates its own specific feedback. While this factor might seem to complicate the ability of the system to adjust to change, it also has positive implications for the system's survival. A lack of support generated in one sector of the system will generally be counterbalanced by policies that satisfy demands and maintain support in another sector. For example, while a specific foreign-policy output might be creating resistance from some groups, developmental policies may be maintaining support from others. Most specific outputs, in fact, create support from some groups at the same time that they fail to satisfy other groups. Furthermore, the needs of the individual citizen are so varied that even if he is adversely affected by some policies, he may still benefit from others. An active member of a labor union, for example, might not support the government's policies toward labor while he continued to support other policies that maintain the parks or improve his economic welfare.

Thus, a safe balance of demands and support for the system as a whole is generally maintained in the feedback segment of the policy-making cycle. If, however, this balance is threatened by excessive resistance or non-support from many sectors at a given time, policy-makers may try to create support through some means other than specific outputs. An instance of this occurred when, during the early years of the Nixon administration, protests against the Vietnam War gathered such momentum that the administration waged an active campaign of appealing to the "silent majority" to maintain support.

In an extreme instance, if the political system failed to produce outputs that maintained a safe balance of demands and support, violent feedback threatening the system's very existence might result. Such an instance occurred in the United States during the nineteenth century. When the policies of the federal government seemed to threaten the entire economic and social life of the South, the failure of the system to find solutions that maintained support led to the attempted secession of some states and civil war.

Obviously, it would be impossible to examine all the situations where feedback occurs, or all the forms that feedback takes. Particular types of policies do not always result in the same kinds of feedback. An examination of the feedback engendered by specific protective and maintenance outputs in recent decades does, however, illustrate the complex nature of the feedback process. For many of these outputs, the feedback process is still going on.

Review questions

1. Why is a feedback mechanism necessary in a political system?
2. Why is it sometimes difficult to measure the feedback to a particular policy?

Feedback to Protective Policies

The most recent policies strengthening the rights of individual citizens have come from the Supreme Court which, during the last two decades, has expanded civil liberties and civil rights in several areas. Through broad interpretation of the "equal protection" clause of the Fourteenth Amendment, Court decisions have ruled against discrimination and segregation in public institutions and facilities, and have insisted on the reapportionment of state and congressional election districts according to the principle of "one man, one vote." The Court has also strengthened First Amendment freedoms by barring the recitation of religious prayers from public schools and by curtailing censorship of speech and press. The rights of the accused have also been strengthened through constitutional interpretation.

All of these policies have produced both support and resistance. Feedback reactions to some of the Court's policies resulted in new legislative outputs that have either strengthened or weakened the decisions. Resistance to other decisions has been strong initially but has eventually given way to support and compliance with the original Court output. While all of the decisions have produced new demands on the judiciary in the form of an increased number of cases, feedback to Court policies has been directed primarily at Congress and the President.

Feedback reaction to school desegregation. Never has there been stronger feed-

back reactions to a federal policy than there was after the Supreme Court's 1954 decision in *Brown v. Board of Education*. In that decision, the Court decreed that racial segregation of public schools was unconstitutional. Thus, a federal policy of school integration was established. From groups who had been demanding government action to protect civil rights, there was not only support for the Court's policy but renewed zeal in demanding additional outputs to enforce it. Negative reactions to the policy were also vigorous, and in some cases, violent.

In the years following 1954, demands mounted for new congressional and executive policies to erase other forms of racial discrimination. Gradually, the major political parties responded to the demands of those who supported government protection of civil rights. But, because of the intense and conflicting reactions to the Supreme Court's desegregation policy, the feedback mechanism did not produce a

SO MOMMA AND I GOT ON THIS BUS TO GO TO THE COUNTRY AND SUDDENLY A BUNCH OF COLORED PEOPLE GOT ON AND WE WERE SURROUNDED BY POLICEMEN AND WE ALL GOT ARRESTED.

MOMMA **TRIED** TO TELL THE POLICEMEN WE WERE ONLY GOING TO THE COUNTRY BUT ALL THE COLORED PEOPLE WERE SINGING "**WE SHALL OVERCOME**" SO THE POLICEMEN COULDN'T HEAR US.

SO AFTER DADDY GOT US OUT OF JAIL MOMMA AND I WENT TO GET A **SANDWICH** IN A **DRUG-STORE** BEFORE WE TRIED AGAIN TO GO TO THE COUNTRY—AND SUDDENLY A BUNCH OF COLORED PEOPLE WERE SITTING ON STOOLS ALL AROUND US AND WE WERE SURROUNDED BY POLICEMEN AND WE ALL GOT ARRESTED.

MOMMA **TRIED** TO TELL THE POLICEMEN WE WERE ONLY TRYING TO **EAT** AND **GO TO THE COUNTRY** BUT ALL THE COLORED PEOPLE WERE SINGING "**WE SHALL OVERCOME**" SO THE POLICEMEN COULDN'T HEAR US.

SO AFTER DADDY GOT US OUT OF JAIL WE **RENTED** A CAR TO THE COUNTRY AND MOMMA WAS SO RELIEVED THAT BEFORE EVEN **UNPACKING** SHE TOOK ME DOWN TO THE BEACH TO RELAX AND SUN BATHE AND SUDDENLY A BUNCH OF COLORED PEOPLE WERE SUN BATHING ALL AROUND US AND THE POLICEMEN CAME AND WE ALL GOT ARRESTED.

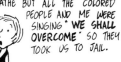

MOMMA **TRIED** TO TELL THE POLICEMEN WE WERE ONLY TRYING TO SUN BATHE BUT ALL THE COLORED PEOPLE AND ME WERE SINGING "**WE SHALL OVERCOME**" SO THEY TOOK US TO JAIL.

I DON'T MIND THE COLORED PEOPLE BUT I WISH THEY'D LEAVE THEIR POLICEMEN HOME.

(This little girl's story shows how bystanders get caught in the political process and its feedback.)

major new policy output on civil rights until ten years after the Supreme Court's decision.

■ *Support and new demands.* From many groups who supported the Supreme Court's desegregation decision came new demands to force compliance of segregated school systems. But the pace of desegregation was slow. As a result, many groups stepped up their pressure on Congress to adopt measures that would accelerate integration. One such demand called for the withholding of federal aid from segregated schools. This proposal was resisted for many years, not only by those who opposed school integration but also by some groups who supported school integration but did not want to jeopardize programs for improving education.

The thrust of the Supreme Court's decision had been against *de jure* segregation—that is, against schools that were actually segregated by state law. In many systems, however, where there had never been *de jure* segregation, schools were often racially segregated in fact because of racially separated neighborhoods, especially in the North and West. This condition of *de facto* segregation complicated the feedback process, as concerned groups initiated school boycotts and demonstrations, and pressed for the busing of students to achieve racial balance in all schools.

Another aspect of the feedback reaction to the Supreme Court's decision was the increase of new demands for ending racial discrimination in other areas. Initial support for the Court's policy was thus transformed into multiple demands on the legislature and the President for new action. Having won one civil rights battle for equal education, these groups pressed for legislation guaranteeing equal employment opportunities, equal access to housing, and the right to vote for all groups in the population. As the federal government delayed

Editorial cartoon by Frank Interlandi.
Copyright, Los Angeles Times, Reprinted with permission.

"Say, isn't this the same group that was for 'law and order' a while back?"

(It is not unusual to find that apparently conflicting feedback reactions are expressed by the same people.)

its response to such demands, the civil rights groups became cynical about the ability of the government to act. Support was withdrawn and demonstrations were organized. This feedback response culminated in the summer of 1963 with an interracial march on Washington of approximately 200,000 people—one of the largest demonstrations ever to be held in the nation's capital.

■ *Resistance.* The Supreme Court's decision also produced resistance. Many conservatives in both the North and South regarded the decision as an intrusion on the rights of the states which, until 1954, had the authority to regulate public educational facilities within their own borders. In some states where resistance was particularly strong, governors tried to block the enforcement of court orders to desegregate schools. Public schools were even closed in a few areas to avoid compliance. For the most part, however, resistance took a more moderate form as school districts sought gradual, rather than immediate, enforcement of the Court's policy.

Token desegregation occurred in some regions. In others, the school districts complied by desegregating one or two grades each year. Ten years after the Court's decision, all states had at least token school integration, but relatively slight progress had been made toward real integration of the nation's schools.

■ *The government's response.* The feedback to the policy of school desegregation was strong and persistent, both from those who supported the policy and those who resisted it. Against this background, new government outputs were slow in coming.

The major political parties were somewhat cautious in their responses to the feedback demands. During the national election of 1956, both the Democratic and Republican platforms included planks supporting the principle of the *Brown* decision. The Democrats also pledged to work toward ending racial discrimination in other areas, but rejected a strong civil rights plank. But by 1960, both parties were ready to take a more positive stand on the issues of school desegregation and civil rights. The two platforms tried to placate both sides of the political reaction by promising to strengthen the ability of the Justice Department to enforce school desegregation while pledging to provide local school districts with federal assistance if they integrated schools.

The greatest amount of pressure for new government action was exerted on Congress. As civil rights bills were proposed in both houses, bipartisan groups developed in Congress on opposite sides of the issue. Some proposals were killed in committees led by chairmen who were against such measures. Other bills succeeded only after extensive alterations had been made.

Although they did not deal specifically with school integration, the Civil Rights Acts of 1957 and 1960 to protect voting rights were essentially new outputs resulting from the feedback response to the 1954 *Brown* decision. They did not, however, satisfy the demands of civil rights groups, or of many labor, religious, special interest, and other groups which continued to lobby for broader civil rights legislation.

The major government response to this continued feedback was the Civil Rights Act of 1964. The Act dealt both with enforcing school desegregation and with protecting other civil rights.

On the school issue, the Attorney General was authorized to sue for the desegregation of public schools and colleges on the complaint of a private citizen. Title VI of the Act barred federal funds from any public program or activity where discrimination was practiced. Thus, the Department of Health, Education, and Welfare could withhold educational funds from school districts that were still racially segregated. At the same time, the Office of Education was authorized to grant, on request, technical, financial and other assistance to help local school systems with desegregation. The Act also barred discrimination in public accommodations, in various types of employment, and strengthened the protection of voting rights. (See also Chapter 19, pages 484–486.)

■ *Continued feedback.* With the passage of the 1964 Civil Rights Act, some of the feedback to the Supreme Court's 1954 decision subsided. The fact that the government's response was ten years in coming illustrates the difficulties that result when an initial policy output produces strong, conflicting reactions.

Furthermore, the feedback reactions did not end in 1964. For example, the matter of de facto segregation in public schools continued to be an important issue. The demands of the desegregationists included

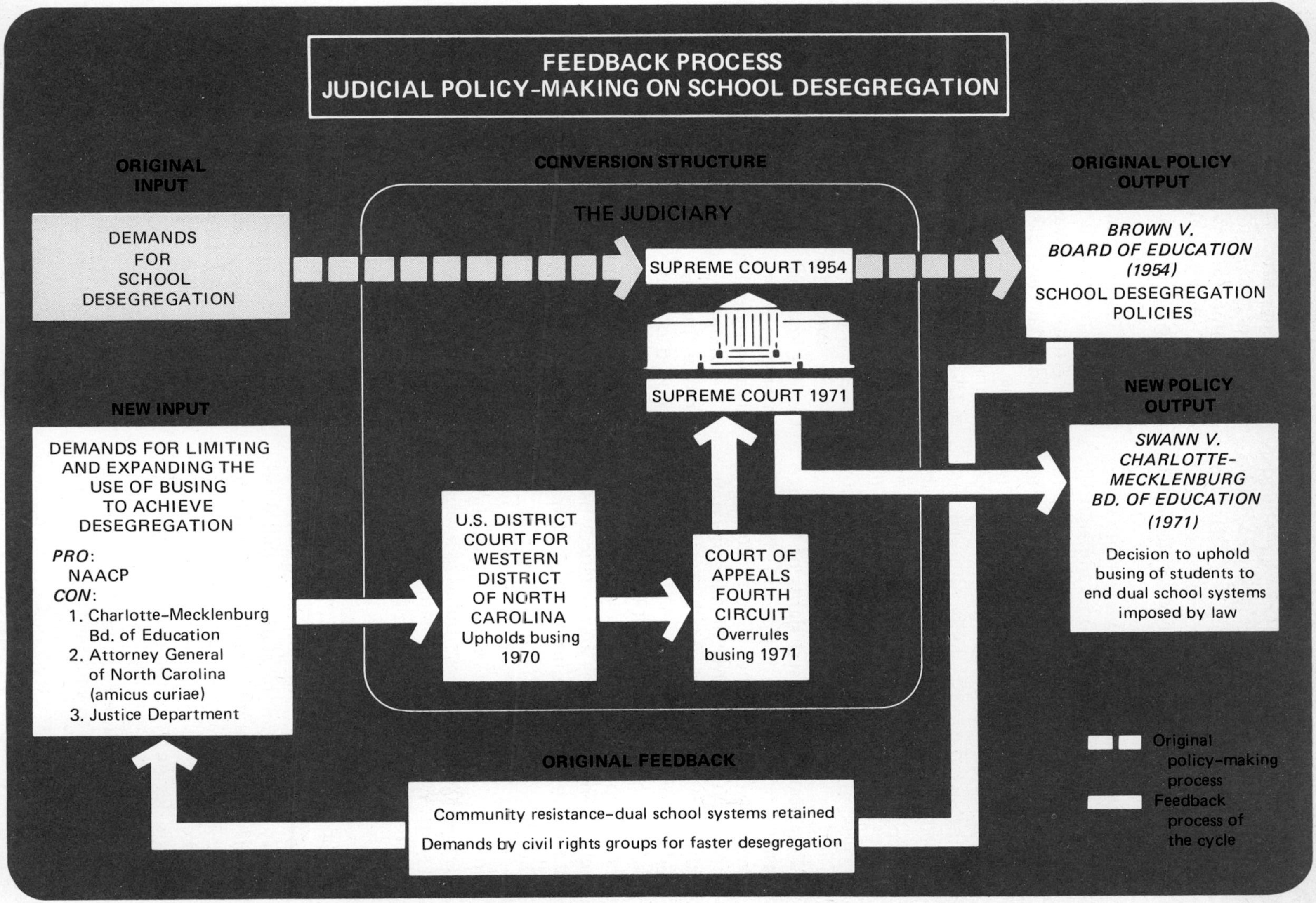

FEEDBACK PROCESS

JUDICIAL POLICY-MAKING ON SCHOOL DESEGREGATION

ORIGINAL POLICY OUTPUT

BROWN V. BOARD OF EDUCATION (1954) SCHOOL DESEGREGATION POLICIES

NEW POLICY OUTPUT

SWANN V. CHARLOTTE-MECKLENBURG BD. OF EDUCATION (1971)

Decision to uphold busing of students to end dual school systems imposed by law

Original policy-making process

Feedback process of the cycle

CONVERSION STRUCTURE

THE JUDICIARY

SUPREME COURT 1954

SUPREME COURT 1971

COURT OF APPEALS FOURTH CIRCUIT Overrules busing 1971

U.S. DISTRICT COURT FOR WESTERN DISTRICT OF NORTH CAROLINA Upholds busing 1970

ORIGINAL FEEDBACK

Community resistance–dual school systems retained

Demands by civil rights groups for faster desegregation

ORIGINAL INPUT

DEMANDS FOR SCHOOL DESEGREGATION

NEW INPUT

DEMANDS FOR LIMITING AND EXPANDING THE USE OF BUSING TO ACHIEVE DESEGREGATION

PRO: NAACP

CON:
1. Charlotte-Mecklenburg Bd. of Education
2. Attorney General of North Carolina (amicus curiae)
3. Justice Department

busing students from one neighborhood to another. Feelings against this viewpoint were strong. Many people felt that the desire to integrate the schools was over-riding the freedom of individuals to select schools for their children.

The question of busing was a major issue in the presidential-election campaign of 1968. In 1969, legislation was introduced in both houses of Congress to allow HEW to continue granting funds to schools where the only means of attaining racial balance was through busing students. Although this legislation did not pass in Congress, its introduction certainly indicates the intensity of new reactions by some people to governmental efforts to enforce desegregation.

Reaction to increased rights of the accused. In the late 1950's and 1960's a number of Supreme Court decisions strengthened the rights of alleged criminals. In such cases as *Mallory v. United States* (1957), *Miranda v. Arizona* (1966), and *United States v. Wade* (1967), the Court decided in favor of the accused by curtailing certain procedures and practices used by law enforcement officials. (See Chapter 18, pages 443–444.)

During the same period, there was a recognizable increase in crime throughout the nation which was attributed to a variety of causes. Some people blamed the pressure of living in cities, some thought it was due to the increase in addicts who had to raise money by any means to pay for drugs; others found fault with permissiveness in raising children; still others thought it might be liberal moral standards that were to blame. Although it would be unfair to trace the increase in crime to any one source, some law-enforcement officials and certain segments of the general public felt that at least part of the increase in crime could be attributed to the Court's more lenient policies toward accused criminals.

Strong demands were put on Congress to pass legislation strengthening the ability of law-enforcement officials to apprehend criminals and to perform their function of protecting people and property. These demands included pressure to counteract the Supreme Court's rulings that had broadened the rights of accused criminals. The concern for crime was so intense that both presidential candidates for the 1968 elections made law and order a major campaign issue.

■ *The Omnibus Crime Control Act of 1968.* Congress' response to these demands was the passage of the Omnibus Crime Control and Safe Streets Act of 1968. In some respects, this Act was a response to completely new demands for strengthening law enforcement. In part, the law was also an answer to the feedback that had been initiated by policies of the Supreme Court.

The major thrust of the Act was not to remove judicial protection from those accused of crime, but to buttress law enforcement officers in the fulfillment of their jobs. Grants were provided to the states for improving the recruitment and training of police officers, for educating the public on the problems of crime, and for training special police units for critical crime areas. Funds were also made available for encouraging neighborhood youth groups to improve police-community relations and for research in law enforcement. Furthermore the Act banned the shipment of hand guns and ammunition in interstate or foreign commerce. (See also, case study Chapter 10, pages 248–253.) And, the Act authorized law enforcement officers to use wiretapping in certain controlled situations to obtain information about suspected criminal activity.

The Omnibus Act dealt with the critical feedback to the Supreme Court's decisions by modifying several Court rulings on the rights of the accused. Normally it is

"COME NOW—THERE IS NO SUCH THING AS A BAD BOY . . ."

(Many people felt that the Supreme Court was coddling criminals when it extended the rights of the accused.)

thought that Congress can not refute a decision of the Supreme Court or the judiciary. Nevertheless, Congress does make laws that determine the organization, jurisdiction, and procedures of the federal courts. Thus, unless a law is unconstitutional, the Supreme Court must adhere to the will of the legislature.

The Omnibus Act included provisions making it permissible for police to hold a suspect for at least six hours before arraignment and to obtain a confession during that time which would be admissible in court. Another part of the Act made it permissible to introduce confessions as evidence in court even if the confessions were obtained without informing suspects of their rights to silence and legal counsel.

In 1970 another law was passed that countered the trend in Court policies of protecting the rights of criminal suspects. Having constitutional authority to govern

the District of Columbia, Congress passed a law permitting police in the District to enter homes of criminal suspects without knocking—provided that such action was approved by a judge. The "no-knock" law was considered by some officials as a model for dealing with crime that should be duplicated by the states. Others saw the law as an infringement of civil liberties.

In the early 1970's, the Supreme Court itself, began to modify its own former position. In 1971, for example, the Court ruled that, to determine the truth in a criminal case, a confession that had been obtained before a suspect had been advised of his rights could be presented at a trial if the testimony and evidence introduced for the defendant were contradicted by the earlier confession.

One reason for this tougher attitude toward the accused might have been the appointment of two new justices whose views were more moderate than those of their more liberal predecessors. While the Court is detached from direct political pressures, the feedback against earlier judicial policies may have had at least an indirect effect on Court outputs by influencing the selection of the new men on the Court.

In spite of a possible new trend in Court decisions with respect to criminal suspects, the Court will no doubt retain its role as the protector of individual rights against excesses of other branches. But with the wide popular concern for crime and for improving law enforcement, feedback against earlier Court decisions in this area will probably continue to influence government outputs during the 1970's.

Feedback on the school-prayer ban and legislative reapportionment. In 1962 the Supreme Court produced two controversial policy decisions that led to vigorous negative feedback. In the case of *Engel v. Vitale,* the Court ruled that the recitation of prayers in public schools was a violation of the First Amendment. In the case of *Baker v. Carr,* the Court held that a state law apportioning representatives to a state legislature was subject to judicial review by federal courts when such a law was alleged to violate the "equal protection" clause of the Fourteenth Amendment.

While both of these decisions were widely supported, vigorous reactions against both rulings led to strong congressional response. In both instances, proposals were introduced in Congress to override the Court by amending the Constitution.

■ *Reactions on school prayers.* In *Engel v. Vitale,* the Court determined that public school recitations of prayers violated the principle of the separation of church and state. (See also Chapter 19, pages 477–479.) There was intense reaction to this decision. Congressmen were bombarded with mail from constituents who sought to have the decision overruled. Responding to this mail and to other expressions of negative feedback, members of Congress introduced more than one hundred resolutions to reverse the Court's decision. The most publicized of these proposals, known as the Becker Amendment, was introduced into the House to amend the Constitution and "put God back into public schools." The proposed amendment read, in part:

"nothing in this Constitution shall be deemed to prohibit the offering, reading from, or listening to prayers or Biblical scriptures if participation therein is on a voluntary basis, in any governmental or public school, institution, or place."

The House Judiciary Committee, however, delayed holding hearings on such proposals because Chairman Emanuel Celler (D, N.Y.) favored the decision of the Supreme Court in *Engel v. Vitale.* Finally, in 1964 the Committee did hold hearings on the Becker Amendment and other proposals, but none of these bills was ever reported out of committee.

The feedback to the Court's prayer decision was less intense and less persistent than the feedback on school desegregation. Opposition to the Supreme Court came primarily from small religious groups around the country. Support for the school prayer decision from major church groups and laymen more than equaled feedback demands to overrule the Court.

■ *Reaction to reapportionment.* Once the Supreme Court determined in *Baker v. Carr,* that state legislative apportionment could be challenged in federal courts, there was immediate feedback directed at legislatures and courts at both state and federal levels. Essentially, the decision paved the way for reapportionment of election districts for state legislatures and for the House of Representatives. In state and federal courts,

Taylor in the Dallas Times-Herald

"The Law of the Land."

(The Supreme Court ruled that state legislatures and congressional districts are bound by this principle.)

suits were started against two-thirds of the states. In some states, new apportionment plans were either adopted or put before the voters for approval.

Because the Supreme Court had provided no guidelines for reapportionment in *Baker v. Carr,* new questions arose about the proper methods of reapportionment. Several new cases involving these questions reached the Supreme Court. In the case of *Wesberry v. Sanders* (1964), the jurisdiction of the courts was extended to the apportionment of congressional districts, and the Court established the principle now referred to as "one man, one vote." In the majority opinion for the *Wesberry* case, Justice Black noted that "the command of Article I, Section 2 [of the Constitution] that Representatives be chosen 'by the people of the several States' means that as nearly as is practicable one man's vote in a congressional election is to be worth as much as another's."

As a result of this doctrine, the apportionment schemes of a number of states proved to be unacceptable to the Court. The Court struck down state apportionment alignments wherever it found that a majority of a state's legislators represented only a minority of the state's population. Similarly, state apportionment of congressional districts was declared unconstitutional in a number of cases.

The most controversial of the Court's decisions on reapportionment was the decision on *Reynolds v. Sims* (1964). In the *Reynolds* decision, the Court ruled that seats in both houses of state legislatures had to be allocated in proportion to the population. As a result of the outcry against the *Reynolds* decision, several constitutional amendments were introduced in Congress that would have allowed the states to apportion at least one legislative chamber on a basis other than population. The late Republican leader Everett Dirksen spearheaded this drive in the Senate, but his efforts were fruitless. In the House of Representatives, a bill was introduced in 1964 to remove jurisdiction from the federal courts in apportionment cases. This bill passed in the House by a roll-call vote of 218 to 175, but it never got through the Senate.

Despite the outcry against the Court's policies on legislative reapportionment, support for the decisions balanced out the demands to change them. As with the issue of school prayers, negative feedback on reapportionment eventually subsided and the Court's policy has retained enough support to survive.

Review questions

1. Why was Congress slow to respond to feedback on school desegregation?
2. How did Congress' eventual response to this feedback differ from its response to feedback on other Court outputs?

579

Maintenance Policy Feedback

Maintenance policies—whether they deal with foreign policy, internal security, or economic policy—generally come from Congress, the President, or the bureaucracy. Thus the feedback to such policies is generally directed at whichever of these conversion structures is responsible for the policy. Reactions to a foreign-policy decision will generally be directed at the President and the State Department. Reactions to legislation on foreign aid or federal economic assistance are normally directed at Congress. Occasionally, the policies of these branches will raise constitutional questions that result in new feedback demands on the judiciary. But by and large, it is the legislature, the President, or the "fourth branch" that must respond to feedback on maintenance policies.

Reactions to foreign policy. The general public is usually less concerned about foreign policy than about domestic issues. When Congress appropriates funds for foreign aid or to maintain defense forces, or when the executive branch promotes collective security pacts, the effects of such outputs are removed from the everyday concerns of most people. Therefore, feedback reactions to maintenance policies of this type usually come from foreign nations.

Of course, some aspects of foreign policy do lead to feedback from special interest groups within the political system. Foreign trade policies, for example, produce feedback not only from abroad but also from domestic groups affected economically by foreign trade. The involvement of the United States in war has also resulted in stronger responses from the general public than other aspects of foreign policy outputs.

■ *Feedback from foreign nations.* Following World War II, it became a major foreign policy objective of the United States to contain or stop the spread of communism abroad. To achieve this objective, the federal government embarked on the most massive foreign aid program ever undertaken by one country and, at the same time, concluded a series of international, anti-communist alliances. (See also, Chapter 20, pages 499–502.) Feedback reactions to these policies have come primarily from foreign governments.

□ *Responses to foreign aid.* Part of America's foreign aid program following World War II was aimed at assisting the economic recovery of the war-torn nations of Western Europe. The program also provided economic and military aid for developing nations in other parts of the globe. It was hoped that such aid would gain support for American policies from those nations receiving aid.

The feedback from Western Europe on American aid has been particularly significant. Initially, the program resulted in the support of these nations, and American economic assistance did succeed in helping the economic recovery of Europe. The success of the European Economic Community or Common Market—an economic alliance of Belgium, France, Italy, Luxembourg, the Netherlands, and West Germany—was made possible, in part, by the start it got from American aid.

As the nations of Europe have become economically stronger, however, they have sought to reassert their independence from American economic domination. Thus, while Europe's initial response to American aid was that of support, the long-range feedback response has been an effort to resist the continued European dependence on the United States.

□ *Support for alliances.* American alliances throughout the world have also engendered numerous reactions from abroad. One of the most significant feedback results was the formation of counter-alliances by communist nations. American alliances also resulted in the support of some countries that have been brought under the protective cloak of American military defense. The refusal of Japan to rearm while pursuing peaceful forms of economic development has been a source of support for American alliances as well as a demand for the maintenance of such policies.

When the United States has provided military and economic aid through its international alliances, feedback has often consisted of support from nations receiving that aid along with demands for more assistance. In the late 1950's and early 1960's, the repeated demands of South Vietnam for more and more American assistance to stave off the communist infiltration from North Vietnam were, in part, feedback responses to the formation of the Southeast Asia Treaty Organization.

■ *Feedback on foreign trade policies.* Reactions to foreign trade policies come both from domestic economic groups and from foreign nations. Protectionist policies, which include high tariffs and restrictive quotas on imports, tend to have the support of some American businesses and labor groups while provoking negative responses abroad. Free trade policies, on the other hand, may lead to support from abroad and to both positive and negative feedback at home.

□ *The Kennedy Round talks.* During the 1960's, the thrust of American policy in foreign trade was toward the expansion of free trade. After considerable pressure from the Kennedy administration, Congress passed the Trade Expansion Act in 1962. This legislation authorized the President to cut protective tariffs on imports by up to 50 percent in return for tariff concessions by other nations.

For the next five years, trade negotiations known as the Kennedy Round were conducted between the United States and numerous foreign nations. In 1967, after years of difficult bargaining, the Kennedy Round produced agreements between the United States and fifty-two other countries. Tariffs on approximately 60,000 imported items were reduced by an average of 35 percent.

□ *Feedback on trade agreements.* The conclusion of the Kennedy Round talks was hailed by the Johnson administration and certain trade groups as a boon for international trade and for American exports. But the agreements met with immediate resistance from some domestic groups. The oil, steel, and chemical indus-

THE ADAMANT CONCIERGE

Yardley, *The Sun* (Baltimore, Md.)

(NATO troops stationed in France were no longer considered necessary by French President de Gaulle in 1966.)

tries saw the accord as a major threat that would permit low-cost imports to drive domestic goods out of the American market. Labor groups also responded with some alarm, fearing that low wages abroad would maintain imported goods at such competitive prices that jobs in American industries would be jeopardized.

Intensive lobbying was undertaken by protectionist groups to pressure Congress into reversing the trend of the Kennedy Round agreements. Most of this feedback consisted of new demands to impose quotas on imports—from oil and textiles to strawberries and baseball gloves. At the same time, diplomats from abroad expressed the intention of their countries to retaliate against any United States protectionist measures by raising tariffs on American exports. The White House responded to this pressure by lobbying to prevent action by Congress.

□ *Government response.* The protectionist drive won considerable support in Congress. Since 1968, a number of bills have been introduced in both houses to place restrictive quotas on various imports. One such attempt would have placed quotas on cotton imports from the Middle East to protect cotton growers in Texas, California, and other states. This measure was eventually passed in Congress but vetoed by the President. While lobbying against congressional action on similar measures, the White House, through diplomatic channels, sought to get foreign nations to limit their exports to the United States voluntarily.

Most of the measures proposed in Congress in the late 1960's to restrict imports were defeated through pressure from the administration or by Presidential veto. However, Congress was able to respond to protectionist demands, in part, by refusing to extend the President's tariff-cutting authority beyond the 1967 limit of the Trade Expansion Act. Concern for the effect of imported goods on the domestic economy in the early 1970's continued to bolster protectionist demands. While feedback to the Kennedy Round agreements is certain to keep flowing back to executive and legislative decision-makers for the next several years, the final result of this feedback is still in question.

■ *Feedback during times of war.* While the general public does not usually respond to most foreign-policy outputs, this attitude changes somewhat during wartime. In such crises, opposing political parties and most segments of the population pull together to support the government and work for victory.

Yet during most wars in which the United States has been involved, there has also been some form of resistance or protest from anti-war groups. This was the case for example, during the War of 1812, the Spanish-American War in 1898, and World War I. Several times during the twentieth century, general support for a war effort has been followed by a negative reaction at the polls. In these instances, the electorate has turned the political party in power out of office when hostilities started. There is little doubt that President Eisenhower's election victory in 1952 was due in part to the identification of the Democratic party with the Korean conflict. Similarly, the victory of the Republicans in the national election of 1968 can be credited in part to the incumbent party's involvement in Vietnam.

□ *Feedback reactions on Vietnam.* At no other time in the past century has the federal government faced such intense feedback against a major foreign policy decision as it faced over the action in South Vietnam. Since the original escalation of the "war" in 1965, such feedback has affected government responses in various ways. As a result of strong, conflicting feedback reactions on Vietnam, the government's response has been to find some compromise between the demands of "hawks" who wanted total military victory and "doves" who demanded immediate withdrawal of American troops.

Under Presidents Eisenhower and Kennedy, military advisers were sent to South Vietnam to help that government resist communist infiltration from North Vietnam. After a report of a North Vietnamese attack on two United States destroyers in 1964, Congress passed the Gulf of Tonkin Resolution giving the President carte blanche to take "all necessary measures to repel any armed attack against the forces of the United States, . . . to prevent further aggression . . ." in Vietnam. When President Johnson sent more American troops to Vietnam, there were immediate feedback reactions.

The first demonstration against Vietnam involvement was on April 17, 1965 when 15,000 demonstrators picketed the White House. The demonstration was sponsored by the Students for a Democratic Society, the Student Non-Violent Coordinating Committee, and Women's Strike for Peace. By the fall of the same year, these groups were joined by other organizations in holding anti-war demonstrations in forty cities. Prominent individuals, such as Dr. Benjamin Spock and the Rev. Martin Luther King, Jr., joined the protests to bring pressure on the government to get out of Vietnam.

Numerous anti-war demonstrations and rallies continued to be held in Washington and around the country at various times between 1965 and 1970. Although there were also counter-demonstrations by people who supported the government's action, the number of individuals aligned with the anti-war protests seemed to grow with each succeeding year. In October 1969, opposition to the Vietnam action was dramatized by the Vietnam War Morato-

"MY COUNTER-ATTACK AT PRINCETON SHOULD RELIEVE THE PRESSURE FROM THE IVY LEAGUE ENOUGH TO ALLOW ME TO DEAL SHARPLY WITH THE WEST COAST GUERRILLA ACTIVITY."

Fischetti, New York Herald Tribune, Inc.

(Anti-war sentiment was particularly strong among the students and faculty members on the nation's campuses.)

rium. The Moratorium included work stoppages in some places, and dismissal of classes in many colleges and universities throughout the country. It was supported by a wide range of people. Hundreds of thousands of people attended rallies in the nation's major cities to protest the war. Over fifty members of Congress spoke at anti-war rallies and more than eighty others endorsed the Moratorium as an effective and peaceful way of demonstrating opposition to the war. Many protesters sent telegrams to President Nixon urging him to end the Vietnam conflict, and thousands of other demonstrators signed similar statements to be forwarded to the President.

At the time of the Vietnam War Moratorium, counter-demonstrations were also held to show support for government policy. In connection with the Moratorium for example, 135 crosses representing the city's war dead were placed on a lawn of the University of Pittsburgh campus. Meanwhile over 200 counter-demonstrators and faculty members at Pittsburgh's Point Park College staged a rally with the theme "victory with honor" in another part of town.

□ *The response of decision-makers*. The response of the government to the anti-war protests, especially in the first few years of the conflict, was to separate the negative feedback of the protesters from the opinions of the less vocal general public. The Johnson administration, like that of President Nixon later, tended to overlook the protesters and to rely on the support of the rest of the public. While the Senate held televised hearings on the Vietnam issue in 1966, Congress continued to appropriate funds for the troops in South Vietnam. At the time of the Vietnam War Moratorium, however, several resolutions were introduced in Congress calling for withdrawal of American troops.

Although the feedback to the United States' involvement did not precipitate an immediate withdrawal, it did contribute to some changes in the government and in the Vietnam operation. After Senator Eugene McCarthy of Minnesota ran a successful anti-war campaign against President Johnson in a Democratic presidential primary in 1968, attention was drawn to the existence of negative feelings about the war within an otherwise silent electorate. The fact that in 1968 President Johnson decided not to seek reelection and that he later halted the bombing of North Vietnam to get peace negotiations underway in Paris certainly indicates that negative feedback was having some effect. In addition, after the election in 1968, the Nixon administration began to focus on turning the war effort completely over to the South Vietnamese, "Vietnamization," and on the gradual withdrawal of American troops.

This new approach to Vietnam policy did not end the protests against the war. In the spring of 1970, a joint effort by American and South Vietnamese troops to weed out enemy sanctuaries in Cambodia threatened to re-escalate the war and did re-escalate the anti-war protests. In an effort to answer this new feedback and to limit any new escalation of the war, Congress passed legislation prohibiting the further use of American ground troops outside of South Vietnamese borders.

□ *Implication of feedback on Vietnam*. The experience of the Vietnam conflict illustrates a dilemma that is always part of the feedback process. To what extent can leaders assume that protest demonstrations represent the wishes of the majority of citizens? In the case of the feedback reactions to the Vietnam policy, the President and Congress were confronted with weighing the vocal reactions against the policy and the unspoken support of the rest of the population.

In a letter written in the fall of 1969 to a student at Georgetown University who had asserted that the President was not taking note of the will of the people, Mr. Nixon stated there was a

"clear distinction between public opinion and public demonstration. To listen to public opinion is one thing; to be swayed by public demonstrations is another . . . if a President . . . allowed his course to be set by those who demonstrate, he would betray the trust of all the rest."

Whatever the ultimate outcome of America's policy in Southeast Asia, it seems obvious that neither the President nor Congress can afford to ignore the kinds of feedback demands that have resulted from actions in Vietnam. There are indications that these demands are gradually leading the government to a policy of more disengagement in world affairs. As a result of the experience in Vietnam, the United States' policy of containment is being increasingly questioned. There is no longer much desire among Americans to be the world's policemen. It may be that during the 1970's there will be a resurgence of isolationism.

Most foreign policy does not raise such strong adverse domestic reaction as occurred with regard to Vietnam. The President remains largely free to lead the American people who are more than willing to follow him as he initiates new foreign policies. Feedback to foreign policy decisions ordinarily takes the form of new supports, rather than demands for change. Certainly most of the important foreign policy decisions of this century have had the public's support rather than its opposition.

Reaction to internal security policies. When the security of the country is threatened from within, the feedback to policies that preserve the system tends to be in the form of support. As threats to internal security subside, however, feedback to such policies is more likely to be negative and there is apt to be a resurgence of demands for the protection of individual freedoms.
■ *Internal security measures.* During the 1940's and 1950's, internal security policies came from all three branches of government. In 1940, Congress passed the Smith Act making it a crime to conspire to overthrow the government by force or violence. In 1947, the President issued an executive order establishing a review board to investigate the loyalty of government employees. And in the *Dennis* case of 1951, the Supreme Court upheld the Smith Act and claimed that Congress was expected to prevent threats that were clearly dangerous to the security of the country. (See also Chapter 20, pages 510–511.)

Reaction to these policies during the post-World War II years was mostly in support of the measures. In some cases there were demands for even more rigid controls of communists. Almost all states decided to adopt their own anti-sedition laws, and the requirements for loyalty oaths instituted by the federal government were copied by many states.

Encouraged by the investigation in the early 1950's led by Senator Joseph McCarthy, many private groups embarked on witch hunts of their own. Over 20 percent of the nation's labor force was asked to take loyalty oaths. The American Legion managed to get the motion picture industry to fire supposed communists. The Daughters of the American Revolution examined textbooks and attacked those they considered to be communist influenced. Still other groups including the Chamber of Commerce of the United States, the Disabled American Veterans, and Veterans of Foreign Wars, supported the government in its endeavors to control subversive activities.

Such feedback from private sectors led first to more severe laws governing internal security. The Internal Security Act of 1950, for example, which was passed by Congress over President Truman's veto, required communist and communist-front organizations to register with the federal government. In 1954 the Communist Control Act backed up the 1950 Act, by subjecting registrants to various penalties. Essentially the Communist party had been outlawed.
■ *Fear for protection of civil liberties.* In the wake of this concern for the nation's internal security was a gnawing fear that civil liberties would be lost during the hunt for communists. Feedback from civil liberties groups was directed at the Supreme Court in the form of demands for stricter interpretations of the Bill of Rights and the freedoms of speech and press. Demands of this nature came from such diverse groups as the American Civil Liberties Union, the AFL-CIO, the American Veterans Committee, Americans for Democratic Action, the Civil Rights Congress, the NAACP, the National Farmers Union, and the National Lawyers Guild.

The Supreme Court reacted to these demands by moderating internal security laws. In the *Yates* case in 1957, for example (see Chapter 20, pages 511–512), the Supreme Court modified its previous position in the *Dennis* case by ruling that the federal government could curb civil liberties only if the security of the nation was threatened by a real danger in the form of concrete action. The *Yates* decision placed a greater burden on the government to prove an immediate threat to its existence.

The Supreme Court also limited the effects of other internal security statutes during the 1950's in order to protect individuals from abridgment of First Amendment rights. In 1958 in *Kent v. Dulles,* for example, the Court held that the Secretary of State could not deny passports solely on the basis of a person's beliefs or associations. During this same period the Court curtailed the use of secret informers in industrial security programs. Each of these Supreme Court decisions represented a negative feedback to congressional and administrative security measures.

In the early 1960's the Supreme Court retreated slightly from its earlier position upholding civil liberties in internal security cases. Congress, in 1961 and 1962, had passed new laws governing internal security, and thereby strengthened certain provisions of the Smith Act and other subversive activity statutes. But the Court did not curb these laws.

■ *Pro and con on internal security.* The ebb and flow of the public's sentiment with regard to internal security is typical of feedback reactions. At certain times, popular feeling seems to be overwhelmingly in favor of rigid control of subversive activities, while at other times reaction is more in favor of protecting civil liberties.

Ordinarily the general public supports Congress, the President, and the Supreme Court in whatever they wish to do to maintain the nation's security. This is even more true if government leaders manage to stir up the public to believe that there is in fact a threat to the safety of the nation. Under such circumstances the patriotic fervor of most Americans rises to the occasion. But as the presence of internal threats to national security seems to diminish, concern for dangers to national security is usually replaced by concern for dangers to individual liberties. At such times, if the government should suddenly decide to embark again on "witch hunts," there would undoubtedly be some strong feedback reactions in opposition to the government policy.

Reactions to economic policies. The federal government's policies to develop and maintain the economy and quality of life touch the lives and livelihoods of just

Drawing by Richter; ⓒ 1968 The New Yorker Magazine, Inc.

"The cost of living sure keeps going up and up and up!"

(Because economic policies affect virtually everyone, reactions to such outputs are quite easy to observe.)

about everyone in the nation. For this reason, there is constant feedback to such policies. Business groups will naturally support any part of government that enacts policies they consider favorable to their interests. Conversely they will react vigorously to change policies they consider detrimental. Groups that receive benefits from the government, such as veterans, usually support those policies that increase the scope and amount of benefits they receive. This is also true of senior citizens who receive benefits from social security.

■ *Expansion of the bureaucracy.* Feedback to government economic policies has frequently led to the creation of new administrative agencies. This type of government response is usually an attempt to satisfy feedback demands on a specific issue. In long-range terms, such agencies eventually become the focus of feedback responses to subsequent government policies.

The creation of regulatory commissions, for example, has generally been the result of feedback from specific economic groups. During the mid-nineteenth century, when the policies of state and federal governments led to the economic domination of some regions by the railroads, strong negative feedback came from farmers in these regions. The creation of the Interstate Commerce Commission (ICC) in 1887 was a government response to the demands of farmers for government regulation of the railroads. The ability of the ICC to eventually curb railroad abuses succeeded in satisfying the demands of the farmers and restored support for the system that had been withdrawn.

While thus answering the feedback to the earlier government policies, the ICC has continued to serve both as a source of government outputs and as a receiver of feedback from a special economic group. When the government failed to produce policies that satisfied the railroads, the industry had a specific conversion structure for registering complaints. Ultimately, through its response to such feedback, the ICC was transformed into an agency that promoted the railroads' interests and thus maintained the industry's support.

■ *Aftermath of the New Deal.* The New Deal era of the 1930's witnessed the introduction of many new economic policies carried out by a host of new administrative agencies. In some respects the New Deal policies were the result of strong feedback against a previous administration for failing to solve the crisis of economic depression. Whether that crisis was in fact solved by the New Deal outputs or by the onset of World War II is still subject to debate. The policies of the New Deal, however, did produce strong and immediate feedback responses. While the complexion of this feedback changed in subsequent decades, many aspects of the New Deal economic and welfare outputs were still producing feedback responses in the early 1970's.

□ *Initial feedback.* During the 1930's, feedback responses both for and against the New Deal of President Franklin Roosevelt were intense. The strongest support came from those groups that received benefits under the economic and welfare measures of the New Deal. Legislation providing minimum wages, the National Labor Relations Act, and other outputs, for example, won support of labor groups. Many farmers were also brought into the New Deal fold through the enactment of the Agricultural Adjustment Act and policies of acreage quotas and price subsidies for crops. These policies were supported by a majority of the farmers who continued to vote for the Roosevelt administration in national elections.

New Deal policies also produced intense opposition. Business groups, for example, resisted the minimum wage law and other measures adopted to regulate their activities toward labor. Such feedback eventually contributed to the passage of the Taft-Hartley Act in 1947 to limit certain practices of labor groups. Another New Deal output that met strong resistance was the establishment of the Securities and Exchange Commission. The most negative feedback to this measure came from brokers and investors whose activities were to be regulated by the Commission.

Feedback reactions to the New Deal were expressed not only through pressure group activities but also in presidential elections. Roosevelt's Democratic administration was returned to office in 1936, 1940, and 1944 largely with the support of labor and farmers at the polls. Many business groups continued to express their dissatisfaction with the New Deal by voting for the Republican party candidates.

□ *Long-term feedback.* Many of the maintenance policies of the New Deal eventually won acceptance as the necessary responsibilities of government. Following World War II, administrations of both political parties continued to support the government's role in providing for unemployment insurance and other social security benefits, and in regulating various aspects of economic life. In recent years, negative feedback to these policies has ceased and been replaced by new demands for the expansion of existing benefits. Congress has responded to these new demands by extending various social security programs to cover additional segments of the population.

The long-range nature of the feedback process can be illustrated by the fact that some New Deal measures are producing new effects and new feedback reactions today. For example, during the New Deal era various programs were enacted to provide financial assistance for the aged, the

sick, and families without a source of income. Like other New Deal measures, these welfare programs became an accepted part of government's responsibility to maintain the general welfare. But in the late 1960's, the number of people receiving such assistance and the costs of the programs skyrocketed. Funded by federal, state, and local governments, the welfare programs became a particularly serious financial burden for city governments whose sources of revenue were dwindling. The programs were also increasingly criticized for failing to deal with the economic problems of families with sources of income too low to maintain a minimum standard of living.

The Nixon administration responded to this growing feedback by proposing a program of family assistance that would include a guaranteed minimum income for all families. Whether Congress accepts the Nixon plan or will respond to this feedback with another alternative promises to be an important issue of the 1970's.

Feedback and public apathy. The preceding illustrations of feedback reveal the many different reactions that occur as a result of government policy. The role of feedback in the political system is to make the government continually responsive to new political demands while taking into account the balance of support that exists for any particular policy.

Feedback need not always be vocal; it may also take the form of simple acquiescence or quiet agreement with government decisions. Whatever its form, there is almost always feedback from some source, particularly from the pressure groups that are directly affected by a policy. The vocal expression of popular feedback reactions, however, is inclined to be fragmented and, thus, may hardly seem to exist at all.

The federal government is deeply involved, for example, in virtually every sphere of economic activity. Its various outputs affect the economic lives of people in agriculture, labor, transportation, defense, communications, atomic energy, housing, and so on. Feedback to any one output comes primarily from the interest groups directly affected. The public as a whole does not seem to be concerned, and does not react directly to most economic policies of government.

When the ICC, for example, determines the rates to be charged for railroad freight, feedback to that agency comes from the railroad industry, not from the public. Even the ICC's decisions to allow railroads to discontinue many passenger trains did not raise significant public reaction. When the Civil Aeronautics Board raises or lowers airline rates, even though some of the public is affected, feedback comes primarily from the airlines themselves.

In recent years, various consumers' and citizens' groups have been organized to serve as pressure groups to force the government to be more responsive to the public's demands and feedback reactions. So far there is little evidence that the existence of such groups will change the apathy of the general public toward government policy-making.

During the late 1960's and early 1970's, the public did seem to be increasingly concerned about problems of environmental pollution. Yet as the government began to develop policies for pollution control, feedback responses came primarily from special interest groups. Thus, when President Nixon proposed a $10 billion program to improve the environment, reactions to the proposal came from leaders of such pressure groups as the American Forestry Association, the Conservation Foundation, the Sierra Club, and the National Wildlife Federation.

In attempting to gauge the degree of support that exists for particular policies,

Well . . . David did it . . .

Le Pelley in *The Christian Science Monitor.* © TCSPS.
Reprinted with permission from The Christian Science Monitor.
1970 The Christian Science Publishing Society. All rights reserved.

(If youth can muster the support of the apathetic segments of society, they could very well slay this Goliath.)

then, the decision-makers within any policy subsystem are faced with the problem of weighing the opinions of active pressure groups with the apathy of the rest of the public. In many instances, particularly with regard to economic policies, the government seems most apt to respond to the important pressure groups that react to the outputs directly affecting them. Yet in the area of foreign policy where international reactions must also be considered, the government in recent years has seemed to bypass the protests of pressure groups in deference to the silent support of the general public. Whatever their accuracy in measuring public opinion in the feedback process, government decision-makers must constantly adjust and readjust their outputs to balance the demands and support of the political system.

Review questions

1. Under what circumstances may feedback to American foreign policies originate within the United States?

2. How has feedback from some groups resulted in an expansion of the bureaucracy? In what ways has such feedback been expressed?

Chapter Review

Terms you should know

de facto segregation	Kennedy Round	*Reynolds v. Sims*
de jure segregation	negative feedback	*Wesberry v. Sanders*
feedback process	political apathy	*Yates* decision

Questions about this chapter

1. Some political scientists suggest that the feedback process is "a series of related occurrences that begins as soon as an output is produced." By referring to a specific policy, show how this statement is true.
2. How might a political system be affected if it failed to maintain a "safe balance of demands and supports"? Has such a failure ever occurred in the United States?
3. How did the existence of *de facto* segregation complicate feedback to the *Brown v. Board of Education* decision?
4. Why is feedback to Supreme Court outputs usually directed at Congress, the President, or the bureaucracy?
5. How was the Omnibus Crime Control Act of 1968 partially a result of feedback to Court decisions? What other factors may have caused its passage by the legislature?
6. If the *Yates* decision had been made in 1952, what kind of feedback probably would have resulted? Why?
7. What has been the result of continued feedback to the economic policies of the New Deal?
8. Why has there been a change in feedback from Europe on American foreign policies since World War II?

Thought and discussion questions

1. List the different channels through which feedback to policy outputs can be expressed. Do you think that one of these ways is more effective than others in getting policy makers to act on demands? Why or why not?
2. Are there provisions in the Constitution which insure the existence of a feedback mechanism in the United States' political system? If so, what are they?
3. Do you think it is possible for any political system to exist without a feedback mechanism? In your answer, consider totalitarian governments as well as democratic ones. Could a democracy exist without some means of expressing and channeling feedback?
4. Both Presidents Nixon and Johnson interpreted the silence of the majority on the Vietnam issue as support of their policies. What dangers and advantages do you see in interpreting silence as positive feedback? What role might political apathy play in such an interpretation?

Class projects

1. Consider several issues both national and local that are important to your own community. For instance, how does the National Railroad Passenger Corporation affect your community? Determine through newspapers, television, etc., what groups and individuals are the sources of feedback to these issues. How are these people trying to channel their opinions to decision-makers?
2. Choose an issue currently being discussed in your school and formulate feedback to it. How is feedback expressed within your school community? What channels to decision-makers are open to you?

Case Study: Feedback on a crime bill

The Supreme Court's insistence on protecting the rights of the accused in recent decades has provoked considerable feedback. Law-enforcement officials reacted by demanding new laws to strengthen their hand in dealing with criminal suspects; civil libertarians supported the Court's rulings and opposed efforts to counteract them.

One result of this feedback was the passage of a new crime control law for the District of Columbia in July 1970. Effective February 1, 1971, the law applies only to residents of Washington, D.C.; but many people see it as a preview of further anti-crime legislation elsewhere.

The 1970 law has itself generated feedback. Supporters of the law praise it as an innovative piece of legislation that should reduce the high crime rate in the D.C. area. One major source of support for the law is the Americans for Effective Law Enforcement (AELE), an organization founded in 1966 to protect the right of American citizens to "secure for themselves [the] domestic tranquility and justice that has been guaranteed in the Preamble to the Constitution of the United States."

Critics, on the other hand, including the American Civil Liberties Union (ACLU), claim that the 1970 law is repressive and that several of its provisions deny American citizens of constitutional rights. Some of these provisions are: preventive detention, "no-knock" police raids on suspect criminal establishments, broader anti-crime wiretapping under court order, the reclassification of some sixteen and seventeen year-old offenders from juveniles to adults, and mandatory minimum sentences of life imprisonment for offenders convicted of a felony for the third time. The ACLU is presently testing the constitutionality of the law in the courts.

This case study includes letters, articles, and testimony from the AELE and the ACLU prior to and following the passage of the controversial D.C. crime control law. The opinions represented here illustrate the kinds of reactions and counter-reactions that emerge in the feedback process and often lead to alterations in government policy.

As you read these opinions, keep the following questions in mind.
1. Why does the AELE support the "no knock" provision of the 1970 law?

2. Why does Frank Carrington maintain that the police must become more vocal in the law enforcement area? According to Carrington, who should the police address if they want to change existing legislation?
3. What apprenhensions does the ACLU have about the D.C. law?
4. How does Carrington feel about "preventive detention" for criminal suspects? On what grounds does the ACLU differ?
5. What indications are there of Washington's inability to control its own political destiny?

Speaking for the Police

FRANK CARRINGTON

Crime is, without doubt, our number one domestic problem, and public demand for protection against society's lawless elements has reached a peak. At the same time, laws and court decisions which prevent the police from affording this protection confront law enforcement on every side.

It is in this area especially that the police must become articulate. They must show to the public, the legislatures, and to the courts, just *how* a given law or decision adversely affects police effectiveness; further, if possible they should present a solution to the problem that has been created.

This article postulates this duty of the police to speak out and give examples of areas where speaking out is most necessary. . . .

The Duty To Speak Out

In October of 1969, a Conference on Preventive Detention was held at the Center for Continuing Education of the University of Chicago. The flier announcing the Conference listed twenty-three panelists for the three day affair. These panelists, to quote from the flier represented: ". . . federal and state legislators and officials concerned with criminal justice; professors of law and political science; and attorneys and members of the judiciary." Not one policeman was listed on the panel!

Preventive detention, the right of a judge to deny bail to an individual who is found to be dangerous, is one of the most crucial and controversial issues facing our criminal justice

system today. It is wholly admirable that such a star-studded panel should be convened to discuss this issue; and the interests of the panelists in this area are beyond question. Why, however, should that group, whose interest in preventive detention is certainly of equal immediacy with that of the listed panelists, be excluded?

It is the policeman on the street who must face the bullets of an armed robber who, free on bail from two previous armed robbery arrests, is committing yet another crime to secure money to pay for attorneys and bondsmen.

The desperation of an addict's need to feed his habit is a substantial factor in the danger that officers must face daily; and, an addict released on bail after several arrests compounds his desperation with each offense and release. . . .

The Attorney General of the United States, the Hon. John N. Mitchell, put the problem squarely before the International Association of Chiefs of Police:

"There has been a tendency to ignore the law enforcement community in favor of social scientists who can explain the motivations of the criminal, but who can do little to protect the innocent against the mugger or armed robber."

The police would be well advised to take a cue from these words of the top law enforcement officer in the United States. . . .

The problem to which the writer is address-

This article has been condensed from The Journal of Criminal Law, Criminology, and Police Science, Vol. 61, No. 2. *Reprinted by permission of the publisher. Copyright © 1970 by Northwestern University School of Law.*

ing himself may be fruitfully considered in the context of recent United States Supreme Court decisions restricting the police and enlarging the rights of criminal defendants and suspects. Does the public agree with this expansion of individual civil liberties while society grows daily more unsafe? If public opinion polls are any indication, the answer is clearly "no.". . .

[A] much more practical aspect of the policeman's duty to himself to speak out concerns those areas of the law where the already dangerous job of a policeman is made more dangerous by laws or court decisions. . . . For example, it is very well to sit in a court room or law class and postulate an absolute requirement that officers must knock on a door and announce their presence before entering forcibly to make an arrest or search. After all, does not fair play to persons in the sanctity of their homes require no less? However, to the officer crouching in a hallway before a door which may conceal an armed and desperate felon the picture may appear slightly different; a knock may be answered by a bullet. There is a certain question, therefore, of fair play to the officer involved also.

Court Decisions

The case of *Chimel v. California,* decided by the United States Supreme Court on the last day of the October, 1968 term is one that should make even the most lethargic policeman wish to speak out; for in this case, the Court delivered an opinion that evidenced a complete and utter disregard of the practical problems that a policeman must face in attempting to do his job. *Chimel* is a classic example of a decision that might have been basically sound, if confined to its facts. . . .

Let us look at *Chimel* from a practical point of view. The facts of the case are simple. The police in Santa Ana, California went to the house of Ted Steven Chimel in the late afternoon of September 13, 1965 to arrest him, with an arrest warrant, for the burglary of a coin shop. The arrest warrant was issued at 10:30 A.M. that morning. Without going into detail, it is sufficient to say that a thorough search of Chimel's house was made, incident to his arrest, and the coins taken in the burglary were found. At Chimel's trial, these coins were introduced into evidence and he was convicted. His conviction was upheld in the California District Court of Appeal, and the California Supreme Court. The California Supreme Court relied on *United States v. Rabinowitz,* to sustain the arrest-based search which revealed the coins. The United States Supreme Court granted certiorari.

In a 6–2 opinion, written by Justice Potter Stewart, the Court reversed Chimel's conviction, overruling *Rabinowitz* and overturning nineteen years of its own precedent. The Court laid down a new rule dealing with searches of premises incident to a lawful arrest. Such searches may encompass only:

". . . the area 'within [the arrestee's] immediate control'—construing that phrase to mean the area from within which he might gain possession of a weapon or destructible evidence.". . .

Now, after *Chimel,* each warrantless search of the premises, where an arrest is made, must be confined to the area within the arrestee's "immediate control". But where are the guidelines for the police? *Chimel* provides no guidelines at all. Every judge who is called upon to review police action can make of it what he will. . . .

Justice John Marshall Harlan concurred in *Chimel* with reservations. He said:

". . . every change in Fourth Amendment law must now be obeyed by state officials facing widely different problems of local law enforcement. We simply do not know the extent to which cities and towns across the nation are prepared to administer the greatly expanded warrant system which will be required by today's decision; nor can we say with assurance that in each and every local situation, the warrant requirement plays an essential role in the protection of those fundamental liberties protected against state infringement by the Fourteenth Amendment.". . .

The Safety of the Policeman

Justice Stewart recognized in *Chimel* that there is a danger to the police from weapons in the immediate area of the arrestee, but he ignored the fact that weapons in other portions of the premises may be equally dangerous if the arrestee *or others on the premises* can get to them. . . .

Legislative Enactments

Turning from court decisions to legislative enactments, the need for police articulation can again be shown. . . .

An example of a provision of the law that restricts police efficiency to an alarming degree may be found in the Colorado Children's Code dealing with questioning of juveniles. The Code prohibits the questioning of any juvenile (a person under eighteen) unless a parent or guardian of the juvenile is present. This sounds fine in theory, but presents great problems in practice. In a recent Denver Case, four young hoodlums attacked six youngsters with chains, bricks, and fists. One of the victims was a twelve-year-old girl. Of the suspects arrested, only one was over eighteen. The 18 year-old was questioned and jailed. The juveniles, two seventeen and one sixteen, had to be released because their parents refused to come to the police building; since there is no flexibility in the Code provision requiring parental presence at any questioning, the refusal of the juveniles' parents to appear stymied the investigation as far as the juveniles were concerned. . . .

Laws and Rules Involving the Officer's Safety

Another area of the law in which the police must become vocal, in their own self-interest, involves provisions of the laws that increase the danger of police work. Two such provisions of the Federal law are illustrative of the problem. Both provisions deal with the execution of search warrants by federal officers; one, a statute, requires officers to knock on a door or otherwise announce their office and purpose before entering to arrest or search; the other, a Federal Rule of Criminal Procedure prohibits the execution of a search warrant at night unless the supporting affidavit is positive that the property sought is on the premises to be searched.

. . . [A] case experience will illustrate the effects of the above mentioned provisions as constituting a threat to an officer's safety in certain cases. [This] description [is] based on the personal experience of the writer who participated in [the] raid.

. . . [S]ix law enforcement agencies participated in a narcotic raid on a motorcycle gang in January of 1969 in Gilpin County, Colorado. Surveillance of the house which was raided indicated that the occupants carried side arms, rifles, and shotguns inside the house and on the premises. It was anticipated that twelve to eighteen persons would be in the house when the raiding party of thirty-six officers "hit" it.

Since the search warrant was issued by a Colorado Court, the federal requirement of knocking and announcement did not, strictly speaking, in this case apply; however, federal agents from the Bureau of Narcotics and Dangerous Drugs, and the Alcohol, Tobacco, and Firearms Division of the U.S. Treasury Department were in the raiding party. It was felt that if the search uncovered any federal violations such as narcotics or firearms, the federal agents might wish to prosecute also. For this reason a decision was made to adhere to the federal standard of announcing the presence and purpose of the officers so that no question could be legitimately raised later that the execution of the search warrant did not meet federal statutory requirements.

At the time of this raid, Colorado Rules of Criminal Procedure required a "positive" affidavit for nighttime searches; and since the affidavit was not positive, the raid had to be made in the daytime.

Thus, under two rules based upon conceptions of "fair play" the officers had to make their approach to the house in full daylight, and the persons in the house had to be alerted to the officers' approach. This despite the fact that the officers knew that the occupants were armed and, further, that they had records for crimes of violence. At 7:30 A.M., the Sheriff of Gilpin County announced the officers' presence over the loudspeaker of his car. Fortunately, all of the violators were asleep; and, due to the element of surprise, the violators were captured in their beds. Most had fully loaded guns in bed with them. All, later told the raiders in no uncertain terms that they would have shot it out with them if they had not been caught asleep. Twenty-nine firearms were seized including a machine gun, sawed-off shotguns, rifles and pistols.

Careful planning of the raid plus a certain amount of luck resulted in an accomplishment of the law enforcement objective without any shooting or killing. The fact remains, however, that the officers were exposed to a greater amount of danger because of the required daylight approach and the required announcement. A fire-fight most certainly would have occurred if an early rising occupant of the house, glancing out the window, had seen the approaching officers; or if the Sheriff's announcement had alerted them before they were covered and subdued. . . .

Illustrative of the fact that, whether or not the police speak out, the civil liberties groups and liberals, in general, will speak out is an article in the (Denver) Rocky Mountain News of July 15, 1969. In this article, entitled, "No-Knock Entry Meets Opposition", the American Civil Liberties Union is reported as opposing a Nixon Administration proposal which would authorize an unannounced entry to arrest or search, provided advance authorization for such entry from a magistrate is secured. Melvin

Wulf, Legal Director of ACLU, objected to such a law because "it offends our notion of what is just and fair." The police should let it be known that what is "just and fair" from the safety of Mr. Wulf's office may seem quite a bit different to an officer going into a house full of armed men. Fortunately, most judges and legislators are reasonable men. . . .

No policeman is above the law, and he must obey the laws and court decisions applicable to his work whether he agrees with them or not. At the same time, it is submitted that a constructive, well reasoned articulation of police problems can be a means of bringing about needed changes in the laws which will, in turn, increase the professional policeman's efficiency without a concomitant loss in an individual's personal liberties or freedoms. The need for this police articulation has never been greater. It is no longer optional. It is a duty!

Americans for Effective Law Enforcement INC.

228 NORTH LASALLE STREET · CHICAGO, ILLINOIS 60601

March 26, 1971

Our position is that unannounced ("no knock") entry should clearly be permitted when it reasonably appears that knocking and announcement by the police would increase the physical danger to police officers or to others or that knocking would enable the violator to dispose of evidence while entry was being sought. . . .

. . . [One] justification for a "no knock" entry, destruction of evidence, is based on the rather obvious principle that violators in possession of contraband will attempt to destroy such contraband, when they are raided, if they are given the opportunity to do so. This can be illustrated in narcotics cases where quantities of narcotics have been flushed down toilets or washed away down sinks while entry is being attempted. . . . The destruction of evidence can be further illustrated by the fairly common practice of bookmakers to use specially treated paper upon which to write their bets. This paper is of two types—"flash paper" which literally explodes when lit with a match or cigarette, burning away in seconds and leaving no ash—and "soluble paper" which, when immersed in water dissolves completely in a matter of seconds. When these special papers are used, all evidence of taking bets can be destroyed in a few seconds. We believe that in cases in which there is a reasonable expectancy of such destruction of evidence the police should not be required to knock and give the violator the few extra seconds which he needs to destroy the evidence, thereby frustrating the purpose of the raid—e.g. the seizure of evidence.

Although we have not put out anything in writing on this matter prior to now we have taken the position described herein in speeches and TV "talk" shows. . . .

Sincerely,

(Signed)

Frank Carrington
Executive Director

Courtesy of Frank Carrington, Executive Director, Americans for Effective Law Enforcement, Inc. Chicago, Ill. March 26, 1971.

American Civil Liberties Union

SUITE 501, 1424 16th STREET, N.W., WASHINGTON, D. C. 20036

March 16, 1970

Dear Congressman:

The House District Committee has just reported H. R. 16196, the District of Columbia Court Reform and Criminal Procedure Act of 1970. Although the bill does contain some welcome and long overdue reforms of the District court system, many of its provisions constitute deeply disturbing inroads on fundamental rights and liberties guaranteed by the Constitution.

Once again a majority of the members of the House District Committee have shown themselves willing to authorize serious invasions of liberty on the voteless residents of the District of Columbia, which they would never tolerate, much less support, against their own constituents.

In discussing the disturbing features of this bill, I should like to begin with the most offensive of them—preventive detention, "no-knock" search warrants, warrants to compel physical evidence, and almost unlimited wiretap authority. . . . Neither the bill's title nor the table of contents, therefore, gives an inkling of the wide-ranging police powers which this single section of the bill would permit in the District of Columbia. . . .

Preventive Detention

Much has already been said and written on the subject of "preventive detention" to demonstrate that it is both unconstitutional and undesirable. The American Civil Liberties Union joins these other voices in urging you to reject this proposal which, in authorizing detention on the basis of mere guesses about future behavior, cannot be distinguished from a sixty-day jail sentence imposed without a crime having been committed. Moreover, the cumbersome hearing procedure written in by the drafters to muffle its otherwise bluntly unconstitutional impact will further clog the already terribly overburdened court system in the District of Columbia.

Thus preventive detention, which its supporters say is necessary because of the present long delays between arrest and trial, will result in even longer delays. The burdens caused by these hearings will sharply reduce the beneficial effects anticipated from the addition of new judges. The risk of police-community friction and potentially explosive confrontation over this provision—which can be so easily interpreted as an attack on Washington's black community—cannot be underestimated. We urge you to resist efforts to undermine the Constitution and to avoid these dangers by rejecting preventive detention and concentrating on improving the courts in order to end once and for all the present long delay between arrest and trial.

Courtesy American Civil Liberties Union, Department of Information, Washington, D.C.

"No-Knock" Warrants

. . . The ACLU firmly believes that all "no-knock" authorizations which expand the traditional common law circumstances under which this has been permitted must be rejected as unconstitutional. . . .

Section 23–591 authorizes "no-knock" searches <u>with or without a warrant</u> where notice "may" result in evidence being destroyed, disposed of, or concealed. Since almost any evidence could fall under this loosely drawn standard, the effect will be to permit "no-knock" searches in almost every case. Moreover, the police are not required to give notice where notice would be "a useless gesture." Nothing prevents the police from concluding that the simple fact that the occupants might object to a police visit makes notice "useless" since they will have to use force anyway.

There is nothing which prevents such unannounced entries from taking place during the middle of the night. Imagine the reaction of even a peaceful law-abiding citizen to the unannounced forcible entry of the police into his home on a quiet evening or in the middle of the night. The danger to police officers who make "no-knock" entries into homes in the middle of the night cannot be minimized.

. . . There can be no doubt that the police will seek to use this authority to deal with any and every violation of the law where they wish to enter without notice. It will indeed become the rule. Citizens, supposedly protected by the Fourth Amendment will be forced to accept the "no-knock" entry into their homes as the normal situation. This cannot be so in a democracy under law. . . .

Wiretapping and Surveillance

. . . The drafters of the bill have totally ignored the 1967 report of the President's Commission on Law Enforcement and Administration of Justice. We urge you to remember its words in considering this provision:

"In a democratic society privacy of communication is essential if citizens are to think and act creatively and constructively. Fear or suspicion that one's speech is being monitored by a stranger, even without the reality of such activity, can have a seriously inhibiting effect. . . ."

Treatment of Juveniles

. . . The bill would exclude altogether from juvenile court jurisdiction any child sixteen or older accused of a serious crime. The result will be to exclude a child simply on the basis of the charge, without any reference to his past record (good or bad) or the strength of the evidence against him. The juvenile court judges will have no discretion since they will not even have jurisdiction over these youths. In addition, the bill provides for waiver of juveniles fifteen or older and accused of a felony to the adult court. In so doing, the bill presumes waiver in each case and places the burden on the defendant to show why he can still be rehabilitated in juvenile court. Once a juvenile is waived to the adult court, the jurisdiction of the juvenile court ends, <u>even with respect to future misconduct of any kind, including minor offenses.</u>

These provisions are totally inconsistent with our concept that juveniles may be more susceptible to rehabilitation than older persons committing crimes and that, as a result, juvenile court treatment of an offender should be highly individualized and geared to his rehabilitation. . . .

In Conclusion: An Overview of the Bill's Impact

As disturbing as each of these provisions is by itself to anyone concerned with the continued existence of civil liberties, even more troublesome to contemplate are the serious inequities and harassment which can and will be inflicted upon District residents as the police begin to realize the uses to which these techniques can be put in combination. Imagine the innocent citizen who, never having even been arrested before, is wrongly suspected of committing a crime. His phone—both home and business—can be tapped. He can be picked up and detained by the police to be fingerprinted and forced to submit to other physical tests even though the police could not arrest him. If the police should wish to search for evidence, they can do so without warning by breaking into his home in the middle of the night. And if the police, knowing full well that they lacked probable cause to arrest, decided to arrest him anyway, this bill would rob him of the right to resist—no matter how illegal or brutal the police's methods. Should he be charged with a so-called "dangerous crime" (which in this bill is defined broadly to include attempted robbery and the sale or even the use of marijuana) and should a judge decide, perhaps because he threatened the officers who broke forcibly into his home, that his release would jeopardize "the safety of any other person," he could be placed in preventive detention.

This sounds disturbingly like a police state, rather than the seat of democratic government—our nation's capital.

*   *   *   *   *

The American Civil Liberties Union urges you to amend H.R. 16196, to eliminate these unconstitutional and dangerous provisions so that the bill focuses its attention primarily on court reform. . . .

In many respects, H. R. 16196, aside from its court reform provisions, reflects a Congressional desire to stop crime in the District, but a complete unwillingness to devote the resources really necessary to make the fight successful. I call upon you to take steps to turn the full attention of the Congress toward the real solutions of the crime problem—more efficient courts, vastly improved penal systems, and elimination of the reasons which cause people to commit crimes.

Sincerely yours,

(Signed)

Lawrence Speiser, Director
Washington Office, ACLU

(Signed)

Allision W. Brown, Jr.
Chairman, National Capital
Area Civil Liberties Union

American Civil Liberties Union

SUITE 501, 1424 16th STREET, N.W. WASHINGTON, D. C. 20036

June 4, 1970

Dear Congressman:

We wish to bring to your attention certain facts concerning the controversy which has surrounded the proposed "no-knock" entry provisions of the D.C. Crime Bill. . . .

[T]he Justice Department . . . claims to clear up what it labeled a "misunderstanding" concerning the "no-knock" provision. This bill, the Department of Justice alleges, does nothing more than codify existing law on no-knock entry. . . .

. . . [T]he "no-knock" provision in this bill goes well beyond these recognized exceptions to the Fourth Amendment requirement. The bill permits "no-knock" entry with or without warrants where "such notice *may* result in the evidence subject to seizure being easily and quickly destroyed, disposed of, or concealed." The common law exception dealing with destruction of evidence contains a very important limitation on permissible "no-knock" entry—that persons within must have been made aware of the presence of someone else outside. The language of this bill will permit the police to decide in advance that certain situations, such as narcotics offenses or others in which evidence could be easily hidden, will always require "no-knock" entry. The common law rule would not have permitted the police to break in on persons asleep in their beds. The D.C. Crime Bill, permitting just such unlimited uses of this power, thus goes well beyond any exception in present common law.

The D.C. Crime Bill also permits "no-knock" entry where "such notice would otherwise be a useless gesture." As existing common law authority is fully covered by other provisions in the "no-knock" section of the bill, this provision serves only to place unlimited authority and discretion in the hands of the police, thus enlarging the common law exception so as to destroy the rule. . . .

The Justice Department's statement also repeatedly cites as a safeguard, an advance to be applauded, the fact that officers are required to obtain a warrant to conduct a "no-knock" search "when the circumstances which would justify such an entry are known in advance." What the statement so carefully fails to point out is that when the circumstances are not known in advance, the police are not precluded from no-knock entry but may conduct the exact same entry without a warrant.

In sum, the police will be able to initiate such unannounced entries without judicial intervention and without any reason to believe that such

Courtesy American Civil Liberties Union, Department of Information, Washington, D.C.

power is required in a particular case. Moreover, the bill makes it a crime to resist the police when they enter.

To secure passage of the "no-knock" bill, the Justice Department is deliberately misstating both the existing law and the impact of the proposed "no-knock" law. The no-knock law itself can only lead to tragedy and will further widen the gulf between citizens and the police. . . .

Sincerely,

(Signed)

Lawrence Speiser
Director
Washington Office

(Signed)

Florence B. Robin
Executive Director
ACLU of the National
Capital Area

End questions

1. What type of feedback do you think the AELE's position on the D.C. Crime Bill will generate? New demands or supports? Contrast this type of feedback with what the ACLU hopes to accomplish by testing the constitutionality of the bill.
2. Who do you think is more qualified to speak out on matters of crime—the social scientist or the policeman? What kind of feedback on the D.C. Crime Bill would you expect from these two types of people?
3. Do Supreme Court decisions mirror the attitudes of the current administration? What are the reasons for your answer? Cite cases. How are these examples of feedback, and what type of feedback are they?
4. What is the significance of the *Chimel v. California* decision reached in the state court of California? Why did the Supreme Court overrule the state decision? Which group, the AELE or the ACLU, would favor the Supreme Court's decision? Why?

Supplementary Reading

COOK, FRED J. *The Nightmare Decade.* New York: Random House, 1971. McCarthyism was not a "temporary aberration of the American spirit," writes journalist Fred J. Cook. Utilizing contemporary sources, Cook recreates the ten years when Senator Joseph R. McCarthy cast his shadow on the halls of Congress, gaining the attention as well as support of many Americans. Cook's book is for those who do not remember the McCarthy era as well as those who lived through it.

DAMERELL, REGINALD G. *Triumph in a White Suburb.* New York: Apollo, 1969. Paperbound. The story of Teaneck, New Jersey and its attempts at school integration is a most interesting one. The authors prove, through tape-recorded testimony by members of the community, that when laws change actions, they change feelings as well.

EBENSTEIN, WILLIAM. *Two Ways of Life: The Communist Challenge to Democracy.* Rev. ed. New York: Holt, Rinehart & Winston, 1966. Ebenstein focuses on a discussion of the Soviet Union as the strongest Communist power and the United States as the main representative of the democratic nations. He writes in an absorbing manner, emphasizing the central roles these two nations play in the continuing struggle for world power.

FULBRIGHT, J. WILLIAM. *The Arrogance of Power.* New York: Random House, 1967. (Also in paper.) The chairman of the Senate Foreign Relations Committee criticizes various aspects of American foreign policy and the behavior and attitudes of Americans in contact with foreigners. Mr. Fulbright comments "America is showing signs of that arrogance of power which has afflicted, weakened, and in some cases destroyed great nations in the past."

LEDERER, WILLIAM J., and BURDICK, EUGENE. *The Ugly American.* New York: Norton, 1958. Paperbound edition, New York: Fawcett World (Crest), 1969. A near classic, this book reveals some of the bunglings that are part of day-to-day activities in the American foreign service. The scene is Southeast Asia, and much of the action centers around one American who is trying to do something for the local inhabitants but is confronted with bureaucratic red tape.

LIPSKY, MICHAEL, ed. *Police Encounters.* Chicago: Aldine Publishing Co., 1970. The book addresses itself to issues of police behavior toward minorities and lower income persons, police responses to mass disturbances, and the limitations of police in preventing crime. The authors try to disprove both public misconceptions about police behavior and police protestations by analyzing many subjects related to law enforcement.

LORD, WALTER. *The Past That Would Not Die.* New York: Harper and Row, 1965. This is the story of James H. Meredith's 1962 enrollment in the University of Mississippi and the civil-rights riot that ensued. The book is a detailed recital of a day of terror and of confrontation between state and federal authorities.

MICHENER, JAMES A. *Kent State: What Happened and Why.* New York: Random House, 1971. Michener analyzes the tragedy at Kent State University in Ohio, where four students died in a student demonstration. The book presents a thorough minute-by-minute account of the events leading up to the confrontation between the students and the National Guard. Michener shows how easily divisions in a community can escalate toward tragedy—how "Kent State could be your community."

MILLER, ARTHUR R. *The Assault on Privacy*. Ann Arbor: University of Michigan Press, 1971. Computers, data banks, and dossiers are the subject of this book. Mr. Miller describes in lucid terms, how their misuse can lead to repression and eventual denial of individual freedom. It is a startling exposé of what is on record already, and of the inadequacy of the present safeguards for keeping this information confidential from unscrupulous snoops. Miller bestirs his readers to demand an end to abuses of computer technology and surveillance techniques.

MOORE, TRUMAN. *The Slaves We Rent*. New York: Random House, 1965. Photographs tell the story of approximately 2 million people, unprotected by any social legislation and not citizens of any state, who live in grinding poverty as migrant farm workers. How and why this has happened is explored, and solutions to the problem are proposed.

SHUTE, NEVIL. *On the Beach*. New York: Apollo, 1964. Paperbound. World destruction by atomic war is Mr. Shute's theme. The fears, trepidations, and last-minute thoughts that go through the minds of the planet's last survivors in Australia, where prevailing winds will soon carry the fatal atomic fallout, adds a chilling ingredient to an already frightening theme.

WATTERS, PAT. *Down to Now*. New York: Pantheon Books, 1971. The author seeks to grasp, in a personal manner, the civil-rights movement's deepest meaning for America. Mr. Watters reflects on the rise and fall of the southern civil-rights movement and its possible re-emergence. Besides presenting the "hard facts," he tries to capture "the change which occurred in the hearts of the people, the dynamics of it, the causes, the effects."

CHAPTER 23

The Role of the Federal Government in Urban Affairs

When the concept of federalism was embodied in the national Constitution in 1787, the Framers had a fairly broad notion of what the role of the states would be. Among the functions left to the individual sovereign states were those that concerned local government. The Constitution established no direct relationship between the local governments and the national government.

According to the original constitutional scheme, the most immediate demands of local communities for governmental action were to be directed either toward the state governments or toward whatever local governing structures the states set up. Yet during the twentieth century, the difficulties faced by state and local structures in meeting local political demands have resulted in a constitutional transition—the development and expansion of a direct role for the federal government in municipal and local affairs. Just how has this development come about?

The Federal Government and Urban Concerns

Like other developments that have occurred within America's political system, the federal government's concern with urban affairs has come about gradually. Although conscious recognition of the federal role in urban affairs did not emerge until the 1960's, the actions of the national government have been affecting urban areas indirectly since the founding of the Republic. Consider the profound impact that national immigration policies have had since the eighteenth century in shaping the growth and character of urban centers. The protective tariffs and other national economic policies of the nineteenth century that promoted the growth of American industry and commerce certainly contributed to the development of cities where these activities thrived.

Governmental responses to needs. As the populations of urban areas have swelled, it has been inevitable that most national policies concerned with people, their social needs, and economic relations, would have a major impact on the patterns of urbanization and on urban populations. In the year 1900, about one-third of the nation's people lived in urban areas; but by 1930 more than half of the total population was concentrated in such regions. When President Johnson delivered the first major Presidential message on cities in 1965, over 70 percent of the United States population lived in urban areas. Thus while many federal programs have been initiated to aid people in both urban and rural communities, a greater proportion of federal resources, services, and facilities have naturally been allocated to urban areas where the majority of people live.

In 1964, for example, the Economic Opportunity Act set up community action programs to attack poverty throughout the nation. Federal funds were pumped directly to local agencies to finance such activities as trips for slum children, day care services, social work counseling, reading instruction, and so forth. While the 1964 Act was directed toward alleviating problems of poverty in both rural and urban areas, by far the bulk of the community action programs existed in urban areas. Since the allocation of federal funds by-

How can harried urban areas make the national government more aware of the innumerable problems they constantly confront? Is the federal government likely to be sympathetic toward urban problems or ignore them?

Table 26.1

Major Federal Programs that Concern Urban Areas	
Highway construction	Airports and air terminal construction
Flood control and prevention	Hospital planning and construction
Water pollution control	General welfare assistance
Services to children with developmental disabilities	Social security
Control of communicable diseases	Vocational education
Health centers and clinics	Vocational rehabilitation
Disaster relief	Employment security
Civil defense	Legal aid programs
School lunches	Community action programs
Special problems of federally impacted areas (where military bases and other federal installations place burdens on local resources)	Housing and urban development
	Crime control and safety in the streets
	Drug abuse control

passed local governments, local officials resisted the establishment of competing centers of power in their community, and the community action programs died out by the end of the 1960's as a result of pressure from local officials.

National programs for highway and airport construction, flood and pollution control, disaster relief, school lunches, housing, and many other purposes also have been directed toward the needs of people in all communities. Although some federal aid for airport construction has gone to rural areas, it is obvious that the major urban population centers with their larger air traffic demands receive the great bulk of such aid. Similarly, the establishment of health programs in rural areas, where they serve a handful of people, does not compare with the impact of such programs in urban areas where they serve many thousands of people.

■ *Differences between urban and rural needs.* It has also become widely recognized since the 1930's that the needs of people in urban areas differ in many ways from the needs of those in non-urban areas. This contrast was highlighted by the Great Depression. The rampant unemployment during the Depression and the problems of finding money to pay for the basic needs of food and shelter were peculiarly urban phenomena. The means of survival for unemployed urban workers were quite different from those of farmers who could usually manage to scrape up something to eat without the intermediate step of securing funds. It was only when these differences were made obvious by an economic crisis that the federal role in cities became more direct and visible.

In contemporary society, the contrasts between urban and rural needs are evident in many ways. Rural regions, which are losing many skilled and younger people to urban communities, are characterized today by relatively sparsely settled territories with dwindling populations. The existence of many thousands of people within limited amounts of space in cities, on the other hand, produce particular problems not found to the same extent elsewhere. Since housing in cities is scarce, for example, many residents must pay exorbitant rents to live in crowded and unsafe dwellings. The high concentration of industrial plants creates high air-pollution levels that are harmful to the health of city residents. The density of the urban population combined with its ethnic and racial diversity make it more likely for intergroup tensions and conflicts to emerge. Obviously, then, federal policies that are formulated to answer people's needs and to promote the general welfare have had to be oriented differently for urban and rural populations.

■ *Federal influence on municipal governments.* The urban role of the federal government has had an impact not only on the people who live in urban areas but also on the functioning of local government. Federal policies today contribute both directly and indirectly to the financial resources of municipalities as well as to the demands made on local structures and the performance of municipal services.

In addition to the federal funds for programs such as social security and unemployment that reach the cities through grants to the states, more than 5 percent of the federal budget is devoted to direct grants-in-aid payments to local governments. Furthermore, many federal projects that affect the conditions of urban life also produce demands on municipal governing structures. The construction of a federal atomic energy installation in a region, for example, revamps the economy of nearby cities and swells the population. These changes in turn contribute to increased demands by the growing population on local school systems and on municipal governments for facilities and services.

Hundreds of national agencies perform services that benefit the cities and municipal governing structures as well. The FBI, for example, provides information to local authorities, trains law enforcement officials, and helps in the investigation and prosecution of criminals—all without charge to the municipalities.

While the activities and policies of the federal government have had a profound impact on urban life and municipal government, most federal programs—like those of the other levels of government—have been responses to particular needs and problems that presented themselves at different times. The purposes and results of each federal output has thus been viewed in isolation rather than in the context of the total urban situation. Only in the last decade has the feedback process begun to force policy-makers at the federal

From *The Herblock Gallery* (Simon & Schuster, 1968)

"HELP"

(By the end of the 1960's, the plight of the cities had worsened to almost catastrophic proportions.)

level to focus on urban needs in a comprehensive way.

Reasons for federal government's interest in urban affairs. The increased activity of the federal government in urban affairs has come about for a number of reasons. First, the financial, territorial, and political limitations on state and local governments for dealing with urban problems have encouraged spokesmen for urban interests to seek outputs from conversion structures in Washington. Another contributing factor has been the fact that most federal maintenance and developmental policies have had a tremendous impact on the cities whether they were specifically directed at urban problems or more generally directed to the total society.

In the past several decades, policy-makers in both local and state governments have become increasingly concerned about meeting demands for improving the urban environment. This concern, however, has been difficult to translate into workable public policies. Both demand-makers and policy-makers in local and state political subsystems are turning increasingly toward the federal government for solutions to urban problems.

■ *Limitations of local and state governments.* Solutions to urban problems at the local level have been hindered by the political fragmentation, limited jurisdiction, and inadequate financing powers of local government. While housing shortages and their political solutions are not confined by municipal boundaries, the territorial jurisdictions of most local governments are. Existing municipalities, furthermore, can barely finance day-to-day functions let alone new policies for urban rejuvenation. Special district governments fail to provide broad and long-term solutions for meeting urban problems. And the process of setting up an effectively operating multi-purpose metropolitan governments is so cumber-

some and has met with so many obstacles that the likelihood of solving urban problems through such structures is small indeed.

Some state governments have not been particularly active in solving urban problems. The states, like the local governments, are limited financially in their ability to cope with the magnitude of urban problems. Furthermore, many urban areas—such as those of Chicago, Detroit, Kansas City, Memphis, New York, Philadelphia, and St. Louis—transcend state boundaries and thus do not fall within the territorial jurisdiction of a single state government.

Another factor that has kept the states from solving urban problems in the past has been the largely rural composition of state legislatures. Before the rulings of the Supreme Court on legislative apportionment in the 1960's, state legislative chambers tended to be dominated by representatives of rural constituencies. (See also, Chapter 18, pages 438, 445 and Chapter 22, pages 578–579.) Thus even when urban communities made demands on state legislatures, their demands were rarely converted into outputs that dealt with urban needs. Ironically, by the time reapportionment rulings began to take effect, so many residents of central cities had fled to the suburbs that suburban representatives made up sizeable segments of the reapportioned legislatures. The possibilities for state legislative action on urban problems, therefore, still remain in doubt.

■ *Prospects for federal solutions.* With all these limitations on state and local policy solutions, it is not surprising that urban communities have turned more and more to the national government for action on their demands. Unlike the municipalities and states, the federal government does have territorial jurisdiction broad enough to encompass multi-municipal and multi-state urban regions. In addition, because of the financial structure of the national political system, Washington is regarded by many persons as the only adequate source of funds for answering urban needs.

Unlike local governments that derive most of their revenues from taxing property owners, the federal government distributes its tax burden more equitably among citizens in proportion to their incomes. This factor tends to make federal solutions more palatable to most people. If a municipality decided to construct public housing for poor families, for example, the financial burden of the project might fall unfairly on a limited segment of municipal residents. Older retired homeowners with limited incomes might be saddled with high property taxes while persons who work inside the city using its services would contribute much less to the project. Since the federal income tax is levied on a wider range of people, the use of federal funds to finance public housing spreads the burden over a greater number of taxpayers. While state and local governments could also provide

for collecting more local income taxes, the resistance of voters has generally thwarted the enactment of such measures.

Another logical reason for channelling urban demands to the federal government is that federal policy-makers have been more responsive than state officials to such demands. In the past, while state legislatures tended to be controlled by rural interests, cities often increased their representation in Congress as their populations grew. The attention of Congress is therefore drawn more easily to urban needs. Furthermore, the support of urban voters is very important to the election of candidates for the Presidency and the Senate. Thus elected officials at the national level—regardless of their political party affiliations—have to take particular notice of the demands of urban voters to maintain their support at the polls.

■ *Urban lobbies in Washington.* Like other interest groups with special needs and problems, people concerned with urban problems make demands on federal

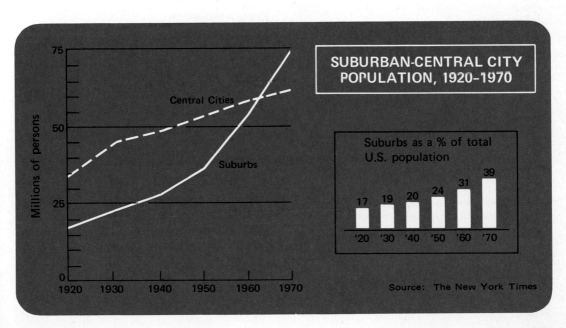

SUBURBAN-CENTRAL CITY POPULATION, 1920–1970

Central Cities

Suburbs

Millions of persons

Suburbs as a % of total U.S. population

'20	'30	'40	'50	'60	'70
17	19	20	24	31	39

Source: The New York Times

"Pecking order"

Haynie in *The Louisville Courier-Journal*

(Urban governments are hampered in responding to their problems by their inability to get enough revenue.)

policy-makers most effectively through organized pressure groups. Lobbying activity on behalf of urban interests is not a new development, but it has become more intensive in recent years.

There are many pressure groups that while representing specific interests within the population, have always been concerned with urban-related issues. Labor organizations like the AFL-CIO, for example, have often supported federal outputs to improve the urban environment. Their support stems, in part, from the fact that urban conditions very much affect the lives of industrial workers concentrated in urban areas. This support is also due to the fact that federal programs provide employment for members of labor organizations in such urban industries as housing construction.

Many other special interest groups, including religious, educational, and veterans' organizations, have also been involved in lobbying activities to support federal programs that would help the cities.

There are also pressure groups that are specifically organized to represent the interests of municipalities and of municipal officials. The National League of Cities, formed in 1924, maintains a registered lobbyist in Washington and has actively supported federal programs that would benefit its members. The United States Conference of Mayors and the National Institute of Municipal Law Officers are other organizations that engage in similar activities.

During the decade of the 1960's, moreover, a number of large American cities set up offices in Washington for the purpose of pressuring the national government to meet various local needs. Mayors and governors are traveling more and more frequently to Washington to represent urban interests before congressional committee hearings and the various agencies of the federal bureaucracy.

Review questions

1. Why has the federal government always been responsive to urban needs?
2. Why have state and local governments turned to the federal government for solutions to urban problems?

Housing and Urban Renewal Policies

Of all the federal policies affecting urban areas, those most specifically and directly designed to have a special urban impact have been in the area of housing and urban renewal. But even national outputs on urban housing have emerged not as part of an overall strategy but as piecemeal responses to specific demands and pressures. Like other federal domestic policies, the widespread impact of housing programs on urban affairs has not been consciously recognized until recent years.

Overview. The federal government's interest in housing has been a very controversial one. In the early part of this century, the focus of government concern was on the unsafe conditions and deteriorated dwellings that housed low-income families in many central cities. Following World War II, concern shifted to the overall shortage of housing for all income groups, particularly in urban regions. While there has been general agreement on the need to rectify slum conditions and housing shortages, there has been bitter disagreement among different interest groups as to how these problems should be solved.

Since the 1930's when the federal government began formulating policy outputs pertaining to housing, certain ideas have been advanced by concerned interest groups that have influenced the government's approach. First, there has been a strong feeling among some groups that housing problems can be solved more effectively by private industry than by direct governmental solutions. This view has been supported by the real estate interests, for example, who have felt that government programs to construct housing would threaten the survival of their industry. Another widely held view, which coincides with the desire of communities to preserve local autonomy, has been that local housing problems will be solved best on the local level rather than by the federal government. At the same time, many groups, interested in improving the lot of the poor and in increasing the supply of decent housing, have felt that nothing substantial could be accomplished without active federal involvement.

The federal outputs to maintain and develop housing and the urban environment generally have been devised through compromise between these points of view. A major thrust of federal housing legislation has been to combine federal funds and guidelines with local government administration and private investment. Over the years, as new housing measures have been added to the framework established during the New Deal period, the emphasis of federal policy has repeatedly shifted. The major aspects of this policy have been: financial assistance for lending institutions and homeowners, public housing, urban redevelopment, urban renewal, and rehabilitation.

Assistance to lenders and homeowners. The first extensive federal legislation on housing grew out of the emergency of the Depression of the 1930's when the scarcity of money intensified the shortage of housing and the deterioration of existing dwellings. Without funds, homeowners could not afford to pay off the mortgages on their homes or to make home improvements and repairs. Banks and other financing institutions were discouraged from lending funds for home construction or for mortgages and repairs, because they were afraid that such loans would not be paid off.

The response of the federal government was to create several government agencies that could bolster the ability of private institutions to finance home buying, home improvements, and housing construction. In 1933, when banks were foreclosing mortgages at a rate of a thousand per day, the government created HOLC—the Home Owners Loan Corporation. HOLC provided money to refinance, at lower interest rates and longer payment terms, mortgages that were about to be foreclosed. The Federal Housing Administration (FHA) was established in 1934 with the authority to insure long-term mortgages and other loans made by private lending institutions for home construction and repairs. Supplementing this action was the creation in 1938 of the Federal National Mortgage Association. Commonly known as "Fannie Mae," this organization repurchases mortgages from the original lenders—banks, insurance companies, and loan associations—when these lending institutions need cash. All of these agencies served to stabilize private lending institutions and indirectly to maintain housing for thousands of home-owners during and after the 1930's.

Another related housing measure was the Servicemen's Readjustment Act of 1944. This Act authorized the Veterans Administration to guarantee credit to veterans who wished to purchase, construct, or improve homes. Known as the G.I. Loan Program, the terms of the Act were subsequently extended and liberalized. Together with the FHA mortgage insurance program, the G.I. Loan Program encouraged the post-war boom in home construction outside of the central cities.

Public housing. The first federal legislation aimed at the construction of public housing was the United States Housing Act of 1937—also an outgrowth of the Depression. The purpose of the Act was to encourage municipal governments to replace deteriorated dwellings in low-income neighborhoods with upgraded housing.

The public housing program of 1937 was not intended to increase the housing supply. Such an objective was considered to belong to private industry. The enactment of the 1937 law was motivated primarily by the need to alleviate high unemployment and to replace slum dwellings with better quality housing. At the same time, it was a response to the demands of social reformers who for decades had been suggesting that the social ills of slums could be cured if safe and sanitary housing were provided and slums were eliminated.

The 1937 Act set up the Federal Public Housing Authority, which was authorized to make loans and contributions to local public housing agencies for slum clearance and public housing projects. The local agencies to handle these projects were created by state and local legislation. The Federal Public Housing Authority was responsible for approving the plans of the local agencies for the sites, costs, and rents of the projects. Once a local agency received federal approval for its plan along with a grant of federal funds, the local agency itself was responsible for building the housing projects which it then owned and operated. One of the conditions attached to all grants was that for every unit constructed, a substandard unit had to be eliminated.

One of the weaknesses of the 1937 Housing Act was that it did not alleviate the housing shortage. Often the program resulted in more acute shortages because, in actuality, more substandard units were removed than there were new units built. The funds appropriated for the program by Congress were limited; and by 1948 only 114,000 units had been built under the 1937 Act.

Urban redevelopment. Following World War II, the federal government began to focus more attention on the nationwide shortage of housing. Home building had fallen off during the Depression and the war; and veterans and defense workers returning to urban communities from defense installations needed shelter. Moreover, the 1940 Census had reported that 49 percent of the nation's existing housing was "substandard"—in other words, dilapidated or lacking plumbing facilities. In his message to Congress in 1945, President Truman noted that 1,500,000 new units would have to be constructed each year for ten years to alleviate the housing shortage.

The Housing Act of 1949 extended the operations of the FHA for insuring mortgages and contained provisions for public housing similar to those of the 1937 law. The Act also included a new emphasis on *urban redevelopment.* Like public housing, the urban redevelopment program was funded primarily by the federal government and administered by municipal agencies. Its purpose, however, was to en-

INTERGOVERNMENTAL POLICY-MAKING
Issue: Public Housing Projects

INPUTS **CONVERSION STRUCTURES** **OUTPUTS**

INTEREST GROUPS

AFL-CIO
League of Women Voters
Urban League
U.S. Conference of Majors
National League of Cities
U.S. Chamber of Commerce
American Municipal
  Association
Mortgage brokers
Apartment owners
Real Estate associations
Education organizations
Religious organizations
Veterans organizations

CONGRESS

1. Sets conditions
2. Appropriates funds

FEDERAL
POLITICAL
SYSTEM

DEPARTMENT OF
HOUSING AND URBAN
DEVELOPMENT (HUD)

| 1. Develops guidelines | 3. Provides funds |
| 2. Approves local plan | |

$
$
$
$

INTEREST GROUPS

Mayor
City council
Labor organizations
Landlords
Construction industry
Business leaders
Social workers
Local residents

| 1. Draws up plan for site, costs, and rents of project | 2. Buys land, relocates families, clears slums, builds, owns, and manages public housing units |

LOCAL PUBLIC
HOUSING AGENCY

Slum
  clearance
Low–rent
  housing for
  low-income
  families

STATE LEGISLATURE
AND
MUNICIPAL GOVERNMENT
Create agency

STATE
AND LOCAL
POLITICAL
SYSTEMS

courage the construction of all kinds of housing by *private* developers.

■ *Opposition and support.* Although the 1949 law was originally sponsored by conservative and liberal Senators of both parties, bitter controversy surrounded its passage. Particularly strong opposition to the public housing provisions was voiced by many business and trade groups engaged in the production and financing of housing. Among the opponents were such groups as the Mortgage Bankers Association, the National Apartment Owners Associations, the National Association of Home Builders, and the National Association of Real Estate Boards. The Council for Constitutional Government and the National Economic Council also joined the opposition.

Support for the bill came from a wide variety of groups. The two major labor organizations, numerous veterans, church, and welfare organizations, the American Municipal Association, the National Public Housing Conference, the United States Conference of Mayors, and others took part in lobbying activities to obtain the bill's passage.

The strength of opposition and support for the legislation kept it floundering in Congress for four years before it was enacted in 1949. The urban redevelopment proposals, however, received more general support than did the more controversial provisions for public housing. Certain provisions of the bill as finally enacted reflected the interests of specific groups that had supported it. Veterans of World Wars I and II were to be given preference in the occupancy of new housing. Labor leaders obtained a provision in the law guaranteeing to workers on public housing projects the same wages as workers in private industry. Moreover, provisions limiting public housing occupancy to low-income families insured that the public projects would

not compete with private dwellings on the regular housing market.

■ *Major provisions of the Housing Act of 1949.* The public housing provisions of the 1949 law preserved the basic features of the 1937 program. A new Public Housing Administration replaced the former Federal Public Housing Authority. Additional funds were authorized for federal loans and subsidies to local public housing agencies. To ensure that public housing projects would house only low-income families, local authorities had to keep rents at least 20 percent below the rents for similar private housing, and families could not occupy a public housing unit once their income passed a specified maximum.

Title I of the 1949 Act was the section on urban redevelopment. The basic strategy behind the urban redevelopment program was that local governments would buy land in blighted areas, clear the land of slum housing, and then resell it at low cost to private developers. The federal government provided funds to local governments to make up the differences between the purchase price and the lower resale price. The low price at which the land was made available to redevelopers was designed to be a financial incentive to improve the property and then sell or rent it at a low rate later.

Under Title I, a local redevelopment agency would submit a plan for redeveloping a blighted area to the federal authorities for approval. While the emphasis of the plan had to be on housing, it could also include provisions for some parks or commercial and industrial land use. Once the plan was approved, the local agency bought and cleared the land with the aid of federal funds and then sold it at a loss. Two-thirds of the agency's loss was reimbursed by a federal grant. The developer who purchased the land had to conform to the redevelopment plan and build safe and sanitary housing at reasonable rents.

Urban renewal and rehabilitation. Amendments to the 1949 Housing Act have been made almost every year since its enactment. In 1954, without greatly altering the structure of the 1949 law, Congress made very few provisions for public housing but added other provisions that significantly broadened the scope of urban redevelopment.

The intent of the 1954 law was to encourage, not only the construction of new housing on cleared slum sites, but also the rehabilitation of existing housing and the *prevention* of urban blight. This shift in emphasis had been recommended in a report by President Eisenhower's Advisory Committee on Housing which introduced the term "urban renewal" to describe these broader objectives.

■ *Workable programs.* The 1954 housing law required that local communities seeking redevelopment aid had to adopt comprehensive "workable programs" in order to receive federal funds. The workable programs had to include a number of features. First, the local redevelopment agency had to provide an adequate plan for relocating people who were displaced by slum clearance at redevelopment sites. To facilitate this aspect of the workable programs, a federal program was established to insure private construction of housing for families so displaced.

Second, workable programs had to include housing codes that set minimum standards for all housing. One aim of such codes was to permit structurally sound dwellings to be *rehabilitated*—that is, to be brought up to minimum standards instead of being torn down. Federal money was also made available to communities to study ways to improve code enforcement and thus prevent the deterioration of existing housing. A third workable-program requirement was that citizens of local communities had to participate in the adoption of urban renewal plans. And finally, the local agency had to show that a proposed redevelopment project fit in with a master plan for community renewal.

One significant departure of the 1954 law from earlier redevelopment legislation was that up to 10 percent of a federal grant could be used toward commercial or industrial rather than housing development. In addition, while federal grants were still used by local agencies to tear down deteriorated buildings and sell land to developers, local communities were encouraged to salvage structurally sound buildings whenever possible.

■ *Operation of urban renewal.* The plan for an urban renewal project is generally initiated by a local redevelopment authority which selects an area in the community for redevelopment. Once a plan is drawn up and approved by the local agency and the regular municipal government, hearings are held to give residents of the community an opportunity to voice support or opposition to the plan. The plan is then submitted to the federal Urban Renewal Administration for approval, and federal funding is arranged.

After federal approval is obtained, city

Ed Fisher. Copyright 1969 Saturday Review, Inc.

"Well, thanks for the look around, Mr. Mayor. I'll let you know whether this area qualifies for federal urban assistance. Offhand I'd say you've got enough blight but not enough sprawl."

(While the federal government encouraged cities to rebuild, money was not granted without some limitations.)

officials start to acquire real estate for the project through their powers of eminent domain. The period that follows is often one of hardship for tenants and business people in the area who are forced to relocate. Financial aid is available for residents whose homes are slated for rehabilitation. Other tenants are relocated so that their buildings can be demolished and the cleared land sold to private developers.

The goals of the urban renewal program have been viewed differently by the various groups that have supported it. Social reformers have looked to redevelopment as an instrument for improving living conditions for the poor. On the other hand, downtown merchants, realtors, and mayors have thought of urban renewal as a means of shoring up property values in the central cities. By demolishing slums, areas near central business districts could be redeveloped to include some middle-income and high-income housing. Wealthier people would be lured back from the suburbs to live and shop in the cities and help pay municipal taxes. In addition, the cleared areas could be used for commercial and industrial purposes which would raise the assessed value of the land compared to its value when it had slum tenements. In turn, the value of properties in nearby areas would be raised and further development by private investors would be stimulated. These economic advantages would enable urban communities to regain lost civic glory and prestige as well as more revenue from taxes.

Some cities such as Boston, Chicago, and Pittsburgh initially used their urban renewal programs to construct monumental commercial buildings and luxury apartments. By the late 1950's, however, the emphasis of many renewal programs shifted to providing moderate and low-income housing and to rehabilitating existing dwelling units.

Feedback on public housing and urban renewal. How did the federal government's public housing and renewal programs affect the nation's cities? There are some indications that between 1949 and 1964, some progress was made in upgrading the conditions of housing. By 1964, there were approximately 576,000 low-rent public housing units in various communities. In addition, close to 160 urban renewal projects had been completed, and approximately 1,300 other renewal plans had received federal approval. The 1960 Census reported that more than 18 percent of the nation's housing was still substandard, but this figure was only half of what it had been in 1950.

In spite of these gains, the housing problems of the nation were far from solved. Between 1960 and 1964, for example, 3.5 million housing units were destroyed for highway construction, renewal projects, or by other causes. Housing experts estimated that close to 2 million new units would have to be constructed in urban areas each year to keep pace with housing needs. In addition, various problems were encountered with the federal programs which aroused much criticism.

■ *Problems with public housing.* Over the years, supporters of public housing have been generally unenthusiastic about the results of the program. A major criticism of the projects has been that they have not solved the social and familial disorders of slum areas but simply transferred these problems to public housing. This factor has been a great disappointment to public housing reformers who had hoped that decent housing would reduce the amount of crime, juvenile delinquency, broken families, and other social ills of slum areas. Yet, once the streets of slums were cleared of refuse and debris and the dilapidated structures were replaced with bright new apartments insulated from the hazards of the streets, the same basic social and economic problems of low-income families remained. Public housing could not cure such problems as family and community disorganization, unemployment, racism, poverty, or disease.

Other criticisms have been directed at the public housing programs. Many critics complain that the design of the projects is too sterile and institutional in character—creating a prison-like atmosphere. There have been other complaints that public housing tends to isolate poor families from the rest of a community and thus insures that many of their problems will persist. Yet residents in middle-class neighborhoods, afraid that low-income projects will reduce the property value of their neighborhoods, often use their political influence to prevent such projects from being built in their areas.

Another flaw in the program has been the stipulation that a family, once its level of income has improved beyond a certain point must move out of a project. Critics argue that tenants threatened with the possibility of eviction have little motivation to improve their economic status. A public housing tenant will not want to earn more money if it will only result in his having to leave his neighbors to live in inferior private housing elsewhere at a higher rent.

■ *Criticisms of urban renewal.* Like public housing, the federal urban renewal programs have also been the target of severe criticism from many quarters. One major criticism has been that the hardship which renewal brings to many residents and proprietors in a renewal area far outweighs any benefits of a program. Small business proprietors who are displaced and relocated are not reimbursed for lost goodwill and clientele. Many give up their businesses instead of attempting to rebuild their trade from the ground up in a new locale. Residents are hit hard, too. In many

A. Cramer. Copyright 1967 Saturday Review, Inc.

"It's a 10 million dollar housing development to rid the city of slums. When it's finished, they'll be able to rent apartments to the poor for $250 a month."

(Although this situation seems incongruous, practicality often takes precedence over people's needs.)

cases they are moved from one blighted area to another, and still have to pay higher rents. Minority groups who have to relocate find themselves excluded from many residential neighborhoods.

Another criticism has been that urban renewal reduced the amount of low-rent housing available to low-income persons. As slums are demolished they are not replaced by enough public housing to make up for the loss in dwelling units. Existing public units are already fully occupied, and new units are usually not ready for occupancy when tenants have to be relocated. Moreover, critics point out that renewal projects have often destroyed neighborhoods that were substandard in appearance, but strong in terms of social and family life. Criticism has been directed also at city officials who are too eager to tear down buildings in an area that might be salvaged if building codes were enforced.

Frequently, the time lag involved in getting projects underway encourages further deterioration to take place. When an area is designated for renewal, owners stop making any property improvements. If the program is then stalled for one reason or another, the neighborhood may deteriorate even faster than it would have if the property had not been designated for renewal at all. In other instances, housing has been swiftly demolished, but then the bulldozed land has been allowed to lie vacant for many years.

■ *Improving the programs.* While the federal government has usually been defensive about these criticisms, it has nonetheless continually responded by revising the housing legislation. When public housing was under attack during the early 1950's, for example, Congress shifted its attention to urban renewal and was slow to appropriate public housing funds authorized by the 1949 law. Subsequent criticisms of renewal programs also resulted in legislative improvements. Special FHA mortgage insurance was made available to facilitate rehabilitation of existing buildings and loans were made available to non-profit groups to build housing for elderly citizens.

The Housing Act of 1961 included some particularly important revisions. It established new categories of FHA mortgage insurance with liberal interest and repayment terms to encourage: (1) the construction of low-rent housing by non-profit organizations such as churches and labor unions; (2) the improvement of existing dwellings within or near urban renewal project areas; (3) experimentation in design and techniques for the construction of housing; and (4) the development of condominium housing—that is, apartments in multi-family dwellings that are individually owned and have separate mortgages.

The 1961 Act also authorized the Public Housing Administration to apply unused funds still remaining from the 1949 law for additional public housing construction. The Act also provided additional loans or grants for such community facilities as college housing, sewage plant improvements, urban mass transit systems, and the creation of "open space" recreational facilities. In spite of the many improvements that were made in the housing programs during these years, however, demands began to mount in the mid-1960's for a more comprehensive federal approach to deal with problems of urban regions.

Review questions

1. List the general programs that the federal government has adopted to improve the nation's housing. What overall need has each of these general programs responded to?
2. What criticisms have been made about public housing and urban renewal?

A New Direction in Federal Urban Policy

By the mid-1960's, many national political leaders, mayors, scholars, and urban planners began to take a broader look at the federal government's role in urban affairs. They began to recognize that while all national domestic programs were having an impact on the cities, there did not seem to be any coordination of these programs that would give a logical direction to urban development. In fact, the objectives of various programs seemed to be in direct conflict with each other and tended to aggravate rather than alleviate many urban problems. In response to mounting pressure from urban residents and their representatives in local and national circles, federal policymakers have begun to view urban needs from a broader perspective.

Contradictions in policy. The objectives of most federal maintenance and developmental policies affecting the cities have seemed quite desirable when considered in isolation. There have been policies to eliminate slums, to increase the supply of housing for the poor and other income groups, and to improve housing design. Other policies have been geared to reducing traffic congestion in central cities, to revitalizing urban business districts, and to increasing municipal tax bases. There have also been programs to improve local planning and to encourage more citizen participation in local decision-making. Few people would quibble with the value of any of these objectives. Yet as put into effect, many of the benefits intended by some policies have been cancelled out by the results of others.

Many contradictions in policy have been noted by critics. The costs of improving housing design, for example, make it difficult to construct dwellings that poor people can afford. The replacement of slums with high-income housing and commercial developments further reduces the supply of low-income housing available. The revitalization of urban business districts, moreover, increases rather than decreases traffic congestion. And effective local planning is often counteracted by increased local citizen participation.

One important objective of urban planners has been to halt the flight of middle-class residents to the suburbs so as to maintain an adequate tax base for the central cities. Thus urban renewal programs have earmarked some funds for the construction of more middle-income and luxury apartments in the central cities. At the same time, however, the FHA mortgage insurance program has made it easier for people to buy houses in the suburbs. The federal funds that have been poured into the construction of highways not only have

Fitzpatrick in the *St. Louis Post-Dispatch*

PROBLEM BEFORE THE ALDERMEN

(Frequently an apparent solution to one urban problem creates another problem that is just as disastrous.)

made it easier for people employed in the cities to live in the suburbs but also have intensified traffic congestion downtown.

The execution of national policy for urban areas has also been inconsistent. Urban renewal has been used for widely divergent purposes in different communities, depending on the local interests that have supported it. In some cities renewal has been used to rehabilitate neighborhoods and add to the supply of low and moderate-income housing. In other cities it has been used to clear sites for parking lots and shopping malls or to erect civic monuments.

Coordinating urban policies. In response to such criticisms, the federal government has begun to take a more searching look at the needs of cities. The scope of this new federal perspective was evident when President Johnson, in 1964, noted that "in

619

the next 40 years we must rebuild the entire urban United States." The shift in thinking was also indicated by the coordination of urban-related policies in the federal bureaucracy and in the kinds of urban programs that Congress has enacted.

■ *Department of Housing and Urban Development.* An important step toward the coordination of national urban policies was the creation of the Cabinet-level Department of Housing and Urban Development (HUD). This step had first been proposed by President Kennedy in 1962 but was not enacted until President Johnson proposed it again in 1965.

The new executive department was authorized to administer federal programs affecting urban communities. A number of existing agencies—the Housing and Home Finance Agency (HHFA), the Federal Housing Administration, the Public Housing Administration, the Urban Renewal Administration, and Fannie Mae—were consolidated under one roof to share administrative costs and leadership.

The initial impact of HUD was symbolic. Elevation of national programs on urban affairs to departmental status called attention to their importance and stimulated a search for a more comprehensive federal policy toward urban areas. Also significant was the appointment of Robert C. Weaver as the first HUD Secretary. Weaver was the first black American to hold a Cabinet post.

■ *Rent supplements.* In addition to the creation of HUD, another major new idea—the *rent supplement* program—was enacted in 1965. The purpose of this program is to enable certain low-income people to obtain housing in private dwellings that rent for more than they can afford with their own incomes. People eligible for rent supplements include the physically handicapped, the elderly, and those displaced by government programs such as urban renewal. Rent supplements are available to persons in these categories who can not obtain adequate private housing at rents equal to or less than 25 percent of their incomes. Under the federal program, such people pay one-quarter of their incomes toward their rents, and the government pays the difference between what the tenants can pay and what the actual rent is.

■ *Model Cities.* A third significant departure from previous legislation was the adoption of the Model Cities program. This plan, which was initiated as part of the Demonstration Cities and Metropolitan Development Act of 1966, is aimed at restructuring the total environment of deteriorated neighborhoods by dealing with social problems as well as the physical manifestations of urban blight. The intent of the program is to demonstrate the success of such coordination in carefully selected localities which will then serve as models for other areas. The term "Demonstration Cities," identified in the title of the 1966 law, was subsequently changed to "Model Cities."

Unlike the Housing Act of 1949, the Model Cities program had the support of a broad spectrum of interests. Groups such as the United States Conference of Mayors, the National League of Cities, the National Governors Conference, the Mortgage Brokers Association, and the National Association of Home Builders—formerly on opposite sides over many housing issues—joined forces to work for the passage of the new program.

The Model Cities program coordinates the funds and policies of all government levels for improving housing, education, transportation, health facilities, and for combating unemployment, and focuses all these programs on the "model" neighborhoods. In order to create well-balanced communities containing residents of different income levels, the Model Cities program also provides for the construction of both public and private housing in these demonstration neighborhoods.

HUD selects cities for the program which can demonstrate that they have adequate programs of their own for providing health care services, schools, employment, recreational facilities, and other urban needs. Federal funds for the demonstration projects are then channelled through special city agencies created for the purpose by the local governments.

It is still too early to tell how successful these programs will be. The success of Model Cities depends on massive funding and it will probably be a number of years before any major progress can be realized.

■ *Council on Urban Affairs.* By the end of the 1960's, as more and more citizens were looking to the federal government for solutions to urban problems, President Nixon created the post of Presidential Advisor on Urban Affairs. The following year, in 1969, he established the President's Council on Urban Affairs as part of the Executive Office. As he signed the Executive Order creating the Council, the President noted that "the establishment of the President's Urban Affairs Council is an historic occasion in American government." The significance with which the President viewed the Council is evident from the fact that he assigned to it people of national importance. The Council's membership includes a wide range of Cabinet members such as the Attorney General; the Secretaries of Commerce; Labor; Agriculture; Transportation; Housing and Urban Development; and Health, Education, and Welfare; as well as the Vice President of the United States.

The President viewed the Council for Urban Affairs as the domestic equivalent of the National Security Council. The Urban Affairs Council has been assigned the tasks of developing a national urban policy including both immediate and long-range goals, coordinating the federal government's urban programs, and encouraging full cooperation between all levels of government.

At the time the President created the Council, he did emphasize the need for fostering responsibility for urban problems in state and local governments. But by establishing the Council he had, in effect, reinforced the orientation of those Americans who had begun to look to the federal structures for meeting urban needs. In doing so, he made it likely that demands on the federal government for outputs maintaining and developing the urban environment would increase significantly in the years ahead.

Effects of national urban policy on other governments. As the federal government has come to grips with developing a coherent policy toward cities, it has also encouraged other changes in local and state governments. Major changes are taking place in the kinds of local techniques being used or devised for coping with urban matters.

■ *Emphasis on planning.* Planning, as a technique for defining problems and drawing up solutions for urban communities, has mushroomed. During the first three years of Boston's redevelopment program, for example, the Boston Redevelopment Authority expanded from a staff of 16 to 440 employees. Of the new employees, 77 percent were professional planners.

Moreover, as the emphasis of the federal housing and redevelopment programs has shifted from the mere construction of buildings to other human and social matters, the training and interests of professional planners have broadened. Planners now study sociology, economics, and political science. Planners no longer confine their activities to drawing sterile designs for buildings and cities and sketching land-use

"It's not going to be all roses, Son. You'll get a lot of bellyaches about irreplaceable landmarks and the desecration of our architectural heritage."

(Planners, too, have to react to complaints by city residents about destruction of the urban landscape.)

maps showing what already exists. They are also suggesting reasons for social change and learning to take advantage of federal regulations to accomplish more within a given program.

Politicians have also learned to use planning as a means of wielding power. The techniques and the mystique of professionalism can sometimes be manipulated by mayors to block proposals they wish defeated and to dress up other proposals as something they are not. A mayor can blunt political opposition to a proposal, for example, by referring to "the technical findings of a planning staff," even if the matter under discussion is not really a "technical" one.

■ *Local governmental reorganization.* Federal policies have also stimulated administrative reorganization within city government, and many mayors and city managers are coordinating and merging departments. As with the federal government, the overall goals and priorities of coordination are not clear in local political systems, but there is now more awareness of the overlap of many municipal functions. Mayor John Lindsay of New York, for example, reorganized the city government by regrouping departments in terms of related functions.

■ *Municipal finances.* Still another impact of federal activity in urban affairs has been the awakening of cities to the need for squeezing out more revenue. Many major cities have capitalized on the new concern for the plight of the cities and pressured for sales taxes in their state legislatures. The states as a result have sought additional ways to reimburse the cities and towns for municipal services. Some cities have been able to institute city income taxes affecting all people who earn their incomes in the city, not just residents or property-owners within the city limits. The concern of city dwellers over suburbanites, who do not pay a share of the central city's property tax but who do use services and facilities provided by those taxes, has encouraged city leaders to find ways to tax commuters.

■ *Effects on state government.* Another result of the federal role in urban affairs has been the diminishing role of state governments as the middlemen between national and local structures. The federal government has been dealing directly with urban communities not only in housing and urban development but through anti-poverty and other programs as well. State politicians and bureaucrats have thus become increasingly concerned about the future role of states in the federal system.

States have played only a minor role in urban programs. They have mostly limited their activities to passing enabling legislation which authorizes the creation of various agencies by municipalities or of special district governments that transcend municipal boundaries. They have shown little inclination to allocate their budgets to aid cities or to use their powers to solve city problems. Of course, state budgets are limited, as are those of cities, and they do have to be distributed in response to rural as well as urban demands.

Review questions

1. What programs has Congress enacted recently to answer urban needs? What are the objectives of these programs?
2. How has national urban policy brought about changes by the state and local governments in dealing with urban problems?

Chapter Review

Terms you should know

community action program	G.I. loans	urban redevelopment
Council on Urban Affairs	HUD	urban rehabilitation
"Fannie Mae"	Model Cities	urban renewal
FHA	rent supplements	"workable program"

Questions about this chapter

1. How have grants-in-aid programs increased the involvement and participation of the federal government in local affairs?
2. Why is there a vast difference in the amount of funds that the federal government allocates to urban areas as compared to rural areas?
3. How have federal responses to urban needs had an influence on municipal governments?
4. How do people who reside in cities make their needs and demands known to the federal government?
5. What has been the consequence of the "piecemeal" approach of the federal government toward housing and urban renewal?
6. Why has the federal government's urban redevelopment program generated so much controversy?

7. How have some of the federal government's urban policies been self-defeating? Give some examples.
8. Why have state officials and politicians resisted to some degree the federal government's participation in urban affairs?

Thought and discussion questions

1. If the federal government relied on property taxes for most of its income as do local governments now, what do you think would be the reaction of most people? Who would favor such a change? Who would oppose it? How might Americans change their way of living as a result?
2. "Only in the last decade has the feedback process begun to force policy-makers at the federal level to focus on urban needs in a comprehensive way." Do you agree with this statement, or do you disagree? Explain your answer.
3. Who do you suppose would support an urban redevelopment plan? Who would oppose it? Explain how and why each of these groups would help or hinder the project.

Class projects

1. Find out how the community services where you live are financed. What sort of taxes are imposed on the residents? What is the assessment on property? How are funds allocated within the community? (Most of this information can be obtained from the local newspaper in the spring when community budgets are prepared, or directly from the local government.)
2. Look at the table on page 606. How many of the programs on that list are available in your community? Have any programs been expanded or cut back within the last year? What do you suppose are the reasons for such expansion or reductions? Can you identify the groups that would support or oppose such expansions and reductions?

Signs of change in the American political system are as much in evidence in the 1970's as they have been in the past. These signs are being felt by many parts of the political system as various groups are pressuring decision-makers to rethink the policies and priorities that have been shaped during the past several decades.

The fact that certain groups—such as Afro-Americans, Mexican Americans, Puerto Rican Americans, American Indians, women's organizations, the poor, and others—have recently become active in making political demands demonstrated evidence of change in the system today. The extension of suffrage to eighteen-year-olds is another sign of change. Now that a new political channel has been opened to young people, questions are being raised about its potential effect on the political system. Will youth follow the paths established by their elders or will voting patterns be dramatically altered? How will political parties and public policies be affected by this younger electoral constituency? These specific questions can be answered only after this new constituency has voted in several elections.

The formal institutions of government are also feeling the impact of change. The development of a direct liaison between urban areas and the national government, for example, has raised questions about the future status of state and municipal governments within the federal system. The relative power of Congress and the Presidency is posing an institutional dilemma at the national level. Concern for domestic problems and the quality of American life, meanwhile, is challenging many aspects of government policy that have emerged in the post-World War II period.

How will these and other changes affect the future of the American political system? Will the fundamental principles of American democracy be altered? Will there be a major recasting of responsibilities within the many formal institutions of government? Can the original constitutional framework continue to remain flexible enough to withstand whatever changes are necessary? In the light of such queries, which confront a political system undergoing the stress of transition, the main question that must be contemplated is "Where do we go from here?"

UNIT SIX
The System in Transition

CHAPTER 24

The Trends in American Politics

The American political system, like all political systems, must be able to maintain continuity while responding to change. Because political activity is based on people's thoughts and actions, it is an ongoing process that is constantly adapting traditions and institutions to the changes demanded by society.

The most significant traditions that provide continuity for America's political system are rooted in America's political ideology. The basic principles of constitutional democracy, and the formal aspects of government that were designed according to these principles, are just as important today as they were in 1787. As the United States has grown from a rural, agrarian nation to a highly industrialized and urban one, the political system has kept pace by adapting to these far-reaching changes. One of the major challenges to the United States in the future will be the need to preserve its fundamental political traditions while reshaping its political system to meet the increasingly complex needs of American society.

Future Trends in Constitutional Democracy

The ideological foundations of America's political system, inherited from political theorists of the past, are still very much part of American political thought. Consciously or unconsciously, most Americans do believe in the principles underlying the concept of constitutional democracy that describes their political system. The principle of popular sovereignty—which holds that government is ultimately answerable to the interests and wants of the people—is still basic to the idea of democracy as Americans understand it. The idea of constitutionalism—by which the power of government must be restrained according to explicit legal standards and limitations—still finds its most obvious expression in the written national Constitution.

During the two centuries since constitutional democracy was established in the United States, however, many changes have occurred within the political system. The powers of some governmental structures have greatly expanded in spite of the provisions in the constitutional document that were designed to limit government power. Major interest groups and political parties have come to play a significant role in government policy-making in spite of the original intent of the Framers to minimize the influence of factions. Because of these developments in the actual operation of the political system in the United States, there will no doubt be increasing concern in the future over whether constitutional democracy can remain a viable form of government.

The theory and practice of democracy. The idea of democracy rests on the belief that people have the capacity as well as the right to govern themselves and thus to determine what government should do for them. To most Americans, democracy also means that every citizen within the political system has the opportunity to voice his or her wants, and that the expressions of all citizens are therefore given equal weight when governmental decisions are made.

In practice, however, democratic political systems have not always conformed to these tenets of democracy. Evidence gathered by political scientists in recent years, for example, suggests that "the peo-

With all the options open to Americans in the future to restructure the political system, will there be any drastic changes? What do current trends indicate that Americans are most interested in changing?

ple" may not be interested at all in what government does. In fact most people may be content to leave political matters to an "elite" group except when policy outputs clearly seem to be adverse to their interests. Yet despite such evidence, many Americans continue to believe that pure democracy is a workable form of government, and that they must actively participate in the political process, have opinions on political issues, and cast their votes in all elections to preserve this democratic ideal.

A reason for these assumptions may be that through the experiences of education and political socialization, people have learned to believe in the democratic ethic without also learning about how democracy functions in practice. Not surprisingly, the contradictions between the theories and practice of the democratic process have produced tensions in American society—particularly as members of the younger generation have observed that government does not live up to the *ideals* of democracy that they have learned to believe in. What are some of these contradictions between theory and practice?

■ *Public versus private interest.* According to the traditional explanations of democratic theory, the decisions of government in a democracy should coincide with a broadly based popular interest. The public policy outputs of American government, however, do not seem to be based on a broad public consensus. Public policy is formulated instead by various pressure groups interacting with certain components of government. Rather than a unified political system that converts a general public will into policy, there are numerous policy subsystems for agriculture, transportation, defense, and so on that determine particular public policy decisions.

One of the most frequently heard complaints about the American political system today is that private interest groups have too much access and wield too much influence over governmental decision-making. These objectors feel that this situation is counter to the basic tenets of democracy because government policy-makers do not take the broader "national interest" into account. Many political scientists respond to such complaints by pointing out that a broad public consensus does not, and probably can not, exist on most issues of public policy. They conclude, therefore, that it is impossible to objectively define a "national interest," and that the attention policy-makers give to pressure groups is only natural in a pluralistic democracy.

■ *Specialization in decision-making.* Another factor that may seem to contradict America's democratic ethic is the growing specialization and expertise in govern-

Fitzpatrick in the *St. Louis Post-Dispatch*

FASCISM IN A NEW TIN SUIT.

(Some people fear that too much specialization might reduce their influence on government decision-makers.)

mental decision-making. As major issues of public policy concern matters of an increasingly technical nature, the knowledge of experts is called on more and more for the formulation of policy outputs. At the same time, it becomes harder to support the notion that all citizens should participate in determining public policy.

This development calls to mind the dilemma posed by Aristotle: Who is the better judge of a feast, the cook or the guests? As this riddle suggests, just because formulation of policy becomes the function of experts does not mean that people will be unable to determine how governmental decisions affect their own interests. Citizens can still participate in the political process by responding to the impact that decisions have on them—even if they do not fully understand the complexities of the policies involved.

Very few citizens, for example, understand the intricacies of modern defense policy, but most citizens certainly feel the impact of the draft and of the vast defense expenditures that drain tax dollars from their pockets and from other desirable projects. A large number of citizens might arrive at the conclusion that defense expenditures should be reduced, even though "experts" may insist that such a course would also reduce national security. Similarly, most citizens may not understand the technicalities of regulatory decision-making; but if they have to pay higher fares for public transportation and higher rates for telephone service, they can make judgments about the effects of regulatory decisions on their own interests.

■ *The future of democratic values.* Just as people in other nations learn to accept and preserve their political ideologies, citizens in the United States—through the process of political socialization—learn to believe in the value of the democratic process. Yet, if the realities of the American political

© 1968 by Jules Feiffer

(Perhaps the best way to obtain changes in the system is to resort to one of the traditional procedures.)

system seem to contradict traditional democratic ideals, can the values of democracy remain meaningful and relevant to Americans? Can citizens continue to believe that government is responsive to them in practice as well as in theory?

It should become increasingly evident in the years ahead that Americans must understand the *practice* as well as the theories of their political system if they are going to be able to make that system responsive to them. The realities of America's political system are not so terrible. At the same time, not everything about the system must be accepted as it is. Nevertheless, unless citizens understand how their political system really functions, they can not make realistic proposals to bring about those changes that ought to be made.

It may be very important, for example, for Americans to recognize the reality and importance of organized interest groups in the policy-making process. As this fact becomes better understood, it is more likely that people concerned about pollution, poverty, consumer protection, urban needs, and other problems will organize effective political groups that will have a significant impact on decision-makers. Such activity could prove to be more effective in counteracting the influence of entrenched interest groups than futile harangues against such interests.

It will also be important for citizens to view their demands realistically within the context of their pluralistic society. While Americans as a whole seem to accept the value of democratic principles, the diversity within the American population makes it inevitable that a wide variety of values and beliefs will be held by the many groups within the system. As judgments are made about public policy—both within and outside of government—they reflect the particular values of whoever is making them.

In such a climate of diversity, a responsive democratic government is naturally confronted with a broad range of demands; and it is impossible for the preferences of every citizen to be implemented at all times. More often than not, consensus on policy matters must be arrived at through compromise between conflicting values and points of view. While the right of each group to express its values and preferences must be preserved in a constitutional democracy, it would be unrealistic—and undemocratic—for any one group representing a minority of the population to expect its demands to be implemented at the expense of all the other groups.

Still the realities of the democratic process do not render the values of democracy obsolete. As long as individuals retain their capacity for rational thought and understand their political environment, and as long as the value of each individual is recognized, it would seem unnecessary for

democratic values to be altered. If the system seems totally unresponsive to the demands that are made on it, this would pose very serious problems for the maintenance of the system. At the same time, it is important that people do not become discouraged when they feel that government is not moving in exactly the directions that they want it to. In the long run, persistent demands do tend to be heard and government does respond to them in some way.

Constitutional trends. Obviously, both the realities of democracy and its theories must be considered together if democratic values are to remain meaningful. In a constitutional democracy, furthermore, even such fundamental principles as those presented in the Constitution itself are subject to reexamination.

Several features in the national Constitution were expressly designed to limit the power of government at the national level. The sovereignty of state governments within the national federation, for example, was intended to check the over-extension of national government power. The separation of powers and shared functions of the three branches of federal government were intended to prevent the excessive use of power by any one branch. The Bill of Rights was added to the original document to restrain the federal government from encroaching on the civil liberties and rights of individual citizens.

These features of the Constitution not only built certain restraints into the operation of government but also made the existence of tensions between certain parts of government inevitable. The tensions between national power and states' rights, between congressional and presidential power, between the national interest and individual rights will continue to characterize America's constitutional government in the future just as they have in the past.

Despite these elements of continuity,

definite trends have already appeared that seem to be reshaping the original constitutional fabric. The power of the state governments in many spheres, for instance, appears to be diminishing in favor of a more dominant role for the national government. The growing pressure on Washington to solve the problems of metropolitan regions today is just one indication of the changing complexion of federalism. Similarly, the expansion of power within the Presidency and the federal bureaucracy seems to have diminished the position of Congress in some policy areas. This trend is particularly notable in foreign affairs with respect to the war power. The President now engages in "police actions" without necessarily consulting Congress. An example of this occurred in 1970 when President Nixon ordered troops into Cambodia, thus widening the Vietnam War without consulting with the Senate Foreign Relations Committee and other appropriate members of Congress. Thus, the effectiveness of the separation-of-powers doctrine has diminished—at least in the area of military engagements abroad. A democratically responsive Congress will have to regain the initiative if the powers of the Presidency and of the administrative branch are to be curbed.

The developments just described will undoubtedly continue to pose a major dilemma for American constitutional democracy in the future. That dilemma is: Are the constitutional checks embodied in the Constitution still sufficient to curb governmental power?

■ *Loose versus strict construction.* Much of the Constitution's meaning has been derived from its interpretation by the Supreme Court. Throughout the history of the Republic, there have been debates over the merits of "loose" versus "strict" constructionist interpretations. The term *strict construction* refers to interpretations that adhere strictly to the letter rather than the spirit of the document. According to a strict constructionist's view, government should not do anything that is not expressly authorized or enumerated in the Constitution. *Loose construction,* on the other hand, refers to interpretations that permit the government to undertake activities *implied* rather than stated by the words of the document.

Since Chief Justice John Marshall first determined that Congress could pass legislation for purposes implied by its enumerated powers in Article I, loose construction has been an important theme in the history of American constitutional law. There have been eras of strict construction, but these have been relatively short-lived. A notable era of strict constructionism occurred during the 1930's when the Supreme Court nullified major New Deal legislation on the grounds that Congress had overstepped the enumerated powers of Article I. Yet before the New Deal era was over, the Court had modified its position to a more loose constructionist one and had approved much of Congress' innovative legislation.

This loose constructionist tendency of the Supreme Court has been largely responsible for the adaptability of the Constitution and of the political system to the pressure of change. But loose constructionist interpretations of the Constitution have also permitted the national government to extend its authority into almost any sphere of activity. It is very likely that this trend will continue to shape constitutional law in the future as much as it has in the past. The Supreme Court will probably continue to support the authority of Congress to pass legislation on any matters it sees fit and to delegate broad authority to the President and the bureaucracy. And the Court will continue, no doubt, to apply constitutional limitations to state governments through its interpretations of "equal protection of the laws" guaranteed by the Fourteenth Amendment.

■ *The future of constitutional restraint.* If the national government can extend its authority into so many spheres of political activity, will any constitutional restraints remain to protect the American people against abuse of that authority? The answer to this question may also be suggested by recent trends in constitutional law. While the Supreme Court has approved the expansion of national authority in many areas, it has also tended to apply rather "strict" limitations on both national and state governments in its interpretations of the Bill of Rights. This was particularly true during the recent tenure of Chief Justice Earl Warren when the Court made a number of strong pronouncements concerning the protection of civil liberties and rights.

Interpretations of the Warren Court in these areas brought about major changes in American society with regard to desegregation of public schools and facilities, the strengthening of the rights of the accused, the separation of church and state, the reapportionment of state and congressional legislative districts, and the limitation of governmental censorship of the press and films. In many of these policy areas, the Court was ahead of the general population; and there was considerable negative feedback in response to its decisions. (See also Chapter 22, pages 571–579.)

The Supreme Court can never get too far ahead of the American people without causing a storm of protest. The announced intention of President Nixon to appoint strict constructionists to the Court and his subsequent appointments of Chief Justice Warren E. Burger and Associate Justice Harry A. Blackmun may result in some modification of the Warren Court's decisions—particularly with respect to the rights of alleged criminals.

It is very difficult to predict the future trends of constitutional law in this area without taking into account popular attitudes and the kinds of demands and supports that are likely to be made on the Court. The decisions of the Warren Court can never be completely reversed; and they will probably remain part of the constitutional law of the country. In any case, the Supreme Court's interpretations of the Bill of Rights will continue to limit governmental intrusions on individual rights in the future as they have in the recent past.

Review questions

1. What basic principles underlie American beliefs about constitutional democracy?
2. Why do the realities of the American political system seem to contradict ideals of democracy?

Future Trends in Public Policy-Making

The future of constitutional democracy in the United States will ultimately depend on how the components of the nation's political system will operate. As in the past, changes in American society will naturally affect the kinds of demands and supports that will reach policy-makers at all levels of government. The nature of political inputs, in turn, will have an impact on the structures of government themselves as well as on the kinds of public policies that emerge from these segments of government.

Trends in political demands and supports. As the American Republic has grown, the sources of political inputs have greatly expanded. One factor contributing to this expansion has been the democratization of the political process. The enfranchisement of more and more citizens has vastly increased potential political inputs. In recent years, civil rights legislation has managed to help close the gap between potential and actual inputs by encouraging and protecting members of minority groups who want to exercise their right to vote. As political parties and interest groups have evolved as channels of political demands and support, the increasingly national scope of these organizations has also expanded political inputs.

With the expansion of the sources of political inputs, the content of inputs has broadened as well. This has been made possible in part by the growth of mass media. Newspapers, magazines, radio, and television inform people in all parts of the country about political issues. Because the mass media deal with national political issues, the attention of the electorate is now focused on national concerns more than ever before. More people have become aware of the connections between national and local policy and recognize that local enclaves can not survive apart from the broader society within which they must function. The intensity and content of political demands and supports as well as the sources of these inputs undoubtedly will differ in future years from those at present.

■ *Political attitudes.* How will the nature of public opinion and political attitudes change in the future? The answer to this question will probably be determined by the fact that more and more people are being drawn into the political system and are becoming aware of the impact of government on them. People in higher educational and income brackets now tend to participate more actively in politics than do people with fewer educational and eco-

Drawing by D. Fradon; © 1968 The New Yorker Magazine, Inc.

"That's the trouble with a truly enlightened electorate."

(As constituents grow in awareness, it becomes increasingly difficult for any politician to deceive them.)

nomic resources. As education reaches greater numbers of people and is buttressed by a rise in the economic level of society in general, it is logical to assume that more people will participate in political activity. Government will have to become responsive to the political expectations of many more people than has been the case until now.

As citizen participation increases, it is possible that polarization will also increase along such lines as urban versus suburban or young versus old and this polarization will be reflected in divergent political attitudes. As the educational and economic levels of more people in the population improve, however, it is also possible that there will be greater similarity in the political attitudes of various groups because of the common experiences from which these attitudes emerge. Such merging of political attitudes may become even more pronounced as more political issues become national in scope. Many pressing problems that society will face in the future, such as protection of the environment, will affect everyone in the society to the same extent and may therefore contribute to the cohesion of attitudes, expectations, and demands that are channelled to government.

■ *Political parties.* The nature of political parties in the future will reflect the same changes in society that will determine political attitudes. As greater numbers of citizens become involved in the political process, the organizations and ideologies of the major parties are bound to be affected.

The history of the party system in the United States points up some general trends that may become even more pronounced in the future. The two major political parties today are "umbrella" parties, encompassing wide-ranging interests and viewpoints that are highly diverse in nature. Yet the party system of the nineteenth century represented a greater degree of diversity than it does today. The two parties in the twentieth century have developed fairly distinct points of view on many major issues of public policy and have evolved more meaningful ideologies than existed previously. As the diversity within the population continues to diminish, it is possible that two political parties with very distinct ideologies will eventually emerge. This development will most likely come about if polarization in political attitudes becomes more intense and thus accentuates the conflicts between the parties.

It is also possible, however, that party ideologies will become even less distinct. Just as educational and economic advancement for more people may reduce the distinctions in political attitudes, these factors may also reduce ideological distinctions between parties. As more people become concerned with overriding political issues, this too may reduce differences. There are some evidences of this trend today. During the 1930's, the increasing role of government in maintaining economic stability and promoting the general welfare produced intense ideological conflicts between the major political parties. Today, however, both major parties have accepted these activities as proper goals because they have become generally accepted by the society at large.

■ *Interest groups.* The political demands of interest groups until now have been determined largely by the views of the leaders of such groups who have generally had a great deal of influence in promoting particular programs. The influence of interest group elites has been possible partly because of the apathy of interest group memberships and partly because of the lack of any common consensus within society about the political responsibility of such groups. Nevertheless, the recent hue and cry over the "military-industrial complex" reflects a growing public concern that the operation of interest groups within major policy subsystems may not be serving the national interest. Perhaps this concern is only the beginning of a trend that may eventually produce counteracting demands on government and a withdrawal of support for policies initiated by such subsystems.

Already public pressure against the major interest groups within some policy subsystems seems to have had a notable impact. Until recently, many major corporations have fought vigorously to prevent any regulations of their activities that were proposed to stop pollution or the production of unsafe products. But public demands for such pressing needs as safety belts, padded dashboards, collapsible steering wheels, and anti-pollution devices in automobiles have produced government regulation of industry in recent years that was never thought possible before. The interest groups affected, such as the automobile manufacturers and the gasoline industries, are now finding it expedient to be responsive to a broader constituency and to pay attention to some of these problems lest government regulation become even more strict.

In the future, more common political attitudes will develop as people perceive critical social, economic, and technological problems, such as pollution, in the same way. Interest groups will probably find it increasingly difficult to maintain their solidarity as their members respond to issues outside of the sphere of any one particular group. Steelworkers interested in preserving their own jobs may recognize that steel mills still contribute to both air and water pollution, thus endangering their own health. Interest group leaders may find it even more difficult to mobilize members than they do today, and they may also find it harder to justify the priority of their own demands in the face of compelling national interests recognized by all.

If society is going to live in perpetual crises, which could be the case in the future due to such forces as the population explosion and destruction of the environment, common concern for overcoming these crises will further weaken the divisions between opposing groups. Demands for government action will tend to be the same regardless of what group expresses them. The unifying impact of a crisis was seen during World War II when party and interest-group differences receded and were replaced by a common effort to win the war.

In the past, the existence of different interest groups in the American political system has been a reflection of the pluralism in American society. According to some political theorists the need to support and encourage various groups with contrasting political attitudes has probably increased rather than reduced the democratic character of the political system. Other political theorists maintain that the broader national interest is of paramount concern and therefore the merging of political attitudes will be beneficial to the future of democracy.

Trends in the structures of government. Predictions about changes in the structures of government have usually been inaccurate. During the 1930's, for example, the growth of the bureaucracy led some commentators to predict that Congress would no longer function as a significant institution but merely as a rubber stamp of the executive branch. The power of Congress in some areas of policy-making has in fact diminished. Yet today, when the power of Congress should have diminished to practically nothing according to forecasters of the 1930's, there is instead a movement toward increasing the responsibilities of Congress. Congress is beginning to reassert its constitutional prerogatives to ward off the threat of executive domination. Nevertheless, the increasing powers of the bureaucracy and the Presidency will continue to threaten congressional power in the future.

■ *Continued expansion of the bureaucracy.* One future trend in governmental structure is almost certain—the growth in the authority of the bureaucracy. As government expands its activities in response

Drawing by Stevenson; © 1968 The New Yorker Magazine, Inc.

"Hofstetter is projecting urban blight in the nineteen-seventies, Dr. Bartley is hypothesizing aftereffects of the Third World War in terms of agronomy, and Fitler, there, is, I'm afraid, wool-gathering."

(The nation's think-tanks have been contributing significantly to the bureaucracy's expertise and growth.)

635

From *The Herblock Gallery* (Simon & Schuster, 1968)

"WHAT'S THE EXCITEMENT ABOUT COMBINING THE DEPARTMENTS OF LABOR AND COMMERCE?"

(In 1971 President Nixon presented a plan for a complete reorganization of the executive departments.)

to increasing demands, the administrative branch will have to assume more responsibility for shaping and implementing government policies. In all probability, the bureaucracy will continue to function with relative independence.

During recent years, many administrative agencies have been coordinated into major departments, and this trend in the organization of the bureaucracy may continue. Such coordination tends to increase the ability of the President to control administrative agencies and bring their activities in line with his own policies.

The administrative branch, however, will still retain a large degree of independence for several reasons. The increasing complexity and scope of government activity will not only make it necessary for Congress to delegate policy-making authority to the bureaucracy, but will also increase the necessity for such authority to be delegated from higher to lower levels within the bureaucracy itself. The President can not possibly keep in touch with everything that goes on in such a vast bureaucratic network of administrative agencies and, in fact, is apt to be more dependent on these agencies than they will be on him. The absence of political cohesion between the Presidency and Congress will also continue to make executive domination of the fourth branch difficult. It is unlikely that the President will be able to dominate the bureaucracy unless he is also able to control Congress.

■ *More specialization.* As the vitality of the bureaucracy increases in the future, certain characteristics that are associated with "administration" will affect many aspects of government. Policy-making will increasingly involve specialists or experts on technical matters. While many political demands will be channelled to policy-makers, decisions will tend to be non-partisan—that is, they will not adhere to the positions taken by any one political party. These characteristics will pertain to the operation of many parts of government within given subsystems—including congressional committees and their staffs working in conjunction with administrative agencies and various offices tied to the Presidency that will be looking for technical solutions to critical problems.

■ *Unity of national structures on policy.* The development of common interests among various government constituencies may also result in more uniformity in the way officials within different branches approach political issues. Congress, the President, the bureaucracy, and even the courts may be dealing with many common problems and may therefore tend to form similar points of view on public policy.

It is conceivable that such uniformity could improve the efficiency with which government operates. In the past, however, the policy conflicts between different branches and subsystems have helped to prevent the arbitrary exercise of power by government. As long as each branch remains essentially independent and responds to different interests for support, citizens are somewhat protected from government intrusion. Thus, the trend toward uniformity between the branches of government may have serious implications for the need to maintain responsible, as opposed to arbitrary, government action.

Perhaps one of the most effective instruments for maintaining responsible government will be the independent judiciary, capable of exercising judicial review over the laws of Congress and the actions of the executive branch. It is probable that the organization and procedures of the judiciary will remain much the same in the future as they have been up to now, because this key institution of government has never changed its procedures significantly. It is true that the judiciary—and the Supreme Court in particular—has changed its interpretations of the law at various times to accommodate changing conditions. The special nature of the judicial function, however, and the judicial procedures that have been developed for carrying out that function, have helped to preserve the independence of the judicial system in the past and will probably continue to do so in the future.

■ *The structure of federalism.* If one had asked a political scientist twenty or thirty years ago to predict the trends in federalism, undoubtedly the political scientist would have noted that a greater concentration of power in the hands of the national government was inevitable. In fact, the role of the federal government has greatly expanded in recent decades to meet a great many needs that have become national in scope.

If the bases of fragmentation in the American political system do gradually break down, sectional, regional, and local interests will probably become more dependent on the national government for both policy guidelines and money. At the present time, however, there is a movement toward decentralization of governmental power and toward strengthening the power of state and local governments. This is known as *new federalism*. A recent example of such decentralization was the urban renewal policy that was carried out under the direction of local governments with the help of federal funds and guidelines. The growing interest in revenue sharing—under which state and local governments would be given complete discretion to use federal funds as they see fit—provides further evidence of a possible trend toward revitalizing the power of state and local structures.

Nevertheless, this decentralization will probably not be carried too far and certainly will not entirely reverse the concentration of power at the national level. It is still too early to determine whether nationalism or localism will be the dominant trend with respect to intergovernmental relations. Only the future will tell.

Trends in the outputs of government. Governmental outputs are determined, of course, by the nature of political demands and supports and by the responses of government structures to these inputs. Since the 1930's, significant changes have come about in the nature of governmental outputs in all areas of policy-making. In the realm of protective policies, the most significant outputs have been those from the national judiciary and other federal branches that have strengthened civil liberties and civil rights.

There have also been broad changes

in maintenance policies dealing with international matters as the United States has increased its involvement abroad through foreign aid programs, military alliances, and active military engagements in such areas as Vietnam. With respect to domestic policies, the greatest change since the 1930's has been the expansion of governmental outputs for maintaining and improving the economic and general welfare of the population. The latter trend has been accompanied by an increasing number of policy outputs that involve cooperation between national, state, and local governments.

These overall changes in the nature of government outputs have been dramatic, but they have generally been forthcoming not as a result of thoughtful policy planning but in response to special interests or events that have demanded immediate government attention at various times. Thus, government policy has been more of a patchwork than a carefully integrated quilt. How will the changes in attitudes and political inputs in the future affect the policy outputs of government?

■ *Future protective policies.* In the areas of civil liberties and civil rights, policy outputs in the future will undoubtedly reflect prevalent community attitudes. During the 1950's and 1960's, the Supreme Court laid the groundwork for a system in which individuals are given maximum protection against government and community encroachment on their rights and freedoms. Congress has contributed further to this development by enacting legislation to protect voting rights and civil rights of citizens.

However, in recent years there has been a slight "backlash" or negative reaction to some of the Court's protective decisions. As a result, a trend may develop of curtailing civil liberties somewhat, particularly with respect to the rights of alleged crimi-

nals, reflecting the basic tension that always exists between individual freedoms and the welfare of the general community.

As political attitudes and demands tend to merge in the future and government structures become more uniform in their political responses, however, it will become increasingly important that individual rights and liberties be protected. Constitutional democracy requires that the freedoms of individuals to express their beliefs and viewpoints be preserved regardless of the beliefs and views of the majority of the community. The Supreme Court has traditionally been used as the final arbiter of individual rights. It should continue to do so.

■ *Future maintenance policies.* The future public-policy concerns of government will certainly differ from those of the past. The nationalization of many issues is bound to result in government outputs that are less local in their scope. Increasing emphasis will be placed on environmental control and on the numerous problems confronting citizens in urban areas such as crime, housing shortages, poverty, and drug addiction. While state outputs for solving these problems will be vital to supplement federal policy, state solutions by themselves will be ineffective. Because these problems are national in impact, national programs will be needed to maintain the welfare of the American community as a whole.

These pressing new concerns may result in greater stress on domestic than foreign policy in the future, and there is apt to be a decreasing emphasis on the need to fight wars to contain any opposing ideologies throughout the world. Certainly the end of the Vietnam action may bring with it a new trend toward isolationism in the United States as the country turns to solving domestic problems that have been neglected.

The growing need for national solutions

Feiffer

VIETNAM IS DEAD AS AN ISSUE. THE REAL ISSUE IS ECOLOGY.

BUT WHAT CAN WE DO ABOUT IT?

WE HAVE TO CONTROL THE ENVIRONMENT.

BUT HOW CAN WE DO THAT?

WE HAVE TO CONTROL POLLUTION.

BUT HOW CAN WE DO THAT?

WE HAVE TO CONTROL INDUSTRIAL WASTE.

BUT HOW CAN WE DO THAT?

WE HAVE TO CONTROL INDUSTRY.

OH, YOU MEAN SOCIALISM.

ECOLOGY IS DEAD AS AN ISSUE.

(Even pressing concerns must be examined from all angles before they can be presented as possible inputs.)

to many problems suggests that more and more outputs will be coming from government structures at the national level. The responsibilities of state and local governments, however, are also expanding at an unprecedented rate; and the expenditures of the state and local governments together far exceed those of the national government. As state and local governments continue to rely on federal government finances to bail them out of difficult situations, it is probable that there will be more coordination of policy outputs coming from all levels of government. Thus, while government outputs become more national in scope, the ratio of responsibility between national and state governments may remain constant as both levels expand their operations into different spheres of activity.

In order for the American political system to remain operable, it is vital that it be able to respond to the new demands that will arise in the future. With the end of the Vietnam conflict, government should be able to concentrate on meeting many of the intense demands that have developed over the last decade, particularly from minority groups and urban dwellers. Governmental structures will have to continue to balance opposing demands before making public policy decisions. But certain basic principles of the Constitution, such as equal rights, must never be compromised. All structures of government will have to take a leadership stance in protecting individual freedom and guaranteeing basic rights to all citizens.

Review questions

1. Does it appear that major changes in government structures will occur in the near future?
2. Can the outputs of government be completely divorced from the nature of inputs? Why or why not?

Chapter Review

Terms you should know

backlash	loose construction	popular sovereignty
democratic values	new federalism	strict construction

Questions about this chapter

1. What elements of continuity and change are evident in the American political system today?
2. Why do most Americans leave decision-making to so-called experts? Does specialized decision-making necessarily eliminate participation in politics by individual citizens? Why, or why not?
3. How have the patterns of constitutionalism changed since 1791? How have debates over the merits of strict versus loose construction been related to these developments?
4. How have the mass media changed the inputs of the American political system? What factors may contribute to other changes in political inputs in the future?
5. Why might uniformity between the different branches of government have serious implications for the political system? What factors might counteract the effects of such uniformity?
6. Is the movement for a "new federalism" consistent with other trends in the American political system? Explain.

Thought and discussion questions

1. Narrow demands of special interest groups may increasingly conflict with the broader needs of their members. Groups representing teachers and other government employees, for example, may bargain for salary increases while their members oppose higher taxes. What similar conflicts might arise within other labor, agricultural, industrial, or professional organizations? Do you feel that you belong to any interest group? How might some of your own concerns conflict with the demands of an interest group to which you yourself might belong?
2. It has been suggested that a new federal framework is needed for the American political system. Some political thinkers have proposed a federal system consisting of regional and city-state governments rather than state governments. Do you think this proposal is a good one? Why or why not?

Class projects

1. Make a chart which is divided into several columns labeled economic, social, technological, international, and political. In each column, list the changes that you think may occur in that category before the year 2000. In the last column, include the responses you think government will make to the other changes you predict.
2. Write a letter to the authors or publisher of this book and explain why you liked or disliked the book. You might note such things as (1) how the book might be improved, (2) information that you learned from reading the book that you did not know before, (3) how the book helped you to understand how the American political system really works.

Supplementary Reading

BRADBURY, RAY. *Fahrenheit 451*. New York: Simon & Schuster, 1967. Paperbound edition, New York: Ballantine, 1969. Mr. Bradbury writes a chilling and suspensful novel about life in the future—a time when the reading of books is a crime against the state. Any citizen found reading a book, or having books in his possession, is subject to arrest; and the books are burned—at the temperature for burning paper, "Fahrenheit 451." The future, for Mr. Bradbury, is the all-powerful state running the lives of all people.

HUXLEY, ALDOUS. *Brave New World*. New York: Harper & Row, 1932. Paperbound edition, New York: Bantam. Huxley unravels a tale about a scientifically run society, where people are created in test tubes, inculcated from birth to be happy with the status quo. It is a regimented existence—individuals are trained not to think, or question, but to be satisfied with their status. This book is a fascinating projection of a utopian world, aspects of which may come to fruition in the future.

MEANS, RICHARD L. *The Ethical Imperative*. New York: Anchor Books, 1971. Paperbound. Mr. Means feels that a reexamination of critical goals and values is in order for all Americans. Simplistic solutions will not work, according to the author, if America is to forge ahead. The problems of today—the decay of the cities, increasing crime rate, controversial foreign policy, the clamor for an improved environment, etc.,—are the result of a breakdown in the basic values of American society.

PHILLIPS, KEVIN P. *The Emerging Republican Majority*. New York: Anchor Books, 1971. Paperbound. To numerous observers it appears obvious that American political trends have veered toward the conservative. Has a new political era begun? Mr. Phillips tries to answer this question by analyzing voting patterns and predicting future voting behavior.

ROSE, ARNOLD M. *The Power Structure: Political Process in American Society*. New York: Oxford Press, 1967. A professor of sociology and a former member of the Minnesota legislature, Mr. Rose sets out to refute the contention that our political lives are dominated by an economically powerful "elite." Power, he argues, is exercised by the interplay of a variety of forces—a point he illustrates from the 1930's to the present.

TOFFLER, ALVIN. *Future Shock*. New York: Random House, 1970. The startling theory of change and adaptation presented in this book has direct implications for anyone concerned with social or personal upheaval. Toffler deals with the future of the family, the pace of daily life, values, violence, decision-making, friendships in the future, and more. He writes with clear insight into the nature of change in contemporary society.

The Constitution
of the
United States
of America

We the People of the United States, in Order to form a more perfect Union, establish Justice, insure domestic Tranquility, provide for the common defence, promote the general Welfare, and secure the Blessings of Liberty to ourselves and our Posterity, do ordain and establish this Constitution for the United States of America.

ARTICLE I.

SECTION 1. All legislative Powers herein granted shall be vested in a Congress of the United States, which shall consist of a Senate and House of Representatives.

See 257−8, 302−3

SECTION 2. The House of Representatives shall be composed of Members chosen every second Year by the People of the several States, and the Electors in each State shall have the Qualifications requisite for Electors of the most numerous Branch of the State Legislature.

See 142−6

No Person shall be a Representative who shall not have attained to the Age of twenty-five Years, and been seven Years a Citizen of the United States, and who shall not, when elected, be an Inhabitant of that State in which he shall be chosen.

See 138−9

[Representatives and direct Taxes shall be apportioned among the

Source: U.S. Government Printing Office, 1968. House Document #308.
[NOTE: *This book presents the Constitution and all amendments in their original form. Items which have since been amended or superseded, as identified in the footnotes, are bracketed.*]

several States which may be included within this Union, according to   See 132, 257
their respective Numbers, which shall be determined by adding to the
whole Number of free Persons, including those bound to Service for a   See 257–9
Term of Years, and excluding Indians not taxed, three fifths of all other
Persons.]* The actual Enumeration shall be made within three Years
after the first Meeting of the Congress of the United States, and within
every subsequent Term of ten Years, in such Manner as they shall by
Law direct. The Number of Representatives shall not exceet one for
every thirty Thousand,** but each State shall have at Least one Repre-
sentative; and until such enumeration shall be made, the State of New
Hampshire shall be entitled to chuse three, Massachusetts eight,
Rhode-Island and Providence Plantations one, Connecticut five, New-
York six, New Jersey four, Pennsylvania eight, Delaware one, Mary-
land six, Virginia ten, North Carolina five, South Carolina five, and
Georgia three.

When vacancies happen in the Representation from any State, the
Executive Authority thereof shall issue Writs of Election to fill such
Vacancies.

The House of Representatives shall chuse their Speaker and other   See 258, 259, 262
Officers; and shall have the sole Power of Impeachment.   See 301,

SECTION 3. The Senate of the United States shall be composed of   See 139
two Senators from each State, [chosen by the Legislature thereof,]***
for six Years; and each Senator shall have one Vote.

Immediately after they shall be assembled in Consequence of the first
Election, they shall be divided as equally as may be into three Classes.
The Seats of the Senators of the first Class shall be vacated at the Expiration of the second Year, of the second Class at the Expiration of the
fourth Year, and of the third Class at the Expiration of the sixth Year,
so that one-third may be chosen every second Year; [and if Vacancies
happen by Resignation, or otherwise, during the Recess of the Legisla-   See 136, 609
ture of any State, the Executive thereof may make temporary Appointments until the next Meeting of the Legislature, which shall then fill
such Vacancies.]****

No Person shall be a Senator who shall not have attained to the Age   See 138–39
of thirty Years, and been nine Years a Citizen of the United States, and
who shall not, when elected, be an Inhabitant of that State for which he
shall be chosen.

The Vice President of the United States shall be President of the   See 262
Senate, but shall have no Vote, unless they be equally divided.

The Senate shall chuse their other Officers, and also a President pro   See 259, 262, 301–2, 347–8
tempore, in the absence of the Vice President, or when he shall exer-
cise the Office of President of the United States.

The Senate shall have the sole Power to try all Impeachments. When   See 86
sitting for that Purpose, they shall be on Oath' or Affirmation. When the
President of the United States is tried, the Chief Justice shall preside:

*Changed by section 2 of the fourteenth amendment.
**Ratio in 1965 was one to over 410,000.
***Changed by section 1 of the seventeenth amendment.
****Changed by clause 2 of the seventeenth amendment.

And no Person shall be convicted without the Concurrence of two thirds of the Members present.

Judgment in Cases of Impeachment shall not extend further than to removal from Office, and disqualification to hold and enjoy any Office of honor, Trust or Profit under the United States: but the Party convicted shall nevertheless be liable and subject to Indictment, Trial, Judgment and Punishment, according to Law.

SECTION 4. The Times, Places and Manner of holding Elections for Senators and Representatives, shall be prescribed in each State by the Legislature thereof; but the Congress may at any time by Law make or alter such Regulations, except as to the Place of Chusing Senators. See 185–6, 257

The Congress shall assemble at least once in every Year, and such Meeting shall [be on the first Monday in December,]* unless they shall by Law appoint a different Day. See 134–5

SECTION 5. Each House shall be the Judge of the Elections, Returns and Qualifications of its own Members, and a Majority of each shall constitute a Quorum to do Business; but a smaller number may adjourn from day to day, and may be authorized to compel the Attendance of absent Members, in such Manner, and under such Penalties as each House may provide. See 289

Each House may determine the Rules of its Proceedings, punish its Members for disorderly Behavior, and, with the Concurrence of two thirds, expel a Member. See 287–9, 293–301, 303–4

Each House shall keep a Journal of its Proceedings, and from time to time publish the same, excepting such Parts as may in their Judgment require Secrecy; and the Yeas and Nays of the Members of either House on any question shall, at the Desire of one-fifth of those Present, be entered on the Journal. See 297

Neither House, during the Session of Congress, shall, without the Consent of the other, adjourn for more than three days, nor to any other Place than that in which the two Houses shall be sitting.

SECTION 6. The Senators and Representatives shall receive a Compensation for their Services, to be ascertained by Law, and paid out of the Treasury of the United States. They shall in all Cases, except Treason, Felony and Breach of the Peace, be privileged from Arrest during their Attendance at the Session of their respective Houses, and in going to and returning from the same; and for any Speech or Dabate in either House, they shall not be questioned in any other Place.

No Senator or Representative shall, during the Time for which he was elected, be appointed to any civil Office under the Authority of the United States, which shall have been created, or the Emoluments whereof shall have been encreased during such time; and no Person holding any Office under the United States, shall be a Member of either House during his Continuance in Office.

SECTION 7. All Bills for raising Revenue shall originate in the House of Representatives; but the Senate may propose or concur with Amendments as on other Bills. See 258

Every Bill which shall have passed the House of Representatives and See 81–83, 85–6, 367

*Changed by section 2 of the twentieth amendment.

the Senate, shall, before it becomes a Law, be presented to the President of the United States; If he approve he shall sign it, but if not he shall return it, with his Objections to that House in which it shall have originated, who shall enter the Objections at large on their Journal, and proceed to reconsider it. If after such Reconsideration two thirds of that House shall agree to pass the Bill, it shall be sent, together with the Objections, to the other House, by which it shall likewise be reconsidered, and if approved by two thirds of that House, it shall become a Law. But in all such Cases the Votes of both Houses shall be determined by Yeas and Nays, and the Names of the Persons voting for and against the Bill shall be entered on the Journal of each House respectively. If any Bill shall not be returned by the President within ten Days (Sundays excepted) after it shall have been presented to him, the Same shall be a Law, in like Manner as if he had signed it, unless the Congress by their Adjournment prevent its Return, in which Case it shall not be a Law.

Every Order, Resolution, or Vote to which the Concurrence of the Senate and House of Representatives may be necessary (except on a question of Adjournment) shall be presented to the President of the United States; and before the Same shall take Effect, shall be approved by him, or being disapproved by him, shall be repassed by two thirds of the Senate and House of Representatives, according to the Rules and Limitations prescribed in the Case of a Bill. See 302

SECTION 8. The Congress shall have Power To lay and collect Taxes, Duties, Imposts and Excises, to pay the Debts and provide for the common Defence and general Welfare of the United States; but all Duties, Imposts and Excises shall be uniform throughout the United States; See 87−8, 96−101, 257−62

To borrow money on the credit of the United States;

To regulate Commerce with foreign Nations, and among the several States, and with the Indian Tribes; See 29, 110−1

To establish an uniform Rule of Naturalization, and uniform Laws on the subject of Bankruptcies throughout the United States; See 43, 443

To coin Money, regulate the Value thereof, and of foreign Coin, and fix the Standard of Weights and Measures;

To provide for the Punishment of counterfeiting the Securities and current Coin of the United States;

To establish Post Offices and post Roads; See 368

To promote the Progress of Science and useful Arts, by securing for limited Times to Authors and Inventors the exclusive Right to their respective Writings and Discoveries; See 414−5

To constitute Tribunals inferior to the supreme Court; See 408−9, 412, 415

To define and punish Piracies and Felonies committed on the high Seas, and Offenses against the Law of Nations;

To declare War, grant Letters of Marque and Reprisal, and make Rules concerning Captures on Land and Water; See 255, 319, 327−32

To raise and support Armies, but no Appropriation of Money to that Use shall be for a longer Term than two Years; See 502, 504

To provide and maintain a Navy; See 368

To make Rules for the Government and Regulation of the land and naval Forces; See 319

To provide for calling forth the Militia to execute the Laws of the Union, suppress Insurrections and repel Invasions;

To provide for organizing, arming, and disciplining the Militia, and for governing such Part of them as may be employed in the Service of the United States, reserving to the States respectively, the Appointment of the Officers, and the Authority of training the Militia according to the discipline prescribed by Congress;

See 120, 515

To excercise exclusive Legislation in all Cases whatsoever, over such District (not exceeding ten Miles square) as may by Cession of particular States, and the acceptance of Congress, become the Seat of the Government of the United States, and to exercise like Authority over all Places purchased by the Consent of the Legislature of the State in which the Same shall be, for the Erection of Forts, Magazines, Arsenals, dock-Yards, and other needful Buildings;—And

See 137

To make all Laws which shall be necessary and proper for carrying into Execution the foregoing Powers, and all other Powers vested by this Constitution in the Government of the United States, or in any Department or Officer thereof.

See 114–5

SECTION 9. The Migration or Importation of such Persons as any of the States now existing shall think proper to admit, shall not be prohibited by the Congress prior to the Year one thousand eight hundred and eight, but a tax or duty may be imposed on such Importation, not exceeding ten dollars for each Person.

The privilege of the Writ of Habeas Corpus shall not be suspended, unless when in Cases of Rebellion or Invasion the public Safety may require it.

See 87, 471

No Bill of Attainder or ex post facto Law shall be passed.

See 87

No capitation, or other direct, Tax shall be laid, unless in Proportion to the Census or Enumeration herein before directed to be taken.*

See 259

No Tax or Duty shall be laid on Articles exported from any State.

No Preference shall be given by any Regulation of Commerce or Revenue to the Ports of one State over those of another: nor shall Vessels bound to, or from, one State, be obliged to enter, clear, or pay Duties in another.

No Money shall be drawn from the Tresury, but in Consequence of Appropriations made by Law; and a regular Statement and Account of the Receipts and Expenditures of all public Money shall be published from time to time.

No Title of Nobility shall be granted by the United States: And no Person holding any Office of Profit or Trust under them, shall, without the Consent of the Congress, accept of any present, Emolument, Office, or Title, of any kind whatever, from any King, Prince, or foreign State.

SECTION 10. No State shall enter into any Treaty, Alliance, or Confederation; grant Letters of Marque and Reprisal; coin Money; emit Bills of Credit; make any Thing but gold and silver Coin a Tender in Payment of Debts; pass any Bill of Attainder, ex post facto Law, or Law impairing the Obligation of Contracts, or grant any Title of Nobility.

No State shall, without the Consent of the Congress, lay any Imposts

See 114, 389

*But see the sixteenth amendment.

or Duties on Imports or Exports, except what may be absolutely necessary for executing its inspection Laws: and the net Produce of all Duties and Imposts, laid by any State on Imports or Exports, shall be for the Use of the Treasury of the United States: and all such Laws shall be subject to the Revision and Controul of the Congress.

No State shall, without the Consent of Congress, lay any duty of Tonnage, keep Troops, or Ships of War in time of Peace, enter into any Agreement or Compact with another State, or with a foreign Power, or engage in War, unless actually invaded, or in such imminent Danger as will not admit of delay.

ARTICLE II.

SECTION 1. The executive Power shall be vested in a President of the United States of America. He shall hold his Office during the Term of four Years, and, together with the Vice-President, chosen for the same Term, be elected, as follows.

See 89—90, 132—3, 316

Each State shall appoint, in such Manner as the Legislature thereof may direct, a Number of Electors, equal to the whole Number of Senators and Representatives to which the State may be entitled in the Congress: but no Senator or Representative, or Person holding an Office of Trust or Profit under the United States, shall be appointed an Elector.

See 139—42, 316—7

[The Electors shall meet in their respective States, and vote by Ballot for two persons, of whom one at least shall not be an Inhabitant of the same State with themselves. And they shall make a List of all the Persons voted for, and of the Number of Votes for each; which List they shall sign and certify, and transmit sealed to the Seat of the Government of the United States, directed to the President of the Senate. The President of the Senate shall, in the Presence of the Senate and House of Representatives, open all the Certificates, and the Votes shall then be counted. The Person having the greatest Number of Votes shall be the President, if such Number be a Majority of the whole Number of Electors appointed; and if there be more than one who have such Majority, and have an equal Number of Votes, then the House of Representatives shall immediately chuse by Ballot one of them for President; and if no Person have a Majority, then from the five highest on the List the said House shall in like Manner chuse the President. But in chusing the President, the Votes shall be taken by States, the Representation from each State having one Vote; a quorum for this Purpose shall consist of a Member or Members from two thirds of the States, and a Majority of all the States shall be necessary to a Choice. In every Case, after the Choice of the President, the Person having the greatest Number of Votes of the Electors shall be the Vice President. But if there should remain two or more who have equal Votes, the Senate shall chuse from them by Ballot the Vice-President.]*

See 133—4

The Congress may determine the Time of chusing the Electors, and the Day on which they shall give their Votes; which Day shall be the same throughout the United States.

Superseded by the twelfth amendment.

No person except a natural born Citizen, or a Citizen of the United States, at the time of the Adoption of this Constitution, shall be eligible to the Office of President; neither shall any Person be eligible to that Office who shall not have attained to the Age of thirty-five Years, and been fourteen Years a Resident within the United States.

See 139

**[In Case of the Removal of the President from Office, or of his Death, Resignation, or Inability to discharge the Powers and Duties of the said Office, the same shall devolve on the Vice President, and the Congress may by Law provide for the Case of Removal, Death, Resignation or Inability, both of the President and Vice President, declaring what Officer shall then act as President, and such Officer shall act accordingly, until the Disability be removed, or a President shall be elected.

See 135, 348-9

The President shall, at stated Times, receive for his Services, a Compensation, which shall neither be encreased nor diminished during the Period for which he shall have been elected, and he shall not receive within that Period any other Emolument from the United States, or any of them.

Before he enter on the Execution of his Office, he shall take the following Oath or Affirmation: — "I do solemnly swear (or affirm) that I will faithfully execute the Office of President of the United States, and will to the best of my Ability, preserve, protect and defend the Constitution of the United States."

SECTION 2. The President shall be Commander in Chief of the Army and Navy of the United States, and of the Militia of the several States, when called into the actual Service of the United States; he may require the Opinion in writing, of the principal Officer in each of the executive Departments, upon any subject relating to the Duties of their respective Offices, and he shall have Power to Grant Reprieves and Pardons for Offenses against the United States, except in Cases of Impeachment.

See 319-21, 344-6

He shall have Power, by and with the Advice and Consent of the Senate, to make Treaties, provided two-thirds of the Senators present concur; and he shall nominate, and by and with the Advice and Consent of the Senate, shall appoint Ambassadors, other public Ministers and Consuls, Judges of the supreme Court, and all other Officers of the United States, whose Appointments are not herein otherwise provided for, and which shall be established by Law: but the Congress may by Law vest the Appointment of such inferior Officers, as they think proper, in the President alone, in the Courts of Law, or in the Heads of Departments.

See 112-4, 315, 321-3, 345, 366-7, 445-6

The President shall have Power to fill up all Vacancies that may happen during the Recess of the Senate, by granting Commissions which shall expire at the End of their next Session.

SECTION 3. He shall from time to time give to the Congress Information of the State of the Union, and recommend to their Consideration such Measures as he shall judge necessary and expedient; he may, on extraordinary Occasions, convene both Houses, or either of them, and in Case of Disagreement between them, with Respect to the Time of

See 287-9, 302, 323-4

See 318-9

**This clause has been affected by the twenty-fifth amendment.*

Adjournment, he may adjourn them to such Time as he shall think proper; he shall receive Ambassadors and other public Ministers; he shall take Care that the Laws be faithfully executed, and shall Commission all the Officers of the United States.

SECTION 4. The President, Vice President and all civil Officers of the United States, shall be removed from Office on Impeachment for, and Conviction of, Treason, Bribery, or other high Crimes and Misdemeanors.

See 8—9

ARTICLE III.

SECTION 1. The judicial Power of the United States, shall be vested in one supreme Court, and in such inferior Courts as the Congress may from time to time ordain and establish. The Judges, both of the supreme and inferior Courts, shall hold their Offices during good Behaviour, and shall, at stated Times, receive for their Services, a Compensation, which shall not be diminished during their Continuance in Office.

See 94—5, 390—1, 407—12

SECTION 2. The judicial Power shall extend to all Cases, in Law and Equity, arising under this Constitution, the Laws of the United States, and Treaties made, or which shall be made, under their Authority;—to all Cases affecting Ambassadors, other public Ministers and Consuls;—to all Cases of admiralty and maritime Jurisdiction;—to Controversies to which the United States shall be a Party;—to Controversies between two or more States;—between a State and Citizens of another State;—between Citizens of different States;—between Citizens of the same State claiming Lands under Grants of different States, and between a State, or the Citizens thereof, and foreign States, Citizens or Subjects.

See 409, 413—4, 436

In all Cases affecting Ambassadors, other public Ministers and Consuls, and those in which a State shall be Party, the supreme Court shall have original Jurisdiction. In all the other Cases before mentioned, the supreme Court shall have appellate Jurisdiction, both as to Law and Fact, with such Exceptions, and under such Regulations as the Congress shall make.

See 413—4

The trial of all Crimes, except in Cases of Impeachment, shall be by Jury; and such Trial shall be held in the State where the said Crimes shall have been committed; but when not committed within any State, the Trial shall be at such Place or Places as the Congress may by Law have directed.

See 417—22

SECTION 3. Treason against the United States, shall consist only in levying War against them, or in adhering to their Enemies, giving them Aid and Comfort. No Person shall be convicted of Treason unless on the Testimony of two Witnesses to the same overt Act, or on Confession in open Court.

See 508—14

The Congress shall have Power to declare the Punishment of Treason, but no Attainder of Treason shall work Corruption of Blood, or Forfeiture except during the Life of the Person attainted.

ARTICLE IV.

SECTION 1. Full Faith and Credit shall be given in each State to the public Acts, Records, and judicial Proceedings of every other State.

And the Congress may by general Laws prescribe the Manner in which such Acts, Records and Proceedings shall be proved, and the Effect thereof.

SECTION 2. The Citizens of each State shall be entitled to all Privileges and Immunities of Citizens in the several States.

A Person charged in any State with Treason, Felony, or other Crime, who shall flee from Justice, and be found in another State, shall on demand of the executive Authority of the State from which he fled, be delivered up, to be removed to the State having Jurisdiction of the Crime.

[No Person held to Service or Labour in one State, under the Laws thereof, escaping into another, shall, in Consequence of any Law or Regulation therein, be discharged from such Service or Labour, but shall be delivered up on Claim of the Party to whom such Service or Labour may be due.]*

SECTION 3. New States may be admitted by the Congress into this Union; but no new State shall be formed or erected within the Jurisdiction of any other State; nor any State be formed by the Junction of two or more States, or parts of States, without the Consent of the Legislatures of the States concerned as well as of the Congress.

The Congress shall have Power to dispose of and make all needful Rules and Regulations respecting the Territory or other Property belonging to the United States; and nothing in this Constitution shall be so construed as to Prejudice any Claims of the United States, or of any particular State.

SECTION 4. The United States shall guarantee to every State in this Union a Republican Form of Government, and shall protect each of them against Invasion; and on Application of the Legislature, or of the Executive (when the Legislature cannot be convened) against domestic Violence.

See 508—14

ARTICLE V.

The Congress, whenever two-thirds of both Houses shall deem it necessary, shall propose Amendments to this Constitution, or, on the Application of the Legislatures of two-thirds of the several States, shall call a Convention for proposing Amendments, which, in either Case, shall be valid to all Intents and Purposes, as part of this Constitution, when ratified by the Legislatures of three-fourths of the several States, or by Conventions in three-fourths thereof, as the one or the other Mode of Ratification may be proposed by the Congress: Provided that no Amendment which may be made prior to the Year One thousand eight hundred and eight shall in any Manner affect the first and fourth Clauses in the Ninth Section of the first Article; and that no State, without its Consent, shall be deprived of its equal Suffrage in the Senate.

See 129—37

ARTICLE VI.

All Debts contracted and Engagements entered into, before the Adoption of this Constitution, shall be as valid against the United

See 536—7

*Superseded by the thirteenth amendment.

States under this Constitution, as under the Confederation.

This Constitution, and the Laws of the United States which shall be made in Pursuance thereof; and all Treaties made, or which shall be made, under the Authority of the United States, shall be the supreme Law of the Land; and the Judges in every State shall be bound thereby, any Thing in the Constitution or Laws of any State to the Contrary notwithstanding. See 108, 114

The Senators and Representatives before mentioned, and the Members of the several State Legislatures, and all executive and judicial Offiers, both of the United States and of the several States, shall be bound by Oath or Affirmation, to support this Constitution; but no religious Test shall ever be required as a Qualification to any Office or public Trust under the United States.

ARTICLE VII.

The Ratification of the Conventions of nine States shall be sufficient for the Establishment of this Constitution between the States so ratifying the Same.

DONE in Convention by the Unanimous Consent of the States present the Seventeenth Day of September in the Year of our Lord one thousand seven hundred and Eighty seven and of the Independence of the United States of America the Twelfth. In Witness whereof We have hereunto subscribed our Names.

Go WASHINGTON
Presidt and deputy from Virginia

New Hampshire.

JOHN LANGDON
NICHOLAS GILMAN

Massachusetts.

NATHANIEL GORHAM
RUFUS KING

New Jersey.

WIL: LIVINGSTON
DAVID BREARLEY.
WM PATERSON.
JONA: DAYTON

Pennsylvania.

B FRANKLIN
ROBT. MORRIS
THOS. FITZSIMONS
JAMES WILSON

Connecticut.

WM SAML JOHNSON
ROGER SHERMAN

New York.

ALEXANDER HAMILTON

Maryland.

JAMES MCHENRY
DANL CARROLL
DAN: OF ST THOS JENIFER

Virginia.

JOHN BLAIR
JAMES MADISON Jr.

North Carolina.

THOMAS MIFFLIN
GEO. CLYMER
JARED INGERSOLL
GOUV MORRIS

WM BLOUNT
HU WILLIAMSON
RICHD DOBBS SPAIGHT.

Delaware.

GEO: READ
JOHN DICKINSON
JACO: BROOM
GUNNING BEDFORD jun
RICHARD BASSETT

South Carolina.

J. RUTLEDGE
CHARLES PINCKNEY
CHARLES COTESWORTH
  PINCKNEY
PIERCE BUTLER

Georgia.
WILLIAM FEW
ABR BALDWIN

Attest:

WILLIAM JACKSON, *Secretary.*

ARTICLES IN ADDITION TO, AND AMENDMENT OF, THE CONSTITU-
TION OF THE UNITED STATES OF AMERICA, PROPOSED BY CONGRESS,
AND RATIFIED BY THE LEGISLATURES OF THE SEVERAL STATES, PUR-
SUANT TO THE FIFTH ARTICLE OF THE ORIGINAL CONSTITUTION.*

AMENDMENT I. (1791)**

Congress shall make no law respecting an establishment of religion, or prohibiting the free exercise thereof; or abridging the freedom of speech, or of the press; or the right of the people peaceably
to assemble, and to petition the Government for a redress of grievances.

See 129–30

AMENDMENT II. (1791)

A well regulated Militia, being necessary to the security of a free
State, the right of the people to keep and bear Arms, shall not be
infringed.

See 18, 248–53

AMENDMENT III. (1791)

No Soldier shall, in time of peace, be quartered in any house, without
the consent of the Owner, nor in time of war, but in a manner to be prescribed by law.

AMENDMENT IV. (1791)

The right of the people to be secure in their persons, houses,
papers, and effects, against unreasonable searches and seizures, shall

See 455–63, 593

*Amendment XXI was not ratified by state legislatures, but by state conven-
tions summoned by Congress.
**Date of ratification.

not be violated, and no Warrants shall issue, but upon probable cause, supported by Oath or affirmation, and particularly describing the place to be searched, and the persons or things to be seized.

AMENDMENT V. (1791)

No person shall be held to answer for a capital, or otherwise infamous crime, unless on a presentment or indictment of a Grand Jury, except in cases arising in the land or naval forces, or in the Militia, when in actual service in time of War or public danger; nor shall any person be subject for the same offence to be twice put in jeopardy of life or limb; nor shall be compelled in any criminal case to be a witness against himself, nor be deprived of life, liberty, or property, without due process of law; nor shall private property be taken for public use, without just compensation.

AMENDMENT VI. (1791)

In all criminal prosecutions, the accused shall enjoy the right to a speedy and public trial, by an impartial jury of the State and district wherein the crime shall have been committed, which district shall have been previously ascertained by law, and to be informed of the nature and cause of the accusation; to be confronted with the witnesses against him; to have compulsory process for obtaining witnesses in his favor, and to have the Assistance of Counsel for his defence.

AMENDMENT VII. (1791)

In suits at common law, where the value in controversy shall exceed twenty dollars, the right of trial by jury shall be preserved, and no fact tried by a jury, shall be otherwise reexamined in any Court of the United States, than according to the rules of the common law.

AMENDMENT VIII. (1791)

Excessive bail shall not be required, nor excessive fines imposed, nor cruel and unusual punishments inflicted.

AMENDMENT IX. (1791)

The enumeration in the Constitution, of certain rights, shall not be construed to deny or disparage others retained by the people.

AMENDMENT X. (1791)

The powers not delegated to the United States by the Constitution, nor prohibited by it to the States, are reserved to the States respectively, or to the people.

AMENDMENT XI. (1795)

The Judicial power of the United States shall not be construed to extend to any suit in law or equity, commenced or prosecuted against one of the United States by Citizens of another State, or by Citizens or Subjects of any Foreign State.

AMENDMENT XII. (1804)

The Electors shall meet in their respective states and vote by ballot for President and Vice-President, one of whom, at least, shall not be an inhabitant of the same state with themselves; they shall name in their ballots the person voted for as President, and in distinct ballots the person voted for as Vice-President, and they shall make distinct lists of all persons voted for as President, and of all persons voted for as Vice-President, and of the number of votes for each, which lists they shall sign and certify, and transmit sealed to the seat of the government of the United States, directed to the President of the Senate;—The President of the Senate shall, in presence of the Senate and House of Representatives, open all the certificates and the votes shall then be counted;—The person having the greatest number of votes for President, shall be the President, if such number be a majority of the whole number of Electors appointed; and if no person have such majority, then from the persons having the highest numbers not exceeding three on the list of those voted for as President, the House of Representatives shall choose immediately, by ballot, the President. But in choosing the President, the votes shall be taken by states, the representation from each state having one vote; a quorum for this purpose shall consist of a member or members from two-thirds of the states, and a majority of all the states shall be necessary to a choice. [And if the House of Representatives shall not choose a President whenever the right of choice shall devolve upon them, before the fourth day of March next following, then the Vice-President shall act as President, as in the case of the death or other constitutional disability of the President.—]* The person having the greatest number of votes as Vice-President, shall be the Vice-President, if such number be a majority of the whole number of Electors appointed, and if no person have a majority, then from the two highest numbers on the list, the Senate shall choose the Vice-President; a quorum for the purpose shall consist of two-thirds of the whole number of Senators, and a majority of the whole number shall be necessary to a choice. But no person constitutionally ineligible to the office of President shall be eligible to that of Vice-President of the United States.

See 132—5

AMENDMENT XIII. (1865)

SECTION I. Neither slavery nor involuntary servitude, except as a punishment for crime whereof the party shall have been duly con-

See 132, 407—10

*Superseded by section 3 of the twentieth amendment.

victed, shall exist within the United States, or any place subject to their jurisdiction.

SECTION 2. Congress shall have power to enforce this article by appropriate legislation.

AMENDMENT XIV. (1868)

SECTION 1. All persons born or naturalized in the Unites States, and subject to the jurisdiction thereof, are citizens of the United States and of the State wherein they reside. No State shall make or enforce any law which shall abridge the privileges or immunities of citizens of the United States; nor shall any State deprive any person of life, liberty, or property, without due process of law; nor deny any person within its jurisdiction the equal protection of the laws. See 60, 129−30, 132, 145, 438

SECTION 2. Representatives shall be apportioned among the several States according to their respective numbers, counting the whole number of persons in each State, excluding Indians not taxed. But when the right to vote at any election for the choice of electors for President and Vice-President of the United States, Representatives in Congress, the Executive and Judicial officers of a State, or the members of the Legislature thereof, is denied to any of the male inhabitants of such State, being twenty-one years of age, and citizens of the United States, or in any way abridged, except for participation in rebellion, or other crime, the basis of representation therein shall be reduced in the proportion which the number of such male citizens shall bear to the whole number of male citizens twenty-one years of age in such State.

SECTION 3. No person shall be a Senator or Representative in Congress, or elector of President and Vice-President, or hold any office, civil or military, under the United States, or under any State, who, having previously taken an oath, as a member of Congress, or as an officer of the United States, or as a member of any State legislature, or as an executive or judicial officer of any State, to support the Constitution of the United States, shall have engaged in insurrection or rebellion against the same, or given aid or comfort to the enemies thereof. But Congress may by a vote of two-thirds of each House, remove such disability.

SECTION 4. The validity of public debt of the United States, authorized by law, including debts incurred for payment of pensions and bounties for services in suppressing insurrection or rebellion, shall not be questioned. But neither the United States nor any State shall assume or pay any debt or obligation incurred in aid of insurrection or rebellion against the United States, or any claim for the loss or emancipation of any slave; but all such debts, obligations and claims shall be held illegal and void.

SECTION 5. The Congress shall have power to enforce, by appropriate legislation, the provisions of this article. See 469−70

AMENDMENT XV. (1870)

SECTION 1. The right of citizens of the United States to vote shall not be denied or abridged by the United States or by any See 132, 142−3, 145−7, 469 −70

State on account of race, color, or previous condition of servitude—

SECTION 2. The Congress shall have power to enforce this article by appropriate legislation.

AMENDMENT XVI. (1913)

The Congress shall have power to lay and collect taxes on incomes, from whatever source derived, without apportionment among the several States, and without regard to any census or enumeration.

See 131–2

AMENDMENT XVII. (1913)

The Senate of the United States shall be composed of two Senators from each State, elected by the people thereof, for six years; and each Senator shall have one vote. The electors in each State shall have the qualifications requisite for electors of the most numerous branch of the State legislatures.

See 136

When vacancies happen in the representation of any State in the Senate, the executive authority of such State shall issue writs of election to fill such vacancies: *Provided,* That the legislature of any State may empower the executive thereof to make temporary appointments until the people fill the vacancies by election as the legislature may direct.

This amendment shall not be so construed as to affect the election or term of any Senator chosen before it becomes valid as part of the Constitution.

AMENDMENT XVIII. (1919)

[SECTION 1. After one year from the ratification of this article the manufacture, sale, or transportation of intoxicating liquors within, the importation thereof into, or the exportation thereof from the United States and all territory subject to the jurisdiction thereof for beverage purposes is hereby prohibited.

See 131

[SECTION 2. The Congress and the several States shall have concurrent power to enforce this article by appropriate legislation.

[SECTION 3. This article shall be inoperative unless it shall have been ratified as an amendment to the Constitution by the legislatures of the several States, as provided in the Constitution, within seven years from the date of the submission hereof to the States by the Congress.]*

AMENDMENT XIX. (1920)

The right of citizens of the United States to vote shall not be denied or abridged by the United States or by any State on account of sex.

See 136

Congress shall have power to enforce this article by appropriate legislation.

Repealed by section 1 of the twenty-first amendment.

AMENDMENT XX. (1933)

SECTION 1. The terms of the President and Vice President shall end at noon on the 20th day of January, and the terms of Senators and Representatives at noon on the 3d day of January, of the years in which such terms would have ended if this article had not been ratified; and the terms of their successors shall then begin.

See 134—5

SECTION 2. The Congress shall assemble at least once in every year, and such meeting shall begin at noon on the 3d day of January, unless they shall by law appoint a different day.

SECTION 3. If, at the time fixed for the beginning of the term of the President, the President elect shall have died, the Vice President elect shall become President. If a President shall not have been chosen before the time fixed for the beginning of his term, or if the President elect shall have failed to qualify, then the Vice President elect shall act as President until a President shall have qualified; and the Congress may by law provide for the case wherein neither a President elect nor a Vice President elect shall have qualified, declaring who shall then act as President, or the manner in which one who is to act shall be selected, and such person shall act accordingly until a President or Vice President shall have qualified.

See 135, 348

SECTION 4. The Congress may by law provide for the case of the death of any of the persons from whom the House of Representatives may choose a President whenever the right of choice shall have devolved upon them, and for the case of the death of any of the persons from whom the Senate may choose a Vice President whenever the right of choice shall have devolved upon them.

SECTION 5. Sections 1 and 2 shall take effect on the 15th day of October following the ratification of this article.

SECTION 6. This article shall be inoperative unless it shall have been ratified as an amendment to the Constitution by the legislatures of three-fourths of the several States within seven years from the date of its submission.

AMENDMENT XXI. (1933)

SECTION 1. The eighteenth article of amendment to the Constitution of the United States is hereby repealed.

See 131

SECTION 2. The transportation or importation into any State, Territory, or possession of the United States for delivery or use therein of intoxicating liquors, in violation of the laws thereof, is hereby prohibited.

SECTION 3. This article shall be inoperative unless it shall have been ratified as an amendment to the Constitution by conventions in the several States, as provided in the Constitution, within seven years from the date of the submission hereof to the States by the Congress.

AMENDMENT XXII. (1951)

SECTION 1. No person shall be elected to the office of the President more than twice, and no person who has held the office of President, or acted as President, for more than two years of a term

See 90, 135, 198

to which some other person was elected President shall be elected to the office of the President more than once. But this Article shall not apply to any person holding the office of President when this Article was proposed by the Congress, and shall not prevent any person who may be holding the office of President, or acting as President, during the term within which this Article becomes operative from holding the office of President or acting as President during the remainder of such term.

SECTION 2. This article shall be inoperative unless it shall have been ratified as an amendment to the Constitution by the legislatures of three-fourths of the several States within seven years from the date of its submission to the States by the Congress.

AMENDMENT XXIII. (1961)

SECTION 1. The District constituting the seat of Government of the United States shall appoint in such manner as the Congress may direct: See 136–7

A number of electors of President and Vice President equal to the whole number of Senators and Representatives in Congress to which the District would be entitled if it were a State, but in no event more than the least populous State; they shall be in addition to those appointed by the States, but they shall be considered, for the purposes of the election of President and Vice President, to be electors appointed by a State; and they shall meet in the District and perform such duties as provided by the twelfth article of amendment.

SECTION 2. The Congress shall have power to enforce this article by appropriate legislation.

AMENDMENT XXIV. (1964)

SECTION 1. The right of citizens of the United States to vote in any primary or other election for President or Vice President, for electors for President or Vice President, or for Senator or Representative in Congress, shall not be denied or abridged by the United States or any State by reason of failure to pay any poll tax or other tax. See 143–5

SECTION 2. The Congress shall have power to enforce this article by appropriate legislation.

AMENDMENT XXV. (1967)

SECTION 1. In case of the removal of the President from office or of his death or resignation, the Vice President shall become President. See 135, 347–51

SECTION 2. Whenever there is a vacancy in the office of the Vice President, the President shall nominate a Vice President who shall take office upon confirmation by a majority vote of both Houses of Congress.

SECTION 3. Whenever the President transmits to the President pro tempore of the Senate and the Speaker of the House of Representatives his written declaration that he is unable to discharge the powers and See 135, 348–9 duties of his office, and until he transmits to them a written declaration to the contrary, such powers and duties shall be discharged by the Vice President as Acting President.

SECTION 4. Whenever the Vice President and a majority of either the principal officers of the executive departments or of such other body as Congress may by law provide, transmit to the President pro tempore of the Senate and the Speaker of the House of Representatives their written declaration that the President is unable to discharge the powers and duties of his office, the Vice President shall immediately assume the powers and duties of the office as Acting President.

Thereafter, when the President transmits to the President pro tempore of the Senate and the Speaker of the House of Representatives his written declaration that no inability exists, he shall resume the powers and duties of his office unless the Vice President and a majority of either the principal officers of the executive department or of such other body as Congress may by law provide, transmit within four days to the President pro tempore of the Senate and the Speaker of the House of Representatives their written declaration that the President is unable to discharge the powers and duties of his office. Thereupon Congress shall decide the issue, assembling within forty-eight hours for that purpose if not in session. If the Congress, within twenty-one days after receipt of the latter written declaration, or, if Congress is not in session, within twenty-one days after Congress is required to assemble, determines by two-thirds vote of both Houses that the President is unable to discharge the powers and duties of his office, the Vice President shall continue to discharge the same as Acting President; otherwise, the President shall resume the powers and duties of his office.

AMENDMENT XXVI. (1971)

SECTION 1. The right of citizens of the United States, who are eighteen years of age or older, to vote shall not be denied or abridged by the United States or any state on account of age.

See 137, 143, 625

SECTION 2. The Congress shall have the power to enforce this article by appropriate legislation.

Index

age of black voters in, 152, *154*; percentage who vote in, *155*; poll tax in, 144–5; primary procedures in, 213

Alaska, delegate selection in, 214; primaries in, 211

American Bar Association, 238–9, 373

American Broadcasting Company, 386

American Civil Liberties Union, 439, 467; and civil rights, *36*

American Farm Bureau Federation, 236

American Federation of Labor-Congress of Industrial Organizations, composition of, 236

American Federation of Teachers, 37

American Independent Party, 189, 199–201

American Jewish Congress, 37

American Legion, 6, 239, 547–8

American Medical Association, 6, 238–9, 241–2, 338, 553; and socialized medicine, 241

American Veterans Committee, 37

American Revolution, 77

American Riflemen's Association, the, 248

American Sugar Refining Company, 30

Americans for Democratic Action, 238

amicus curiae brief, defined, **37**

anti-ballistic missile system (ABM), 504–5

Anti-Federalist Party, 187

Anti-Masons, 212

antitrust laws, Clayton Act, 30; enforcement agencies of, 30; Federal Trade Commission Act, 38, 375; Sherman Act (1890), 30

antitrust policy, actions of bureaucracy in, 39, 441

anti-war demonstrations, 583

ANZUS Council, 499

apathy, *570*; and Congress, 263; and feedback, 570, 588–9; encourages use of personal influence, 8; family influence on, 162; in integration, 127; in presidential elections, *224*; obstacle to democracy, 7; prevents knowledge of rights, 9

appellate jurisdiction, defined, **409**

apportionment, and Supreme Court, 437–8; *Baker v. Carr*

aristocratic constitutionalism, 55

Aristotle, 58

appropriation bills, made by approval of Congress, 258

Arizona, delegate selection in, *214*

"arms of Congress," defined, **40**

Argentina, arms sales from United States, 112

Arkansas, delegate selection in, *214*; 1968 election results in, *154*; nomination procedures in, 210; percentage of black voters in, 152, *154*; percentage who vote in, *155*

arraignment, 421

Articles of Confederation, 65–6, 77, 79, 103;

weakness of central government in, 105

assassination, and gun control, 253; in United States, 249

assimilation, defined, **16**, 45

Atchison, Topeka, and Santa Fe Railway, 40

Atomic Energy Commission, 362

Attorney General, origin of, 368

Australia, federalism in, 103; immigration to, 43

authority, defined, **10**; limits in political system, 13; overlapping in government, 27

Avena, J. Richard, 48

Aztecs, 3

balance of payments, defined, **507**

balance of power, 498

Baker, Howard, 307

Baker v. Carr, 438, 578

Baldwin, Hanson, on defense policy, 530–2

ballot, 221

Baltimore, percentage of black voters in, 151

Banfield, Edward, 10

Bank of the United States, 536–7

Barkley, Allen, keynote address of, 215

Barragan, Rev. Miguel, 45

Barron v. Baltimore, 473

Becker amendment, 578

behavorial research, and political campaigns, 219

Bell, John, *141*

Bentley, Edith, 513

bicameral framework, purpose of, 257–8

bicameral legislature, defined, **79**

Bigart, Homer, 47

bill of attainder, defined, **87**

Bill of Rights, 54, 86–7, 129–30; and Fourteenth Amendment, 474–6; and procedural rights, 468–9; and rights of defendants, 444, 452–3, 455–62, 469; and school program issue, 478–9 arbitrary government actions limited in, 469; as source for judicial procedures, 417; as source of civil liberties, 452–3, 455–62, 467–9; disputed meanings of, 434, 470–1; early interpretations of, 472–3; extended to movies, 519; extended to states, 132, 471–6; imprecise language in, 469; individual rights upheld in, 129–30, 132, 245–6; jurisdiction of, 473; on treaties, 115; roots of, 60; states rights protected in, 104, 129–30, 469; wartime restrictions of, 509–12; *see also* civil liberties, civil rights, individual amendments

Bills, and committee procedures, 289–93; and

319–21; *see also* Presidency

Commerce, Department of, as public interest groups, 39, 235, 369

"Commerce Compromise," 80

Commission on Law Enforcement and Administration of Justice, 251

committee chairman, functions of, 290–3

Committee for Constitutional Government, 238

Committee of the Whole, procedures of, 294, 297

Committee on Standards of Official Conduct, 289

Committee on Un-American Activities, 289

Committee System, *288*, 289–93, 384–5; procedures in, 289–93, reform of, 293, Rules Committee in, 294; seniority rule in, 291–3; specialization in, 289

Commodity Credit Corporation, 547

common law principle, defined, **131**, 407

communications, 166, 168

communications-satellite bill, 300

communism, and nationalism, 502; and U.S. security, 512–4; as ideology, 15

Communist Control Act of 1954, 110, 514, 585

Communist party, and Smith Act, 510–11

Community Action program, 344

community needs versus individual rights, 470–2, 517–21

compartmentalization of executive departments, 371

concurrent powers, 120–1, defined, **108**, 411

concurrent resolutions, defined, **287**

conference committees, defined, **289**; duties of, 301–2, 306–13

conflict of branches, **27–8**

conflicts of interest, defined, **304**

Congress, 16, 148, 257–9, 262, 302; and bureaucracy, 39, 242–3, 271, 365–7, 384–5; and conference committees, 301–2; and conflict with President, 302; and controls on lobbying, 245–6; and court system, 408–9, 412; and crime legislation, 444; and desegregation, 574; and field trips, 290; and foreign aid, 322; and Gulf of Tonkin Resolution, 321; and gun control legislation, 253; and House calendars, 294; and interest groups, 245, 272; and legislative function of Presidency, 302, 323–4; and mass media, 303; and Presidency, 338–9, *351–3*; and presidential disability, 349–50; and presidental succession, 447–8; and presidential veto power, 367; and Supreme Court appointments, 445; and undeclared wars, 319; appropriation bills in, 258; as a conversion structure, 25; as subsystem, *18*; bicameral framework in, 257–8, 302–3; calendar of, 290; commerce power of, 29; committee system of, *17*, 195, *288*, 289–96, *295*, 301, 306–13; conflicts of interest in, 304; constituent demands on, *33*; constitutional basis of, 257–62; control over judiciary by, 412, 442–8; control over military of, 319; delegation of powers by, 387–90, 395; delegation of trade powers, 30; District of Columbia administration by, 137; dual role of, 14; early dominance of, 257; early presidential nominations in, 212; (enumerated) powers of, 87–8, 257; ethics in, 304; evolution of, 148, 257, 302, 307; foreign policy role of, 322–3; fragmentation in, 302–3; implied powers of, 114–5; officers of, 259–62; political constituencies of, 339; procedures of, *287–9*, 293–4; qualifications for, 258; reforms of, 300, 303–4; role in Civil Rights, *36*; seniority in, 292; sources of demands on, *269*, 271–2; specialization in, 289; structure of, 257–62; war power of, 255, 319, 327–32

Congress of Industrial Organizations (CIO), 37

Congress of Racial Equality (CORE), 6

congressional districts, **139**

congressional intent, **388–9**

congressmen, as investigators, *266*; functions of, 262–7; party identification of, 264; staff of, 266–7

Connecticut, delegate selection in, *214*; nominating procedure in, 210; percentage of black voters in, 151

Connecticut Compromise, 80

Consent Calendar, defined, **294**

constituencies, *33*, *34–5*, *36*, 37, 40; *see also* political constituencies

constituency demands, channels of, *33*

constituents, defined, **32**

Constitution of the United States, 14, 577–95; amendment procedures, 129, *130*; and bureaucracy, 323, 365–6, 378; and democratization, 129; and political parties, 184; checks on presidency in, 315–6, 321–2; commerce clause in, 89; compromises in, 78–80; Connecticut Compromise in, 80; controversial interpretation in, 434; District of Columbia in, 137; durability of, 130; enumerated powers in, 108; evolution of, 51, 129, 148–9, 255; flexibility of, 129, 149; government limitations in, 85–7; implied powers in, 107; interpretation of, 89; judicial interpretation of, 107–8; modern trends of, 630–2; national supremacy in, 108; on census, 259; on congressional powers, 87–9, 257–62, 318; on constitutional counts, 411–2; on contracts, 538; on election procedures, 133, 138–9, 212; on electoral col-

defendant, **411**, 419

Defense Department, *17*, 35, 86; as interest group, 234; liaison staff of, 243; origin of, 369

defense policy, 544, and 'ABM, 504–5; and disarmament, 505, 507; budget of, *504*; problems of, 502, 504–5, 507

De Gaulle, Charles, 499

de jure segregation, 573

Delano, California, 48

Delaware, delegate selection in, 214; nominating procedure in, 210

delegate-at-large, **213**

demands, 11; and interest groups, 243; on bureaucracy, 381–6; as inputs, *12–3*; channels of, 14–5; elections as, 223–4; in pluralistic system, 27; in subsystems, *17, 18, 19*; of interest groups, 233; of political constituencies, 32; similarities of, 14

democracy, 4, 9, **53**–54; advantages of, 71–5; and congressional procedures, *303*; and congressmen, 263–4; and election systems, 137–8; and interest groups, 233, 242; and internal security, 508–14; and judicial review, 435; and nominating procedures, 209–10; and political campaigns, 218–21; and specialization, 628–9; Anglo-American concepts of, 16; as ideology, 15; channels of demands in, 15; citizen participation in, 5; demands of, 243–4; elections in, 4–5, 221–2, 257–8; forms of, 116; future of, *629*–30; growth in United States, 129–37, 148–9; in practice, 627–8; interest groups in, 243–4; interpretations of, 16; in town government, 619–20; in United States, 129, 627–8; legislative function in, 387–90; loyal opposition in, 196; nonvoters in, 9; organized citizen participation in, 5–6; pluralism in, 42; political parties in, 183; problems of minorities in, 7–8, 45; public versus private interest in, 628; purpose of, 467; role of media in, 171–2; types of, 16; versus republic in United States, 138

Democracy in America, 69

Democratic party, 212; and New Deal, 195; character of, 336; contemporary dominance of, 223; delegate selection in, 213; diversity within, 187; support for Wallace in, 200

Democratic-Republican party, 187

democratization, 129; and presidential power, 316–7; in nominating procedures, 209

dēmokratía, defined, 53

demonstrations, against the war, 583–4; as withdrawal of support, 573

demos, **53**

Dennis v. United States, 510–11

de novo trial, **374**

Denver, 47–8

Derthick, Martha, 719

despotism, 116

Detroit, nonwhite voting in, 151, 165

desegregation, and *de facto* segregation, 573; feedback to, 571–6; resistance to, 573–4; *see also* civil rights

developmental policies, 535; and domestic programs, 557–8; and income maintenance, 556–7; and revenue sharing, 558; and space program, 555–6

deviating elections, **223**

Dewey, Thomas, 141, *161*, 357, nomination of, 207

Dietrich, Frank S., 443

direct demands, **386**

direct democracy, **138**

direct lobbying, **246**

Dirksen, Everett, 248, 445

disarmament, 502, 504–5, 507

Discharge Calendar, **294**

discharge petition, **296**

discharge rule, **298**

dissenting opinion, defined, **422**; *440*

district courts, 409; creation of, 412; powers of, 413

District of Columbia, delegate selection in, *214*; franchise in, 136–7; primary procedures in, 213

District of Columbia courts, 415

District of Columbia Crime Control Act, 591–600

dockets, **435**

Dodd, Thomas, 249–51

Domestic Affairs Council, 342

Douglas, Mike, 227

Douglas, Stephen, 141

Douglas, William, 246, 516

draft laws, criticism of, *134*

drugs, and individual rights, 471; federal control of, 554

due process of law, 469; and rights of defendants, 475–6; extended to states, 474–5; in quasi-judicial action, 392; *see also* civil liberties, Fourteenth Amendment

Dulles, John Foster, 331, 357

Eastland, James, 37, 299

Economic Opportunity Act, 699

economic policy, and business interests, 544–5; and interest groups, 235; and labor, 541, 543–4; and tariffs, *544*; during World War II, 540; early forms of, 536–7; feedback to, 586–

8; history of, 535–40; philosophy of, *536*; reaction to, *586*; trends in, 540

economic security, 541

editorialize, **167**

education, aid to, 21, 195; and church-state separation, 477–9; and civil rights, 20–3, 48, 123–7; and drug use, 493; and Supreme Court, 477–8; as developmental policy, *553*; as political subsystem, 18; busing in, 21, 125, 574, 576; constituencies in, 35; discrimination in, 48–9; federal aid to, 551, 553; human relations training in, 22; in Bristol Township, 21–3; in democracy, 7–9; motivation in, 126–7; political socialization in, 16

Education Act of 1965, 553

Education Department, 371

Ehrlichman, John, 342

Eisenhower, Dwight David, 83, 85, 135, *164*, 339; and civil service, 384; and desegregation action, 340; and deviating elections, 223; and Little Rock crisis, 438; and Sherman Adams case, 9; and transferral of power, 351, 354–63; as party leader, 324; disability of, 348; internal security actions of, 512; popular image of, 318; Supreme Court appointments of, 446

elections, 5; and constitutional amendments, 132–5; and multiple choice ballot, 221; and political parties, 185, 196; and two-party system, 185; as demands, 223–4; as feedback, *12*–13; classification of, 222; control of officials through, 8; differing terms of office in, 138; evaluation of, 223–4; indications of trends in, 222–3; informal factors in, 4–5; in United States, 137–41; interest groups in, 242–3; nominations in, 5, 209–17; primaries as, 210; requirements for, 142–4; riding on coattails in, 199; single choice ballot in, 221; state variations of, 210; structure of, 137; types of, 185–6, 221–2, *224*, 257; uniqueness of, 222; universal suffrage in, *143*; *see also* voting rights

electoral college, 139–42, 212; and minority presidents, 140, *141*; and strengthening of Presidency, 316–7; criticism of, *134*, 140; function of, 132–3; members of, 90–1, 139–40; origin of, 133; reform of, *141*; southern votes in, 151; ties in, 140

elitism, 210, 239–40, 243

Ellsworth, Oliver, 79

Emancipation Proclamation, 132

Employment Act of 1946, 342

Engle v. Vitale, 478–9, 578

Eniwetok Atoll, 362

environmental policies, *557*, 589

"equal protection" clause, 132, 137, 470; and poll tax, 145, 147

"equal time" rule, 167–8

equality, 4, 6–9, 417–8; *see also* democracy

Ervin, Sam, 491–5

Espionage Act of 1917, 509–10

ethnic groups, and political attitudes, 164–5; assimilation of, 45; attraction to politics of, 44–5; foreign ties of, 43; identity of, 45; Mexican-Americans as, 47–9; pluralism among, 166

Europe, immigration from, 43; political parties in, 183–4

Everson v. Board of Education, 477–8

executive agencies, 341–4; Bureau of the Budget as, 342; Central Intelligence Agency as, 344; Executive Office as, 341; National Aeronautics and Space Council as, 344; National Security Council as, 344; organization of, *370*; structure of, 367–8; *see also* administrative agencies

executive agreement, 112–3, 322

executive branch, 67; and political parties, 196; as interest group, 234; as presidential constituency, 338–41; bureaucracy, 39; increasing power of, 148; organization of, 341–6; presidential leadership of, 327

Executive Calendar, **298**

executive departments, development of, 368–9; within federal bureaucracy, 367; organization of, 369, *370*, 371; *see also* Cabinet, administrative agencies

executive functions, **381**

Executive Office, 323, 341–2, *343*, 344, 358, 382

executive power, 315

executive sessions, **289**

ex post facto, **87**

extraordinary majority, **86**

factions, 62–4, 148

"factories in the fields," 547

Fair Labor Standards Act, 542

fair play, **8**

family, and political attitudes, 161; as social systems, 11–12; conflict within, *161*

Family Assistance Program, 556–7

family farmer, 547

Farm Bureau Federation, 238

"farm bloc," 546

Farm Credit Administration, 377

farm subsidies, 30, *547*

farm surpluses, 547

6; extended to states, 475

first reading, defined, **289**

Fischer, John, 692

fixed term, of Presidency, 316

flexibility, 9, 12–5; in Constitution, 149; in federalism, 116; in law enforcement, 7; through constitutional amendments, 129

Florida, delegate selection in, *214*; 1968 election results in, *154*; origin of poll tax in, 137; percentage of black voters in, 152, *154*; percentage who vote in, 155

Food and Drug Acts, 554

Food and Drug Administration, 371, 554

Food Stamps Program, 563, 566

Ford, William, 307

Ford Foundation, 48

foreign aid, 502, 580

foreign policy, 167; and collective security, 499–502; and containment policy, 498–9; and defense policy, 502, 504–5, 507; and disarmament, 505, 507; and federalism, 119–20; and foreign aid, 502; and industrialization, 498; and trade policy, 507; and world balance of power, 498; as political subsystem, 497; attitudes toward, 193; current trends in, 502; executive agreement in, 322; in Supreme Court cases, 112, 114–5; internationalism in, 498–502; role of Presidency in, 321–3

foreign trade, growth of, *508*

foreign trade policy, *506*; and balance of payments, 507; and free trade, 507; and protectionism, 507; and war feedback, 582–3; feedback to, 581–2; of United States, 507

formal hearings, defined, **391–2**

Fourteenth Amendment, 60, 132, 145; and apportionment clause, 438; and civil liberties, 467, 469–70; and civil rights, 479–80; and First Amendment, 473–6; and illegal searches, 452–3, 455–62, 468–9; and "liberty of contract," 538; and *Slaughter-House Cases*, 473; and Supreme Court, 434; Bill of Rights included in, 474–6; extended to states, 474–6

Fourth Amendment, extension to states of, 475–6

Fowler, Henry (Secretary of Treasury), 98–9

fragmentation, and Supreme Court, 446–7; in Congress, 302–3; in federal bureaucracy, 377–8

Framers, and government bureaucracy, 323, 365–6; and judicial review, 435–6; and power of war, 319; and Senate foreign-policy powers, 321; attitude toward President, 315–6; influence of Great Britain on, 407; intentions of, 434; intention toward judiciary of, 407; on Congress, 256–62

France, elections in, 222; political parties in, 184–5; proportional representation in, 185–6

franchise, defined, **136**

Frankfurter, Felix, on judicial process, 430–1

Franklin, Ben A., 491

Franklin, Benjamin, on Presidency, 332

freedom of speech, limitations on, 516–7; restrictions on, 509–12

Freeman, Orville, 564

free trade, defined, 507

Fremont, John, *140*

Freund, Paul, on judicial policy making, 433

Fritscher, A. Lee, 395

Fugitive Slave Law, *121*

Fulbright, J. William, 56, 293, 339

"gag rule," defined, **295**

Galbraith, John, on the "military-industrial complex," 525–30

Gallagher, Cornelius, 494–5

Gallup Poll, 160; on black voting, 152

Gandhi, Mohandas K.; 48

Garfield, James, *141*, 383; Cabinet of, *369*

Garment, Charley, 228–9

Garment, Leonard, 228

General Services Administration, 377

Georgia, delegate selection in, *214*; 1968 election results in, *154*; nominating procedure in, 210; percentage of black voters in, 152, *154*; percentage who vote in, *155*

Georgia v. Chisholm, 131

gerrymandering, 48

Gettys, R. H., 125

ghettos, voting patterns in, 153

ghost writers, *219*

Gibbons, Thomas, 29

Gilbert, William B., 454

GI Loan Program, 612

Ginzburg v. United States, 518

Gitlow v. New York, 474–5

Glidden Company v. Zdanok, 414–5

Goldwater, Barry, *164*

Gonzalez, Rudolfo (Corky), 47–8

government, action and reaction in, 568; action in, 569; administrative lobbying in, 242–3; and bureaucracy, 365–78; and executive duties, 318–9; and private interest groups, 235; and public opinion, 159–60; and strengthening factors of Presidency, 316–8; aid to agriculture, 545–7; aid to business firms, 544–5; and civil liberties, 467–8; and civil rights, 468; and needs of the people, 535; as collective action, 3; as countervailing force, 38; as customer, 544; as mediator, 3; as organizer, 3; as part of political science, 10; as political system, 1; as protection, 468; as social instrument, 3; as unique political system, 13; authority in, 10; balancing role of, 540; bureaucracy in, 381; changing outputs of, 637–9; citizens participation in, 5; citizen participation elections, 4–5; complexity of, 243; conflict of branches in, 27–8; conflicts within, 38–42; congressional functions in, 257–62; constituencies of, 338–41; continuity in, 148; conversion structure in, 255; corruption in, 8; democratic process in, 4; dynamics of democracy in, 1; economic intervention of, 540; economic role of, 535–40; elected officials in, 209; electoral constituencies in, 32, *33*; ethnic groups in, 3; evolution of policy in, 1; federalism in, 377–8; feedback system in, 569–70; formal forces in, 10; formal mechanism of, 4; function of, 373; function of elections in, 223–4; geographical boundaries of, 25; independent regulatory agencies in, 39–41; inequality of application to citizens in, 7; influences of human behavior in, 1; intricacy of, 35; involvement in private enterprise of, 537–40; judicial interpretation of, 30–2; lawmaking procedures in, 287; lobbying in, 7; military system of, 3; need for, 3; need for moderation in, *516*; news management by, 168; organized citizen participation in, 5–6; overlapping authority of, 25; part of political science in, 10; pluralism in, 41–2; policy-making spheres of, 244; political constituencies in, 32; power of interest groups in, 244; power of taxation in, 27; presidential constituencies in, 335–41; procedures of, 1; purpose of, 1–3; reasons for independent regulatory commissions in, 373; relationship of branches in, 255; representation in, 1; representative, 4; restraint of, 467–8; role of political parties in, 183, 194–6; role of the citizen in, 1; rules for society in, 3; sets standards of, 3; settles disputes in, 3; specialization in, 195; theoretical basis in, 3; types of, 25; types of functions of, 408; unofficial considerations of, 1; will of the people in, 1

government agencies, and interest groups, 235; Council of Economic Advisors to, 342; Domestic Affairs Council in, 342

Government Corporation Control Act, 377

government corporations, **367**; examples of, 377; purpose of, 377; *see also* administrative agencies, federal bureaucracy

governmental authority, 10, 28–9

governmental constituencies, types of, 338–41

governmental interest groups, defined, **233**

governmental restraint, 467–8

grand jury, procedures of, 421

Great Britain, democracy in, 16; political parties in, 183–4; unwritten constitution of, 77; wildlife treaties with United States, 114

Great Northern Railroad, 40

Great Society, 324

Greblen, Leo, 49

Greece, federalism in, 103

Green, Marlon D., 110–1

groups; *see* ethnic groups, interest groups, organized groups, social groups

Guam, 25

Guitierrez, Angel, 49

Gulf of Tonkin Resolution, 331

gun control, **18**; and assassination in United States, 253; and interest group activity, 248–53; legislation for, 248–53

Hamilton, Alexander, 62; advocacy of federal government by, 105; and Federalist party, 187; economic policy of, 536–7; listing factors favoring states rights, 106; on bureaucracy, 323; on composition of Constitution, 58; on control of bueaucracy, 365–6; on electoral college, 139–40; on *Federalist Papers*, 67; on judicial review, 435–6; powers of central government in federalism, 105

Hancock, John, *141*

Harlan, John Marshall, on "separate but equal" doctrine, 481

Harper v. Virginia State Board of Elections, 145, 147

Harris Poll, 160

Harrison, Benjamin, *141*

Hatch Act of 1939, 137

Hawaii, delegate selection in, *214*

Hawthorne, Charles, 126

Hayes, Rutherford B., 140–1

Health, Education, and Welfare, Department of, 35; civil rights enforcement by, 123, 125; organization of, 371; origin of, 369; welfare programs of, 28

health insurance, conflict over, 241

health programs, 553–5

hearings of congressional committees, 289–90

Henderson, Robert P., 494

Henry, Laurin, 354–63

ulation of Lobbying Act of 1946, 245; and health programs, 553–4; and hunger, 563–7; and mass media, 168, 242; and political campaigns, 236, 242–3; and political constituencies, 233–4; and political parties, 195, 233; and popular participation, 243–4; and Presidency, *234*, 336–8; and public interest, 234–5, 628; and public opinion, 159, *244*; and separation of powers, 244; and specialization, 235–6; as channels of demands, 15; as information spreaders, 242; case study of, 248–53; categories of, 233–5; coalitions among, 244; conflicting loyalties in, 240–*241*; controls on, 24, 243–7; defined, **233**; demands of, 238, 241–2, 386–7, 439; direct lobbying by, 246; dishonesty within, 244; elitism in, 239; function of, 241–2; in agriculture, 236–8, 545–7; in business, 544–5; in organized labor, 236–7; in professional groups, 238–9; interaction of, 233–5; investigations by, 566–7; political ideology of, 238–9; power of, 6–7; public relations in, 241–2; size of, *237*; trends in, 634–5; types of, 159

Intergroup Education Committee, 22
Interior, Department of, 368, 391
Internal Revenue Service, 245, 391, 441
internal security, 508–14; and clear and present danger, 509–10; feedback to, 585–6; oppressiveness of, *511*; see also civil liberties
Internal Security Act of 1950, 110, 513, 585
Internal Security Division, 441
International Ladies Garment Workers, 242
internationalism, 507
International Telephone and Telegraph, 386
interstate commerce, **30**; and gun control, 249–53; and national preemption, 110–1
Interstate Commerce Act, 538
Interstate Commerce Commission, 39–41, 234, 382, 587; and Act to Regulate Commerce, 371–2; and Hepburn Act, 374–5; and railroad interests, *372*; and Transportation Act of 1958, 373; as promotional agency, 375; as prototype, 371; as punitive agency, 374–5; early problems of, 374–5; evolution of, 372, 374–5; functions of, 373; jurisdiction of, 235, 374; origin of, 371
Iowa, delegate selection in, *214*
isolationism, 497–8
issue familiarity, 170

Jackson, Andrew, *140*
Jackson, Robert H., 246
Japan, elections in, 222

Javits, Jacob, 563–4
Jay, John, 58
Jefferson, Thomas, 71, 133–4; and Declaration of Independence, 59–61; and Democratic-Republicans, 187; and Louisiana Purchase, 322; economic policy of, 537; on executive power, 66–7
Jewish voting patterns, 164; *see also* ethnic groups
Job Corps, 344
John Birch Society, 238
Johnson, Andrew, 86
Johnson, Lyndon, 96–9, 147, *164*, 213, 331, 339; and gun control, 249–53; and New Hampshire primary, 336; and non-germane amendments, 298; and open housing, 486; as party leader, 195, 324; image of, 227, 319; news management by, 168; resentment toward, 200; Supreme Court appointments of, 445–6
Johnson, U. Alexis, 493
joint committees, 289
Joint Economic Committee, 98
joint resolutions, 287
judicial procedure, concurring opinion in, 422; dissenting opinion in, 422; hearings in, 418; in civil cases, 419–21; in criminal cases, 420–2; notice of the proceeding in, 418; presumption of equality in, 417–8; problems of, 422–3; right to appeal in, 418, *419*; sources of, 416–7
judicial process, 30–2; Benjamin Cardozo on, 428–9; Felix Frankfurter on, 430–1; formal demands on, 439; policy-making in, 434, 437–8; role of legal profession in, 439–40
judicial review, 29, 83, 95, 435; establishment of, 435–7; implications of, 437; in *The Federalist*, 436
judiciary, and federal courts, 408–9; and interest groups, 238; and precedents, 408; and private interest groups, 233; and statutory interpretation, 434; appellate jurisdiction in, 409; as political system, 439–47; as presidential constituency, 340; as subsystem, 19; authority of, 28–9; civil law in, 409; common law tradition in, 131, 407; constitutional courts in, 411–2; constituency demands on, *33*–4; control over bureaucracy of, 385; criminal law in, 409; demands on, 439–41; function of, 408; Holmes, Oliver Wendell, on, 425–8; independence of, 407; interpretive function of, 30–2, 390, 408, 433–5; jurisdiction in, 408–9; legislative control of, 443–4; legislative courts in, 411–2; policy-making role of, 433–4, 437–8; pressure group demands on, 439; self-re-

loyalty oaths, 514
Loyalty Review Board, 512
Lucey, Reverend Robert E., 47

Maddox, John, 229
Madison, James, 58, 62, 67, 71, 81, 436; on factions, 62–4, 133; on republic, 138–9; on separation of powers, 64–5
magazines, influence of, 167; popular use of, *170*
Magna Carta, 55
Maine, delegate selection in, *214*
maintaining elections, defined, **222**; examples of, 222
maintenance policies, and community standards, 517–21; feedback to, 579; subsystem of, *503*; trends in, 744–5; types of, 497
majority rule, constitutional obstacles to, 85–7; in U.S. democracy, 69–71
major total counts, 611–2
Malcolm X, 21
Mallory v. United States, 444
malnutrition in United States, 561–7
management, and political parties, 187
Mansfield, Mike, opposition to filibuster, 301
Marbury v. Madison, 95, 435–7
Marshall, Chief Justice John, 95, 631; and "national supremacy," 107–8; on *Barron v. Baltimore*, 473; on *Gibbons v. Ogden*, 29; on judicial policy-making, 433; on *McCulloch v. Maryland*, 107–8; on *Marbury v. Madison*, 435–7; on state immunity from Bill of Rights, 473
Marshall Plan, 502
Maryland, delegate selection in, *214*; *McCulloch v. Maryland*, 107–8; primary procedures in, 214
Massachusetts, 145; delegate selection in, *214*; nominating procedures in, 210–1; percentage of black voters in, 151
mass media: *see* media
McCarthy, Eugene, 584; and New Hampshire primary, 336
McCarthy, Joseph, 293, 513
McClellon, John L., investigation of labor racketeering by, 293
McClosky, Herbert, 193
McCollum v. Board of Education, 478
McCormack, Edward T., 210
McGiniss, Joe, 226
McKinley, William, and changes in voting patterns, 222
McLaurin v. Oklahoma State Regents, 482

McLuhan, Marshall, 227
McReynolds, Justice James C., 458
Meat Inspection Act of 1906, 554
media, 633; and censorship, 517–21; and changing image of Nixon, 228–9; and internationalism, 498; as used by interest groups, 242; bias in, *167*; campaign expenditures in, 219–20; combatting corruption in, 8–9; control by Federal Communications Commission in, 8; control of, 168; dilution of information in, 171–2; editorialization in, *171*; effect of, 170–1; effect on Congress of, 303; effect on public opinion in, 169; government news management in, 168; impact of, 166; information selection in, 167; involvement with administrative agencies, 243; mergers in, 168; monopolies in, 168–9; news management in, 168; political socialization through, 16; popularity of, 169, *170*; role of, 171; Sherman Adams case with, 9; types of, 166–7; unifying influence of, 172
Medicaid, 553–4
Medical Information Bureau, 490
Medicare, 195; American Medical Association interest in, 6; and interest groups, 238
medicine, professional groups in, 238–9
mercantilism, defined, **536**
merit system, 383–4; operation of, 384
mestizos, defined, 47
Metropolitan Water District of Southern California, 25
Mexican-American Legal Defense and Educational Fund, 48
Mexican-American Youth Organization, 49
Mexican-Americans, 166; *see also* Chicanos
Mexico, and Organization of American States, 499; federalism in, 103
Michels, Robert, 183
Michigan, delegate selection in, *214*; percentage of black voters in, *151*; presidential voting in, 153; primaries in, 211
migrant workers, 47
military-industrial complex, 525–30
military intelligence, and domestic surveillance, 491–2
Miller, Chester, 125
Mills, Representative Wilbur D., 97, 101, 307
minimum income, 556–7
minimum wage laws, 538
Minnesota, delegate selection in, *214*; "gag law," 475; percentage of black voters in, 151; primaries in, 211
minority, lobbying, 6–7; power of, 5–7
minority groups, political views of, 336
minority Presidents, *140, 141*

as minority President, 200–1; budget message of, 555; campaign of, 227–30; deviating election of, 223; on space program, 556; overturned vetoes of, 367; staff of, 342; style of, 319; Supreme Court nominations of, 445; television debates of, 167; use of television by, 226–31; votes for, 153–*154*

"no knock" law, 476, 577, 594–600

nominating procedures, and primary elections. 210–1, 213–4; and state party committees, 214; caucuses in, 209–10; elitism in, 210; history of, 209–10; *see also* national nominating conventions

non-germane amendments, 298

North Atlantic Treaty Organization (NATO), 499–*500*; and France, *581*

North Carolina, delegate selection in, *214*; nonwhite voters in, 152, *154*; presidential election returns in, *154*; voting percentages in, *155*

North Dakota, delegate selection in, *214*; populism in, 118; primaries in, 211

Nossiter, Bernard, 526

notice of the proceeding, defined, 418

Nuclear Test Ban Treaty, 505

nullification, defined, 105

occupations, and political activity, 162–4

Office of Economic Opportunity, 344, 563

Office of Emergency Preparedness, 344, 382

Office of Management and Budget, 271, 342, 382

Office of Price Administration, 390

Office of Science and Technology, 344

Office of the Special Representative for Trade Negotiations, 344

Ogden v. Gibbons, 29

O'Hara, Rosemary, 193

Ohio, delegate selection in, *214*; nonwhite voters in, 151

oil industry, 545

Oklahoma, delegate selection in, *214*

Olmstead v. United States, 450–62

Olney, Richard S., on ICC, 375

Omnibus Crime Control Act, 252, 443–4, 576–7

one-ballot tradition, 217

"one man, one vote," 579; *see also* reapportionment

one-party regions, 187

open housing, 486

open rule, 295

operating agencies, 344

Organization of American States, 499

Oregon, 145; delegate selection in, *214*

original jurisdiction, 409

Orth, Franklin, 252

outputs, and feedback, 569–70; changes in, 744; in pluralistic system, 27; in subsystems, 17, 18, *19*; in Congress, 287; of Judiciary, 441; *see also* feedback, political systems

Pacifica Foundation, 520–1

Pacific Telephone and Telegraph, 457

parliamentary government, 91–2

parliamentary supremacy, 257

parochial education, court decisions on, 477–8

Paterson, William, 79

patronage, 120

Peace Corps, 502

Pendleton Act; *see* Civil Service Act

Pennsylvania, nonwhite voters in, 151

Pennsylvania v. Nelson, 109–10

Perkins, Charles, 375

Permanent Investigations Subcommittee of the Senate Committee on Government Operations, 293

Pink, Louis H., 112–4

plaintiff, 409, 411, 419

platform, 209, *216–7*

Plato, 51, 58

pleadings, 419

pledged delegates, 213–4

Plessy v. Ferguson, 480–1

pluralism, 27, 45, 197, 238, 352, 476, 570–1, 630; and interest groups, 233; and media, 172; in Cabinet, 345–6

plurality, 185

pocket veto, 85

police action, 255; *see also* Congress, war power of

Polk, James, *140*, 329

policy-making, 1, *17*, 34–5, 38–9, 244; and feedback process, 569–70; and interest groups, 7, 233, 242; trends in, 639–40

political attitudes, *159*, 570, 633, 639; as expressed in elections, 227; as personal interests, *163–4*; determinants of, 161; effect of media on, 169; ethnic influence on, 164–5; family influence on, 161–2; interest group influence on, 234; religious influence on, 164; *see also* political socialization

political bosses, 190, 210

political campaigns, 219; and Corrupt Practices Act, 219; and election procedures, 221; and interest groups, 236, 242–3; finances of, 219–20, 245; modern methods in, 218, *219*, *220*

-1, 226–31; Semantic Differential Test in, 229

political constituencies, **32**, *264*, 291; and feedback system, 571; and interest groups, 234; and separation of powers, 138; of administrative agencies, 382–3; of congressmen, 257, 339; of judiciary, 441–2; of Presidency, 316–7, 324–5, 335–41; of Supreme Court, 446–7; opposing views of, 35

political parties, 148, *183*–5, 190, 193–*197*, 264; and congressmen, 264; and desegregation, 574; and election procedures, 221; and electoral college, 140; and interest groups, 233; and multi-party system, 184–5; and Presidency, 185–7, 317–8, 324–*325*, 338, 352; and religion, *164*; and state government, 214; and third parties, 188–9, 199–201; and unit rule, 140; coalitions in, 185–*186*; constituencies of, 336; conventions of, 209–11, 212–*216*, 217; differences in, 193–5, 202–6; elitism in, 210; factions in, 187, *194*, *216*; ideology in, 184, 634; in agriculture, 546; influence of federalism on, 190; in urban areas, 336; leadership in, 190, 193; loyalty in, 161; machine organization of, 190; objectives of, 183; origin of, 133; pluralism in, *188*, 197; reform of, 197–8; structure of, 183–4, 189–91; tradition of, 187–8; trends in, 634; unity in, 194–6; whips of, 262

political philosophy, 58–62, *536*; *see also Federalist Papers*

political science, 9–11

political socialization, 16–17; by interest groups, 242; failure among blacks, 45; political parties in, 196

political subsystems, 10; education as, 18, *553*; foreign policy as, 497; interrelation of, *26*, 35; judiciary as, 439–47; labor as 541–4; maintenance policy as, *503*; presidency as, 335–41 of developmental policy, 535; voting rights as, 485

political systems, 255; authority in, 4, 10; bureaucracy in, 38–40, 365–78; citizen participation in, 5, 209, 253; cultural influences on, 16; developmental policies in, 535; elections in, 209–11, 218–24; ethnic groups in, 164–5; external threats to, 497–507; family influence in, 161–2; federalism in, 103–4; feedback process in, 568–90; forces in, 5–6, 8–9, 227; formation of attitudes in, 161; fragmentation in, 38; historical examples, 3; ideology in, 15–6; initiatives in, 320; internal threats to, 508–14; judicial function in, 30–2, 407, 439–47; legislative functions in, 257–62;

lobbying in, 242–3; maintenance policies of, 497–514; media role in, 171–2, 226–31; moderation in, *516*; outputs of, 465; participation in, 170; personal values in, 4; pluralism in, 27; policy making in, 244; political constituencies in, 32, 34; political parties in, 183, 194–6; President in, 319–25, 335–41; public opinion in, 159–60; seat of power in, 190; self preservation of, 497; statuatory law in, 30; subsystems in, *17, 18, 19*; trends in, 632

polls, 159–60, 174–9

poll tax, 132, 137, 143–*145*

Pollach, Herbert, 566

pollution, 1, *589*

Poor People's March, 48

popular sovereignty, **62**–4, 627

populism, development of, 118–*119*

Port of New York Authority, 25, *26*

Postmaster General, 345

Post Office, Department of the, 368

poverty, *549*, 564, 569

prayers, in schools, 478–9

Presidency, 14, 16; and assassination, 347–51; and bureaucracy, 39, 323, 365–8, *369*, 382; and Cabinet, 344–*346*; and Central Intelligence Agency, 344; and Congress, 268, 287–9, 321–2, *338*–9, *351*–2; and decision-making, *320*; and democratization, 317; and electoral college, 139–42, 316–7; and election of 1968, 199–201; and elections, 90–1, 141, 151, 153–4, *211*, 218–23, *224*, 335–6; and executive agencies, 323, 341–2, 344; and governmental constituencies, 338–41; and individual personalities, 315, 318–9; and interest groups, *234*, 336–8; and legislative mandates, 324; and media, 171–2; and minority Presidents, *140*, *141*, and political constituencies, 234; and political parties, 190, 216–7, 317–8, 324–*325*, 352; and popular expectations, 352–3; and Senate advice and consent, 315, 321–2; and State of the Union, 323–4; and Supreme Court appointments, 445–6; and two-party system, 185–7; and Vice President, 350; and White House Staff, 341–2; as chief executive, 323; as chief legislator, 287–9, 302, 323–4; as Chief of State, 318–9; as Commander in Chief, 319–21; as conversion structure, 318; as political subsystem, *17*, 335–41; checks on, 28–9, 315–6, 320, 324–5, *340*; constituencies of, *33*, *164*, 316–7, 325, 335–41; constitutional powers of, 85, 89–94, 315–9, 321–4, 366; disability of, 135, 348–9; evolution of, 148, 315–*316*, 318; executive agreements of, 322; executive office

separation of powers, **54**–5, 57, 81, 83–4, 129, 138, 258, 319, 327, 332; and limitation on Presidency, 352–3; and political powers, 194–6; and public interest, *435*; education of, 148, 255, 302; in Congress, 258; in Constitution, 59; in foreign policy, 322–3; judicial-legislative conflicts in, 44–5; Montesquieu, 61–2; problems of, *338*

Servicemen's Readjustment Act, 612

Shakespeare, Frank, 228–9

Shays, Daniel, 78

Sherman Act, 30, 32

Sierra Club, 6

silent majority, 352, 571

single-choice ballot, **221**

single-member districts, defined, **185**

Sipuel v. University of Oklahoma, 482

Sixth Amendment, 444, 469, 476

slaughter house cases, 473

slavery, 80, 132

Small Business Administration, 377, 545

Smith, Al, 164

Smith, Walter Bedell, 359

Smith Act, 109, 510–11, 514

Smith v. California, 517–8

"smoke-filled rooms," 210

social groups, 4; and voting patterns, 152

social security, 9, 30; expanding benefits of, 551; organization of, *550*

Social Security Act, 541, 551

Social Security Administration, 371

social welfare, 548–55; and social security, 550–1; aid to education, 551, 553; and health programs, 553–5

socialism, 184

socialized medicine, 241

society, 3, 7

Society for the Prevention of Cruelty to Animals (ASPCA), 6

Soil Conservation Service, 547

Solicitor General, function of, 440–1

"Solid South," 2–3, 335–6

Sorensen, Theodore, 342; on presidential limits, 325

South, percentage of black voters in, 151–2; percentage who vote in, *155*; populism in, 118

South Carolina, choice of elections in, 140; delegate selection in, *214*; 1968 election results in, *154*; nominating procedures in, 210; percentage of black voters in, 152, *154*; percentage who vote in; 155; segregation in, 123–7

South Dakota, delegate selection in, *214*; populism in, 118

Southeast Asia Treaty Organization (SEATO),

331; history of, 499–500

southern states, and nominating conventions, 213; discrimination in voters registrations, 146; poll tax in, 137

Soviet Union, communism in, 16; elections in, 222; relations with United States, 113; totalitarianism in, 53–4

sovereignty, and states, 77–8; defined, **4**; in a democracy, 53

space program, 555–6; and domestic needs, *556*

Spain, elections in, 222

Spanish-American War, 329

Speaker of the House, *259*, 262; and calendars, 294; and presidential succession, 347–8; conference committee members appointed by, 301; exclusion from Rules Committee of, 295

specialization, and committee system, 289; and independent regulatory agencies, 373; and interest groups, 234–236; effects on government, 148; in administrative agencies, 242–3; increase in, 638; in government, *628–9*; in judiciary, 416; in subsystems, **17**

Speiser, Lawrence, 494

Spirit of the Laws (Montesquieu), 61

Super Sonic Transport (SST), *339*

standard committees, defined, **289**

standing vote, defined, **297**

State, Department of, *17*, 358; organization of, *370*; origin of, 368

state governments, and civil rights, *36*; and urban problems, 608; early dominance of, 104; overlapping authority in, 25–8

state sovereignty, 473

state courts, and "due process" in criminal cases, 475–6

state laws, first declaration of unconstitutionality of, 474–5

State of the Union, 323–4

states, absentee voting laws in, 144; and presidential elections, 335–6; and segregation, 480; and Social Security, 551; and the railroads, 537–9; and unemployment insurance, 541; control of nominating procedures in, 210–11; decreasing power of, 148–9; elections chosen by, 140; exempted from Bill of Rights, 473; included in "due process" clause, 474–5; literacy tests used by, 145; moral character tests in, 145; power to create courts of, 409; primary systems of, 213–4; requirements for voting, 143–4; selection of delegates from, *214*; structure of courts in, 409; voting requirements set by, 142–3

States Rights, and *Barron v. Baltimore*, 473-4; and fugitive slave laws, *121*; and slaughter